W9-BLH-426

During the first six of the ten months covered by this volume, Madison completed his initial period of service as a delegate from Virginia in the Congress of the Confederation. His correspondence with Thomas Jefferson and Edmund Randolph, as well as his other papers, reveal the mounting difficulties besetting him and his fellow nationalists who sought to preserve a union among the thirteen states. The major problems, which included demobilizing the discontented army, obtaining public revenue, funding the Confederation debt, pressing the British to evacuate their military posts, enforcing the preliminary articles of peace, creating a public domain in the West, locating a provisional or permanent capital of the Confederation, and negotiating commercial treaties with European powers, fostered sectionalism, factionalism, and an emphasis upon state sovereignty. As a prominent member of Congress, Madison sought legislative and constitutional remedies for this menacing divisiveness.

Early in December, after an absence of over three years, Madison returned to Montpelier, his father's estate. There during the winter of 1783–1784, he studied law, renewed old friendships, and canvassed the residents of Orange County for support of his candidacy for election to the House of Delegates of the Virginia General Assembly.

THE PAPERS OF

James Madison

SPONSORED BY

The University of Chicago

AND

The University of Virginia

VIEW OF SEVERAL PUBLIC BUILDINGS IN PHILADELPHIA

From left to right: Protestant Episcopal Academy, County Courthouse, State House (Independence Hall), Hall of American Philosophical Society, Hall of Library Company of Philadelphia, Carpenter's Hall.

THE PAPERS OF
James Madison

VOLUME 7

3 MAY 1783—20 FEBRUARY 1784

EDITED BY

William T. Hutchinson and William M. E. Rachal

EDITORIAL STAFF

Jean Schneider Robert L. Scribner

THE UNIVERSITY OF CHICAGO PRESS

CHICAGO AND LONDON

International Standard Book Number: 0-226-36300-7
Library of Congress Catalog Card Number: 62-9114

The University of Chicago Press, Chicago 60637
The University of Chicago Press, Ltd., London

Published 1971
Printed in the United States of America

CONTENTS

1784

ILLUSTRATIONS

INTRODUCTION

During the first six of the approximately ten months covered by this volume, James Madison completed the first period of his service as a delegate to the Congress of the Confederation. The tenor of his life was markedly affected late in June 1783 by a mutiny of troops in Philadelphia. Concluding that the soldiers imperiled its safety as well as its "honor," Congress changed its place of meeting from the State House in that city to Nassau Hall on the campus of the College of New Jersey at Princeton. There Congress initially convened on 30 June and remained until two days after Madison's term expired on 2 November. Immediately following the mutiny, he discontinued taking his invaluable notes on debates and stopped writing, or apparently even signing, any of the letters frequently posted by the Virginia delegation to Governor Benjamin Harrison.

Although from 20 March 1780, when he entered Congress, until late in June 1783, the methodical and conscientious Madison rarely had been absent, he attended only about forty of ninety-four sessions of Congress between 30 June and 1 November 1783. During most of that time he remained in his commodious quarters in Mrs. House's boardinghouse in Philadelphia, probably enjoying the companionship of men who shared his own tastes, and certainly engaged in research and writing on a subject or subjects not positively identified. He was irked by his cramped accommodations in Princeton. Sharing with Joseph Jones in that village a room so small that the bed had to serve as a table, Madison found it difficult enough to maintain his correspondence with Jefferson, Pendleton, and Randolph without compounding his discomfort by continuing his notes on congressional debates.

This striking change in Madison's customary conduct as a delegate admits of a more plausible explanation than a resolve to subordinate his duty to Virginia to his personal convenience. Although his keen disappointment early in August because Catherine (Kitty) Floyd withdrew from her engagement to marry him may have briefly caused his interest in public affairs to flag, his letters make clear that he kept abreast of the news as reported in the Philadelphia press and from Princeton. What he read or heard seldom warranted good cheer. The continental treasury remained virtually empty. The plan for restoring public credit, of which Madison was the chief author, was disregarded, only partially approved, or wholly rejected by Virginia and all the other states except Delaware and Pennsylvania before the close of 1783. Moreover, on many days at Princeton, Congress failed to muster a quorum—either the minimum of two delegates from each of nine states required for deciding important issues, or even the minimum of the same number of delegates from each of seven states needed for transacting routine business. This circumstance largely justified Madison in spending so many days in Philadelphia, especially since he was always ready to board the "Flying Machine" stagecoach for Princeton whenever the number of Virginia delegates there fell below the necessary two or Congress rallied a sufficient quorum to determine a course of action on major problems.

Those problems which principally engaged the attention of Madison, as manifested by his papers in the present volume, were (1) the failure of the individual states on the one hand and of the British commanders-in-chief in North America on the other to enforce the provisions of the preliminary treaty of peace; (2) the delay by the American peace commissioners and their British counterparts in Paris in concluding the definitive treaty of peace; (3) the restrictions imposed by Great Britain and to a lesser extent by France upon American cargoes and ships trading especially with their respective West Indian colonies; (4) the policies which the United States should adopt toward European powers, including the exchange of diplomatic and consular agents, the negotiation of treaties of amity and commerce, and the advisability of subscribing to a pact defining "neutral rights"; (5) the extent of Congress' power under the Articles of Confederation to create a "peace establishment" including policies relating to an army and navy, Indian affairs and the government, defense, and public-land administration of the territory north and west of the Ohio River; (6) the differences between Congress and Virginia upon the terms of cession of Virginia's claims to that area; (7) the resistance of Massachusetts and Connecticut to honoring Congress' pledge to reward officers of the continental army with full pay for five years after their demobilization; and (8) the selection of the temporary and permanent site or sites for the meeting of Congress after its expected departure from Princeton.

Each of these issues, to a greater or lesser extent, had arisen, intensified, and long remained unsolved because of lack of money; interstate and sectional rivalries; enmity toward the British and former Loyalists; cooling of affection for the French; a growing desire to be isolated from European politics; increasing emphasis by most of the states upon their sovereignty; neglect by several states to maintain an effective delegation in Congress or, for many months, to be represented at all; and the declining influence in that body of the small band of arch-nationalists, led by Hamilton, and of the more numerous moderate nationalists for whom Madison was often a spokesman.

From early in June 1783, when Robert R. Livingston returned to New York, until near the close of the next year, the position of secretary for foreign affairs remained unfilled. Robert Morris, superintendent of finance, had indicated his intention of resigning on 1 May 1783 but continued in that office for eighteen months thereafter, in spite of the vexing financial crisis and repeated harassment by his political enemies both within and outside of Congress. Having almost no army to administer after the discharge or furloughing of the continental troops in May and June 1783, General Benjamin Lincoln, secretary at war, retired on 12 November of that year. Congress left the office vacant until March 1785. The frustrated Hamilton withdrew from Congress near the close of July 1783. Madison was briefly so pessimistic about the outlook of public affairs that he believed he could retire to Virginia before the close of his term without sacrificing the interests of his state in its relations with Congress. By the last week of August, however, he became more sanguine, probably because each of ten states had two or more delegates in Congress on the twenty-seventh of that month, and several issues of prime concern to his state seemed to be ripe for decision.

Although Madison in his congressional committee reports and motions set forth his views about some of the issues and tendencies mentioned above, he revealed them more explicitly and in greater detail in his private letters to Jefferson and Randolph. By construing as broadly as possible the powers delegated to Congress by the Articles of Confederation, and urging the amendment of that document in the two particulars emphasized in the plan for restoring public credit, Madison displayed his eagerness as a nationalist to strengthen the union and provide Congress with an adequate revenue. Unlike Hamilton and a few other leaders, he was not ready to conclude that only a new constitution, drafted by a convention, could save the United States from dissolution, probably attended by civil war and foreign invasion. He believed that the economic interests and political institutions of the New England states contrasted too sharply with those of states south of Pennsylvania, for example, to permit them to dwell together in amity under the roof of a highly centralized government.

To reinforce the weakening bonds of union by giving all the states a common territorial possession, to provide the Confederation with a potential source of large income from land sales, to prevent the secession of the increasing number of people settling west of the Appalachian Mountains by promising eventual statehood to the areas in which they lived, and to relieve Virginia, financially much embarrassed, of administrative and military obligations in a region too distant from the seat of government for her to discharge successfully, Madison urged that his state cede all of the Northwest Territory to Congress, except a "District" adequate in size for honoring the bounty-land warrants issued to Virginia's continental troops. At the same time he opposed those men, including some ultra-nationalists both within and outside Congress, who held that, because Great Britain in the preliminary articles of peace had relinquished its sovereignty over that vast area to the United States, Congress could govern its inhabitants and dispose of its soil without giving heed to Virginia's antecedent title. To Madison's gratification, Congress on 13 September 1783 abandoned its long-continued intransigence by resolving to accept a cession by Virginia upon terms calculated to gain the approval of that state's General Assembly. It fulfilled his expectation in December, soon after his return to Montpelier. The formal transfer to the United States of Virginia's title to the Northwest Territory, except the "District" mentioned above, took place in Congress on 1 March 1784.

During the nine months immediately preceding this event, other aspects of the situation in the Northwest Territory became more ominous. Its southern fringe along the Ohio River lured many unauthorized settlers from western Pennsylvania and Virginia, including Kentucky. Lacking money, and without a military force west of the Appalachian Mountains, except for a feeble garrison at Fort Pitt, Congress was frustrated in its hope that the Indians in the Ohio country could be induced to keep the peace and surrender land to the United States. Agents dispatched there in the summer of 1783 returned with discouraging reports. In September a congressional proclamation, wholly futile in its effect, warned the whites from trespassing north of the Ohio River. Relations between Virginia and Pennsylvania temporarily cooled as each state charged that the citizens of the other composed most of the interlopers. Pennsylvania, suffering from raids into her western counties by Indians who, although living in the Ohio country, claimed land within her limits, found members of Congress, including Madison, opposed to her request to negotiate a purchase of those claims from the marauding Indians. The Articles of Confederation warranted this reply to Pennsylvania. The situation was similar in western New York. The possession of a constitutional right without the power to exercise it frequently characterized the history of Congress during Madison's last six months as a delegate.

This impotency was starkly shown by the inability of Congress to compel either the British commanders-in-chief in North America or the state governments to abide by the provisions of the preliminary articles of peace. With good reason, Madison and other leaders believed that General Sir Frederick Haldimand, commanding the British military forces in Canada and along the southern shores of Lakes Ontario and Erie in the United States, maintained the garrisons at Niagara and Detroit in order to supply arms to the Indians, to influence them to cede no land, and to maintain their traffic in furs with the British. General von Steuben, who had been sent by Washington to receive possession of those forts from the British, returned to the headquarters at Newburgh, New York, foiled in his efforts to accomplish his mission. At the same time, probably anticipating this outcome, Washington inspected the installations of American troops at Albany and in the Mohawk Valley.

Bringing a copy of Steuben's report and another much lengthier one detailing the advisable composition of a United States regular army, Washington arrived at Princeton on 23 August in response to Congress' request that he make himself available for consultation about "the military peace establishment." Four days later, having no money and also grave doubts about its constitutional power to create a standing military force in peacetime, Congress, including Madison, voted to postpone a decision on the issue. Madison and Washington, who continued to reside near Princeton as long as Congress remained there, had met briefly several times before, but their association that autumn probably marked the beginning of their noteworthy friendship.

One matter of mutual interest to them, as well as to many other leaders, was the continuing occupation of New York City and its environs by General Sir Guy Carleton and his troops. At the behest of Congress, Washington had tried—at first by a conference with Carleton and later by commissioners in New York—to induce his British counterpart to hand over the public records and the privately owned slaves being held within the lines of his army. Owing to the prolonged invasions of Virginia by the enemy in 1780 and 1781, these were matters of particular concern to residents of that state. Besides basing his refusal to relinquish the slaves upon a technicality relating to their status, Carleton contended that he had no obligation to do so until the conclusion of the definitive treaty of peace, and, even if this were not so, he was amply justified by the Americans' flagrant violations of the preliminary articles of peace. He finally completed his slow evacuation of New York City on 25 November. Washington's commissioners reported that during the summer and autumn of 1783, slaves were aboard almost every transport or other ship carrying British troops and Loyalists out of New York Harbor to Canada or the Bahama Islands.

While deploring Carleton's conduct, Madison could not deny that many of the state and local governments, as well as informal groups of citizens, were openly flouting guarantees of the preliminary treaty to British creditors and Loyalists. Executive proclamations, of which Governor Harrison's of 2 July was a conspicuous example, bade the returned Loyalists to depart forthwith; legislatures refused to repeal acts confiscating the property of British subjects or Loyalists; courts were barred to their use; and state officials permitted townspeople and rural folk to harry Loyalists who sought to reoccupy their former homes and resume their prewar means of livelihood. Although inability to pay old debts, unwillingness to return confiscated real estate, and a desire to retaliate for extensive devastation by enemy troops and Loyalist guerrillas probably accounted for much of this display of hostility, the official justification was the same as that used by Carleton—the war would not end until the ratification of the definitive peace treaty. Although Madison had never evinced sympathy for the Loyalists, he became convinced that these violations of the preliminary articles of peace handicapped the commissioners of Congress in their negotiations of a definitive treaty in Paris, rendered the attainment of "domestic tranquility" impossible, and delayed the creation of a "peace establishment." For these reasons, he moved in Congress on 18 October that the "honor of the Confederacy" and "principles of good faith" required that the states refrain from acts contravening the "stipulations" in the preliminary articles.

In contrast with the insistence that Loyalists and British creditors must wait to receive their due until the ratification of the definitive peace treaty, Americans with raw materials for export, with funds to purchase foreign products, or with ships hastened to resume trading with Great Britain and its West Indian colonies as soon as news of the signing of the preliminary articles reached the United States. British merchantmen appeared simultaneously in Atlantic coastal ports, eager to re-engage in the customary pre-Revolutionary traffic. In Virginia, for example, the pressure of planters and merchants for the restoration of commerce with the erstwhile enemy was so heavy upon Governor Harrison that he proclaimed its reopening even before the Virginia General Assembly on 24 May repealed all laws prohibiting economic intercourse with Great Britain. Earlier in the same month, Madison became a member of a committee instructed by Congress to recommend what terms a commercial treaty with that country should include.

This subject particularly interested Madison. The economic well-being of his most influential constituents in Virginia depended upon the English market for their tobacco. Their relations with New England owners of cargo ships before 1776 were not always cordial, but they nevertheless had been an important economic link between those colonies which, as states, were joined within a common union. The recommended import duty of 5 per cent on goods of foreign origin was a cardinal provision of the plan devised by Madison for restoring and maintaining the solvency of the Confederation. His hope of having Great Britain agree to a commercial treaty embodying provisions of "perfect reciprocity" quickly faded because of circumstances beyond his control. Unlike Great Britain, the United States possessed neither colonies nor a navy able to protect a merchant marine. The premature avidity displayed by Americans for selling their products to the mother country and for buying her goods in return naturally convinced the British ministers that no modifications of the restrictive Navigation Acts need be tendered in order to enjoy all the prewar advantages of trade with the United States. As a result, the congressional instructions to the American commissioners at Paris for negotiating a commercial treaty with Great Britain could not be fulfilled during 1783 or for a long time thereafter. Madison was further disappointed to find that, notwithstanding the intimate military and financial association of the United States with France during the Revolution, French merchants were unprepared to extend to American exporters as favorable terms of credit and merchandising as those available in Great Britain. In addition, the government of Louis XVI was scarcely more generous than that of George III in opening its West Indian ports to American cargo ships.

Madison's desire that the United States widen its economic relations with the countries of western Europe was not unlimited. He felt no regret because Tsarina Catherine II of Russia, by refusing to recognize the independence of the United States, thwarted the efforts of Francis Dana, the minister-designate to her court, to conclude a commercial treaty with her. Congress concurred with the recommendation of Madison, as chairman of a committee, to postpone replying to a request by merchants of Hamburg for the establishment of a consulate there. Although in January 1783 he shared prominently in congressional actions attending the ratification of the treaty of amity and commerce with the States-General of the Netherlands, six months later he opposed its proposal that the United States join it, and perhaps other European countries, in a "league of armed neutrality." On that occasion Madison expressed his own and the majority opinion of Congress by writing, "the true interest of these states requires that they shd. be as little as possible entangled in the politics & controversies of European Nations."

When the commercial treaty drafted in Paris by Benjamin Franklin and the ambassador of Gustavus III of Sweden reached Congress, Madison, as chairman of a committee, reviewed its terms, recommended its approval, and drafted both "the form of ratification" and the proclamation of the president of Congress declaring the treaty to be in effect. More as evidence that the United States, in spite of its weak government, was attracting wider attention overseas than that American exporters would soon enjoy a much larger market for their products, Madison was happy to inform Jefferson in September 1783 of Austria's, Denmark's, Portugal's, Prussia's, Tuscany's, and Spain's apparent readiness to negotiate commercial treaties with commissioners of Congress. At Princeton on the last day of October, when Madison's tenure as a delegate was about to end, Congress formally greeted the first minister to the United States from the States-General of the Netherlands. Madison, along with other members of Congress who were sensitive to its "honor" and "dignity," regretted that the village and its inadequate accommodations barred a ceremony of reception sufficiently elaborate to please the Dutch minister.

Although Madison seems to have agreed during the mutiny in June that the evident inability or unwillingness of the government of Pennsylvania to shield the delegates from the insults and threats of the soldiers obliged Congress, for the maintenance of its own self-respect and safety, to leave Philadelphia, he was much disappointed during the summer and autumn by the refusals of Congress to return, at least temporarily, to that city, especially since its prominent residents and the state authorities repeatedly extended cordial invitations, accompanied with assurance of adequate protection.

By July 1783 Madison had come to realize that the problem of determining a location for the Confederation's capital was singularly complex, involving personal rivalries often economic in basis, state pride, sectional jealousies, and considerations of financial costs, defensibility in case of hostile invasion, and accessibility to the territory west of the Appalachian Mountains. Most of the delegates agreed, more or less willingly, that the slow pace and expense of travel in a Union extending nearly fifteen hundred miles along the Atlantic Ocean obliged the site to be no farther south than the Potomac River and no farther north than the Hudson River. Although this decision limited the issue geographically, it intensified the competition among communities large and small within that area. Some delegates, including Arthur Lee and his Massachusetts allies, viewed the many advantages of Philadelphia as minor compared with the menace to Congress from Robert Morris' domination of that city. Other members of Congress, especially those from New England, were satisfied either to remain in Princeton or to remove to some other town where living was similarly homespun and untainted by the wealth and ostentation of a metropolis such as Philadelphia or New York City.

State governments offered sites: New York, at Kingston; New Jersey, at Trenton; Pennsylvania, at Philadelphia or Germantown; Delaware, at Wilmington; and Maryland, at Annapolis. Numerous small communities in New Jersey also sought the prize. President Elias Boudinot believed that Elizabethtown, his place of residence in that state, would be an excellent choice. It perhaps was a circumstance of good omen to Madison, during a period when he found little cause to be happy about public affairs, that New York, New Jersey, and Delaware, which for weeks at a time had no effective delegations in Congress, were nevertheless eager for the capital of the Confederation to be within their borders. Receiving so many invitations from established communities, Congress was unable to muster a majority in favor of having any one of them become eventually the site of the "permanent" capital.

The question of jurisdiction increased the difficulty of making a selection. The General Assembly of Virginia, for example, hoped that the residents of Williamsburg, where public buildings were available, would co-operate in presenting their town as an attractive site for Congress to choose. The lack of initial enthusiasm manifested by most of the delegates toward that proposal became even greater upon hearing of the hesitation by Williamsburg residents to subject themselves to the degree of governmental control desired by Congress. With this aspect of the problem Madison was much interested. Although in September, as a member of a committee on the subject, he favored an entire exclusion of state authority from any "district" ceded by a state to Congress for its "permanent residence," he differed from his committee colleagues by contending that Congress should concert with the inhabitants of "the district" before deciding about the organization and administration of their government. The matter was not settled during the remainder of his term.

On 7 October Congress went far toward defining the meaning of "district" by deciding to locate "a federal town" for its permanent residence near the falls of the Delaware River, close to Trenton. Thereby the issue of jurisdiction over numerous inhabitants was made less acute, and the irresolvable competition between cities was ended by an act of avoidance. The outcome left the southern bloc, including all the delegates from Maryland, Virginia, North Carolina, and South Carolina, unappeased. On 20 October, a day on which Madison was not present, they succeeded, with the help of the Massachusetts and Rhode Island delegations, in having Congress authorize the erection of a second "federal town"—this one to be "at or near the lower falls of Potomac or Georgetown." That location had been strongly recommended by both the Virginia and Maryland legislatures. The next day a similar sectional compromise enabled a resolution to pass, declaring that Congress, as a place of temporary residence, would meet at Annapolis for about six months, beginning on 26 November, and thereafter for a period of similar duration at Trenton. Although disappointed because Congress had not returned to Philadelphia in July, Madison probably was gratified by these decisions, for they signified that by compromise the Union could be held together, even when confronted with an unusually divisive issue. Obviously unable to foresee the culmination of one of these plans seventeen years later in the establishment of the capital of the United States fairly close to his home in Virginia, he at least could include those plans, as he prepared to return to that state, among the few constructive actions of Congress during his last six months as a delegate.

Although in August and the first two months of autumn Madison's indecision about the time of his return signified mainly his doubt about whether or when the outstanding public issues would come to a head in Congress before the end of his tenure, it also reflected his eagerness to see Jefferson and his uncertainty about where they could meet. On 6 June, the General Assembly of Virginia had elected Jefferson to head its delegation in Congress during the three years beginning on 3 November. From 29 October, the date of Jefferson's arrival in Philadelphia, until he and Madison parted at Annapolis on 27 November, they were together almost continually. The subjects of their conversations surely included, with Madison taking the lead, congressional problems and personnel, and, with Jefferson to the fore, the latter's elaborate program of desirable constitutional and legal reforms for Virginia. The subject of books read or worth purchasing could hardly have been avoided when they diverted their discussions from public affairs. On 22 November, as they were leaving Philadelphia, the official copy of the definitive treaty of peace, signed on 3 September, reached that city.

Madison spent the unusually cold and stormy winter of 1783–1784 at Montpelier, his father's estate in Orange County, Virginia. His papers, written or received in that season, are fewer than for any other consecutive three-months' period of his life subsequent to 1779. Studying law, visiting and being visited by kinsfolk and other neighborhood friends, and canvassing for sufficient votes to be cast on the polling days late in April to assure him of a seat in the Virginia House of Delegates occupied much of his time. Soon after the date of the final letter in this volume, Edmund Randolph was told by Madison that his expected service as a delegate would be "most noxious" to a continuation of his recent companionship with Sir Edward Coke's *The First Part of the Institutes of the Lawes of England; or, A Commentary upon Littleton.*

EDITORIAL NOTE

Of the two hundred and sixteen items in this volume, seventy-one have been printed either in whole or in part, but seldom with any annotation, in earlier editions of the writings of James Madison. Ninety-one of the documents, including one written by him on behalf of all the Virginia delegates in Congress, are altogether or largely in his hand. The manuscripts of four others by him are missing. The partial contents of two of these, including a second letter written for the Virginia delegation, are known from printed excerpts. The remaining two are, respectively, a transcript and a copy made soon after the date of the original. Among the seventy-one papers addressed solely to him were twenty letters from Edmund Pendleton. Only eight of these survive. An acquaintance with the contents of the others is limited to what appears in printed extracts or in brief topical summaries made by Peter Force's clerk. Except for one letter and a printed excerpt from another, all of Madison's letters to Pendleton during this period have disappeared. Prior to the expiration of Madison's term in Congress, there were fifteen letters and one other paper, besides the two letters mentioned above, written on behalf of the Virginia delegation by one or another of its members. That delegation received twenty-one letters and eight instructions. The present volume also includes five miscellaneous items, consisting of four editorial notes and a letter, meant for JM but addressed by John Beckley to Edmund Randolph. Among these notes are two bearing upon missing letters from the Virginia delegation in Congress to Governor Benjamin Harrison, one upon a letter from Alexander Hamilton, probably never posted to JM, and one upon the anonymous essays entitled "North-American, No. 1" and "North-American, No. 2."

In preparing the manuscript of this volume for publication, the editors benefited from courtesies extended by Whitfield J. Bell, Jr., Librarian, American Philosophical Society; Julian P. Boyd of the Papers of Thomas Jefferson; Atcheson L. Hench of the University of Virginia; Edmund S. Morgan of Yale University; Paul R. Wagner of the Princeton University Library; Nicholas B. Wainwright of the Historical Society of Pennsylvania; and Karl J. Weintraub of the University of Chicago. The editors also gratefully record their thanks to Miss Cheryl Seaman, project assistant, for many tedious chores performed efficiently and in good spirit.

EDITORIAL METHOD

ABBREVIATIONS

FC File copy. Any version of a letter or other document retained by the sender for his own files and differing little if at all from the completed version. A draft, on the other hand, is a preliminary sketch, often incomplete and varying frequently in expression from the finished version.

JM James Madison.

LC Library of Congress.

MS Manuscript. A catchall term describing numerous reports and other papers written by Madison, as well as items sent to him which were not letters.

NA National Archives.

PCC Papers of the Continental Congress, a collection in the National Archives.

RC Recipient's copy. The copy of a letter intended to be read by the addressee. If the handwriting is not that of the sender, this fact is mentioned in the headnote.

Tr Transcript. A copy of a manuscript, or a copy of a copy, customarily handwritten, made considerably later than the date of the manuscript and ordinarily not by its author or by the person to whom the original was addressed. The "Force Transcripts," made under the direction of Peter Force in the mid-nineteenth century, are those most frequently used in the present series.

SHORT TITLES FOR BOOKS

Only those books used very frequently, and a few whose titles are so long as to necessitate an abbreviation, have been given short titles. This list applies only to Volume VII.

Boyd, *Papers of Jefferson.* Julian P. Boyd *et al.*, eds., *The Papers of Thomas Jefferson* (18 vols. to date; Princeton, N.J., 1950——).

Brant, *Madison.* Irving Brant, *James Madison* (6 vols.; Indianapolis and New York, 1941–61).

Burnett, *Letters.* Edmund C. Burnett, ed., *Letters of Members of the Continental Congress* (8 vols.; Washington, 1921–36).

Cal. of Va. State Papers. William P. Palmer *et al*., eds., *Calendar of Virginia State Papers and Other Manuscripts* (11 vols.; Richmond, 1875–93).

Fitzpatrick, *Writings of Washington*. John C. Fitzpatrick, ed., *The Writings of George Washington, from the Original Sources, 1745–1799* (39 vols.; Washington, 1931–44).

Gwathmey, *Historical Register of Virginians*. John H. Gwathmey, *Historical Register of Virginians in the Revolution: Soldiers, Sailors, Marines, 1775–1783* (Richmond, 1938).

Hansard's Parliamentary Debates. William Cobbett, ed., *The Parliamentary History of England from the Earliest Period to the Year 1803* (36 vols.; London, 1806–20; continued as *Hansard's Parliamentary Debates*).

Heitman, *Historical Register Continental*. F. B. Heitman, *Historical Register of Officers of the Continental Army during the War of the Revolution* (Washington, 1914).

Hening, *Statutes*. William Waller Hening, ed., *The Statutes at Large; Being a Collection of All the Laws of Virginia, from the First Session of the Legislature, in the Year 1619* (13 vols.; Richmond and Philadelphia, 1819–23).

JCC. Worthington Chauncey Ford *et al*., eds., *Journals of the Continental Congress, 1774–1789* (34 vols.; Washington, 1904–37).

JCSV. H. R. McIlwaine *et al*., eds., *Journals of the Council of the State of Virginia* (4 vols. to date; Richmond, 1931––).

JHDV. *Journal of the House of Delegates of the Commonwealth of Virginia; Begun and Held at the Capitol, in the City of Williamsburg*. Beginning in 1780, the portion after the semicolon reads, *Begun and Held in the Town of Richmond. In the County of Henrico*. The journal for each session has its own title page and is individually paginated. The edition used is the one in which the journals for 1777–1786 are brought together in two volumes, with each journal published in Richmond in 1827 or 1828, and often called the "Thomas W. White reprint."

JHDV (1828 ed.). *Journal of the House of Delegates of Virginia, Anno Domini, 1776* (Richmond, 1828).

McIlwaine, *Official Letters*. H. R. McIlwaine, ed., *Official Letters of the Governors of the State of Virginia* (3 vols.; Richmond, 1926–29).

Madison, *Letters* (Cong. ed.). [William C. Rives and Philip R. Fendall, eds.], *Letters and Other Writings of James Madison* (published by order of Congress; 4 vols.; Philadelphia, 1865).

Madison, *Papers* (Gilpin ed.). Henry D. Gilpin, ed., *The Papers of James Madison* (3 vols.; Washington, 1840).

Madison, *Writings* (Hunt ed.). Gaillard Hunt, ed., *The Writings of James Madison* (9 vols.; New York, 1900–1910).

New Jersey Archives. William S. Stryker *et al*., eds., *Documents Relating to the Revolutionary History of the State of New Jersey* (2d ser.; 5 vols.; Trenton, 1901–17).

Papers of Madison. William T. Hutchinson, William M. E. Rachal, *et al*., eds., *The Papers of James Madison* (7 vols. to date; Chicago, 1962––).

Pa. Archives. Samuel Hazard *et al*., eds., *Pennsylvania Archives* (9 ser.; 138 vols.; Philadelphia and Harrisburg, 1852–1949).

Swem and Williams, *Register*. Earl G. Swem and John W. Williams, eds., *A Register of the General Assembly of Virginia, 1776–1918, and of the Constitutional Conventions* (Richmond, 1918).

Syrett and Cooke, *Papers of Hamilton*. Harold C. Syrett and Jacob E. Cooke, eds., *The Papers of Alexander Hamilton* (15 vols. to date; New York, 1961——).

Va. Gazette. *Virginia Gazette, or, the American Advertiser* (Richmond, James Hayes, 1781–86).

Wharton, *Revol. Dipl. Corr*. Francis Wharton, ed., *The Revolutionary Diplomatic Correspondence of the United States* (6 vols.; Washington, 1889).

MADISON CHRONOLOGY

1783

1 May–2 November	JM, delegate in Congress, continues to reside in Philadelphia.
2 May	JM returns to Philadelphia from trip with family of William Floyd to New Brunswick, N.J.
6 May	JM elected to committee *in re* British evacuation of western posts.
6 May	JM elected to committee *in re* treaty of commerce with Great Britain.
6 (or 7) May	Joseph Jones, a delegate to Congress from Virginia, leaves Philadelphia to attend session of Virginia General Assembly.
9 May	JM successfully moves that plan for restoring public credit and address to states, both documents mainly drafted by him, be presented by executives of states to their respective legislatures with "all possible expedition."
9 May	JM and fellow Virginia delegates induce Congress not to assume power of garrisoning posts in Northwest Territory claimed by Virginia.
12 May	JM elected chairman of committee *in re* Washington-Carleton negotiations on enforcement of preliminary articles of peace.
12 May	Arthur Lee, a delegate to Congress from Virginia, leaves Philadelphia to attend session of Virginia General Assembly.
13 May	Society of the Cincinnati formed by continental army officers.

15 May	JM elected to committee *in re* enforcement of articles of preliminary treaty of peace with Great Britain.
20 May	JM moves with partial success that American commissioners seek to have preliminary articles revised in definitive treaty of peace.
21 May	Congress further debates report of Madison committee *in re* instructions to Francis Dana, minister-designate to Russia.
21 May	JM seconds Alexander Hamilton's motion, "generally concurred in," *in re* League of Armed Neutrality.
22 May	JM moves unsuccessfully to postpone negotiations of commercial treaty with Russia.
23 May	JM moves unsuccessfully to recommit report advocating discharge of troops enlisted for duration of war.
23–24 May	Virginia General Assembly instructs delegates in Congress *in re* commercial treaty with Great Britain.
24 May	Virginia General Assembly repeals all acts prohibiting trade with Great Britain.
26 May	Congress unanimously resolves to furlough troops enlisted for duration of war.
26 May	Congress instructs American peace commissioners to remonstrate against British retention of American slaves.
27 May	JM expresses hope Jefferson will return to Virginia General Assembly or to Congress.
30 May	New committee of Congress replaces that elected 15 May.
1 June	JM receives from Jefferson notes on debates in Congress in 1776 and annotated, handwritten copy of Declaration of Independence.

4 June	JM elected to committee to consider report and other proposals *in re* Virginia's offer to cede claims to Northwest Territory.
4 June	Virginia General Assembly instructs delegates in Congress to procure copies of all vouchers relating to financial dealings of agents of Congress with Virginians.
4 June	Virginia General Assembly enacts law prohibiting members thereof from serving concurrently in Congress.
5 June	Robert L. Livingston serves last day as secretary for foreign affairs.
6 June	JM elected chairman of committee *in re* "Rights of Neutral Nations."
6 June	Congress receives report on Virginia offer to cede claims to Northwest Territory.
6 June	Virginia General Assembly elects Jefferson to head delegation to Congress for term beginning 3 November.
8–21 June	Washington issues circular letter to executives of states urging adoption of congressional plan for restoring public credit.
11 June	JM elected to committee to consider resolution to furlough troops and letter of Washington *in re* discontent in ranks over demobilization without pay.
11 June	Virginia House of Delegates rejects impost provision of plan for restoring public credit.
12 June	JM submits, and Congress amends and adopts, report on neutral rights.
12 June	Congress refers to JM and committee elected on 4 April data *in re* needs of peacetime military establishment.
17 June	JM receives from Jefferson copy of "Thoughts" on new constitution for Virginia.

17 June	Virginia General Assembly instructs delegates in Congress *in re* leveling fortifications at Yorktown and Gloucester.
18 June	JM elected to committee *in re* treaty of commerce with Sweden.
19 June	As recommended by committee elected 11 June, Congress resolves to send to each state executive copy of Washington's letter and of congressional resolutions *in re* furloughing of troops and urgent need of Congress to give them three months' overdue pay.
19 June	JM elected to committee to report upon vote required in Congress for admission of new states to Confederation.
19–26 June	Contingents of Pennsylvania continental troops mutiny in Philadelphia.
20 June	Virginia General Assembly instructs delegates in Congress *in re* guards for state public buildings.
21 June	Congressional plan to restore public credit adopted in entirety by Delaware. Only Pennsylvania thereafter in 1783 sanctions complete plan.
24 June	Congress adjourns, to convene at Princeton on 26 June.
24 June	JM signs for last time letter of Virginia delegates to Governor Benjamin Harrison.
26 June	Massachusetts General Court protests pledge of Congress to reward demobilized officers with full pay for five years or half pay for life.
26–27 June	Virginia General Assembly instructs delegates in Congress *in re* demobilization of troops.
26–27 June	Virginia General Assembly instructs delegates in Congress *in re* ships of state navy.

27 June	House of Delegates of Virginia General Assembly defers until October session consideration of bill to levy imposts for use of Congress.
27 June	Virginia General Assembly instructs delegates in Congress *in re* cession of claims to Northwest Territory.
28 June	Virginia General Assembly instructs delegates in Congress *in re* offer of Williamsburg and "land adjoining," or of location "on the river Potomac," as permanent site for Congress.
28 June	Virginia General Assembly adjourns.
30 June	Congress reconvenes at Princeton, where between *ca.* 25 August and 25 October JM, although retaining his quarters in Philadelphia, shares room with Joseph Jones.
30 June–2 November	JM attends only about 40 of 94 sessions of Congress.
1 July	JM elected to committee to report on protest of Robert Morris against Maryland's paying own continental troops.
2 July	JM elected to committee to consider advisability of withdrawing American commissioners sent to New York City to recover American public and private property held by British.
2 July	King George III issues proclamation dashing hopes of Congress to negotiate advantageous treaty of commerce with Great Britain.
3 July	JM elected chairman of committee *in re* Washington's recommendation that General von Steuben be sent to receive possession of western posts from British.
6 July	JM asked by Hamilton to state in writing latter's attitude concerning departure of Congress from Philadelphia.

11 July	Massachusetts General Court repeats protest of 26 June.
16 July	Arthur Lee resumes attendance in Congress.
23 July	JM added to committee elected 18 July to report on jurisdiction of Congress over place of permanent residence.
23 July	JM elected chairman of committee *in re* memorial of merchants of Hamburg.
23 July	JM elected to committee *in re* "establishment of a mint."
23 July	Congress receives "address" of citizens of Philadelphia asking return to their city.
24 July	JM reports to Congress on treaty with Sweden.
26 July	JM reports to Congress on memorial of merchants of Hamburg.
ca. 27 July	Hamilton quits Congress.
28 July	Virginia delegates move in Congress according to instructions of 26–27 June *in re* ships of state navy.
28 July	JM submits to Congress report *in re* Maryland's payment of continental troops.
29 July	Congress ratifies treaty of commerce with Sweden.
ca. 1 August	JM's engagement to marry Catherine Floyd broken.
5 August	Committee, including JM, on establishment of mint, recommends that Robert Morris submit estimate of cost.
14 August	Congress rejects proposed return to Philadelphia.
23 August	Washington arrives in Princeton.
25 August	JM elected to committee *in re* offer of Elizabethtown, N.J., for permanent site of Congress.

26 August	Committee, including JM, appointed 6 May *in re* treaty of commerce with Great Britain, discharged.
26 August	Washington formally received by Congress.
27 August	JM votes for Congress to postpone consideration of its power to create "a military peace establishment."
ca. 27 August	Joseph Jones resumes attendance in Congress.
3 September	Definitive treaty of peace with Great Britain signed at Paris.
5 September	Committee, including JM, reports on jurisdiction of Congress over place of permanent residence.
13 September	Congress adopts report on Virginia cession of claims to Northwest Territory, and copy of the report is sent to executive of Virginia.
18 September	JM elected chairman of committee on protests of Massachusetts General Court *in re* pay for demobilized continental officers.
19 September	JM elected to committee *in re* commercial and financial relations with France.
19 September	JM submits report on protests of Massachusetts General Court.
19 September	JM opposes request of Pennsylvania to treat with Indians beyond state boundaries.
22 September	JM moves that the extent of powers of Congress over permanent site be "concerted" with "inhabitants thereof."
23 September	Congress adopts proclamation restricting purchase of or settlement on Indian lands beyond limits of any state.
25 September	JM's draft of proclamation, submitted 24 July, announcing ratification of treaty with Sweden, signed by President Elias Boudinot.

25 September	JM's report of 19 September on protests of Massachusetts General Court amended and adopted by Congress.
3 October	Congress adopts Virginia delegates' motion of 28 July *in re* ships of state navy.
7 October	Congress decides permanent site for "federal town" be "near the falls" of Delaware River.
14 October	Joseph Jones leaves Philadelphia to return to Virginia.
15 October	JM elected to committee on Northwest Territory.
16 October	JM elected to committee *in re* "state of affairs" with southwestern Indians.
18 October	JM moves that state governments be requested to prevent violations of preliminary articles of peace.
20 October	Congress decides to locate second "federal town" near lower falls of Potomac River.
20 October	Virginia General Assembly reconvenes in Richmond.
21 October	Congress decides to reconvene at Annapolis on 26 November.
22 October	Morris submits to Congress elaborate report on public credit.
29 October	JM's motion of 18 October amended and adopted by Congress.
29 October–22 November	JM and Jefferson are together in Philadelphia.
31 October	Congress receives minister to United States from Netherlands.
2 November	JM's term as delegate to Congress ends.
4 November	Congress adjourns at Princeton to reconvene at Annapolis.
22 November	JM and Jefferson leave Philadelphia.

22 November	Official copy of definitive treaty of peace with Great Britain reaches Philadelphia.
25 November	British troops complete evacuation of New York City.
25 November	JM and Jefferson arrive at Annapolis.
26 November	Scheduled to reconvene in Annapolis, Congress fails to muster quorum.
27 November	Homeward-bound, JM leaves Annapolis.
27 November	Harrison re-elected governor of Virginia.
ca. 3 December	JM converses with George Mason at Gunston Hall.
5 December	JM reaches Montpelier, his first day at home since 6 March 1780, and resides there during remainder of period spanned by present volume.
13 December	Congress, mustering quorum, receives official copy of definitive treaty of peace with Great Britain.
22 December	Virginia General Assembly, acceding to terms of congressional report of 13 September, authorizes delegates in Congress to convey to Congress state claims to Northwest Territory.
22 December	Virginia General Assembly adopts impost amendment, subject to adoption by all other states.
23 December	Washington resigns as commander-in-chief of continental armies.

1784

14 January	Congress ratifies definitive treaty of peace with Great Britain.
1 March	Congress accepts Virginia deed ceding most of state's claims to Northwest Territory.

THE PAPERS OF

James Madison

From Jacquelin Ambler

RC (LC: Madison Papers). Cover missing. Docketed by JM, "May 3d. 1783."

RICHMOND VIRGA. 3. May 1783

DEAR SIR

Another Week is elapsed, and Mr. Newton has failed to forward the thousand pound Bill which he informed me is due to this State from some Gentlemen in Philad. & both he & the other Commissioners were anxious to pay into the Treasury.[1] I regret exceedingly having given you reason to expect it. You cannot be more disappointed than I am on this score. As the Assembly *should* meet the day after tomorrow I must conclude Mr. Newton means to bring up the Bill himself;[2] if he does, I know no mode so likely of your availing yourself soon of a part of the balance due you from the State than by drawing a greater proportion than others from that remittance.[3] I hint this because Mr. Jones will be here & expects to receive Money while at Richmond I am told, & most of the other Gentlemen are of so much shorter standing at Congress that I presume the State cannot be much if at all in arrears to them;[4] however you can judge better of this than I can & will write your sentiments freely. We are told several British Merchantmen are arrived but it seems they are not allowed to break bulk until the Law is repealed[5]

Yrs

J. A.

[1] For Colonel Thomas Newton, Jr., and the two other commissioners of the navy, see *Papers of Madison*, VI, 278, n. 3. The nature of the transaction is not known, but two bills of exchange of £500 were forwarded by Lacaze and Mallet of Philadelphia. See Ambler to JM, 17 May 1783, and n. 2.

[2] Although the Virginia General Assembly convened on 5 May and mustered its first quorum one week later, Colonel Newton, the delegate from Norfolk Borough, is not mentioned in the journal of the session until 2 June (Swem and Williams, *Register*, p. 18; *JHDV*, May 1783, pp. 3, 12, 30). By 17 May, Ambler had received from Newton two bills of exchange, each for £500 Virginia currency, which he mailed to JM on that day (Ambler to JM, 17 May; Statement of Receipts, 28 May 1783).

[3] This JM did. See Delegates to Auditors, 28 May 1783. The receipt was initialed by JM, Theodorick Bland, Jr., and John Francis Mercer. The balance due JM on that date in Virginia currency was £726 8*s*. 3*d*., or $2,420 (Statement of Receipts, 28 May 1783).

[4] Joseph Jones and Arthur Lee, the two other members of the Virginia delegation in Congress, were also delegates from King George County and Prince William

County, respectively, in the Virginia General Assembly (Swem and Williams, *Register*, p. 18). Jones first attended the May session on 20 May and Lee four days later (*JHDV*, May 1783, pp. 19, 21; Jones to JM, 25 May 1783). While in Richmond Jones probably received from Ambler his equitable proportion of the money available for the five delegates in Congress. For Lee in this regard, see Ambler to JM, 7 June 1783. In order of duration of service, their ranking was Jones, JM, Bland, Lee, and Mercer.

[5] For example, Governor Benjamin Harrison on 28 April had written to Commodore James Barron, Sr., to permit the British merchant ship "Hansford" to proceed to Smithfield, provided that no cargo should be discharged until authorization was granted by the naval officer at Hampton, Va. (Executive Letter Book, 1783–1786, p. 104, MS in Va. State Library). Convinced that the General Assembly would sanction a resumption of trade with the British, Harrison on 14 May issued to all the naval officers a general directive of the same tenor as that in his letter to Barron (*ibid*., p. 122). Ten days later the General Assembly repealed "All acts and ordinances prohibiting importation of British goods" (*JHDV*, May 1783, pp. 14, 20; Hening, *Statutes*, XI, 195). See also Randolph to JM, 9 May 1783, and n. 14.

Benjamin Harrison to Virginia Delegates

FC (Virginia State Library). In the hand of Thomas Meriwether, assistant clerk of the Council of State. Addressed to "Virginia Delegates in Congress."

RICHMOND May 3d. 1783.

GENTLEMEN

I duely received your favor of the 22d. of last Month, and anxiously wait for the News by the French Frigates,[1] a report prevails here that Lord Shelburne has said in the House of Lords that as there is no Time fixed by the Treaty for the evacuation of New York, he means not to do it till the Americans shall have given Satisfaction to the Refugees, can this possibly be true?[2]

British Vessels are arrived from the West Indies with valuable Cargoes which cannot be landed under our present Laws as I suppose there are some of them at Philadelphia you will oblige me by letting me know whether they are permitted to trade or not.[3]

Please to inform my Friend Charles Thomson that I will send him a Copy of the Cession of the back Country by the next Post and with it a Copy of another Resolution repealing it, which may perhaps be a lesson in future not to refuse a good Offer when Men are in the Humor for giving.[4]

I am Gentlemen with respect Yrs: &c.

B. H.

[1] *Papers of Madison,* VI, 479, and n. 3.

[2] In a debate of 17 February in the House of Lords on the terms of the preliminary articles of peace, the Earl of Shelburne is reported, with regard to the Loyalists ("Refugees"), only to have expressed deep regret at "the unhappy necessity of our affairs, which induced the extremity of submitting the fate of the property of these brave and worthy men to the discretion of their enemies" (*Hansard's Parliamentary Debates,* XXIII, cols. 411–13). According to the *Pennsylvania Packet* of 26 April, Richard Brinsley Sheridan spoke on 3 March 1783 in the House of Commons in favor of delaying the evacuation of New York City until the signing of the definitive treaty of peace gave the Loyalists added assurance that their confiscated property would be returned, but *Hansard's Parliamentary Debates* omits mention of a speech by him on that date. In the rumor referred to by Harrison, "Sheridan" may have become confused with "Shelburne." See also *Papers of Madison,* VI, 458, n. 3; 499; 500, n. 6.

[3] Ambler to JM, 3 May 1783, and n. 5. On 26 April 1783 a merchant vessel from New York City had apparently been permitted to unload her cargo at Philadelphia (*Papers of Madison,* VI, 471, n. 1).

[4] Except for this statement of intention, there appears to be no evidence that Governor Harrison sent to Charles Thomson, secretary of Congress, a copy of the resolutions of cession of 2 January 1781. For this offer, see Hening, *Statutes,* X, 564–67; *Papers of Madison,* V, 116; 117, n. 9; 118, nn. 14–17; 119, nn. 19–20; 290, n. 8; 292, n. 19. Before Harrison wrote to the delegates on 9 May (*q.v.*), he had been informed of his mistake in assuming that the Virginia General Assembly at its session of October 1782 had repealed the offer of cession. The governor's misapprehension illustrates the lack of communication between the legislative and executive branches of the government, partly resulting from delay in printing the laws. For the public printer's shortage of money and paper as late as 16 June 1783, see *JHDV,* May 1783, pp. 50, 60.

Thomas Walke to Virginia Delegates

RC (NA: PCC, No. 78, XXIV, 367–70). Addressed "To the Honble The Virginia Delegates in Congress." Docketed, "Letter from Thos Walke to the Delegates of Virga. May 3d 1783. Read May 8th, 1783 (copy of the within sent to the Commander in Chief Agreeably to an order of Congress of this day.)"

PHILADELPHIA May 3d 1783.

GENTLEMEN[1]

In consequence of the 7th: article of the treaty between America, and England;[2] I, with a number of others, have been to New-York; in order to reclaim our slaves that were wrested from us by the British enimy; supposing there cou'd be no obstacle to our recovering, at least such of the slaves as we cou'd find and prove to be our property, but contrary to our expectations, the event has proved the reverse, in as much as, that having discover'd the numberless difficulties attending this matter, we thought it most expedient to apply to Sir Guy Carlton, that through his means the business might be rendered more practicable, than we had before found it;[3] upon which application, we recieved for answer, from his aid de camp,[4] that no slaves were to be given up, who claimed the benefit of their former proclamations for liberating such slaves as threw themselves under the protection of the British government,[5] and that he thought it unnecessary for us to wait longer on business of that nature. This appears to me to be such a glareing piece of injustice, and open violation of the above mentioned article of the treaty, that I think it my duty as well as interest to acquaint you of this matter, that you may lay it before Congress, who will I flatter myself as speedily as possibly, take the necessary steps for preventing a further injury being done to the citizens of this country:[6] if there is not an immediate check put to the proceedings of the British General in this matter, the injury will be inconcieveable, as I am well assured several hundreds of the above mentioned slaves sailed during the last weik to Nova Scotia.[7] I am with the utmost respect and regard

Your Most Obedt. Servt:

THOS WALKE

1 Theodorick Bland, Joseph Jones, Arthur Lee, JM, and John Francis Mercer.

2 The relevant passage of the preliminary articles of peace, ratified by Congress on 15 April 1783, reads: "his Britannick Majesty shall, with all convenient speed, and without causing any destruction, or carrying away any negroes or other property of the American inhabitants, withdraw all his armies, garrisons and fleets from the said United States and from every port, place and harbour within the same" (*JCC*, XXIV, 249).

3 On 28 April 1783 Thomas Walke (*ca.* 1740–1797), a justice of the peace of Princess Anne County, Captain John Willoughby, Jr., sheriff of Norfolk County, and "others" submitted to General Sir Guy Carleton a "Memorial" on their own behalf and that of "sundry inhabitants" of the two counties, asking to be aided in recovering "at least 300 negroes" (*Norfolk Herald*, 6 Apr. 1797; *Papers of Madison*, V, 90, n. 2; Historical Manuscripts Commission, eds., *Report on American Manuscripts in the Royal Institution of Great Britain* [4 vols.; London, 1904–9], IV, 61–62; *Lower Norfolk County Virginia Antiquary*, I [1896], 17; *Va. Mag. Hist. and Biog.*, I [1893–94], 450; XV [1907–8], 187, 188, 192; XXVI [1918], 412–13). Walke was also a member of the House of Delegates from his county during most of the sessions from 1782 to 1788, and of the Virginia convention of 1788 which ratified the Constitution of the United States (Swem and Williams, *Register*, pp. 16, 20, 27, 29, 441). In a letter of 30 August 1782 Governor Benjamin Harrison informed the Virginia delegates in Congress that Willoughby had lost ninety slaves and was "thereby ruin'd" (*Papers of Madison*, V, 90, and n. 2; 111; 112, n. 2; 113; 148; *Cal. of Va. State Papers*, III, 266).

[4] Perhaps Major George Beckwith (1753–1823) (Fitzpatrick, *Writings of Washington*, XXVII, 240, n. 62; Worthington Chauncey Ford, comp., *British Officers Serving in the American Revolution, 1774–1783* [Brooklyn, N.Y., 1897], p. 26).

[5] On 30 June 1779 General Sir Henry Clinton, Carleton's immediate predecessor as commander-in-chief of the British military forces in North America, issued a proclamation in which "negro deserters" were "promised liberty to follow any occupation." In June 1782 Lieutenant General Alexander Leslie, commanding the British army in South Carolina and Georgia, promised freedom to the "many Negroes" who had rendered services to his troops (Historical Mauscripts Commission, eds., *Report on American Manuscripts*, I, 463; II, 544; Burnett, *Letters*, VII, 175–76).

While or soon after Walke and Willoughby were told not "to wait longer," Captain Hugh Walker, a merchant shipowner of Richmond and Urbanna, Middlesex County, came to Carleton's headquarters on a similar mission from Governor Harrison, and was also rebuffed (Historical Manuscripts Commission, eds., *Report on American Manuscripts*, IV, 39; *JCSV*, III, 246; McIlwaine, *Official Letters*, I, 34; III, 55). On his return to Virginia, Walker reported to Harrison, "I waited on Sir Guy Carleton's Secretary every Day, till I got the answer." Maurice Morgann, the "Secretary," continued Walker, told him "I was not allowed to take any slaves without their own concent; & they are taught not to come here" (*Cal. of Va. State Papers*, III, 491).

On 5 May, in compliance with instructions from Congress and also with a request from Harrison who had forwarded "a List and description of Negroes," Washington conferred with Carleton without much hope of enlisting his co-operation in recovering slaves. Carleton declared that "the 7th: article" obliged him to sequester, for return to their masters, only those Negroes who were still "*Property*" at the time of embarkation; that he could not violate the pledges of freedom made to the Negroes by "his Predecessors in Command," and that, unlike in the case of "archives, records, deeds and papers belonging to any of said states, or their citizens," he was not required by the seventh article to deliver the Negroes to the "persons to whom they belong." If, concluded Carleton, his interpretation was incorrect, the alleged owners of the slaves could seek reparations from "the Crown of Great Britain" through the normal diplomatic channels (Fitzpatrick, *Writings of Washington*, XXVI, 370, 402–6; *JCC*, XXIV, 249–50). The next day Washington, in a letter to Harrison, expressed his conviction "that the Slaves which have absconded from their Masters will never be restored to them. Vast numbers of them are already gone to Nova Scotia" (*Papers of Madison*, VI, 462, n. 2; 479; 480, n. 7; Fitzpatrick, *Writings of Washington*, XXVI, 364–65, 369–70, 401–6).

[6] On 8 May, upon receiving from the Virginia delegates the present letter, Congress ordered that a copy of it should be forwarded to Washington (JM Notes, 8 May; *JCC*, XXIV, 333). That copy was docketed by Lieutenant Colonel Jonathan Trumbull, Jr., military secretary of Washington, "Superceeded by Measures already taken" (Fitzpatrick, *Writings of Washington*, XXVI, 430, and n. 57).

[7] Walke had been correctly informed. A registry book, kept by Carleton's orders, reveals that Negroes were aboard ships leaving New York Harbor as early as 23 April and as late as 30 November 1783. The destination of many of these vessels was Halifax, Nova Scotia (Historical Manuscripts Commission, eds., *Report on American Manuscripts*, IV, 471). In the *Pennsylvania Packet* of 26 April, under a New York City date line of 19 April 1783, is a news item to the effect that British headquarters had warned all shipmasters against harboring Negroes, "without obtaining a legal right to them."

Virginia Delegates to Bernardo de Gálvez

Copy (Sección Cuba 2370, Archivo General de Indias, Seville). Addressed to "His Excellency don Bernardo de Galvez, Governor of the Havana." This copy, including the signatures and the enclosure, appears to have been made by a clerk. For a suggested explanation of the copy's origin, see n. 3.

EDITORIAL NOTE

Oliver Pollock, a merchant of New Orleans, had rendered important service to both Congress and Virginia as commercial agent. To pay for military supplies, Pollock had used his own money or loans secured by his notes from business acquaintances. By the spring of 1782 he desperately needed remuneration to satisfy his impatient creditors.

At the request of Governor Jefferson in 1779, Governor Gálvez, who was a friend of the American cause and of Pollock, had advanced him $74,087 from the Spanish provincial treasury. In the same year Jefferson authorized Pollock to draw bills for nearly $66,000 on Penet, d'Acosta Frères et Cie, the commercial agent of Virginia at Nantes, France. Unknown to Pollock, J. Pierre Penet by 1782 was bankrupt, partly at least because Virginia had been unable to furnish him with the cargoes of tobacco promised in return for his shipments of military matériel. In the meantime Pollock had drawn bills on the Penet Company and used them as security for the repayment of additional loans.

Threatened with suits by his creditors who were holding his worthless bills of exchange drawn on Penet, Pollock late in April 1782 was granted permission by Don Estavan Miró, who was acting as governor in Gálvez' absence, to go to Richmond and Philadelphia to seek payment by the Virginia General Assembly and by Congress. Both bodies already had acknowledged their heavy indebtedness to Pollock, but neither they nor he knew the exact sums owed. Some of his vouchers had been lost; some of his consignments evidently had been priced in specie, others in paper currency; some goods shipped on the continental account had been diverted to the use of Virginia and vice versa; and some had been forwarded to military or civilian officials of Virginia in the Ohio country who had no legal authority to order them. Adding to the baffling complexity, some of the bills of exchange issued by Pollock had been purchased by Simon Nathan. These two men, being creditors of the bankrupt Penet Company, expected its debtor, Virginia, to cover their losses. See NA: PCC, No. 50, fols. 285, 331; *Papers of Madison*, I, 277, n. 7; III, 98; 99, n. 1; 256, n. 1; IV, 349, and n. 5; James Alton James, *Oliver Pollock: The Life and Times of an Unknown Patriot* (New York, 1937), pp. 74, 81, 270–72, 276; Lawrence Kinnaird, ed., *Spain in the Mississippi Valley, 1765–1794* (3 vols.; Washington, 1946–49), II, 8–12; John Walton Caughey, *Bernardo de Gálvez in Louisiana, 1776–1783* (Berkeley, Calif., 1934), pp. 85–93, 98.

From August 1782, when he arrived in Philadelphia, until the date of the present letter, Pollock found that the controversial nature of many of his claims and the empty state of both the continental and Virginia treasuries combined to thwart him from gaining immediate cash payments. On 31 October 1782 President John Hanson wrote Miró that Congress was well disposed toward Pollock and would deal justly with him "as soon as possible." About four months later President Elias Boudinot affirmed this promise by sending Miró a duplicate of Hanson's letter. In Richmond, where Pollock tarried for almost three months, the legislature adjourned on 28 December 1782 after adopting the resolution, of which a copy was enclosed in the present letter, postponing further action upon his claim until the session of May 1783. By then the report of the commissioners on western accounts, including their judgment of the validity of many of Pollock's bills, would probably have been submitted. Also the Virginia delegates in Congress were expected to gain from Pollock, who had returned to Philadelphia in February, adequate guarantees to assure Virginia against paying twice the sum covered by the protested bills of exchange which he had drawn on the Penet Company and given as security for loans from businessmen in New Orleans.

In their letter of 29 April 1783, the delegates informed Governor Harrison, "Mr. Pollock has declined offering any security for the present, as he expects the returned Bills themselves, which he says will be the best Vouchers in his power to give." In other words Virginia obviously would not assume for payment the amount of the bills of exchange unless they were surrendered to her treasury. Only Pollock's creditors in New Orleans, who held these bills, could submit them. Virginia, therefore, was amply protected against any claim by him in their regard. See Lawrence Kinnaird, ed., *Spain in the Mississippi Valley*, II, 55, 63–64, 71, 75–76; *Papers of Madison*, III, 345, n. 5; V, 208, n. 5; 287, n. 19; 455, n. 10; VI, 474; 475, nn. 3–5; 476, n. 6; 478, n. 3; 502; *JCC*, XXIV, 149, n. 1, 234–38; James A. James, *Oliver Pollock*, pp. 276, n. 9, 280, 282, 288; John W. Caughey, *Bernardo de Gálvez*, pp. 99–100.

PHILADA. May 4th. 1783

SIR

We have the honor of Enclosing to your Excellency[1] a Resolution of the General Assembly of our State, by which your Excellency will see that the Accounts of Mr. Oliver Pollock, are Liquadated, and the balance put into a due Course of payment.[2]

We think it proper to give your Excellency this Information for the benefit of such of the subjects of the King of Spain as are in Possession of the Bills drawn by the said Mr Pollock on Penette, Dacosta, Freres & Co[.] these Bills will be paid agreeable to the Inclosed Resolve, upon thier being presented at the Treasury of Virginia.

We beg leave to recommend Mr Pollock to your Excellency's protection, as one who has suffer'd much and who has discharged his duty both to the Publick & to his Creditors with Zeal & Integrity

We have the honor to be with sentiment of the highest respect Your Excellencys Most Obedient and Humble Servts.

(Copy) Sign'd
ARTHUR LEE
J. MADISON JUR.
THEOD. BLAND JR
JOHN F. MERCER
delegates in Congress from the State of Virginia[3]

[1] When the present letter was written, the positions held by Don Bernardo de Gálvez (*ca.* 1746–1786) were far more impressive than merely "Governor of the Havana." Ever since early in 1777, after military service in Europe, Africa, and against the Indians in Louisiana, he had been the governor of that province. On 12 November 1781, in recognition of his success in capturing Pensacola from the British and driving them from the rest of West Florida, Charles III of Spain issued him a patent of nobility, promoted him to the rank of lieutenant general, and added West Florida to the vast area of which he was governor. In May 1782, although the decisive naval victory of Sir George Brydges Rodney on 9–12 April in the Battle of the Saints had effectively ruined Gálvez' plan to mount an expedition against the British in Jamaica, he brought the Bahama Islands under the flag of Spain.

At the time of the Virginia delegates' letter to Gálvez, he had sailed, or was about to sail, for Spain. When he finally reached Havana again on 4 February 1784, he was captain general of Cuba as well as the governor of Louisiana and West Florida. Early the next year he became viceroy of New Spain with his seat of authority in Mexico City. His residence in Mexico began with his arrival at Vera Cruz on 21 May 1785 and closed with his death from fever on 30 November 1786 (John W. Caughey, *Bernardo de Gálvez*, pp. 61–68, 210–11, 214, 244–46, 251, 252, and n. 36, 253, 257; *Papers of Madison*, I, 218, n. 6; II, 39 and n. 1; 110, n. 2; III, 83, n. 1; 183, n. 21; IV, 36, n. 16; 113, n. 6; 239, n. 14).

[2] By "Liquadated," the delegates meant that the "Resolution" embodied only a schedule for payments by Virginia to Pollock. Assuming that the resolution quoted below is an accurate copy of the enclosure by the delegates and that they had faithfully reproduced the copy received by them from Governor Harrison, the latter varies occasionally in phraseology, as well as in abbreviations, punctuation, and capitalization, but not in meaning, from the resolution entered in the journal of the House of Delegates (*JHDV*, Oct. 1782, pp. 83–84; *Papers of Madison*, VI, 13; 15, n. 5; 474; 475, n. 5).

IN THE HOUSE OF DELEGATES

The 27th Decem: 1782

Resolv'd, that the Accounts of Oliver Pollock be liquidated agreeable to the recommendation of the Executive upon the Settlement made by their Commissioners, Sampson Mathews and Merriwether Smith Esqrs. and paid in Manner following. ten Thousand Dollars immediately, and Certificates passed for the remainder of his Accounts bearing Interest at the rate of six pCent per annum to wit, ten Thousand dollars payable the first day of January, One thousand seven Hundred & eighty four, Ten thousand Dollars the first day of January, One Thousand seven Hundred and Eighty five and the Ballance in Certificates with the like Interest payable in four years from the date thereof Provided that the Issuing of Certificates for one half the Amount of the said Accounts be postponed untill the said Oliver Pollock finds such security as may be approved of by the delegates representing this State in Congress for the Indemnification of the state from any demand for the bills drawn by him on Penette, Dacosta, Freres & Coy.

Test

JOHN BECKLY C H D

1782 Decem: 28th
Agreed to by the Senate
Will. Drew Ck. a Copy

Test

For the commissioners on western accounts, including Matthews and Smith, see *Papers of Madison*, II, 40, n. 2; III, 329, n. 3; 345, n. 5; IV, 378, n. 5; V, 263; 265, n. 9; *JCSV*, III, 188. The stipulation about paying Pollock "ten thousand Dollars immediately" was delusive, for he discovered by calling upon Jacquelin Ambler, the treasurer, that "I could not get as much as paid my expenses to Virginia" (Lawrence Kinnaird, ed., *Spain in the Mississippi Valley*, II, 77–78). The editorial note above explains why the resolution closed with a proviso. See also n. 3. For John Beckley and William Drew, the clerks, respectively, of the House of Delegates and the Senate of the Virginia General Assembly, see *Papers of Madison*, II, 318, n. 2.

3 The delegates gave their letter and its enclosure to Pollock for delivery, upon his return to New Orleans or Havana, to Gálvez. Two days before the date of the letter. Congress resolved that "as soon as the situation of the finances will permit," Pollock should be paid as much of his claim as had already been authenticated, except the $74,087 loaned him by Governor Gálvez from the Spanish treasury at New Orleans (ed. note). At the same time, Congress instructed Robert Morris to ascertain from New Orleans whether Gálvez had advanced that money to enable Pollock to provide military supplies for the United States or for Virginia (*JCC*, XXIV, 323). On 8 May Congress agreed to hang on the wall of its meeting room Pollock's gift of a portrait of Gálvez, "an early and zealous friend of the U. S." (NA: PCC, No. 50, fol. 289; *JCC*, XXIV, 333, and n. 2). Although refusing on 22 April, in spite of the unanimous vote of the delegates of Virginia and five other states, to pay Pollock $10,000 for his five years' labors as commercial agent at New Orleans, Congress eight days later rewarded him with half that sum for his "extra-ordinary services." On 30 May without a recorded vote, Congress appointed him to be the unsalaried American commercial agent "at the port of Havannah" (*JCC*, XXIV, 266, 318, 372, 376–77).

Pollock delayed his departure from the United States until early in August. By then he almost certainly knew that on 25 June the Virginia General Assembly had instructed the treasurer "until further orders" to cash none of the warrants which had been issued to him. Ill fortune pursued him to Cuba. Upon arriving there in mid-August, he found not only that Gálvez was in Spain but that he could expect few commissions as commercial agent because the port of Havana was closed to all foreign shipping. On 18 August Pollock wrote to Governor Miró at New Orleans, enclosing what apparently is the present copy of the Virginia delegates' letter and its enclosure. In his acknowledgment of 18 October 1783 Miró blamed Pollock for not recognizing while in the United States that one of his "principal and most sacred obligations" had been to assure the repayment of those "generous citizens" of New Orleans who, by lending money on the security of bills of exchange drawn on the Penet Company, "have suffered enough by bearing with you for the long time of four years." Miró apparently did not realize that the promises to pay, which were almost all that Pollock had been able to gain in Philadelphia and Richmond, applied to his creditors in New Orleans as well as to himself. The Virginia General Assembly had agreed to honor the bills on Penet as soon as their holders presented them in person or through their authorized agent. See ed. note above; also, Harrison to Speaker of the House of Delegates, 5 May 1783, in Executive Letter Book, 1783–1786, pp. 110–11, MS in Va. State Library; *JHDV*, May 1783, pp. 83, 85; Lawrence Kinnaird, ed., *Spain in the Mississippi Valley*, II, 77–78, 87–88, 91–92; James A. James, *Oliver Pollock*, pp. 280–92, 297, and n. 1, 306, n. 16, 335–37, and nn., 346. From 9 January to 10 November 1783, inclusive, Virginia paid to Pollock £3,608 9*s*. 10*d*. (Treasurer's Book or Account of Payments Made Publick Creditors by the Treasurer, Jany. 1783 to Decr. 1785, unpaginated MS in Va. State Library).

From Edmund Pendleton

RC (Historical Society of Pennsylvania). Cover missing.

VIRGA.[1] May 4. 1783

DEAR SIR

I am now to acknowledge the rect. of yr. two favrs. of the 8th. & 22d. past,[2] Mr. Jones being, as I suppose from his letter, by this time in Virginia: this circumstance will increase your trouble, but I must reiterate former injunctions, that when it will be particularly inconvenient to you to write, you make free in leaving me unaddressed.[3] The doubt whether the War is discontinued until the signing of the definitive treaty, has reached our Executive, & suspended the admitting to Entry a British Ship arrived here, until that event, or until our Assembly, who meet tomorrow, shall alter the Law.[4] we are told that an embargo on all ships for America, is laid in London, probably on Acct. of this doubt, tho' that circumstance, & their manifesting no preparation for the evacuation of New-York, excites Suspicions of some intentions not honourable on their part.[5] Congress will no doubt be on their guard, & I hope the Assemblies will not take up the Subject of the Treaty in any part until it has it's definitive force.[6]

I am sorry to hear that Congress in the final adjustment of their plan have rejected any thing wch. had a tendancy to sooth the Minds of our Assembly, who I am afraid wanted not provocatives to relish the whole but badly:.[7] I find a fix'd Aversion in some Gentn. to putting an independent Revenue into the hands of Congress, which say they, is necessary for no other purpose than to give them the appointment of a number of Officers dependent on them, & so to gain an undue Influence in the States: besides that the Nature of Man & former experience justifies a suspicion that a Number of unnecessary Offices may be created, to make room for Relations and favourites, by wch. much of the Revenue may be diverted from the payment of our debts. The impost they approve, but can't be perswaded but that it may be collected & remitted to the Continental Treasury, by our Naval Officers & Treasurer, without the Intervention of any new Officer.[8] these are the sentiments of most of the few Members[9] I have conversed wth., what will be the result of a full discussion of the Subject, I can't pretend to foretel, but you'l perceive it was rather unlucky for the Plan, to withhold any part that had an aspect favourable to Us. My hopes of any thing good from that unhappy youth C. T., have been for some time at an end, & therefore I am the less affected by his last Imprudent step, for such I have no doubt it will turn out to be.[10] I am

My Dr. Sir Yr. mo. Affe. & Obt.

EDMD PENDLETON

[1] Edmund Pendleton had arrived in Richmond on 25 April (*Papers of Madison*, VI, 500; 501, n. 10).

[2] These "favrs" are missing, but at least some of their contents, according to Pendleton's remarks in the present letter, were very similar to those in JM's letters to Randolph on the same dates (*Papers of Madison*, VI, 439–40; 483).

[3] Joseph Jones apparently left Philadelphia on the evening of 6 May to return to Virginia (JM to Randolph, 6 May 1783). He and JM customarily alternated week by week in writing to Pendleton, but when Jones was in Virginia or was ill, his turn was taken by JM (*Papers of Madison*, V, 97; 98, n. 12; 157; 192–93; 194, n. 2).

[4] *Ibid.*, VI, 471, n. 1; 481; 500, n. 6; Ambler to JM, 3 May, and n. 5; Harrison to Delegates, 3 May 1783.

[5] Pendleton probably either read or heard a rumor set afoot by the *Maryland Gazette* (Annapolis) of 1 May, which printed an extract of a purported letter from Lorient, dated 14 March 1783, stating that "An embargo is laid in England upon all the vessels which were fitting out for America, of which there were many, till the treaty of commerce is settled, or till it is known they will be admitted into the ports of the United States." The last British troops did not leave New York City until 25 November 1783.

[6] That is, until the definitive treaty became effective. It was signed by the representatives of Great Britain and the United States on 3 September 1783, ratified by Congress on 14 January 1784, by George III on 9 April 1784, and ratifications exchanged on 12 May 1784 (Wharton, *Revol. Dipl. Corr.*, VI, 673–74, 756, 806). The official news of the exchange reached Charles Thomson, secretary of Congress, on 27 July of that year (Burnett, *Letters*, VII, 575).

[7] *Papers of Madison*, VI, 481; 482, nn. 10, 11; 483.

[8] The plan for restoring public credit, which had been adopted by Congress on 18 April, was not sent to the executive of each state until 9 May. The plan recommended a schedule of duties on specific imports, to be collected by men "appointed by the states, within which their offices are to be respectively exercised" (*JCC*, XXIV, 257–58; Burnett, *Letters*, VII, 160–61). See also *Papers of Madison*, VI, 311–14. A naval officer supervised shipping in each of the seven districts comprising tidewater Virginia. There were also three deputy naval officers (McIlwaine, *Official Letters*, III, 355–56; Hening, *Statutes*, XI, 258–64).

[9] That is, of the Virginia General Assembly. See Ambler to JM, 3 May 1783, n. 2.

[10] Craddock Taylor (*Papers of Madison*, II, 262, and n. 1). The name of Taylor's wife and the date and place of the marriage have not been determined. See Pendleton to JM, 16 June 1783.

Notes on Debates

MS (LC: Madison Papers). For a description of the manuscript of Notes on Debates and a discussion of JM's reasons for recording what was said and done in Congress, see *Papers of Madison*, V, 231–34.

No. XIV[1]

Monday May 5.

Mr. Bland & Mr. Mercer moved to erase from the Journal the resolution of Friday the 2d. inst. applying for an addition of three Millions to the grant of six millions by H. M. Xn Majesty, as in part of the loan of four Millions requested by the Resolution of Sepr. 14. 1782.[2] As the resolution of the 2d. had been passed by fewer than nine States, they contended that it was unconstitutional. The reply was that as the three Millions were to be part of a loan heretofore authorized, the sanction of nine States was not necessary.[3] The motion was negatived The two movers alone voting in the Affirmative.[4]

[1] For a probable explanation of this Roman numeral, see *Papers of Madison*, V, 231.

[2] *JCC*, XXIII, 577–79; XXIV, 325–26; *Papers of Madison*, V, 127; 129, nn. 8–10. His Most Christian Majesty was Louis XVI of France.

[3] The journal of 2 May does not record the vote whereby Congress adopted the resolution offered by Alexander Hamilton and seconded by James Wilson. JM was absent from Congress on that day (*Papers of Madison*, VI, 498, and n. 2). To "borrow money on the credit of the united states" was one of the twelve powers granted to Congress which, according to the ninth article of the Articles of Confederation, required for their exercise the affirmative vote of at least nine state delegations. By the same article, "a question on any other point, except for adjourning from day to day" depended for an affirmative answer upon the concurrence of only seven state delegations (*JCC*, XIX, 220). On 28 February 1783 Congress had taken an opposite stand on a similar issue (*Papers of Madison*, VI, 301, and nn. 2, 4).

[4] The journal records that Benjamin Hawkins of North Carolina also voted "ay." Only eight states were effectively represented in Congress when the tally was taken (*JCC*, XXIV, 328–29).

Notes on Debates

MS (LC: Madison Papers). For a description of the manuscript of Notes on Debates, see *Papers of Madison*, V, 231–34.

Tuesday May 6.

A motion was made by Mr. Lee, to recommend to the several States to pass laws indemnifying Officers of the Army for damages sustained by individuals from Acts of such officers rendered necessary in the execution of their military functions: It was referred to Mr. Lee, Mr. Williamson & Mr. Clarke.[1]

He proposed also that an Equestrian Statue should be erected to General Washington[2]

A report from the Secy. of For: Affairs of a Treaty of Commerce to be entered into with G. Britain, was referred to Mr. Fitzimmons, Mr. Higginson, Mr. Rutlidge, Mr. Hemsley, & Mr. Madison[3]

[1] During the war Congress occasionally empowered continental officers to impress food, vehicles, and other military supplies, even though many of the delegates had doubted the constitutionality of those authorizations. On 18 May 1781, for example, Congress adopted JM's motion directing Brigadier General Anthony Wayne, in case of need, to impress "provisions and forage," and "report the amount thereof to the executives of the states within which the same shall be taken" (*Papers of Madison*, III, 124, and n. 2). See also *ibid.*, III, 227–28, 229, n. 10; 326, n. 5; IV, 72, n. 2; 287.

Although the right to impress might be inferred from the war power delegated by Articles VI and IX of the Articles of Confederation, Congress had no courts in which citizens, aggrieved because they had been deprived of property for military use, could sue the impressment officers. Only the states had the power to render these officers immune from prosecution for damages. For the report of the Lee committee, see JM Notes, 7 May. See also *Papers of Madison*, IV, 91–92; Instruction to Delegates, 4 June 1783, n. 1.

[2] *JCC*, XXIV, 330, and n. 1. See also JM to Randolph, 12 August 1783.

[3] In a dispatch of 5 February 1783 from Paris to Robert R. Livingston, John Adams discussed various aspects of United States foreign relations, especially the advisability of concluding a treaty of commerce with Great Britain (Wharton, *Revol. Dipl. Corr.*, VI, 242–47). See also *Papers of Madison*, V, 476, and nn. 1, 2; 477, nn. 4, 5; VI, 452–53, and n. 7; JM to Jefferson, 6 May 1783, and n. 5. In accordance with Alexander Hamilton's report of 29 April on behalf of a committee appointed the day before to consider Adams' dispatch, Congress on 1 May "*Ordered*, That a commission be prepared" authorizing Adams, Franklin, and Jay to negotiate a treaty, subject to revision by Congress, "and in the mean time to enter into a commercial convention" of one year's duration. Congress also adopted the committee's recommendation by instructing Livingston to "lay before Congress, without delay, a plan of a treaty of commerce and instructions relative to the same" for transmittal to the three commissioners (NA: PCC, No. 186, fol. 97; *JCC*, XXIV, 320–21). Upon receiving Livingston's "plan" and "instructions" on 6 May, Congress referred them to the FitzSimons' committee (NA: PCC, No. 185, III, 64). Its report of 19 June was evidently tabled. On 15 August 1783, eleven days before discharging this committee as reconstituted on 5 August, Congress transferred its assignment to a new committee, of which neither FitzSimons nor JM was a member (NA: PCC, No. 186, fols. 99, 116, 118; *JCC*, XXIV, 404–5).

To Theodorick Bland

MS (Virginia State Library). On the same small page, above JM's receipt for pay as a delegate, appears one signed by Joseph Jones on behalf of himself and John Francis Mercer, and another signed by Arthur Lee. On a second small page, which originally may have been joined with the other to form a single folio, Bland wrote his own receipt, followed by: "The Auditors will be pleased to debit the delegates respectively for the sums opposite to their names in the Margin and to Issue Warrants for the same to the treasurer." In the left margin Bland listed \$332 15/90 for Lee, Madison, and himself, respectively, and \$664 30/90 for Jones, who was to give one-half of that amount to Mercer. Below Bland's writing, Jacquelin Ambler, the treasurer of Virginia, made two one-line entries which apparently are irrelevant to the present item. See Statement of Receipts, 28 May 1783, hdn. The auditors were John Boush, Harrison Randolph, and Bolling Stark.

May 6. 1783

Recd. of Col: Bland three hundred thirty two dollars fifteen ninteenths, being one fifth of five hundred pounds Virginia Currency remitted in a bill drawn by David Ross of Virga. on John Ross of Philada. in favor of J. Madison & by him endorsed to Col: Bland,

J Madison Jr.[1]

---

[1] *Papers of Madison*, VI, 473; 474, n. 1. In the Charles Campbell Collection of Theodorick Bland Papers in the Virginia Historical Society is an undated document written by Bland and entitled: "Copy of Receipts from the Gentn. of the Delegation for their Proportion of a Bill of 500£ Virga. Currency drawn by D: Ross on J: Ross in favor of J. Madison—& remitted by J: Ambler Esqr. treasurer for the use of the delegates which Bill was negotiated by me T. B." Below this title Bland copied for his own records the receipts and the request to the auditors mentioned in the headnote. Bland docketed his retained copy: "Copy of Rects. & memdms. the original delivd. to the Honble J: Madison to be transmitted to the treasy." Joseph Jones, who left Philadelphia on either 6 or 7 May to return to Virginia, may have carried the recipient's copy of these receipts to Richmond and delivered them to Ambler (JM to Randolph, 6 May 1783).

Since each of the five delegates received \$332 15/90 (\$332.17), they together were paid \$1,660.83, even though at the exchange rate of 3⅓ to 1 the total of the £500 bill of exchange was \$1,666.67. The discount was therefore \$5.83—a fee assumed, proportionately, by the delegates rather than *in toto* by the treasury of Virginia. See Statement of Receipts, 28 May 1783.

Virginia Delegates to Benjamin Harrison

RC (Historical Society of Pennsylvania). Cover missing. Docketed, "Lr. from the Delegs: in Congress: May 6th. 1783." Although only JM signed it, he obviously was writing on behalf of all members of the delegation.

PHILADA. 6. May 1783.

SIR

Your Excellency's favor of the 25th. Ulto.[1] came duly to hand yesterday. A commercial intercourse is under present circumstances carried on freely from other States with our late Enemy, and as far as an advantage can be drawn from it, Virginia must certainly be equally entitled to share in it.[2]

Congress have recd. no further intelligence relative to the final treaty of peace, nor any other material intelligence from Europe.

The plan to be recommended to the states for funding the national debt, has been at length concluded, and with the documents proper to explain & urge it, will be forwarded as soon as the whole can be duly prepared.[3]

We inclose your Excelly. a letter addressed to us from Coulougnac & Cie, representing their transactions with Penet.[4]

We have the honor to be with sentiments of due respect Yr. Exclly's Obt. & hbl serts.

J. MADISON JR.

[1] Not found. Perhaps Archibald Blair, clerk of the Council of State, was absent, and for that reason the letter was not "registered" in the Executive Letter Book, MS in Va. State Library.

[2] *Papers of Madison,* VI, 471, and n. 1; 481; 499; 500, n. 6; Ambler to JM, 3 May, and n. 5; Harrison to Delegates, 3 May 1783.

[3] *Papers of Madison,* VI, 471; 473, n. 7; 488; 494, n. 1. Elias Boudinot, president of Congress, forwarded the "plan" and "the documents" on 9 May 1783 (Burnett, *Letters,* VII, 160–61).

[4] The letter of Coulignac et Cie to the delegates has not been found, but judging from the references to it by Harrison in his letter of 29 May 1783 to the company, the Coulignac firm in Nantes was again seeking reimbursement by Virginia of money loaned in 1780 to Penet, d'Acosta Frères et Cie for the purchase of military supplies ordered by Governor Jefferson on behalf of his state (Harrison to Coulignac and Company, 29 May, in Executive Letter Book, 1783–1786, pp. 140–41, MS in Va. State Library). Harrison enclosed this letter in his letter to the delegates on 31 May 1783 (*q.v.*).

Subsequent to the bankruptcy of Penet in 1782, the remaining partners of his commercial company and Louis Auly (Lewis Abraham Pauly) also claimed that they had helped to finance the same shipments as those for which Coulignac and Company loaned money. For the background and amount of these claims, see *Papers of Madison*, VI, 342, and n. 1; 353; 412–13; 413, n. 3; 414–15 nn.; also *Cal. of Va. State Papers*, III, 260, 390; Harrison to Thomas Barclay, 29 Mar. and 10 May 1783 in Executive Letter Book, 1783–1786, pp. 83–86, 121–22, MS in Va. State Library.

To Thomas Jefferson

RC (LC: Madison Papers). Address on cover is no longer legible, except for "Thomas Jefferson Esqr." Docketed by him, "Madison Jas. May 6 1783."

On the verso of the cover Jefferson deciphered the passages written in the JM-Jefferson Code No. 2, and here italicized. This code was first used by Jefferson in his letter of 14 April 1783 to JM (*Papers of Madison*, VI, 459). In his old age JM docketed the page, "decypher of letter May 6. 1783."

PHILADA. May 6. 1783.

DEAR SIR

Your favor of the 21. Ult.[1] written at Col: Pendleton's[2] was brought to hand by the post of last week. Col: Floyd's family did not set out untill the day after it was received. I accompanied them as far as Brunswick, about 60 miles from this, and returned hither on friday evening.[3] Mr. Jones will attend the Assembly, and proposes to begin his journey this afternoon, if the present rain should cease. Mr. Lee also means to set out for the same purpose in a few days.[4]

Congress have received a long and curious epistle from Mr. Adams dated in February addressed to the president not to the secretary for foreign affairs.[5] *He animadverts on the revocation of his commission for a treaty of commerce with Great Britain*[,][6] *presses the appointment of a minister to that court with such a commission*[,] *draws a picture of a fit character in which his own likeness is ridiculously and palpable studi*[e]*d*[,] *finaly praising and recomending Mr. Jay for the appointment provided injustice must be done to an older servant.*[7]

Letters from the Marquis de la Fayette and Mr. Carmichael shew that the Court of Spain has become pretty tractable since the acknowledgment of our Independence by G. B. The latter has been treated with due respect, and the Court has agreed to accede to the territorial limit fixed for W. Florida in the provisional Articles. The navigation of the Mississippi remains to be settled.[8]

My absence from Congs. the past week disables me from giving you the exact information of their latest proceedings.[9] I am told that in consequence of *Mr. A—— letter the secretary of foreign affairs has been instructed to project a treaty of commerce with Great Britain* which will *probable bring the attention of Congress to the general department of foreign affairs*[10]

Under the same cover with this are two letters for Miss Patsy[,] one from Mrs. Trist, and the other from Miss Floyd[11] with the copy of a song. I beg that my compliments may be accepted along with them.

I am Dear Sir your sincere friend

J. MADISON JR.

[1] Not found.

[2] At Edmundsbury, the estate of Edmund Pendleton. He had been the colonel of the militia of Caroline County in 1772 (David John Mays, *Edmund Pendleton, 1721–1803* [2 vols.; Cambridge, Mass., 1952], I, 266; T[homas] E. Campbell, *Colonial Caroline: A History of Caroline County, Virginia* [Richmond, 1954], p. 370).

[3] *Papers of Madison*, VI, 498, and n. 2. Early in the war William Floyd had served as a colonel of militia (E[dmund] B. O'Callaghan and B[erthold] Fernow, eds., *Documents Relative to the Colonial History of the State of New-York* [15 vols.; Albany, 1853–87], XV, 287).

[4] Ambler to JM, 3 May, n. 4; Pendleton to JM, 4 May 1783, n. 3. Arthur Lee left Philadelphia on the afternoon of 12 May to return to Virginia (*JCC*, XXIV, 339; JM to Randolph, 13 May 1783).

[5] JM Notes, 6 May 1783, and n. 3. JM was misinformed. John Adams' letter of 5 February was addressed to Robert R. Livingston, secretary for foreign affairs (NA: PCC, No. 104, IV, 347–55). See also Wharton, *Revol. Dipl. Corr.*, VI, 242–47; JM to Jefferson, 13 May 1783.

[6] The resolution of 12 July 1781, revoking Adams' commission and instructions of 27–28 September 1779 for negotiating a treaty of commerce with Great Britain, had been drafted by JM (*Papers of Madison*, III, 188, and nn. 1, 2; 189, nn. 6, 16). See also JM to Jefferson, 10 June 1783.

[7] Although JM obviously meant "palpably" rather than "palpable," he found no cipher for "bly" in the code. He underlined the four ciphers required to encode the word "provided." Adams named Francis Dana second only to John Jay as the best qualified minister to be sent by Congress to "the court of Great Britain, provided that injustice must be finally done to him who was the first object of his country's choice" (Wharton, *Revol. Dipl. Corr.*, VI, 246).

[8] Unnoted in the journal, Congress on 25 April had received from William Carmichael, chargé d'affaires at the court of Madrid, five dispatches, and also Lafayette's letter of 2 March to Livingston, enclosing copies of his correspondence with José Moñino y Redondo (1728–1808), Conde de Floridablanca, prime minister of Spain and minister of foreign affairs (NA: PCC, No. 185, III, 63). In his dispatch of 21 February, Carmichael reported that the court of Charles III had at last received him "formally as the *chargé des affaires* of the United States," thanks largely to Lafayette's influence and that of Armand Marc, Comte de Montmorin Saint Hérem, the French ambassador in Madrid.

Lafayette in his letter of 2 March, after describing his own activities during his stay of about a week in or near Madrid, added: "Mississippi is the great affair. I think it is in the interest of America to be well with Spain, at least for many years, and particularly on account of the French alliance; so that I very much wish success to Mr. Jay's negociations. I have advised Mr. Carmichael to continue his conferences, and I think they will be of service." In an audience with Charles III, Lafayette was assured: "With respect to the limits, his Catholic majesty has adopted those that are determined by the preliminaries of the 30th of November, between the United States and the court of London. The fear of raising an object of dissensions is the only objection the king has to the free navigation of the river Mississippi." On 22 February, in the presence of the French ambassador, Lafayette induced Floridablanca to give "his word of honor" (which later proved to be fragile) that he would not oppose "the general principle" of the boundaries "established by the treaty between the English and Americans" (Wharton, *Revol. Dipl. Corr.*, VI, 256–57, 259–61, 268–70; Louis Gottschalk, *Lafayette and the Close of the American Revolution* [Chicago, 1942], pp. 397–99, 405–13). See also Wharton, *Revol. Dipl. Corr.*, V, 710–11, 783–85; VI, 184–87, 215–18.

9 See references cited in n. 3.

10 This statement makes clear that JM wrote this letter before Congress convened on 6 May. See JM Notes, 6 May 1783, and n. 3. For the final syllable of "probable," see n. 7, above.

11 Miss Martha Jefferson, Mrs. Nicholas Trist, and probably Miss Maria Floyd rather than her sister, Catherine. See *Papers of Madison*, VI, 182, n. 28; 222, n. 16; 234–35; 235, n. 2; 255, and n. 1.

To Edmund Randolph

RC (LC: Madison Papers). Unsigned but in JM's hand. Cover franked by "J. Madison Jr." and addressed by him to "Edmund Randolph Esqr. Richmond." Docketed by Randolph, "J. Madison, 6th. May 1783." Many years later JM or someone at his bidding placed a bracket at the close of the fourth paragraph, probably to designate that the letter to that point should be published in the first comprehensive edition of JM's papers. See Madison, *Papers* (Gilpin ed.), I, 529–30. Henry D. Gilpin, without using ellipses, excised all the first sentence of the second paragraph after the words "Mr. Adams." This omission may have conformed with Dolley Madison's wishes, expressed after her husband's death in 1836. See *Papers of Madison*, I, xvii.

PHILADA. 6 May. 1783.

MY DEAR FRIEND

After a silence of 4 weeks your favor of the 26. Ult: was particularly welcome.[1] Your conjecture was but too well founded as to the compiler of the Proclamation. The offensive passages were adverted to by some, but the general eagerness on the occasion, increased by some unavoidable delays, rendered all attempts to draw the attention of Congress to smaller inaccuracies unacceptable.[2]

We have no late despatches from Paris, except a letter from Mr. Adams which affords a new & signal exemplification of those qualities which have so much distinguished his correspondence with Congress.[3]

We are informed from Madrid by Mr. Carmichael & the Marquis de la Fayette, that that Court, since the British acknowledgmt. of our Independence has dismissed its hauteur & reserve towards the U. S. has treated the American Chargé d'Affaires with due attention & has signified its acquiescence in the limits fixed by the provisional articles between the U. S. & G. B. The navigation of the Mississippi remains to be discussed.[4]

Yesterday was fixed for an interview between Genl. W. and Sr. G. Carlton for the purpose of taking arrangements for carrying the stipulations of the provisional articles into effect. The interview was proposed by the former, who intimated that as the evacuation of the post of N. Y. was particularly interesting to the State of N. Y., Govr. Clinton would accompany him on the interview.[5] The answer of Carlton imputed that he did not decline the proposition, but suggested that as Genl. Gray was expected with final orders it might be best to postpone the conference; adding that he should be attended by *Lt. Govr. Elliott* and *Chief Justice Smith*.[6]

The sample you give of the new Assembly is a flattering one.[7] The plan of revenue with an address & sundry documents enforcing it is in the press & will soon be ready for them.[8] Mr. Jones proposes to set out this evening, & will make but a very short stay at home. Mr. Lee enters on his journey tomorrow & proceeds without a halt to Richmond.[9]

[1] Randolph's duties as attorney general of Virginia, and probably his efforts to reach an accommodation with his father's creditors, explain why his customary weekly letters had not been written to JM between 31 March and 26 April 1783. See *Papers of Madison*, VI, 415; 416, nn. 1, 3; Pendleton to JM, 4 May 1783, n. 1.

[2] On 11 April 1783 Congress adopted the proclamation of a "cessation of arms," of which Robert R. Livingston, secretary for foreign affairs, was the draftsman (*Papers of Madison*, VI, 450, and n. 1; 451, n. 4; 499).

[3] JM to Jefferson, 6 May 1783, and nn. 5–7.

[4] *Ibid.*, 6 May 1783, and n. 8.

[5] For the relevant "stipulations of the provisional articles" of peace, see *Papers of Madison*, VI, 465; 466, n. 3; 466, and n. 1; 479; 480, nn. 6, 7; also Walke to Delegates, 3 May 1783, and n. 2. Having been instructed by Congress on 15 April, Washington wrote six days later to General Sir Guy Carleton proposing a conference. The letter's closing sentence reads, "Should an Interview be consented to on your part, the Governor [George Clinton] of this State, being particularly interested in Any Arrangements which respect the Restitution of the Post of N York, will attend me, on this Occasion" (Fitzpatrick, *Writings of Washington*, XXVI, 345–48).

[6] In his reply of 24 April to Washington, Carleton stated that, although he could not "decline the personal interview proposed" to be held at Tappan, N.Y., on 5 May, Washington might prefer to postpone the meeting until Major General Sir Charles (later Earl) Grey (1729–1807), who had been appointed to succeed to Carleton's command, arrived from Great Britain with more detailed instructions concerning

"the final arrangements"–including presumably the evacuation of New York City. Carleton, however, eagerly accepted Washington's suggestion that all prisoners of war should be exchanged immediately (NA: PCC, No. 152, XI, 245–47). For Carleton's probable reason favoring haste in this regard, see *Papers of Madison*, VI, 465; 466, n. 3; 466, n. 1.

The Tappan conference, which lasted only "some Hours" on 5 May because of Carleton's "Indisposition," confirmed Washington's belief that very few of the Negro slaves sequestered by the British would be returned. Although Carleton promised to withdraw his troops from Westchester County, N.Y., at once, he declined to pledge as early an evacuation of Long Island and the Penobscot River area of Massachusetts. The relinquishment by the British of their posts in the Old Northwest appears not to have been a subject of discussion (Fitzpatrick, *Writings of Washington*, XXVI, 401–6; Walke to Delegates, 3 May 1783, and nn. 2, 3, 5, 7). The "Lt. Govr." was Andrew Elliot (1728–1797). Although the Crown had appointed William Smith (1728–1793) "Chief Justice" on 4 May 1779, he never served, because those portions of New York held by the royal forces remained under military control. From 1785 until his death he was chief justice of Canada. For Smith's history of New York, see *Papers of Madison*, VI, 103.

7 *Papers of Madison*, VI, 499; 500, nn. 2, 3.

8 *Ibid*., VI, 471, 473, n. 7; 488–94; 494–98 nn.; Delegates to Harrison, 6 May 1783, and n. 3.

9 Although Joseph Jones probably left Philadelphia on 6 May, Arthur Lee delayed his departure until six days later (JM to Jefferson, 6 May 1783, and n. 4). Lee resumed his attendance in Congress on 16 July and Jones on or shortly before 27 August 1783 (*JCC*, XXIV, 435, 525).

Notes on Debates

MS (LC: Madison Papers). For a description of the manuscript of Notes on Debates, see *Papers of Madison*, V, 231–34.

Wednesday May 7.

The Resolution moved yesterday by Mr. Lee for indemnifying military Officers, being reported by the Committee was agreed to[1]

The Committee on a motion of Mr. Dyer, reported "that the States which had settled with their respective lines of the army for their pay since Aug. 1. 1780, should receive the Securities which would otherwise be due to such lines."[2]

The report was opposed on the ground that the settlements had not been discharged in the value due. The notes issued in payment by Connecticut were complained of, as being of little value.[3]

The Report was disagreed to. see Journal.[4]

1 JM Notes, 6 May 1783, and n. 1; *JCC*, XXIV, 330.

2 On 2 May 1783 the motion of Eliphalet Dyer (Conn.) was referred to a committee comprising Stephen Higginson (Mass.), chairman, Abraham Clark (N.J.), and John Lewis Gervais (S.C.) (NA: PCC, No. 186, fol. 99; *JCC*, XXIV, 327). JM had not attended Congress on that day (JM Notes, 5 May 1783, n. 3).

JM summarized rather than quoted the committee's report, drafted by Higginson. The report recommended that, upon receiving "proper vouchers" from a state which had "settled with the officers and soldiers" of its continental line, Robert Morris, superintendent of finance, should issue to that state "public securities, payable in the same manner and for the same sums as would have been otherwise given" by the treasury of the United States to those troops for their service between 1 August 1780 and the date on which they were paid by their state (*JCC*, XXIV, 330–31). Contrary to ordinances of Congress, several states had paid the wages overdue to their discontented continental troops with money deducted from the financial quotas requisitioned from those states by Congress. See *Papers of Madison*, V, 173–75; 175, n. 11; 366, n. 26; VI, 128, n. 39; 171, n. 1; *JCC*, XXIII, 624–25; 629–31.

[3] If a state paid its troops in the old continental paper currency or in state-issued paper currency at a ratio of 40 to 1 of that continental currency, as stipulated by the ordinance of 18 March 1780, the real value of the money the soldiers received would have been far less than Congress had guaranteed to them by a resolution of 10 April 1780 (*JCC*, XVI, 264, 344–45). See also Burnett, *Letters*, VI, 386, 413, 546; VII, 20, 153; Charles J. Hoadly *et al.*, eds., *The Public Records of the State of Connecticut* (11 vols. to date; Hartford, 1894——), III, 21–22, 41, 189–90, 254, 310–12, 523–24; IV, 12–14, 20.

[4] *JCC*, XXIV, 331. The delegates from Massachusetts, Rhode Island, Connecticut, and New Jersey voted unanimously in favor of the recommendation. Except for Arthur Lee, those from Virginia, North Carolina, and South Carolina were unanimously against it. New Hampshire and New York each had only one delegate in attendance, while Delaware, Maryland, and Georgia had none. The two delegates from Pennsylvania deadlocked in the tally.

From Thomas Jefferson

RC (LC: Madison Papers). Unsigned but in Jefferson's hand. Docketed by JM, "From Ths. J. to J.M. May 7, 1783." On the docket page someone unknown wrote, "Ths. Jefferson May 7. 1783." Using the JM-Jefferson Code No. 2, Jefferson enciphered the words which are here italicized. Interlineated on the manuscript is JM's decoding of these ciphers. Filed with the manuscript are two pages entitled by JM "as decyphered from letter of May 7. 1783" and docketed by him, "to J Madison 7. May 1783." Except that JM replaced all coding with the words it symbolized, he copied on those pages that part of Jefferson's first paragraph beginning with the words "This is the view I form at present of *the leaders*" and also the whole of the two succeeding paragraphs. In the manuscript of the letter, he bracketed these portions, placed an asterisk beside the first bracket, repeated the asterisk in the bottom margin of Jefferson's first page, and wrote, "see the paper decyphering what is in [ ]."

TUCKAHOE[1] May 7: 1783.

DEAR SIR

I rec[eived] your favor of Apr. 22. and am not a little concerned at the alterations which took place in the Report on the impost &c. after

I left you. the article which bound the whole together was I fear essential to get the whole passed; as that which proposed the conversion of state into federal debts was one [pa]latable ingredient at least in the pill *we* were to swallow.[2] this proposition being then hopeful, I never consulted you whether The paiment of our Western expenditures, annexed as a condition to our passing the articles recommended, would not be acceded to by Congress; more especially when one of those articles is the cession of that very territory for the acquisition & defence of which these expenditures have been incurred.[3] if I recollect rightly, Congress offered this in their first proposition for a cession.[4] I beg your sentiments however on this subject by return of the first post.[5] notwithstanding the unpromising form of these articles,[6] I have waited a fortnight in the neighborhood of Richmond that I might see some of the members. I passed yesterday *in associating* & *conversation with as* many of them *as I could the attorny*[7] has *cooperated* in this work. This is the view I form at present of *the leaders. A. Lee R. H. Lee M. Page Taylar* will be *against* them. so will *Thruston* and *White if elected* and even an *Arthur Cambel*[l] is thought *worthy of being named* with these as having some *infloence in the south west* quarter.[8] In their *favor will probable be Tylar Taz*[e]*well General Nelson W Nelson Nicholas* & a *Mr. Stewart* a *young man* of *good talents* from the *West*[9] *Henry* as usual is *involved in mistery* Should the *popular tide run strongly* in either *direction*, he will fall *in with it* Should it *not* he will have a *struggl*[e] *between his enmity to the Lees & his enmity* to every *thing which may* give *influence to Congress*[10] *T Mason* is a *meteor* whose *path can not* be *calculated*[11] all the powers of *his mind* seem at present *concentrated* on one *singl*[e] *object* the *producing* a *convention* to *new model* the *Constitution*[12] this *is a subjec*[t] much *agitated* and seems the *only one* they will have to *amuse themselfs* with *til* they shall *receive* your *proposetions These should* be *hastened as* I think the session will be short.[13]

I have seen mr. Wythe. he has none of his amendments or notes on the Confederation.[14]

Mr. Short has desired me to suggest *his name* as that of a *person willing* to become a *legatine secretary* should these *offices be continud. I have apprized him of* the possibility that they may not. you know *my high opinion of his ableties and merits* I will therefore only add that a *peculiar talent* for *prying into facts* seems to mark *his character as proper for* such a *business He is young* & little *experienced in business* tho well *prepared for it* these defects will *lessen dayly* should *persons* be *proposed less proper* on the whole, you *would* on motives of public good, *knowing his willingness* to *serve give him* a *nomination* & do justice to *his character.*[15]

I rejoice at the information that *Miss K. and yourself concur* in *sentiments* *I rejoice* as it will *render you happier* and will give *to me a neighbor on whom I shall set high value* *You* will be continued in *your* delegation[16] till the end of three years from the completion of the Confederation.[17] *You* will therefore *model your measures accordingly* You say nothing of the time when you shall pay your visit to *Virginia.* I hope you will *let me know* of your *arrival* as soon as *it happens* should the *call* be made *on*[18] *me*, which was sometimes the subject of *our conversation* and be *so timed with your* visit *as that you may* be the *bearer of* it *I shall* with great pleasure accomodate *my movements to yours* so as to *accompany you on your return to Philadelphia*[19]

I set out this morning for Monticello. my affectionate compliments to the ladies & gentlemen of the house and sincere friendship to yourself. Adieu[20]

[1] The estate of Thomas Mann Randolph (1741–1793) on the James River in Goochland County, about thirteen miles west of Richmond (Frances Archer Christian and Susanne Williams Massie, eds., *Homes and Gardens in Old Virginia*, rev. by Ella Williams Smith *et al.* [3d ed.; Richmond, 1962], pp. 180–85). In 1790 Randolph's eldest son married Jefferson's daughter Martha (Patsy).

[2] *Papers of Madison*, VI, 481; 482, nn. 9–11. Jefferson had left Philadelphia on 12 April 1783 to return to Virginia (*ibid.*, VI, 396). By "we," which is underlined and not encoded, Jefferson signified Virginia or, more precisely, its General Assembly. The congressional proposals for restoring public credit could not become effective until ratified by the legislature of every state.

[3] While Jefferson was in Philadelphia, he had shared JM's expectation that Congress would accept the general pledge, incorporated in the proposed plan for restoring public credit, to assume every state's unauthorized but reasonable war expenses, including the cost of Virginia's military operations in the Old Northwest. Congress, however, excised that provision before adopting the plan on 18 April and refused later that month to reinstate it, in spite of efforts by JM and delegates from other states with similar claims (*ibid.*, VI, 291; 296, n. 40; 310; 312–13; 315, n. 14; 316, n. 16; 317; 318, n. 2; 324, n. 7; 400–401; 403, nn. 11–13; 404, nn. 14–16, 18; 406; 440; 441, n. 6; 442–43; 445, n. 11; 468, and n. 1; 469; 470, nn. 4, 5; 471; 477; 478, n. 1; 502, and n. 3; 503, nn. 4, 5).

Attached to the offer of the Virginia General Assembly on 2 January 1781 to cede the territory north and west of the Ohio River to the United States were several provisos, including the stipulation that Congress must reimburse Virginia for "all the charges she has incurred, on account of the country, on the northwest side of the Ohio river, since the commencement of the present war" (*JHDV*, Oct. 1780, p. 80).

[4] On 10 October 1780 Congress rejected the committee report which included

that guarantee (*JCC*, XVII, 806–7; XVIII, 915–16; *Papers of Madison*, II, 138, n. 2).

5 JM to Jefferson, 20 May 1783.

6 Jefferson, of course, had not seen the final form of the plan for restoring public credit, since Elias Boudinot did not post it from Philadelphia to Governor Harrison until 9 May (Delegates to Harrison, 6 May, and n. 3). Jefferson's comment reflected his reading of JM's letter of 22 April 1783 (*Papers of Madison*, VI, 481–83).

7 Edmund Randolph. See *Papers of Madison*, VI, 440.

8 Jefferson probably knew Arthur Lee's views from talking with him in Philadelphia, for his brother Richard Henry Lee did not arrive in Richmond until 8 May. See JM to Jefferson, 6 May, and n. 4; Randolph to JM, 9 May 1783. For Mann Page, Jr., and John Taylor, delegates in the Virginia General Assembly from Spotsylvania and Caroline counties, respectively, see *Papers of Madison*, IV, 137, n. 3; VI, 423, n. 8.

Charles Mynn Thruston and Alexander White of Frederick County were both re-elected (Swem and Williams, *Register*, p. 17). For Thruston, see *Papers of Madison*, V, 283, nn. 2, 3. White (1739–1804) was a British-trained lawyer who served in the House of Delegates, 1782–1786 and 1788, in the Virginia Convention which ratified the Federal Constitution, and in the United States House of Representatives from 1789 to 1793. Between 1788 and 1796 he occasionally corresponded with JM. In 1795 he was appointed by President Washington one of three commissioners to lay out the city of Washington, D.C. (Swem and Williams, *Register*, pp. 20, 22, 28). For Arthur Campbell, see *Papers of Madison*, IV, 126, n. 1; V, 454; 456, n. 12.

9 For John Tyler, speaker of the House of Delegates, from Charles City County; Henry Tazewell, the delegate from Williamsburg; Thomas Nelson, Jr., from York County; William Nelson from James City County; George Nicholas from Albemarle County; and Archibald Stuart from Botetourt County, see Swem and Williams, *Register*, pp. 17, 18; *Papers of Madison*, I, 225, n. 5; III, 197, n. 1; IV, 30, n. 2; V, 219, n. 10; 400; 403, n. 12; VI, 417, n. 6; 500, n. 2.

Stuart (1757–1832) left the College of William and Mary in 1780 to serve under the command of his father in the Carolina campaign. He later studied law under Jefferson. He was also a delegate from Botetourt County between 1784 and 1786, from Augusta County between 1786 and 1788, and a state senator, 1797–1800 (Swem and Williams, *Register*, pp. 17, 19, 21, 23, 26, 49, 52). During his long public career Stuart also participated in the Virginia Convention which ratified the Federal Constitution in 1788 and served as a judge of the General Court of his state. He was a correspondent of JM between 1787 and 1793.

10 For the "enmity" of Patrick Henry toward the Lees, see *Papers of Madison*, II, 199; 269–70; IV, 225; 306; 355–56; V, 79, n. 16; 339; 340, n. 11; 404, n. 18; 453. For Jefferson's dislike and distrust of Henry, see Boyd, *Papers of Jefferson*, VI, 85 n., 144 n., 205, and nn. In the General Assembly of May 1783 Henry was present at least by the twelfth of that month, when the House of Delegates mustered its first quorum of the session. On that day Henry and his supporters succeeded by a vote of 61 to 20 in having John Tyler elected speaker over the opposition of the advocates of Richard Henry Lee for that position (*JHDV*, May 1783, p. 4). See also Randolph to JM, 9 May 1783, and n. 4.

11 In his retained copy of the letter, Jefferson began this sentence: "The Attorney [Edmund Randolph] thinks T.M. [Mason]" (Boyd, *Papers of Jefferson*, VI, 267, n. 3). The youthful Stevens Thomson Mason (1760–1803), a resident of Loudoun County, a nephew of George Mason, an alumnus of the College of William and Mary, a Revolutionary veteran, and a lawyer, was at the beginning of his political career. Again a delegate from Loudoun County in 1794, he was a member of the Virginia Convention of 1788 which ratified the Federal Constitution, a state senator from 1787 to 1790, and a United States senator from 1794 to 1803. Jefferson came

to number Mason among his close friends and, after 1790, as an ardent supporter in national as well as in state politics (Swem and Williams, *Register*, pp. 18, 27, 30, 32, 34, 42). Thomson Mason set forth his views in a letter to the freeholders of Stafford County, 10 June 1783 (*Va. Gazette*, 14 June 1783).

12 On a separate page which has much of Jefferson's writing deciphered, JM interlineated "[State]" between "the" and "Constitution" at some time after the adoption of the Federal Constitution. Jefferson was also eager to "*new model*" the Form of Government of Virginia and had devoted much thought to what the changes should be. See *Papers of Madison*, VI, 319; 320, n. 7; 321, n. 8; 441, n. 10; Jefferson to JM, 17 June 1783; Boyd, *Papers of Jefferson*, VI, 278, 294–306. Probably late in the spring of 1783 Stuart procured a copy of Jefferson's draft for a new constitution (*An Occasional Bulletin*, Virginia Historical Society, XV [1967], 8).

13 On 22 May Governor Harrison submitted to the House of Delegates a pamphlet containing an address and recommendations of Congress that the states authorize "a System for the Support of public Credit" (Executive Letter Book, 1783–1786, p. 33, MS in Va. State Library; *JHDV*, May 1783, p. 16). The May session of the General Assembly adjourned on 28 June, thereby being of about the usual duration (*ibid.*, pp. 93, 99). If the delegates "*to amuse themselfs*" prior to 22 May talked about "*producing a convention*," no mention of the fact appears in their journal (*ibid.*, pp. 3–16). See Jones to JM, 25 May 1783.

14 For Chancellor George Wythe, see *Papers of Madison*, II, 49; 51, n. 6; III, 20; 22, nn. 3, 4; 80; 81, n. 8; IV, 307, n. 5; V, 263. JM, who apparently hoped to write a history of civil affairs during the Revolution, or at least to edit primary sources relating thereto, seems to have asked Jefferson, when they were together in Philadelphia, to inquire of Wythe whether he could supply documents for the period 1775–1776 during his service in the Continental Congress (*Papers of Madison*, V, 232–33). See also *JCC*, II, 199; IV, 402, and n.; VI, 1071–73; Jefferson to JM, 1 June 1783, and nn. 5–7.

15 For William Short and a summary of his long service overseas, beginning in 1784 as private secretary of Jefferson in France, see *Papers of Madison*, III, 269–70, n. 2; Boyd, *Papers of Jefferson*, VII, 363, and n., 384, 521, 534; *William and Mary Quarterly*, 3d ser., XXI (1964), 516–33; *Proceedings of the American Philosophical Society*, CII (1958), 596–612.

16 At some undetermined time, but hardly before late in July or early in August 1783, when Catherine Floyd withdrew from her engagement to marry him, JM canceled this paragraph with heavy, wavy lines of ink as far as "delegation." The decipherment by the present editors agrees with that of Boyd, *Papers of Jefferson*, VI, 267. See also Brant, *Madison*, II, 284.

17 *Papers of Madison*, VI, 464, and n. 6. For JM's response to Jefferson's suggestion, see JM to Jefferson, 20 May; Randolph to JM, 24 May; and JM to Randolph, 3 June 1783.

18 JM inadvertently wrote 108, the symbol for "commerce," instead of 1080, signifying "on."

19 *Papers of Madison*, VI, 440. On 6 June the Virginia legislature elected Jefferson a delegate to Congress for the year beginning on the first Monday of November (*JHDV*, May 1783, p. 39). Jefferson left Monticello on 16 October and first attended Congress, then assembled at Princeton, N.J., on 4 November 1783 (Boyd, *Papers of Jefferson*, VI, 349 n.; *JCC*, XXV, 803). He had stopped at Philadelphia on 29 October for nearly a week. During that period and also thereafter until late in November, when Jefferson and JM were fellow travelers to Annapolis, the new meeting place of Congress, they were frequently together (Boyd, *Papers of Jefferson*, VI, 355 n., 377, 381).

20 *Papers of Madison*, VI, 182, nn. 28, 29.

Notes on Debates

MS (LC: Madison Papers). For a description of the manuscript of Notes on Debates, see *Papers of Madison,* V, 231–34.

Thursday May 8.

Mr. Bland suggested that the Prisoners of War should be detained, until an answer be given as to the delivery of slaves, represented in a letter from Mr. Thomas Walke, to be refused on the part of Sr. Guy Carlton.[1]

On his motion seconded by Mr. Williamson it was ordered that the letter be sent to Gen: Washington for his information, in carrying into effect the Resolution of Apl. 15; touching arrangements with the British Commander for delivery of the posts, negroes &c.[2]

A Portrait of Don Galvez was presented to Congress by Oliver Pollock.[3]

[1] *Papers of Madison,* VI, 456; 458, n. 3; 462, and n. 2; 466, and n. 1; 479; 480, n. 7; Walke to Delegates, 3 May 1783, and hdn., nn. 2–3, 5–7.

[2] *Papers of Madison,* VI, 462, and n. 2; 466, and n. 1; JM to Randolph, 6 May 1783, and n. 5; *JCC,* XXIV, 333.

[3] Delegates to Gálvez, 4 May 1783, and ed. n., n. 3; *JCC,* XXIV, 333, and n. 2.

Motion of Instruction to the President

MS (NA: PCC, No. 36, II, 111). Docketed, "Motion of Mr. Madison Seconded by Mr. Holten passed May 9th 1783."

EDITORIAL NOTE

Closely following the tally of votes by which the plan for restoring public credit was adopted on 18 April 1783, there is printed in the Gaillard Hunt edition of the journals of Congress John Rutledge's undated and undocketed motion of almost the same tenor as the present one of JM. Rutledge probably did not offer his resolution on 18 April, for otherwise he would not have left that date to be inserted in his opening clause, "That the resolutions of the instant be transmitted to the several states" (NA: PCC, No. 36, II, 23; *JCC,* XXIV, 261–62). Rutledge's motion may also date on 9 May. If he did introduce it, he probably withdrew it after being reminded that, although he was a strong advocate of state rights, he had confined the role of state legislatures only to taking "the measures necessary for complying with the requisitions of Congress."

[9 May 1783]

That the Presidt. at the time of transmitting copies of the recommendations of Congs. of the day of &c. to the Executive authorities of the several States,[1] inform them that it is the earnest desire of Congress, that such of the Legislatures as are neither sitting, nor about to meet in a short Time, may be convened with all possible expidition.[2]

[1] See ed. n. Before offering the motion, JM probably substituted for "&c" the phrase "and the address of the same month" (*Papers of Madison*, VI, 488; 498; Delegates to Harrison, 6 May 1783, and n. 3).

[2] Having received from Elias Boudinot a printed copy of the "recommendations" and its appended documents, Governor Harrison on 22 May 1783 referred them to the Virginia House of Delegates (Executive Letter Book, 1783–1786, p. 133, MS in Va. State Library; Harrison to Delegates, 7 June 1783). See also JM to Jefferson, 13 May 1783, and n. 11.

Notes on Debates

MS (LC: Madison Papers). For a description of the manuscript of Notes on Debates, see *Papers of Madison*, V, 231–34.

Friday May 9.[1]

A question on a Report relating to the occupying the Posts when evacuated by the British was postponed by Virginia in right of a State.[2]

Mr. Dyer moved a recommendation to the States to restore confiscated property conformably to the Provisional Articles. The motion produced a debate which went off without any positive result.[3] Adjourned to Monday

[1] Neither of the proceedings noted by JM is mentioned in the journal of Congress for this date (*JCC*, XXIV, 335–37).

[2] On 15 April Congress had included among its instructions to Washington a request that he "make the proper arrangements with the Commander in Chief of the British forces, for receiving possession of the posts in the United States occupied by the troops of his Britannic Majesty" (*JCC*, XXIV, 242; *Papers of Madison*, VI, 462, and n. 2; 466, and n. 1). In his reply of 3 May, Washington asked for "some more particular Explanation of the Intentions of Congress," especially since negotiations for the evacuation of "the Northern and Western Posts" would "take much time," because they were under the military jurisdiction of General Sir Frederick Haldimand, "who commands in the District of Canada," rather than of General Sir Guy Carleton in New York City. Washington also emphasized that, if there should be an interim between evacuation by British and occupation by American troops, the vacated posts probably would be "burned or destroyed by the Indians, or some other evil minded persons" (Fitzpatrick, *Writings of Washington*, XXVI, 398–400).

On 6 May Congress appointed a committee, Alexander Hamilton, chairman, and

JM and Oliver Ellsworth (Conn.) among the other four members, to recommend a reply. Because entries in the journal of Congress are lacking, doubt is warranted whether the committee submitted versions of the report on both 8 and 9 May. Charles Thomson's committee book makes clear only that Congress received "a Report" on 8 May (NA: PCC, No. 186, fol. 99). The docket of Hamilton's draft of a report includes the notation, "Delivered May 8, 1783." The docket of Ellsworth's variant draft reads, "May 9, 1783—postponed by the State of Virginia" (NA: PCC, No. 38, fol. 303; No. 19, VI, 431–33).

If the Hamilton draft was debated on 8 May, the Virginia delegates almost surely opposed its recommendation that Congress have full power to decide how long the troops dispatched by Washington to garrison the posts should remain there. The territorial claim of Virginia to the Old Northwest, as well as her military operations in that area, would impel her delegates to resist an assumption of so much authority by Congress. Although the report may have been returned on 8 May to the committee for revision, the Ellsworth draft of the next day could hardly have been more acceptable to the Virginia delegates. The offending passage had been excised, but the wording of the report still implied that Congress had complete military jurisdiction in the Old Northwest, at least over the posts. If for this reason the Virginians induced Congress on 9 May to postpone a vote on the report, they evidently were no better satisfied three days later when they alone, but with JM absent, opposed the adoption of a slightly amended version of the Ellsworth draft (*JCC*, XXIV, 337–39).

On the manuscript below the report appears the following canceled passage, also in Ellsworth's hand: "Resolved that the Expence of such Garrisons shall be charged to the particular State to whom the Property of the Posts so garrisoned, shall be finally adjudged" (NA: PCC, No. 19, VI, 433). Whether this resolution was suggested only within the committee or offered in Congress as an amendment during the debates on 9 or 12 May cannot be determined.

3 Congress had ratified the preliminary articles of peace with Great Britain on 15 April 1783 (*JCC*, XXIV, 242–51). For discussion of the stipulation of those articles providing for the return of the confiscated property to Loyalist or British owners, see *Papers of Madison*, VI, 15, n. 5; 48, n. 1; 328; 330, n. 2; 334–35; 337, n. 12; 340; 370; 456; 458, n. 3; 499; 500, n. 6. For renewed debates of the issue, see JM Notes, 14 and 20 May 1783.

Benjamin Harrison to Virginia Delegates

FC (Virginia State Library). In the hand of Thomas Meriwether. Addressed to "Virginia Delegates in Congress."

RICHMOND May 9th. 1783.

GENTLEMEN

I duly received your favor of the 29th. of last Month.[1] In my last I requested you to let Mr. Thompson know I would send by this Post an Act of Assembly repealing the Cession of the Western Teretory. I then thought there had been one, but the Clerk of the Delegates informs me I was mistaken, which you'l please to let him know, if you have delivered the Message.[2]

I find private Letters frequently full of interesting Intelligence respecting the Politics of Europe, and the fears and expectations of Congress from that quarter, and many other things of Moment which would be of advantage to the State if known to the Executive, to obtain such Communications, appears to me to have been the principal Intention in establishing a weekly Correspondence between the Governor and the Delegates, and that without them it is scarcely worth the Continuance. I would not be understood to entertain a wish to be let into Secrets which ought not to be devulged, or to trespass so far on your Time, as to take you from the Duties of your Appointment, but I think as you write in turn, the Member to whose lot it falls might spend a few Minutes each Day between the Posts, in such Communications, which would be particularly useful to me during the setting of the Assembly as I am frequently applied to by the Members for Intelligence on Subjects which they know have been received by particular Gentlemen and on which they expect at least as full Information from their Governor as they can obtain from others.[3]

There are not Members of Assembly enough met to proceed to Business, nor will there be before Munday,[4] from the Tember[5] of those I have conversed with it is to be apprehended, the Article of British Debts in the Treaty, will be but illy digested, tho' I have my Hopes they will not enter on that Subject this Session.[6]

I am with respect Gentlemen Yrs: &c.

B. H.

[1] *Papers of Madison*, VI, 501.

[2] Harrison to Delegates, 3 May 1783, and n. 4. The clerk of the Virginia House of Delegates was John Beckley (*JHDV*, Oct. 1782, p. 89; E. Griffith Dodson, *Speakers and Clerks of the Virginia House of Delegates, 1776–1955* [Richmond, 1956], pp. 19, 140). For Beckley, see *Papers of Madison*, I, 318, n. 2.

[3] In letters of 6 April 1782 and 15 February 1783, Governor Harrison had also chided the delegates either for the sparseness of their letters or for failure to enclose a Philadelphia newspaper with them (*ibid.*, IV, 139–40; VI, 241; 242, n. 3). Only in a limited sense did the delegates write in turn, although their ideal seems to have been that one delegate should draft four letters in succession before being relieved of the task by another delegate.

Taking, for example, the sixteen letters of which the draftsmen are known, posted by the delegates to Harrison between 1 January and 30 April 1783, Mercer and Bland each wrote five; JM, three; Lee, two; and Jones, one. Harrison's criticism may have been especially directed at Bland, who had drafted the four letters most recently received by the governor. The response of the delegates to his criticism is in their letter of 20 May 1783, of which only a printed extract is available to the editors (*q.v*). The delegates could also have partially justified the brevity of their letters in April by remarking that Lee and Jones, soon returning to Richmond for the session of the Virginia General Assembly, would inform Harrison as fully about the proceedings of Congress as their discretion permitted (Ambler to JM,

3 May, n. 4; Pendleton to JM, 4 May, n. 3; JM to Randolph, 6 May, n. 9; Delegates to Harrison, 27 May 1783). Among the "private Letters," the governor may have included not only those written to him, but also those sent by JM to Randolph and perhaps to Pendleton, who was then in Richmond.

[4] Ambler to JM, 3 May 1783, n. 2.

[5] For the sake of clarity, the clerk should have placed a period rather than a comma after "Munday" and capitalized the first letter of "from." By "Tember" he probably meant "Timbre" or "Tembre."

[6] Article IV of the preliminary articles of peace stipulated "that creditors on either side shall meet with no lawful impediment to the recovery of the full value in sterling money, of all bona fide debts heretofore contracted" (*JCC*, XXIV, 248). See also *Papers of Madison*, VI, 47; 48, nn. 2, 4; 334; 340; 341, n. 5; 370; 439; 440, n. 2.

Although the governor had submitted a copy of the preliminary articles of peace to the speaker of the House of Delegates on 5 May, he omitted mention of the debts issue until 3 June 1783. On that day he sent the speaker an account of debts owed to British creditors, "which this Moment came to hand" (Executive Letter Book, 1783–1786, p. 149, MS in Va. State Library). Two petitions from residents of Essex County and one from Fairfax County, protesting against the procedure which probably would be used if that article of the treaty were enforced, were received by the House of Delegates and referred to the committee of the whole house on the state of the Commonwealth. The session adjourned, however, without either resolutions or a statute relating directly to the subject being offered or adopted by the General Assembly (*JHDV*, May 1783, pp. 12, 37, 65).

From Edmund Randolph

RC (LC: Madison Papers). Unsigned but in Randolph's hand. Docketed by JM, "May 9th. 1783." Cover addressed by Randolph to "The honble James Madison jr. esq of congress Philadelphia." The right margin of the second of the three folios comprising the letter was trimmed so carelessly as to excise portions of the text.

RICHMOND May 9. 1783.

MY DEAR SIR

The due arrival of your friendly attention by every post[1] has not been requited, in the manner most agreeable to my own feelings. My engagements in the forum from the 1st. Ulto. to this day,[2] and the barrenness of intelligence must serve as my apology.

Monday last was the day appointed for the meeting of the assembly: and a larger number of members appeared, than has been seen for some years on the first day of the session.[3] Among them was Mr. Henry. He is earnest in the reduction of the taxes; alledging the inability of the people, and scarcity of cash.[4] These facts have received strong support from the motions, made at the last general court, against delinquent sheriffs to the amount of about £50,000. Their excuses in general consisted of the impracticability to find purchasers for the property seized.[5]

Whether this temper predicts much in favor of the recommendations of congress, now on the road, I have not yet determined. It does not of necessity become an Obstacle to them, as the impost in most parts is supposed to fall heaviest upon men of opulence, for whose sakes the diminution of the taxes is by no means intended.[6]

Some of those, with whom I have conversed, argue thus: "Our consumption exceeds our ability [in?] annual income: that of the other states does not: these therefore will by the impost pay according to their wealth, while we thereby render the yearly excess of our yearly revenue still more ruinous." This objection shall not long keep its ground.[7]

The cession of our western country, as recommended, beyond the assignment already made to the U. S, when connected with the delivery of a capital fund into the hands of congress, gives birth to difficulties of every complexion. It revives in the minds of some the ardor of congress to grasp that territory, and the possibility of this fund being diverted to offensive measures again[st] it. It is supposed to diminish our power, wealth and importan[ce] at the same time, that the impost itself will daily lessen our pecu[niary] talents.[8] The labour will be severe indeed, which shall ex[pel?] the conviction of some individuals: for with them argument derived from the posture of our affairs, and the necessity of yielding something, altho' to our disadvantage, to the cause [of] peace and the harmony of the union, pass under the appe[lla]tion of misdirected zeal, or ill-founded fears.

Mr. R. H. Lee arrived yesterday without his brother the Dr.[9] My business has prevented me from conversing with him at all, and indeed with a[ny] other member, as fully as I wish.

We are much alarmed at the purpose of sending the definitive treaty to the imperia[l] courts before its completion.[10] We have been too muc[h] injured by the war, not to dread its return. Perhaps i[t] would not be easy to find precedents of the abortion o[f] a treaty of peace, which has been carried as far as the ra[ti]fication of preliminaries:[11] but a fresh opposition may b[e] artfully excited in these courts by G. B, who is now per[haps] led to hope something from Morris's letter[12] and the spir[ited] movements of the army.[13]

Several british vessels have a[rri]ved in our rivers: some of which affect to intitle themsel[ves] to an entry by distress, and others in right of commerce upon t[he] cessation of hostilities. The executive have adjourned thei[r] cases to the assembly; before whom several zealous

Scotch will appear, as I am told, urging the indulgence.[14] An indulg[ence] it must be called; for a final consummation of the war dep[ends] as it would seem to me, upon the definitive treaty alone. I [am] somewhat surprized at the difficulties, which you sugges[t] in the construction of the phrase "*during the war.*" Howsoever active enmity may have been suspended by the preliminaries, the *state* of war appears still to exist.[15]

[1] Except for his letter of 26 April, Randolph had not written to JM since 29 March. During the same period, JM had written to him on 1, 8, 10, 15, 22, and 29 April 1783 (*Papers of Madison,* VI, 429–30; 439–40; 449–50; 465; 483; 503–4). By 9 May Randolph obviously could not have received JM's letter dated three days earlier (*q.v.*).

[2] As attorney general of Virginia, Randolph was obliged to attend sessions of the General Court, which convened its spring term on 1 April; of the Court of Admiralty, "so often as there shall be occasion" for that tribunal to "sit"; and of the High Court of Chancery and the Court of Appeals (Hening, *Statutes,* X, 99, 455; Pendleton to JM, 4 May 1783). He also was expected to be available during each session of the General Assembly for consultation on constitutional and other legal matters. See *JHDV,* May 1783, p. 36.

[3] Ambler to JM, 3 May 1783, and n. 2.

[4] Jefferson in his letter of 4 May to JM (*q.v.,* and n. 10) had been less certain of the course Patrick Henry would pursue. Although Henry returned to his home two weeks before the adjournment of the Virginia General Assembly on 28 June, he shared prominently in the proceedings of the House of Delegates during the month beginning on 12 May (*JHDV,* May 1783, pp. 4–53; Randolph to JM, 21 June 1783).

The most important of the several measures reflecting "the present distressed state" of many Virginians was an act of 28 June entitled "An act to suspend the operation of the act, intituled, An act to amend and reduce the several acts of assembly for ascertaining certain taxes and duties, and for establishing a permanent revenue, into one act." Besides postponing "to a future day" the enforcement of the "act to amend and reduce . . . ," this stay law stipulated "That no distress for any tax imposed by the said act shall be made before the twentieth day of November next" (*Papers of Madison,* V, 454, n. 2; *JHDV,* May 1783, p. 99; Hening, *Statutes,* XI, 194). The House of Delegates on 13 May, having been informed by "a committee of the whole House" of the need for this relief, appointed a committee, including Henry among its twelve members, to draft an appropriate bill. He continued to support the measure as long as he attended the session (*JHDV,* May 1783, pp. 6, 9, 21; Randolph to JM, 24 May 1783).

[5] Sheriffs, as tax collectors, were subject to heavy penalties upon conviction by the General Court of failing to collect taxes in money or "commutables" when due or neglecting to render an accounting of them to the tax commissioners or auditors of public accounts, or transmitting the tax money to the treasury (Hening, *Statutes,* X, 172, 199–202, 252–53, 255–56, 507–8). Inability to convert into cash the "commutables" acceptable as taxes or, more usually, the private property seized for nonpayment of taxes also was penalized. See *Papers of Madison,* VI, 379. For the law of 28 June 1783 "for the relief of sheriffs," see *ibid.,* VI, 500; 501, n. 8.

[6] Included in the plan for restoring public credit, adopted by Congress on 18 April, were recommendations that each state levy import duties for the support of the government of the Confederation. Upon receiving a copy of "the plan," Governor Harrison submitted it immediately to the General Assembly (*Papers*

of Madison, VI, 312; 322; 350; 471; Jefferson to JM, 7 May, and n. 13; Instruction to President, 9 May 1783, n. 2).

[7] In summarizing the argument which Randolph did not find persuasive, he probably would have added clarity by inserting "our spending over" between "excess of" and "our." Randolph soon expressed concern lest a majority of the members of the House of Delegates reject the recommended imposts (Randolph to JM, 24 May and n. 6). See also Pendleton to JM, 4 May 1783, and n. 8.

[8] Harrison to Delegates, 3 May, and n. 4; Jefferson to JM, 7 May, and n. 3; JM Notes, 9 May 1783, and n. 2. For the long background of the "cession" problem, see the indexes of *Papers of Madison*, Vols. II–VII, under Western lands.

[9] For Arthur Lee's arrival in Richmond, see Ambler to JM, 3 May, n. 4; JM to Jefferson, 6 May 1783, n. 4.

[10] *Papers of Madison*, VI, 504, and n. 2.

[11] JM Notes, 9 May 1783, n. 3.

[12] Randolph probably referred to the published letter of 24 January from Robert Morris informing Congress of the desperate state of the Confederation treasury and of his intention to resign as superintendent of finance on 31 May (*Papers of Madison*, VI, 439; 440, n. 3).

[13] *Ibid.*, VI, 286; 348; 349, nn. 1, 2; 355–56; 375; 377, n. 2; 392, and n. 6; 440; 486, n. 2; 499, 500, n. 4.

[14] Delegates to Harrison, 6 May 1783 and citations in n. 2. In his message of 5 May to the Virginia House of Delegates, Governor Harrison mentioned the arrival of several British merchant vessels and requested an early "Determination" whether they should be permitted to discharge or load cargoes (Executive Letter Book, 1783–1786, pp. 115–16, MS in Va. State Library). On 12 May, even before this message was "laid before the House," it appointed a committee, Patrick Henry chairman, to prepare a bill "to repeal the several acts of Assembly, for seizure and condemnation of British goods, found on land." The House, having received the committee's proposal on 13 May, amended and adopted the measure on that day. Tardiness in assembling and insistence by the Senate upon amendment explain why the bill was not enacted into law until 24 May (*JHDV*, May 1783, pp. 4, 5, 6, 14, 20). This brief statute closes by making its effective date 13 May, thus exonerating the governor and the naval officers for sanctioning trade with the British before the repeal of the several prohibitory laws (Ambler to JM, 3 May 1783, n. 5; JM to Jefferson, 13 May, and n. 9; *Va. Gazette, and Weekly Advertiser*, 9 May 1783; Hening, *Statutes*, XI, 195).

[15] *Papers of Madison*, VI, 449–50; 465; and esp. 483. See also *ibid.*, VI, 450, and n. 3; 456; 458, n. 3.

From Jacquelin Ambler

RC (LC: Madison Papers). Cover addressed to "The Honobl. James Madison of Congress Philadelphia." Docketed by JM, "May. 10. 1783."

RICHMOND, VIRGA. 10th. May 1783

DEAR SIR

To my great mortification Mr. Newton is not yet come to the Assembly and, altho' I wrote pressingly to him last week to send me the Bill,

I have received no Answer. I hinted in my last the probability of your drawing from Mr. Newton's Bill a part of the Arrears due to you, supposing some of the Gentlemen of the Delegation to have received nearly the amount of their Salaries: will you write me your Opinion as to the practicability of your being ava[i]led in this way. I find Mr. Mercer, as well as Mr. Jones, has given directions to their friends here to draw in their behalf when the Treasury is in Cash; by this it should seem they prefer this mode to that which I had adopted of purchasing Bills on the joint Accot. & remitting them to Philada. it must be obvious to them that both cannot be done.[1]

Bills, such as I approve, are become scarce, if this was not the case, I confess I should be at a loss to know how to act, as some of the Gentlemen prefer the receiving their proportions here. Yours[,] Mr. Randolph will remit,[2] unless you direct the contrary, whenever the Circumstances of the Treasury will enable me to make a dividend.[3]

Yr friend & Servt

J. A.

[1] Ambler to JM, 3 May 1783, and nn. 1–4. James Monroe, a member of the Council of State, had probably been asked by his uncle, Joseph Jones, "to draw" for him. Monroe was acting in behalf of John Francis Mercer, a friend since their student days at the College of William and Mary (*Papers of Madison*, V, 192, and n. 6; VI, 43; George Morgan, *The Life of James Monroe* [Boston, 1921], p. 27; *Va. Mag. Hist. and Biog.*, LIX [1951], 99, 184, 185).

[2] Edmund Randolph and JM had helped each other on matters of personal finance for over a year (*Papers of Madison*, IV, 194, and n. 2; 195, nn. 6, 8; 262; 417; 448; V, 19, and n. 3; 70; 73; 91; 95; 96, n. 3; 104; 128; 266, and n. 1; VI, 182; 183, n. 4). See also Randolph to JM, 24 May 1783.

[3] Ambler to JM, 17 May 1783.

From Edmund Pendleton

Tr (LC: Force Transcripts). In the left margin at the top of the transcription, Peter Force's clerk wrote "MSS. [M]cGuire's." See *Papers of Madison*, I, xxii, xxiii. Addressed to "The Honble James Madison, Esqr Philadelphia."

Richmond, May 10, 1783

Dr Sir

I have no favr from you to acknowledge since my last,[1] but have one from our friend Mr Jones of the 29th past, who from former Lres

I expected had left Philada before that Period.[2] I am sorry to learn from him, that determinations in the British Courts of Admiralty (I suppose at N. York) have extended the period of legalising Captures at Sea to two Months from the ratification of the Preliminary Articles, which appears to me wholly unwarrantable by the terms of those Articles; besides the loss of much American property, such a glaring stretch of Judicial Rapacity gives an impression unfavourable to the Spirit of Conciliation held out by their King,[3] which meeting with something of the same impression in the revival of Committees in the East for sending back Refugees as fast as they appear, has not that healing Aspect, wch Peace was expected to produce, and may suddenly rekindle the flames of War, even before the definitive treaty is signed;[4] an event the British Parliament do not, from their debates, seem very averse to: It is a serious subject, but I will suppres further thoughts on it, leaving it to those to whom it belongs and who from a view of the whole are better enabled to form a Judgment on it.[5] We yet want 11 members to make an House of Delegates, which they expect will be compleated on Monday next.[6] many Projects of a Political nature, as well as relating to finance, are in Embryo, but I will not trouble you with the Indigested heap, which even the authors do not appear to have brought to any Point. my future letters will probably state them, as they shall be brought forth. In the mean time our trade is almost at a stand, many Vessells lying in the Rivers, not yet permitted to an Entry.[7] We have had some fine Rains—which has relieved us from the dread of a famine, from a remarkable drought in April.

I am My D Sr yr very Affe

EDMD PENDLETON

[1] Pendleton to JM, 4 May 1783, and n. 1.

[2] *Ibid.*, and n. 3.

[3] Jones appears to have been misinformed. See *Papers of Madison*, VI, 391, n. 4; 420–21, and n. 4; 422, n. 6; 430; 440; 441, n. 4; 449; 450, and nn. 1, 3; 451, n. 4; 456; 458, n. 3.

[4] With his letter of 29 April Jones may have included the *Pennsylvania Packet* of 26 and 29 April. These issues tell of town meetings in New Haven, Boston, and "a number of other towns to the eastward" adopting resolutions to bar Loyalists "and traitors" who seek "to return or remain among them." Several of the towns appointed committees to enforce these prohibitions, in spite of Articles IV and V of the preliminary articles of peace (*JCC*, XXIV, 248; Delegates to Harrison, 23 Aug. 1783).

[5] The issues of the *Pennsylvania Packet*, mentioned in n. 4, and also the issue of

24 April, printed extracts of proceedings in the House of Commons on 18 and 24 February and 3 March 1783 with regard to the provisional articles of peace. Several of their opponents called them "disgraceful and wicked, and treacherous," "shameful and extravagant concessions" which had "tarnished our splendid victories" and "diminished our grandeur." In the debate of 3 March, the reply to several speakers who advocated the retention of New York City until the definitive treaty of peace had been signed was that a withdrawal so long delayed would certainly lead to more armed conflict. See also *Va. Gazette*, 26 Apr.; Pendleton to JM, 4 May 1783, n. 5.

6 Ambler to JM, 3 May, n. 2; Harrison to Delegates, 9 May 1783.

7 Harrison to Delegates, 3 May; Randolph to JM, 9 May 1783, and n. 14.

Notes on Debates

MS (LC: Madison Papers). For a description of the manuscript of Notes on Debates, see *Papers of Madison*, V, 231–34.

Monday May 12. See Journal[1]

1 On 12 May, besides adopting instructions to Washington about the military posts in the Old Northwest and referring to a committee, JM, chairman, the Washington-Carleton correspondence about, and Washington's report on, the Tappan conference, Congress appears to have decided nothing of importance (JM Notes, 9 May, n. 2; *JCC*, XXIV, 337–40, 340, n. 1). See also Delegates to Harrison, 20 May 1783.

Tuesday May 13. No Congress.

Virginia Delegates to Benjamin Harrison

Letter not found.

EDITORIAL NOTE

13 May 1783. In a letter of 20 May to Edmund Randolph (*q.v.*), JM mentioned a "letter from the Delegation by the last post to the Govr.," asking him to inform the General Assembly of the expected negotiations "for a Treaty of Commerce" with Great Britain and of the delegates' wish to know "the final sense of the State" on that subject. Governor Harrison referred the letter to the House of Delegates on 22 May (*JHDV*, May 1783, pp. 16, 17). See also Instruction to Delegates, 23–24 May 1783.

To Thomas Jefferson

RC (LC: Madison Papers). Cover franked by JM and addressed to "Thomas Jefferson Esqr." Many years later, after recovering the letter, JM docketed the cover page, "Madison Jas May. 13, 1783." Henry D. Gilpin printed all of the letter except the last paragraph (Madison, *Papers* [Gilpin ed.], I, 531–32). The passages written in the JM-Jefferson Code No. 2 have been italicized by the present editors. In the left margin of a separate page, on which Jefferson decoded the first two paragraphs of the letter, JM wrote, "Decypher of May 13–1783."

PHILADA. May 13. 1783.

DEAR SIR

Marbois lately took occasion in our family[1] *to complain of ungenerous proceedings of the British against individuals as well as against their enemies at large and* finally signified that *he was no stranger to the letter transmited to Congress which he roundly avered to be spurious* His *information came from Boston* where [the] *incident is said to be no secret* but *whether* [it] *be the echo of letters from Philadelphia or has transpired from the correspondence of Mr. Adams to his private friends is* uncertain.[2] This *conversation passed during my absence in New Jersey*[3] *but was related to me by Mr. Carrol*

A project for a treaty of commerce with Britain has been reported by Secretary foreign affairs and is now[4] *in the hands of a committee*[5] *The objects most at heart are first a direct trade between this country & the West Indies Second a right of carrying between the later and other parts of the British empire Thirdly a right of carrying from West Indies to all other parts of the world*[6] *As the price of these* advantages *it is proposed that we shall ad*[mit] *British subjects to equal privileges with our own citizens As to the* [first] *object it may be observed that the bil*[l] *lately brought in British parliament renders it probable that it may be obtained without such a cession*[7] as to the *second that it concerns eastern states* cheifly and as *to the third that it concerns them alone*[8] Whilst the *privilege to be ceded* will cheifly if not alone *affect the southern states* The interest of these *seems to require that they should retain at least the faculty of giveing any* encouragement *to their own merchants ships or mariners which may be necessary to prevent relapse under scotch monopoly* or *to* acquire *a maritime importance* The *eastern states need no such precaution*[9]

Genl. Washington & Genl. Carlton have had an interview on the subject of arrangements for executing the provisional Treaty. It was interrupted by the sudden indisposition of the latter. In the conversation which took place he professed intentions of evacuating New York & all the posts in the U.S. held by British Garrisons as soon as possible, but did not authorize any determinate or speedy expectations. He confessed that a number of Negroes had gone off with the Refugees since the arrival of the Treaty, and undertook to justify the permission by a palpable & scandalous misconstruction of the Treaty, and by the necessity of adhering to the proclamations under the faith of which the Negroes had eloped into their service. He said that if the Treaty should be otherwise explained, compensation would be made to the owners and to make this the more easy, a register had been & would be kept of all Negroes leaving N.Y. before the surrender of it by the British Garrison. This information has been referred by Congs. to a Committee. But the progress already made in the discharge of the prisoners, the only convenient pledge by which fair dealing on the other side could be enforced, makes it probable that no remedy will be applied to the evil.[10]

I have sent Mr. Randolph a pamphlet comprehending all the papers which are to be laid before the States relative to the National debt &c. and have desired him to let you have the reading [of] it. The fewness of the copies made it impossible for me to get one for each of you.[11]

I am Dr Sir your sincere friend

J. MADISON JR.

[1] JM's fellow lodgers in the boardinghouse of Mrs. Mary House. Among them was Daniel Carroll, whom JM mentioned at the close of this paragraph. See *Papers of Madison*, VI, 180; 182, n. 29.

[2] On 13 March 1782 the Marquis de Barbé-Marbois, consul general of France in Philadelphia, wrote to Vergennes criticizing the terms of peace sought by Congress. Having intercepted this dispatch, the British made a copy of it available to the American peace commissioners. They forwarded it to Congress. See *Papers of Madison*, V, 436–37; 441; 443, nn. 2, 3; 444, n. 5; 466; VI, 6, and n. 2; 383; 385, n. 12. Although the commissioners' dispatches were intended by Congress to be confidential, they no doubt had been shown to Jefferson upon his arrival in Philadelphia on 27 December 1782 as a peace commissioner expecting to sail to France (*ibid.*, V, 171, n. 7; 393, n. 5). Adams commented on the Marbois letter in a copy of his "Peace Journal" sent to his wife. She showed or read portions of the journal to "Friends" and may have given it to Jonathan Jackson, who possessed a letter announcing its transmittal (L[yman] H. Butterfield *et al.*, eds., *Diary and Autobiography of John Adams* [4 vols.; Cambridge, Mass., 1961], III, 41–43, 55, 59, n. 4, 64). The letter, in spite of Marbois' insistence to the contrary, had been written by him (Richard B. Morris, *The Peace Makers: The Great Powers and American Independence* [New York, 1965], p. 325).

[3] *Papers of Madison*, VI, 498, and n. 2.

[4] In the manuscript, the ciphers for "affairs and is now" have become illegible. The decoding is taken from Madison, *Papers* (Gilpin ed.), I, 531.

[5] JM Notes, 6 May, and n. 3; JM to Jefferson, 6 May 1783, and n. 5. Livingston's "*project*" has not been found.

[6] The first two of these objects were rights or privileges which Americans had enjoyed as colonists, while the third, except for non-enumerated commodities, was a type of commerce barred to them by the British navigation acts. For a more comprehensive discussion of commerce by JM, see his letter of 20 May 1783 to Randolph.

[7] JM uses "cession" in the sense of "concession." He of course did not know that on 8 May the British House of Commons had debated ineffectually, and for the last time before Parliament adjourned on 16 July 1783, a bill introduced early in March "for the provisional establishment and regulation of trade and intercourse between the subjects of Great Britain and those of the United States of North America." Discussions of the measure or of amended versions of it on 7 and 11 March, 11 and 15 April, and 8 May revealed that it was much more vigorously opposed than supported (*Hansard's Parliamentary Debates*, XXIII, cols. 602–15, 640–45, 728–30, 762–65, 894–96, 1121–22). JM most probably had read the terms of the bill and a summary of the debate on 11 March in the *Pennsylvania Packet* of 8 and 13 May 1783. The bill seems to have been doomed from the outset, for its most influential proponent, the Earl of Shelburne, had been obliged to resign as prime minister on 24 February (*Hansard's Parliamentary Debates*, XXIII, col. 571; *Papers of Madison*, VI, 504, and n. 3).

In the course of a long speech in the House of Lords on 17 February 1783, defending the provisions of the preliminary articles of peace and advocating unhampered commerce with the United States, Shelburne had said: "Situated as we are between the old world and the new, and between the southern and northern Europe, all that we ought to covet upon earth is free trade, and fair equality. With more industry, with more enterprize, with more capital than any trading nation upon earth, it ought to be our constant cry, let every market be open, let us meet our rivals fairly, and we ask no more" (*Hansard's Parliamentary Debates*, XXIII, cols. 409–10).

[8] Ships owned and manned by New Englanders, rather than by citizens of the middle or southern states, carried most of the cargoes comprising American commerce with ports in the West Indies, the British Isles, and Europe. See *Papers of Madison*, VI, 288, n. 16; 291–92.

[9] In contrast with New England, the principal exports of the southern colonies had been staples, such as tobacco, rice, and indigo. The navigation acts obliged these commodities to be marketed only in England. This commerce, including that of the imports received in return, was often controlled by Scottish merchants and their factors resident in southern ports. Besides being charged with driving hard bargains, they had usually refused to join the patriot cause at the outbreak of the Revolution. See *Papers of Madison*, I, 115; III, 69, n. 2; 120, n. 1; V, 98, n. 4.

[10] *Ibid.*, VI, 462, and n. 2; 465; 466, n. 3; 466, and n. 1; 479; 480, nn. 6, 7; Walke to Delegates, 3 May, and nn. 2, 3, 5, 7; JM to Randolph, 6 May, and nn. 5, 6; JM Notes, 8 May; 9 May 1783, and n. 2. On 12 May Washington's letter of 8 May, enclosing copies of his correspondence with General Carleton and an account of their conference on 6 May, was referred to a committee, JM chairman (*JCC*, XXIV, 340, n. 1). This committee returned these documents to Charles Thomson on 21 May but apparently never submitted a report to Congress (NA: PCC, No. 186, fol. 101).

[11] JM to Randolph, 13 May 1783. The pamphlet is entitled *Address and Recommendations to The States by The United States in Congress assembled* (printed

by David C. Claypoole, Philadelphia, 1783). No doubt reflecting the "fewness of the copies," a second and slightly variant edition was published by Claypoole later in 1783. Other editions appeared during the same year in Massachusetts, Connecticut, New Jersey, Virginia, and England (*JCC*, XXV, 986–87). See also JM to Jefferson, 20 May 1783, and to Randolph on the same day.

To Edmund Randolph

RC (LC: Madison Papers). Cover missing. Randolph's surname is written in an unknown hand at the bottom of the letter's second page. Internal evidence permits no doubt that he was the addressee.

PHILADA. 13. May. 1783.

DEAR SIR

By Mr. Lee who set out yesterday afternoon I sent you a pamphlet collecting into one view all the acts & documents relative to the National debt &c which Congress have prepared for the Legislatures.[1] For still more minute information on the subject, I refer you to Mr. Jones who is now on his way to Virga. and will be at Richmond a few days after Mr. Lee.[2] I refer you to him rather than to the latter gentleman because the task will coincide more with his sentiments as to the measure.[3]

Genl. Washington & Genl. Carlton have had an interview on the subject of the provisional treaty which was interrupted by the indisposition of the latter. It wd. seem from the conversation which passed that altho' a sincere intention is professed of evacuating N.Y. & all the other posts, the time at which it may be expected is very uncertain; and that a shameful evasion of the article for restoring the slaves will be practiced. Carlton did not deny that numbers of them were going off from N.Y. and attempted to justify the indulgence by a most outrageous misconstruction of the Treaty; and by the [professed?] necessity of adhering to the tenor of the proclamations under which the Negroes had resorted within the British lines. He said that in case a different construction of the Treaty sd. be established a compensation would be made to the suffering owners, and that the precaution of keeping Registers of all Negroes which should leave N.Y. would be accordingly observed. An ominous sample of candor & good faith in our New friends![4]

We have no further advices of the definitive Treaty.[5] The sweets of peace begin to be amply enjoyed notwithstanding its delay. All foreign commodities have fallen to a price almost below example whilst the produce of the Country has proportionally risen beyond former prices. Salt is already down at ¼ Dr. per bushel & wheat up at 8/. perdo.[6] I hope a removal of all legal obstacles to a share of these blessings, will claim the first attention of the Assembly.[7] Their proceedings on that & other matters will furnish you with ample means I trust for resuming your correspondence as soon as your forensic labours will admit of a respite.[8] With great affection I am Dr. Sir Yr. fr[i]end & Sert.

J. MADISON JR.

The letter from the Govr. signifies that the territorial cession of Virga. has been revoked. Is this the fact? ascertain it & let me know.[9]

[1] JM to Jefferson, 6 May, and n. 4; 13 May 1783, and n. 11.

[2] Ambler to JM, 3 May, and n. 4; Pendleton to JM, 4 May, and n. 3; Randolph to JM, 24 May 1783.

[3] Arthur Lee, who in contrast with Joseph Jones opposed many of the provisions of the plan for restoring public credit, had not been in Congress on 18 April when the plan was adopted by an almost unanimous vote (*Papers of Madison*, VI, 430; 431, n. 9; *JCC*, XXIV, 261).

[4] JM to Jefferson, 13 May 1783, and n. 10.

[5] Pendleton to JM, 4 May, and n. 6; Randolph to JM, 9 May 1783, and n. 15.

[6] Although the issues of Philadelphia newspapers during the first half of May do not mention the price of salt or wheat and rarely give the price of any commodity, they contain abundant evidence of increasing amounts and varieties of French and British wares available for purchase.

[7] Randolph to JM, 9 May 1783, and n. 14.

[8] *Ibid.*, and nn. 1, 2.

[9] Harrison to Delegates, 3 May, and n. 4; Randolph to JM, 24 May 1783.

Notes on Debates

MS (LC: Madison Papers). For a description of the manuscript of Notes on Debates, see *Papers of Madison*, V, 231–34.

Wednesday May 14.

Mr. Hamilton & Mr. Elseworth moved a call on the States, to fulfil the recommendation relative to the Tories. After some remarks on the subject, the House adjourned.[1]

[1] Hamilton's motion, seconded by Oliver Ellsworth, is not noted in the official journal for 14 May. The "remarks" clearly related to Articles IV, V, and VI of the provisional articles of peace and foreshadowed the appointment the next day of a committee, Hamilton, chairman, and Ellsworth and JM among the other four

members: "To take into consideration & report to Congress what further steps are proper to be taken by them for carrying into effect the stipulations contained in the articles between the United States & Great Britain dated 30 November 1782" (NA: PCC, No. 186, fol. 102; *JCC*, XXIV, 248–49). See also JM Notes, 30 May 1783, and nn. 1, 2.

Notes on Debates

MS (LC: Madison Papers). For a description of the manuscript of Notes on Debates, see *Papers of Madison*, V, 231–34.

Thursday May 15. see Journal.

The Report relating to the Dept. of For: Affairs taken up and after some discussion of the expediency of raising the Salary of the Secy, Congress adjourned.[1]

[1] JM's original entry for this date probably was only "see Journal" (*JCC*, XXIV, 343–45). Upon discovering that the journal failed to mention the committee's report concerning the "Dept of For: Affairs," he crowded his sentence on that subject in tiny handwriting within the small space he had left above his entry, "Friday May 16. see Journal."

On 7 May Congress had appointed a committee, Arthur Lee, chairman, to consult with Robert R. Livingston "respecting his continuance in Office" as secretary for foreign affairs (NA: PCC, No. 186, fol. 100). The committee's report of 9 May consisted only of a letter of that date from Livingston, explaining again why he felt obliged to resign. On earlier occasions he had pointed out that his salary of $4,000 was about $3,000 less than his living expenses in Philadelphia as secretary for foreign affairs. See *Papers of Madison*, V, 342–43; 449; VI, 223; 224, n. 7; 281, n. 9; 418–19, and n. 4.

Probably few of the delegates on 15 May favored an increase in Livingston's salary, for Congress on 9 May had appointed a committee, Hamilton, chairman, "to consider and report the means of reducing expenditures in all" executive departments (*JCC*, XXIV, 337). See JM Notes, 23 May 1783.

From Edmund Randolph

RC (LC: Madison Papers). Unsigned but in Randolph's hand. Docket lacking. JM did not receive this letter until 9 June. See JM to Randolph, 10 June 1783.

Richmond May 15. 1783.

My dear friend

The assembly have plunged into business without delay;[1] and the important question of the impost has occupied their first attention. Mr. Henry is its strenuous supporter, and was the author of the resolution, by which an impost is declared to be fit for adoption under certain limitations and restrictions. What those limitations & restrictions shall be remain unknown, as they are left to the preparation of the committee, appointed to bring in the bill, to be founded on that resolution. It is unfortunate that this subject has been discussed under the aspect, in which congress formerly presented it to the different legislatures. The odious parts of the scheme, which the new recommendations will correct, furnish a topic of declamation, if not of solid argument against it. The committee will therefore probably defer their report, until the arrival of Mr. Jones, or some other bearer of the late proposals, relative to the impost.[2]

Mr. H—y being fixed in his opinion, little need be apprehended from the *Lee*ward quarter. I am informed, that much was said of the danger of introducing continental officers for the collection of the impost, and much was complained of this alteration for supplying the treasury of the U. S. against the provisions of the confederation. To these objections Mr. Henry ludicrously offered an easy remedy, by drawing the teeth and cutting the nails of the officers of revenue. The incroachment on the confederation met no serious answer.[3]

I wish for the sake of national honor, that the legislature had not been so rapid as they have been in repealing the acts against british merchandize. You will perceive, how eagle-winged they were in this business. I should be sorry for the eagerness after these proscribed commodities, if they did not tend to shew a determination to conform to the spirit of the treaty.[4]

The wiser opinion concerning the offensive branches of the treaty seems to be, at least to postpone any steps concerning them until the whole is laid open by the definitive one. Some ill-digested minds are daily belching out crude invectives, and determinations to oppose the collection of british debts. These however are checked by the moderation of better heads, which, howsoever they lament the recovery of these debts, will not violate the treaty; or in other words will not subject british executions to other impediments, than are imposed on those of our own citizens.

An exclusion of certain refugees is popular with some.[5] Mr. H—y rejects with indignation every resentment against petty objects, as being unworthy of legislative enmity, and being too likely to put aside from the view of the members of the assembly the wide-extended field of legislation.

Religion, which has been hitherto treated with little respect by the assembly, was yesterday incorporated into their proceedings. Mr. H—ry moved for a chaplain; and that a prayer should be composed adapted to all persuasions. The prayer has not been reported, tho' several trials, I am told, have been made.[6]

I have denied the mission of Payne to Rhode Island by an act of congress, as far as I was authorized so to do by the information, which I have as yet received. I wish to be authorized to go farther, even to a positive contradiction. For it carries an unfavourable impression. It leads the adversaries of congressional powers to declaim roundly against tampering &c.[7]

Colo. Nicholas has obtained leave to bring in a bill against the eligibility of members of congress to the assembly. It will succeed.[8]

I shall send you a copy of the journal, of every week, if the industry of the printer will suffer me. This second sheet is the only one relating to real business.[9]

1 Ambler to JM, 3 May 1783, n. 2.

2 On 16 December 1782, after being apprised of Rhode Island's refusal to approve the proposed 5 per cent impost amendment to the Articles of Confederation but before receiving word of the Virginia General Assembly's recision of its ratification of that amendment, Congress adopted a long report, drafted by Hamilton, urging the Rhode Island legislature to reverse its action. By May 1783 the coming of peace, attended with a growing stress upon the sovereignty of each state, rendered Hamilton's insistence upon the constitutional power of Congress to tax "the commerce of these states" and to appoint the collectors of the levy far more "odious" than it had been five months earlier (*JCC*, XXIII, 798–810; *Papers of Madison*, V, 385, n. 12; 407, and n. 1; 442; 445, nn. 16–18; VI, 8–9).

In January 1783 Governor Harrison, who deplored the repeal of the ratifying resolution by his state's legislature, received a copy of the Hamilton report from the Virginia delegates in Congress (*ibid.*, VI, 11; 12, n. 1; 14; 20). In his message of 5 May, submitting the Hamilton report and other documents to the House of Delegates, Harrison implicitly criticized the General Assembly for its act of recision by referring to Rhode Island's refusal as a severe blow to the credit of "the rising nation" (Executive Letter Book, 1783–1786, p. 106, MS in Va. State Library). Nine days later, following a recommendation by the "committee of the whole House on the state of the Commonwealth" that "an impost of five per cent on certain goods, imported, ought to be granted to discharge certain engagements made by Congress, under proper regulations," the House of Delegates appointed a committee, Mann Page, Jr., chairman, and Patrick Henry among the other nine members, to prepare a bill for that purpose (*JHDV*, May 1783, p. 7).

The qualifications of "certain goods," "certain arrangements," and "under proper regulations," if insisted upon by the General Assembly, obviously would render its adoption of the recommendations less than an equivalent of ratifying the impost amendment. See Jameson to JM, 24 May, and n. 3; Jones to JM, 25 May 1783. Furthermore, as Randolph remarked, the supporters of the bill were handicapped by being obliged to argue for it in the context of Hamilton's nationalistic report rather than in that of the plan for restoring public credit. For the arrival of Joseph Jones bringing a copy of that plan together with JM's "Address to the States," see Ambler to JM, 3 May, n. 4; Pendleton to JM, 4 May, n. 8; Jefferson to JM, 7 May,

n. 13; Instruction to President, 9 May, and n. 2; Randolph to JM, 9 May 1783, and n. 7.

[3] For the opposition of Arthur Lee and Richard Henry Lee to the proposed impost and their political rivalry with Patrick Henry, see *Papers of Madison*, V, 401; 404, n. 18; 453; VI, 12, nn. 3, 4; 55; Jefferson to JM, 7 May, and n. 8; JM to Randolph, 13 May 1783, and n. 3.

[4] Ambler to JM, 3 May, and n. 3; Delegates to Harrison, 6 May; Randolph to JM, 9 May, and n. 14; 24 May 1783.

[5] Pendleton to JM, 4 May, n. 6; 10 May, and n. 4; JM Notes, 9 May, and n. 3; Harrison to Delegates, 9 May, and n. 6; Randolph to JM, 9 May, nn. 4–5. Articles signed "Decius" and "A Whig" in the *Virginia Gazette* of 3 and 10 May 1783, respectively, also support Randolph's reference to "crude invectives."

[6] Although Henry's motion of 14 May is not recorded in the journal, the House of Delegates the next day adopted a resolution stipulating: "That the chaplain do compose a form of prayer, to be approved by the committee for Religion, fit and proper to be used in this House; and that it be a standing order, that divine service be performed every day, by using the said form or any other as the House may from time to time direct; and that service begin in the House immediately after the bell shall be rang for calling the House" (*JHDV*, May 1783, p. 7). The chaplain was the Reverend Benjamin Blasgrove (1746–1793), who on 28 June 1783 was voted £80 for his services during the session (*ibid.*, p. 96; *Va. Gazette, and Weekly Advertiser*, 13 Sept. 1793). The House of Delegates elected the standing "committee for Religion," William Cabell of Amherst County, chairman, on 13 May (*JHDV*, May 1783, pp. 4–5; Swem and Williams, *Register*, p. 17).

At the opening of each session from 1777 through 1780 the House of Delegates had appointed a chaplain. Henry's motion, therefore, was not original in asking for a resumption of the practice but in recommending that "a form of prayer" be composed and that the daily session open with a "divine service." Although the journal of the session of May 1783 omits further mention of the matter, the terms of the resolutions presumably became effective. Until 1806 the "standing order" remained unrepealed in spite of protests that it invaded liberty of conscience, united church and state, and obliged tax money to be spent for religious purposes (Sadie Bell, *The Church, the State, and Education in Virginia* [Philadelphia, 1930], pp. 151–56).

[7] What Randolph had heard about Thomas Paine was accurate, except that Congress did not pass a resolution authorizing him to go to Rhode Island at Confederation expense to urge the General Assembly of that state to adopt the proposed impost amendment. After engaging in a newspaper controversy in Philadelphia on behalf of the amendment, Paine went to Rhode Island in December 1782 and had at least five articles of the same tenor published in the *Providence Gazette* (William R. Staples, *Rhode Island in the Continental Congress, with the Journal of the Convention that Adopted the Constitution, 1765–1790* [Providence, 1870], pp. 428, 558; *Papers of Madison*, V, 375, n. 12). There is no doubt that Robert Morris employed Paine "to write for Continental measures" (Clarence L. Ver Steeg, *Robert Morris: Revolutionary Financier with an Analysis of His Earlier Career* [Philadelphia, 1954], p. 172). See also JM to Randolph, 10 June 1783. By the reprinting in the *Virginia Gazette* on 3 and 10 May 1783 of his "The Last Crisis, No. XIII," attention in Richmond had been drawn again to Paine, whom many Virginians heartily disliked because of his pamphlet in 1780 opposing the claim of their state to western lands. See *Papers of Madison*, III, 14, n. 17; VI, 498, n. 38.

[8] On 15 May the House of Delegates appointed George Nicholas and Thomas Smith of Gloucester County as a committee to prepare a bill "to repeal so much of any act, or acts of Assembly, as allows the delegates in Congress to be eligible to either House of Assembly" (Swem and Williams, *Register*, p. 17; *JHDV*, May

1783, p. 7). The bill, which Nicholas introduced the next day, was adopted in amended form by the House of Delegates on 21 May and by the Senate three days later. Upon being signed by the speaker of the House on 4 June 1783, the bill became a law (*ibid.*, pp. 9, 16, 18, 19, 34; Hening, *Statutes*, XI, 249–50). See also Jones to JM, 25 May 1783, and n. 4.

9 Enclosure not found. Lack of money and paper made the task of James Hayes, Jr., printer to the Commonwealth, very difficult. See *Papers of Madison*, VI, 9; 10, n. 11; 218, n. 1. In view of Randolph's comment in his letter of 24 May to JM (*q.v.*, and n. 9), he probably did not mean a printed version by "second sheet" but rather a handwritten copy made in the office of John Beckley, clerk of the House of Delegates.

Notes on Debates

MS (LC: Madison Papers). For a description of the manuscript of Notes on Debates, see *Papers of Madison*, V, 231–34.

Friday May 16. see Journal[1]

1 In the journal edited by Gaillard Hunt the entries for 16 May and the editorial augmentation thereof make clear that the session was almost wholly devoted to a consideration of petitions or to other particular rather than general issues (*JCC*, XXIV, 345–47, and nn.). Unmentioned in the journal was an inconclusive debate on the funds in Robert R. Livingston's custody. See *Papers of Madison*, VI, 418–19, and nn. 1, 3, 4.

Saturday May 17. no Congress.

From Jacquelin Ambler

RC (LC: Madison Papers). Letter unsigned but in Ambler's hand. Cover addressed to "The Honobl. James Madison of Congress Philadelphia." Docketed by JM, "May 17. 1783."

Richmond Virga. 17. May 1783

Dear Sir

Mr. Newton has at length sent the first Bills which I now transmit you, two of £500. each.[1] I was alarmed at the first view of them, being drawn at a very long period after sight, but I observe they were accepted as long ago as September last & of course payable immediately. As Mr. Mercer's order for £100. has been paid here; & Mr. Jones, I presume, will also expect to draw Money out of the Treasury on his arrival, I think it highly reasonable you should draw, in addition to your share of the present Remittance, a part of the arrears due to you.[2] this I hope you will be able to effect. in aid of this Mr. Attorney has drawn by warrants upon the Auditors £300. on your Accot. which he has commissioned Mr. Webb to remit to you.[3] I had procured three Bills of £100. each on Messrs. Inglis & Co. not doubting but the Auditors would on Mr. Randolph's first application issue warrants for £300. on your Accot. but it seems they have lost the Account I was at so much trouble to state for them & they now fancy the Balance due to you even to this time does not exceed the £200.[4] I kept no Copy of that Accot. but I hope you have & shall be obliged to you to send it by next post.[5] I hope on sight of it to be able to satisfy the Gentlemen that you are under the Mark. The extreme hurry of business must apologize for this *scrawl*.

Be so good as forward an acknowledgment from the Gentlemen of the Sums each have drawn in the several Genl. Dividends & request the favor of them to state their Accots. to the 31st March inclu. & transmit them to the Auditors directing warrants to be made out.[6] there is no other mode of adjusting their Accounts

1 Ambler to JM, 3 May 1783, and nn. 1, 2.

2 Ambler to JM, 10 May 1783, and n. 1. These bills were drawn on Lacaze and Mallet, merchant-importers, on Water Street, between Arch and Race streets, Philadelphia (Delegates to Auditors, 28 May; *Pennsylvania Journal*, 8 Mar. 1783). For Jones's arrival in Richmond on 20 May, see Jones to JM, 25 May 1783.

3 Ambler to JM, 10 May, and n. 2; Randolph ("Mr. Attorney") to JM, 24 May 1783. Foster Webb, Jr., was commissioner of the state treasury of Virginia (*Papers of Madison*, IV, 173, n. 12; V, 266, n. 1).

4 On 31 December 1782 the balance due JM had been £865 8*s*. 3*d*. Including the £200 which he would take as his share from the bills of exchange enclosed in the present letter, he had been paid £475. Thus there was still owed to him £390 8*s*. 3*d*. and his daily stipend of £2 3*s*. ($8.00) since 1 January 1783 (*Papers of Madison*, VI, 326, n. 3; 379; 455, n. 2; JM to Bland, 6 May, hdn., and n. 1; Statement of Receipts, 28 May 1783).

5 Statement of Receipts, 28 May 1783.

6 The Virginia delegates were obligated by a statute of 1 July 1782 to submit quarterly financial statements (Hening, *Statutes*, XI, 31–32).

Benjamin Harrison to Virginia Delegates

FC (Virginia State Library). In the hand of Thomas Meriwether. Addressed to "Virginia Delegates in Congress."

In Council May 17th. 1783.

Gentlemen

I have nothing of Consequence to communicate to you by this Post[.] a sufficient Number to constitute an Assembly met on Munday last, but the great Business of the Session is not sufficiently open'd to enable me to form a conclusive Judgment on the Steps that will be taken to improve the present happy Moment.[1]

I could wish you to hasten the determinations of Congress on the Subject of a revenue as much as possible or they may come too late for the necessary discussion and therefore go perhaps unattended to.[2] You some Time ago promised to send me a Copy of the Offer made by N. York of a Teretory to Congress, for the purpose of building a Town for their reception, and to hold their meetings in[,] which has slip'd your Memory, I wish you again to think of it and to send it forward with any proposal that may be made by Maryland, as I like the Idea of fixing it at George Town and have no doubt of our Assembly's coming into any reasonable Proposition that shall be made to them.[3]

I am with respect Gentlen: yrs: &c.

B. H.

[1] Ambler to JM, 3 May, n. 2; Randolph to JM, 15 May 1783.
[2] Jefferson to JM, 7 May 1783, nn. 6, 13.
[3] *Papers of Madison*, VI, 447; 448, nn. 4–7. See also Jones to JM, 28 June 1783.

From Edmund Pendleton

Tr (LC: Force Transcripts). In the left margin at the top of the transcription, the clerk wrote "MSS McGuire's." See *Papers of Madison*, I, xxii, xxiii. The second paragraph, copied from the original manuscript, appears in Stan. V. Henkels Catalogue No. 694 (1892).

RICHMOND May 17th 1783

DR SIR

Your favr of the 6th reached me here in the usual course, for which I am now to make my Acknowledgements.[1]

I think with you that there appears no reason to suppose either of the Imperial Courts will at all concern themselves with the terms of a compromise in which they are not Interested, but considering it as a mere Compliment, will soon return the Preliminaries with their courtly approbation.[2] Nor do I think the Financial circumstances of Britain afford any ground to suppose they would wish to depart from the Accommodation, the terms of which are as favourable as they could desire, granting, as they seem to have long agoe admitted, that the Independence of America was to form the Basis of it;[3] a circumstance however which Sr. G. Carlton seems to have forgot in his answer to Genl. Washington upon the subject of a proposed Interview, had the Genl. proposed to be accompanied by Mr Clinton in his Official Character. At[4] any time during the Contest, the opposition of a like Character under the King, as the companion of Sir Guy, would have been witty, & not exceptionable; but according to the Provisional & Prelimy. Articles, the Sovereignty of the United States, being acknowledged, the official Character of Mr Clinton stands Recognized even by themselves, and his attendance on Such a meeting within the state of which he was Chief Majestrate, was a measure pointed out & justified by the Strictest propriety. To make a proposition therefore to drag into life a burried officer of former opposed Rank, but now no more, & add another who to keep up the Metaphor scarcely deserved Xstian burial, and that by their names of Office; to meet Govr Clinton smels strongly of a designed Insult; Sir Guy may however explain himself into some Innocent meaning, & I wish he may.[5]

The House of Delegates have Passed a law for admitting to entry sevl Vessels now in our ports, but who could not be admitted to Entry by our prohibitory Laws, wch are considered as in force until the Signature of the definitive treaty, as the only Act wch terminates the War—but we have not yet a Senate to give this New law a Sanction, to the great mortification of some Gentlemen, who seem to long for the Flesh Pots of Egypt, particularly some cheese & Porter in a Vessel from Ireland.[6]

Mr Jones is not yet arrived with yr propositions,[7] but as they are represented, an opinion favourable to them appears to be gaining ground, tho' the impost only has been the Genl. Subject of conversation. the various Projects for the Session, still remain in an Indegested state, so that I must still suspend any account of them to a future day. it is sd Mr H—y is all powerful hitherto.[8] I am as usual

Dr Sr Yr. very Affe & obt Servt

EDMD. PENDLETON

[1] The next paragraph suggests that JM in his missing letter of 6 May to Pendleton had included information contained in his letter of that date to Randolph (*q.v.*).

[2] *Papers of Madison*, VI, 504, and n. 2; Randolph to JM, 9 May 1783. The word "return," which Peter Force's clerk omitted in the transcript, is taken from Henkels' excerpt mentioned in the headnote.

[3] *Papers of Madison*, V, 418, n. 17; VI, 354, n. 4; 449, n. 10; Pendleton to JM, 10 May, and n. 5; JM to Jefferson, 13 May 1783, and n. 7.

[4] If the Henkels excerpt from the original letter is accurate, Pendleton placed a dash rather than a comma after "Interview" to indicate, even though he did not capitalize the "h" in "had," that the remainder of the present sentence was equivalent to a new one. The excerpt, furthermore, has Pendleton place a comma rather than a period after "character" and follow that word with a lower case "A" in "at." These alterations help to clarify Pendleton's meaning.

[5] Before being officially informed by King George III of his recognition of the independence of the United States, General Carleton would have appropriately designated Andrew Elliot as the royal lieutenant governor of New York and taken him to the Tappan conference of 6 May as a "witty" or shrewd offset to the attendance of Governor George Clinton. Holding that the recognition of independence had in effect canceled the commission of that British civil official, Pendleton did not so much object to his presence at the conference as to Carleton's continued use of his obsolete title in his letter to Washington. In his reply to Carleton and report to Congress, Washington apparently ignored that "use" as a possibly "designed Insult." See JM to Randolph, 6 May, and n. 6; JM to Jefferson, 13 May 1783, and n. 10; Fitzpatrick, *Writings of Washington*, XXVI, 370, 402–6, 410–12.

[6] Randolph to JM, 9 May, and n. 14; Pendleton to JM, 10 May, and n. 4. The unidentified "Vessel from Ireland" was probably the seemingly unnamed one mentioned in a letter of 8 May from Williamsburg to Governor Harrison. Only a brief summary of this letter has been found by the present editors (*Cal. of Va. State Papers*, III, 481). The craft may have been an "Irish cutter" of the design described by Pendleton in an earlier letter to JM (*Papers of Madison*, V, 96; 98, n. 4). See also Randolph to JM, 24 May 1783.

[7] Ambler to JM, 3 May, n. 4; Instruction to President, 9 May 1783, n. 2.

[8] Jefferson to JM, 7 May, and n. 10; Pendleton to JM, 10 May; Randolph to JM, 15 May, and nn. 2, 3; Harrison to Delegates, 17 May 1783.

Notes on Debates

MS (LC: Madison Papers). For a description of the manuscript of Notes on Debates, see *Papers of Madison*, V, 231–34.

Monday May 19.

Spent in debating the Report recommending provision for Tories according to the Provisional Artics. of peace.[1]

[1] The session of 19 May is not noted in the journal (*JCC*, XXIV, 347, n. 1). On 20 March Congress referred an instruction from the Virginia General Assembly regarding the confiscated property of British subjects, and resolutions of the Executive Council of Pennsylvania regarding private debts owed to Loyalists or other British subjects, to a committee composed of Samuel Osgood, chairman, John Francis Mercer, and Thomas FitzSimons (*Papers of Madison*, VI, 370; 371, n. 3). The committee's report, submitted on 1 April, apparently was not debated until 19 May. By then Osgood had left Congress. For the report and the reconstituted committee, see Instructions to Peace Commissioners, 20 May, and nn. 1, 3; JM Notes, 14 May, n. 1; 20 May, and n. 5; 26 May 1783, and n. 1.

Motion of Instructions to Peace Commissioners

MS (NA: PCC, No. 69, II, 433–34). In JM's hand and docketed by him, "Motion of Mr. Madison May 20. 1783."

[20 May 1783]

That the sd. Ministers[1] be instructed also to endeavor to insert in the Difinitive Treaty of peace between U. S. & G. B, reasonable provision for the interests of such of the Inhabitants of Canada as may have suffered by confiscations or sequestrations of their effects, in Consequence of their engaging in the service of the U. S.[2]

That the sd. Ministers be further instructed to contend for an express stipulation in the difinitive Treaty of peace providing for a fair liquidation of all charges for subsistance of prisoners of war and other just purposes, & for discharge of the balances which may appear to be due.[3]

1 These opening words suggest that while Congress was in session on 20 May, JM drafted the motion as an addendum to the report of the committee to which the memorial of the Pennsylvania Supreme Executive Council and the instruction of the Virginia General Assembly to its delegates in Congress had been referred on 20 March. See JM Notes, 19 May 1783, and n. 1. The "Ministers" were Franklin, John Adams, and Jay.

2 This recommendation recalls the memorials of Thomas Wiggans and Moses Hazen. See *Papers of Madison*, VI, 191, n. 16; 442; 443, n. 1; 445, n. 10. Although this first paragraph of the motion is canceled with crosshatches in ink, JM's notes for 20 May (*q.v.*) are warrant for concluding that the paragraph had been referred to a committee before the deletion was made.

3 JM Notes, 19 May, and n. 1; 20 May 1783, and n. 5. The issue of inducing the British to recompense Congress for subsisting their many troops held as prisoners of war by the Americans had been of long duration. See *Papers of Madison*, II, 277, n. 1; IV, 172, n. 6; 330–31; 331, n. 5; V, 105, n. 8; 191, n. 27; VI, 457. For the embodiment of JM's second recommendation in instructions adopted by Congress on 30 May, see JM Notes, 30 May 1783, n. 3.

Notes on Debates

MS (LC: Madison Papers). For a description of the manuscript of Notes on Debates, see *Papers of Madison*, V, 231–34.

Tuesday May 20.

On the proposal to discharge the troops who had been enlisted for the war (amounting to ten thousand men) from the want of means to support of them.

Mr. Carroll urged the expediency of caution, the possibility that advantage might be taken by G. B. of a discharge both of prisoners and of the army, and suggested the middle course of furloughing the troops.[1]

Mr. Dyer was strenuous for getting rid of expence; considered the war at an end: that G. B. might as well renew the war after the definitive Treaty as now; that not a moment ought to be lost in disburdening the public of needless expence.

Mr. Rutlidge viewed the conduct of G. B. in so serious a light that he almost regretted having voted for a discharge of Prisoners.[2] He urged the expediency of caution, and of consulting the Commander [in] chief. He accordingly moved that the Report be referred to him for his opinion & advice. The motion was seconded by Mr. Izzard.

Mr. Clarke asked whether any military operation was on foot that the Commander in Chief was to be consulted. This was a national question, which the National Council ought to decide. He was agst. furloughing the men because they would carry their arms with them:[3] He said we were at peace, & complained that some could not separate the idea of a Briton from that of cutting throats.

Mr. Ellsworth enlarged on the impropriety of submitting to the Commander in Chief a point on which he could not possess competent materials for deciding. we ought to discharge the men engaged for the war or to furlough them. He preferred the former.

Mr. Mercer descanted on the insidiousness of G. B. and warmly opposed the idea of laying ourselves at her mercy, that we might save fifty thousand dollars; altho' Congress knew that they were violating the Treaty as to Negroes.[4]

Mr. Williamson proposed that the Soldiers be furloughed. Mr. Carroll seconded him, that the two modes of furlough & discharge might both lye on the table.

By general consent this took place.

The Report as to confiscated property, on the Instructions from Virga. & Penna. was taken up, & agreed to be recommitted,[5] together with a motion of Mr. Madison to provide for the case of Canadian refugees, & for settlement of accts. with the British, and a motion of Mr. Hamilton to insert, in a definitive Treaty a mutual stipulation not to keep a naval force on the Lakes.[6]

[1] The journal of Congress does not mention the proposals about troops noted by JM (*JCC*, XXIV, 348). On 24 April Congress resolved that although the war would not officially end until the signing of the definitive peace treaty, Washington

should use his discretion in furloughing or discharging troops enlisted for the duration of the war (*Papers of Madison*, VI, 486, and nn. 1–3). Prior to the date of the present item, Washington authorized at least one commanding officer to grant furloughs to the most discontented among his troops but apparently decided against discharging those enlisted for the duration of the war (Fitzpatrick, *Writings of Washington*, XXVI, 384, 429, and n. 53, 430).

[2] *Papers of Madison*, VI, 457; 458, nn. 3, 10; 462, and n. 2; 465; 466, n. 3; 466, and n. 1; 479; 480, n. 5. For the vote on 15 April 1783 by John Rutledge, see *JCC*, XXIV, 243.

[3] Although Abraham Clark may have assumed correctly that duration-of-war troops on furlough would "carry their arms" to their homes, he could not defend his statement by quoting the resolutions of 24 April. They obviously were a compliance with Washington's suggestion of 18 April that "at the Discharge" those soldiers should be complimented by giving them their "Arms and Accoutrements" (*JCC*, XXIV, 270; Fitzpatrick, *Writings of Washington*, XXVI, 332–33; *Papers of Madison*, VI, 486, and n. 1). On 26 May 1783, however, Congress adopted Hamilton's motion to furlough duration-of-war troops and allow them "to take their arms with them" (*JCC*, XXIV, 364). See also *JCC*, XXIV, 390.

[4] Walke to Delegates, 3 May, and nn. 2, 3, 5, 7; JM to Randolph, 6 May 1783, n. 6.

[5] JM Notes, 19 May 1783, and n. 1. The report of the committee, Osgood, chairman, apparently exists no longer in its original form. During the debate on 20 May, the report may have been amended before it was referred to a committee comprising Mercer, chairman, FitzSimons, and Bland (*JCC*, XXIV, 375 n.). The report, as printed in the journals (*JCC*, XXIV, 372–76), is no doubt a mixture of the recommendations of the Osgood committee, the Hamilton committee, the Mercer committee, and still later the Wilson committee, and probably also of amendments made during the debates in Congress on 19, 20, 29, and 30 May. Since separate documents written by each of these committees and detailed records of the debates are no longer extant, the evolution of the report from its first to its final form cannot be traced. The much corrected manuscript of the ultimate report is in NA: PCC, No. 20, II, 153–56.

[6] Instructions to Peace Commissioners, 20 May 1783, and n. 2, *JCC*, XXIV, 348, and nn. 1, 2; Syrett and Cooke, *Papers of Hamilton*, III, 361; JM Notes, 29 May, and n. 1; 30 May 1783, and n. 3.

Virginia Delegates to Benjamin Harrison

Printed extract (*Cal. of Va. State Papers*, III, 485). The style of the paragraph quoted in this abstract suggests that the letter was written by JM, except for the signatures of Bland and Mercer.

[20 May 1783]

They had recd. his letter of the 9th and had made the correction therein indicated, to Mr. Thompson, in regard to the territorial cession.[1]

"If an official & joint correspondence with your Excelly. be less circumstantial than that which individual delegates may enter into with their private friends, we persuade ourselves that your Excelly. is too sensible both of our public & private respect for your character to impute to any defect of either. The difference can only proceed from the necessity in the former case of confining ourselves, not only to such matters as are worthy of the public, & for which we can be officially responsible, but to such also, with respect to which no diversity of private opinions may exist."[2]

No further news from Europe—Sir Guy Carleton in reply to a letter from Genl: Washington had expressed his former sentiments regarding the negroes, uttered at the conference held at Orange Town, &c.[3]

[1] Harrison to Delegates, 3 May, and n. 4; 9 May 1783.

[2] Harrison to Delegates, 9 May 1783, and n. 3.

[3] Walke to Delegates, 3 May, and nn. 3, 5; JM to Randolph, 6 May, and n. 6; 13 May; JM Notes, 8 May, and 12–13 May 1783, n. 1. On 19 May Congress received a letter, written five days earlier by Washington, enclosing a dispatch of 12 May from General Carleton (*JCC*, XXIV, 347, n. 1; Fitzpatrick, *Writings of Washington*, XXVI, 430). In his letter Carleton repeated that although many Negroes, who had been freed before he became commander-in-chief, had sailed with Loyalists and British troops from New York City late in April for Nova Scotia, the name of each and of his "original proprietor" had been carefully entered in a "register." Thus, continued Carleton, if he had violated the preliminary articles of peace, Congress could seek reparation on behalf of the owners through the usual diplomatic channels (NA: PCC, No. 152, XI, 279–85; Jared Sparks, ed., *The Writings of George Washington* . . . [12 vols.; Boston, 1834–37], VIII, 543–45). See also Delegates to Harrison, 27 May 1783.

"Orange Town," now Orangeburg, is near the Tappan Zee, the portion of the Hudson River by which "the conference" is usually designated.

To Thomas Jefferson

RC (LC: Madison Papers). Unsigned but in JM's hand. Addressed to "Thomas Jefferson Esqr." Following the return of this letter to JM, he docketed it "Madison Jas." above the date. Many years after the letter was written, he or someone at his bidding placed a bracket at the beginning of the second paragraph and another bracket at the close of the third paragraph to designate them for inclusion in the first comprehensive edition of his writings. See Madison, *Papers* (Gilpin ed.), I, 538–40.

PHILADA. May 20. 1783.

DEAR SIR

In obedience to your request I am to answer by this post your favor of the 7. inst:[1] recd yesterday. My brevity will therefore be excused.

For the tenor of the conditions on which Congs. were formerly willing to accept the cession of Virga. I beg leave to refer to their resolutions of the 6 of Sepr. & 10 of Ocr. 1780.[2] I take it for granted you have their Journals. The expunging of the article relative to State expences was a subject of no less regret with me than it is with you & for the same reason,[3] but I acknowledge that considering the probable defect of vouchers in Virga.[4] & the ardor with which the clause was supported from some other quarters, mine was much diminished in the course of the discussion. On the last trial there were but two or three States besides Virga. that favored it. *S. Carolina's* opposition to it had great weight.[5] After this clause was expunged it was thought improper to retain the connective clause as Virga. will now be at liberty to confine her accession to the revenue part of the plan, without enlarging her territorial Cession or being deprived of the opportunity of annexing any Conditions she may think fit. The connective clause however could not have been carried I believe either before or after the mutilation of the plan.[6] Notwithstanding this disappointment I adhere to my wishes not only that the revenue may be established, but that the fœderal rule of dividing the burdens may be changed,[7] and the territorial disputes accomodated. The more I revolve the latter subject, the less inducement I can discover to a pertinacity on the part of Virga. and the more interesting it appears to the Union.[8]

I am sorry your departure from Richmond became necessary before more of the members were assembled. I make no doubt that useful impressions have been left with those who were so & were susceptible of them. I shall keep in mind the intimation relative to Mr. Short.[9] The idea of adding the fraction of a year to my Congressial service is totally new, and even if it sd. prevail, will not as far as I can now see, coincide with my private conveniency.[10]

Since my last I have been able to procure for you a copy of pamphlet which I herewith enclose. If in consequence of the provisional steps I before took it sd. prove a duplicate I shall thank you to forward one of them to my father.[11] The ladies & gentlemen join me in complimts. to Miss Patsy & to your self.[12]

Adieu.

1 *Q.v.* See also *Papers of Madison*, VI, 502, and n. 3.

2 *Papers of Madison*, II, 77–78; 78, n. 2; 136–37; 138, n. 2; VI, 315, n. 14.

3 Jefferson to JM, 7 May, and n. 3; Randolph to JM, 9 May 1783.

4 The defective vouchers were both those which were nonexistent because they had been destroyed by the British during their invasions of Virginia and those supporting the controversial claims of Oliver Pollock and Simon Nathan for military supplies furnished to Virginia troops in Kentucky and the Illinois country. See *Papers of Madison*, VI, 14; 15, n. 8; 30, n. 8; 54, and n. 2; 154; 155, n. 2; 192; 212; 215, n. 14; 474; 475, nn. 3–5; 476, nn. 6, 7; 502; Delegates to Gálvez, 4 May 1783, and ed. n., nn. 1–3.

5 The italicization of "*S. Carolina's*" signifies that JM underlined it. The South Carolina delegates, including the influential John Rutledge, had favored expunging

the article, even though the state had incurred heavy expenses in resisting the British. The Pennsylvania delegates, also contrary to expectation, had voted to retain the article. On 21 April, the date of the "last trial," only New York and Pennsylvania joined Virginia in an effort to reinstate the article in the plan for restoring public credit. See *Papers of Madison*, VI, 291; 292; 310; 314, n. 1; 316, n. 16; 317–18, and n. 2; 400–401; 403, nn. 11–13; 404, nn. 14, 18; 442–43; 444, nn. 2, 6–8; 468, and n. 1; 469; 470, nn.; *JCC*, XXIV, 256, n. 1.

JM's "ardor" may have been "much diminished" by finding the Pennsylvanians ranged on his side. Their state had usually obtained the prior consent of Congress before going into debt for war purposes and had consistently opposed Virginia's claims to the territory north and west of the Ohio River. He almost certainly knew that James Wilson, the ablest member of the Pennsylvania delegation, as well as Robert Morris and other leading residents of Philadelphia, was a shareholder in western land companies based on grants deemed invalid by Virginia (Thomas Perkins Abernethy, *Western Lands and the American Revolution* [New York, 1937], pp. 216, 239, 263; *Papers of Madison*, VI, 443; 444, nn. 7, 8; 471; 472, n. 4).

6 *Papers of Madison*, VI, 440; 441, n. 6; 471; 472, nn. 2–4; 481; 482, nn. 10, 11.

7 *Papers of Madison*, VI, 327; 402; 404, n. 22; 405, n. 27; 406; 408; 440; 481; 482, n. 10.

8 In the report on restoring public credit, JM had stated that a cession of the western lands to Congress would be "a further mean[s] as well of hastening the extinguishment of the debts, as of establishing the harmony of the U. States" (*Papers of Madison*, VI, 312–13; 442–43; 502, and n. 3). JM also believed that for Virginia to retain title to, and jurisdiction over, most of her western territory would be to her disadvantage both politically and economically. If Congress was ceded the West, it would become the common possession of all the states, thus serving as a much needed bond of union among them (*Papers of Madison*, V, xvii; 116; 119, n. 19; 276; 292, n. 19).

9 Jefferson to JM, 7 May 1783, and nn. 8–11, 14, 15. Following "so," JM obviously meant the word "assembled" to be interpolated.

10 *Ibid.*; also *Papers of Madison*, VI, 464, and n. 6. JM's "private conveniency" probably related either to his expected marriage to Catherine Floyd in the autumn or to his plan to study and to collect primary sources on the American Revolution (*Papers of Madison*, V, 232). JM inadvertently wrote "coinincide" instead of "coincide" and an "I" between "far" and "as."

11 JM to Jefferson, 13 May 1783, and n. 11.

12 *Papers of Madison*, VI, 182, nn. 28, 29; JM to Jefferson, 6 May 1783, and n. 12.

To Edmund Randolph

RC (LC: Madison Papers). Unsigned but in JM's hand. Docketed by Randolph, "Js. Madison, Jr. May 1783." Many years later, after the letter was returned to JM, he wrote below the date line, "Randolph, Edm." In another hand "[20?]" was inserted between "May" and "1783." Apparently the same person wrote "96 Vol. I" at the top of the right margin of the first page of the letter. The reference beyond doubt is to JM's letter of 20 August 1784 on American commerce as printed in Madison, *Letters* (Cong. ed.), 1, 90–99. Bracketed letters and words denote blurring in the manuscript to the point of illegibility.

PHILADA. [20] May 1783

MY DEAR SIR

Your favor of the 9th. inst:[1] was duly brought by yesterday's Mail. My impatience is great to know the reception given to the propositions of Congress,[2] by the Assembly. I foresaw some of the topics which are employed against them, & I dread their effect from the eloquent mouths which will probably enforce them; but I do not despair. Unless those who oppose the plan, can substitute some other equally consistent with public justice & honor, and more conformable to the doctrines of the Confederation, all those who love justice and aim at the public good will be ad[v]ocates for the plan. The greatest danger is to be apprehended from the difficulty of making the latter class sensible of the impracticability or incompetency of any plan short of the one recommended; the arguments necessary for that purpose being drawn from a general survey of the fœderal system, and not from the interior polity of the States singly.[3]

The letter from the Delegation by the last post to the Govr. apprised the legislature thro' him that negociations for a Treaty of Commerce with G. B. might be expected soon to take place and that if any instructions should be deemed proper no time ought to be lost in giving the subject a legislative discussion. For my own part I wish sincerely that the commercial interests of Virginia were thoroughly investigated & the final sense of the State expressed to its representatives in Congress.[4]

The power of forming Treaties of Commerce with foreign nations is among the most delicate with which Congs. are intrusted, and ought to be exercised with all possible circumspection. Whilst an influence might be expected from them on the event or duration of the war, the public interest required that they should be invited with all the respectable nations of Europe, and that nice calculations of their tendency should be dismissed. The attainment of the object of the war has happily reversed our situation and we ought no longer to enslave ourselves to the policy of the moment. The State of this Country in relation to the Countries of Europe it ought to be observed, will be continually changing, and regulations adapted to its commercial & general interests at present, may hereafter be directly opposed to them. The general policy of America is at present pointed at the encouragement of Agriculture, and the importation of the objects of consumption. The wid[er] therefore our ports be opened and the more extensive the privileges of all competitors in our Commerce, the more likely we shall be to buy at cheap & sell at profitable rat[es.] But in proportion as our lands become settled, and spare hands for manufactures & navigation multiply, it *may* become our policy to favor those objects by peculiar privileges, bestowed on our own Citizens; or at least to introduce regulations inconsistent with foreign engagements suited to the present state of things.[5]

The relative situation of the different States in this respect is another motive to circumspection. The variance of their policy & interests in the article of commerce strikes the first view, and it may with great truth be noted that as far as any concessions may be stipulated in favor of foreign nations they will cheifly be at the expence of those States which will share least in the compensations obtained for them. If for example, restrictions be laid on the Legislative rights of the States to prohibit, to regulate or to tax as they please their imports & exports, & to give such preferences as they please to the persons or vessels employed in them, it is evident that such restrictions will be most felt by those States whi[ch] have the greatest interest in exports & imports. If on the other side the Citizens of the U.S. should in return for such a stipulation be [ob]l[ig]ed to navigate & carry, in forbidden channels, is it not equally evident [that] the benefit must fall to the share of those States which export & consume least, and abound most in resources of ships & seamen.[6]

Nor should it be overlooked that as uniform regulations of the Commerce of the different States, will so differently affect their different interests, such regulations must be a strong temptation to measures in the aggrieved States which may first involve the whole confederacy in controversies with foreign nations, and then in contests with one another. I may safely suggest also to your ear, that a variety of circumstances make it proper to recollect that permanent engagements entered into by the Confederacy with foreign powers, may survive the Confederacy itself;[7] that a question must then arise how far such engagements formed by the States in their fœderal character are binding on each of them separately, and that they may become pretexts for quarrels with particular States, very inconvenient for the latter, or for a general intrusion into American disputes. On the other hand candor suggests that foreign connections, if founded on principles equally corresponding with the policy & interests of the several States might be a new bond to the fœderal compact.

Upon these considerations I think it would be advisable to form all our commercial Treaties in future with great deliberation, to limit their duration to moderate periods, & to restrain our Ministers from acceding finally to them till they shall have previously transmitted them in the terms adjusted, for the revision & express sanction of Congress. In a Treaty of Commerce with G. B. it may be the policy of Virga. in particular to reserve her right as unfettered as possible over her own commerce. The monopoly which formerly tyrannized over it,[8] has left wounds which are not yet healed, & the numerous d[eb]ts due from the people, & which by the provisional articles they are immediately liable for, may possibly be made instruments for reestablishing their dependence.[9] It cannot therefore be for the interest of the State to preclude it from any regulations which experience may recommend for its thorough emancipation. It is possible that experience may never recommend an exercise of this right, nor do my own sentiments favor in general, any restrictions or preferences in matters of commerce, but those who succeed us will have an equal claim to judge for themselves and will have further lights to direct their judgments. Nor ought the example of old & intelligent nations to be too far or too hastily condemned by an infant & inexperienced one. That of G. B. is in the science of commerce particularly worthy of our attention: And did she not originally redeem the management of her Commerce from the monopoly of the Hanse towns by peculiar exemptions to her own subjects? did she not dispossess the Dutch by a like policy? and does she not still make a preference of her own Vessels & her own mariners the basis of her maritime power?[10] If Holland has followed a different system the reason is plain. Her object is not to exclude rivals from her own navigation but to insinuate herself into that of other nations.[11]

The leading objects in the proposed Treaty with G. B. are 1. a direct commerce with the W. Indies. 2. the carrying trade between the different parts of her dominions. 3. a like trade between these & other parts of the world. In return for these objects we have nothing to offer of which we could well deprive her, but to secure to her subjects an entire equality of privileges with our own Citizens.[12] With regard to the 1. object it may be observed, that both the temper & the interest of the nation leave us little ground to apprehend an exclusion from it. The French have so much the advantage of them from the facility of raising food as well as the other produce of their Islands, that the English will be under the necessity of admitting supplies from the U.S. into their Islands, and they surely will prefer paying for them in commodities to paying for them in cash.[13] With regard to the 2 & 3 objects it may be observed that altho' they present great advantages, they present them only to those States which abound in maritime resources. Lastly with regard to the concession to be made on the part of the U.S. [it] may be observed that it will affect cheifly, if not solely, those States which will share least in the advantages purchased by it. So striking indeed does this contrast appear that it may with certainty be inferred that If G. B. were negociating a Treaty with the former States only, she would reject a mutual communication of the privileges of natives, nor is it clear that her apprehensions on this side, will not yet lead her to reject such a stipulation with the whole.[14]

If this subject should be taken up by the Legislature, I hope that altho' not a member, your attention & aid will be given to it. If it sh. not be taken up publickly, I wish for your own private sentiments & those of the most intelligent members which you may be able to collect.[15]

We have no European intelligence. Sr. G. Carlton in a letter to [Gel.] W. avows the same sentiments as were expressed in the conference relative [to the] negroes, but repeats his caution agst. their being understood as the national construction of the Treaty.[16]

I send you herewith three more copies of the pamphlet of Congress which I have procured since my last.[17] If Majr. Moore[18] & Mr. F. Strother[19] sd. be in the Assembly, I beg the favor of you to present one with my compliments to each of them. The third you will dispose of as you may think best.

In reviewing the freedom of some of the remarks which I have hazarded above, I am almost induced to recall them till I can cover them with [cyph]er.[20] As there is little danger attending the mail at present, and your own [discretion?] will take care of such as may be improper to be reverberated to this place, I shall upon the whole let them stand.

1 *Q.v.*

2 Instruction to President, 9 May 1783, n. 2.

3 Randolph to JM, 24 May; 14, 21, and 28 June; Jones to JM, 25 and 31 May; 8, 14, 21, and 28 June; Pendleton to JM, 2 June 1783; James Mercer to John Francis Mercer, 6, 21 May, 4 June 1783, *Va. Mag. Hist. and Biog.*, LIX (1951), 97–99, 100–102, 185–86.

4 Delegates to Harrison, 13 May, ed. n.; Instruction to Delegates, 23–24 May 1783. JM's comments in the present letter reflect the prominence of commercial treaties in the proceedings of Congress for over a month. On 12 April JM became chairman of a committee instructed to report on the general problem of commercial treaties and on the particular issue of negotiating one of them with Russia. The report on Russia drafted by FitzSimons, a member of the committee, was submitted on 22 April, debated on 21 May, and superseded the next day by proposals made during the debate (*JCC*, XXIV, 267, and n. 11; *Papers of Madison*, VI, 453, nn. 3, 7; JM Notes, 21–22 May; Instruction to Dana, 22 May 1783). On 6 May Congress transferred the other assignment of this committee to a new committee which also was to submit a plan of a treaty with Great Britain and "instructions to the minister

for negotiating it" (JM Notes, 6 May, and n. 3; JM to Jefferson 6 May 1783, and n. 7). For JM's earlier views of commercial treaties, see *Papers of Madison*, V, 476; VI, 452.

5 JM underlined "may." Article IX of the Articles of Confederation conferred upon Congress "the sole and exclusive right and power" to enter into treaties, "provided that no treaty of commerce shall be made whereby the legislative power of the respective states shall be restrained from imposing such imposts and duties on foreigners, as their own people are subjected to, or from prohibiting the exportation or importation of any species of goods or commodities whatsoever." Article VI forbade the states to lay any imposts or duties which traversed the stipulations of a commercial treaty with France or those of a proposed treaty with Spain (*JCC*, XIX, 216, 217).

Although JM necessarily had these provisions in mind, his discussion centers upon the place of commercial treaties in shaping the peacetime foreign policies of the United States and as being shaped by the divergent economic interests of the thirteen states. Even if free trade were beneficial to an agricultural nation, the rise of American manufacturers and shipping might make protective tariffs and preferential tonnage duties desirable. Because of changes to be anticipated in both international and interstate economic relationships, the provisions of a commercial treaty should be applicable during a short term only.

6 JM had often stressed the prime interest of the New England states in shipping and hence in high freight rates as opposed to the need of the southern states to market their surplus staples overseas as inexpensively as possible. See *Papers of Madison*, VI, 287; 288, n. 16; 290–92; 298–99; 431, n. 2.

7 *Ibid*., IV, xviii–xix; 6–7; 56, 57, n. 7; V, xviii–xix; VI, 258, n. 4; 293, n. 15; 327; 392; 429.

8 JM to Jefferson, 13 May 1783, n. 9.

9 *Papers of Madison*, VI, 47; 48, n. 4; 340; 341, n. 5; 370; 416; 418, n. 10; 422–23; 439; 458, n. 3; Randolph to JM, 15 May, and n. 5; JM Notes, 19 May 1783, and n. 1.

10 In 1578 Queen Elizabeth of England had abolished the special privileges which merchants of the Hanse towns (Hamburg, Lübeck, Bremen, etc.) had enjoyed in the "Steelyard" of London for over three centuries (W[illiam] Cunningham, *The Growth of English Industry and Commerce during the Early and Middle Ages* [reprint of 5th ed., New York, 1968], p. 195; W. Cunningham, *The Growth of English Industry and Commerce in Modern Times* [reprint of 4th ed.; New York, 1968], p. 74). The English Navigation Acts, enacted by Parliament in the third quarter of the seventeenth century and still in force in 1783, had been directed mainly against the Dutch. The Anglo-Dutch naval wars of 1652–54, 1665–67, and 1672–74 largely resulted from their rivalry in trade and navigation.

11 *Ibid*., pp. 7–8, 675, n. 4; Pierre Daniel Huet, *A View of the Dutch Trade in all the States, Empires and Kingdoms in the World* (trans. from the French; 2d ed.; London, 1722), pp. 13, 17, 19, 32; George Masselman, *The Cradle of Colonialism* (New Haven, 1963), pp. 30, 44–69, 468–69. These references support JM's generalization. The Dutch premise, as Huet expressed it, was that trade "has not any Enemy so Mortal as Constraint." Producing little from their own soil, the Dutch were obliged to secure the raw materials for their manufacturing industries from the sea, foreign countries, or their own colonies. Obviously, therefore, they favored free trade. To "insinuate" themselves into the carrying trade, they charged lower freight rates than their rivals.

12 JM Notes, 6 May, and n. 3; JM to Jefferson, 13 May, and nn. 6, 7; *JCC*, XXIV, 320–21, 404. See also *Papers of Madison*, IV, 476, and nn. 2, 3; 477, nn. 4, 5.

13 JM was overly sanguine in expecting Great Britain, because her West Indian islands were not self-sufficient in food, to allow foreigners to trade with them. See *Papers of Madison*, VI, 334; 337, n. 13; 340; 356; 357, n. 17.

[14] Great Britain's desire to be again the principal market for American agricultural staples, produced mainly in the South, and to pay for them with her manufactured goods might induce her to permit American merchantmen to engage in her carrying trade, both between her colonies and the mother country and between them and foreign countries. If so, the southern states would be the cause but not the beneficiary of a concession chiefly advantageous to New England.

[15] Randolph apparently did not accede to JM's request (Randolph to JM, 14, 21, and 28 June).

[16] Delegates to Harrison, 20 May 1783, and n. 3.

[17] JM to Jefferson, 13 May, and n. 11; 20 May; JM to Randolph, 13 May 1783.

[18] For William Moore, a member of the House of Delegates from Orange County, see *Papers of Madison*, I, 147; 148, n. 2.

[19] French Strother (1733–1800) of Culpeper County served as a member of the Virginia Convention of 1776, of the House of Delegates from 1776 to 1791, and of the Senate of the Virginia General Assembly from 1791 to 1800. He was also a member of the Convention of 1788 in Virginia which ratified the Federal Constitution. In 1783 he owned 26 slaves (*Va. Herald* [Fredericksburg], 4 July 1800; Swem and Williams, *Register*, pp. 1–54, *passim*, 242, 243; Augusta B. Fothergill and John Mark Naugle, comps., *Virginia Tax Payers, 1782–87, Other Than Those Published by the United States Census Bureau* [n.p., 1940], p. 121). JM and Strother probably became friends when they were fellow members of the Convention of 1776, as they held similar views on religious liberty.

[20] JM had encoded the paragraph in his letter of 13 May 1783 to Jefferson (*q.v.*) relating to the proposed treaty of commerce with Great Britain. In that communication, however, he had not clearly signified that he was expressing his own views of the subject.

Notes on Debates

MS (LC: Madison Papers). For a description of the manuscript of Notes on Debates, see *Papers of Madison*, V, 231–34.

Wednesday May 21.

Thursday. May 22.

See the secret Journal for these two days.

The passage relating to the armed neutrality was generally concurred in for the reasons which it expresses.

The disagreements on the questions relating to a Treaty of Commerce with Russia, were occasioned chiefly by sympathies particularly in the Massachusetts Delegation with Mr. Dana; and by an eye in the navigating & Ship building States to the Russian Articles of Iron & Hemp. They were supported by S. Carolina who calculated on a Russian market for her rice.[1]

[1] On 12 April 1783 Congress referred to a committee, composed of JM, chairman, Nathaniel Gorham (Mass.), and Thomas FitzSimons, the dispatch of 16 December 1782 from Francis Dana, minister-designate at the court of St. Petersburg. Before FitzSimons on 22 April reported for the committee, its members were directed

also to consider Dana's dispatch of 19 December 1782, enclosed in a covering letter from Robert R. Livingston, secretary for foreign affairs. The committee recommended that Dana should be permitted "to return to America so soon as he can with propriety"; should be instructed to decline Russian proposals for a commercial treaty unless negotiations had advanced so far as to injure "the faith and honor of the United States" by withdrawing; and, in that event, should insist on limiting the duration of the treaty to a maximum of fifteen years (*Papers of Madison*, VI, 427, n. 13; 452; 453, nn. 1–3; *JCC*, XXIV, 267).

Reaching no decision on 22 April except that the treaty must also provide for "exact reciprocity" and should not go into effect until approved by Congress, further consideration of the committee's report was "postponed" until 21 May. On that day the report was replaced by Hamilton's lengthy motion, seconded by JM, which, save for a paragraph on the "armed neutrality," chiefly constituted a rephrasing of the committee's terse recommendations so as to render them less offensive to Dana and his friends in Congress. JM suggested that although the rejection of the motion by a vote of 6 to 3 signified that one too few state delegations agreed with the proposals regarding the commercial treaty, the members "generally concurred" with Hamilton's statement about the "armed neutrality." JM implicitly included the latter subject in his motion of 22 May (*q.v.*). On 21 and 22 May, in five of the six tallied polls taken on issues connected with the commercial treaty, the Massachusetts and South Carolina delegations all voted alike (*JCC*, XXIV, 348–57; Instruction to Dana, 22 May 1783, and n. 3).

After pointing out that the "primary object" of Dana's mission was to treat for the admission of the United States to the League of Armed Neutrality, and that the peace treaty with Great Britain had greatly lessened the importance of this "object" as a support of American independence, Hamilton continued: "That though Congress approve the principles of armed neutrality, founded on the liberal basis of a maintenance of the rights of neutral nations and of the privileges of commerce, yet they are unwilling, at this juncture, to become a party to a Confederacy which may hereafter too far complicate the interests of the United States with the politicks of Europe" (*JCC*, XXIV, 350, 351–52). For Dana and the League of Armed Neutrality, see *Papers of Madison*, II, 56, n. 3; 165; 167, nn. 2, 3; III, 45, n. 9; 221, n. 14; IV, 10–11; 16, n. 24; 182, n. 14; 388, n. 11; V, 189, n. 13; *JCC*, XVIII, 1166–73, and esp. 1169; Rights of Neutral Nations, 12 June, and nn. 7, 8; JM Notes, 12 June 1783, and n. 3; David M. Griffiths, "American Commercial Diplomacy in Russia, 1780 to 1783," *William and Mary Quarterly*, 3d ser., XXVII (1970), 397–410.

Motion of Instruction to Francis Dana

MS (NA: PCC, No. 36, II, 121).

[22 May 1783]
MR MADISON MR CARROLL[1]

That Mr. Dana be informed that the Treaties lately entered into for restoring peace, have caused such an alteration in the affairs of these States, as to have removed the primary object of his mission to the Court of Russia, the acquisition of new supports to their Independence[2]

That he be instructed, in case he shall have made no propositions to the Court of Russia on the subject of a Treaty of Commerce to decline making such untill he shall receive further instructions from Congress: that in case he shall have made such propositions, he be informed that it is the desire of Congress, that as far as will consist with the honor of the U. S. he insist on a limitation of the Treaty to the period of 15 years, and that the same be subject to the revisal & approbation of Congress before they shall be obliged to accept or ratify it.

That a Come: be appointed to prepare & report a plan of a Treaty proper to be transmitted to Mr. Dana.[3]

[1] The journal entry for 22 May begins: "Congress resumed the consideration of the subject under debate yesterday; and the report of the committee being again postponed," JM offered a motion, seconded by Daniel Carroll. For "the report of the committee," see JM Notes, 21–22 May 1783, and n. 1.

[2] Near the top of the manuscript JM started the draft of his motion beginning with what is now the second paragraph. Evidently having sharpened his quill, he wrote beneath this paragraph so much of his new introductory paragraph as begins with "that the Treaties lately entered into" and ends with "supports to their Independence," and preceded the whole with an asterisk. He then wrote at the top of the page, "That Mr. Dana be informed." and placed an asterisk at each end of the phrase. This odd separation indicates that the paragraph relating to the "primary object" of Dana's mission, although first in the text as introduced, was drafted later than the rest of the motion (*JCC*, XXIV, 354). For the "primary object," see JM Notes, 21–22 May 1783, and n. 1.

[3] *Ibid.* The effort of Oliver Ellsworth of Connecticut and Nathaniel Gorham of Massachusetts to have Congress postpone consideration of JM's motion was supported only by the delegates of their own states and Rhode Island. JM's motion was then lost by a vote of 5 to 3. The delegates of New Jersey, Pennsylvania, Maryland, Virginia, and North Carolina were unanimously for the proposal; those of Massachusetts, Connecticut, and South Carolina unanimously against; the two of Rhode Island deadlocked; New York's single vote not counting, and New Hampshire, Delaware, and Georgia unrepresented. Thereupon, Congress unanimously adopted Ellsworth's motion: "That Mr. Dana be instructed, in case he has not already proceeded too far in the commercial treaty," to "stipulate, that the treaty be limited to the term of fifteen years; and that the same be subject to the revisal and approbation of Congress, before they shall be under obligations to accept or ratify it." FitzSimons was named chairman of a committee to "report a plan of a commercial treaty proper to be transmitted to Mr. Dana" (*JCC*, XXIV, 355–57). See also Rights of Neutral Nations, 12 June, and nn. 5–7; JM Notes, 12 June 1783.

Notes on Debates

MS (LC: Madison Papers). For a description of the manuscript of Notes on Debates, see *Papers of Madison*, V, 231–34.

Friday May 23

The Report from Mr. Hamilton Mr. Gorham and Mr. Peters, in favor of discharging the soldiers enlisted for the war, was supported on the ground that it was called for by Economy[1] and justified by the degree of certainty that the war would not be renewed.[2] Those who voted for furloughing the soldiers, wished to avoid expence, and at the same time to be not wholly unprepared for the contingent failure of a definitive treaty of peace.[3] The view of the subject taken by those who were opposed both to discharging and furloughing, were explained in a Motion by Mr. Mercer seconded by Mr. Izard to assign as reasons, first that Sr. Guy Carlton had not given satisfactory reasons for continuing at N. York. second, that he has broken the articles of the provisional Treaty relative to the negroes, by sending them off.

This motion appeared exceptionable to several, particularly to Mr. Hamilton, & rather than it should be entered on the Journal by yeas & nays, it was agreed that the whole subject should lye over.[4]

The Report relating to the Department of For: Affairs being taken up: Mr. Carroll seconded by Mr. Williamson moved that no public Minister should be employed by the U. S. except on extraordinary occasions.[5]

In support of the proposition it was observed that it would not only be economical, but would withold our distinguished Citizens from the corrupting scenes at foreign Courts, and what was of more consequence would prevent the residence of foreign Ministers in the U. S. whose intrigues & examples might be injurious both to the Govt. & to the people.[6]

The considerations suggested on the other side were that Diplomatic relations made part of the established policy of Modern Civilized nations, that they tended to prevent hostile collisions by mutual & friendly explanations, & that a young Republic ought not to incur the odium of so singular & as it might be thought disresp[ect]ful innovation. The discussion was closed by an adjournment till Monday.[7]

[1] *JCC*, XXIV, 358. On 23 April Congress resolved that, even before the signing of the definitive treaty of peace, Washington should furlough or discharge soldiers enlisted for the duration of the war, "if circumstances shall" so "require" (*Papers of Madison*, VI, 486, and n. 2). By mid-May "the mutinous dispositions" of some of the troops led him to sanction "Furloughs for any length of time they wish; we are better without them than with them" (Fitzpatrick, *Writings of Washington*, XXVI, 429–30, 443). Of the 10,399 troops in Washington's main army, composed of the continental lines of the four New England states, New York, and New Jersey, 6,022 were of duration-of-war status (NA: PCC, No. 137, II, 451).

Another of the compelling circumstances was lack of money. Acceding to a request of 9 May from Robert Morris, superintendent of finance, Congress appointed a committee, composed of Hamilton, chairman, Gorham, and Richard Peters (Pa.), to consult with him. Following their conference six days later, Morris addressed to them a long "State of my Department and the Resources I can command," supporting his conclusion that the army, except for a garrison at West Point, must be "disbanded immediately." If the "Army is kept together," Morris warned, "they will consume as much in one Month as the Taxes will produce in two and Probably much more. To make them three Months Pay will require I suppose at least six hundred thousand Dollars and every Day they continue in the Field lessens the Practicability of sending them Home satisfied." With his statement Morris enclosed extracts from the records of his office showing that, from 1 January to 15 May 1783, the outgo had exceeded the income by $583,599.78. Of the $941,609.57 in receipts, slightly over one-fourth had come from the seven states which had been able and disposed to pay at least part of their requisition quotas. Most of the rest had been derived from drafts on loans to the United States by Louis XVI of France and Dutch bankers, or from additional drafts on them for money which it was hoped they had made or would make available (NA: PCC, No. 137, II, 433–55; Syrett and Cooke, *Papers of Hamilton*, III, 356–61).

2 After remarking that "all the other beligerent Powers have been disarming for months past," Morris commented in his letter to the committee: "To express Doubts of the Sincerity of Britain on this Subject is I know a fashionable but in my Opinion a very foolish Language. We have the best Evidence of their Sincerity which the Nature of Things will admit for we know they are unable to carry on the War and we see & feel that they are passing every Act and doing everything in their Power to conciliate our Affections" (Syrett and Cooke, *Papers of Hamilton*, III, 360).

3 Except for FitzSimons and Wilson of Pennsylvania, all the delegates who favored "furloughing" represented the states providing the troops in Washington's army. For this reason a sectional distribution of votes defeated JM's motion, seconded by Carroll, to recommit the committee's report and, later in the session, the motion to adopt the report. These tallies also reveal that Peters, a member of the committee, had not agreed with its recommendation (*JCC*, XXIV, 359, 360–61).

4 Walke to Delegates, 3 May, and nn. 2, 5; JM to Randolph, 6 May, and nn. 5, 6; 13 May; JM to Jefferson, 13 May; Delegates to Harrison, 20 May 1783, and n. 3. Although Ralph Izard drafted the motion, Mercer introduced it and later wrote "withdrawn" below the text (NA: PCC, No. 36, II, 127; *JCC*, XXIV, 361, and n. 1). Hamilton evidently believed it to be impolitic to make "discharging and furloughing" depend upon the continuing occupation of New York City by the British and their refusal to surrender the slaves there to their alleged owners. Regarding these as three separate issues, he supported the wish of Washington and Morris to reduce the size of the main army; introduced on 26 May a motion protesting "the British seizure of Negroes belonging to citizens of the United States"; and, three days later, a motion informing Washington of Congress' desire that "the evacuation of New York and its dependencies may not be retarded by a preference to that of any other place" (*JCC*, XXIV, 363–64, 368; JM Notes, 26 May 1783, and nn. 1, 2).

5 Neither the "Report" nor the motion is mentioned in the journal for 23 May. See JM Notes, 15 May 1783, and n. 1.

6 *Papers of Madison*, VI, 223; 224, n. 7; 272; 287.

7 In a letter of 20 May 1783, Stephen Higginson, a delegate from Massachusetts, informed Samuel Adams: "There are those also among us who wish to keep up a large force, to have large Garrisons, to increase the navy, to have a large diplomatic Corps, to give large Sallaries to all Our Servants. Their professed view is to strengthen the hands of Government, to make us respectable in Europe, and I believe, they might add to divide among Themselves and their Friends, every place of honour and of proffit. but it is easy to see where all this will lead us, and Congress I think is not yet prepared for such Systems" (Burnett, *Letters*, VII, 167). Hamilton surely was one of "those among us" to whom Higginson referred (Syrett and Cooke, *Papers of Hamilton*, III, 351–53). See also JM to Jefferson, 10 June 1783.

Instruction to Virginia Delegates *in re* Treaty of Commerce

FC (Virginia State Library).

EDITORIAL NOTE

On 22 May 1783 the Virginia House of Delegates referred to the Committee of Commerce the letter of 13 May from the delegates in Congress to Governor Benjamin Harrison (Delegates to Harrison, 13 May 1783, ed. n.; *JHDV*, May 1783, p. 16). On 23 May, instead of the committee's recommendation, the House of Delegates unanimously adopted a resolution of instruction drafted by Joseph Jones. The Senate concurred the next day (*JHDV*, May 1783, pp. 17–18, 19; Jones to JM, 25 May 1783).

In the House of Delegates

Friday 23d. of May 1783

Resolved that the Delegates from this State to Congress be instructed that the Legislature approve a treaty of Commerce with Great Britain upon principles of reciprocity desiring however that no treaty of Commerce between these States and any power whatsoever may be finally concluded on, before the same shall have been sent to Congress for approbation and the different States have had an opportunity of considering it, that in the mean time the Legislature approve of a provisional treaty with Great Britain whereby the Commercial intercourse between the two Countries may be facilitated.[1]

Teste

John Beckley Clk HD[2]

1783 May 24h.
Agreed to by the Senate.
Will Drew. C. S[3]

[1] The recommendation of the Committee of Commerce, which was discussed in "a committee of the whole House," read: "That it be recommended to the members of Congress of this State, in the instructions they are about to give to our plenipotentiaries abroad, respecting a treaty of commerce to be entered into by them with Great Britain, that it is the desire of the legislature of this State to act upon liberal and generous principles, allowing to that nation the same advantages in point of commerce, which they are willing to allow us, reserving to ourselves the right of giving any bounty in tonnage or otherwise, to vessels built within this State." Perhaps the most striking contrast between this proposal and the resolution of instruction adopted by the committee of the whole House and thereafter by the House of Delegates was in the matter of preferential tonnage duties. By a statute

of the Virginia General Assembly, enacted in the session of October 1782, all vessels, no matter whether owned by Virginians, residents of other states, or by foreigners, were obliged, upon entering or clearing from a Virginia port, to pay a tax of 1*s*. 3*d*. per ton (Hening, *Statutes*, XI, 121). This tonnage tax, insofar as it applied to vessels of under "the burthen of sixty tons" owned by citizens of Virginia or Maryland, was abolished by the Virginia legislature on 28 June 1783 (*ibid*., XI, 289; *JHDV*, May 1783, p. 99).

A copy of the instruction, with which the Senate had concurred on 24 May, was enclosed by Governor Harrison to the Virginia delegates in his letter of 31 May (*q.v*., and n. 4). On 10 June JM commented in his letter to Randolph (*q.v*.) that "The principle on which" the resolution "is founded corresponds precisely with my idea." By then JM almost certainly knew that Joseph Jones had drafted the instruction (Jones to JM, 25 May 1783). No evidence has been found that the Virginia delegates submitted the resolutions to Congress. They probably regarded the instruction as a standing order to guide their actions in the event that a provisional commercial treaty should be received by Congress.

2 Clerk of the House of Delegates.

3 Clerk of the Senate.

From Jacquelin Ambler

RC (LC: Madison Papers). Docketed by JM, "May 24. 1783."

RICHMOND VIRGA. 24. May 1783

DEAR SIR

The Auditors have at length found the Accot. and are now satisfyed that I did not exceed the mark when I assured them the Bal. due to you on the 1st. Jany last was upwards of £800. in consequence of which they have given Mr. Webb a Warrt. on your Accot. for £100. which he will transmit you in addition to the £200. sent last Post.[1] I must repeat my request that the Gentlemen of the Delegation will forward to the Auditors States of their several Accots. with directions to them to issue Warrants for the respective sums they have divided. their directions to the Auditors to issue the Warrts. may be sent altho they may not have time to adjust & send the Accots. I am about to settle the affairs of the Treasury with a Committee of the Assembly & without Warrants I cannot accomplish it.[2]

Yrs. affect'ly,

J. AMBLER

If any Vessel Offers to James River from Philal. I will be particularly obliged to you to send us two Rheam of best Office writing Paper one pound Sealing Wax. six boxes Wafers & 500 best Dutch Quills. Money

shall be repaid immediately on your sending the Accot.[3]
Paper & wax Certificates acct.

[1] JM to Bland, 6 May, hdn.; Ambler to JM, 17 May 1783, and n. 4.

[2] Statement of Receipts, 28 May 1783. Although the "Committee" to which Ambler referred has not certainly been identified, it may have been a subcommittee of the standing Committee for Courts of Justice, Thomson Mason, chairman, elected by the Virginia House of Delegates on 13 May. On 26 May the Mason committee introduced an omnibus bill embracing among other provisions several for continuing in effect a number of temporary laws relating to the treasury (*JHDV*, May 1783, pp. 5, 21). For later comments by Ambler on the Virginia "Gentlemen in Congress" and their "Warrants," see his letter to JM of 5 July 1783.

[3] For the probable outcome of this request, see Ambler to JM, 14 June 1783.

From David Jameson

RC (LC: Rives Collection of Madison Papers). Docketed by JM, "May 24. 1783."

Richmond May 24. 1783

Dr Sir

I heartily congratulate you on the return of Peace—an event that places every thing within our reach to give us as a people human Felicity. I have the pleasure of being informed by Mr. Jones that you enjoy a good state of health—a close & constant application to business seems not to have been so prejudicial to you as I feared it would.[1] You have had much to do and not a little remains still to be done beside other matters of great moment that of establishing or rather of drawing the great outlines of an universal Commerce will require much deliberation. You will receive a short resolution of the Assembly in answer to your request on that head[2]

A Bill is under consideration to lay Duties &ca. agreable to the recomendation of Congress for a National Revenue, which I doubt not will pass.[3] the mode of collecting those duties is not fixed but I suppose Congress will have the appointment of some officers on the occasion. I take the liberty to offer my services should you think me worthy of an appointment. the injury I have suffered by the depredations of the British and the much greater by depreciation (having recd. considerable sums in paper money for debts due to me before the war); will make it necessary to turn my attention to something:[4] And as I have formerly mentioned to you, the giving a constant or very frequent attendance at this place is very inconvenient to me. An act has passed to repeal the act for seizure & condemnation of British goods—And to permit the entry of British Vessels[5] with the highest esteem

I am Dr Sir Yr obt. hume Ser

David Jameson

[1] David Jameson was a senator from the district which included Yorktown, his home (*Papers of Madison*, I, 217, n. 2). Joseph Jones was also attending the Virginia General Assembly as a delegate from King George County (Ambler to JM, 3 May 1783, and n. 4). While Jameson and JM were fellow members of the Council of State in 1778–1779, JM's health had been precarious but was much improved after March 1781 (*Papers of Madison*, I, 215; II, 56, n. 7; 84, n. 1; 143; 163; III, 13, 25–26).

[2] Instruction to Delegates, 23–24 May 1783, and n. 1.

[3] Jameson was overly sanguine. See Randolph to JM, 15 May and n. 2. The committee, which the House of Delegates had appointed on 14 May to prepare a bill for levying a qualified 5 per cent impost on behalf of Congress, made no report and was "discharged" from its assignment on 3 June (*JHDV*, May 1783, pp. 7, 33). See also Randolph to JM, 24 May, and nn. 5, 6; Pendleton to JM, 26 May 1783, and n. 11. The congressional plan for restoring public credit included provisions for impost duties. For this reason the receipt of the plan by the House of Delegates on 22 May 1783 rendered largely irrelevant the bill which the committee was considering.

[4] For Jameson's heavy losses of slaves and other property during the British occupancy of Yorktown and its environs in 1781, see *Papers of Madison*, III, 215; V, 392. Prior to the Virginia statute of 5 January 1782 abolishing the legal-tender quality of the state's depreciated paper currency, Jameson evidently had been obliged to accept much of it from his prewar debtors (*ibid.*, III, 29, n. 17; 336, nn. 3, 4).

[5] Hening, *Statutes*, XI, 195; Ambler to JM, 3 May, n. 5; Randolph to JM, 15 May 1783.

From Edmund Randolph

RC (LC: Madison Papers). Unsigned but in Randolph's hand. Cover missing.

Richmond May 24. 1783.

My dear friend.

The address of congress has at length arrived, and received the commendations to which it is so justly intitled, and some of which I should enumerate here with cordiality, did I not perceive the marks, which it bears of your pen.[1] Dr. Lee, who came yesterday, delivered me the copy, intrusted by you to him for my use.[2]

A nice division took place about three days ago, whether the taxes should be postponed in their collection until october or december. The majority was in favor of the latter day but was too small to furnish a decided opinion, as to the final issue. The numbers were, I believe, 53 & 50.[3] One of the reasons against the postponing of the collection was, that the revenue from the impost could not reach congress early enough for those immediate demands of money, which their necessities daily create. This fell from an unauspicious mouth, not well addicted to the impost itself. It was answered by Mr. Henry, who remains the firm friend of this measure, that it was unavoidable, it being out of the power of the people to pay the taxes so quickly, and that his favorite scheme of the impost must supply congress from the pockets of the wealthy consumer.[4] But there is a considerable hesitation, when the impost is urged to be irrevocable: and with some the objection can never be subdued, unless credit should be allowed for the surplus of our just quota:[5] I find it difficult to repel the false reasoning of those, who use this language by the clear doctrine on this head: and it is now a cant phrase on the tongues of the disaffected to the impost, that we cannot rate our ability to pay by our consumption, as the other states fairly may.[6] After all, I trust the recommendation of congress will work its way.

Œconomy is driven at by every member of the assembly: and a bill is now before the committee of the whole house for reducing the salaries of the different officers. The governor's 1000£ per annum keeps its ground by a majority of 5, the council have lost 100£ per annum, & the judges have received by addition 100£ per annum. Thus far the change has gone by shifting from the council to the judges 100£ per annum.[7] A bill for the reduction of the number of members of congress has miscarried.[8] It is presumed that you will not object to remain in Philadelphia until the completion of the term, allotted for your existence by the confederation. It is the general wish, that you should continue until March 1784.[9]

Our ports are fully open to British ships: and I am sorry to see a general ardor after those commodities which public acts have so lately proscribed. For our national reputation is too dear to be lost in the opinion of those people, who beyond the water have admired our self-denial, by a hunger and thirst after cheese and porter.[10]

The exclusion of members of congress from seats in the legislature will, I believe, certainly take effect.[11]

I inclose to you two sheets of the journal: the first, which I omitted to send to you last week and the third. I shall go to Wmsburg. for a week, but shall instruct George Hay to apply to the clerk, who has promised me to transcribe every thing, occurring in the day worthy of notice, and to supply my absence.[12]

At Mr. Ambler's request I drew a warrant the other day in your name for £300, 200£ of which he has already remitted to you, and the balance goes on this week, as I am informed.[13]

Adieu: for at present I can add nothing certain as to the repeal of the cession:[14] the being wholly new to me; and I have not time this morning to satisfy myself. This is the last day of the court and they are urgent for my attendance.[15]

1 Delegates to Harrison, 6 May, and n. 3; Instruction to President, 9 May 1783, n. 2.

2 JM to Randolph, 13 May 1783.

3 Jones to JM, 25 May, and n. 3; Pendleton to JM, 26 May 1783. The close "division" probably occurred during a debate in a "committee of the whole House on the state of the Commonwealth" and therefore was not entered in the journal of the Virginia House of Delegates (*JHDV*, May 1783, pp. 16, 17). For the measure to which Randolph referred, see also *Papers of Madison*, VI, 500; 501, n. 8; Randolph to JM, 9 May 1783, and n. 4.

4 *Ibid.* For the impost, see Randolph to JM, 15 May, and n. 2; Jameson to JM, 24 May, and n. 3; Jones to JM, 25 May 1783.

5 In the plan for restoring public credit, adopted by Congress on 18 April, the first five paragraphs dealing with impost duties and financial requisitions upon the states were declared by the sixth paragraph, once they had been adopted by all the states, to be "irrevocable by any one or more of them without the concurrence of the whole, or of a majority of the United States in Congress assembled" (*JCC*, XXIV, 257–59). The third paragraph, contrary to what the opponents of the plan speciously argued, provided that if Congress should receive in any year more revenue from a state than its just proportion, the excess would be refunded (*JCC*, XXIV, 258).

6 Randolph to JM, 9 May 1783, and n. 7. The argument could certainly be advanced that Virginians, as compared with the residents of most other states, had so much property destroyed during the British invasions of 1780 and 1781 that they would be obliged to repair their losses by purchasing goods abroad on credit. Hence their "consumption" in this regard would be an unfair gauge of their "ability to pay" Congress.

7 This bill, which had been introduced on 19 May by George Nicholas, was passed by the House of Delegates in amended form on 4 June but failed of acceptance by the Senate (*JHDV*, May 1783, pp. 11, 12, 18, 30, 33).

8 On 14 December 1782 the House of Delegates voted to postpone until the General Assembly's session of May 1783 further consideration of a bill to reduce the number of Virginia delegates in Congress from 5 to 3 (*Papers of Madison*, V, 401, and nn. 18, 19). Being among the matters "depending and undetermined," this bill was referred on 13 May to the "Committee for Courts of Justice." Four days later all these matters were transferred for decision to the "committee of the whole House on the state of the Commonwealth." It was this committee that quashed the bill (*JHDV*, May 1783, pp. 5, 9; Jones to JM, 25 May 1783).

9 *Papers of Madison*, VI, 464, n. 6; JM to Jefferson, 20 May 1783, and n. 10.

10 Randolph to JM, 9 May, and n. 14; 15 May; Pendleton to JM, 17 May 1783, and n. 6.

11 Randolph to JM, 15 May 1783, and n. 8.

[12] *Ibid.*, and n. 9. See also the Rev. James Madison to JM, 4 June 1783. George Hay (1765–1830), son of a former proprietor of the Raleigh tavern in Williamsburg, and brother of Charles Hay, was reading law under Randolph (*Papers of Madison*, V, 340, n. 14; 426, n. 3). In 1803, having distinguished himself as a lawyer, political polemicist, and ardent Republican, he was appointed by President Jefferson United States attorney for the district of Virginia. In that capacity he served as prosecutor in the trial of Aaron Burr for treason. After representing Henrico County in the Virginia House of Delegates during the session of 1816–1817, Hay was a state senator for four years (Swem and Williams, *Register*, pp. 93, 97, 100, 102, 105). In 1825 he became United States judge for the district of eastern Virginia (*Journal of the Executive Proceedings of the Senate of the United States of America* [Washington, 1828——], I, 458, 459; III, 449, 525; *Va. Advocate* [Charlottesville], 1 Oct. 1830). His second wife, whom he married in 1808, was Eliza, a daughter of James Monroe (*Virginia Argus* [Richmond], 7 Oct. 1808). It is said of Hay that he was a "man of fine personal appearance, of very dignified manners and withal, rather pompous" (Samuel Mordecai, *Virginia, Especially Richmond, in By-Gone Days* . . . [2d ed.; Richmond, 1860], pp. 90–91). JM and Hay occasionally exchanged letters between 1804 and 1823.

[13] Ambler to JM, 10 May, and n. 2; 17 May, and n. 3; JM to Randolph, 27 May 1783.

[14] Harrison to Delegates, 3 May, and n. 4; Randolph to JM, 9 May, and n. 8; 14 June; JM to Randolph, 13 May 1783.

[15] Randolph to JM, 9 May 1783, and n. 2. The High Court of Chancery was in session. Before "being" Randolph surely meant to write "this," not "the."

From Joseph Jones

RC (LC: Madison Papers). Cover missing.

RICHMD: 25th. May 1783.

DR. SIR,

After resting at home[1] two days I set out for this place where I arrived on Tuesday last and took my seat in the House some days before my Colleague, who made his appearance for the first time yesterday.[2] my arrival was seasonable with respect to a Bill then before the House for Postponing the collection of the Taxes for the ease of the people untill December next, that, as it was said by Mr. H——y who supported the measure, they might enjoy a short respite from bearing the burthen of Taxes a kind of holy day to rejoice more cheerfully on the glorious termination of the War. this Bill was by order to be considered that day in a Comitee of the whole and I was in time to give such information to the Comtee: as to induce them to come to no conclusion *then* but to rise and ask leave to sit again that they might have an opportunity before they determined the que[sti]on to hear the contents of the proceedings relative to that subject which might be daily expected from Congress.[3] A Bill which was called by some an exclusion bill was also before the House and has since passed the Delegates its object is the rendering Members of Congress in future ineligible to the legislature. I expect it will also obtain the assent of the Senate. You will be under no difficulty in discovering the policy of this Bill.[4] It was proposed in the Comtee. of the House to reduce the number to three but the question was determined in the negative.[5] the Laws agt. the importation of British merchandize are repealed and their Vessells have been permitted to land their Cargoes.[6] A revision of the Salaries of the officers of Government was under considerat[ion] of a Committee yesterday. a small majority continued the 1000. £ P ann. to the Governor, the privy Councillors reduced to 2400. £. The Judges of the Court of Chancery could in the Com: be raised to only 400 each whether as much will be allowed the Judges of the General Court and of the Admirilty I have some doubt especially the latter as Z––h J––hn––n and his adherents are for reductions.[7] The plan of Congress for obtaining funds from the States was laid before the House and read the day before yesterday.[8] this System appears to me at present to have more friends than Enemies, and I think the former will increase the latter diminish. I may however be mistaken in my Conjecture and the result of our deliberations on it may prove that I am so, for you are not to learn how fickle and variable the conduct of this Body has been in this business. as a further proof of it I will only mention that when I came here I found a bill had been ordered in to *reenact the 5 PCt. Some, R. H. L. and his adheren*[*ts*] are opposed to the measure. others, who are opposed in part, dislike the clause declaring the act irrevocable and that the State is not to have credit for the surplus of Tax beyond her quota of the annual demand, if there shod. be a surplus. these are a kind of neutrals upon the whole, which each side hopes to gain. they express their wish to support the measure, but these objects repel them. the chief of these I have yet found out are J. T––yl––r and G––e N––l ––s.[9] these are also strong advocates for a revision of the scale for loan office certificates. for the measure P. H––y, the Sp––k––r and several other respectable members.[10] That part of the Delegates Letter as respected the Treaty of Commerce with Great Britain was refd. to the Com: on Trade with instruction to make a speedy report, which was done yesterday morning as an instruction to our Delegates in Congress. It proposed only entering into a treaty upon liberal & generous principles reserving a right to give bounties on Tonnage &c.: the Rept. not pleasing the House a debate ensued, which terminated in a Commitm[ent] of it to a Com: of the whole, into which the House was immediatly resolved. a large field was then opened and great commercial knowledge or rather a want of it displayed. finding the business taking the turn it did, and likely to be delayed and at last, perhaps, produce instructions rather hurtfull than usefull I took the liberty to recommend a short instruction to the purport of that you will receive I did this from a knowledge that something similar was the object of Congress and the best that at present and speedily could be given. a general concurence ensued, the other motions withdrawn and the one sent you passed immediately and unanimously.[11] The Officers of our line and of Genl. Clarks regiment have presented Memorials stating that they understand the Lands on the Cumberld. reserved for the Officers has been great part of it (the best of the lands) taken up by others, that it was greatly short of the quantity necessary to answer the purpose and requesting a district of Country on the N. Wt. of the Ohio to be assigned them. th[ere] appears a general disposition to gratify them.[12] I could wish if any thing is or is meant to be done in Congress respecting our Cession we shod. be informed of it withot. delay.[13]

Sr. Guy Carletons conduct respecting the Negro prop[erty] is considered by many here as a departure from the provision[al] articles, and will be made use of to justify a delay in paying the British debts.[14]

The Treasurer informs me a remittance to the Delegates has been made since I came away of £100[0] also of £200 to yourself on acct. of the balance due. un[til] an account is returned to him of the distribution of the sums remitted our accouts cannot be closed. you w[ill] therefore attend to this.[15] pray make my Complts. to the Gent: of our Delegation and the Ladys of your fami[ly.][16] with real esteem

I am Yr. friend

Jos: Jon[es]

P.S. No letter from you this post. the notion of a Convent[ion] seems for the present to be laid aside.[17] the Seal & Letter for the president of the College is committed to the care of Mr. Wyt[he] who takes his departure for Williamsburg today being the last of the Chancery Session.[18]

[1] At his estate of Spring Hill in King George County.

[2] "Tuesday last" was 20 May, four days before his "Colleague" Arthur Lee first attended the House of Delegates (*JHDV*, May 1783, p. 19).

[3] Randolph to JM, 24 May, and n. 3. Governor Harrison submitted the con-

gressional plan for restoring public credit to the House of Delegates on 22 May (Instruction to President, 9 May, n. 2; *JHDV*, May 1783, p. 16).

4 Randolph to JM, 15 May, and n. 8. The "policy," which had been embodied in law from 28 June 1777 to 11 June 1779, was revived in order to weaken the Lee faction in the Virginia General Assembly by making Arthur Lee ineligible for re-election to the House of Delegates as long as he continued to be a delegate in Congress. See *JHDV*, May 1777, p. 112; May 1779, p. 42; Hening, *Statutes*, IX, 299; X, 75.

5 Randolph to JM, 24 May 1783, and n. 8.

6 Randolph to JM, 9 May, and n. 14; 24 May; Pendleton to JM, 17 May 1783, and n. 6.

7 Randolph to JM, 24 May 1783, and n. 7. The £2,400 was the annual total allotted to the eight "privy Councillors" to be apportioned among them on the basis of how often each of them attended the meetings of the Council of State (*Papers of Madison*, IV, 29, nn. 2, 6; 232, n. 8).

Zachariah Johnston (1742–1800), a captain of militia in the Revolutionary War, was a delegate from Augusta County in the House of Delegates in 1778–1791, and from Rockbridge County in 1792, 1797, and 1798. He supported the ratification of the Constitution of the United States in the Virginia Convention of 1788, and was a presidential elector in 1788–1789. Among his correspondents were Jefferson, John Marshall, and George Mason. Johnston owned much land in Augusta and Rockbridge counties and in Kentucky. In Virginia politics he was conspicuous for his dislike of slavery and his support of religious liberty. He seems always to have tried to shape his policy in conformance with what he believed would best help the "common man" (Swem and Williams, *Register*, pp. 5–38 *passim*, 49; *Tyler's Quarterly Historical and Genealogical Magazine*, V [1923–24], 185–92; Howard McKnight Wilson, *The Tinkling Spring, Headwater of Freedom: A Study of the Church and Her People, 1732–1952* [Fisherville, Va., 1954], pp. 222–36).

8 Jones should have written 22 May rather than "day before yesterday" (*JHDV*, May 1783, p. 16). See n. 3, above.

9 Jones was not wholly accurate in stating that the bill was "to reenact the 5 PCt." See Randolph to JM, 15 May, and nn. 2, 3; 24 May, and nn. 5, 6; Jameson to JM, 24 May, and n. 3; Pendleton to JM, 26 May 1783, and n. 5. "R. H. L." was Richard Henry Lee; J. T--yl--r and G--e N--l--s, John Taylor and George Nicholas.

10 "P. H--y, and the Sp--k--r" were Patrick Henry and John Tyler. On 16 and 20 May two remonstrances and petitions of similar purport were submitted to the House of Delegates. The one from "sundry inhabitants" of Amelia County, after complaining that "want of system, rather than the want of ability" probably explained why the state had defaulted in paying the interest due on "Loan Office certificates and other public" securities, asked that they be made "negotiable" so as to "add new motion and vivacity to the wheels of circulation and commerce" by increasing the money supply. On 22 May the House of Delegates referred these petitions to a committee and instructed Jacquelin Ambler, the treasurer, to report the amount of outstanding loan-office certificates and unpaid interest due on them, using the "table of depreciation" so as to equate the total in terms of specie (*JHDV*, May 1783, pp. 8–9, 16).

The law which the General Assembly enacted on 28 June 1783 left the scale of depreciation unaffected (*JHDV*, May 1783, pp. 84, 85, 89, 90, 99; Hening, *Statutes*, XI, 268–69). This omission is explained by the preamble of the resolutions, which noted that "from the destruction of some of the public books and papers by the enemy, the monies borrowed on public account cannot be ascertained with precision." For this reason, the resolutions called upon holders of loan-office certificates to enable the Board of Auditors to write on each certificate its specie value and the amount of interest due and unpaid. The auditors were further instructed to provide "the next session of Assembly" with "an alphabetical list" of the holders (*JHDV*, May 1783, pp. 95–96, 98). Although the plea of the petitioners to have the evidences of debt made "negotiable" was not granted, the statute relieved their immediate economic distress by delaying until 1 February 1784 the due date of those taxes for which at least some of the petitioners had hoped that loan-office certificates could be tendered (Hening, *Statutes*, XI, 268).

11 Instruction to Delegates, 23–24 May 1783, and n. 1.

12 Separate memorials, one from the officers of the Virginia line on continental establishment, the other from those of Brigadier General George Rogers Clark's former "Illinois regiment," both being on behalf of themselves and their men, were received by the House of Delegates on 21 May (*JHDV*, May 1783, p. 15). The continental officers noted the "insufficiency" of an act of 5 January 1782 which had set aside for them and their men "all that tract of land included within the rivers Mississippi, Ohio, and Tenissee, and the Carolina boundary line" (*ibid.*, Nov. 1781, p. 74; Hening, *Statutes*, X, 465), and asked the legislature to replace that tract with lands "on the north westerly side of the Ohio." The "Illinois" officers requested that they and their men might be permitted to locate the 150,000 acres, previously promised them, "opposite to the town of Louisville," and establish a town there. On 28 May the House received a third memorial, from the officers of the state line, who, on behalf of themselves and their men, set forth that they were "in the same predicament with the officers and soldiers of the Virginia continental line, with respect to their claims to the bounty of land." All three memorials were committed to the Committee of Propositions and Grievances, Patrick Henry chairman (*JHDV*, May 1783, p. 24).

For the reply to the memorial from the officers of the Virginia line on continental establishment adopted by the House of Delegates and Senate, see Instruction to Delegates, 27 June 1783. See also *JHDV*, May 1783, pp. 32, 53, 78, 90, 93; Jones to JM, 31 May; 8 June 1783, and n. 14.

13 JM to Jefferson, 20 May, and n. 8; JM to Randolph, 10 June 1783.

14 JM to Jefferson, 13 May, and n. 10; Randolph to JM, 15 May, and n. 5; JM Notes, 19 May, and n. 1; Delegates to Harrison, 20 May 1783, and n. 3.

15 Ambler to JM, 17 May, and n. 2; 24 May; Randolph to JM, 24 May; Delegates to Auditors, 28 May 1783.

16 JM, Bland, and Mercer were the Virginia delegates in Philadelphia. The "Ladys" to whom Jones referred certainly included Mrs. Mary House and Mrs. Nicholas Trist (*Papers of Madison*, VI, 429; 460, n. 8).

17 Jefferson to JM, 7 May 1783, and nn. 12, 13.

18 The "president" of the College of William and Mary was the Reverend James Madison (*Papers of Madison*, VI, 49; 50, n. 4; Rev. James Madison to JM, 4 June 1783). For Chancellor George Wythe, see Jefferson to JM, 7 May, and n. 14. See also Pendleton to JM, 4 May 1783, n. 1.

The "Seal" was for the college. See Receipt of Robert Scot, 16 June 1783. This new seal, of a design unlike that employed during the colonial period and long since returned to use, caused confusion when impressed by the faculty of the college on an official document in January 1784 (Benjamin Harrison to the Reverend James Madison "and other professors of the university of William and Mary," 27 Jan. 1784, Executive Letter Book, 1783–1786, p. 264a, MS in Va. State Library).

Notes on Debates

MS (LC: Madison Papers). For a description of the manuscript of Notes on Debates, see *Papers of Madison*, V, 231–34.

Monday May 26.

The Resolutions on the Journals instructing the Ministers in Europe to remonstrate agst. the carrying off the Negroes;[1] Also those for furloughing the troops passed *unanimously*.[2]

[1] The resolutions of instruction concerning "the Negroes," which were largely drafted by John Rutledge but introduced by Alexander Hamilton, directed the American peace commissioners in Europe "to remonstrate thereon to the Court of Great Britain, and take proper measures for obtaining such reparation as the nature of the case will admit." The commissioners were to be sent copies of the letters between Washington and Carleton on the subject, while Washington, armed with a copy of the above resolutions, was directed "to continue his remonstrances to Sir Guy Carleton, respecting the permitting negroes belonging to the citizens of these states to leave New York and to insist on the discontinuance of that measure" (NA: PCC, No. 36, II, 129–30; *JCC*, XXIV, 363–64). Robert R. Livingston dispatched a copy of the resolutions to the peace commissioners on 28 May (Wharton, *Revol. Dipl. Corr.*, VI, 453). For Washington's fulfillment of the direction to him, see Fitzpatrick, *Writings of Washington*, XXVI, 465. For the background of the reso'utions, see Jones to JM, 25 May 1783, and citations in n. 14.

[2] By underlining "unanimously," JM apparently meant that each of the two motions on "furloughing" received a unanimous vote. The first resolution, drafted and introduced by Hamilton, directed Washington to furlough "the noncommissioned officers and soldiers," who had enlisted "to serve during the war," and also "a proportionable number of commissioned officers of the different grades." He should assure them that they would "be discharged as soon as the definitive treaty of peace is concluded." Washington and Benjamin Lincoln, secretary at war, were instructed to have those troops escorted "to their respective homes" in a manner "most convenient to themselves and to the states through which they may pass," and to permit them "to take their arms with them" (*JCC*, XXIV, 364; Syrett and Cooke, *Papers of Hamilton*, III, 364 and the second n. 1). See also JM Notes, 20 May, and nn. 1, 3; 23 May, and nn. 1–3; 19 June 1783, n. 10.

In the second motion, offered by Hugh Williamson, which instructed Nathanael Greene to furlough the troops of North Carolina who had enlisted for a term of eighteen months and a proportional number of officers, the privilege of retaining their arms was not included. Greene and Lincoln were also to "take measures for conducting such troops to their respective homes" (*JCC*, XXIV, 365, and n. 1; JM Notes, 11 June 1783, n. 1). The troops under Greene's command from Virginia, Maryland, and Pennsylvania had already been similarly favored (*Papers of Madison*, VI, 190, n. 13).

From Edmund Pendleton

Tr (LC: Force Transcripts). In the left margin at the top of the transcription, Peter Force's clerk wrote "MSS. [M]c. Guire's." See *Papers of Madison*, I, xxii, xxiii. Addressed to "The Honble James Madison, Esq Philadelphia."

EDMUNDSBURY, May 26th. 1783

MY DEAR SIR

I am just returned from Richmond much fatigued by the Courts, which for the first time have found full emploiment for their whole terms.[1] The manner of doing business, hearing causes in Court for 6 hours, & employing the mornings & evenings in dijesting & settling Opinions, however proper and necessary to be observed in Courts which are, or nearly approach to, the de[r]nier resort of Justice, are a heavy tax upon my advanced age; howe[ve]r when I find it insupportable, I must quit the Office, as I can't think of relaxing in the other point.[2]

I am to thank you for your favr of the 13th and for the Pamphlet inclosed,[3] which I read over, tho' for want of time, not with the Attention I wish to give it, & then delivered it to Mr Jones who was before at Richmond.[4] Our debt indeed is heavy, & added to our own peculiar demands, will require taxes difficult to be paid; however a radical System, well dejested & strictly pursued; and the practice of Industry & Oconomy, (which so far from being an evil, may produce the greatest good, if it prevents our return to that Indolence & extravagance that was Our Character formerly) will carry us thro' it in a reasonable time. I am told the 5 pct & other impost, tho' warmly opposed, will be granted, tho' perhaps with some modulation wch may not affect the genl principle, particularly to direct the portions allotted annually to our Citizens to be paid them here, to save the carriage & recarriage of the money, & avoid another inconvenience of drawing such quantities of Specie from all the States, to circulate only in the Vortex of Phila. or what other place Congress may sit in. This last seems to be made a great objection, & on that ground some Gentln seem to wish that besides what may be due to our Citizens, we might be allowed to pay good Bills of Exchange to answer our proportion of foreign remittances & prevent the drain of our Specie—however nothing is yet determined on in this business, which the House of Delegates have not taken up.[5] Besides repealing the laws which prevented the importation or consumption of British goods (at length passed by the Senate with a clause to make it retro-active from the day it pass'd the other House)[6] they have been emploied in a new tobacco Law,[7] in a new regulation of Salaries in the civil department, and in Suspending the payment of taxes 'til December next.[8] The ground of this last is the short crop, & present unsettled State of trade, which I am satisfied would have made the collection of the whole alarmingly distressing, if not wholly impossible; but I am not so,[9] that part of it might not have been received without any great inconvenience, and am certain that Procrastination, by which increased accumulation of Payments are made necessary, is very hurtful to public as well[10] as private Debtors; not to take notice of the embarrassment wch may be thrown upon the general System by the delay, perhaps when they have the recommendations of Congress under deliberation, they may find it necessary to revive the collection of part of the taxes, which, as mentd before, I think the true Interest of the people.[11] I had almost forgot to mention that they have made their Members again ineligible to Congress.[12] A Letter from the Governor will bring on another great constitutional question, the end & consequences of which cant be foreseen. An Act of Assembly has authorised the Executive Upon complaints against County Majistrates to hear them, and if they think it just to remove from office the person complained of. Such a complaint in writing being lodged with the Governor, he laid it before the Council, & proposed the party should be summon'd to answer, & a day fix'd for the hearing, four of the Council determined, & it is so entered in their journal, but the law was against the principles of the Constitution, the general tenor of the Laws, and the liberty of the Citizens, and therefore they would not Execute it. The Govr having several times in vain endeavour'd by remonstrance, to procure a change in their Opinion, at length sent a Copy of the Articles exhibited and of their order, to the House of Delegates, who have not yet discuss'd them; & when they have done so, I do not see how they can mend it, and remove the Objection to their power, which is not increased since they gave force to the former Law, if the Legislature can to any on the Subject. If this branch of the Executive may dispute the force of the law on this ground, it would seem to run thro the whole department, since no line is drawn, to limit the power of Judging on the Subject; a constable may therefore refuse to obey & Execute his Warrant on the same pretence, and so the legislature are at once made subject to the control of the Executive, a Position which I believe is not Supportable by any thing wch can be drawn from the constitution, Law, or the principles of liberty.[13]

Some Gentn have received wth. great pleasure the Account of Sr Guy Carleton's tergivisatious conduct respecting the restitution of Our slaves, considering it as a proper excuse for not paying British debts, which, they say, may now Consistent with good faith, be set off against each other, as they ought to have been by the Treaty. This however is at present only common tab[l]e talk, & hath not yet reach'd the Assembly, nor will it be canvassed there, I suppose, until they have the definitive Treaty.[14] Mr Jones is better after his journey, than he expected to be.[15] I am

Dr Sr Yr mo. affe. & obt. Servt

EDMD PENDLETON

[1] *Papers of Madison*, VI, 500; Pendleton to JM, 4 May 1783, n. 1. See also *Papers of Madison*, V, 220, n. 6. By law the number of days the High Court of Chancery might sit was limited to eighteen in May and eighteen in November, annually; but the sessions could not begin until "business depending before" the Court of Appeals, which convened late each April and October, was completed (Hening, *Statutes*, IX, 390; X, 89–90, 455). Pendleton was a judge on both tribunals.

[2] Pendleton would be sixty-two years of age on 9 September 1783. Upon the reorganization of the judicial system of Virginia, he resigned on 2 March 1789 as senior judge of the High Court of Chancery to accept election by the General Assembly as a judge of the reconstituted Court of Appeals, the supreme tribunal of Virginia. He served on the bench of this court until his death on 26 October 1803 (David J. Mays, *Edmund Pendleton*, I, 6; II, 274, 345).

[3] The "Pamphlet inclosed" in the missing letter of 13 May from JM was undoubtedly a copy of the one mentioned by him in his letter of that day to Jefferson (*q.v.*, and n. 11).

[4] Jones to JM, 25 May 1783, and n. 2.

[5] By "5 pct & other impost," Pendleton almost certainly referred not to the original impost amendment of 3 February 1781 but only to the impost provisions of the plan for restoring public credit, adopted by Congress on 18 April 1783. Those provisions modified and in effect superseded the earlier proposed amendment, for they specified varying ad valorem duties on wines, liquors, teas, coffee, cocoa, pepper, sugars, and molasses, as well as "a duty of five per cent. ad valorem" on "all other goods" (*JCC*, XIX, 112–13; XXIV, 257). The "plan" probably presumed, although it did not explicitly stipulate, that the money derived from the tariffs would be sent to the Philadelphia "Vortex." Pendleton's dislike of any arrangement which depleted Virginia's meager supply of specie had been often manifested. See *Papers of Madison*, IV, 50; 151–52; 277; 346–47; V, 110; VI, 344.

In mentioning "recarriage," Pendleton referred to the third paragraph of the plan for restoring public credit, wherein it was provided that when "the revenues established by any State shall at any time yield a sum exceeding its actual proportion, the excess shall be refunded to it" (*JCC*, XXIV, 258). The "foreign remittances" by Congress would be to pay the interest on, or the principal of, loans from Louis XVI and Dutch bankers as well as the cost of maintaining American diplomatic and consular officials overseas. Foreign consignees of Virginia's exports, including possibly the tobacco and other "commutables" received in payment of state taxes, paid for them in bills of exchange or in European wares purchased by the Virginia exporters.

[6] Ambler to JM, 3 May, n. 5; Randolph to JM, 9 May 1783, and n. 14.

[7] On 13 May the House of Delegates appointed a committee to prepare a bill

"to amend and reduce the several acts of Assembly, for the inspection of tobacco, into one act." The measure, which the committee submitted on 21 May, was debated for the first time on 27 May. The lengthy bill was not enacted into law until 28 June 1783 (*JHDV*, May 1783, pp. 6, 14, 16, 18, 23, 98; Hening, *Statutes*, XI, 205–46).

[8] Randolph to JM, 24 May, and nn. 3, 7; Jones to JM, 25 May 1783, and n. 7.

[9] After "so," Pendleton may have intended to write, or Peter Force's clerk neglected to copy, "satisfied," "sure," or another word of similar import.

[10] Either Pendleton in his letter or the clerk in his transcription inadvertently repeated "as well."

[11] Three tax bills were introduced in the House of Delegates during the session of May 1783, but only one of them became a law. On 18 June a committee reported a measure "to ascertain certain duties and imposts, and to establish adequate funds for the discharge of this State's quota of the principal and interest of the debt of the United States." Eight days later the House adopted this proposal, but it was not acted upon by the Senate (*JHDV*, May 1783, pp. 63, 65, 70, 82, 84–85, 86). On 27 June the House voted to hold over until the autumn session a bill introduced the preceding day "to levy certain duties for the use of Congress" (*ibid.*, May 1783, pp. 86, 93). On 28 June the General Assembly enacted a statute "to amend the act for appropriating the public revenue." This measure, which was introduced two days earlier in fulfillment of a resolution adopted on 11 June, was adopted by the House of Delegates on 27 June and by the Senate the next day (*ibid.*, May 1783, pp. 48–49, 68, 70, 87, 88, 90, 93, 96, 99). This law stipulated that a part of the proceeds from the tax on land "shall be applied to the use of congress, towards paying this state's quota of the interest of the debt due by the United States"; and that a part of the proceeds from the tax on slaves "shall be applied towards making good to congress any deficiency which may arise in this state's quota of interest due on the debts of the United States, so as to make good to congress the annual sum of four hundred thousand dollars" (Hening, *Statutes*, XI, 247–48). These sources, however, would provide no income until late in 1783 at the earliest, for the same session suspended the collection of taxes until 20 November in that year (Randolph to JM, 9 May 1783, and n. 4).

On 10 September 1782 Congress had asked Virginia to furnish $174,000 as its share of "the interest of the domestic debt." On 18 October of that year, Congress requisitioned Virginia for $290,000 "for the service of the year 1783" (*JCC*, XXIII, 564, 571, 666). If the General Assembly replaced the latter sum with the $256,487 allotted to Virginia in the plan for restoring public credit (*JCC*, XXIV, 259), the total of that amount and the $174,000 would still be over $400,000. Robert Morris, superintendent of finance, reported to Congress that between 1 December 1782 and 30 June 1783 Virginia forwarded, omitting fractions of dollars, $104,403. Between 1 July and the close of 1783 the state paid an additional $68,444 (NA: PCC, No. 137, II, 757–61; *Va. Gazette*, 4 Jan., 8 Feb., 5 Apr., 7 June, 5 July, 2 Aug., 6 Sept., 4 Oct., 1 Nov., and 6 Dec. 1783; 3 Jan. 1784). The sources of revenue enabling Virginia to make these payments seem mainly to have been the sale of tobacco and hemp received in payment of taxes in 1782 and the surplus in the fund hitherto used to meet the expense of recruiting soldiers. For that fund, see *Papers of Madison*, VI, 280, n. 7; 282, n. 3; 303, n. 4; 439. Morris also agreed that Virginia should count as a part of its requisitioned quota the money spent to subsist continental troops of the state upon their return from the southern army (*JCSV*, III, 195, 199, 200; *Cal. of Va. State Papers*, III, 415, 510; *JHDV*, May 1783, p. 40; Ambler to JM, 1 June 1783).

[12] Randolph to JM, 15 May 1783, and n. 8.

[13] *Papers of Madison*, VI, 346–47; 347, n. 5. On 20 February 1783 at a meeting of the Virginia Executive, the four privy councilors who attended, including John Marshall, differed from Governor Harrison by holding that the statute of 2 Decem-

ber 1778 delegating to the Executive the power, after a conclusive hearing, to remove a justice of peace for "misconduct, neglect of duty, or malpractices" violated the Form of Government by unconstitutionally delegating judicial power to the Executive (Hening, *Statutes,* IX, 478; *JCSV*, III, 221–22). Instead of "but" after "journal," Pendleton probably wrote "that." On 21 and 26 May 1783 the governor and dissident privy councilors, respectively, submitted their contrasting views to the House of Delegates. Although the documents were referred to the committee of the whole house on the state of the commonwealth, it cannot be demonstrated that the matter was discussed therein (*JHDV*, May 1783, pp. 14, 22; Pendleton to JM, 2 June 1783). Pendleton appears to have agreed with the governor.

[14] *Papers of Madison,* VI, 422; Walke to Delegates, 3 May, and nn. 2, 3, 5–7; JM to Randolph, 6 May, n. 6; 13 May; JM Notes, 8 May; 26 May, and n. 1; Harrison to Delegates, 9 May, and n. 6; Randolph to JM, 15 May, and n. 5; Delegates to Harrison, 20 May, and n. 3; Jones to JM, 25 May 1783.

[15] Ambler to JM, 3 May, n. 4; Pendleton to JM, 4 May, and n. 3; Jones to JM, 25 May 1783, and n. 1.

Notes on Debates

MS (LC: Madison Papers). For a description of the manuscript of Notes on Debates, see *Papers of Madison,* V, 231–34.

Tuesday 27 May

No Congress[1]

[1] Although in the manuscript JM wrote "No Congress" at the right of a bracket with which he united "Tuesday 27 May" and "Wednesday 28 May," the editors have separated the two entries, for others of his papers are dated on the earlier of those days. In a letter of 28 May the Rhode Island delegates informed Governor William Greene of that state: "There have been for some time past, but Eight States represented. This confines the business to a very narrow Circle, as a principal part of it, which should now engage their Attention, requires the voices of Nine States" (Burnett, *Letters,* VII, 174).

Virginia Delegates to Benjamin Harrison

Printed copy (Burnett, *Letters,* VII, 172, and n. 1). John F. Mercer probably wrote the letter, with the exception of the other two signatures. An abstract, emphasizing the third paragraph, is in *Cal. of Va. State Papers,* III, 493.

PHILADA. 27 May 1783.

SIR,

We have been honored with your Excellency's favor of the 17th instant.[1] Mr. Jones we believe carried with him a copy of the offer of a Seat for Congress in the State of N. York. Lest it should have happened otherwise, we will endeavor to provide one for the next mail.[2] The propositions of Congress with regard to Revenue have long since been transmitted to your Excellency by the President. Relying on the full explanations of our two Colleagues who will attend the General Assembly, we have supposed it unnecessary to trouble you with any less perfect remarks on that subject in our correspondence.[3]

The state of our information from Europe remains precisely as at the date of our last;[4] the progress of the definitive Treaty, of the British bill relative to a commerce with the United States, and of the arrangements for a new administration, being left in the utmost uncertainty by the latest arrivals in this port.[5]

Congress have received no further communications from the Commander in chief, with respect to the Conduct of the British Commander at New York, touching the evacuation of that port, or the execution of the other articles of the provisional Treaty. The breach of that which stipulated a restoration of the Negroes, will be made the subject of a pointed remonstrance from our Ministers in Europe to the British Court; with a demand of reparation; and in the mean time General Washington is to insist on a more faithful observance of that stipulation at N. York.[6]

We have the honor to be with great esteem and respect yr Excelly's Obt. Hble Servts.

John F. Mercer
J. Madison Jr.
Theok. Bland Jr.

1 *Q.v.*

2 *Papers of Madison,* VI, 447; 448, nn. 4, 7. In their missing letter, probably dated 3 June, the delegates sent Governor Harrison a copy of New York's "offer" and of the "much more advantageous" one made by Maryland of a site in Annapolis. On 12 June he submitted these documents to the Virginia House of Delegates (Executive Letter Book, 1783–1786, p. 152, MS in Va. State Library; *JCSV,* III, 268; *JHDV,* May 1783, p. 50). The offer of 30 May of the Maryland General Assembly was received by Congress on 2 June (NA: PCC, No. 186, fol. 105; *JCC,* XXIV, 378, n. 2; Burnett, *Letters,* VII, 180). See also JM to Randolph, 10 June, and n. 14; Instructions to Delegates, 28 June 1783.

3 Delegates to Harrison, 6 May, and n. 3; Instruction to President, 9 May, and n. 2. The "two Colleagues" were Joseph Jones and Arthur Lee (Ambler to JM, 3 May, n. 4; Jones to JM, 25 May 1783, and n. 2).

4 Delegates to Harrison, 20 May 1783. Except for a brief letter from John Adams recommending a consular appointment, no dispatch from Adams, Franklin, Jay, or Henry Laurens was received between 10 April and 10 June 1783 (NA: PCC, No. 185, III, 61–66).

5 *Papers of Madison,* VI, 440, n. 2; 449, n. 10; 504, and n. 3; JM to Jefferson, 13 May, and n. 7; Instruction to Delegates, 23–24 May 1783, and n. 1.

6 Delegates to Harrison, 20 May, and n. 3; JM Notes, 26 May 1783, and n. 1.

To James Madison, Sr.

RC (LC: Madison Papers). Docketed "May 27. 1783" by the recipient. Probably some years after writing the letter, JM wrote "Madison Js" above the date line.

PHILADA. May 27. 1783.

HOND. SIR

I duly recd. yours of the 16th. inst:[1] yesterday by the post, and hope as you are fixing a communication with Fredg.[2] that I shall hear often from you during my stay here thro' the same channel, as I shall be attentive on my side to fulfil your wishes on that subject. How long my stay will be continued here is uncertain, but longer probably than my last indicated. I wish for this reason, that tho' I shall attend to the bark & Vitriol[3] for my mother, an intermediate supply may be procured within the State. I shall endeavor to provide a chair for you, on a convenient model, perhaps with a top to it if such an addition will not too much augment the price.[4] I have hitherto not been inattentive to the request of Mos: Joseph,[5] but shall in consequence of your letter renew my efforts for the books, which the return of peace, renders more likely to be attainable for him. I see few books in the Catalogue which you have sent[6] which are worth purchasing, but I will peruse it more carefully & send you the titles of such as I may select.

I rcd. a letter from Mr. Jos: Chew a few days ago by which & the information of Col: Wadsworth who brought it & is a friend of his, I find that he is in N.Y. with his family, that they are all well, that he continues as yet to hold a post which supports them comfortably, that altho' he has enjoyed opportunities of honestly laying up profits, his generosity of temper has prevented it. I can-not learn whether he proposes to remain in this country or not, but am inclined to think he will go to Canada, where he has some little expectations.[7] He seems to be exceedingly anxious to hear of his friends in Virga. and I have written as fully to him on the subject as my knowledge would admit. I wish some of his friends on the spot & particularly yourself would write to him. Besides the information he wd. receive, it would be a pleasing proof to him that he still retained a place in their remembrance & regards.

We are without information of late as to the progress of the difinitive Treaty, and of the bill in the British Parliamt. for opening trade with the U. States. The confusions produced in their councils by the long suspension of the Ministry seem to put every thing to a stand.[8] The paper which I inclose will give you the latest information on that subject.[9] Remember me affectionately to all the family & be assured that I am

Yr. dutiful son

J. MADISON JR.

P.S. I have got a piece of silk for Sally which I shall send by the first opportunity if any offers before I set out myself. Perhaps I may make an addition to it. Fanny I suppose too must not be overlooked.[10]

[1] Not found.

[2] JM's letter of 5 June to his father (*q.v.*) makes clear that the father's letter of 16 May 1783 had been sent to James Maury, a merchant of Fredericksburg, which was on the postrider's route from Richmond to Philadelphia. For Maury, see *Papers of Madison*, I, 114, n. 8; VI, 388.

[3] The "bark" was cinchona bark (quinine) or a substitute for it. See *Papers of Madison*, IV, 126; 127, n. 3. "Vitriol," as adapted for medicinal use, was an astringent salt (sulphate). Taken internally, it served as a cathartic; applied externally to a wound it helped to stanch bleeding. Vitriol in liquid form (oil of vitriol) appears among other medicines advertised in the *Pennsylvania Packet*, 27 May 1783.

[4] A chair was a light, one-horse, open, two- or four-wheel chaise or gig.

[5] Moses Joseph (d. *ca.* 1788) was a small-scale farmer of Orange County (Orange County Court Records, Personal Property Tax Books, 1782–1788; Land Tax Books, 1782–1788, both in Va. State Library).

[6] JM's letter of 5 June 1783 to his father designates this work as "Docr. Hamilton's." No doctor with either that surname or the variant spelling "Hambleton" appears to have been a resident of Orange or any contiguous county in 1783. The "Catalogue" may have been a manuscript compiled, or a printed work purchased, by a "Doctor Hamilton" who lived far distant from Virginia.

[7] For Joseph Chew, Loyalist and merchant, see *Papers of Madison*, I, 69, and n. 5. Refinement of the date of his birth, given as *ca.* 1725, in that footnote, is permitted by the remark of James Madison, Sr., that both he and Chew were born in April 1723 (James Madison, Sr., to Chew, 19 Feb. 1783, MS in College of William and Mary Library). Chew had returned to America by 1779 and, as secretary of Indian affairs, was attached to British headquarters in New York, where he interested himself in the plight of Loyalist refugees, "many" of whom were his "old neighbours" (Historical Manuscripts Commission, eds., *Report on American Manuscripts*, I, 30, 422; IV, 282; Chew to JM, 6 Nov. 1783). "Wadsworth" probably was Colonel Jeremiah Wadsworth (1734–1804), a resident of Hartford, Conn., and formerly continental commissary of purchases. He and his partner John Carter had contracted with Robert Morris to supply food to Washington's army (*Papers of Madison*, V, 227, n. 11).

[8] Delegates to Harrison, 27 May 1783, and n. 4.

[9] The *Pennsylvania Packet* of 27 May 1783, which was the "paper" probably enclosed by JM, informed his father of the course of the Franco-British war in India during the early autumn of 1782; of the St. Patrick's Day "Ceremonial" in Dublin on 17 March 1783; and of the members of the Portland-Fox-North coalition ministry, as listed by an unauthenticated report dated 1 April in London. See *Papers of Madison*, VI, 504, n. 3.

[10] JM's sisters Sarah ("Sally"), eighteen years of age, and Frances ("Fanny"), nine (*Papers of Madison*, I, 76, n. 3; "The Madison Family Tree," following p. 212, nos. 1, 3; III, 206; 208, n. 4).

To Edmund Randolph

RC (LC: Madison Papers). Cover franked by "J. Madison Jr" and addressed to "Edmund Randolph Esqr. Richmond." Docketed by Randolph, "J. Madison Jr. May. 27 1783."

PHILADA. May 27th. 1783

MY DEAR SIR

A letter recd. yesterday from Mr. F. Webb,[1] inclosing bills in my favor for £200 Virga. Curny. informed me of the successful effort of your friendship for my relief. Mr. Ambler informed me that your attempt was for £100 more, but was abridged on a doubt as to the balance due to me.[2] My answer to him by this conveyance will shew that you would have been sufficiently under the mark.[3]

The next post I hope will bring me your remarks on the Budget of Congress, with the pulse of the Assembly with regard to it.[4] The example of Virga. will have great & perhaps decisive influence on the event of it. In Rhode Island they are attacking it in the News papers before it has appeared. But this State is swayed by a party which has raised & connected its importance with an opposition to every Contl. measure. The bulk of the people are taken in by a belief that if no general impost on Trade be levied, their State will be able to tax the neighbouring States at pleasure.[5] Should all the other States unite heartily in the plan, I do not think any single State will take upon itself the odium & the consequences of perseviring in a veto upon it.

I wish much to know how far your hope was well founded of an introduction of Mr. Jefferson into the Legislature.[6] The hopes of some I find extend to his Mission to Congress.[7] The latter would be exceedingly fortunate & if his objections are not insuperable ought & I trust will be urged upon him by his friends. I have been also indulging a hope that your return for such periods as would be most interesting, & wd least interfere with the exercise of your profession, might be reconciled to your views. Unless temperate & experienced members come in for the ensuing year, I foresee that the exclusions reqd. by the Confederation will make way for a change in the fœderal Councils not favorable to those catholic arrangements on which the harmony & stability of the Union must greatly depend.[8]

We have recd. no accession of intelligence either as to the progress of the definitive Treaty, of the bill in the British Parlt. for commerce with the U-S. or of the negociations among the hungry suitors for the loaves & fishes of the Administration.[9]

I am Dr. Sir Yr sincere friend

J. M.

[1] Not found. For Foster Webb, Jr., see Ambler to JM, 17 May, and n. 3; 24 May 1783.

[2] Ambler to JM, 10 May, and n. 2; 17 May, and n. 4; 24 May; Randolph to JM, 24 May 1783.

[3] Summary of Accounts, 28 May 1783.

[4] The "Budget" was the plan for restoring public credit. See Randolph to JM, 24 May, and nn. 5, 6; Jones to JM, 25 May, and n. 3; Pendleton to JM, 26 May 1783, and nn. 5, 11.

[5] *Papers of Madison*, VI, 131, n. 7; 168, nn. 25, 28; 169, n. 38; 226, n. 3; 262, nn. 4, 5; 268, n. 14; 291; 294, n. 23; 495 n. 10.

[6] Randolph had expressed this "hope" in his letter of 26 April 1783 (*Papers of Madison*, VI, 499).

[7] On 6 June 1783 Jefferson was one of the five men elected by joint ballot of the Virginia House of Delegates and Senate to serve as delegates in Congress for "one year from the first Monday in November next" (*JHDV*, May 1783, p. 39).

[8] Delegates in Congress who had gained experience by serving the maximum term of three consecutive years permitted by Article V of the Articles of Confederation were necessarily, and often eagerly, returning home (*JCC*, XIX, 215). The legislatures of New Hampshire, Rhode Island, Connecticut, New York, Maryland, and Georgia seemed either indifferent about being represented in Congress or content to have only one delegate there. That delegate, of course, counted neither in making a quorum nor in voting. JM also noticed that some of the new members, however well qualified they were in other respects, often evinced more determination than their predecessors to advance the particular interests of their constituencies to the detriment of "the harmony & stability of the Union." See *Papers of Madison*, VI, 16; JM Notes, 27 May 1783, n. 1.

[9] Delegates to Harrison, 27 May, and n. 4. By "the Administration" JM meant the new ministry in Great Britain (JM to James Madison, Sr., 27 May 1783, and n. 9).

Notes on Debates

MS (LC: Madison Papers). For a description of the manuscript of Notes on Debates, see *Papers of Madison*, V, 231–34.

Wednesday 28 May

No Congress[1]

[1] JM Notes, 27 May 1783.

Summary of Accounts with Virginia

FC (LC: Madison Papers). In JM's hand.

[28 May 1783]
Virga. Curry.

Balance due as per lettr. from Tresr. Der. 31. 1782	£865–8–3[1]
Accruing from Der. 31. to May 28. 140 days at 8 drs. 1120 Drs eql. to	336[2]
	1201–8–3
Rece[i]pts since Dr. 31. £50 £100.[3] May 6th £125[4] £200	475[5]
Balance due May 28	£726–8–3
	10
	3/7260[7]
	2420 Dollrs.

J. M. 2420
T. B. 826
J. F. M. 221[6]

1 *Papers of Madison*, VI, 375. For an itemization of the amount owed to JM at the close of 1782, see *ibid.*, VI, 211, n. 3.

2 Dollars in Virginia currency were equated in pounds by dividing the dollars by 3.333. JM recorded the result in round numbers, omitting approximately 8*d.* From 1 January to 28 May, inclusive, there were 148 days, but he claimed pay for only 140. By accompanying the family of William Floyd from Philadelphia to New Brunswick, N.J., JM had been absent from Congress for four days (*ibid.*, VI, 498, n. 2). For reasons unknown, he and the other Virginia delegates apparently had not attended Congress on 3 January. JM seems also to have been absent on 12 May 1783 (*JCC*, XXIV, 35–36, 339). The incompleteness of the journals of Congress is such that the other two days of his nonattendance cannot be established.

3 For the £50 and £100, see Statement of Receipts, 28 May 1783. Instead of £50, JM's account with Virginia, 1783, shows £50 18*s.* 11*d.* (Settlement of Accounts, 31 Dec. 1783). In that account, he probably added the discount he had been obliged to accept when he cashed the bill of exchange. See *Papers of Madison*, VI, 405.

4 *Ibid.*, VI, 473; 474, n. 1. On 6 May 1783 JM acknowledged receipt from Theodorick Bland of \$332 15/90 (\$332.17). Although at 3⅓ for 1 he should have received \$333.33, the difference of \$1.17 was his share of the discount totaling \$5.85 paid on the bill of exchange for £500 (\$1,666.67) by the five Virginia delegates (JM to Bland, 6 May 1783, and hdn., n. 1). JM in his account with Virginia, 1783, correctly entered £100 rather than £125.

5 Although in this summary for his own files, JM may have intended to record all "Rece[i]pts" between 1 January and 28 May 1783, his total of £475 contrasts sharply with the corresponding figure of £947 18*s.* in his Statement of Receipts, 28 May 1783 (*q.v.*). The probable explanation of the difference of £472 18*s.* is as

follows. The entry of £125 should have been £100 (n. 4). The entry of £200 covered only his portion of one of the two bills of exchange, each for £500, on Lacaze and Mallet (Delegates to Auditors, 28 May 1783). JM's total share of those bills of exchange was £697 18*s*. (Statement of Receipts, 28 May 1783). Therefore, by changing in the present item the £125 to £100, and the £200 to £697 18*s*., the total of his receipts becomes a correct £947 18*s*. See Ambler to JM, 17 May 1783, and n. 4.

6 "T. B." and "J. F. M." are Theodorick Bland, Jr., and John Francis Mercer, respectively. The figure opposite the name of each is the amount owed to him in dollars.

7 JM disregarded the 8*s*. 3*d*.

Virginia Delegates to Virginia Auditors of Public Accounts

MS (Virginia Historical Society). Copy in the hand of Theodorick Bland. Initialed by him for JM and John Francis Mercer. The present copy is prefaced with the statement, "Copy of the negotiation of 3333 1/3 dollars drawn on Lacaze & Mallet the original of which is in Mr. Madisons handwriting." JM's "original" has not been found.

PHILADELPHIA May 28th 1783

J Ambler Esqr. having remitted to James Madison for use of the Virga. Delegates two Bills of Exchange for five hundred Pounds Virga. Curcy drawn on Messrs. Lacaze & Mallet[1] in favor of Paul Loyal[l] and Compy[2] we have in consequence thereof, received the following proportions respectively viz J. Madison 2326 1/3 T B. 794 1/3 J.F. 212 2/3[3] for which sums the auditors of the Commonwealth will please to issue warrants on our accts respectively in favor of J Ambler Esqr[4]

Signed J. M
T. B
J F M

1 JM to Bland, 6 May, and n. 1; Ambler to JM, 17 May, and n. 2; 24 May; Statement of Receipts, 28 May 1783.

2 A firm at Norfolk, Va. (Norfolk City Court Records, Order Book 2, p. 30, microfilm in Va. State Library). See also *Papers of Madison*, VI, 279, n. 3.

3 The "J. F." should be "J. F. M." These three sums are in dollars rather than pounds. In his Statement of Receipts, 26 May 1783 (*q.v.*), JM entered £697 18*s*. "Virga. Curry." instead of $2326 1/3. The latter figure is obtained by multiplying the pounds by 10 and dividing the result by three.

4 Bland to JM, 6 May, hdn.; Ambler to JM, 5 July 1783.

Statement of Receipts from Treasurer of Virginia

RC (Virginia State Library). In JM's hand. Although docketed: "Nov. 26. 1783 Jas. Madison £947.18.0 On account," the statement limits JM's receipts to those during the first five months of 1783. The November date appears to be that on which Jacquelin Ambler sent all of JM's vouchers to the Board of Auditors. At the close of the receipts of the Virginia delegates dated 6 May 1783, Ambler wrote above the initials of his name: "Nov. 26. 83 Rec'd. also Mr. Madisons proportion includ[ed] in warrt of £947.18" (JM to Bland, 6 May 1783, and hdn., n. 1). See also n. 6, below.

In LC: Madison Papers is JM's retained copy of this statement. Except for several abbreviations and capitalizations, its text is that of the recipient's copy.

[28 May 1783]

Philada. Received from Jaquelin Ambler Esqr. Treasurer of Virginia on account of my Salary as a Delegate to Congress the sums following, to wit,

1783		
March 29.	out of money from Wm. Satchel Sheriff of Northampton County	£50. Virga. Curry.[1]
	out of two bills of exchange one for £300 on Saml. Inglis & Co. and the other for £200 on Wm. Turnbul & Co	100.[2]
May 6.	out of a bill of exchange on Jno. Ross for £500	100.[3]
28.	out of two bills of exchange each for £500 on Lacaze & Mallet	697.18[4]
		£947.18[5]

For which several receipts amounting as above to nine hundred forty seven pounds eighteen Shillings Virginia currency I hereby request the Auditors of public accounts to issue a warrant or warrants placing the same to my debit.[6]

J. Madison Jr.

[1] *Papers of Madison*, VI, 183, and nn. 6, 7; 211. In his account with Virginia, December 1783 (Settlement of Accounts, 31 Dec. 1783), JM's entry for 29 March reads: "To cash recd. of Mr. Jones out of a sum recd by him for use of the Delegates to Congs. from the Sheriff of N. hampton," £50 18*s*. 11*d*.

[2] *Papers of Madison*, VI, 379, and n. 2; 405; 455, n. 2. In his account with Virginia, December 1783, JM's entry for "April" reads: "To do. [cash] recd. out of bills of exchange on Inglis & Co. for one thousand dollars & Trumbul & Co. for 666 2/3 remitted by J. Ambler Esqr. for use of the [Delegates]," £100. JM should have written "Turnbull" rather than "Trumbul."

[3] *Ibid.*, VI, 473; 474, n. 1. In his account with Virginia, December 1783, JM's entry for "April" also reads: "To do. [cash] recd. out of do. [bill of exchange] on Jno. Ross & Co. for 1666 2/3 remitted by J. Ambler Esqr. for use of do. [Delegates]," £100. In the present item JM evidently entered this sum under the date when he negotiated rather than received the bill of exchange.

[4] Ambler to JM, 17 May, and n. 2; Delegates to Auditors, 28 May 1783, and n. 3. In his account with Virginia, December 1783, JM entered under "May" as follows: "To do. [cash] recd. out of 2 bills for £500 each on Lacaze & Mallet remitted by J. Ambler Esqr. for use of the Delegates," £697 18*s*.

[5] Also under "May" in JM's account with Virginia, December 1783, is an entry reading: "To do. [cash] recd on two bills dated 12 & 14 May 1783 for £100 each on S. Inglis & Co. by D. Cochran in favr. of J. Ambler Esqr & remitted by Foster Webb in consequence of warrants issued on my account," £200. Why JM did not list this sum in the present item is not clear. He had received the two bills of exchange on 26 May but perhaps neglected to include them because they were still unnegotiated. See JM to Randolph, 27 May 1783. David Cochrane (1740–1792), a native of Glasgow, Scotland, was a prosperous merchant at Newcastle in Hanover County, Va. (Miriam Margaret Cochrane Hunter, "The Cochrane Family" [mimeographed, n.p., 1943], pp. 1, 24; *Va. Gazette, and General Advertiser* [Richmond], 10 Oct. 1792).

[6] In the Virginia State Library is a manuscript entitled "Remittances made to Delegates in Congress from 27 March 1783 to 28th May following—for which no Warrants have issued . . . £2,203. 15. 9." Then follows the portion of this total received by each of the five delegates. The sum opposite JM's name is £947. 18. Below this listing is the notation "26th Novr. & 2d. Decr. 1783—Warrants were obtained from the Auditors for the several sums above mentioned." The manuscript is docketed, "Genl. Acct. of money advanced Delegs. without Warrts."

Notes on Debates

MS (LC: Madison Papers). For a description of the manuscript of Notes on Debates, see *Papers of Madison*, V, 231–34.

Thursday May 29.

The report of the Committee concerning Interest on British debts was committed after some discussion.[1]

[1] The submission of the report is not mentioned in the journal for 29 May (*JCC*, XXIV, 368–69). For the appointment of "the Committee" headed by John Francis Mercer, see JM Notes, 20 May 1783, and n. 5. The portion of the report relating to private debts owed by Americans to Loyalists or other British subjects was referred on 29 May to a committee, James Wilson, chairman, Gunning Bedford, Jr. (Del.), and Mercer. To the Mercer committee, which had rendered the report, was recommitted the portion relating to Loyalists' or other British property confiscated

by the separate states (NA: PCC, No. 20, II, 156; JM Notes, 20 May, and n. 5). In effect this division of assignment discharged the Mercer committee, for confiscations was the subject of a report on 16 May by another committee, Hamilton, chairman. This report was accorded further consideration on 30 May. See JM Notes, 30 May 1783, and nn. 1, 2.

Notes on Debates

MS (LC: Madison Papers). For a description of the manuscript of Notes on Debates, see *Papers of Madison,* V, 231–34.

Friday May 30

The debates on the report recommending to the States a compliance with the 4th. 5. & 6th. of the provisional articles were renewed;[1] the report being finally committed nem: con: see Secret Journal[2]

The Report including the objections to interest on British debts; was also agreed to nem: con: not very cordially by some who were indifferent to the object; and by others who doubted the mode of seeking it by a new stipulation.[3]

[1] For the appointment of, and instruction to, the committee which submitted this "report," see JM Notes, 14 May 1783, and n. 1. The report was made on 16 May, first debated three days later, and spread on the journal on 30 May (NA: PCC, No. 186, fol. 102; Syrett and Cooke, *Papers of Hamilton,* III, 366). For the fourth of the provisional articles of peace with Great Britain, see Harrison to Delegates, 9 May 1783, n. 6. The fifth and sixth articles pledged Congress to "earnestly recommend" to the state legislatures "the restitution of all estates, rights and properties" taken from Loyalists who had not "borne arms" against the United States, to allow Loyalists who had fought in the British army "to remain twelve months unmolested" while trying to regain their confiscated property, and to "immediately set at liberty" persons "in confinement" or under prosecution for "the part which he or they may have taken in the present war" (*JCC,* XXIV, 248–49).

The committee prefaced its recommendation by affirming the desire of Congress, and its trust that King George III shared that desire, to give "speedy and full effect to all the stipulations" of the treaty so as to hasten "the blessings of peace." The resolution "required" the states to "remove all obstructions" preventing the Loyalists or British from being released, if in jail, or from being paid their just debts, and "earnestly recommended" that the states, "with that spirit of moderation and liberality, which ought ever to characterise the deliberations and measures of a free and enlightened nation," enable the Loyalists to recover their confiscated properties (*JCC,* XXIV, 371).

[2] On a motion of Richard Peters, seconded by Ralph Izard, the eight states effectively represented in Congress voted unanimously to commit the report to a committee composed of James Wilson, chairman, Bland, and Abraham Clark (*JCC,* XXIV, 371–72; NA: PCC, No. 186, fol. 105). Hamilton, the only delegate in attendance from New York, had been chairman of the committee submitting the report. He voted against its commitment. The Wilson committee seems never to

have rendered a report, possibly because of the interruption of public business by the flight of Congress to Princeton. See JM Notes, 21 June 1783, and n. 7; Motion *in re* Preliminary Peace Treaty, 18 Oct. 1783.

[3] The report of the Wilson-Bedford-Mercer committee, appointed on 29 May, was adopted without a tallied vote. These resolutions, which embodied two instructions and one expression of "desire," were for the guidance of the American peace commissioners. One instruction required them to seek an amendment to Article IV of the preliminary articles of peace, guaranteeing that "no execution shall issue for any debt contracted before the war, in less than three years after the signing of the definitive treaty." On this subject Congress also expressed the "opinion" that it would be "highly inequitable and unjust" if British creditors charged their American debtors with interest for the war years when they had suffered "depredations of private property" and been "excluded in a great measure from a commercial intercourse with foreign nations, and consequently deprived of all mart for their produce." Congress "farther instructed" the peace commissioners "to contend for an express stipulation in the definitive treaty of peace providing for a fair liquidation of all charges for subsistence of prisoners of war, and other reasonable demands," together with a pledge to pay "in a reasonable period" the "balances" which may be "justly due" (*JCC*, XXIV, 374–76). See also Instructions to Peace Commissioners, 20 May, and n. 3.

Robert R. Livingston, secretary for foreign affairs, dispatched a copy of these resolutions on 31 May 1783 to the American peace commissioners (Wharton, *Revol. Dipl. Corr.*, VI, 458–59). For discontent over the prospects of an early demand by British creditors for American citizens to pay their pre-Revolutionary debts, see *Papers of Madison*, VI, 422–23, and n. 7; 439; 440, n. 2; 458, n. 3; Randolph to JM, 15 May, and n. 5; Jones to JM, 25 May; Pendleton to JM, 26 May 1783.

Benjamin Harrison to Virginia Delegates

RC (Virginia Historical Society). In the hand of Archibald Blair but signed by Harrison. The cover, enveloping several enclosures, is missing. The verso of the present letter is docketed in an unknown hand, "Gov: Harrisons Letter May 31st. 1783." The original text, clipped on the edges, is internally mutilated or has deteriorated. Obliterated words or letters are supplied, as shown in brackets, from the file copy (Va. State Library) in the hand of Thomas Meriwether. Exceptions are letters bracketed in the postscript, written by the governor. These have been taken from Charles Campbell, ed., *The Bland Papers* (2 vols. in 1; Petersburg, Va., 1840), II, 109.

VIRGINIA IN COUNCIL May 31st. [1783].

GENTLEMEN

A few days ago an Express from Baylors Regiment delivered the enclosed by which you will [find] they have mutinied and the [Cause] they assign for their conduct. General Morgan & two of the Supernumerary Officers of the Corps were sent the n[e]xt Day to meet them & carry them to Winchester, which [w]e understand from Doctor L[e]e was agreeable to the determination of Congress who proposed to order th[em into t]he State to be [dis]banded; you will please [to la]y the Letter before them for their Directions. I wrote to the Mutineers and sharply reprimande[d] them for their conduct but promised in consideration of their past Services to overlook it as far as it related to me. They are really a band of heroes who have performed great & meritorious Services, and I am Satisfied would not have taken this rash Step if their Sufferings had not been very great.[1] [En]closed you have an open Letter [to] Coulougnac & co. in answer to one [wro]te to you which youl please to forward[2] with the one to Mr. Mazzie.[3]

I am with great respect Gentlemen Your mo: ob: Humble Servant

BENJ: HARRISON

P. S. You have inclosed a resolve of the Genl Ass[embly app]roving of a Tre[aty of Com]merce[4] N. C.[5]

[1] On 29 May the governor and Council deliberated on a memorial signed seven days earlier at Moravian Town (now Winston-Salem), N.C., on behalf of about one hundred troopers of the consolidated First and Third Continental Dragoons ("Baylor's Regiment") by Sergeant Major William Daingerfield, four sergeants, and five corporals. They frankly admitted that although their corps had received "the greatest Aplause of Any men that Belong'd to the Southering Army," they had been obliged to desert their post on the Congaree River in South Carolina because of hunger, lack of money, and a rumor that General Nathanael Greene "Intended to Dismount Us and Leave us to Shift for Our Selves." The memorial added that their slow march would enable the state government to have food and pay ready for them on their arrival in Richmond. By addressing their plea to Thomas Nelson, who had not been governor since 30 November 1781, the malcontents revealed how completely out of touch they were with affairs in their native state (NA: PCC, No. 18, XVII, 357–60).

William Daingerfield (*ca.* 1759–1826), a native of Fredericksburg, Va., returned after the war to South Carolina, where from 1811 until his death he was "manager of the planting interest upon and in the neighborhood" of St. John's Parish, Berkeley County. In the War of 1812 he was captain of a cavalry troop and subsequently lieutenant colonel of the Eighth South Carolina Regiment of Cavalry until "old age" forced his retirement (Louis A. Burgess, comp. and ed., *Virginia Soldiers of 1776* [3 vols.; Richmond, 1927–29], III, 1222; *City Gazette* [Charleston, S.C.], 2 June 1826; reprinted in *South Carolina Historical Magazine*, LXII [1961], 55).

On 29 May Harrison addressed the ailing Colonel George Baylor at Fredericksburg, requesting that he resume active command of his regiment (*Papers of Madison*, V, 320, n. 9; *Cal. of Va. State Papers*, III, 417; Executive Letter Book, 1783–1786, p. 140, MS in Va. State Library). On the same day the governor informed the House of Delegates of the crisis and of his dispatch by "express" to the mutineers urging them to proceed to Winchester, a continental depot that could quarter and victual them. He recommended that the General Assembly immediately authorize Jacquelin Ambler to provide enough money for a commissary, so that the dragoons would not resort to impressing food from farmers before reaching their destination. On 30 May the Assembly complied, but instead of imposing on Baylor, instructed Harrison to request Brigadier General Daniel Morgan, then in Richmond, to take command of the dragoons, "attended by such officers as he may think necessary, and a commissary" (Executive Letter Book, 1783–1786, p. 139; *JHDV*, May 1783, pp. 25, 26; *JCSV*, III, 263; *Papers of Madison*, II, 95, n. 4).

With the approval of the Council, Harrison later in the day wrote to the mutineers, acknowledging that their sufferings had been "great," regretting that they had felt impelled to "tarnish all their glorious Actions," and promising, "I shall send an officer that you love and respect who has fought and conquer'd with you and who will conduct you to Winchester" (Executive Letter Book, 1783–1786, p. 142). The fact that on this same day the governor wrote to General Greene on an unrelated subject (*ibid.*, pp. 144–45) is convincing evidence that he had not received the southern commander's letter penned at Charleston nine days before. In that dispatch Greene denounced the mutineers, denying that they lacked food and charging that their "principal object" was to sell their stolen mounts. Greene warned Harrison that if the ringleaders should not be punished "capitally," it would be impossible in the future "ever to keep an Army from mutiny" (*Cal. of Va. State Papers*, III, 486, 493–94).

Arthur Lee evidently reminded Harrison of what neither Greene nor the dragoons seem to have heard, that Congress on 24 April had instructed Benjamin Lincoln, secretary at war, and Robert Morris, superintendent of finance, to "take immediate measures" for moving the Virginia, Maryland, and Pennsylvania continental lines, "together with the corps of artillery and cavalry," back "within their respective states" (*JCC*, XXIV, 275; *Papers of Madison*, VI, 486, n. 3; JM Notes, 26 May 1783, n. 2). See also Fitzpatrick, *Writings of Washington*, XXVI, 441–44. On 10 June Congress referred the dragoons' memorial to Lincoln and Morris. Six days later they advised that Lincoln be empowered either to pardon the troopers if they would surrender themselves and "deliver up" their horses by an unspecified date, or if they refused, to deal with them as "the articles of war prescribe." Charles Thomson noted that the recommendation was "obsolete" (*JCC*, XXIV, 389, n. 2, 400–401; NA: PCC, No. 137, II, 557).

2 *Papers of Madison*, VI, 412; 414, n. 7; Delegates to Harrison, 6 May 1783, and n. 4. In his letter of 29 May to Coulignac et Cie of Nantes in regard to its controversial bill of £85 14*s.* 9*d.* for goods shipped to Virginia in 1781, Harrison asked the firm to supply a duplicate invoice to replace the one destroyed by the British. He added that if the claim was found to be valid, it would be honored as soon "as the exhausted Situation of the State will admit" (Executive Letter Book, 1783–1786, pp. 139–41; *Cal. of Va. State Papers*, III, 260).

3 On 8 January 1779 Philip Mazzei had been appointed Virginia's commercial agent in Tuscany (*Papers of Madison*, I, 287, n. 1). On 31 August 1782 Mazzei received Governor Harrison's letter of 31 January in that year terminating the assignment (Howard R. Marraro, ed., *Philip Mazzei, Virginia's Agent in Europe* [New York, 1935], p. 101). In his dispatch of 31 May 1783, enclosed in the present letter, the governor reminded Mazzei that his commission had expired three months after the notification of recall reached him, that is, on 30 November 1783. Regretting Mazzei's distressed situation, as described in his letter of 31 December 1782, Harrison assured him that a warrant for £200 sterling had been drawn in his favor and urged him to return to Virginia as soon as possible (*JCSV*, III, 252; Executive Letter Book, 1783–1786, pp. 146–47). See also *Papers of Madison*, VI, 243; 244, n. 5.

4 Instruction to Delegates, 23–24 May 1783.

5 Nemine Contradicente, or, unanimously.

From Joseph Jones

RC (LC: Madison Papers). Undocketed and cover missing.

RICHMD. 31 May 1783

DR. SIR.

I should have been uneasy on account of your health had I not heard Letters were received from you by the last Post as I had none myself this or the last week.[1] If you wrote as I suppose you did the letters must have either miscarried or been stopt at Fredericksburg.[2] We have not yet been in a Com: on the papers from Congress, and I begin to fear the opposition will be more powerfull, than the last week I apprehended.[3] individual and local considerations appear to me to be too general and so fixed as to afford but small consolation to those, who wish the policy of the State to be governed by more enlarged & liberal principles.[4] I do not however, yet, dispair of the Assemblys adopting the plan recommended by Congress for establishing funds to discharge the national debt, although a fact mentioned to me yesterday evening (that P. H.[5] was deserting the measure) alarms my fears. Since my last the Bill for postponing to the 20th. of Nov. next the making distress for the Taxes has passed the Delegates by a Majority of 13 and was the day before yesterday assented to by the Senate.[6] hurtfull and dangerous as this step will I fear prove, it was warmly espoused by Mr. H—y, opposed by his Antagonist[7] and every effort made to fix the day to an earlier period, but in vain. It is true the people are in many places distressed for Indian corn. Tobacco flour and hemp have greatly increased in their price while imported articles have considerably decreased yet such was the rage for giving ease to the people nothing could be offered sufficiently forceable to prevent the suspension taking place.[8] The Memorial of the Officers of the Virga. line has been reported by the Com: reasonable and the several resolutions reported by the Com: in consequence stand refd. to the Com: of the whole on the State of the Commonwealth. this proceeding is repugnant to the Cession of the lands beyond the Ohio, and giving a preference to the Offs: of our line to those of other States, will excite discontints in the Army, as well as involve us in controversy with Congress. these obstacles, if they shall not ultimately defeat, will at least delay our determination. whatever is meant to be done respecting the Cession shod. be hastened, and the result communicated as soon as possible.[9] A voluminous Tobacco Bill has taken up great part of this week we got rid of it yesterday and have sent it to the Senate.[10] A Bill to repeal an act of the last Session "to prohibit intercourse with and the admission of British Subjects into this State" and another Bill in consequence to repeal the law "declaring who shall be deemed Citizens" and for declaring who shall be deemed Citizens, are before the House.[11] *the two great leaders of the House*[12] are Upon these bills united both concuring in the repeal of the former and opposing the passage of the Latter; but I think upon different princip[les,] the one P. H. conceiving it the true interest of the State to adm[it] all Classes of people withot. distinction, the other not only perh[aps] for the same reason but for others also and in particular that he thinks the Articles of the Treaty preclude us from discrimination.[13] The Citizen bill may come under consideration to day the Advocates for it are disposed to exclude all Natives who have left the Country since April 75, all who having taken the Oath of Allegiance to the States or held offices under either from that period who have gone over to the Enemy. these matters are premature and I could have wished them to have been delayed to a future day. they may probably be yet postponed.[14] Sr. Guy Carletons conduct respecting the Negros is considered here as evasive of the articles of the Treaty and confirms in their opinions if it does not increase the number opposed to the payment of British debts. time for payment and deduction of the interest during the War seems to be generally the Sentiment, and to be desired by many of those, who are supposed to be most attached to the British interest.[15] The day before yesterday we were informed that abt. 100 of Baylors Regiment of Cavalry were on their way in N. Carolina to this State withot. any officer above subalterns to command them. the reasons assigned by them for their conduct—want of provision for themselves and Horses. I suspect the true ground of their desertion to be the order for their remaining when [t]he Infantry were to march to this State which I think took place before I left Philadelphia. That they might not distu[rb] the inhabitants in their rout by plunder and probably occasion the sheding of blood in consequence, Genl. Morgan who was here with some other officers were sent to ta[ke] the command of them and conduct them to Winchester.[16] pray inform me what has been done respecting the Indians since I left Congress. whr. any steps have be[en] taken in consequence of the orders given the Comr. in Chie[f] concerning them.[17] Tell Mr. Mercer I must leave him fo[r] the present to his friend Monroe and other Correspond[ents.][18] The bill rendering Delegates to Congress ineligible in future to the legislature has passed the Senate. do you come in and when?[19] I am,

Yr. Friend & Servt.

Jos: Jones

[1] While Jones was in Virginia, JM probably wrote to him for the first time on 3 June. That letter and JM's other letters to him, dated 6, 10, 17, and 30 June, and 7 July, and perhaps several more of which no mention has been found, are missing. See JM to Randolph, 3 and 17 June; Jones to JM, 8, 14, 21, and 28 June, and 14 and 28 July 1783.

[2] The site of the post office nearest to Jones's plantation in King George County.

[3] Jones to JM, 25 May 1783, and nn. 3, 8.

[4] JM to Randolph, 27 May 1783, and n. 8.

[5] Patrick Henry. See Jefferson to JM, 7 May, and n. 10; Randolph to JM, 9 May 1783, and n. 4.

[6] Randolph to JM, 9 May, and n. 4; 24 May, and n. 3; Pendleton to JM, 26 May 1783, and n. 11. It probably was JM who drew a line in ink along the left margin of the text from near the beginning of the sentence, "Since my last," to near the end of the sentence closing with the words "Indian corn."

[7] Richard Henry Lee in particular. See Jefferson to JM, 7 May, and n. 10; Randolph to JM, 15 May 1783, and n. 3.

[8] JM to Randolph, 13 May; Randolph to JM, 24 May; Jones to JM, 25 May 1783.

[9] Jones to JM, 25 May, and n. 12; 8 June, and n. 14. See also *Papers of Madison*, VI, 502, and n. 3; 503, nn. 5, 6; Jefferson to JM, 7 May, and n. 3; JM Notes, 9 May, and n. 2; 5 June, and n. 1; Randolph to JM, 9 May; JM to Jefferson, 20 May 1783, and n. 8.

[10] Pendleton to JM, 26 May 1783, and n. 7.

[11] The first and second of these bills came before the Virginia House of Delegates for the first time on 24 and 26 May, respectively (*JHDV*, May 1783, pp. 19, 21).

[12] The words are italicized to signify that they were underlined probably by Jones but possibly by JM after receiving the letter. Jones refers to Patrick Henry and Richard Henry Lee.

[13] There is no specific statement in the preliminary articles of peace forbidding "discrimination," but Lee probably was correct in believing that the guarantee was necessarily implied by Articles V, VI, and VII (*JCC*, XXIV, 248–49).

[14] On 21 June the House of Delegates decided to postpone further consideration of both bills until the session of October 1783 (*JHDV*, May 1783, pp. 76, 77).

[15] *Papers of Madison*, VI, 416; 418, nn. 8, 10; Walke to Delegates, 3 May, and nn. 2, 5–7; JM to Randolph, 6 May, n. 6; JM to Jefferson, 13 May, and n. 10; Delegates to Harrison, 20 May, and n. 3; 27 May; Jones to JM, 25 May; JM Notes, 26 May, and n. 1; 29 May, and n. 1; 30 May, and n. 3; Pendleton to JM, 26 May 1783. See also *JHDV*, May 1783, pp. 12, 20, 65.

[16] Harrison to Delegates, 31 May 1783, and n. 1.

[17] JM Notes, 9 May, and n. 2. Between 6 May, when Jones left Philadelphia, and the close of that month neither Congress nor Washington took any important action "respecting the Indians." On 10 May Washington had written Lafayette: "The Indians on the Frontiers of Virginia and Pensylvania have lately committed Acts of hostility, murdering and Scalping many of the innocent Settlers, who were returning to their former habitations in hopes of possessing them in Peace. It is much to be doubted whether these wretches will ever suffer our Frontiers to enjoy tranquility till they are either exterminated, or removed to a much greater distance from us than they now are" (Fitzpatrick, *Writings of Washington*, XXVI, 421).

[18] Jones apparently meant that he would stop writing to Mercer, perhaps because

the number of his committee obligations in the House of Delegates had increased and the information in his letters to JM could be, if JM so chose, relayed to his colleague in Congress. For James Monroe, see Ambler to JM, 10 May 1783, n. 1.

[19] Randolph to JM, 15 May, and n. 8; JM to Jefferson, 20 May, and n. 10; Jones to JM, 25 May 1783, and n. 4.

From Jacquelin Ambler

RC (LC: Madison Papers). Docketed by JM, "June 1. 1783." Cover addressed by Ambler to "The Honobl. James Madison of Congress Philadelphia."

RICHMOND VIRGA. 1st. June 1783.

DR. SIR

As Colo. Bland was the only Member left at Congress, beside yourself, to whom any considerable Arrears could be due,[1] I made no doubt of your being able to draw a part of yours on the receipt of the £1000. last sent, without any difficulty on yours, or inconvenience on the part of your Colleagues;[2] and therefore did not mention the matter in a general letter to them, which perhaps I ought to have done. I hope, however, the business has been settled to your satisfaction, and that the surplus of the general remittance and the £300. sent on your own particular Accot. by Mr. Webb will have rubbed off a good part of the Score of Arrears.[3] I am the more anxious on this head because there is very little probability of the Treasurys being in such Circumstances soon as to enable me to make any considerable payment on this or any other Accot.[4] The Assembly have passed a Law for postponing the collection of the Taxes for the present Year, so that no supplies will get into the Treasury til April next.[5] We have nothing to depend on for support of Government, and to answer pressing Claims made every hour of the day to the amount of hundreds of thousands of pounds but the deficiencies of the Taxes of the last, Year; which, if paid in Commutables, in Hemp particularly, as I expect they will, there will be scarce sufficient raised to pay the bal. of the £80000 ordered at the last Session to be paid to the United States.[6] I know not what will be the consequence

God bless you

J. A.

[1] John Francis Mercer, the only one of JM's colleagues besides Bland in Philadelphia, had been in Congress for less than four months (*JCC*, XXIV, 110). Jones and Arthur Lee were in Richmond attending the House of Delegates (Ambler to JM, 3 May, and n. 4). See also Summary of Accounts, 28 May 1783, and nn.

[2] Ambler to JM, 17 May, and n. 2; Delegates to Auditors, 28 May, and n. 3; Statement of Receipts, 28 May 1783, and n. 4.

[3] Ambler to JM, 17 May, and n. 3; 24 May; Randolph to JM, 24 May; Statement of Receipts, 28 May, and n. 5; JM to Randolph, 3 June 1783.

[4] Except for a payment of £346 15*s*. in September, JM received no more from the treasury of Virginia until after he returned to the state in December (Settlement of Accounts, 31 Dec. 1783).

[5] Randolph to JM, 9 May, and n. 4; Jones to JM, 25 May 1783.

[6] *Papers of Madison*, VI, 501, n. 8. If, as seems certain, Ambler was referring to the resolution of the General Assembly on 28 December 1782, he should have written £50,000 rather than £80,000 (*ibid*., VI, 174, n. 2; *JHDV*, Oct. 1782, p. 86). See also Randolph to JM, 9 May, and n. 5; 14 June, and n. 9; Pendleton to JM, 26 May 1783, and nn. 5, 11.

From Thomas Jefferson

RC (LC: Madison Papers). JM docketed the letter, "June 1. 1783," and probably at a later date, "Tho. Jefferson 1. June 1783."

Monticello June 1. 1783.

Dear Sir

The receipt of your letter of May 6.[1] remains unacknoleged. I am also told that Colo Monroe has letters for me by post tho' I have not yet received them.[2] I hear but little from our assembly. mr. Henry has declared in favour of the impost. this will ensure it. how he is as to the other questions of importance I do not learn.[3]

On opening my papers when I came home I found among them the inclosed cyphers which I had received from either mr. Morris's or mr. Livingston's office. will you be so good as to return them for me? the confusion into which my papers had got going to & from Baltimore & left there for some time will I hope apologize for my having overlooked them when I returned the other papers.[4] I send you inclosed the debates in Congress on the subjects of Independance, Voting in Congress, & the Quotas of money to be required from the states.[5] I found on looking that I had taken no others save only in one trifling case.[6] as you were desirous of having a copy of the original of the declaration of Independance I have inserted it at full length distinguishing the alterations it underwent.[7]

Patsy increases the bundle inclosed with her correspondence. my compliments attend my acquaintances of the family. Patsy's letter to Miss Floyd will need a safe more than a speedy conveyance for which she trusts to your goodness. our friendship for that family as well as your interest in it will always render any news of them agreeable.[8] I am with the sincerest esteem Dr. Sir

Your affectionate friend

TH: JEFFERSON

P.S. I inclose for your perusal the account of the Pain de singe which I mentioned. be so good as to communicate it to Dr. Shippen who had not heard of it. my compliments attend him &[9]

[1] *Q.v.*

[2] Ambler to JM, 10 May 1783, n. 1.

[3] Jefferson was overly sanguine about the fate of "the impost" in the Virginia General Assembly during its session of May 1783. See Jefferson to JM, 7 May, and n. 10; Randolph to JM, 9 May, and n. 4; Jones to JM, 25 May; 31 May; 8 June; Pendleton to JM, 26 May 1783, and n. 11.

[4] The "cyphers" no doubt were the printed encoding and decoding pages which Robert R. Livingston and possibly Robert Morris had furnished to Jefferson after his arrival in Philadelphia on 27 December 1782 expecting to proceed to Paris as one of the American peace commissioners (*Papers of Madison*, VI, 4, nn. 2, 4; 132, n. 1; 180, n. 2; 243, n. 5; 327, n. 6).

[5] Jefferson to JM, 7 May, and n. 14. After receiving Jefferson's record of "the debates" JM noted at the top of the forty-nine-page manuscript: "Furnished to JM by Mr. Jefferson in his hand writing; as a copy from his original notes" (LC: Jefferson Papers). This copy is printed in Madison, *Papers* (Gilpin ed.), I, 9–18, 27–39, and in *JCC*, VI, 1087–93, 1098–1106. Julian P. Boyd concluded that Jefferson, using his rough memoranda, prepared the original copy of his notes on the debates in "the late summer or early autumn of 1776" (Boyd, *Papers of Jefferson*, I, 299–308, 327 n.). Fourteen folios of the manuscript comprise a copy of the Declaration of Independence.

[6] Jefferson probably was referring to his "Outline of Argument Concerning Insubordination of Esek Hopkins," made while he was a delegate to the Second Continental Congress (Boyd, *Papers of Jefferson*, VI, 274 n.; XV, 578–82; Harrison to Delegates, 20 June 1783, and nn. 1, 2).

[7] For a facsimile of the copy of the Declaration of Independence made for JM by Jefferson and now among Jefferson's papers in the Library of Congress, see Julian P. Boyd, *The Declaration of Independence: The Evolution of the Text as Shown in Facsimiles of Various Drafts by its Author, Thomas Jefferson* (Princeton, N.J., 1945), p. 28, plate VIII. See also Boyd, *Papers of Jefferson*, I, 315–19, 416 n., 429. Before this same manuscript was transferred from the collection of Madison papers to that of Jefferson, it was printed in Madison, *Papers* (Gilpin ed.), I, 19–27, and in *JCC*, VI, 1093–98. In each of these printings, the editor indicated the differences between the Jefferson text furnished to JM and that of the engrossed copy of the Declaration of Independence signed by delegates in Congress chiefly on 12 July and 2 August 1776.

JM, probably in 1783 or within a few years thereafter, transcribed the copy of the Declaration sent to him in the present letter. He docketed the transcription, "Dec. Independence" and wrote above the title: "*Original* draught of declaration of Independan. by Mr. J." (LC: Madison Papers). Besides numerous variations in abbreviation, capitalization, punctuation, and indentations between the two manuscripts, JM inadvertently placed Jefferson's paragraph beginning "He has constrained others taken captive on the high seas" immediately before the paragraph beginning "He has waged war against human nature itself" rather than immediately after the paragraph beginning "He is at this time transporting large armies of mercenaries." In their editions, the foregoing editors corrected this mistake in JM's copy without comment.

8 Martha ("Patsy") Jefferson's correspondent in the family of William Floyd was probably Maria Floyd. JM's particular focus of "interest" was Catherine Floyd. See *Papers of Madison*, VI, 235, and nn. 1, 2; 254; 255; Jefferson to JM, 7 May 1783, and n. 16. The Floyds had been among the lodgers in Mrs. Mary House's boardinghouse during Jefferson's stay there. For other members of Mrs. House's "family," see *Papers of Madison*, VI, 182, n. 29.

9 "Pain de singe," or "monkey bread," is the popular name of the gourdlike and edible fruit of the African baobab tree, or of the tree itself. For Dr. William Shippen, Jr., see *Papers of Madison*, VI, 41, n. 8. Perhaps after the ampersand, Jefferson intended to write "his lady," nee Alice Lee of Stratford Hall, Va. (*ibid*).

Notes on Debates

MS (LC: Madison Papers). For a description of the manuscript of Notes on Debates, see *Papers of Madison*, V, 231–34.

Monday. . .June 2. . . see Journals[1]

1 JM's entry reads "Monday & Tuesday June 2 & 3. see Journals." There is correspondence of JM dating on 2 June. For this reason the present editors have divided his entry between the two days.

The Journal of Congress for 2 June principally records two actions: (1) agreement upon the form of commission to be issued to Oliver Pollock "as commercial agent of the United States at the Havannah" (Delegates to Gálvez, 4 May 1783, n. 3; *JCC*, XXIV, 376–77); and (2) the adoption of a resolution instructing Robert Morris, agent of marine, upon the procedure he should follow "whensover complaints are exhibited of public abuses or private injuries committed by the captains or commanders of any privateers or armed vessels sailing under the authority of the United States" (*JCC*, XXIV, 377–78).

From Edmund Pendleton

Tr (LC: Force Transcripts). In the left margin at the top of the transcription, Peter Force's clerk wrote "MSS. McGuires." See *Papers of Madison*, I, xxii, xxiii. Addressed to "The Honble. James Madison, Eqr. Philadelphia."

VIRGA. June 2d 1783

DEAR SIR

I have yr favr of the 20th past[1] and find Sir Guy Carleton, tho' he still avows his strange interpretation of the Provisional Articles respecting the Slaves, has yet the caution to guard agt. the consequences of being directed so to Act by his Superiors, and to represent the evasion as his own private opinion, a subterfuge of the same Character with the construction,[2] for if he is not authorised to Act in the Execution of the Treaty, to what purpose did he meet Genl Washington? was it to deliver his private opinions how the treaty might be evaded, for amusement, whilst the negroes were carrying away out of his & the owners power?[3]

We have several arrivals, but they are of the old Bristol kind, the Capts can tell no more news than the ships can; they have however got goods down to a tolerable price & 40/ pr hundred hath been given for tobacco at Richmond, which is not considered as the ne plus Ultra of the market, and at the same time our fine Merchts on Rappa. talk of only 20/. 25/ has been offered by others for Rappa tobacco.[4]

Nothing conclusive is determined as to the impost, upon a considerable debate, a Majority gave leave to bring in the Bill, but it begins to be doubted whether it will pass, and it is said that even Mr H—y, the great Patron of it, begins to cool on the Subject. what will become of our credit & the public debts, if it fails, I don't know. the Suspension of our taxes 'til December, appears a very bad succedaneum for the imposts: I am willing to hope the matter is misrepresented to me & that you will have a more favourable prospect from Richmond.[5]

The Council have replied to the Governor's charge, & so the matter rests, no determination hath yet been made between them, & I am told there are diversity of opinions which is right; sure I am something should be *done* it, and if they doubt whether the Act in question be constitutional or not, they ought to repeal it and establish a mode of removal of Justice wch is unexceptionable, since the Act of Government ought not to be violated on the one hand, nor on the other unworthy Majistrates immoveably fixed on the state.[6]

I am Dr Sir Yr mo. affe friend

EDMD PENDLETON

[1] Not found.

[2] This first paragraph of the letter, as written in the original manuscript, appears in Stan. V. Henkels Catalogue No. 694 (1892), p. 93. That copy renders the word as "construction" rather than "constitution," as written by Force's clerk. JM had used the word "construction" in the same context in his letter of 20 May to Randolph (*q.v.*) and hence had probably done so in his missing letter of that day to Pendleton.

[3] Walke to Delegates, 3 May, and n. 5; Delegates to Harrison, 20 May, and n. 3; 27 May; Jones to JM, 25 May; 31 May; JM Notes, 26 May, and n. 1; Pendleton to JM, 26 May; 16 June 1783. In conformance with instructions from Congress, Washington took the initiative in seeking a conference with Carleton. Carleton seems to have accepted the invitation reluctantly, for he professed to be uninformed

by the British ministry about how he should interpret the preliminary articles of peace on subjects requiring his participation. Commenting in his letter of 12 May 1783 to Washington upon the issue of the Negroes, Carleton reiterated, "after all I only give my own opinion" (NA: PCC, No. 52, fol. 164). Since he lacked instructions, his emphasis in this regard was not an "evasion." See also *Papers of Madison*, VI, 462, n. 2; 466, n. 3; 479; 480, n. 7; Fitzpatrick, *Writings of Washington*, XXVI, 347–49, 370, 403–5, 409.

[4] The *Virginia Gazette* of 7 June announced the arrival in the James River at Richmond of the "brig Harmony, Captain Caton, in eight weeks from Bristol." See also the issues of that weekly for 24 and 31 May; JM to Randolph, 13 May, and n. 6; Pendleton to JM, 17 May, and n. 6; Jones to JM, 31 May 1783. Tobacco grown in the Richmond neighborhood rarely was of as high quality as the best which came to market along the Rappahannock River. Forty shillings a hundredweight was nearly twice the price offered in February 1783. See *Papers of Madison*, VI, 244, n. 3; 248, n. 3; 282, n. 3; 462, n. 7; Pendleton to JM, 9 June 1783. On 24 May the Virginia state "Agent for Commutables" was offered 25 shillings a hundredweight for the tobacco received for taxes (*Cal. of Va. State Papers*, III, 601).

[5] "H—-y" was Patrick Henry. Pendleton should have written "'til 20 November" rather that "'til December." See Pendleton to JM, 26 May, and nn. 5, 11; Jones to JM, 31 May 1783, and n. 5.

[6] Pendleton to JM, 26 May 1783, and n. 13.

Notes on Debates

MS (LC: Madison Papers). For a description of the manuscript of Notes on Debates, see *Papers of Madison*, V, 231–34.

. . . Tuesday June. . . 3. see Journals[1]

[1] JM Notes, 2 June, n. 1. The entries in the journal of Congress of 3 June 1783 chiefly bear upon details relating to Indian affairs of "the eastern department," that is, eastward of the Connecticut River (*JCC*, XXIV, 379–80).

To Edmund Randolph

RC (LC: Madison Papers). Cover missing. Many years later, after recovering this letter, JM wrote "Randolph" below the text.

PHILADA. June 3d. 1783.

MY DEAR FRIEND

I thank you cordially for the narrative of legislative proceedings contained in your favor of the 24th ulto[1] In return for the Journal of the House of Delegates I inclose herewith a copy of the proceedings of Congs. since Novr. last.[2] There is a chasm in the Journal you have sent arising from the miscarriage of yr. letter which ought to have come by the preceding mail.[3]

The idea of protracting my service in Congs. into a part of the ensuing year does not coincide with the plans which I have in view after Novr. next. I had rather therefore not stand in the way of another Gentleman whom it might suit better, and whose attendance would be more certain. If a reduction of the number of Delegates should take place it will be still more essential not to include me.[4]

I have recd. from Mr. Webb £100 refd. to in yours. The remittance of £1000 havg. been shared not equally as heretofore but according to our respective arrears, this sum will somewhat overpay me. You will therefore not apply for other warrants in my behalf. I wish you had reserved the £50 which you advanced for me sometime ago & that you wd. now draw on me for it if it be more convenient for you to receive it here, or you can readily sell a bill where you are. It will be perfectly convenient for me to pay it.[5]

Being somewhat indisposed in my head & also pressed for time I beg leave to refer to Mr. Jones instead of repeating what I have written to him.[6]

Adieu My dear sir & be assured that I am yr. sincere friend

J. M.

I have a letter from a Correspondt. of Mazzei at Nantz, which informs me that [he] was at Paris in Feby. and wd. sail for America in March or April.[7]

[1] *Q.v.*

[2] The enclosure is missing.

[3] Randolph to JM, 15 May, and 24 May 1783. The earlier of these letters, enclosing a brief portion of the journal of the Virginia House of Delegates, evidently had not reached JM.

[4] *Papers of Madison*, VI, 464, n. 6; JM to Jefferson, 20 May, and n. 10; Randolph to JM, 24 May, and n. 8; Jones to JM, 25 May; JM to Randolph, 27 May 1783, and n. 7.

[5] Ambler to JM, 17 May, and n. 3; 24 May; 1 June; JM to Randolph, 27 May; Statement of Receipts, 28 May 1783, n. 5.

[6] JM's letter of 3 June, now missing, had been received by Jones before he wrote to JM on 14 June 1783 (*q.v.*). Many years later JM recorded in his "Autobiographical Notes" (MS in Princeton University Library) that he had not volunteered for military service at the onset of the Revolution because of "feeble health, and a constitutional liability to sudden attacks, somewhat resembling Epilepsy, and suspending the intellectual functions" (*Papers of Madison*, I, 164). These "attacks" had become far less frequent, but he may have been suffering from a brief recurrence. See Jameson to JM, 24 May, and n. 1; Jones to JM, 31 May 1783.

[7] JM evidently referred to the letter of 15 February 1783 from Mark Lynch, a merchant in Nantes (*Papers of Madison*, VI, 243, and n. 1; 244, n. 5).

Notes on Debates

MS (LC: Madison Papers). For a description of the manuscript of Notes on Debates, see *Papers of Madison*, V, 231–34.

Wednesday June 4.

The Report of the Committee for giving to the army certificates for land was taken up. After some discussion of the subject, some members being for and some agst. making the certificates tra[n]sferrable it was agreed that the Report should lie on the table.[1]

For what passed in relation to the Cession of vacant territory by Virga. see the Journal.[2]

Whilst Mr. Hamiltons motion relating to Mr. Livingston Secretary of For: affrs. was before the House, Mr. Peters moved, in order to detain Mr. Livingston in office,[3] that it be declared by the Seven States present that the Salary ought to be augmented. To this it was objected 1. that it would be an assumption of power in 7. States[4] to say what 9 States ought to do. 2. that it might ensnare Mr. Livingston.[5] 3. that it would commit the present States, who ought to be open to discussion when 9 States should be on the floor. The motion of Mr. Peters being withdrawn, that of Mr. Hamilton was agreed to.

[1] By an ordinance of 16 September 1776, as supplemented by other ordinances or resolutions in 1778 and 1779, Congress pledged bounty lands "to be provided by the United States," at the close of the conflict, to officers and soldiers who should engage to serve in the continental army for the duration of the war. The promised acreage varied from 10,000 acres for the commander-in-chief and 3,000 acres for a major general to 100 acres for a private (*JCC*, V, 763; XII, 1117; XV, 1336–37). Although the nearest of kin would be issued the bounty-land warrants of men who died while in service, an "officer or soldier" was forbidden to transfer his warrant (*JCC*, V, 788). This prohibition was expected to prevent engrossment of bounty lands by speculators. Congress had no land of its own in 1776 but relied on some of the states to provide the requisite tracts within their own borders or to cede their trans-Appalachian claims to the United States (*Papers of Madison*, II, 74–75; 78; III, 305, n.; IV, 10; V, 306, n. 2).

On 30 May 1783, in compliance with its adoption of a motion by Alexander Hamilton, Congress elected a grand committee of ten members "to consider of the best manner of carrying into execution the engagements of the United States for certain allowances of land to the Army at the conclusion of the war" (*JCC*, XXIV, 376, and n. 2). On behalf of the committee, Hamilton on 4 June recommended that until the needed acreage could be located and surveyed, every officer and soldier entitled to bounty land should receive, upon being "furloughed or discharged," a certificate bearing his name and specifying the amount of land to which he was entitled. Congress decided that this "Report should lie on the table" (*JCC*, XXIV, 383, and n. 1). Further extended debate on the subject of bounty lands apparently was not resumed until 14 October (*JCC*, XXV, 677–80). See JM Notes, 5 June 1783, n. 1.

2 Congress resumed discussion of a committee report submitted on 25 April by John Rutledge, chairman. The committee recommended postponing a decision on Bland's motion of 23 April 1783 that Congress accept the terms of Virginia's offer of 2 January 1781 to cede her territory north and west of the Ohio River, until after the Boudinot committee's report of 3 November 1781 on the western lands had been considered. See *Papers of Madison*, VI, 502; 503, nn. 4, 5, 6. On 4 June Congress adopted the Rutledge committee report and referred so much of the Boudinot committee's proposals as "relates to the cession made by the Commonwealth of Virginia" to a committee comprising Rutledge, chairman, and JM among the other four members (*JCC*, XXIV, 381). See also JM Notes, 5 June, n. 1; 6 June 1783.

3 Congress adopted two resolutions introduced by Hamilton. The first provided that the papers of the office of the secretary for foreign affairs should be placed in the custody of Charles Thomson, secretary of Congress, until a successor to Robert R. Livingston "can be appointed." The second resolution, passed unanimously, thanked Livingston "for his services" and assured him of Congress' "high sense of the ability, zeal and fidelity with which he hath discharged the important trust reposed in him" (*JCC*, XXIV, 382). See also *JCC*, XXIV, 336–37. Although Congress on 4 June evidently expected that a new secretary for foreign affairs would soon be elected, the vacancy continued until John Jay became Livingston's successor on 21 December 1784 (*Papers of Madison*, VI, 224, n. 7). See also JM Notes, 10 June 1783, and n. 11.

4 Of the eight states effectively represented in Congress on 30 May, Massachusetts, Rhode Island, Delaware, and North Carolina had two delegates each, or the minimum required to permit their vote to count in a poll, and then only if the two were in agreement. What delegate from one of these states had left Philadelphia or was unable for some other reason to attend Congress on 4 June is unknown, but he probably was either Nathaniel Gorham of Massachusetts or Jonathan Arnold of Rhode Island. The next tallied vote entered in the journal was on 20 June 1783. By then, the total number of delegates attending Congress was twenty, or three less than on 30 May, and the only states effectively represented were Massachusetts, New Jersey, Pennsylvania, Delaware, Virginia, North Carolina, and South Carolina (*JCC*, XXIV, 372, 407; Burnett, *Letters*, VII, 176, 178).

5 To increase Livingston's salary obviously required Congress to "appropriate money" and possibly also "to ascertain" the sums and expenses necessary for the defense and welfare of the United States. Article IX of the Articles of Confederation required the assent of "nine states" for either of these actions to be taken (*JCC*, XIX, 220). Insufficient salary to pay his expenses had been emphasized by Livingston as a principal cause of his resignation (*Papers of Madison*, VI, 418–19, and nn. 2, 4; JM to Jefferson, 10 June 1783). Had Livingston been led to expect a higher salary by the favorable action of seven states, he could have been doubly "ensnared," for not only might the increase subsequently have failed to gain the assent of nine states, but he might also have sacrificed his office as chancellor of New York (*Papers of Madison*, V, 337, and n. 2).

From the Reverend James Madison

RC (LC: Madison Papers). Docketed by JM: "Madison Js Revd June 4. 1783 June 4 1783. Presidt. Madison. inclosing Ret. from Scott for engraving seal." Cover addressed to "The Honb. James Madison Esqr Member of Congress Philadelphia or In his Absence To The Hon J. F. Mercer Esqr."

June 4th 1783.

Dear Sir

I recd. the Seal by Mr. Jones & am much obliged to you for the Trouble you have given yourself relative to it.[1] The offer you made of having the Bill safely lodged with *Scott* the *Engraver*,[2] has induced me to inclose it to you or in your Absence to Mr. Mercer.[3] I ought to apologize for calling the Attention of either of you from more important Business, but am persuaded you will not require one.

Believe me to be Yrs. sincerely

J. Madison

Your Friends, the Atty & Lady[4] are now here. I wish you were of the Party.

If Mr. Mercer, in the Absence of Col.[5] Madison shd. open this, he will oblige me much by sending the inclosed to *Scott the Engraver*

[1] *Papers of Madison*, VI, 49; 50, n. 4; Jones to JM, 25 May 1783, n. 18.

[2] See Receipt of Robert Scot, 16 June 1783. Robert Scot (1744–1823), a native of Edinburgh, was both watchmaker and silversmith before devoting himself exclusively to engraving. A resident of Fredericksburg by 1775, he engraved currency for the Commonwealth of Virginia and in 1780 was awarded £2,103 8*s*. "for his Services & expences in detectg some persons concerned in counterfietg the paper currency." He also made for the state several Indian medals that Governor Thomas Jefferson pronounced "extraordinarily good." By May 1781 Scot had moved to Philadelphia, where he advertised himself as "Late Engraver to the State of Virginia." His name is listed with various addresses in the Philadelphia directories from 1785 to 1822. On 30 December 1793 President Washington, with the approval of the Senate, appointed him engraver to the recently established United States mint—a position which he held for the rest of his life (*Journal of the Executive Proceedings of the Senate of the United States*, I, 143–44; Boyd, *Papers of Jefferson*, IV, 35–37; *Va. Mag. Hist. and Biog.*, LXVIII [1960], 84; George Barton Cutten, *The Silversmiths of Virginia, Together with Watchmakers and Jewelers, from 1694 to 1850* [Richmond, 1952], p. 41; David McNeely Stauffer, *American Engravers upon Copper and Steel* [2 vols.; New York, 1907], I, 242–43; II, 471–74).

[3] John Francis Mercer.

[4] Edmund Randolph, attorney general of Virginia, and Mrs. Randolph. The members of "The Visitors and Governors" of the College of William and Mary had met on 2 June "upon business of importance" (*Va. Gazette*, 24 and 31 May

1783). Randolph implied in his letter of 4 June to JM (*q.v.*) that he also had come to Williamsburg to attend a session of the Court of Admiralty. On 4 June the Virginia House of Delegates granted Randolph "leave to be absent from the service of this House, until Wednesday se'nnight" (*JHDV*, May 1783, p. 36).

[5] *Papers of Madison*, I, 163; 164, n. 1.

From Edmund Randolph

RC (LC: Madison Papers). Unsigned but in Randolph's hand. Cover addressed by him to "The honble James Madison jr. Esqr of congress Philadelphia." Docketed by JM, "June 4. 1783." JM also jotted on the cover: "Dana La: Hol: Md. Peace Estabt. New Delegation Fairfax Instrons. Claypoole for Int. opn. of Gl. W. on proceedings of Congs. Mutinous Men? of Sergts? W. Territory Secy. F. Affrs." These jottings were written by JM on either 16 or 17 June. They were the days, respectively, on which he received the present letter and wrote to Randolph. In his letter to Randolph (*q.v.*), JM discussed most of the topics comprising the memorandum.

WMSBURG. June 4. 1783.

MY DEAR SIR

George Hay has, I hope, complied with my directions in transmitting the operations of the assembly.[1] From this place I can forward nothing new, except the folly of a french captain, who refused to enter with the naval officer[2] on his arrival, insisting that some protection or other, which he possessed under his king, was paramount to any internal regulation here. The naval officer went on board of his vessel in company with another Frenchman;[3] and both of them remonstrated with him on the folly of his obstinacy; but neither could prevail. By this means he has exposed himself or rather his ship to Seizure and condemnation[4] must be his lot.

These foolish events irritate much: and will doubtless be handed to you in Philadelphia with some exaggeration, which it may acquire from the narrative of the party, who is likely to sustain loss.[5] But I cannot be mistaken, because I made it a point to represent the case in its just colours to a Mr. La croix in this town.[6] He answered, that he had stated it in the same light to his countryman, but his labours to recover[7] him were ineffectual.

[1] Randolph to JM, 24 May 1783, and n. 12.

[2] Beverly Dickson (d. 1787) was the naval officer of the Williamsburg district (*Va. Gazette, and Weekly Advertiser*, 6 Sept. 1787; *JCSV*, III, 42, 81; McIlwaine,

Official Letters, III, 356 n.; Pendleton to JM, 4 May, n. 8). Probably Randolph referred to Peter (Pierre?) Heron, master of the "Lark," a French brigantine which had arrived in the James River from Morlaix, France, on 27 May. In that case, the Frenchman was less intractable than supposed. In a petition for relief, submitted on 4 June to the Virginia General Assembly, he declared that "ignorance of the law" and the inaccuracy of his interpreter, who had checked with the naval officer, led him to discharge cargo without paying the required duties. For this offense "the marshal of the admiralty" had seized the "Lark" as a "forfeiture" to the state. Finding Heron's plea to be reasonable, the General Assembly on 9 June 1783 passed a private act returning the vessel to him "upon paying the customary duties, office fees, and the expenses of the seizure" (*JHDV*, May 1783, pp. 37, 38, 42–45; Hening, *Statutes*, XI, 254).

3 Possibly "Mr. La Croix," mentioned in Randolph's next paragraph.

4 That is, by the Court of Admiralty which convened at Williamsburg (*Papers of Madison*, V, 16; 17, n. 2; Randolph to JM, 9 May 1783, n. 2).

5 Heron's acceptance of the action of the General Assembly in answer to his petition would seem to explain the lack of any evidence that the issue was carried to Congress.

6 Peter de La Croix seems to have resided in Virginia as early as 1779. Either in that year or in 1780 his ship was looted and burned by parties unknown. Denying that the court of Accomack County, and later the General Court of Virginia, had jurisdiction over issues between foreigners, "he refused to make any defence" in separate suits brought against him by three members of his crew for nonpayment of their wages. The sailors' claims were sustained by three tribunals, and for a time La Croix was imprisoned for debt. In 1779 and again on 18 June 1783, he petitioned the Virginia General Assembly for redress. The House of Delegates on 20 June, and the Senate four days later, decided that although the state should assume the cost of the "several prosecutions," La Croix had been accorded "two fair and full judiciary hearings." For that reason "it would be inconsistent with the constitution and laws of this country for the Legislature to re-consider the subject" (*JHDV*, Oct. 1779, pp. 96, 100; May 1783, pp. 65, 71, 79). See also Boyd, *Papers of Jefferson*, III, 162–66, 197–98, 213–14; *Cal. of Va. State Papers*, III, 253–54). If the individual in question was the Pierre La Croix who in 1831 died in Fredericksburg at the age of eighty-eight, he had been a drummer boy in Montcalm's army at Quebec, and some service has been claimed for him in the American army during the Revolution (*Records of the American Catholic Historical Society of Philadelphia*, LX [1949], 166).

7 That is "to regain his senses or ability to judge sanely."

Instruction to Virginia Delegates *in re* Contracts

FC (Virginia State Library).

In the House of Delegates

Wednesday the 4th of June 1783

Resolved that the Delegates representing this State in Congress be instructed to take proper Steps for procuring and transmitting to the Executive of this State copies of all Accounts and Vouchers relative to disbursements and Contracts made with the Individuals of this State by any person acting under the authority of Congress in order that a proper inquiry may be made into their conduct.[1]

Teste
JOHN BECKLEY CHD[2]

1783 June 7th.
Agreed to by the Senate.
WILL DREW. C. S[3]

[1] On 17 May 1783 Colonel William Finnie petitioned the Virginia General Assembly for relief from impending legal judgments against him for unpaid debts incurred on behalf of Congress when he had been deputy quartermaster general of the southern department for Virginia (*JHDV*, May 1783, p. 10; *Papers of Madison*, III, 59, n. 6). His petition was in harmony with the resolution drafted by JM and passed by Congress on 13 March 1783 (*ibid*., IV, 91–92). On 7 May of that year Congress adopted Arthur Lee's further resolution on the subject, recommending that the state legislatures provide for the indemnification of continental officers penalized by state courts for acts necessitated by "military operations" (*JCC*, XXIV, 330). In the General Assembly on 30 May, Lee introduced a bill of similar tenor. Following referral of his proposal to the committee of the whole house, the House of Delegates on 17 June resolved to defer further consideration of the measure until "the second Monday of September next" (*JHDV*, May 1783, pp. 27, 62). This postponement had been foreshadowed on 4 June, when Patrick Henry, chairman of the Committee of Propositions and Grievances, successfully moved that Finnie's petition be rejected and that the present instruction to the delegates be adopted (*JHDV*, May 1783, pp. 34–35). Harrison almost certainly enclosed a copy of the instruction in his letter to the delegates of 20 June (*q.v.*). See also Delegates to Harrison, 14–15 Aug. 1783, n. 2.

[2] Clerk of the House of Delegates.

[3] Clerk of the Senate.

Notes on Debates

MS (LC: Madison Papers). For a description of the manuscript of Notes on Debates, see *Papers of Madison*, V, 231–34.

Thursday June 5. see Journal.[1]

[1] The journal records the adoption of a resolution introduced by Hugh Williamson to vacate the commission of any "captain or commander" who, without authorization of Congress or the agent of marine, should transport "goods and merchandise" aboard a "vessel in the service of the United States."

Following the adoption of this proposal, Bland, seconded by Hamilton, offered a motion designed to promote domestic tranquillity; placate and reward the discontented veterans of the continental army; resolve the long-extended controversy over Virginia's land claims north and west of the Ohio River; assure the settlement, defense, and making of states in that area; and provide large revenues for the use of the nearly bankrupt Congress. If Congress adopted the motion, it was not to become effective until approved by "the army of the United States" and until the Virginia General Assembly had rescinded from its offer of cession the stipulation requiring Congress to guarantee to that state its remaining territory west of the Appalachian Mountains. Should Virginia acquiesce in this regard, the motion recommended that Congress accept Virginia's offer of cession with its other provisos.

These proposals were followed by others in the Bland-Hamilton motion: (1) repeal of the resolution pledging full pay for five years to the officers of the continental army; (2) in lieu thereof and of all other money owed to officers and soldiers who had served for the duration of the war, a grant to each of them, for every dollar due him, of thirty acres in the Northwest Territory in addition to the promised bounty lands; (3) a guarantee that the acreage would be free of all taxes and quitrents for seven years; (4) extension of the provisions of No. 2 and No. 3 to apply to officers and soldiers who served for at least three years; (5) a regulation that surveyors of the United States lay off for the above purposes a sufficiently large tract divided into districts, subdivided into townships; (6) admission of a district, containing "20,000 male inhabitants" as a state, equally "Independent free and Sovereign" as any of the original thirteen states; (7) reservation as the unalienable property of the United States of ten thousand acres "out of every hundred thousand acres so granted"—the "rents, issues, profits and produce" of the reserve to be used only for "the payment of the Civil List of the United States, the erecting frontier forts, the founding Seminaries of larning, and the surplus after such purposes (if any) to be appropriated to the building and equiping a Navy" (*JCC*, XXIV, 384–86, 386, n. 1). Congress referred this motion to the grand committee appointed on 30 May (JM Notes, 4 June 1783, n. 1). See also *Papers of Madison*, II, 72–78; VI, 371, n. 4; 375; 435; 436–37; 471; 472, nn. 2–4; Randolph to JM, 9 May; JM to Jefferson, 20 May, and nn. 5, 8; Jones to JM, 25 May, and n. 12; 31 May 1783.

To James Madison, Sr.

RC (LC: Madison Papers). Docketed "5 June 83" by the recipient. After recovering the letter, JM added "Madison Js June 5. 1783." On a fragment of the cover, in JM's hand, is "Col: James Recommended to the care of Mr. J. Maury Fredericksburg."

PHILADA. June 5. 1783.

HON[?]D SIR.

By the post preceding the last I answered yours of the 16th. addressing it to the care of Mr. Maury.[1] I was prevented by more necessary writing from inclosing the papers again by the lasts post as I had intended. I now supply the omission by two Gentlemen[2] going to Fredericksbg. All the news we have recd. is contained in them, and respects solely the arrangement which is at length made of a British Ministry.[3]

Having sent several copys of the pamphlet of Congress on the subject of Revenue &c. which I suppose will be transcribed in the Virga. gazettes, I shall add nothing on that subject presuming that you will thro' some channel or other obtain a sight of these proceedings.[4] I inclose a memorandum of the books which I wish you to select from Docr. Hamilton's Catalogue.[5] I shall take care not to disappoint you of the chair* which I promised to bring with me.[6] The time of my setting out is as uncertain as at the date of my last; but it will certainly take place before the fall.[7] Remember me affecy. to my mother & all the family & be assured that I am yr. dutiful son

J. MADISON JR.

I have the promise of the books for Moses Joseph & expect to bring them with me.[8]

[1] JM to James Madison, Sr., 27 May 1783, and n. 2.

[2] Unidentified.

[3] The *Pennsylvania Journal* of 4 June and the *Pennsylvania Packet* of the next day printed "the arrangement."

[4] *Papers of Madison*, VI, 471; 473, n. 7; 487–94. The plan for restoring public credit and the accompanying "Address to the States" by JM were submitted by Governor Harrison to the House of Delegates on 22 May. Only the plan appeared in the *Virginia Gazette* of 14 June. It is possible that the address was printed the next week, but no copy of the issue of 21 June 1783 has been found. Neither the plan nor the address appears in the extant issues of the *Virginia Gazette, and Weekly Advertiser*.

[5] JM to James Madison, Sr., 27 May 1783, and n. 6.

[6] *Ibid.*, and n. 4. JM's asterisk refers to the postscript even though he did not precede it with a second asterisk.

[7] JM did not arrive home until early in December 1783. See Jefferson to JM, 7 May 1783, n. 19.

[8] JM to James Madison, Sr., 27 May 1783, and n. 5.

Notes on Debates

MS (LC: Madison Papers). For a description of the manuscript of Notes on Debates, see *Papers of Madison*, V, 231–34.

Friday June 6.

The report as to the territorial Cession of Virga. after some uninteresting debate was adjourned.[1]

[1] JM Notes, 4 June, and n. 2. See also *ibid.*, 5 June, and n. 1. The journal of Congress omits mention of a session on 6 June. The report, again debated on 10 June, was not adopted by Congress until 13 September (*JCC*, XXIV, 406–9, 559–64; JM Notes, 10 June 1783).

From Jacquelin Ambler

RC (LC: Madison Papers). Docketed by JM, "June 7. 1783." Cover missing.

VIRGA. RICHMOND 7th. June 1783.

DEAR SIR

My last will have informed you of the recovery of the Accos. in the Auditor's Office.[1]—nothing necessary now but a full state of the division of the several Remittances among the Gentlemen Delegates, and orders on the Auditors to issue Warrants for the respective sums.[2] Mr. A. Le[e] was at the Treasury yesterday lamenting his having left Phila. before the two last Remittances got to hand.[3] I imagined all the Members were there and that all would come in for a share. I am sorry Mr. Lee did not & the more so as we have it not in our power to supply the deficiency here at this time.

I can send you nothing for your Amusement this week unless the Journals of the Assembly as far as they have been published will afford it.[4]

I am Dear Sir with great esteem Yr. affect Servt

J. AMBLER

[1] Ambler to JM, 24 May 1783.

[2] *Ibid*., and n. 2. See also JM to Bland, 6 May, and hdn., n. 1; Summary of Accounts, 28 May, and n. 5; Delegates to Auditors, 28 May; Statement of Receipts, 28 May 1783, and nn.

[3] Arthur Lee had left Philadelphia on 12 May, before the remittances of 17 and *ca*. 24 May had reached the delegates (JM to Jefferson, 6 May, n. 4; Ambler to JM, 17 May; 24 May; Randolph to JM, 24 May; Jones to JM, 25 May; JM to Randolph, 27 May; 3 June 1783).

[4] Randolph to JM, 15 May, and n. 4; 24 May 1783.

Benjamin Harrison to Virginia Delegates

FC (Virginia State Library). In the hand of Thomas Meriwether. Addressed to "Virginia Delegates in Congress."

IN COUNCIL June 7th. 1783.

Gentlemen

I have rec'd. your favor by the last Post,[1] and have no official Communications to make you. We are anxiously waiting for the definitive Treaty,[2] some of our People can hardly persuade themselves that Peace is yet certain and our Merchants wish to Keep them in that Opinion.[3] I beg the favor of you to send me the address of Congress &ca. the one sent me by your President was immediately forwarded to the Assembly[4] without reading so that I dont know any of it's Contents.

I am Gentlen. &c.

B. H.

[1] Delegates to Harrison, 27 May 1783.

[2] The definitive treaty of peace was not received by Congress until 13 December 1783 (Pendleton to JM, 4 May 1783, n. 6; *JCC*, XXV, 812).

[3] If the merchants were able to do so convincingly, they could continue to buy staples for export at low prices and to charge high prices for imported goods, especially since the demand for them in Virginia was heavy. See Randolph to JM, 9 May, and n. 14; 24 May; JM to Randolph, 13 May, and n. 6; Pendleton to JM, 17 May; 2 June 1783, and n. 4.

[4] Instruction to President, 9 May, n. 2; JM to James Madison, Sr., 5 June, n. 4; Delegates to Harrison, 17 June 1783.

From Joseph Jones

RC (LC: Madison Papers). Lacks docket and cover.

EDITORIAL NOTE

Although Joseph Jones clearly dated this letter "8th June," he either wrote portions of it on 7 June or else mistakenly used the term "yesterday" to date certain proceedings of the House of Delegates which had taken place on 6 June. Thus at the outset of his third paragraph he mentions as happening "Yesterday" an election which had occurred on 6 June. Again, in his final paragraph, which is on a half-folio of the letter that has become separated in the Madison Papers (LC) from the other four folios, he referred to a petition from Hanover County as having been presented "yesterday." The House of Delegates received that document on 6 June 1783. See Worthington C. Ford, ed., *Letters of Joseph Jones of Virginia* (Washington, 1889), pp. 115–16, 116 n.

RICHMOND 8th. June 1783.

DR. SIR.

I am still deprived of the pleasure of hearing from you, no letter having arrived by this Post.[1] Col. Taliaferro[2] informs me he directed Smith to send forward any letters for me to Fredericksburg where I suspect they are stoped.[3] I shall write to Smith upon the subject by this post. your letters will find me here till the last week or at least the 25th of this month[4]

We have not yet taken up the plan of Congress for general revenue. it is agreed to do it next monday or Tuesday.[5] Mr. R. H. L. is opposed to it in toto.[6] Mr. H—y, I understand thinks we ought to have credit for the amount of the Duty under an apprehension we shall consume more than our proportion or in other words that we shall by agreeing to the impost as recommended pay more than our quota of the debt.[7] J. Taylor wholly agt. the plan G. N—l—s thinks with H—y. The Speaker is for it B—x—n I am told is so too, but he has not said as much to me. the two first named being in the opposition is what alarms me.[8] Mr. H—y I am told was at first in favor of the impost and had early in the Session concurred in bringing in a bill to revive the former Law, but has since changed his opinion. the Members seem to be very much divided. I wish we could hear whether any of the States have adopted it.[9]

Yesterday our Delegates to Congress were elected[:] Jefferson, Hardy, Mercer, Lee, Monroe.[10] Mr. Griffin was voted for and had near fifty votes, but three objections were started agt. him which I am told had weight or were made so to keep him out, his Seat in the Court of appeals, his residence in Philadelph[ia] and just before the ballot was taken some wispers were spread he was withdrawn for the reasons above, which it is said lost him some votes. the two first mentd. reasons were the chief obstacles one was publicly mentd. in the House which gave me an opportunity of endeavouring at least to obvia[te] the objection.[11] My compliments to Mr. Mercer and inform him what he had heard of a report circulat[ed] to his prejudice either never existed or has died away so as not to be mentioned or even whispered.[12] Mr. Short is elected to supply the vacancy in the Council.[13] In consequence of the Memorial of the Officers of the Virga. line a report from the Com: of prop: & G: to whic[h] it was refd. has been under consideration. It was proposed to allow our line the whole of their land on the N. W. side of the Ohio, with an additional quantity as a gratuity on pretence the Cumberland Tract was greatly deficient in quantity and quality, also to bear the expence of the location. this report was so repugnant to the cession to Congress and to the remonstrance in 1779 whereby the legislature promised to furnish lands beyond the Ohio to the States wanting lands for their lines that I could not help opposing it, which has given it a check for the present, and upon consideration I am convinced a great majority will disapprove the report. Mr. H—y warmly espoused the report R. H. L when it was discussed unable to attend being somewhat indisposed. what side he may take on the next discussion of the report I can not learn. be it as it may, I think if they unite in this business, they cannot carry it.[14] Congress having not accepted the cession and declined to assign their reasons for delay, will produce *at least* a determination fixing the time, when, if the cession is not accepted, it shall become void, if not an immediate revocation of it. I am not withot. hopes this business may yet be concluded so as to answer the views of Congress, and I think nothing but resentment for not accepting by Congress, or assigning reasons for not accepting the cession of this State, will operate agt it.[15] Our people still retain their opinions of the importance of this State, its superiority in the Union, and the very great exertions and advances it has made in preference to all others. their views are generally local, not seeing the necessity or propriety [o]f general measures now the War is over. these notions are great obstacles to the adoption of the 5 P Ct. duty as a general revenue.[16] It is impossible to estimate the individu[al] debt of the State with any precision. by some computati[ons] we shall have to provide for raising £300,000 annual[ly] to discharge the interest of our continental quota and State debt.[17] The Comrs. appointed have settled as far as they were able the expence of the Illinois country they have disc[overed] great frauds and impositions, and reduced the debt very considerably, but it is still enormous. The accts. are not yet returned so that I cannot give you the bal[ance][18] Nathans demand is refd. to the Com: of the whole.[19] strong suspicions prevail agt. Pollocks integrity, and it is said proofs can be adduced to shew the injustice of his claim upon the State.[20] in short the prejudices he[re] are so great agt. those who have demands for money or necessaries furnished on the public account to the Westward, that it is to be feared injury may result to individuals. at the same time it must be confessed many circumstances authorize a suspicion of the fairness of their claims. a Mr. Pollard formerly of th[is state?][21] is just arrived from Bristol. He brings papers so late a[s] the 8th. apr:. an adm: appears to have been then formed as w[as] stated in the packet of the last week. North and Fox by the coalit[ion] had lost their influence & were generally reprobated. It was doubted [whether?] the last wod. be reelected in westminster.[22] Caermarthen was to go to Fr[ance] to put the finishing hand to the Treaty but had not departed and it was un[certain?] when he wod.[23] the Nation exceedingly divided by the Whig and Tory p[arties] abt. the peace. the bill for opening the Commerce with Am: had gone through th[ree] different modifications and not likely to pass.[24]

Yr. friend

Jos: Jone[s]

The bill declaring who shall be Citizens has not yet been considered in a Com: of the whole. P. H—y, R. H. L. agt. any discrimination.

I cannot concur, and must when the matter comes in take part with those who are for some discrimination so as not to trench upon the Treaty.[25] A long pet. from Essex drawn by M.S.[?]. has been presented questioning the right of Congress to make the peace as it stands, asserting the 4th. article interferes with the legislation of the states.[26] yesterday a pet. from Hanover with near 300 subscribers was presented praying the refugees may not be allowed the right of Citizenship[27] I am pretty confident there is a majority of the House in favor of the sentiments of the last petition.

1 Jones to JM, 31 May 1783, n. 1.

2 Francis Taliaferro (*Papers of Madison*, III, 51, n. 4).

3 William Smith (*ibid.*, II, 124, n. 8), for many years postmaster at Fredericksburg (*Va. Herald* [Fredericksburg], 9 Mar. 1802). Jones would have been clearer had he written "at" rather than "to" Fredericksburg.

4 Jones left Richmond on 28 June. See Jones to JM, 28 June 1783.

5 Pendleton to JM, 4 May, and n. 8; Jefferson to JM, 7 May 1783, n. 13. On Wednesday, 11 June, the Virginia House of Delegates adopted four resolutions relating to the revenue provisions of the congressional plan for restoring public credit and to compliance with the financial quota allocated by Congress to the state. The first two resolutions designated as "inadmissible" the request that Congress be enabled to collect duties on Virginia imports or on any other "particular branches of the revenue of the State." The third and fourth resolutions, which were assigned to a committee to embody in a bill, declared that Virginia should provide revenue for discharging its "quota of the continental debt" by levying and collecting "duties and imposts," by allotting some or all of the proceeds of "the land tax" and, if necessary, "the tax arising from slaves" (*JHDV*, May 1783, pp. 48–49). For the bills introduced in pursuance of these resolutions, see Pendleton to JM, 26 May, and n. 11; 2 June 1783.

6 For Richard Henry Lee, see Jefferson to JM, 7 May 1783, and n. 8.

7 For Patrick Henry's shift of position on the issue of the impost, see Randolph to JM, 9 May, and nn. 4, 7; 24 May, n. 6; Pendleton to JM, 26 May, and n. 5; 2 June; Jefferson to JM, 1 June 1783.

8 For John Taylor of Caroline County, see *Papers of Madison*, VI, 423, n. 8; Jefferson to JM, 7 May 1783, and n. 8. For George Nicholas, see *Papers of Madison*, VI, 417, n. 6. For John Tyler and the contest between followers of R. H. Lee and Henry over Tyler's re-election as speaker of the House of Delegates, see *ibid.*, IV, 30, n. 2; VI, 417, n. 6; Jefferson to JM, 7 May 1783, and n. 10. For Carter Braxton, a delegate from King William County, see *Papers of Madison*, I, 164, n. 2; 169, n. 16; II, 180; 181, n. 3; 248; 269.

9 Jefferson to JM, 7 May 1783, and n. 2. On 21 June Delaware, and on 25 August and 23 September Pennsylvania, approved the entire plan for restoring public credit (NA: PCC, No. 75, fols. 213–16, 217–20, 282–84, 287–92). On 8 May Connecticut had agreed to the proposed change in the base for allocating tax quotas but withheld its approval of the recommended imposts (*ibid.*, No. 75, fols. 77–80; *JCC*, XXV, 529–30). For other partial sanctions before the close of 1783 by New Jersey, Maryland, and Massachusetts, see JM to Jefferson, 11 Aug. 1783, and nn. 14, 17–19.

10 *JHDV*, May 1783, p. 39. For Jefferson, Arthur Lee, and Mercer, the action of the Virginia General Assembly on 6, not on 7, June was a re-election, although Jefferson had not served as a delegate since 1776. For Samuel Hardy of Isle of

Wight County, see *Papers of Madison*, IV, 429, n. 3; V, 263; 265, n. 9. For James-Monroe, see *ibid.*, IV, 152–53, n. 14; 192, n. 6. The one-year term of these delegates began on 3 November 1783.

[11] The Virginia General Assembly of May 1783 was composed of 25 senators and 152 delegates. Thus, in the unlikely event that there were no absentees, a bare majority would have been eighty-nine votes (Swem and Williams, *Register*, pp. 17–18). Arthur Lee stated that, besides the seventy-six delegates who voted for him, fifteen others had originally intended to do so but defected to Isaac Zane because of the "whispering" of Lee's opponents. They also unsuccessfully tried to defeat him by nominating his brother, Richard Henry Lee, so as to split the vote. The latter foiled this effort by withdrawing his name (Charles Campbell, ed., *Bland Papers*, II, 110).

For Cyrus Griffin, see *Papers of Madison*, II, 13, n. 3; 40. The Virginia General Assembly viewed Griffin's election by Congress on 28 April 1780 to be a judge of the Court of Appeals as "vacating his Seat in Congress" and "rendering him ineligible" as long as he held that office (*ibid.*, II, 52–53; 54, n. 5; V, 252, n. 2). Griffin did not resign until 1787. Although Jones revealed the nature of only two of the "three objections" to Griffin, these two apparently occasioned the "wispers" and were the "chief obstacles" to his election.

In a letter on 13 June 1783 to Theodorick Bland, Arthur Lee remarked: "There was great manoeuvring on the election of delegates for congress. When it was found that you and Mr. Madison, being in the nomination, interfered with some of their candidates, they persuaded the members that you should not be balloted for; and a resolution to that purpose being obtained, both were withdrawn" (Charles Campbell, ed., *Bland Papers*, II, 110).

[12] In his letters James Mercer claimed that his younger brother John Francis Mercer largely owed his defeat in April 1783 for election as a delegate from Stafford County in the General Assembly to malicious rumors concerning his share in an allegedly unsavory transaction relating to "tob[acc]o Lan[d]s." These rumors probably comprised the "report," mentioned by Jones, which James Mercer charged Arthur Lee and his "Gang" with reviving in the May session of the General Assembly to discredit both the Mercer brothers (*Va. Mag. of Hist. and Biog.*, LIX [1951], 94, 97, 98, 100–101).

[13] Jefferson to JM, 7 May 1783, and n. 15. On 10 June William Short "took his Seat at the Board" of the Council of State for the first time (*JCSV*, III, 267). He had been elected four days before by the Virginia General Assembly to fill the vacancy caused by the resignation of Robert Lawson (*JHDV*, May 1783, pp. 36, 39–40).

[14] Jones to JM, 25 May, and n. 12; 31 May 1783. For the "remonstrance" by the Virginia General Assembly on 10 and 15 December 1779 and the resolutions of 18 December 1778, upon which that protest was based, see *JHDV*, Oct. 1778, pp. 124–25; Oct. 1779, pp. 84, 90. See also *Papers of Madison*, II, 75–76.

[15] Jones to JM, 14 June 1783. See also *Papers of Madison*, VI, 400–401; 441, n. 6; JM Notes, 4 June, and n. 2; 5 June, n. 1; 6 June 1783, and n. 1.

[16] *Papers of Madison*, VI, 139, n. 13; 144–45; 208, n. 3; 210, n. 3; 285; 291–92; 327; 344; 494, n. 7; Pendleton to JM, 4 May; Randolph to JM, 9 May; 15 May, n. 2; 24 May, and nn. 5, 6; Jones to JM, 25 May; 31 May 1783.

[17] *Papers of Madison*, VI, 21, n. 5; 139, n. 13; 172; 174, n. 2; 262, n. 6; 292; 432; 434, n. 6; 488.

[18] *Ibid.*, IV, 378, n. 5; V, 229, nn. 4, 5; VI, 476, n. 6; Delegates to Gálvez, 4 May, ed. n., and n. 2.

[19] *Papers of Madison*, VI, 474; 475, nn. 3, 5; Delegates to Gálvez, 4 May, ed. n.; JM to Jefferson, 20 May, and n. 4. On 12 May 1783 the House of Delegates had

referred a letter from Governor Harrison, enclosing papers concerning the financial claim of Simon Nathan, to a committee of the whole house on the state of the commonwealth (*JHDV*, May 1783, pp. 4, 58, 71, 72–75, 81–82, 84). See Randolph to JM, 28 June 1783.

[20] *Papers of Madison*, VI, 474; 475, nn. 3, 4, 5; 476, nn. 6, 7; 478, n. 3; 502; Delegates to Gálvez, 4 May, and hdn., nn. 2, 3; JM to Jefferson, 20 May, n. 4; *JHDV*, May 1783, pp. 68, 77–78, 83, 85.

[21] Pendleton to JM, 2 June 1783, n. 4. The Pollard alluded to was possibly William (d. 1829?), at this time or later of Hanover County, Va. His friends in 1779, having had "no Intelligence" of him were "inclined to apprehend" that he was either imprisoned for debt in France or had "died in some obscure Situation where his connexions were not known" (Frances Norton Mason, ed., *John Norton & Sons, Merchants of London and Virginia* [Richmond, 1937], p. 430). Before 1788 he removed to Georgia (Lucian Lamar Knight, *Georgia's Landmarks, Memorials and Legends* [2 vols.; Atlanta, 1913–14], I, 1058; Greene County, Ga., Court Records, 1803, photocopy in Va. Historical Society).

[22] *Papers of Madison*, VI, 504, n. 3. The doubt respecting Charles James Fox was unwarranted. On 7 April 1783 he had been re-elected to the House of Commons by voters of his constituency, the city of Westminster, "without opposition, though amid some hissing." The coalition ministry precariously remained in office until 19 December 1783 (A. W. Ward, G. W. Prothero, Stanley Leathes, eds., *Cambridge Modern History* [13 vols.; Cambridge, England, 1902–12], VI, 467).

[23] David Hartley, well disposed toward the United States and a personal friend of Franklin, was the commissioner of King George III who signed the definitive treaty of peace. See Pendleton to JM, 4 May, n. 6; JM to Jefferson, 10 June 1783, and n. 8. "Caermarthen" was Francis Osborne (1751–1799), Marquis of Carmarthen and later the Duke of Leeds, who had been ambassador at the court of Versailles and who was from 1783 to 1789 the British foreign secretary.

[24] Pendleton to JM, 10 May, and n. 5; JM to Jefferson, 13 May, and n. 7; Instruction to Delegates, 23 24 May 1783, and n. 1.

[25] Jones to JM, 31 May 1783, and nn. 11, 13, 14.

[26] Although at first glance Jones would seem to have written "Mr. I.," a comparison between what appears to be "I" and the undoubted capital "S" in "Speaker" in his second paragraph makes clear that they are identical in form. "M.S.," who obviously would be someone well known to JM, almost certainly signified Meriwether Smith, a resident of Essex County, a member of the Virginia Council of State, a former colleague of JM in Congress, and an opponent of the hard-money policies championed by Arthur and Richard Henry Lee (*Papers of Madison*, II, 40, n. 2; 149, n. 4; IV, 225; 227, n. 4; V, 341, n. 5; 427, n. 7; Brant, *Madison*, II, 27; *JHDV*, Oct. 1782, p. 72). In harmony with this opposition, the petitioners, assuming that the General Assembly could set aside burdensome provisions of the preliminary peace treaty with Great Britain, asked that both the fourth and fifth articles relating to "the payment of Debts Contracted before the Revolution" and the return of Loyalists to Virginia remain unenforced within the state (Petition, Essex County, MS in Va. State Library). Upon receiving the petition on 4 June, the House of Delegates tabled it (*JHDV*, May 1783, p. 37). See also Harrison to Delegates, 9 May, and nn. 6, 7; Randolph to JM, 15 May, and n. 5; Jones to JM, 25 May; 31 May 1783.

[27] This petition "of sundry inhabitants of the county of Hanover" was received by the House of Delegates on 6 June and referred on that day to the "committee of the whole House" on the citizenship bill, which Jones mentioned at the outset of the paragraph (*JHDV*, May 1783, p. 41).

Notes on Debates

MS (LC: Madison Papers). For a description of the manuscript of Notes on Debates, see *Papers of Madison*, V, 231–34.

Monday June 9th.

Not States enough assembled to make a Congress.[1] Mr. Clarke signified to those present, that the Delegates of N. Jersey being instructed on the subject of the Back lands,[2] he should communicate the Report thereon to his Constituents.[3]

[1] JM Notes, 4 June 1783, and n. 4. Complying with "positive instructions," Elias Boudinot, president of Congress, wrote on 3 June to the governors of New Hampshire, Connecticut, New York, Maryland, and Georgia, urging them to send delegates so that at least the required minimum of nine states would be able to vote effectively on issues making "the present conjuncture of affairs" of "great importance" (Burnett, *Letters*, VII, 178). This plea, which Boudinot repeated on 3 and 22 July, did not bring an adequate representation until 7 August 1783 (*ibid.*, VII, 210, 231; *JCC*, XXIV, 493).

[2] Abraham Clark referred to resolutions of the New Jersey General Assembly dated 16 June 1778 and 29 December 1780–3 January 1781, claiming for the state a proportionate share of the western lands and opposing the provisos included in the offer of Virginia to cede lands north and west of the Ohio River to Congress (*JCC*, XI, 649–50; NA: PCC, No. 69, fols. 565–71). See also *Papers of Madison*, VI, 291. Clark's colleagues from New Jersey in Congress were Boudinot and Silas Condict.

[3] For the "Report," see JM Notes, 4 June, n. 2; 5 June, n. 1; 6 June 1783, and n. 1. Clark's "Constituents," the "legislative council and general assembly of New Jersey," adopted a "representation and remonstrance" on 14 June, reaffirming their earlier resolutions on the subject and urging Congress to "press" Virginia "to make a more liberal surrender of that territory of which they claim so boundless a proportion." This document was laid before Congress on 20 June (*JCC*, XXIV, 407–9). See also JM Notes, 10 June 1783.

From Edmund Pendleton

Tr (LC: Force Transcripts). In the left margin at the top of the transcription, Peter Force's clerk wrote "MSS. McGuires." See *Papers of Madison*, I, xxii, xxiii.

VIRGA. June 9th. 1783

DEAR SIR

In answer to yr favr of the 27th past, I should be glad to give you a full detail of the Sentiments of the Assembly, upon the Budget before them,[1] but having left Richmond a fortnight,[2] I can say nothing as to individual Opinions, and they have not made any Public determination, except to order in a Bill for the 5 P Cent as mentd. in my last, since which I have heard nothing from them on that subject.[3] You'l probably be informed from thence of the Election of Mr. Jefferson, Mr. Hardy, Mr Mercer, Dr Lee & Mr Monroe for our next years Delegates to Congress.[4] I was a deal disappointed in not finding you continued, that we might have had yr services 'til February, a point wch seemed agreed on when I left Richmond, but perhaps some letter from you prevented it.[5]

We are just told of a considerable number of arrivals from Europe, but not the particulars, the price of our tobacco will soon be fix'd.[6]

Have you yet found out what sort of a wife C. T. has? I want to hear, & yet I fear the Account will be disagreeable—should it be otherwise, my concern will be for her.[7] I am

Dr Sir Yr affe & obt Servt

EDMD PENDLETON

[1] Although the letter of 27th May to Pendleton has not been found, it probably included a sentence similar to that in JM's letter of the same day to Randolph: "The next post I hope will bring me your remarks on the Budget of Congress, with the pulse of the Assembly with regard to it" (JM to Randolph, 27 May 1783, and n. 4).

[2] On 26 May Pendleton had "just returned from Richmond" to his estate of Edmundsbury (Pendleton to JM, 26 May 1783).

[3] *Ibid.*, and nn. 5, 11; 2 June; Jones to JM, 8 June 1783, and n. 5.

[4] Jones to JM, 8 June 1783, and n. 10.

[5] *Papers of Madison*, VI, 464, n. 6; JM to Jefferson, 20 May, n. 10; Randolph to JM, 24 May 1783.

[6] Pendleton to JM, 2 June 1783, and n. 4. Pendleton meant that with peace assured and the law of supply and demand restored to normal operation, the price of tobacco would "soon" be stabilized.

[7] Pendleton to JM, 4 May, and n. 10; 16 June 1783.

Notes on Debates

MS (LC: Madison Papers). For a description of the manuscript of Notes on Debates, see *Papers of Madison*, V, 231–34.

Tuesday June 10.

The Report on the Cession of Virga. was taken up.[1] Mr. Elseworth urged the expediency of deciding immediately on the Cession. Mr. Hamilton joined him, asserting at the same time the right of the U. States.[2] He moved an amendment in favor of private claims.[3] Mr. Clarke was strenuous for the right of the U. S. and agst. waiting longer.[4] (this had reference to the absence of Maryland which had always taken a deep interest in the question)[5] Mr. Gorham supported the policy of acceding to the report. Mr. Fitzimmons recommended a postponement of the question, observing that he had sent a copy of the Report to the Maryland Delegates. The President was for a postponement till the sense of N. Jersey be known.[6] The Delaware Delegates expecting instructions were for postponing till Monday next. It was agreed at length that a final vote should not be taken till that day[7] Mr. M. yielding to the sense of the House, but warning that the opportunity might be lost by the rising of the Legislature of Virga.[8]

Mr. Hamilton & Mr. Peters with permission moved for a recommitment of the Report, in order to provide for Crown titles within the territory reserved to the State.[9] Mr. Madison objected to the motion, since an amendment might be prepared during the week & proposed on Monday next. This was acquiesced in. It was agreed that the President might informally notify private Companies & others as well as the Maryland Delegates of the time at which the Report would be taken into consideration[10]

The Order of the day for appointing a Secretary of For: Affairs, was called for, & none having been put in nomination, the order was postponed.[11] Mr. Bland then nominated Mr. Arthur Lee, Mr. Gorham nominated Mr. Jefferson, but being told he would not accept, then named Mr. Tilghman, Mr. Higginson nominated Mr. Jonathan Trumbull. Mr. Mongomery nominated Mr. George Clymer. It was understood that Genl. Schuyler remained in nomination[12]

1 *Papers of Madison,* VI, 503, n. 4; JM Notes, 4 June, and n. 2; 5 June, n. 1; 6 June 1783, and n. 1. The journal of Congress for 10 June omits mention of the "Report."

2 *Papers of Madison,* VI, 400–401; 441, n. 6; 442–43; 444, n. 2; 472, n. 4; 482, n. 10; 491; 503, n. 5.

3 The land speculators' "private claims" to large areas north and west of the Ohio River were usually based on grants from Indians or titles, real or alleged, conferred by the Crown of Great Britain. See the entries, Illinois Company, Indiana Company, Land companies, Vandalia Company, and Wabash Company, in the indexes of *Papers of Madison,* II, III, IV, and V.

4 *Ibid.,* VI, 442; 444, n. 6.

5 JM Notes, 4 June, n. 4; 9 June, and n. 1. For Maryland's "deep interest," undeviatingly hostile to Virginia's claim to the Old Northwest, see *Papers of Madison,* II, 72–77; 81–82; 101; 301, n. 4; IV, 179, nn. 7, 8; 201; 221, n. 11; V, 50; VI, 291; 296, n. 38.

6 JM Notes, 9 June, nn. 2, 3. JM, in the feeble hand of his old age, interlineated "[Mr. Boudinot" above "President." As a delegate from Maryland, James McHenry presented his credentials to Congress on 11 June (*JCC,* XXIV, 389; *Papers of Madison,* VI, 485, n. 1). He was the only delegate from his state in attendance until the return of Daniel Carroll on 7 August 1783 (*JCC,* XXIV, 492).

7 JM Notes, 6 June 1783, n. 1. Congress did not meet on Monday, 16 June. The

instructions expected by Gunning Bedford, Jr., and Eleazar McComb, the delegates from Delaware, were not adopted by the General Assembly of their state until 21 June, the final day of the session (*Papers of the Historical Society of Delaware*, VI [1887], 828, 834, 837, 839–41). There appears to be no evidence that these instructions opposing the reservations of land made by Virginia in its offer of cession were laid before Congress.

8 "Mr. M." is JM. See *Papers of Madison*, VI, 502; 503, nn. 5, 6.

9 For the stipulation in the proposal of cession by Virginia requiring Congress to guarantee the title of the state to the western lands excluded from the offer, see JM Notes, 5 June 1783, n. 1. "Crown titles" were grants of land made directly by the king to individuals or corporations (*William and Mary Quarterly*, 2d ser., X [1930], 52–55).

10 Charles Carroll and Samuel Chase of Maryland, and Bernard and Michael Gratz, Robert Morris, William Murray, and Samuel Wharton of Philadelphia were among the prominent shareholders in "private Companies" (*Papers of Madison*, III, 47, n. 2; 344, n. 2; 346, n. 14; IV, 179, n. 8; 221, n. 11; 228, n. 7; Thomas P. Abernethy, *Western Lands and the American Revolution*, pp. 234–35).

11 *JCC*, XXIV, 382, 390. See also *Papers of Madison*, VI, 224, n. 7; 419, n. 4; JM Notes, 4 June 1783, and nn. 3, 4; JM to Randolph, 17 June 1783.

12 Although the journal for 10 June does not refer to the "Order of the day" and omits mention of these nominations, Charles Thomson, the secretary of Congress, recorded them on a prefatory page of one of his committee books. Lee's name was withdrawn on 26 August at his own request; Jefferson's was immediately canceled when Congress was informed, probably by JM, of his friend's unwillingness to serve. On 18 June Silas Condict nominated his fellow citizen of New Jersey, William Churchill Houston (*Papers of Madison*, I, 44, n. 5). On that day Boudinot, who on 18 December 1782 had proposed Hamilton's father-in-law, Major General Philip John Schuyler (1733–1804), re-nominated him. Thereafter no further nominations were made until 25 and 26 February 1784 (NA: PCC, No. 186, fol. 2).

Lieutenant Colonels Tench Tilghman (1744–1786), a Baltimore merchant in civilian life, and Jonathan Trumbull, Jr. (1740–1809), of Hartford, were, respectively, Washington's aide-de-camp and military secretary. Trumbull later had a distinguished political career: four years as speaker during his service of six years (1789–1795) in the United States House of Representatives; two years (1795–1796) in the federal Senate; two years (1796–1798) as lieutenant governor of Connecticut; and eleven years (1798–1809) as governor. Clymer's nomination, first offered by FitzSimons on 18 December 1782 and renewed by Joseph Montgomery on the present occasion, was canceled on an unspecified date.

To Thomas Jefferson

RC (LC: Madison Papers). Many years later after recovering the letter, JM wrote "Madison, Jas." above the date line. The words italicized in the present copy were written in the JM-Jefferson Code No. 2.

PHILADA. 10 June 1783

MY DEAR SIR

Congress have recd. two letters from Mr. *Laurens* dated *London*[,] one the *fiveteenth of March* the *other fiveth of April*.[1] In the former he *persists in* the *jealousy* expressed in *his letter of* the *thirtieth of December of* the *British Councils.*[2] *He says* that *Shelburne* had *boasted of his success* in *gaining the provisional treaty without the concurrence of France and of the good effects he expected to draw from that advantage.* Mr. *Ls remark was* that *admitting* the *fact which he did not* altho' it *might disgrace* and even *prove fatal to the American Ministers,* it *could have no such effects on the United States.*[3] His *second letter* expresses more *confidence in the D. of Portland and Mr. Fox.* These *ministers have*[4] withdrawn the subject of commerce with the U. S. from Parliamt. and mean to open negociations for a Treaty with their ministers in Europe.[5] Mr. Fox asked Mr. L. whether these had powers for that purpose: his answer was that he believed so, that he had seen a revocation of Mr. Adams' commission noticed in the Gazettes but that he considered the paragraph as spurious. From this it would seem that *Mr A had never communicated this* diminution of *his powers to his colleagues.*[6] These letters leave us in the suspence in which they found us as to the definitive Treaty. Mr. L. thinks that no such event could have been relied on under Shelburnes administration.[7] He was on the 5th. of Apl. setting out for Paris with Mr. David Hartley successor to Mr. Oswald, from whence he sd. proceed to America unless a definitive Treaty was near being concluded.[8] Notwithstand the daily arrivals from every quarter we get not a line on the subject from our Ministers at Versailles.[9]

Mr. Dumas has inclosed to Congs. sundry papers from which it a[p]pears that the *Dutch indulge a* violent animosity *against the French court* for *abandoning their interests and the* liberty of *navigation by a premature concluding of the preliminaries.* Complaints on this head are *made through Dumas to Mr. Adam*[s] with *enquiries whether the American ministers had powers to* concert engagements *with the United Provinces,*[10] *his M C Majy, and his Cat Majy*[11] *for maintaining the rights asserted by the neutral confederation*[12] or if the two last *decline with United Provinces alone the answer of Mr A* is not *included but references to it import* that *it was satisfactory and* that *negociations were to be opened accordingly* It is certain notwithstanding that no *powers equal to such a transaction* were *ever given generally to the ministers*[13] and that as far as they were given they were *superceded by the commission to Mr Dana*[14] This correspondence commenced in Jany. & is brought down to late in March and yet no *intimation whatever* concerning it has been *received from* the *ministers themselves*

Congress have lately sent instructions to the Ministers in Eur[ope] to *contend* in *the final treaty for such* amendment of the *article relating to British debts* as will *suspend payment for* [three] *years after the war and expressly exclude interest during the war*[15]

Mr. Livingston has taken his final leave of the department [of] Foreign affairs, He wd. have remained if such an augmentation [of] his Salary had been made as wd. have secured him agst. future expence. But besides the disinclination of several members to augment salaries, there was no prospect of a competent number of States for an appropriation of money until he must have lost the option of the Chancellorship of N.Y.[16] No successor has been yet nominated, altho' the day for a choice has passed. I am utterly at a loss to guess on whom the choice will ultima[tely] fall. *A L* will be *started* if the *defaction* of a respectable *competitor* shd. be *likely to force votes upon him*[17] No such has yet *been made a subject of conversation in my presence*[18]

The general arrangement of the foreign System has been suspended by the thinness of Congs. in part,[19] and partly by the desire of further information from Europe.[20] I fear much the delay will be exceedingly protracted. Nothing but final resignation of the Ministers abroad[21] & the arrival of Foreign Ministers here, will effectually stimulate Congs. into activity & decision on the subject.[22] How far & at what time the first cause will operate is precarious. The secd. seems less so. Mr. Van Berkel has sent directions for proper provisions for his reception in the next month.[23] A Sweedish Gentleman recommended by Dr. Franklin as a Philosopher, and by the Ct. de Vergennes as an intended Minister has been here for some time.[24] From the temper of Spain, a mission from that Court also is not improbable.[25]

The Treaty of Commerce with G. B. is another business suspended by the same cause. The Assembly have instructed us to reserve to Congs. a revisal after it shall have been settled in Europe.[26] This will give force to the doctrine of caution hitherto maintained by us.[27] The time of my setting out for Virga continues to be uncertain, but cannot now be very distant. The prospect of seeing you, I need not assure you, enters much into the pleasure I promise myself from the visit. Mrs. House & Mrs. Trist char[ge] me with their very sincere & respectful compliments to you & beg that they may be remembered very affectionately to Miss Patsy.[28]

I am Dear Sir your sincere friend

J. MADISON JR.

1 Wharton, *Revol. Dipl. Corr.*, VI, 303–5, 360–61. These dispatches, addressed to Robert R. Livingston, were received by Congress on 10 June, five days after he had ceased to be secretary for foreign affairs (NA: PCC, No. 185, III, 66).

[2] JM probably should have referred to Henry Laurens' letter of 24 December 1782. Its contents support JM's remark, and no dispatch of "the *thirtieth*" from Laurens has been found. He began his letter of 9 January 1783 to Livingston by writing, "I had the honor of addressing you on the 15th and 24th ultimo" (Wharton, *Revol. Dipl. Corr.*, VI, 138–40, 164–65, 200). See also Pendleton to JM, 10 May 1783, and n. 5.

[3] In his dispatch of 15 March, Laurens stated that he had "come to London about eighteen days ago, in order to avail myself of opportunities for urging a definitive treaty between Great Britain and the United States, as well as the necessity for removing the British troops from New York." JM virtually quotes two sentences of Laurens' second paragraph concerning the satisfaction derived by the Earl of Shelburne from enticing the American peace commissioners, in spite of their instructions, to negotiate a preliminary peace treaty with Great Britain without consulting Vergennes (Wharton, *Revol. Dipl. Corr.*, VI, 303–4). For the belief of many members of Congress that thereby the commissioners had alienated France at a time when the United States desperately needed further financial aid from King Louis XVI, see *Papers of Madison*, VI, 328–30; 331, n. 4; 332, n. 9; 335; 358–65; 382–84; 394–95; 462, n. 2. JM probably still mistrusted Laurens as being pro-British (*ibid.*, VI, 355; 356, n. 10).

[4] JM inadvertently wrote "have" immediately after enciphering the word. The ministry of the Earl of Shelburne, which had resigned on 24 February, was succeeded on 1 April 1783 by that of the Duke of Portland, leading an uneasy coalition of adherents of Charles James Fox and Lord North (*ibid.*, VI, 504, n. 3; Delegates to Harrison, 27 May, and n. 4; JM to Randolph, 8 Sept. 1783, and n. 4).

[5] Laurens wrote that, "being pressed" by "different members" of the House of Commons, he framed on 22 March "a supposed American bill for regulating commerce with Great Britain, and suggested that it had been received by a courier. This I held up as a mirror to some of the most active men in that House." Since then, Laurens added, "their own bill, which was to have been finished on the 23d, has slept with very little interruption, and is now to all appearances dead" (Wharton, *Revol. Dipl. Corr.*, VI, 360). See also *Papers of Madison*, V, 476; JM to Jefferson, 13 May, and n. 7; JM to Randolph, 20 May, and nn. 4, 5, 14; 17 June 1783, n. 6.

[6] In a dispatch of 14 April to Livingston, Adams commented that the American peace commissioners, lacking powers to make a "durable" commercial treaty, would seek to conclude "a temporary arrangement" (Wharton, *Revol. Dipl. Corr.*, VI, 373). The instructions authorizing such an "arrangement," which Congress adopted on 1 May before receiving Adams' dispatch, reached Franklin on 6 September, three days after the signing of the definitive peace treaty (JM Notes, 6 May 1783, and n. 3; L. H. Butterfield *et al.*, eds., *Diary and Autobiography of John Adams*, III, 141–42, 142, n. 2).

For the adoption by Congress on 12 July 1781 of JM's motion to revoke the commission and instructions issued on 27 and 29 September 1779 to Adams empowering him to negotiate a treaty of commerce with Great Britain, see JM to Jefferson, 6 May 1783, and nn. 5, 6. In his autobiography Adams attributed this "revocation" to Vergennes' "Intrigues with Congress," using La Luzerne and Barbé-Marbois as his "Instruments" (L. H. Butterfield *et al.*, eds., *Diary and Autobiography of John Adams*, IV, 252–53). Because of Laurens' very late arrival to participate in the peace negotiations, Adams may not have thought to inform him of the "revocation." It is probable that Adams communicated the information orally to Franklin and Jay; certainly he had not hesitated to do so in writing to correspondents whom he was not likely soon to see (Page Smith, *John Adams* [2 vols.; Garden City, N.Y., 1962], I, 504–5). Benjamin Vaughan, a British agent, when told by Adams on 12 January 1783 of the "revocation," remarked that the information was "entirely new" and "very important" (L. H. Butterfield *et al.*, eds., *Diary and Autobiography of John Adams,* III, 104–5, 105, n. 1). See also *Papers of Madison,* VI, 132, n. 1; 331, n. 4.

[7] JM reverts to the letter of 15 March in which Laurens had blamed Shelburne for delaying the conclusion of the definitive treaty and the withdrawal of British troops from New York City. In the letter of 5 April, Laurens expressed confidence that the Duke of Portland and Charles James Fox were disposed to effect those ends "with liberality" and "without delay" (Wharton, *Revol. Dipl. Corr.*, VI, 304, 361, 366).

[8] Laurens arrived in Paris on 16 April, and David Hartley eight days later. Hartley's commission for negotiating a peace treaty and a treaty of commerce was not signed until 14 May 1783 (*ibid.*, VI, 366, 385–86, 428–29, 435–36, 442; L. H. Butterfield *et al.*, eds., *Diary and Autobiography of John Adams,* III, 112, n. 1). For Richard Oswald, see *Papers of Madison,* V, 154, n. 2. Laurens, who was in Great Britain at the time of the signing of the definitive treaty of peace in Paris, did not reach the United States until 3 August 1784 (*ibid.*, VI, 427, n. 15; Wharton, *Revol. Dipl. Corr.*, VI, 640–41, 693).

David Hartley (1732–1813), graduate of Oxford University (1750), member of the House of Commons (1774–1780, 1782–1784), and close friend of Franklin, was a Rockingham Whig who had supported the American cause and endeavored to abolish the slave trade. He wrote numerous political tracts, edited some of his father's philosophical writings, published *Letters on the American War* (London, 1778, 1779), and, later in life, devised methods of reducing the hazard of fire in buildings and on ships.

[9] The slowness of communication between Paris and Philadelphia was frustrating both to Congress and the peace commissioners. On 15 April Franklin wrote Livingston, "It is now near three months since any of us have heard from America." On 28 May Livingston commented in a letter to the peace commissioners: "We have been much embarrassed by your silence, not having had a line from you since the provisional articles took effect, nor being at all acquainted with the progress of the definitive treaty; though the earliest information on this subject becomes very important" (Wharton, *Revol. Dipl. Corr.*, VI, 377, 453). See also Delegates to Harrison, 27 May 1783, and n. 4.

[10] Rights of Neutral Nations, 12 June, and nn. 1, 3. In his letter of 28 January 1783 to John Adams, Charles G. F. Dumas commented that government officials of the United Provinces regarded the French desertion of them in the negotiations of a preliminary peace treaty with Great Britain as an "immense and unpardonable fault" (Wharton, *Revol. Dipl. Corr.*, VI, 232, 233–34). For Dumas, see *Papers of Madison*, V, 136, n. 16.

[11] Louis XVI of France and Charles III of Spain, respectively.

[12] League of Armed Neutrality.

[13] Rights of Neutral Nations, 12 June, and n. 4. See also JM to Randolph, 20 May 1783, and nn. 10, 11.

[14] Rights of Neutral Nations, 12 June, and nn. 4–8. See also JM Notes, 21–22 May, n. 1; Instruction to Dana, 22 May 1783, and n. 3.

[15] JM underlined the ciphers for "expressly." The bracketed syllables and words in this and later paragraphs of the letter denote excisions in the manuscript as a result of overly close trimming along the right edge of the text. For the "instructions," see *Papers of Madison,* VI, 440, n. 2; JM Notes, 30 May 1783, and n. 3.

[16] JM Notes, 15 May, and n. 1; 4 June 1783, and nn. 3, 4. For Livingston's position as chancellor of New York State and its effect upon his continuance as secretary for foreign affairs, see *Papers of Madison,* V, 337, n. 2; 353, n. 8. In a letter of 19 March 1783, Governor George Clinton had warned Livingston that there was

"a prevailing opinion in the Senate" of the New York General Assembly that the office of chancellor had become "vacant" as a result of his prolonged absences (Hugh Hastings and J. A. Holden, eds., *Public Papers of George Clinton, First Governor of New York* . . . [10 vols.; Albany and New York, 1899–1914], VIII, 91; also 61, 110).

17 "*A L*" is Arthur Lee. JM used the word "*defaction*" in the sense of "lack of." See *Papers of Madison*, VI, 224, n. 7; JM Notes, 10 June 1783, and n. 12.

18 Although JM almost surely intended to encode "my," requiring 830 as its cipher, he wrote 820, signifying "particular."

19 JM Notes, 23 May, and n. 7; 9 June 1783, and n. 1.

20 On 17 and 18 June Congress received three dispatches from Francis Dana, dated 31 January, 14 and 24 February; one of 27 March from Dumas; one of 15 April from Franklin; and one of 29 October 1782 from William Carmichael (NA: PCC, No. 186, III, 67, 68).

21 For Dana's arrival in Boston on 12 December 1783 from his unsuccessful mission as minister-designate to the court of St. Petersburg, see *Papers of Madison*, VI, 427, n. 14. For the return of Laurens to the United States, see n. 8. Committing American interests at Madrid to the charge of Carmichael, John Jay, minister-designate at the court of Charles III, had left that city early in the summer of 1782 to serve as one of the American peace commissioners at Paris. Following an unsuccessful effort with Adams and Franklin to negotiate a commercial treaty with Great Britain, Jay left Paris on 16 May, sailed from Dover on 1 June, and disembarked at New York City on 24 July 1784, approximately a year after he had written Congress signifying his wish to resign. On 7 May 1784 Congress had elected him secretary for foreign affairs (*Papers of Madison*, V, 20; 22, n. 10; Wharton, *Revo*[l]. *Dipl. Corr.*, VI, 389, 576, 801, 816).

Notwithstanding Franklin's repeated requests, beginning late in 1782, to relinquish his position as minister plenipotentiary at the court of Versailles, Congress delayed until 7 March 1785 before acceding to them. He left Paris on 12 July and reached Philadelphia on 14 September of that year (*ibid.*, VI, 585, 746–47; *Papers of Madison*, VI, 342, n. 12; Burnett, *Letters*, VIII, 25–26, 44, n. 5, 219, and n. 4).

22 JM Notes, 23 May 1783, and n. 7.

23 Rights of Neutral Nations, 12 June 1783, and n. 1. JM also referred to Dumas' dispatch of 5 March, read in Congress on 2 June, reporting that Pieter Johan van Berckel (1724–1800), burgomaster of Rotterdam and "minister-plenipotentiary from their high mightinesses the States-General of the United Netherlands," wished made available for him a house to rent and a coach and horses to buy. Arriving at Chester on 9 October, two days later he reached Philadelphia and was received by Congress at Princeton on 31 October (NA: PCC, No. 185, III, 66; Wharton, *Revol. Dipl. Corr.*, VI, 271, 272, 713–14, 715, 716; *JCC*, XXV, 780; *Pa. Packet*, 11 Oct. 1783).

24 *Papers of Madison*, V, 167–68; 168, n. 3; VI, 335; 338, n. 21; *JCC*, XXV, 613–14. The "Gentleman" was probably the Baron de Kermelin, about whom Franklin had written to Livingston on 7 November 1782 (Wharton, *Revol. Dipl. Corr.*, V, 861–62). By 24 June 1784 the baron had arrived in Philadelphia "from his Swedish Majesty with letters of Credence which he is at liberty to use, provided the United States send a Minister to that Court" (Burnett, *Letters*, VII, 559). The source of JM's knowledge of Vergennes' opinion has not been determined, but it may have been in a dispatch from Vergennes to La Luzerne.

25 JM to Jefferson, 6 May 1783, and n. 8. JM's sanguine view of Spain's more friendly attitude toward the United States probably reflected his reading of Carmichael's dispatches. Congress had not heard from him since 6 May. In a dispatch of 7 May 1783, Livingston commented to Carmichael: "No people in the world

are more governed by their feelings than the Americans, of which the late war was a striking proof, and those feelings have been long sported with in Spain. Yet men of reflection see the propriety of overlooking the past and forming in future a durable connexion. We are necessary to each other, and our mutual friendship must conduce to the happiness of both" (Wharton, *Revol. Dipl. Corr.*, VI, 408). The court of Madrid in 1784 empowered Don Diego de Gardoqui to proceed to the United States in the capacity of *encargado de negocios*. He was received by Congress on 2 July 1785 (Burnett, *Letters*, VIII, 163, n. 7).

26 Instruction to Delegates, 23–24 May 1783, and n. 1. The Virginia General Assembly also expressed the desire that no treaty of commerce should be "finally concluded" with Great Britain until "the different States" as well as Congress had "had an opportunity of considering it."

27 JM to Jefferson, 13 May; to Randolph, 20 May 1783.

28 *Papers of Madison*, VI, 182, n. 29; JM to Jefferson, 6 May, and n. 11; Jefferson to JM, 7 May 1783, and nn. 16, 19.

To Edmund Randolph

RC (LC: Madison Papers). Unsigned but in JM's hand. Docketed by Randolph, "J Madison June 10. 1783." Apparently when he penned the letter, rather than when he recovered it many years later, JM wrote "Edmd. Randolph Esqr." at the bottom of the first of three folios. Cover missing.

PHILADA. June 10th. 1783

MY DEAR FRIEND

Yesterday's mail brought me two letters from you one of the 15 Ulto.[1] inclosing the intervening sheet of the Journals which ought to have come two weeks ago, the other of the 29th. from Williamsbg. inclosing Mrs. Randolphs letter to Mrs. Trist.[2] I have recd. no copy of the Journal from your assistant.[3]

Mr. Jones will have informed you that the Mission of Payne to R. Island by Congs. was a fiction of malice. If the trip was not a spontaneous measure of his own, I am a stranger to its origin.[4]

I am told by one of the Judges of appeal that no case has yet required from them a construction of the epochs which are to limit captures. The 3d. of March was generally applied at first to the American seas, but that opinion has rather lost ground.[5] In N. York it is said that the 3d. of Apl. is adhered to.[6] As the like phraseology is said to have been used in former Treaties, the true construction might be found I sd. suppose in Admiralty precedents.[7]

We have recd. the instruction relative to Commercial Treaties. The principle on which it is founded corresponds precisely with my idea. But I know not how far the giving an opportunity to the States of exercising their judgments on proposed Treaties, will correspond in all cases with the doctrine of the Confederation which provides for secrecy in some such cases.[8] The deviation how ever if there be any is trivial, and not being an intended one can have no ill consequences. No progress has been made towards a Treaty with G. B. owing partly to a desire of hearing further from Europe & partly to the paucity of States represented in Congs. It would seem that the plan of regulating the Trade with America by a Parliamentary Act has been exchanged by the present Ministry for an intended Treaty for that purpose. Mr. Laurens was asked by Mr. Fox whether the American Ministers had powers for a commercial Treaty. his answer was that he believed so; that a revocation of Mr. Adam's powers had appeared some time ago in print, but he considered the publication as Spurious. From this it wd. seem that this act of Congs. had never been communicated by the latter to his colleagues.[9] He lately complained of this revocation in a very singular letter to Congs.[10] I consider it as a very fortunate circumstance that this business is still within our controul, especially as the policy of authorizing *conditional* Treatys only in Europe is so fully espoused by Virga.[11]

Mr. Livingston has taken his final leave of the departmt. of F. Affairs. No nomination for a successor has yet been made though the time assigned for the election has passed, nor does the conversation center on any individual.[12] I have forborne on various accts. to hold forth our friend McLurg.[13] I can form no conjecture on whom the choice will ultimately fall.

The offers of N. Y. & Maryld. of a seat for Congs. are postponed till Ocr. next in order to give time for other offers & for knowing the sense of the States on the subject. Copies of those acts are to be sent to the Executives of each State.[14]

I have forgotten the request of Mr. Mercer for several weeks to make his apology for failing to open a correspondence with you. The regular one maintained between yourself & me, he supposes, would leave little but repetition to him, and his other correspondents, I suppose give him competent employment.[15]

Congress have resumed at length the Cession of Virga. the old obnoxious report was committed, and a new report has been made which I think a fit basis for a compromise. A copy of it is inclosed for the Govr. I have also transcribed it in my letter to Mr. Jones. As it tacitly excludes the pretensions of the Companies,[16] I fear obstacles may arise in Congs. from that quarter. Clarke from N. Jersey informed Congs.

that the Delegates from that State being fettered by instructions, must communicate the plan to their constituents.[17] If no other causes of delay should rise the thinness of Congs. at present will prove a material one.[18] I am at some loss for the policy of the Companies in opposing a compromise with Virga. They can never hope for a specific restitution of their claims, they can never even hope for a cession of the Country between the Alleghany & the Ohio by Virga.[19] as little can they hope for an extension of a jurisdiction of Congs. over it by force. I should suppose therefore that it wd. be their truest interest to promote a general cession of the vacant Country to Congress, and in case the titles of which they have been stript sd. be deemed by them reasonable, and Congs. sd. be disposed to make any equitable compensation, Virga. wd. be no more interested in opposing it than other States.

I inclose different papers to you & to Mr. Jónes & recommend an interchange.[20]

1 *Q.v.*

2 Randolph's letter of 29 May has not been found. For Mrs. Randolph's intention to write to Mrs. Nicholas Trist, see *Papers of Madison*, VI, 381.

3 Randolph to JM, 24 May, and n. 12; 4 June 1783; Beckley to Randolph, 20 June 1783.

4 Randolph to JM, 15 May 1783, and n. 7.

5 The judges of the Court of Appeals in Cases of Capture were Cyrus Griffin, John Lowell, and George Read (*Papers of Madison*, V, 252, n. 2; 368; *JCC*, XXIV, 186, n. 2, 212). The court convened annually at Philadelphia on the first Monday in May, at Hartford on the first Monday in August, and at Richmond on the first Monday in November (*JCC*, XXIV, 185). At least two of the judges had to be present for the court to hear and decide cases. Having been elected by Congress on 5 December 1782, Lowell accepted on 12 February 1783, with the proviso that he need not sit as a judge until the court had decided several pending cases involving clients whom he had earlier guaranteed to represent as their lawyer. He apparently began his service on the bench of the court at its session of May 1784 (*Papers of Madison*, V, 300; 301, first n. 1; 368; 369, n. 2; NA: PCC, No. 78, XIV, 531; *JCC*, XXIV, 186, n. 2, 212; Burnett, *Letters*, VI, 560–61; VII, 91).

For "the epochs" see *Papers of Madison*, VI, 391, n. 4; 450 and n. 1; 451, nn. 2–4. The court seems to have avoided "a construction" of these as late as October 1783 (*JCC*, XXV, 627; Burnett, *Letters*, VII, 317).

6 By "N. York" JM signified the British naval headquarters there. Congress, reflecting the provisions of the preliminary treaties of peace agreed upon by Great Britain with the United States and France, adopted a proclamation on 11 April 1783 declaring that in the Atlantic Ocean north of the latitude of the Canary Islands hostilities had legally ceased on 3 March, which was one month subsequent to the exchange of ratifications between Great Britain and France. For the area of the Atlantic Ocean south of that latitude to the equator the time of cessation had been 3 April 1783. All the eastern coastline of the United States as then constituted was north of the latitude of the Canaries ([David] Hunter Miller, ed., *Treaties and Other International Acts of the United States of America* [8 vols.; Washington, 1931–48], II, 112–14).

[7] Article XXIV of the Treaty of Paris of 1763, although not specifically stated in terms of parallels of latitude, used the word "epochs" and obviously staggered the duration of each of them in direct proportion to the distance in travel time from Paris or London to the designated place (George Chalmers, ed., *A Collection of Treaties between Great Britain and Other Powers* [2 vols.; London, 1790], I, 481–82).

[8] Instruction to Delegates, 23–24 May, and n. 1; Jones to JM, 25 May; JM to Jefferson, 10 June 1783. For the problem of preserving secrecy with regard to confidential matters before Congress, see *Papers of Madison,* V, 397, and n. 1; 398, and n. 10; 420, n. 4; 421, n. 10.

[9] JM to Jefferson, 10 June 1783, and nn. 4–6.

[10] JM to Jefferson, 6 May 1783, and nn. 5–7.

[11] JM to Jefferson, 10 June 1783, and n. 26.

[12] *Ibid.*, and n. 16. On 12 June Livingston left Philadelphia for his home in New York (*Pa. Packet,* 14 June 1783).

[13] For suggestions of nominating Dr. James McClurg, see *Papers of Madison,* VI, 185; 186, n. 8; 223; 281, n. 9.

[14] *Ibid.*, VI, 447; 448, nn. 4, 6, 7; Harrison to Delegates, 17 May; Delegates to Harrison, 27 May, and n. 2. With a circular letter of 10 June 1783 to the executive of each state, President Elias Boudinot sent a copy of the offers by New York and Maryland of a "permanent residence" for Congress (Burnett, *Letters,* VII, 182).

[15] Although the occasion upon which John Francis Mercer had promised to correspond with Randolph is unknown, an expected exchange of letters between Mercer and Joseph Jones had also failed to take place. No doubt Mercer and his friend James Monroe wrote to each other (Ambler to JM, 10 May, n. 1; Jones to JM, 31 May 1783, and n. 18).

[16] Neither the enclosure for Harrison nor JM's letter and enclosure to Jones have been found. For the "new report," see JM Notes, 4 June, n. 2; 5 June, n. 1; 6 June, and n. 1. The sixth and especially the seventh numbered paragraphs of the report warrant JM's statement about the "Companies." The report was amended and adopted on 13 September 1783 (*JCC,* XXV, 559–64).

[17] JM Notes, 9 June, and nn. 2, 3; 10 June 1783, and nn. 3, 10.

[18] JM Notes, 9 June, and n. 1; JM to Jefferson, 10 June 1783.

[19] *Papers of Madison,* II, 53, n. 3; 75–76; III, 138, n. 7; 313, n. 2; VI, 133–34; 138, n. 6; 444, n. 8; 502, n. 3.

[20] Perhaps the *Pennsylvania Gazette* of 4 June, the *Pennsylvania Journal* of 7 June, and the *Pennsylvania Packet* of 7 and 10 June 1783.

Notes on Debates

MS (LC: Madison Papers). For a description of the manuscript of Notes on Debates, see *Papers of Madison,* V, 231–34.

Wednesday June 11. see Journals. secret & public.[1]

[1] The journals of 11 June 1783, both "secret & public," record the adoption of a resolution further postponing the election of a secretary for foreign affairs, and the adoption of a revised report of a committee (Ralph Izard, chairman) on procedures to be followed by Congress in receiving ministers of foreign powers (*JCC,* XXIV, 390, n. 1, 390–91). In addition, the "public" journal notes the presen-

tation of his credentials by James McHenry, a delegate from Maryland; receipt of a letter from Benjamin Lincoln, secretary at war; and the passage of a resolution in response thereto, authorizing him to furlough the continental troops of Pennsylvania, Delaware, Maryland, and Virginia still in service (*JCC*, XXIV, 389–91).

Report on Rights of Neutral Nations

MS (NA: PCC, No. 79, III, 255). In JM's hand. Docketed: "Report of Mr Madison Mr Ellsworth Mr. Hamilton On a report of Secy for forn. Affairs on a letter of 20 March from Mr Dumas Delivered June 11, 1783. read Entd." Designated by JM for inclusion in this report is part of a report dated 3 June, a minor portion of which is in the hand of, and signed by, Robert R. Livingston, secretary for foreign affairs. The report is docketed: "Report of Secy for foreign Affairs on Mr Dumas' letter of 20 March 1783 Delivered June 4. Entd Read. June 6 1783 Referred to Mr Madison Mr Ellsworth Mr Hamilton" (NA: PCC, No. 79, III, 247–53).

[12 June 1783]

The Come. to whom was referred the letter & papers from Mr. Dumas[1] with the Report of the Secy. of F.A. thereon report that it appears from the sd papers as stated in the said Report.

1st. that it appears[2] from them, that propositions have been made on the part of the States General to the ministers of the United States at Paris, (in order to render an express stipulation in favor of the freedom of navigation less necessary in the treaty of peace between great Britain & the United Provinces of the Netherlands,) either to accede to the treaty of the armed neutrality already concluded between some powers of Europe, or to enter into similar engagements with France, Spain and the United Provinces of the Netherlands[3]—or in case France & Spain should refuse to enter into a convention founded on the principles of the armed neutrality, or wish to delay it till after the general peace, to form a separate convention for similar purposes between the United Provinces of the Netherlands & the United States of America.

That the answers to these propositions do not appear from the papers transmitted, tho' there is room to infer from Mr Dumas's Letter of the 4th. and 18th. of February, that the two first of these propositions were encouraged by our Ministers, and that the states general proposed to act in consequence thereof, & had made the last proposition in order to be prepared in case either or both of the two first should fail.[4]

It appears to Mr. Livingston that no powers are at present vested in any person in Europe to agree to any treaty similar to that entered into by Russia, Sweden, Denmark & the United provinces of the Netherlands after the peace shall be concluded The resolution of the 5th. of October 1780, empowers the ministers of those states, if invited thereto, to accede to such regulations conformable to the spirit of the declaration of the Empress of Russia as may be agreed upon by the Congress expected to assemble in pursuance of the invitation of her Imperial Majesty. our ministers received no invitation[5] & special powers were afterwards given to Mr. Dana, which in their nature superseded that resolution. Mr. Dana was by his commission & instruction empowered to sign *the* treaty or convention for the protection of commerce in behalf of the United States either with her Imperial Majesty in conjunction with the other neutral powers, or if that shall be inadmissible, separately with her Imperial Majesty or any of *those* (that is those neutral) powers.[6]

The Treaty being only made to continue during the war, his powers terminated with the war, or at most extended only to sign it with the neutral powers & not to form a new & separate treaty.[7]

Whereupon the Come. observe that as the primary object of the Resolution of Ocr. 5. 1780 & of the Comon. & instructions to Mr. Dana relative to the accession of the U.S. to the Neutral Confederacy, no longer can operate,[8] and as the true interest of these States requires that they shd. be as little as possible entangled in the politics & controversies of European Nations,[9] it is inexpedient for Congs. to renew the said powers either to Mr. Dana[10] or to the other Ministers in Europe; But inasmuch as the liberal principles on which the said confederacy was established are conceived to be in general favorable to the interests of Nations, & particularly to those of the U.S. & ought in that view to be promoted by the latter as far as will consist with their fundamental policy. Resolved journal [?] amendmt[11] that the Ministers Plenipoy. for peace be instructed to endeavor if it can be done without delaying the definitive Treaty to comprise therein a mutual recognition & establishment of the Rights of Neutral Nations conformable to the principles of the said Confederacy, so far as the same can be done without entering into stipulations which may involve these States in contests or wars for the maintanence of those principles.[12]

[1] See hdn.; also *Papers of Madison,* VI, 480, n. 3. Charles G. F. Dumas was nominally chargé d'affaires of the United States at The Hague. His brief dispatch of 20 March to Livingston served principally as a covering letter for copies of

eighteen of his letters, dating between 24 January and 14 March, bearing mostly on the subject of the committee's report (NA: PCC, No. 93, II, 220–32, 241–66, 291–92). Of these letters, Dumas had directed one to Benjamin Franklin, nine to John Adams, minister-plenipotentiary to the Netherlands but then in Paris with Franklin as an American peace commissioner, four to the Duc de La Vauguyon, ambassador of France to the Netherlands (*Papers of Madison*, IV, 291, n. 19), and four to officials of the Dutch government, including two to van Berckel (JM to Jefferson, 10 June 1783, and n. 23). For seven of Dumas' letters to Adams, see Wharton, *Revol. Dipl. Corr.*, VI, 229–30, 232, 233–34, 235–36, 255–56, 272, 273.

[2] JM copied "1st" through "appears" from Livingston's report of 3 June. He then interlineated "Cp"[copy?] over "appears" and followed this word with "&c [see beginning to page 4, line 3]." The present editors have conformed with these instructions by inserting Livingston's report from the place JM designated through folio 4, line 3. Whenever Livingston wrote "United Provinces" or "united provinces," JM in his copying added "of the Netherlands."

[3] To this point the passage from Livingston's report either paraphrases or quotes verbatim from the proposal made by the grand pensionary of Holland, Pieter van Bleiswyck, and transmitted by Dumas to Adams in a letter of 24 January 1783 (Wharton, *Revol. Dipl. Corr.*, VI, 229–30). The preliminary treaty of peace between Great Britain and the Netherlands was signed on 2 September 1783 and the definitive treaty on 20 May 1784 (*Papers of Madison*, IV, 388, n. 11; VI, 449, n. 9). For the "treaty of the armed neutrality," agreed to by Russia, Norway, and Denmark on 9 July 1780 and later that year by the Netherlands, a membership almost immediately rendered nugatory by the Anglo-Dutch war, see *ibid.*, II, 56, n. 3; 167, n. 2; III, 45, n. 9; IV, 16, n. 24.

[4] Adams, five days after receiving Dumas' letter of 24 January, responded that he, Jay, and Franklin, although not expressly instructed by Congress on the proposals of the United Provinces, desired to hasten the conclusion of the definitive treaty of peace. To that end "we should not hesitate to pledge the faith of the United States to the observance of the principles of the armed neutrality" (Wharton, *Revol. Dipl. Corr.*, VI, 233). In letters of 4 and 18 February 1783 Dumas assured Adams that his reply had pleased the Dutch officials; that they were determined not to accept treaty proposals from Great Britain unless they included guarantees concerning "navigation" similar to those in the commercial treaties of the United States with France and the Netherlands; and that they hoped, if France and Spain should be unwilling before the conclusion of the definitive treaty to sign a convention with the United States and the Netherlands "founded on the principles of the armed neutrality," Francis Dana, or Adams, or the American peace commissioners would be willing on behalf of the United States "to sign such a provisional convention" with representatives duly commissioned by "the United Provinces" (*ibid.*, VI, 235–36, 255–56).

[5] For the resolution of 5 October 1780, see n. 8, below. Tsarina Catherine the Great issued a proclamation of armed neutrality on 29 February 1780 (*Papers of Madison*, II, 56, n. 3). By extending an "invitation" during the war, the tsarina would in effect have recognized the independence of the United States, thereby countenancing rebellion and deeply offending Great Britain (*ibid.*, V, 124, n. 6; 189, n. 13; VI, 427, n. 13).

[6] In the left margin of Livingston's report appears in an unknown hand, "Comon: 18 Decr. 1780 4th Art: Instruct." For the commission and instructions to Dana, minister-designate to the court of St. Petersburg, see *JCC*, XVIII, 1164, 1166–73. Referring to the "treaty of the armed neutrality," the fourth article of the instructions directed Dana to "use every means which can be devised to obtain the consent and influence of that Court that these United States shall be formally

invited, or admitted. to accede as principals and as an independent nation to the said convention. In that event, you are authorized to subscribe the treaty or convention for the protection of commerce in behalf of these United States, either with her Imperial Majesty conjunctly with the other neutral powers, or if that shall be inadmissible, separately with her Imperial Majesty, or any one of those powers."

[7] The portion of the committee's report taken from that of Livingston ends with the words "separate treaty." In the left margin of his report, alongside these words, there is written, "9th Article Treaty between Russia &c." The ninth article of the "convention for an Armed Neutrality," concluded on 9 July 1780 by Russia, Norway, and Denmark, begins, "This convention shall be in full force as long as this present war shall last." Statements of the same tenor open the same article of the convention of 1 August 1780 between Russia and Sweden, and the treaty of 10 July 1781 "relative to Armed Neutrality" between Russia and the Holy Roman Emperor ([James Brown Scott, ed.], *Official Documents Bearing on the Armed Neutrality of 1780 and 1800* [Washington, 1917], pp. 51, 64, 123).

[8] At least by implication, those documents became obsolete at the conclusion of the war. For the resolution of 5 October 1780, see *Papers of Madison*, II, 167, n. 3; also *JCC*, XVIII, 905–6; JM Notes, 21–22 May 1783, and n. 1.

[9] *Papers of Madison*, VI, 224, n. 7; 272; 287; 495, n. 11; JM to Randolph, 20 May; JM Notes, 23 May 1783, and n. 7.

[10] Instruction to Dana, 22 May, nn. 1, 3; JM Notes, 12 June 1783.

[11] Immediately following "policy," JM interlineated "Resolved journal [?] amendment" and canceled with a diagonal ink line the remainder of the report. His interlineation and deletion reflect the outcome of the debate on the report (JM Notes, 12 June 1783).

[12] *Ibid.*, and n. 3.

Notes on Debates

MS (LC: Madison Papers). For a description of the manuscript of Notes on Debates, see *Papers of Madison*, V, 231–34.

Thursday June 12.

The Instruction in the *Secret* Journal touching the principles &c of the Neutral Confederacy, passed unanimously.[1]

The Resolution as reported by the Committee being in a positive style, and *eight* States only being present, the question occurred whether nine States were not necessary.[2] To avoid the difficulty a negative form was given the Resolution; by which the preamble became somewhat unsuitable. It was suffered to pass however, rather than risk the experiment of further alteration.[3]

[1] Rights of Neutral Nations, 12 June 1783; *JCC*, XXIV, 392–94. The tallied vote is not shown in the journal.

[2] Georgia was unrepresented in Congress. Rhode Island, Connecticut, New York,

and Maryland, each having only one delegate in attendance, could not cast effective votes. Article IX of the Articles of Confederation included entering "into any treaties or alliances" among the powers of Congress which could be exercised only with the assent of at least nine states (*JCC*, XIX, 220).

[3] Rights of Neutral Nations, 12 June 1783, and n. 11. The committee had recommended that the peace commissioners endeavor to include in the definitive treaty a qualified "recognition & establishment of the Rights of Neutral Nations." Congress replaced this suggestion with an instruction to the commissioners, in the event that the treaty should contain "stipulations amounting to a recognition of the rights of neutral nations," to avoid concurring with "any engagements which shall oblige the contracting parties to support those stipulations by arms." The constitutional doubt was thus resolved by agreeing that, although nine or more states were required to determine what a treaty must "include," eight or less were competent to decide what a treaty must not "include." This change in the resolution obviously rendered "somewhat unsuitable" the "positive style" of the preamble of the committee's report following the words "Ministers in Europe" (*JCC*, XXIV, 394).

Notes on Debates

MS (LC: Madison Papers). For a description of the manuscript of Notes on Debates, see *Papers of Madison*, V, 231–34.

Friday June 13.

The mutinous memorial from the Sergeants was recd. & read.[1] It excited much indignation & was sent to the Secretary at war.

[1] Although the manuscript of the memorial has not been found, its contents were summarized in a number of contemporary letters, including JM's letter of 17 June to Randolph (*q.v.*). The noncommissioned officers of several companies of continental infantry and one company of artillery, stationed at the Philadelphia barracks and composed chiefly of recruits who had experienced no arduous service, voiced in threatening language a demand for their overdue pay before being furloughed in conformance with the resolution of Congress of 26 May (*The Diplomatic Correspondence of the United States of America, from . . . September 10, 1783, to . . . March 4, 1783* [3 vols.; Washington, 1837], I, 9; Burnett, *Letters*, VII, 189, n. 4; Varnum Lansing Collins, *The Continental Congress at Princeton* [Princeton, 1908], pp. 9–11).

Benjamin Lincoln, secretary at war, temporarily warded off the threatened mutiny by having Brigadier General Arthur St. Clair, commanding officer of the Pennsylvania troops, continental line, transfer most of those in Philadelphia to the barracks at Lancaster. Anticipating similar discontent among the soldiers commanded by Major General Anthony Wayne, who were daily expected to arrive in Philadelphia by ship from the southern army, Lincoln arranged for them to disembark at Wilmington and proceed directly to Lancaster for furloughing (*Pa. Archives*, 1st ser., X, 55; William Henry Smith, *The St. Clair Papers: The Life and Public Service of Arthur St. Clair* [2 vols.; Cincinnati, 1882], I, 586, and n., 587, n. 2).

From Jacquelin Ambler

RC (LC: Madison Papers). Cover addressed by Ambler to "The Honobl: James Madison of Congress Philadelphia." Cover docketed by JM, "June 14, 1783."

RICHMOND VIRGA 14 June 1783

DEAR SIR

I am afraid I shall find it difficult to settle my Accounts with the Committee,[1] without obtaining Warrants from the Auditors[2] in favor of the Gentlemen of the delegation to the *full* amount of the *genl.* Remittances made since the first of the present Year. in order to obtain these, I must entreat you to interest yourself with the Gentlemen who now remain at Phila. to sign a Certificate some what similar to the one inclosed. Mr. Jones & Mr. Lee I doubt not will sign here.[3] I am at a loss to discover how the deficiency arises which you mention:—if in negotiating the Bills,—the same I apprehend would have happened had the Bills been sent by any other person;—if actual money had been paid here, which is what the Act requires of me, & this money sent in Specie to Phila., the loss must have been still [?] more considerable.[4] I am, however, very unwilling the Gentlemen should lose a shilling of their right, & therefore take the liberty of pointing out the proper mode of preventing it, which is, by giving the Treasury credit in each of their Accounts for the full amount of their proportion of the several Genl. Remittances, and charging the State with the proportion of loss sustained by each in negotiating the Bills—this will effectually save them. You will readily observe the loss must fall on me if the Certificate to the Auditors do not express the full amount, because they will issue Warrants for no greater sum than the Certificate mentions.

there has not issued a single Warrant for any of the Remittances I have made on the Genl. Account in this year; these amount to   . [I] cannot precisely ascertain the sum, because I am not informed what was paid by the Sheriff of Northampton.[5] You will be so good as return me the Certificate as soon as possible, that I may be enabled to settle my Accounts before the rising of the Assembly.[6]

if you have not purchased the Stationary please to think no more of it.[7] perhaps it may be had on as good terms here.

Yrs.

J.A.

Me[nti]on the Sum paid by the Northampton Shff in yr. next that I may give him credit for it

The Certificates before sent acknowledging the receipt of monies for the several Remittances[8] shall be returned to you as soon as I get the genl. one requested above

[1] Ambler to JM, 24 May 1783, and n. 2.

[2] JM to Bland, 6 May 1783, hdn.

[3] Enclosure not found. JM, Theodorick Bland, and John Francis Mercer were the delegates from Virginia then in Philadelphia. The other two, Joseph Jones and Arthur Lee, were in Richmond attending the Virginia General Assembly. See Ambler to JM, 7 June 1783.

[4] The present editors have not found any of the letters written by JM to Ambler in 1783. Possibly in a note enclosing his Summary of Accounts with Virginia, 28 May (*q.v.*, and nn. 3, 4), JM mentioned his "loss" or "deficiency" caused by having bills of exchange from Virginia cashed in Philadelphia. See also JM to Bland, 6 May 1783, and n. 1. By the law, strictly construed, Ambler was obliged to pay the delegates, "whenever congress shall be sitting," in money rather than in bills of exchange (Hening, *Statutes*, IX, 299).

[5] *Papers of Madison*, VI, 183, and n. 6; 211; Statement of Receipts, 28 May 1783.

[6] Ambler cou'd not have received JM's reply before the adjournment of the Virginia General Assembly on 28 June (*JHDV*, May 1783, p. 99). See also Ambler to JM, 5 July 1783.

[7] Ambler to JM, 24 May 1783.

[8] Statement of Receipts, 28 May 1783.

From Joseph Jones

RC (LC: Madison Papers). Cover missing.

Richmond 14th. June 1783

Dr. Sir.

I have your favors of the 3d. & 6th. with the papers inclosed.[1] since my last[2] the plan of revenue recommended by Congress has been considered in a Comtee. of the whole, and the result contained in the inclosed resolutions which were agreed to withot. a division [;] the number appearing in support of the plan of Congress being so few as not to require it.[3] Mr. B—xt—n and young Mr. Nelson only supported it.[4] In the course of the debate Mr. R. H. L. & Mr. C. M. T. spoke of Congress as lusting after power.[5] the Idea in the Letter to Rhode Island, that Congress having a right to borrow & make requisitions that were binding on the States, ought also to concert the means for accomplishing the end, was reprobated in general as alarming, and of dangerous tendency. In short some of the Sentiments in the letter to Rhode Island tho' argumentative only, operated so powerfully on peoples minds here, that nothing could induce them to adopt the manner recommended by Congress for obtaining revenue.[6] If the 5 PCt is granted to be credited to the States quota, which is the prevailing opinion, it will defeat that revenue unless all the States consent, and N. H. Cont Jersey & N. Car: never will I expect agree to it.[7] Our people have great jealousy of Congress and the other states, think they have done more than they ought, and that the U. S. owe them at least one million pounds.[8] these notions they will not relinquish tho' they acknowledge they are not ready to settle the account.[9] after the two first resolutions had passed P. H. separated from R. H. L. & his party and warmly supported the granting the duties to Congress and the other revenue to make up this State's quota.[10] I will make an attempt to obtain the 5 Pct. as a general revenue, and to authorize the payment of the other revenue by the Collectors to the Continental receiver, instead of the State Treasurer.[11] if these can be effected the funds will be on a tolerable footing, but for the delay which a departure from the plan of Congress must occasion.[12] The disposition to oblige the Officers of our line with lands beyond the Ohio in the room of thos[e] on Cumberland, which are said to be insufficient and very generally barren, has occasioned several leading memb[ers] to press for withdrawing our cession to Congress, that no obstacle might remain to gratifying the Officers. hitherto we have been lucky enough to delay a determination, which however cannot be many more days postponed.[13] A. L. proposed a resolution two days ago to withdraw it. an amendment was proposed to fix a time (the 1st. Sept. next) when it shod. stand revoked if not accepted by Congress. the Committee rose withot. coming to a resl[14] something of this sort will I think ultimately take place. if a secret instruction to our Delegates was practicable to relax, if necessary, any of the Conditions, I shod. like it, as I wish heartily to relinquish that Country to the U. States.[15] the expence attending that Country I shall soon know as the Commissioners who have been out to settle the accoun[ts] are just returned.[16] the proposed alteration for ascertaining the proportions of the States, from the conversations I have had with Gentlemen on the subject will be approved.[17] I entertain however no sanguine expectation of any thing I hear in conversation since the great Majority agt the plan of revenue, which from conversation when I first arrived I was led to believe wod. be adopted.[18] many now say the reading the pamphlet of Congress determined them agt. the measure, disapproving the Sentiments conveyed in the letter to R. I. You cannot well conceive the deranged state of affairs in this Country. there is nothing like system or order. confusion and embarrasmt. must ever attend such a state of things.[19] The two great Commanders[20] make excellent harrangues, handsome speeches to their men but they, want executive Officers or shod. be more so themselves to be usefull, indeed, so far as I am able to judge from the short time I have been here,[21] we are much in want of usefull men, who do business as well as speak to it. a Pendleton and Jefferson wod. be valuable acquisitions to this assembly. we want too a Fitzsimons or some men of his merchantile knowledge and experience.[22]

The Citizen bill remains in the Situation as when I last wrote.[23] before we rise it is probable something may be done in it, especially if the definitive Treaty arrives, which it is probable, as a Ministry has been formed, will soon take place.[24] To divest those who appeared to oppose the payment of the British debts from any attempt of that sort so repugnant to the article of the Treaty and as an alternative less offensive[25] I have intimated that it wod. be better to giv[e] an instruction to our Commrs. for settling the Treaty of Commerce to propose a suspension of payment for some years to make it more convenient to the Debtors and it is probable something may be done in that way as an instruction to our Delegates in Congress.[26] In a Com: on the State of the Commonwealth yesterday, Nathans demand in consequence of the arbitration was taken up but Mr. N—l—s insisting there was a Comr. in Town employed in settling the accots. agt. the public of the Illinois Country who could give information abt. that claim, and shew there had been fraud in the transaction, the Com[ee]. rose withot. coming to a conclusion. it is to be brot. on again today when the Comr. (Col. Fleming) is to be examined.[27] It is asserted great impositions have taken place in polloc[k's] affair, which is also before the House and to come on next Tuesday.[28] I have sold my Chariot and I think shd my Phaeton, in which case, and if I get the money for them I may spend two or three months this fall in Philadelphia as I must get a carriage made there.[29] of this you shall be informed. Complimts. to Bland & Mercer hope they will be content to rece[ive] from you an accot. of what we are doing if not otherwise informed.[30]

Yrs.

Jos: Jones

[1] Jones to JM, 31 May 1783, and n. 1.

[2] Jones to JM, 8 June 1783.

[3] The resolutions, of which Jones enclosed a copy, are summarized in his letter of 8 June to JM, n. 5. See also Jefferson to JM, 7 May, n. 13; JM to Randolph, 20 May; 27 May; Jones to JM, 31 May 1783.

[4] Carter Braxton and William Nelson.

[5] JM Notes, 23 May, n. 7. "R. H. L." is Richard Henry Lee. For "C. M. T.," Charles Mynn Thruston, see Jefferson to JM, 7 May 1783, and n. 8.

[6] For Hamilton's "Letter to Rhode Island," which was among the copies of documents appended by Congress to the plan for restoring public credit, see Randolph to JM, 15 May 1783, and n. 2.

[7] Being proposals to amend the Articles of Confederation, the 5 per cent impost and several other recommendations in the plan for restoring public credit could not become effective without the approval of every state legislature. The proceeds from the imposts were designed to be a main source from which each state should fill its financial quota requisitioned by Congress. In considerable measure, the goods of foreign origin purchased by citizens of the four states mentioned by Jones, respectively, had been transshipped from ports in Massachusetts, Rhode Island, New York, and Virginia. These four states, and Pennsylvania as well, would gain part of their revenue for the supply of Congress at the indirect expense of their less fortunate neighbors. See *Papers of Madison*, VI, 168, n. 28; 290–91; 294, n. 23; Jameson to JM, 24 May, and n. 3; Jones to JM, 8 June 1783, n. 9.

[8] Randolph to JM, 24 May, and n. 5; Jones to JM, 25 May; Pendleton to JM, 26 May 1783, and n. 5.

[9] *Papers of Madison*, VI, 210, n. 3; 214, n. 4; 262, n. 6; 296, n. 40; 310; 344; 469, n. 5; Instruction to Delegates, 4 June 1783, and n. 2.

[10] "P. H." is Patrick Henry. See Randolph to JM, 15 May, and n. 3; Jones to JM, 25 May; 31 May; 8 June; Pendleton to JM, 2 June 1783.

[11] Pendleton to JM, 26 May, n. 11; Jones to JM, 21 June 1783. The continental receiver general in Virginia was George Webb; the treasurer, Jacquelin Ambler.

[12] The Virginia General Assembly refused to sanction the collection of imposts by congressional appointees, as requested in the plan for restoring public credit. The Assembly, however, appeared certain to designate for the use of Congress the proceeds from some taxes to be channeled by agents of the state into its own treasury and then transmitted to Philadelphia. Obviously a "delay" must occur, because citizens would not be required to pay their taxes until 20 November 1783 (Randolph to JM, 9 May, and n. 4; Jones to JM, 25 May; 31 May; 8 June, and n. 5; Pendleton to JM, 26 May 1783, n. 11).

[13] Jones to JM, 25 May, and n. 12; 31 May; JM Notes, 4 June 1783, and nn. 1, 2.

[14] Arthur Lee's motion and the amendatory motion were probably offered during a meeting on 12 June of the committee of the whole house on the state of the commonwealth (*JHDV*, May 1783, p. 51). For this reason they were not entered in the journal of the House of Delegates for that day. For the "cession" issue in Congress, see Jefferson to JM, 7 May, and n. 3; JM to Jefferson, 20 May, and n. 8; JM Notes, 5 June, and n. 1; 6 June, and n. 1; 9 June, and nn. 2, 3; 10 June, and nn.; JM to Randolph, 10 June 1783.

[15] Jones to JM, 21 June; 28 June; Instruction to Delegates, 27 June. See also Randolph to JM, 9 May, and n. 8; Jones to JM, 8 June 1783.

[16] For the Virginia commissioners to settle western accounts, see Delegates to Gálvez, 4 May 1783, ed. n., n. 2.

[17] *Papers of Madison*, VI, 440; 492; 496, n. 27. The session of May 1783 of the Virginia General Assembly adjourned without approving the recommendations by Congress to change the base for allocating financial quotas from comparative state-by-state land values to population. See Jones to JM, 8 June, n. 9; 21 June 1783.

[18] Pendleton to JM, 17 May; Jones to JM, 25 May 1783.

[19] Jones to JM, 25 May 1783, n. 10.

[20] Patrick Henry and Richard Henry Lee.

[21] Jones to JM, 25 May 1783, and n. 2.

[22] JM to Randolph, 27 May, and n. 7. As Jones knew, the Virginia General Assembly eight days earlier had elected Jefferson to be a delegate in Congress.

See Jones to JM, 8 June, and nn. 10, 11. Edmund Pendleton would never again be a member of the Virginia House of Delegates (Pendleton to JM, 26 May 1783, nn. 1, 2). Thomas FitzSimons, a delegate in Congress from Pennsylvania, was a banker and merchant in Philadelphia (*Papers of Madison*, VI, 20, n. 4; 263, n. 14; 471, n. 1).

[23] Jones to JM, 31 May, and nn. 13, 14; 21 June; 28 June 1783.

[24] Harrison to Delegates, 7 June, and n. 2; Jones to JM, 8 June, and nn. 22, 26; JM to Jefferson, 10 June 1783, and n. 8.

[25] Before "offensive" there is an asterisk, probably added either by Jones with the unfulfilled purpose of appending a footnote, or by JM to call his own particular attention to the sentence. For the "debts" in their relation to the preliminary treaty of peace, see Harrison to Delegates, 9 May, and n. 6; Randolph to JM, 15 May, and n. 5; JM Notes, 30 May 1783, and nn. 1–3.

[26] Delegates to Harrison, 13 May, ed. n.; JM to Randolph, 20 May; 10 June; Instruction to Delegates, 23–24 May, and n. 1; Jones to JM, 25 May; JM to Jefferson, 10 June 1783, and nn. 6, 21.

[27] "N--l--s" was George Nicholas. For Colonel William Fleming, one of the Virginia commissioners on western accounts, see *Papers of Madison*, III, 139, ed. n.; V, 229, n. 4. For Simon Nathan and his financial claim against Virginia, see Delegates to Gálvez, 4 May, ed. n.; JM to Jefferson, 20 May, and n. 4; Jones to JM, 8 June, and n. 19; Randolph to JM, 28 June 1783.

[28] For Oliver Pollock and his financial claim against Virginia, see *Papers of Madison*, VI, 474; 475, nn. 4, 5; 476, n. 6; Delegates to Gálvez, 4 May, ed. n., and nn. 2, 3; Jones to JM, 8 June. Action by the House of Delegates on the Pollock claim was delayed until Monday, 23 June 1783 (*JHDV*, May 1783, pp. 76–78).

[29] A "Chariot" was a light pleasure carriage with four wheels. For Jones's return to Philadelphia, see JM to Randolph, 18 Aug. 1783.

[30] Jones to JM, 31 May 1783, and n. 18.

From Edmund Randolph

RC (LC: Madison Papers). Unsigned but in Randolph's hand. Cover addressed by him to "The honorable James Madison jr. esq. of congress. Philadelphia." Cover docketed by JM, "June 14, 1783."

Richmond. June 14. 1783.

My dear friend

It is with real mortification, that I find an abortion of the scheme of impost. By some unaccountable revolution the zealous patrons have cooled, and seem united with its enemies to deal it out through our own treasury, without subjecting it to congress.[1] Perhaps however the most considerable terror which was played off against the proposition, was the furnishing beyond the quota from an excessive consumption in this country.[2] A certain party, which has been adverse to the plan in more *places* than one, appear to have remained uniform in the most bitter opposition.[3] As I write with a despondency on this subject I shall leave the particulars of what passed within the walls of the assembly to Mr. Jones, especially too as I have been employed for a week past in another general court.[4]

A great clamour will probably be excited against the legislature for having voted the payment of their own wages out of a fund, already plighted for other uses.[5] At first sight the measure seems very reprehensible: and indeed there is scarcely an excuse, unless it be the danger, which the nonpayment of those wages, would introduce, of an aristocratical, or at least an opulent representation alone.[6]

It is probable, that the half blood will be rendered heritable in the course of the session. A good measure, dictated by bad motives.[7]

The sum of 50,000£ is directed to be paid to congress:[8] but Mr. Webb, the receiver, informs me, that they exact the price of 40s [?] per hundred for tobacco. He will be obliged to submit to this valuation, or lose his chance of payment, as tobacco is the fund of the principal reliance.[9]

I am now able to say, that the cession to congress has never yet been formally repealed, however it may be in the power of the assembly to consider it so, from the refusal of congress to accept.[10]

[1] Jones to JM, 8 June, n. 5; 14 June, and n. 12. See also Randolph to JM, 15 May; 24 May, and n. 5; Pendleton to JM, 26 May 1783, and n. 5.

[2] Randolph to JM, 9 May 1783, and n. 7.

[3] Randolph probably referred to Arthur Lee. For Lee's opposition to the plan for restoring public credit, see *Papers of Madison*, VI, 12, n. 3; 149; 154, n. 45; 225; 263, n. 15; 399; Jefferson to JM, 7 May, and n. 8; JM to Randolph, 13 May 1783, and n. 3.

[4] Jones to JM, 14 June 1783. By "another general court," as distinguished from the General Court, Randolph must have meant a session of the Court of Admiralty, before which he had been involved in a case only ten days before (Randolph to JM, 4 June 1783).

[5] Randolph to JM, 24 May, and n. 7. On 11 June the House of Delegates adopted by a vote of 43 to 40 a resolution directing the treasurer to "pay the wages of the members attending this present General Asssembly, to wit: a sum not exceeding 1,800£. out of the fund heretofore appropriated for the defence of the Bay of Chesapeake, and a sum not exceeding 1,200£. out of the fund arising from the recruiting law." Five days later, after deciding by a vote of 43 to 26 to embody the resolution in a bill, the House of Delegates appointed Arthur Lee and Richard Henry Lee to be the draftsmen. Their proposal, upon being amended and adopted by the Senate and House of Delegates, as certified by the signature of the speaker of each, became a law on 28 June 1783 (*JHDV*, May 1783, pp. 49, 59, 61, 63, 66, 79, 96, 98, 99). Only three-fourths of the wages of each member was to be derived

from the two funds. The remainder should be paid in tobacco at a valuation fixed by a grand jury impaneled by the General Court (Hening, *Statutes*, X, 137–38, 228–29; XI, 280). See also *Papers of Madison*, VI, 224, n. 3; Pendleton to JM, 26 May 1783, n. 11.

6 The membership of the Senate and House of Delegates, unless assured of a per diem wage and traveling expenses, would necessarily be confined to men of independent means. The preamble of the act of 28 June 1783 begins by affirming: "Whereas it is essential to the independence of the members of the general assembly, and to the due discharge of their duty, that they should receive the money deemed by law necessary for their subsistence while on public service."

7 On 14 May the House of Delegates had instructed the Committee for Courts of Justice "to prepare and bring in a bill to make the half blood inheritable to land and slaves, descended from or given by their common ancestors." Although the bill was presented by Stevens Thomson Mason on 30 May and read a second time the next day, it remained thereafter on the speaker's table until 19 June. On that day a resolution passed to delay until "the third Monday in October next" before debating the measure in "a committee of the whole House" (*JHDV*, May 1783, pp. 6, 26, 27, 69).

Persons of "the half blood" are those with only one parent in common. Although younger brothers and sisters of the half blood were entitled to inherit personal property (*Papers of Madison*, I, 181; 183, n. 5), not until 7 January 1786, with the passage by the General Assembly of "an act, directing the course of descents" (one of the Revised Code of Laws, introduced by JM), were they permitted to share in real estate (*JHDV*, Oct. 1785, p. 132; Hening, *Statutes*, XII, 138–40). Why in 1783 Randolph should have judged this "good measure" to have been "dictated by bad motives" is unclear. He may, however, have seen in it a device to thwart the provision of Article V of the provisional treaty of peace with Great Britain, whereby Congress was obligated to recommend to the states the restoration of Loyalist estates (*JCC*, XXIV, 248–49). A bill could easily have been designed to lead to protracted litigation and otherwise to allow for the fragmentation of large landed estates by dividing them among many legal heirs (*Papers of Madison*, VI, 499; 500, n. 6; Jones to JM, 31 May; 8 June 1783, and nn. 26, 27).

8 This instruction of 6 June to Jacquelin Ambler, treasurer, in fulfillment of a resolution adopted by the Virginia legislature on 28 December 1782, directed him to pay the £50,000 "out of the first money that may come to his hands" (*JHDV*, May 1783, pp. 27, 40, 41; *Papers of Madison*, V, 457–58; VI, 155, n. 2; 172; 174, n. 2).

9 By a resolution adopted by the House of Delegates on 6 June, the treasurer was forbidden to "sell the tobacco of the best quality under forty shillings for every hundred weight, and that of inferior quality at prices proportionable thereto." He was further directed to discharge no debts in tobacco to individuals until the £50,000 pledged to Congress had been paid. A committee of six men, including Patrick Henry, Joseph Jones, and Richard Henry Lee, were appointed to embody the resolutions in a bill but probably never rendered a report (*JHDV*, May 1783, p. 40; Ambler to JM, 1 June, and n. 6; Pendleton to JM, 2 June, and n. 4; 9 June, and n. 6). Legislation for paying the financial quota to Congress was confined to a single bill enacted on 28 June and entitled, "An act to amend the act for appropriating the public revenue" (*JHDV*, May 1783, p. 99; Hening, *Statutes*, XI, 247–49; Pendleton to JM, 26 May 1783, n. 11).

10 Harrison to Delegates, 3 May, and n. 4; JM to Randolph, 13 May; Randolph to JM, 24 May; Jones to JM, 14 June 1783, and n. 14.

Notes on Debates

MS (LC: Madison Papers). For a description of the manuscript of Notes on Debates, see *Papers of Madison*, V, 231–34.

Monday June 16

no Congress

From Edmund Pendleton

Tr (LC: Force Transcripts). In the left margin at the top of the transcription, Peter Force's clerk wrote "MSS. McGuire's." See *Papers of Madison*, I, xxii, xxiii.

VIRGA. June 16th 1783

DEAR SIR

I thank you for yr very Polite concern for my health express'd in yr favour of the 3d.[1] Rest has restored the decay produced by fatigue in the last term, but how shall I remove that Radical one the effect of 62? no matter, let time with all its consequences take its course.[2]

Your observations that the drain of Specie from this State will depend on the ballance of our trade, rather than on the mode of collecting the State's quota of the Continental debt, are judicious, solid & indeed unanswerable.[3] we have it in our power to secure a very large Ballance in commerce, and live elegantly, but whether we have virtue, industry & Œconomy enough to adopt the means, I can't help doubting & shall be very agreably disappointed, in an eventual Solution of these doubts—of which the crowds of people to the Stores newly opened give an unfavourable prospect.[4] I have yet to learn the progress of yr revenue scheme in the Assembly, as our delegates are at present absent, & I have not lately heard what they are about. you'l probably hear [from] some of yr City correspondents.[5]

The motive was obvious for the Gents. saying they rejoiced at the slaves having been sent away from New-York as an infraction of the treaty wch would justify the non-payment of British debts; however this was only private conversation.[6] I believe the Assembly will say nothing on the subject, wch indeed seems improper until the definitive Treaty is communicated, the delay of wch. I suppose chargeable to the want of an Administration in Britain, and not to their disinclination to Peace; so that if your Intelligence be true of the formation of that body, we may now soon expect the Treaty and their American trade Act.[7]

I heard nothing at Richmond of the proposal concerted between you and the Maryland Delegates for removing the Seat of Congress to George Town. Mr Jefferson mentioned when here, a kind of competition for that honr. between George Town & Esopus in New York, who had severally made considerable Offers in Jurisdiction & property, to induce congress to hold their Sessions with them.[8] the Assembly of Maryland were no doubt influenced in the change to Annapolis, by a respect to their Metropolis, the ready provision at that place for the Accommodation of Congress, and perhaps from an inclination to preserve the whole benefit to themselves, of which Virginia at George Town would have participated.[9] For my own part I care not, since tho' no doubt there are advantages in the great circulation of money wherever Congress sit, yet I am so old fashioned as to think that overballanced by another thing wch Circulates with it & need not be named. so that I doubt if Philadelphia would not have a good bargain to give up all advantages on this head to be restored to the Morals her citizens possessed in 1775. don't let me be misunderstood as insinuating the smallest reflection on the Morals of the members of Congress: 'tis not from them, but the company which they draw to them, that I suppose the evil to be apprehended:[10] As Maryland has thus changed her ground, I suppose Virginia will have nothing more to do in it.[11]

I don't understand the effect of Furloughing the Soldiers, as a saving measure; I suppose their pay continues, and as to their provisions, tho' it be saved to the Public, yet if I am not mastaken in my Conjecture that most of them are foreigners, without property & without relations to support them. Individuals where they go will have a bad bargain of this mode of supplying the Provisions which they must & will have. however I mean not to find fault with the measure, for which I doubt not there were reasons that Overballanced this small objection;[12] I wish the British Troops were gone from the States that we might put an end to the expence of the Army altogether.[13]

Crad. T's Marriage has perhaps produced one good effect in driving him to Sea, where, if at all, he may do something. You don't say how he married, & I suppose it imprudent enough. he left considerable property in the hands of his brother T. but on what terms I know not, tho' have heard that the latter purchased it. I have communicated C's sailing to his mother, who wishes to know the sort of wife he has got.[14] I am with the greatest esteem & regard

Dr Sir Yr Affe friend

EDMD PENDLETON

[1] Not found.

[2] Pendleton to JM, 26 May 1783, and nn. 1, 2.

[3] In his missing letter of 3 June, JM evidently had made these "observations" in reply to Pendleton's comments in his letter of 26 May (*q.v.*, and n. 5) about the adverse effect upon Virginia of sending specie to the Philadelphia "Vortex" to meet the annual financial requisitions of Congress.

[4] Randolph to JM, 24 May; Pendleton to JM, 26 May; Jones to JM, 31 May; Harrison to Delegates, 7 June 1783, and nn. 2, 3. A comparison of the issue of the *Virginia Gazette* of 12 April with that of 14 June 1783 reveals how fast business activity and the variety of manufactured goods available for purchase were increasing in Richmond.

[5] Pendleton, who was writing from his estate of Edmundsbury in Caroline County, correctly assumed that Jones and Randolph, then in the "City" of Richmond, had informed JM about the "progress" of the "revenue scheme." See Jones to JM, 8 June, and n. 5; 14 June, and nn. 12, 14, 17; Randolph to JM, 14 June 1783, and n. 9. The delegates from Caroline County attending the session of the Virginia General Asssembly were Robert Gilchrist and John Taylor (Swem and Williams, *Register*, p. 17).

[6] Pendleton had mentioned these unidentified "Gents." in his letter to JM on 26 May (*q.v.*, and citations in n. 14). See also Jones to JM, 25 May; 31 May; JM Notes, 26 May, and n. 1; 30 May 1783, and nn. 1, 3.

[7] JM to Jefferson, 13 May, and n. 7; 10 June, and nn. 3–8; Pendleton to JM, 17 May; JM to Randolph, 20 May, and nn. 13, 14; 10 June; JM to James Madison, Sr., 27 May, and n. 9; Jones to JM, 8 June 1783, and nn. 22, 23.

[8] *Papers of Madison*, VI, 447; 448, nn. 4, 5, 7. For Jefferson's visit at Edmundsbury about 21 April, see JM to Jefferson, 6 May 1783, and n. 2.

[9] Delegates to Harrison, 27 May, and n. 2; JM to Randolph, 10 June 1783, and n. 14; Burnett, *Letters*, VII, 180, 182, and second n. 2.

[10] In "the company" Pendleton probably included speculators, lobbyists, and place-seekers. The presence of diplomatic representatives had encouraged, if not obligated, the entertainments of a frequency and extravagance which to his regret had displaced the laudable Quaker sobriety characterizing society in Philadelphia before the Revolution. For examples supporting Pendleton's comment, see Burnett, *Letters*, III, 333–34, 451–52, 535; VI, 3, 250, n. 3; William Emmett O'Donnell, *The Chevalier de La Luzerne, French Minister to the United States, 1779–1784* (Bruges, 1938), pp. 180, 218–19.

[11] Instructions to Delegates, 28 June 1783.

[12] JM Notes, 23 May, nn. 1, 3. Although foreigners comprised most of the personnel in Hazen's regiment and Armand's partisan legion, they by no means totaled a majority of the continental troops and officers. See *Papers of Madison*, IV, 25, n. 5; V, 237, n. 1; VI, 443, n. 1.

[13] Pendleton to JM, 4 May 1783, n. 5.

[14] Craddock Taylor's "brother T." was Thornton Taylor (d. 1832). His grave may be an unmarked one in the Maysville cemetery, Mason County, Ky. (*Lineage Book of the National Society of the Daughters of the American Revolution*, CXLI [1918], 202; Mrs. W. T. [Ila Earle] Fowler, comp., *Kentucky Pioneers and Their Descendants* [Frankfort, n.d.], p. 230). In that state Thornton had been awarded 2,666 acres of land for service as a lieutenant in the continental army, Virginia line (Gwathmey, *Historical Register of Virginians*, p. 762). The Virginia records include no evidence of Craddock's leaving "considerable property in the hands of his brother T." or of anyone else, or, in fact, of possessing property to leave. The Taylor brothers' mother was Alice Taylor, nee Thornton (d. *ca.* 1786) (Caroline County Land-Property Tax Books, 1785–1787, MSS in Va. State Library).

Receipt of Robert Scot

MS (LC: Madison Papers). In JM's hand, except for Scot's signature.

Philada. June 16. 1783. Recd of J. Madison an order on Messrs. Biddle & Co.[1] for eight pounds fifteen shillings, which on being paid, shall be a discharge in full of the sum due for a seal by me engraved for the University at Williamsburg[2]

Rot Scot[3]

[1] Rev. James Madison to JM, 4 June 1783. The brothers Biddle, Owen (1737–1799) and Clement (1740–1814), merchant-importers of Philadelphia, were birthright members of the Society of Friends; but as militant patriots, they were in 1775 "disowned" by their religious colleagues for "promoting warlike preparation & instructing in the art of war" (William Wade Hinson, *Encyclopedia of American Quaker Genealogy* [Thomas W. Marshall and John Cox, Jr., comps., 5 vols.; Ann Arbor, 1936–46], II, 464). In that year Owen was a delegate to the Pennsylvania Provincial Conference; a member of the colony-state Committee of Safety, 1775–1776; of the Council of Safety, 1776–1777; and of the Board of War, 1777. In 1777 he was continental deputy quartermaster of forage. Of "philosophical" bent, he was instrumental in the promotion of scientific and literary societies, but his introspective nature, perhaps abetted by heavy inroads on his fortune, led him to a "depression of spirits." On 30 May 1783, acknowledging that his "past deviations" had been "contrary to the peaceable principles of Christianity" and brought him only "remorse and sorrow," he begged to "be restored again to membership" in the Quaker congregation (*Pa. Mag. Hist. and Biog.*, XVI [1892], 299–329; LVIII [1934], 312–41). See also *JCC*, VI, 863, n. 1, 968; VII, 296, n. 3; XVI, 238; Boyd, *Papers of Jefferson*, IV, 544.

Apparently never uncertain of the rectitude of his own course, Clement Biddle in 1775 helped raise a company of volunteers known as the "Quaker Blues." In July 1776 he was appointed, with the rank of colonel, deputy quartermaster general for a select group of militia from his own state and New Jersey; in November of the same year, aide-de-camp to General Nathanael Greene; and in 1777, commissary general of forage. Three years later he resigned to attend to his private affairs, but in September 1781 he became quartermaster general of the state militia. He served as justice of the Court of Common Pleas of Philadelphia County, 1788–1789, and as United States marshal for Pennsylvania, 1789–1793. He was business agent for many prominent contemporaries, including George Washington (*Coloniel Records of Pa.*, XIII, 53; *Pa. Archives*, 1st ser., IX, 129–30; *JCC*, III, 329; V, 527; X, 353; XVII, 716; Burnett, *Letters*, III, 62, n. 9; Fitzpatrick, *Writings of Washington*, XXVII, 101–2, 198, 397–98, 426–30; *Journal of Executive Proceedings of the Senate of the United States*, I, 29, 31).

[2] Jones to JM, 25 May, and n. 18; Rev. James Madison to JM, 4 June 1783.

[3] Rev. James Madison to JM, 4 June 1783, and n. 2.

Notes on Debates

MS (LC: Madison Papers). For a description of the manuscript of Notes on Debates, see *Papers of Madison*, V, 231–34.

Tuesday June 17

The day was employed chiefly in considering the Report on the Journal relative to the Department of Finance.[1] Some thought it ought to lie on the files: some that it ought to receive a vote of approbation, and that the Superintendant, should, for the period examined, be acquitted of further responsibility.[2] Mr. Gorham particularly was of that opinion. Finally the Report was entered on the Journal without any act of Congress thereon, by a unanimous concurrence.[3]

[1] The "Report," in the hand of Thomas FitzSimons, had been rendered on 10 June on behalf of a committee, Nathaniel Gorham, chairman, appointed on 6 January and renewed on 31 March 1783, "to enquire fully into the proceedings of the Department of Finance, including the several branches of the same, and report the result of their enquiry." The appointment of the committee with this directive was in pursuance of a resolution written by JM and adopted by Congress on 17 June 1782 (*JCC*, XXII, 334; XXIV, 37, and n. 2, 222, and n. 2, 387, 396–99, 399, n. 1; *Papers of Madison*, IV, 343–44).

[2] The "period examined" was from 14 May 1781, when Robert Morris signified to Congress his willingness to accept appointment as superintendent of finance, to 1 January 1783 (*ibid.*, III, 137, n. 4; *JCC*, XXIV, 398). The number of states effectively represented in Congress on 17 June is unknown, but there were seven on 20 June. If a motion to thank Morris for his services had been introduced on that day, it probably would have been adopted by a vote of five to two. See *Papers of Madison*, VI, 304–5; 305, n. 4; 306, n. 6; 347, n. 4; 409, n. 1; *JCC*, XXIV, 407; Burnett, *Letters*, VII, 184, and n. 5.

[3] *JCC*, XXIV, 396–99.

Virginia Delegates to Benjamin Harrison

RC (Pierpont Morgan Library, New York City). In the hand of John Francis Mercer, except for JM's signature. Docketed, "Virga Delegates Letter recd June 27. 83, June 17th 1783."

Philadelphia June 17th. 1783

Sir

Since our last to Yr. Excellency,[1] little has occurr'd worthy of communication. A Letter from General Washington encloses a very feeling address from the Officers of that part of the Army, comprehended in the late Resolution of Congress hertofore transmitted to Yr Excelly. Their minds too much agitated by the contemplation of prospects, cruel & dispiriting, gave way to suspicions (founded on the indefinite terms of the furlough.) that this mode was adopted to disperse them, & to avoid a compliance with that part of their request which, related to paymt on their discharge. they lamented but in strong & manly terms that they were to end their toils & hardships by returning to inevitable distress, without any aleeviation of their present wants. They implor'd his interference as their General & as their friend. The Commander in Chief then explained to them, that this measure was calculated to promote their interest, without endangering the safety of the States. That by this means the money which must otherwise be expended in their subsistance, woud now be appropriated to the paymt. of part of their dues. He said, that in justice to Congress, he could not but declare his sentiments. That they had made every exertion within their Power to obviate the present distresses of & to procure final justice to the Army. By this prudent, wise & noble conduct of General Washington gathered discontents, which now seemed again ready to burst forth, were on[c]e more happily assuaged, & the Resolution of Congress were quietly complied with.[2]

A Spirit of Mutiny discovered itself in the Troops immediately in Phila. that at first wore an alarming aspect, but by timely exertion it terminated without any ill consequences.[3]

Yr. Excellency will receive the Pamphlett you require.[4]

We have the honor to be &c. Yr. Excellency's most obt. humble Servants

J. MADISON JR.
JOHN F. MERCER

[1] The reference is to a missing letter, probably dated 10 June. This letter, which Harrison submitted on 19 June to the Virginia House of Delegates, enclosed copies of the "report of a Committee of Congress relative to the Offers made by sundry States to that Body to induce them to hold their Sessions in them" and of another congressional committee on the proposed cession by Virginia of lands beyond the Ohio River (Executive Letter Book, 1783–1786, p. 157, MS in Va. State Library; *JCSV*, III, 271; *JHDV*, May 1783, p. 68). See also Delegates to Harrison, 27 May, and n. 2; JM Notes, 6 June, and n. 1; 10 June, and nn. 7, 9; Instructions to Delegates, 27 June; 28 June 1783.

[2] On 7 June Washington forwarded to Congress with his endorsement a copy of the "Address of the Generals and Officers Commanding the Regiments and Corps," signed and presented to him by Major General William Heath, and also of his reply on 6 June to Heath. Mercer well summarized the contents of these documents (NA: PCC, No. 152, XI, 295–315; Fitzpatrick, *Writings of Washington*, XXVI, 472–75, 478–79). The "late Resolution" was that of 26 May regarding the

furloughing of officers and troops in the main army who had engaged "to serve during the war." See JM Notes, 26 May, and n. 2; 11 June 1783, n. 1. When a copy of that resolution was sent to Harrison is unknown.

Having received Washington's letter and enclosures, Congress on 11 June referred them to a committee composed of Hamilton, chairman, JM, and Bland (*JCC*, XXIV, 392, n. 1). Although not noted in the official journal, Hamilton's report on behalf of the committee was submitted to Congress and adopted on 19 June 1783. Thereby Congress agreed to have a copy of Washington's letter and its enclosures sent to the executive of each state, together with a reminder of the resolutions of 2 May "to facilitate the punctual payment of the notes issued to the army on account of their pay" (Syrett and Cooke, *Papers of Hamilton*, III, 398–99). See also *JCC*, XXIV, 325–26. Under a covering letter of 20 June, Elias Boudinot, president of Congress, complied with the resolution (MSS in Va. State Library; Burnett, *Letters*, VII, 192–93).

[3] JM Notes, 13 June, and n. 1; JM to Randolph, 17 June 1783.

[4] Harrison to Delegates, 7 June 1783.

From Thomas Jefferson

RC (LC: Madison Papers). Docketed by JM, "Ths. Jefferson 17 June. 1783," also "June 17. 1783. ideas of Constitution." Many years later William Cabell Rives, author of a detailed biography of Madison's career to 1797, as well as an editor of his papers, added to the docket, "Mr. Henry's course as to the Impost Act."

MONTICELLO June 17. 1783.

DEAR SIR

Your favours of the 13th. & 20th. Ult. came to hand about a week ago.[1] I am informed the assembly determined against the capacity of reelection in those gentlemen of the delegation who could not serve a complete year. I do not know on what this decision could be founded.[2] my hopes of the success of the Congressional propositions here have lessened exceedingly. mr. Henry had declared in favor of the impost: but when the question came on he was utterly silent. I understand it will certainly be lost if it be not already.[3] instead of ceding more lands to the U.S. a proposition is made to revoke the former cession. mr. Henry is for bounding our state reasonably enough, but instead of ceding the parts lopped off he is for laying them off into small republics. what further his plan is I do not hear.[4] however you get the parliamentary news so much more directly from Richmond that it is idle for me to give it you from hence.[5]

A Convention for the amendment of our Constitution having been much the topic of conversation for some time, I have turned my Thoughts to the amendments necessary. The result I inclose to you.

you will have opportunities during your stay in Philadelphia of enquiring into the success of some of the parts of it which tho' new to us have been tried in other states. I shall only except against your communicating it to any one of my own country, as I have found prejudices frequently produced against propositions handed to the world without explanation or support. I trust that you will either now or in some future situation turn your attention to this subject in time to give your aid when it shall be finally discussed. the paper inclosed may serve as a basis for your amendment, or may suggest amendments to a better groundwork.[6] I further learn that the assembly are excluding members of Congress from among them. whether the information they may derive from their presence, or their being marked by the confidence of the people, is the cause of this exclusion I cannot tell.[7]

Be pleased to present me with affection to my acquaintances of the house[8] & to receive yourself the sincerest assurances of the esteem with which I am Dr. Sir

Your friend & servt

TH: JEFFERSON

P.S. I will take the first opportunity of forwarding the pamphlet to your father.[9]

[1] *Qq.v.*

[2] *Papers of Madison*, VI, 464, n. 6; Jefferson to JM, 7 May; JM to Jefferson, 20 May; Randolph to JM, 24 May; JM to Randolph, 3 June, and n. 4; Pendleton to JM, 9 June 1783.

[3] Randolph to JM, 15 May; 24 May, 14 June, and n. 3; Jameson to JM, 24 May, and n. 3; Jones to JM, 31 May; 8 June; 14 June; Jefferson to JM, 1 June; Pendleton to JM, 2 June 1783.

[4] Randolph to JM, 9 May; JM to Jefferson, 20 May, and n. 8; Jones to JM, 8 June; 14 June 1783, and n. 14.

[5] Jefferson had left Richmond on 7 May (Jefferson to JM, 7 May 1783). Except for hearsay, Jefferson may have had to rely mostly upon Isaac Zane for "parliamentary news" (Boyd, *Papers of Jefferson*, VI, 317; Roger W. Moss, Jr., "Isaac Zane, Jr., a Quaker for the Times," *Va. Mag. Hist. and Biog.*, LXXVII [1969], 291–306).

[6] For Jefferson's earlier criticism of the Form of Government of Virginia, adopted in June 1776 by a convention which simultaneously served as the legislature, see *Papers of Madison*, VI, 319; 320, n. 7; 321, n. 8; 441, n. 10; Jefferson to JM, 7 May, and nn. 12, 13. In the present letter Jefferson enclosed nine and a half closely written folios, entitled by him, "To the citizens of the Commonwealth of Virginia & all others whom it may concern, their Delegates of the said Commonwealth send greeting" (LC: Rives Collection of Madison Papers). This was a caption that might be used if his draft of a new Form of Government had been the work of a constitutional convention obliged to refer the document to the sovereign citizens of Virginia for approval or rejection. Although Jefferson wrote "[1783. May–June]" at the top of the first folio, JM some years later evidently forgot when he had received the document and docketed the ninth folio, "Constitution

1784 of Virginia." To his docket William Cabell Rives added, "Drawn by Mr. Jefferson." Julian P. Boyd's edition of the document carefully annotates its contents, places it in its earlier and later contexts, and demonstrates that Jefferson's suggestion of a "Council of Revision" was derived from the New York constitution of 1777 (Boyd, *Papers of Jefferson*, VI, 278–84, 294–308; *An Occasional Bulletin*, Va. Historical Society, XV [1967], 7–8). See also JM to Jefferson, 17 July 1783.

7 Randolph to JM, 15 May, and n. 8; 24 May; Jones to JM, 25 May 1783, and n. 4.

8 JM to Jefferson, 13 May 1783, and n. 1.

9 JM to Jefferson, 20 May 1783.

To Edmund Randolph

RC (LC: Madison Papers). Unsigned but in JM's hand. Cover franked by "J. Madison Jr" and addressed by him to "Edmund Randolph Esqr. Richmond." Cover docketed by Randolph, "J. Madison. June 17. 1783."

PHILADA. 17 June 1783.

MY DEAR FRIEND,

Your favor of the 4th., the second from Williamsburg,[1] was rcd. yesterday. I have recd. nothing from Mr. Hay during your absence from Richmond, but the omission has been supplied by Mr. Ambler whose letter by yesterday's mail inclosed the Journals from the beginning. perhaps this supply was known to Mr. H.[2]

The[3] definitive Treaty is not yet on this side the wat[e]r; nor do we yet hear what stage it is in on the other side.[4] Mr. Dana informs us in a letter of the 17 Feby. that in consequence of proper encouragement he had finally announced himself at the Court of Petersbg. but does not gratify us with a single circumstance that ensued.[5] The gazette of this morning inclosed contains the latest intelligence from the British Parliamt. which I have seen.[6]

The measure of furloughing the troops enlisted for the war has been carried into effect with the main army, and will save a great expence to the public. The prospect which it presented to the officers who were to retire from their subsistance with out receivg. the means of subsistance [elsewhere][7] produced a very pathetic representation to the Commander in chief. His answer by rectifying some errors on which it dwelt, and explicitly giving it as his opinion that Congress had now done every thing wch. could be expected from them towards fulfilling the engagements of their Country, had the effect to which it was entitled.[8] The troops in the barracks at this place, emboldened by the arrival of a furloughed Regt. returning to Maryland, Sent in a very mutinous remonstrance to Congress, signed by the non-commissioned officers in behalf of the whole. It painted the hardships which they had suffered in the defence of their country & the duty of their Country to reward them, demanding a satisfactory answer the afternoon on which it was sent in, with a threat of otherwise taking such measures as would right themselves. The prudent & soothing measures taken by the Secy. at war & Gl. Sinclair have I believe obviated the embarrassment.[9]

Another embarrassment, and that not a small one will soon be laid before them by a Committee. Genl. Washington, the Secy. at war and all the professional men who have been consulted, report, that at least 3 or 4 Regts. will be essential as a peace establishmt. for the U States, & that this establishmt. ought to be a Continental one. West point, the fronteir forts to the Westward, and a few garrisons on the Sea Shore, are conceived by them to be indispensable. Some Naval force is deemed at least equally so, with a few docks & protections for them.[10] on looking into the articles of Confederation, the military power of Congress in time of peace, appears to be at least subject to be called in question. If Congress put a construction on them favorable to their own power, or even if they ask the States to sanction the exercise of the power, the present paroxism of jealousy may not only disappoint them, but may exert itself with more fatal effect on the Revenue propositions. On the other side to renounce such a construction, and refer the establishment to the separate & internal provision of the States will not only render the plan of defence either defective in a general view or oppressive to particular states, but may hereafter when the tide of prejudice may be flowing in a contrary direction, expose them to the reproach of unnecessarily t[hrowing] [a]way a power necessary for the good of the Union, and leaving the whole at the mercy of a single State. The only expedie[nt] for this dilemma seems to be delay;[11] but even that is pregnant with difficulties equally great; since on the arrival of the definitive Treaty Congs must in pursuance of such a neutral plan suffer the whole military establishmt. to be dissolved, every garrisoned-post to be evacuated, and every strong hold to be dismantled; Their remaining ships of war too must be sold, and no preparatory steps taken for future emergencies on that side.[12]

I am exceedingly pleased to find Mr. Jeffersons' name at the head of the new Delegation. I hope it has been placed there with his knowledge and acquiescence.[13]

The order of the day for electing a Secy. of F. Affairs was called for on Teusday last, but no nominations having been then made, the business was put off till the present day. The nominations since made are Mr. A. Lee by Mr. Bland—Mr. Jonathan Trumbell Jnr. by Mr. Biggenson—Col: Tilghman by Mr. Ghorum—Mr. George Clymer by Mr. Montgomery. Genl. Schyler has remained on the list since the fall, but was withdrawn by the Delegates of N. Jersey at the instance of Mr Hamilton. Mr. Jefferson was nominated by Mr. Ghorum, but withdrawn also on intimation that he would not undertake the service.[14]

If Mr. Jones sd. have quitted Richmond forward if you please his letter. It is addressed to you in his absence. It contains little which is omitted in this, but you may open it. If he sd. not be gone you will let him see this, as it is somewhat fuller than his.[15]

[1] Randolph to JM, 4 June. His earlier letter from Williamsburg, written on 29 May 1783, has not been found. See JM to Randolph, 10 June 1783, and n. 2.

[2] Randolph to JM, 24 May, and n. 12; Ambler to JM, 7 June. The "beginning" was 5 May 1783, "the day appointed by law, for the meeting of the General Assembly" (*JHDV*, May 1783, p. 3).

[3] Many years later JM or someone at his direction placed a bracket at the outset of this paragraph and another at the close of the next to last paragraph, thus designating the portion of the letter to be published in the first edition of his papers. See Madison, *Papers* (Gilpin ed.), I, 547–50.

[4] Pendleton to JM, 4 May, n. 6; JM to Jefferson, 10 June 1783, and n. 8.

[5] Although the fact is not mentioned in its journal, Congress on 17 June received dispatches dated 10 February, 25 February, 7 March, and 12 March 1783 from Francis Dana, minister-designate of the United States at the court of St. Petersburg (NA: PCC, No. 186, III, 67; Wharton, *Revol. Dipl. Corr.*, VI, 248–50, 263–64, 275–76, 286–87). In his letter of 25 February, Dana stated he would follow the advice of the ambassador of King Louis XVI of France and delay seeking to be received in his official capacity by Tsarina Catherine the Great. On 7 March, however, trusting in what turned out to be delusive "assurances directly from the private cabinet of her Imperial Majesty that the way was perfectly clear," Dana requested of Count Ivan Andreievich Osterman, the tsarina's vice chancellor for foreign affairs, an audience for the purpose of presenting a copy of his letter of credence. If JM had read the dispatch of 12 March, he probably would have informed Randolph of the opening of the Lenten season in Russia as the reason given Dana by Osterman for delaying the submission of the letter of credence to the tsarina. Unknown to Dana, she had assured Sir James Harris, ambassador from the court of St. James, that she would not accord diplomatic recognition to the United States until the ratification of the definitive treaty of peace or until his own sovereign had received a minister from Congress (*ibid.*, VI, 276 n.).

[6] JM no doubt enclosed the *Pennsylvania Packet* of 17 June, for he was writing on Thursday, and the *Pennsylvania Gazette*, a weekly, appeared only on Wednesdays. That issue of the *Packet* printed an account of a debate, led by Charles James Fox, on 23 April in the House of Commons on a measure to vest in "his majesty in council" for six weeks the power to determine the "mode of entry of American vessels," pending the conclusion of a treaty of commerce. Those who participated in the discussion differed only on matters of detail rather than on "the immediate necessity" of removing all prohibitions on trade with the Americans. See JM to Jefferson, 10 June 1783, and nn. 5, 6.

7 A tear in the fold of the manuscript has obliterated this word. It is taken from Madison, *Papers* (Gilpin ed.), I, 547.

8 Delegates to Harrison, 17 June 1783, and n. 2.

9 JM Notes, 13 June 1783, and n. 1. The "furloughed Regt. returning to Maryland" was a contingent of the state's Third Regiment, commanded by Major Thomas Lansdale, which had left the main army on 5 June and arrived in Philadelphia a week later en route to Baltimore. Other Maryland troops, from the southern army, disembarked in Philadelphia on 15 June (Fitzpatrick, *Writings of Washington*, XXVI, 468, 470; Burnett, *Letters*, VII, 189, n. 4, 247). JM soon discovered that his optimism was not warranted. See JM Notes, 19 June 1783.

10 On 4 April 1783 Congress had appointed a committee, Hamilton, chairman, and JM one of its other four members, to propose "the proper arrangements to be taken in consequence of peace." These arrangements included the "military & naval peace establishments" (*Papers of Madison*, VI, 432–33; 434, n. 9). Among the other "professional men" consulted by Hamilton on behalf of the committee were Major General Benjamin Lincoln, secretary at war, Governor George Clinton of New York, and Washington. On 2 May Washington sent Hamilton a document entitled "Sentiments on a Peace Establishment," written after he had asked at least nine army officers or civil leaders with military experience to share their views with him (Syrett and Cooke, *Papers of Hamilton*, III, 321, 322, 331–32; Fitzpatrick, *Writings of Washington*, XXVI, 374–98, 398, n. 31). To the committee on 12 June Congress referred Washington's letter of 7 June urging that priority in western garrisons be given to the forts at Oswego, Niagara, and Detroit, and enclosing Brigadier General Louis Lebègue Duportail's "Observations Respecting the Fortifications Necessary for the United States" (NA: PCC, No. 185, III, 67; No. 186, fol. 107; Fitzpatrick, *Writings of Washington*, XXVI, 479–80; 480, n. 25).

Although the committee's report, drafted by Hamilton was submitted to Congress on 18 June, it was not spread on the journal until 23 October 1783 (Syrett and Cooke, *Papers of Hamilton*, III, 378–97, 378, n. 1; *JCC*, XXV, 722–44). By then Hamilton had long since returned to New York, Washington had expressed disagreement with some of the recommendations, and JM was about to leave Congress until February 1787. See also Delegates to Harrison, 1 Nov. 1783 (1st letter), and n. 8.

The committee recommended a "Military peace establishment" of "four regiments of infantry" and "one of Artillery incorporated in a corps of Engineers, with the denomination of the corps of Engineers." The personnel of each infantry regiment should total 601; of the corps of engineers, 636; and of a "corps of Artificers," 189 (Syrett and Cooke, *Papers of Hamilton*, III, 383, 384–87). The committee favored the establishment of "Arsenals and magazines," equipped to outfit 30,000 men for three years, at Springfield, Mass., "West Point & its dependencies," Carlisle, Pa., Camden, S.C., and at "Some convenient position on James River to be reconnoitered for that purpose" (*ibid.*, III, 391). Neither Hamilton's draft of the report nor the extended version of 23 October was explicit as to the number of warships required, but both deemed "a fleet of the United States" to be "indispensable," as well as "fortified harbors" for its "reception and protection" (*ibid.*, III, 382; *JCC*, XXV, 725).

11 The bracketed letters are taken from Madison, *Papers* (Gilpin ed.), I, 549. Although the first four paragraphs of the committee's report are almost exclusively devoted to a defense of the constitutional power of Congress, based on the sixth and ninth articles of the Articles of Confederation, to have an army and navy in peacetime, the last of these paragraphs closes by stating: "The Committee however submit to Congress, (in conformity to that spirit of Candour and to that respect for the sense of their constituents, which ought ever to characterize their proceedings) the propriety of transmitting the plan which they may adopt

to the several states to afford an opportunity of signifying their sentiments previous to its final execution" (Syrett anl Cooke, *Papers of Hamilton*, III, 380–81).

[12] Following a defense of the constitutionality of a peacetime army and navy, the committee continued its report with the words: "if there is a constitutional power in the United States" there are "conclusive reasons in favour of fœderal in preference to state establishments." These "reasons" were then set forth in a sequence of six numbered paragraphs, but they did not include the persuasive ones conveyed by JM to Randolph (*ibid.*, III, 381–82).

[13] Jefferson to JM, 7 May, and n. 19; Jones to JM, 8 June, and n. 10; Randolph to JM, 28 June 1783.

[14] JM Notes, 10 June 1783, and n. 12.

[15] JM's letter, probably dated 17 June, reached Jones in Richmond but has not been found (JM Notes, 19 June, and n. 9). Among the topics mentioned in it, other than those in the present letter, may have been a reference to Henry Laurens' dispatch of 15 March, received by Congress on 10 June. Jones left Richmond on 28 June (Jones to JM, 28 June 1783, and n. 15).

Instruction to Virginia Delegates *in re* Fortifications

RC (NA: PCC, No. 20, II, 313–14). Docketed: "Resolve of genl Assembly of Virginia That an application be made to Congress for 750 £ to level works at York Town July 31. 1783 Referred to Mr Read Mr Ellery Mr Williamson."

In the House of Delegates

The 17th June 1783

Resolved that it be an instruction to the Delegates representing this State in Congress to make application to Congress to obtain an order on the Continental Treasurer in this State[1] for a sum of Money not exceeding seven hundred and fifty Pounds for the purposes of levelling the fortifications erected by the Troops of His Most Christian Majesty at York Town in the County of York and at Gloucester Town in the County of Gloucester[2]

June 17th 1783 Teste
Agreed to by the Senate John Beckley CHD
Will Drew CS.

A Copy Teste
John Beckley CHD

[1] George Webb, continental receiver general in Virginia (*Papers of Madison*, IV, 182, n. 6; Jones to JM, 14 June 1783, and n. 11).

[2] The fortifications were those occupied and in part constructed by the French troops, commanded by the Comte de Rochambeau, during the Franco-American siege in September and October 1781 that resulted in the surrender of the British

army led by Earl Cornwallis. The French troops had left Virginia in July and August 1782, and their place in the fortifications was taken by contingents of the Virginia state line or militia (*Papers of Madison*, III, 253, n. 2; 268, n. 2; 276, n. 1; 280, nn. 6, 8, 9; 288, n. 1; 292, and n. 1; IV, 229, n. 18; 395, 397, n. 7; 401, nn. 3, 6, 7; 405–6, 406, nn. 1, 2; 446; *Cal. of Va. State Papers*, III, 280).

On 1 August 1782 Governor Harrison, apparently under a misapprehension that Major General Benjamin Lincoln, secretary at war, intended to have the fortifications destroyed, protested to the Virginia delegates in Congress that many of the defense works were "built by the State, & are necessary for the defence of" the York River "and its Trade" (*Papers of Madison*, V, 6, and n. 2; 7, nn. 5, 6; 25; 46; 47, n. 2; 74). On 16 June 1783 the House of Delegates rejected a bill to have "the works around" Yorktown leveled "at public expense" (*JHDV*, May 1783, pp. 13, 21, 22, 59). The next day the present instruction, seeking to have Congress assume the expense of the demolition, passed both houses of the General Assembly (*ibid.*, May 1783, pp. 62, 63). See also the letter from David Jameson, probably to JM, favoring the instruction (Jameson to JM, 16 July 1783).

The instruction, which Governor Harrison forwarded in his letter of 20 June (*q.v.*), was read to Congress on 31 July and referred to a committee composed of Jacob Read (S.C.), chairman, William Ellery (R.I.), and Hugh Williamson (NA: PCC, No. 185, III, 70; *JCC*, XXIV, 483, n. 2). On 3 September 1783 Read reported that even though Confederation funds had never before been sought to pay for the type of work mentioned in the instruction, and even though the request of the Virginia General Assembly should be deemed "consistent with justice," Congress could not comply in view of the depleted "state of the public finances" (*JCC*, XXV, 533).

Notes on Debates

MS (LC: Madison Papers). For a description of the manuscript of Notes on Debates, see *Papers of Madison*, V, 231–34.

Wednesday June 18.

Nothing done.[1]

[1] The entry in the journal for 18 June is confined to a report of the "Committee of the Week," recommending the disposition of a memorial and each of six letters addressed to Congress on matters of individual concern to their signators (*JCC*, XXIV, 401–2, 402, n. 1). By his comment, JM obviously meant that Congress neither debated nor decided any issue of general importance.

Notes on Debates

MS (LC: Madison Papers). For a description of the manuscript of Notes on Debates, see *Papers of Madison*, V, 231–34.

EDITORIAL NOTE

Following his terminal entry of 21 June 1783, JM inserted a folio considerably larger in size than the pages on which he had recorded his notes on debates. On this folio, which he covered with a folded half-page and inscribed "June 19. 1783," he copied Hugh Williamson's motion, mentioned in the first paragraph of his notes for that day. Although JM did not designate the insertion as a footnote to the paragraph, he obviously meant the motion to be a supplement thereto. For this reason the editors have added JM's copy of the motion as the second paragraph of his notes.

Thursday June 19.

A motion was made by Mr. Williamson seconded by Mr. Bland, to recommend to the States to make it a part of the Confederation, that whenever a *fourteenth* State should be added to the Union, *ten* votes be required in cases now requiring nine. It was committed to Mr. Williamson, Mr. Hamilton and Mr. Madison.[1] The motion had reference to the foreseen erection of the western part of N. Carolina into a separate State.[2]

Motion of Mr. Williamson[3] 2ded. by Mr. Bland June 19. 1783 commited to Mr. Williamson, Mr. Hamilton & Mr. Madison

Whereas the safety and peace of the U.S. are greatly interested in the no. of States that may be reqd. to vote on Questions of a particular class: and whereas it is provided by the 9th. article of the Confederation that the U S in C. asd. shall never engage in a war nor grant letters of marque & reprisal in time of peace, nor enter into any Treaties or Alliances nor coin money, nor regulate the value thereof, nor ascertain the sums & expences necessary for the defence & welfare of the U.S. or any of them, nor emit bills nor borrow money on the Credit of the U.S., nor appropriate money nor agree upon the no. of Vessels of war to be built or purchased or the no. of land or Sea forces to be raised, nor appt. a Commander in chief of the army, or navy, unless nine States assent to the same. It is also provided by the eleventh art: that no Colony except Canada shall be admitted into the Union unless such admission be agreed to by nine States,[4] but no provision is made for the no. of States that may be reqd. to agree in determining such questions when the prest. no. of States shall have been increased: and Whereas the determination of those great questions by 9. States alone when the origl. no. may be considerably increased wd. be a manifest departure from the Spirit of the Confederation & might prove dangerous to the Union. Therefore

Resd. that whenever a 14. State shd. be admitd. into the prest. Union the vote & agreetn. [agreement] of 10 Sts. shall become necessy. for

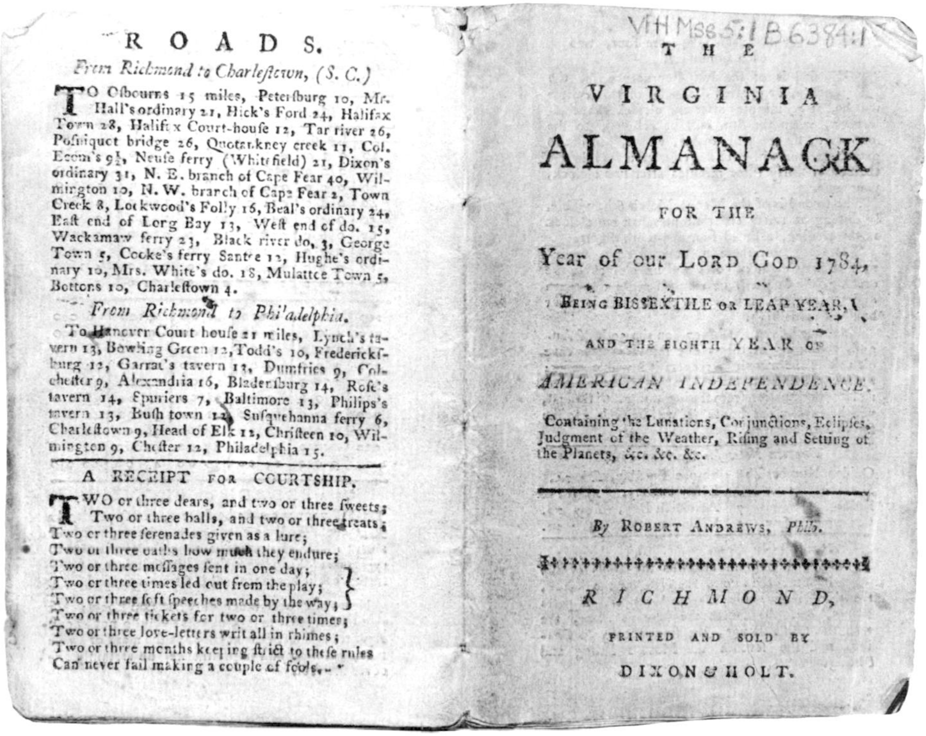

ROADS.

From Richmond to Charlestown, (S. C.)

TO Osbourns 15 miles, Petersburg 10, Mr. Hall's ordinary 21, Hick's Ford 24, Halifax Town 28, Halifax Court-house 12, Tar river 26, Posiquet bridge 26, Quotankney creek 11, Col. Eeom's 9½, Neuse ferry (Whitefield) 21, Dixon's ordinary 31, N. E. branch of Cape Fear 40, Wilmington 10, N. W. branch of Cape Fear 2, Town Creek 8, Lockwood's Folly 16, Beal's ordinary 24, East end of Long Bay 13, West end of do. 15, Wackamaw ferry 23, Black river do. 3, George Town 5, Cooke's ferry Santee 12, Hughe's ordinary 10, Mrs. White's do. 18, Mulattoe Town 5, Bottons 10, Charlestown 4.

From Richmond to Philadelphia.

To Hanover Court house 21 miles, Lynch's tavern 13, Bowling Green 12, Todd's 10, Fredericksburg 12, Garrat's tavern 13, Dumfries 9, Colchester 9, Alexandria 16, Bladensburg 14, Rose's tavern 14, Spurriers 7, Baltimore 13, Philips's tavern 13, Bush town 12, Susquehanna ferry 6, Charlestown 9, Head of Elk 12, Christeen 10, Wilmington 9, Chester 12, Philadelphia 15.

A RECEIPT FOR COURTSHIP.

TWO or three dears, and two or three sweets;
Two or three balls, and two or three treats;
Two or three serenades given as a lure;
Two or three oaths how much they endure;
Two or three messages sent in one day;
Two or three times led out from the play;
Two or three soft speeches made by the way;
Two or three tickets for two or three times;
Two or three love-letters writ all in rhimes;
Two or three months keeping strict to these rules
Can never fail making a couple of fools.

THE

VIRGINIA

ALMANACK

FOR THE

Year of our LORD GOD 1784,

BEING BISSEXTILE OR LEAP YEAR,

AND THE EIGHTH YEAR OF

AMERICAN INDEPENDENCE.

Containing the Lunations, Conjunctions, Eclipses, Judgment of the Weather, Rising and Setting of the Planets, &c. &c. &c.

By ROBERT ANDREWS, *Philo.*

RICHMOND,

PRINTED AND SOLD BY

DIXON & HOLT.

BACK PAGE AND TITLE PAGE OF
"THE VIRGINIA ALMANACK FOR THE YEAR OF OUR LORD GOD 1784"
BY ROBERT ANDREWS

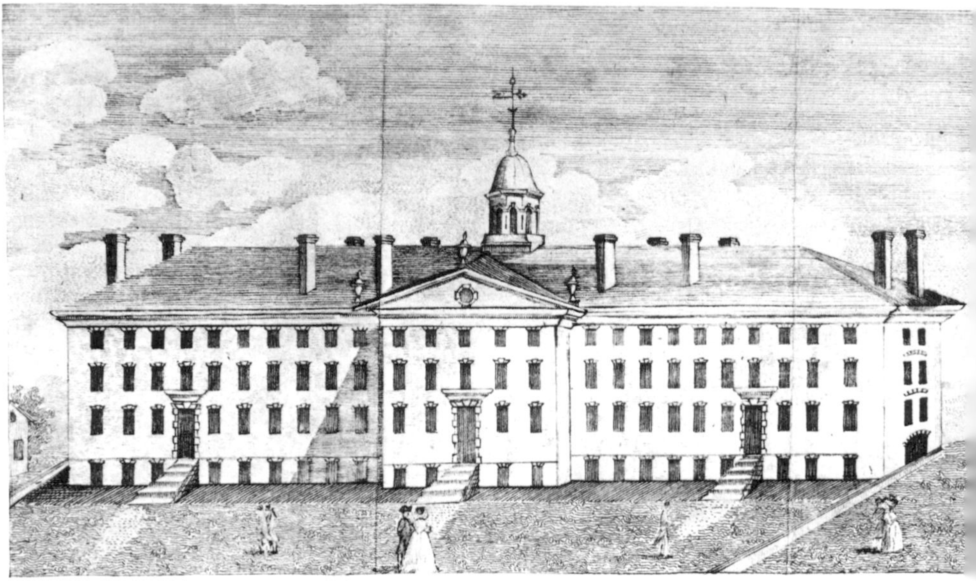

VIEW OF NASSAU HALL, COLLEGE OF NEW JERSEY, PRINCETON

determg all those quests. in the Congs. of U.S. wch. are now determd. by no less than 9.

Resd. that the asst. of 3 addl. States shall be necessy. in determg those questions for every 4 addl. Sts tht. may be admd. into the Union

Resd. that the sevl. Sts be advised to authorise their respective Delegs. to subscribe & ratify the above Resolves as part of the instrumt. of Union.[5]

Information was recd. by Congress from the Executive Council of Pennsylvania, that 80 Soldiers, who would probably be followed by the discharged Soldiers of Armand's Legion were on the way from Lancaster to Philadelpa. in spite of the expostulations of their officers, declaring that they would proceed to the seat of Congress and demand justice, and intimating designs agst. the Bank.[6] This information was committed to Mr. Hamilton, Mr. Peters, and Mr. Ellsworth for the purpose of conferring with the Executive of Pennsylvania and taking such measures as they should find necessary. The Committee after so conferring informed Congress, that it was the opinion of the Executive that the militia of Philadelpa. would probably not be willing to take arms before their resentments should be provoked by some actual outrage; that it would hazard the authority of Govt. to make the attempt, & that it would be necessary to let the soldiers come into the City, if the officers who had gone out to meet them, could not stop them[7]

At this information Mr. Izard Mr. Mercer & others being much displeased, signified that if the City would not support Congress, it was high time to remove to some other place. Mr Wilson remarked that no part of the U. States was better disposed towards Congs than Pennsylvania, where the prevailing sentiment was that Congress had done every thing that depended on them. After some conversation and directing Genl. St. Clair, who had gone out of Town, to be sent for, and it appearing that nothing further could be done at present, Congress adjourned.[8] The Secy. at War had set out for Virginia yesterday.[9] It was proposed to send for him, but declined as he had probably gone too great a distance, and Genl. St. Clair, it was supposed would answer.[10]

[1] *JCC*, XXIV, 403–4. On 5 August 1783 Congress reconstituted the committee by appointing Samuel Huntington (Conn.) and Stephen Higginson in the stead of Hamilton and JM (NA: PCC, No. 186, fol. 109).

[2] The customary frontier grievances of the eight thousand or more white settlers in the mountain valleys of North Carolina were heightened in 1783 by an act of the state's General Assembly opening a land office for the sale of public lands, including that in the Watauga-Holston area, upon which the westerners were squatters and from which the Indian titles had not wholly been cleared. This

statute, by threatening the frontier folk with economic dominance by absentee landlords and increased ravages by the Cherokees, added force to the earlier efforts of leaders in the back country to create an independent republic. Among these leaders were Arthur Campbell of southwestern Virginia and John Sevier and John Donelson of western North Carolina. They eagerly sought wealth from land speculations as well as public office.

Williamson and other men prominent in the government of North Carolina viewed its western lands much as JM did those of Virginia. To govern and defend them was a task too large for a state with an empty treasury, while to convey their title to Congress would result in reducing the state's annual financial quota. From these discontents, which were deepened by North Carolina's proviso in its short-lived offer of cession in April 1784 requiring Congress to confirm the speculators' land titles, arose later that year the abortive state of Franklin or Frankland, named for Benjamin Franklin and centered at Jonesborough and Greeneville, now in Tennessee (George Henry Alden, "The State of Franklin," *American Historical Review*, VIII [1902–3], 271–89; Samuel Cole Williams, *History of the Lost State of Franklin* [Johnson City, Tenn., 1924], pp. 5–33; Thomas P. Abernethy, *Western Lands and the American Revolution*, pp. 191, 290 ff.).

[3] See ed. n.

[4] Except for abbreviating words and altering capitalization and punctuation, Williamson copied all the relevant portion of the sixth paragraph of Article IX and paraphrased the brief Article XI (*JCC*, XIX, 220, 221).

[5] Although the provision in the motion for enlarging the Confederation was of liberal tenor, the motion also increased the degree of acquiescence required to enact ordinances dealing with important issues, thereby making less likely that ultra-liberal delegates from new "frontier" states could work their will.

The report of the reconstituted committee, submitted on 15 September 1783, altered Williamson's second and third proposed resolutions to read: "Whenever a fifteenth state is admitted the assent of eleven states shall become necessary; whenever a sixteenth State is admitted the assent of twelve states shall become necessary and thus onward, in such manner that the assent of at least three fourths of all the states in the union, shall ever be necessary" in deciding questions which in 1783 required the assent of at least nine states. Congress took no action on this report except to have it "entered and read" (*JCC*, XXV, 570–71). Vermont, of course, became the fourteenth state, but its admission on 4 March 1791 accorded with Article IV, section 3, paragraph 1, of the Constitution of the United States rather than with an amended Articles of Confederation.

[6] For Armand's Legion, see Pendleton to JM, 16 June 1783, n. 12; for the Bank of North America, *Papers of Madison*, III, 175, n. 16; IV, 19; 20, n. 7; 23, n. 3; 104, n. 1; 405, n. 11; VI, 494, n. 7. The "80 Soldiers" were of the Third Pennsylvania Regiment commanded by Colonel Richard Butler (*Pa. Archives*, 1st ser., X, 69). For Butler, see *Papers of Madison*, II, 281, n. 4. On 19 June the Pennsylvania Supreme Executive Council, meeting in the State House, transmitted to the state's delegates in Congress, which was also housed in that building, two letters of 17 June from Lancaster, one written by Butler and the other by Colonel William Henry, "containing information of the march, temper, and intentions, of part of the troops stationed at Lancaster" (*Colonial Records of Pa.*, XIII, 603). Butler emphasized his belief that the mutiny had been instigated from Philadelphia "& that the flame is supported by inimical or unconsiderate people." In his letter, Henry mentioned the rumors, current in Lancaster, that the mutineers intended "to rob the Bank, Treasury, &c. &c." and that they probably would be joined by the troops of Armand's Legion, then stationed in York (NA: PCC, No. 38, fols. 37–38, 123; *Diplomatic Correspondence of the United States*, I [1837], 14–17).

[7] James Ewing, vice president of Pennsylvania, rather than President John Dickinson, presided at the meetings of the Executive Council on 19 and 20 June. JM's account of the outcome of the conference, based upon an oral report of the Hamilton committee, contrasts with that given in the following excerpt from a footnote to the minutes of the Executive Council for 19 June: "the Committee and Council concurred in opinion that from the good order observed in their march, the tranquil temper of the troops already here, and the measures pursued by government to make them all easy and contented, the language of invitation, and good humour became more advisable than any immediate exertion of authority" (*Colonial Records of Pa.*, XIII, 603 n.; Syrett and Cooke, *Papers of Hamilton*, III, 400, n.1).

In his letter of 17 June, Butler informed President Dickinson that Captain James Christie would overtake the mutineers on their march toward Philadelphia and seek once again to have them abandon their plan. On 19 June Hamilton, on behalf of the committee, requested Major William Jackson, assistant secretary at war, to meet the marchers before they reached Philadelphia "and endeavor by every prudent method to engage them to return to the post they have left" (Syrett and Cooke, *Papers of Hamilton*, III, 397; *JCC*, XXIV, 415–16). Neither of these efforts succeeded. See JM Notes, 20 June 1783, and n. 1.

[8] General Arthur St. Clair, commander of the continental troops of Pennsylvania, was probably at his residence in Pottsgrove, Philadelphia County (William H. Smith, *St. Clair Papers*, I, 556, n. 2).

[9] Benjamin Lincoln, secretary at war, reached Richmond on the morning of 27 June. His baggage included a letter from JM to Joseph Jones, probably dated 17 June (Jones to JM, 28 June; Randolph to JM, 28 June 1783).

[10] On 19 June Congress also adopted the report of a committee (Hamilton, chairman, JM, and Bland), appointed eight days earlier, recommending that the state executives should be sent copies of Washington's correspondence, dated between 2 and 7 June, with his officers who had protested on their own and their troops' behalf against being furloughed or discharged before receiving at least part of their long overdue pay (NA: PCC, No. 152, XI, 295–305; JM Notes, 26 May 1783, and n. 2; Fitzpatrick, *Writings of Washington*, XXVI, 472–75; *JCC*, XXIV, 392, n. 1, 402–3).

Notes on Debates

MS (LC: Madison Papers). For a description of the manuscript of Notes on Debates, see *Papers of Madison*, V, 231–34.

Friday June 20.

The Soldiers from Lancaster came into the City under the guidance of Sergeants. They professed to have no other object than to obtain a settlement of accounts, which they supposed they had a better chance for at Philadelphia than at Lancaster. [see the Report of the Committee on that subject][1]

The Report of the Committee [see the Journal] on the territorial Cession of Virga. being taken up,[2] & the amendment on the Journal proposed by Mr. McHenry & Mr Clarke, being lost,[3] Mr. Bedford proposed that the second condition of the Cession be so altered as to read "that in order to comply with the said Condition, so far as the same is comprized within the Resolution of ocr. 10. 1780. on that subject," Commissioners as proposed by the Committee, be appointed &c. and that instead of "for the purposes mentioned in the said Condition," be substituted "Agreeable to that Resolution."[4] In support of this alteration, it was urged by Mr. McHenry, Mr. Bedford & Mr. Clarke that the terms used by Virga. were too comprehensive & indefinite.[5] In favor of the Report of the Committee, it was contended by Mr. Ellsworth that the alteration was unreasonable inasmuch as *Civil* expences were on the same footing of Equity as Military and that a compromize was the object of the Committee. Sundry members were of opinion that Civil expences were comprized in the Resolution of ocr. 10. 1780. Mr. Bland & Mr. Mercer acceded to the alteration proposed. Mr. Madison alone dissented, and therefore did not insist on a Call for the votes of the States. Mr. McHenry moved, but without being seconded "that the Commissioners instead of deciding finally should be authorized to report to Congress only.["]

In the course of debate Mr. Clarke laid before Congress the Remonstrance of New Jersey as entered on the Journal.

As the Report had been postponed at the instance of the President & other Delegates of N. Jersey, in order to obtain this answer from their Constituents, and as the Remonstrance was dated on the 14th. of June,[6] and was confessed privately by Mr. to have been in possession of the Delegates on Monday last, an unfairness was complained of.[7] They supposed that if it had been laid before Congress sooner the copy which would have been sent by the Virga. Delegates, might hasten the opening of the Land Office of that State.[8] Mr. Clarke said there were still good prospects, and he did not doubt that the time would yet come when Congress would draw a line limiting the States to the westward & say thus far shall ye go & no farther.[9] Mr. Bedford moved that with respect to the 4th & 5th. Conditions of the Cession "it be declared, that Clarke & his men, & the Virginia Line, be allowed the same bounty beyond the Ohio as was allowed by the U. S. to the same Ranks." This Motion was seconded by Congress adjourned without debating it; there being seven States only present and the spirit of compromise decreasing.[10]

From several circumstances there was reason to believe that R. Island, N. Jersey Pennsylvania & Delaware, if not Maryland also retained latent views of confining Virginia to the Alegheny Mountains[11]

Notice was taken by Mr. Madison of the Error in the Remonstrance, which recites "that Congress had declared the Cession of Virginia to be a partial one["][12]

[1] JM Notes, 19 June 1783, and n. 7. The brackets are JM's. The Hamilton committee's written report, submitted on 20 June, following the arrival of the mutineers in Philadelphia, advised Congress that John Pierce, the paymaster general of the army, who would soon return to the city from Washington's headquarters, had complete charge of arranging financial settlements with continental troops. In every instance the settlement could be reached only at the various posts where the troops were stationed. For this reason the mutinous "detachment" must return to Lancaster before having its demands considered. Money "will immediately be sent" there, continued the report, "to be paid to the troops on account of the month's pay heretofore directed to be advanced to them, the payment of which has hitherto been delayed by particular circumstances; together with notes for three months' pay intended to be advanced to the men when furloughed" (Syrett and Cooke, *Papers of Hamilton*, III, 400, and n. 1; *JCC*, XXIV, 413–15). For Pierce, see *Papers of Madison*, III, 115, n. 2; Fitzpatrick, *Writings of Washington*, XXVII, 53, and n. 87.

[2] For the appointment of "the Committee," including JM, and its report, see JM Notes, 4 June, n. 2; 5 June, n. 1; 6 June, and n. 1; 10 June; JM to Randolph, 10 June 1783, and n. 16; *JCC*, XXIV, 406–7.

[3] The report recommended that Congress, upon accepting the offer of Virginia to cede its lands north and west of the Ohio River to the United States, agree to assume the "necessary and reasonable expences" of both a military and civil nature incurred by Virginia in that area "since the commencement of the present war." The McHenry-Clark motion, if adopted, would have limited this pledge to cover solely the military costs. Of the seven states effectively represented in Congress only New Jersey, Pennsylvania, and Delaware favored the motion (*JCC*, XXIV, 406–7).

[4] The journal omits mention of the motion of Gunning Bedford, Jr. See JM Notes, 10 June 1783, n. 7. Strictly interpreted, the resolution of 10 October 1780 bound Congress financially to reimburse Virginia only for its military expenses "in subduing any of the British posts, or in maintaining forts or garrisons within and for the defence, or in acquiring any part of the territory that may be ceded or relinquished to the United States" (*JCC*, XVIII, 915). Therefore the McHenry and Bedford motions, although differently phrased, were similar in purpose. The committee's report recommended that three commissioners—one appointed by Congress, one by "the State of Virginia," and the third by those two—"should be authorised and empowered to adjust and liquidate the account of the necessary and reasonable expences incurred by the said State" for military operations and civil government in the Old Northwest (*JCC*, XXIV, 406–7). See also *Papers of Madison*, II, 138, n. 2.

[5] The "second condition" of the offer of cession of 2 January 1781 provided "That Virginia shall be allowed and fully reimbursed by the United States, her actual expenses in reducing the British posts at the Kaskaskies, and Saint Vincents; the expense of maintaining garrisons, and supporting civil government there, since the reduction of the said posts; and in general all the charges she has incurred, on account of the country, on the northwest side of the Ohio river, since the commencement of the present war" (*JHDV*, Oct. 1780, p. 80).

[6] JM Notes, 9 June, and nn. 2, 3; 10 June 1783; *JCC*, XXIV, 407–9.

[7] "Monday last" was 16 June. The blank left by JM after "Mr." should perhaps be filled with "Boudinot."

[8] Although the New Jersey delegates could not have known when the May session of the Virginia General Assembly would close, their delay in submitting the representation and remonstrance of their own state legislature to Congress prevented a copy of that document from reaching Richmond before the General Assembly adjourned on 28 June 1783 (*JHDV*, May 1783, p. 99).

[9] *Papers of Madison*, III, 304, n. 1.

[10] The acreage, either in the district of Kentucky or in the territory north of the Ohio River, pledged by the Virginia General Assembly to its officers and troops on "State establishment," including George Rogers Clark and those under his command, and to its officers and troops "upon the continental establishment," was more generous than that stipulated in the bounty-land ordinances of Congress (Hening, *Statutes*, XI, 559–65). See also *Papers of Madison*, II, 53, n. 3; 74; 75; V, 119, n. 20; JM Notes, 4 June 1783, and n. 1. The motion of Bedford, therefore, demanded in effect that Virginia break its contracts with the members of its armed forces. As JM suggests, by noting the decrease in "the spirit of compromise," Bedford aimed only to goad the Virginia delegates rather than to suggest an amendment which Congress would accept.

[11] *Papers of Madison*, II, 74–77; 176–77; 178 nn.; 196, n. 2; IV, 35, n. 10; 179, nn. 7, 8; 201; V, 200; 201, n. 8; VI, 291–92; 296, n. 38; 472, n. 4.

[12] *Papers of Madison*, VI, 471; 472, n. 3.

John Beckley to Edmund Randolph

RC (McGregor Library of University of Virginia Library). Cover addressed to "Edmund Randolph Esq:."

EDITORIAL NOTE

Absence from Richmond for ten days and inability to fulfill JM's request for a copy of the Virginia General Assembly's printed journal covering the recent sessions led Randolph to ask John Beckley, clerk of the House of Delegates, to prepare a summary of its proceedings for JM's information (JM to Randolph, 3 June; 10 June). Beckley's reply is included among JM's papers, for although addressed to Randolph, it was enclosed in and obviously was meant to be a part of Randolph's letter of 21 June 1783 to JM (*q.v.*).

friday evening [20 June 1783]

DR: SIR,

Always disposed to oblige yo. I will endeavor to give the information you request, in a hasty & deranged statement of Legislative proceedings promising that upon the view of closing the Session on Saturday Sevenight[1] they are drawing the Business to a finish. This day two Bills—for the relief of Debtors & for reforming County Courts were put off 'til next Session.[2] And on yesterday the Bill "respecting half Blood inheriting in common &c."—met the same fate.[3] A Bill passed to day for paying the principal & interest of the army debt in 8 years commencing in 1785. it contained Imposts of 9d: pr. Bushel of Salt; 4d. Beer, Ale, Cordage, Hemp, Snuff &c.[4] Congress Impost Bill is put off 'till Monday[.] it adopts the duties recommd. by Congress to be collected &c. by our own Officers & pd. ½ yearly to Congress Receiver and appropriates in aid thereof the Land & pole tax, as far as may be necessary—to continue only until principal & interest of debt is pd. as future Assembly shall after paying the yearly Interest, direct—other States to adopt the Impost also—& Govr. upon official information by Congress to declare it in force by proclamn. This Bill in its present shape, appears to me to be liable to this objection, that other states upon a view of their own particular Circumstances, will, or will not adopt a similar plan. if one State, only, refuses, it falls & thus prevents for the present a System to sink the National Debt. And on the other hand, withholding from Congress the power of collecting at the same time they reserve the right to divert this revenue after paying their annual proportion of principal & Interest, appears to me right: they sacredly pledge the faith of Virginia to pay that annual proportion.[5] The Citizen Bill comes on to morrow & will *I think* be put off.[6] As also a Bill to suspend Confiscations.[7] The report of a Committee of Congress on our Cession, not being acted on by Congress, will also be postponed unless the next post brings their ultimate decision.[8] A bill to fund the whole domestic Debt is in contemplation, but I think will be put off, because no collecting of revenue can be made 'till an other Session.[9]

They have adopted *your* resoltn. to revise Laws &c. since 1769. expence not exceeding 750£ & to be corrected &c. by two Judges of Chancery.[10] A resotn. to pay £50,000 to Congress receiver is also passed & they have admitted hemp to be recd. of defaulting s[heri]ffs and allow a discount of 10 pr. Centum for taxes becoming due under Revenue Act paid in advance.[11] They propose to pass an Appropriation Law & to amend Revenue Act so far as to repeal the duties laid by that & take off the tonnage &c.—also to preclude the receiving Commutables.[12]

I recollect nothing else National & wish yo. may be able to Decypher this.

Your respectful & obed. Servt.

John Beckley

[1] 28 June 1783 (*JHDV*, May 1783, pp. 93, 99).

[2] *Ibid.*, May 1783, p. 70; Jones to JM, 21 June 1783, and n. 3.

[3] *JHDV*, May 1783, p. 69; Randolph to JM, 14 June 1783, and n. 7.

[4] This bill, entitled, "an act to establish certain and adequate funds for the redemption of certificates granted to the officers and soldiers for their arrears of pay and depreciation," was approved by the Senate on 27 June, and signed the next day by the speaker of each house of the General Assembly (*JHDV*, May

1783, pp. 90, 98, 99). Besides omitting mention of an export duty of 4 shillings per hogshead on tobacco, Beckley's lists of "Imposts" would have been more precise if he had written: "On every bushel of salt, the sum of nine pence; on every gallon of distilled spirits, the sum of four pence; on every gallon of wine, the sum of four pence; on every hundred pounds of hemp, the sum of two shillings; on every hundred pounds of cordage, the sum of one shilling; on every gallon of beer, ale, or porter, the sum of four pence; on every pound of snuff the sum of one shilling" (Hening, *Statutes*, XI, 197, 201).

[5] Pendleton to JM, 26 May, n. 11; 2 June; Jones to JM, 8 June, and n. 5; 14 June, and n. 12; Randolph to JM, 14 June 1783, and n. 9.

[6] Beckley's surmise was accurate (*JHDV*, May 1783, p. 76). See also Jones to JM, 31 May, and n. 11; 8 June; 14 June; 21 June 1783, and n. 20.

[7] JM Notes, 30 May, n. 1; Randolph to JM, 14 June 1783, n. 7. Although a "bill for suspending the farther sale of confiscated property" had been introduced in the House of Delegates on 16 May and passed its second reading the next day, it thereafter was laid aside, possibly because the British military officers in the United States showed no inclination to enforce the terms of the preliminary peace treaty by returning slaves and other property (*JHDV*, May 1783, pp. 7, 9, 24). The journal of the House of Delegates during the rest of the session omits mention of an effort to revive the bill. See Delegates to Harrison, 4 Oct. 1783, and n. 7.

[8] Jones to JM, 25 May; 31 May; 8 June; 14 June; JM to Randolph, 10 June, and n. 16; Randolph to JM, 14 June; Instruction to Delegates, 27 June 1783.

[9] Randolph to JM, 24 May; Jones to JM, 25 May; 31 May; Pendleton to JM, 26 May; 2 June, n. 5; Ambler to JM, 1 June 1783. Again Beckley's prediction proved to be accurate. On 23 June the House of Delegates tabled a bill "to amend an act to amend and reduce the several acts of Assembly, 'for ascertaining certain taxes and duties, and for establishing a permanent revenue, into one act' " (*JHDV*, May 1783, p. 78).

[10] Randolph to JM, 18 July 1783, and n. 8.

[11] Pendleton to JM, 26 May, n. 11; Randolph to JM, 14 June 1783, and nn. 8, 9; *JHDV*, May 1783, pp. 27, 40, 44, 46, 52, 63; Hening, *Statutes*, XI, 189–91. The "Congress receiver" was George Webb.

[12] Pendleton to JM, 26 May 1783, n. 11; Hening, *Statutes*, XI, 247–49, 289–91.

Benjamin Harrison to Virginia Delegates

RC (NA: PCC, No. 71, II, 365–67). In Harrison's hand. Addressed to "The Honble: Virginia Delegates in Congress." Docketed, "Letter 20 June 1783 Govr. B. Harrison of Virginia to Honble. delegates of that state on a claim of Edward Cowper July 3 1783 Referred to the Agent of marine to report." The FC in the Virginia State Library varies from the original only in a few instances of punctuation and capitalization.

RICHMOND, June 20th: 1783.

GENTLEMEN:

I enclose you a Letter from mr. Cowper who with a Mr. Ballard were employ'd by me at the repeated request of Col. Richard H: Lee and the other Members of the Navy board at Philedelphia as Pilots to carry Hopkins's fleet round to this Country to attack Lord Dunmore[1] they empower'd me to make the most liberal promises of reward if they would undertake the Business, which they did do and arrived in Philedelphia in three Day[s] after they were apply'd to, where they remain'd six Weeks and were at last sent Home with no more Money than would bear their expences, but were promis'd their reward if they would keep a look out and be ready to go on Board the Fleet as soon as it should arrive here, this Service they also perform'd as far as it related to them being constantly on the look out till they were inform'd the Fleet had stear'd another Course.[2] They have made several applications for their Money but without Success, and have now called on me to use my Endeavours to obtain them that Justice they are so well entitled to; indeed they look to me for it declaring that my Promises alone induced them to undertake the Business, which I verily believe to be true. You will readily determine what a Man of Sensibility must feel when he is call'd on to make Satisfaction for Services render'd the public at his request that he is not able to comply with, and I dare say will use your endeavours to have them paid they expect a Hundred pounds each tho' I think they ought to be satisfied with Sixty.[3] You have also two resolutions of the Assembly which were sent to me to be forwarded.[4]

I am with respect Gentlemen Your most Obedient Servant

Benj Harrison

[1] The enclosure was a letter from Edward Cowper (Couper) (1736–1810) of Elizabeth City County, dated 27 May 1783, sent in the care of Commodore James Barron, Sr., to Governor Harrison (*Papers of Madison*, II, 84, n. 7; NA: PCC, No. 71, II, 369–70; *Lineage Book of the National Society of the Daughters of the American Revolution*, CVIII [1914], 183). Cowper, a Chesapeake Bay pilot, requested "at least £100" as compensation for his "Fatiguing Journey to and From Philadelphia" in December 1775 and January 1776, made as a result of an urgent appeal from Harrison to Archibald Cary of Chesterfield County, Va. For Cary, see *Papers of Madison*, III, 162, n. 3.

At that time Harrison and Richard Henry Lee were among the Virginia delegates attending the Second Continental Congress. By November and early December 1775, although the effective rule of Lord Dunmore, the royal governor of Virginia, had been reduced on land to Portsmouth and Norfolk at the mouth of the James River, British sea power enabled him to control Chesapeake Bay and the navigable rivers flowing into it. The Virginia Committee of Safety, in a letter of 11 November 1775, informed the Virginia delegates in Congress that the patriots did not "have a single Armed Vessell to give the exports & imports even the Shadow of Protection" (David J. Mays, *Edmund Pendleton*, II, 50).

About five weeks before the delegates received this letter, Richard Henry Lee had urged Congress to "advise Virginia and Maryland to raise a force by sea to destroy Lord Dunmore's power" (*JCC*, III, 482, 483). In December 1775 Lee became the member for Virginia on the newly created standing committee on the navy and Esek Hopkins was appointed "commander in chief of the fleet." On 2 December Congress resolved to dispatch two vessels to take or destroy Lord Dunmore's ships in Chesapeake Bay and to have Harrison go at once to Maryland to procure, "in conjunction with the delegates of that colony," additional ships for the same purpose (*JCC*, III, 311–12, 395–96, 420, 443). Probably while on this mission, Harrison wrote to Cary, asking him to send posthaste to Philadelphia two pilots to serve on the vessels which were expected to sail from that port to Chesapeake Bay. Without mentioning William Ballard (d. 1784), also of Elizabeth City County, Cowper stated in his letter to Harrison that he began his trip to Philadelphia on 14 December 1775 and did not reach home again until "38 Days" later.

2 If Cowper and Ballard reached Philadelphia "in three Day[s]," they obviously did so by sea. In his letter of 27 May 1783 to Harrison, Cowper complained that he had "never as Yet Rec'd One Shilling," even though Harrison had promised pay "to my Hearts Content." Instead of proceeding to Chesapeake Bay, the "Fleet" of Commodore Hopkins sailed to New Providence in the Bahama Islands (*JCC*, IV, 285, 333; Boyd, *Papers of Jefferson*, XV, 578–82; Jefferson to JM, 1 June 1783, and n. 6).

3 In his report to Congress on 9 July 1783, accepted a week later, Robert Morris stated that the Ballard-Cowper claim was not within his immediate jurisdiction, for their alleged services had been rendered prior to 1782. He suggested that they should be told to apply to "the Commissioner appointed to settle the Accounts of the United States in Virginia" (NA: PCC, No. 137, II, 611–14). The claims were finally settled under provision of a federal statute of 27 March 1792 whereby Cowper and Ballard's estates on 27 April 1792 were each awarded $172.95, including interest from 21 January 1776 (*American State Papers: Documents, Legislative and Executive, of the Congress of the United States . . . Class IX. Claims* [Washington, 1834], pp. 387, 388). On 28 June 1783 the Virginia General Assembly appointed both Cowper and Ballard among the examiners of Chesapeake Bay pilots. Cowper served long in this capacity, but Ballard was murdered in 1784, allegedly by a French seaman (*JHDV*, May 1783, p. 98; Hening, *Statutes*, XI, 185–89, 299–303; *JCSV*, III, 390).

4 These resolutions were the instruction of 17 June 1783 *in re* fortifications (*q.v.*), and that of 4 June 1783 *in re* contracts. On 3 July Congress referred the latter "to the Superintendant of Finance to take Order" (*JCC*, XXIV, 425; Delegates to Harrison, 5 July 1783). In a letter of 21 July to Harrison, Morris returned the resolution to Harrison and asked him to specify "what particular papers" the General Assembly had in mind. Morris added that many clerks would be required to work a year to make copies of "all the accounts and vouchers." By letter on 9 August Harrison assured Morris that the resolution and a request for a definition of its scope had been sent to John Tyler, speaker of the House of Delegates (Executive Letter Book, 1783–1786, pp. 181, 183, 218, MS in Va. State Library). In a letter of 15 August to Morris, enclosing a copy of Tyler's explanation, Harrison urged compliance with the resolution, for he was convinced that "some discoveries" of "great misconduct in the officers" would be uncovered (*ibid.*, p. 187). See also Delegates to Harrison, 14 Aug.; 23 Aug. 1783, and n. 9.

Instruction to Virginia Delegates *in re* Guards for Public Buildings

RC (NA: PCC, No. 75, fols. 384–85). Docketed: "An act of the State of Virginia for the enlisting Guards June 20. 1783 Recd in Congress July 23 Referred to the Secretary at War."

[20 June 1783]

General Assembly begun and held at the City of Richmond on Monday the fifth Day of May in the year of our Lord 1783

An Act directing the enlistment of Guards for the public prison & Stores

Whereas it is necessary that proper Guards should be kept at this time over the public prison and certain places where public Stores are deposited and it is meant by this Assembly to take measures for relieving the militia from such Duty as soon as possible Be it therefore enacted that it shall and may be lawful for the Governor with Advice of Council to cause as many men not exceeding twenty five with proper Officers to be enlisted as Guards for public Service as he the said Governor with advice of Council may deem necessary and may retain the same in Service so long as the public exigencies may require Provided always that if the Delegates representing this State in General Congress shall on application procure such a number of the soldiers of the line of this State enlisted for three years in the Continental Army as may be sufficient for the purposes aforesaid then the said Guards and Officers enlisted to command the same shall be discharged[1]

1783 June 20
Passed the House of Delegates
John Beckley CHD

June 20th 1783
Passed the Senate
Will Drew CS[2]

A true Copy Teste John Beckley CHD[3]

[1] On 6 June, after agreeing to this proposal of the committee of the whole house on the state of the commonwealth, the Virginia House of Delegates appointed William Ronald of Powhatan County chairman of a committee of six members, including Richard Henry Lee, Joseph Jones, and Patrick Henry, to draft an appropriate measure. They submitted a bill on 18 June (*JHDV*, May 1783, pp. 40, 41, 65, 68, 69, 72). The preamble, besides justifying the law as a means of "relieving the militia," might aptly have added the saving of expense by shifting the cost of the "Guards" from the treasury of Virginia to that of Congress. In his letter to the delegates, forwarding a copy of the act, Governor Harrison stated that he viewed it with "Mortification" (Harrison to Delegates, 4 July). Its supporters may have held that the "public stores" included some property owned

by the Confederation, and that the inmates of the "public prison" included or in the future would include alleged offenders against the ordinances of Congress. On 30 June 1783, with the advice of the Council of State, Harrison directed Lieutenant David Mann to recruit twenty-five men as guards, promising each of them the wages and rations assured to soldiers in the continental service (Executive Letter Book, War Office, 1783–1786, p. 57, MS in Va. State Library).

[2] William Drew and John Beckley, clerks of the Senate and House of Delegates, respectively.

[3] In his report on 28 July, Benjamin Lincoln, secretary at war, pointed out that "it would be inexpedient to order any of the Troops of the Virginia line, inlisted for three years" to perform the requested guard duty, for they would be discharged from service shortly after a copy of the definitive treaty of peace, which was "hourly expected," had reached Congress. Lincoln added that if "Congress approve these sentiments," it "will please to resolve" that, in its opinion, the number of troops proposed by Virginia as "Guards for the public prisons and stores" was "not more" than was necessary for that purpose (*JCC*, XXIV, 455). Lincoln's recommendation reflected his interpretation of the following portion of Article VI of the Articles of Confederation: "nor shall any body of forces be kept up by any state, in time of peace, except such number only, as in the judgment of the united states, in congress assembled, shall be deemed requisite to garrison the forts necessary for the defence of such state" (*JCC*, XIX, 216). For the outcome of Lincoln's proposal, see Motion *in re* Armed Vessels, 28 July 1783; also *JCSV*, III, 338, 363.

Notes on Debates

MS (LC: Madison Papers). For a description of the manuscript of Notes on Debates, see *Papers of Madison*, V, 231–34.

EDITORIAL NOTE

These notes, comprising the final entry made by JM of the deliberations of Congress until he resumed his records in 1787, are dated only 21 June, though they summarize occurrences relating to the mutiny as late as 26 June. After its sessions on 21 June, Congress was adjourned until it reconvened at Princeton, N.J., on 30 June 1783. At least the last three paragraphs of the present notes, which closely resemble the wording of JM's letter to Randolph on 30 June, were written after the Virginia delegates' dispatch of 24 June to Governor Harrison (*qq.v.*).

Saturday June 21. 1783

The mutinous soldiers presented themselves, drawn up in the Street before the State House where Congress had first assembled.[1] The Executive Council of the State sitting under the same roof, was called on for the proper interposition. President Dickinson came in, and explained the difficulty under actual circumstances, of bringing out the militia of the place for the suppression of the mutiny. He thought that without some outrages on persons or property the temper of the militia could not be relied on. Genl. St. Clair then in Philada. was sent for; and desired to use his interposition, in order to prevail on the troops to return to the Barracks. His report gave no encouragement. In this posture of things It was proposed by Mr. Izard that Congs. shd. adjourn. It was proposed by Mr. Hamilton that Genl. St. Clair in concert with the Executive Council of State should take order for terminating the mutiny. Mr. Reed moved that the Genl. shd. endeavor to withdraw the troops by assuring them of the disposition of Congs. to do them justice. It was finally agreed that Congs. shd. remain till the usual hour of adjournment, but without taking any step in relation to the alledged grievances of the Soldiers, or any other business whatever. In the mean time the Soldiers remained in their position, without offering any violence, individuals only occasionally uttering offensive words and wantonly pointing their muskets to the Windows of the Hall of Congress.[2] No danger from premeditated violence was apprehended, But it was observed that spirituous drink from the tipling houses adjoining began to be liberally served out to the Soldiers, & might lead to hasty excesses.[3] None were committed however, and about 3 oC. the usual hour, Congs. adjourned; the Soldiers, tho' in some instances offering a mock obstruction, permitting the members to pass thro' their ranks. They soon after retired themselves to the Barracks.[4]

In the Evening Congress re-assembled and passed the Resolutions on the Journal, authorizing a Committee to confer anew with the Executive of the State and in case no satisfactory grounds shd. appear for expecting prompt & adequate exertions for suppressing the mutiny & supporting the public authority, authorizing the President with the advice of the Committee, to summon the members to meet at Trenton or Princeton in New Jersey.[5]

The Conference with the Executive produced nothing but a repetition of doubts concerning the disposition of the militia to act, unless some actual outrage were offered to persons or property. It was even doubted whether a repetition of the insult to Congress would be a sufficient provocation.[6]

During the deliberations of the Executive, and the suspense of the Committee, Reports from the Barracks were in constant vibration. At one moment the Mutineers were penitent & preparing submissions: The next they were meditating more violent measures. Sometimes the Bank was their object; then the seizure of the members of Congress with whom they imagined an indemnity for their offence might be stipulated. On Tuesday about 2 OClock the efforts of the State authority being despaired of, & the Reports from the Barracks being unfavorable, the Committee advised the President to summon Congress to meet at Princeton which he did verbally as to the members present, leaving behind him a general Proclamation for the Press.[7]

After the departure of Congs. the Mutineers submitted, and most of them accepted furloughs under the Resolution of Congress, on that subject. At the time of submission they betrayed their leaders. the chief of whom proved to be a Mr. Carberry a deranged officer, and a Mr. Sullivan a lieutenant of Horse; both of whom made their escape. Some of the most active of the Sergeants also ran off.[8]

[1] JM Notes, 19 June, and nn. 6, 7; 20 June 1783, and n. 1. The mutinous soldiers from Lancaster, having marched into Philadelphia "in a very orderly manner" on the morning of 20 June, took possession of the arsenal and "powder House" in the city and were joined by many of the soldiers quartered in the barracks. There, the next day, on the pretense that they had been "deserted" by their officers, they chose a committee primarily composed of sergeants to convey an unsigned petition to the Pennsylvania Supreme Executive Council in session at the State House. Although Congress on Friday, 20 June, had decided not to reconvene until the following Monday, President Boudinot succeeded in assembling in the same building delegates from six states by 1:00 P.M. on Saturday. Even before that hour the State House was surrounded by armed and mutinous soldiers to a number varying in the several primary sources from 280 to about 500 (Burnett, *Letters*, VII, 193, 195, 197, 199).

[2] Before President John Dickinson of Pennsylvania came to the "Hall of Congress," he and the Executive Council had been faced with the "petition" threatening them with armed force if they did not within "twenty minutes" empower the mutineers to elect their own commissioned officers with authority to redress the grievances. While the president and Council were deliberating, they were presented with Congress' request, borne by General Arthur St. Clair, that the Pennsylvania executive adopt measures "to draw the soldiers off to their barracks." Reflecting either their trust that a conciliatory course would be sufficient or their fear that the militia in the city would not oppose the mutineers, the president and Executive Council rejected the ultimatum, directed Dickinson to convey it to Congress, and agreed to a mildly worded resolution promising to receive a statement of the soldiers' claims, "if decently expressed and constitutionally presented" (*Colonial Records of Pa.*, XIII, 605). "Mr. Reed" was Jacob Read, a delegate from South Carolina.

[3] The State House was in the Middle Ward of Philadelphia. The nearest of the "tipling houses" was the State House Inn, directly across Chestnut Street. The business enterprises of the ward in 1783 included at least eighteen inns, numerous shops of "grocers," who usually sold liquor, and a few breweries and "beer houses" (*Pa. Archives*, 3d ser., XVI, 789–808; Penn Mutual Life Insurance Company, *The Independence Square Neighborhood* [Philadelphia, 1926], p. 17).

[4] Elias Boudinot's correspondence makes clear that the mutineers, who had kept the members of Congress "Prisoners in a manner near 3 hours," marched back to their barracks at "half past 3 O'clock" in the afternoon. At four o'clock he wrote a letter, to be sped to Washington by a mounted courier, briefly describing the course of the mutiny until that hour, expressing fear that "the worst is not yet

come" and stating that the members of Congress who had convened that afternoon, although lacking one member of being numerous enough to comprise a quorum, "unanimously directed" him to request that Washington initiate "a movement of some of your best troops, on whom you can depend, under these circumstances, toward this City." Boudinot also suggested to Washington that if he could induce the paymaster general "to close the Accounts of the Soldiery with more expedition," the dangerous situation would be greatly eased (Burnett, *Letters*, VII, 193–94, 195). Upon receiving this letter at 3:00 P.M. on 24 June, Washington took immediate steps to hasten about 1,500 troops, commanded by Major General Robert Howe, to Philadelphia by way of Princeton and Trenton (Fitzpatrick, *Writings of Washington*, XXVII, 32–37; JM to Randolph, 30 June 1783, n. 6).

[5] *JCC*, XXIV, 410. The committee was still the one with Hamilton as chairman. He drafted the resolutions. In the third, which is not embraced in JM's summary, Congress issued a pro forma direction to Benjamin Lincoln, secretary at war, who was then two days' journey from Philadelphia on his way to Richmond, to acquaint Washington with "the state and disposition" of the mutinous troops so that he "may take immediate measures to dispatch to this city, such force as he may judge expedient." This directive, of course, had been mostly anticipated by Boudinot in his four o'clock letter to Washington. Writing again to him at eleven o'clock that evening after Congress adjourned, Boudinot enclosed a copy of the resolutions, mentioned that they were "secret till we see what the issue of the conference with the Supreme Executive Council will produce," and emphasized that "it has become absolutely necessary that this wound to the dignity of the Fœderal Government should not go unpunished" (Burnett, *Letters*, VII, 194).

[6] On Sunday, 22 June, at a meeting of the Executive Council in President Dickinson's home, Hamilton and Ellsworth presented a copy of the resolutions of Congress adopted the night before and explained that by "effectual measures" for "supporting the publick authority" Congress meant the use of militia to "reduce the soldiers to obedience," provided that the "temper of the city," secretly ascertained, should sustain the use of force. Although the Council agreed to canvass the feeling "with all possib'e secrecy and dispatch," its members pointed out that no "ammunition was to be procured." Hamilton retorted that "any quantity of musquet and cannon cartridge might be commanded in fifteen minutes" (*Colonial Records of Pa.*, XIII, 606–7).

On 23 June, when Hamilton again appeared before the Executive Council, he was informed that the militia should not be called out, for its field officers and leading citizens of the city relied upon the willingness "of the soldiery" to be "pacific" if they were granted what was "just and reasonable." The next morning the Executive Council reiterated this conclusion (*ibid.*, XIII, 609–10). In a letter of 29 June 1783 to Governor George Clinton of New York, Hamilton characterized the conduct of the executive of Pennsylvania as "to the last degree weak & disgusting" (Syrett and Cooke, *Papers of Hamilton*, III, 402–7, 408; Hamilton to JM, 6 July 1783, and nn. 3, 5).

[7] President Boudinot's decision on the afternoon of 24 June to put into effect the resolution of Congress, passed three days earlier, reflected not only the accumulating evidence of the determination of the Pennsylvania Supreme Executive Council to refrain from employing force, but also the rumor current that afternoon of an imminent attack by the mutineers upon the Bank of North America. At the same time this rumor finally induced the Executive Council to take immediate steps for calling out the militia (*Colonial Records of Pa.*, XIII, 611).

In his proclamation, President Boudinot summoned the members of Congress to convene at Princeton on 26 June 1783 (Burnett, *Letters*, VII, 195–96, 199–200). The *Pennsylvania Packet*, which together with the other newspapers of Philadelphia had omitted all mention of the mutiny, printed a copy of the proclamation, misdated 25 June, in its issue of 26 June. Boudinot in a letter of 23 June 1783 had expressed confidentially his gratification to his brother Elisha that Congress would almost certainly "adjourn to Princeton" in their own state. "I wish Jersey," the president continued, "to show her readiness on this occasion as it may fix Congress as to their permanent residence" (Burnett, *Letters*, VII, 195). The College of New Jersey (Princeton College), of which he was a trustee, quickly offered the use of its buildings to Congress.

8 Although not recognized at once, the subsidence of the mutiny began almost simultaneously with Boudinot's issuance of his proclamation. That morning, in compliance with the request of the Executive Council three days before, many of the soldiers at the barracks made known that they had elected a committee of officers to present their claims. They also abandoned their plan, if it existed, to attack the bank. On 25 June, after failing to induce the Council to accept a statement of their grievances, signed on their behalf by Sergeant James Bennett, and probably realizing that they could not resist the militia and the troops summoned from Washington's army, the mutineers empowered a committee of officers to submit to the Council a petition praying for pardon. At the same time "6 of the leading Serjeants" came to President Dickinson and "put the blame" for the uprising upon Henry Carberry (d. 1822), a supernumerary captain of the Third Pennsylvania Regiment, and John Sullivan, a lieutenant of Colonel Stephen Moylan's dragoons. On the evening of 25 June President Dickinson wrote to President Boudinot, "I am informed by Officers in whom I am persuaded I may confide, that the Mutiny is suppress, except among some of the Lancaster Soldiers." By noon of the following day these too, had made their submission and by nightfall were on the road back to Lancaster (*Colonial Records of Pa.*, XIII, 610–13; *Pa. Archives*, 1st ser., X, 60–62; *Diplomatic Correspondence of the United States*, I, 22–25, 35–36). For the course of the mutiny as described on 18 August 1783 to the Pennsylvania General Assembly by President Dickinson and the Supreme Executive Council, see *Colonial Records of Pa.*, XIII, 654–66.

Carberry and Sullivan succeeded in boarding a British ship at Chester, Pa., and reaching England. In the spring of 1784 Carberry returned to his native state of Maryland and, arrested in Baltimore, was jailed in Annapolis. Pleading guilty and throwing himself upon the mercy of the court, he apparently escaped without penalty. In 1791 he served as a captain under General Arthur St. Clair in the Northwest Territory; in 1792–1794 was a captain of United States infantry; and in 1813–1815 was colonel commanding the 36th United States Regiment of Infantry (Varnum L. Collins, *Continental Congress at Princeton*, p. 12, n. 1; Burnett, *Letters*, VII, 499, 507, 531, 599–600; VIII, 2–4, 397, 531, 852–53).

Soon after the mutiny, a number of noncommissioned officers and privates who had been prominent participants, were tried by a military court at Lancaster. Two were sentenced to death and the others to varying degrees of corporal punishment. They, as well as several officers who had been less directly implicated, received congressional pardons in September 1783. By the summer of 1785 Lieutenant Sullivan had returned to Philadelphia but was not arrested. His attempt to procure back pay was frustrated when on 27 June 1786 his military records were closed with the notation that he had quit the continental service "without leave." Two years later he seems to have shared in an abortive movement to drive the Spanish from the lower Mississippi River valley (*Pa. Archives*, 1st ser., X, 63, 67, 69, 72, 74, 290–93, 320, 323–25, 575–80; *Diplomatic Correspondence of the United States*, I, 37–38; Burnett, *Letters*, VII, 208, n. 3, 227, and n. 2, 293, and n. 4, 297, 499, 517, 531, 599; VIII, 2–4, 397, 643, n. 5, 852; Delegates to Harrison, 5 July, and n. 4; JM to Jefferson, 20 Sept. 1783; Varnum L. Collins, *Continental Congress at Princeton*, p. 13, n. 1).

From Joseph Jones

RC (LC: Madison Papers). Cover missing.

RICHMOND 21st. June 1783

DR. SIR.

Yours of the 10th.[1] I have duly received by the Post this week. we are now as usual puting to sleep many of the bills that have employed our time and attention for great part of this Session[2] among them, two —one for the benefit of Debtors—the other for regulating the proceedings in the County Courts. these were thought to have some connection and ought to rest together. Mr. Mason introduced and patronised the Debtors bill. I was not in the House when it was read but understand it allowed all Creditors to obtain Judgment, but suspended Execution, rather permitted it for a fifth of the debt annually, for five years comprehending as well foreign as domestic Creditors I came into the house during the debate and from the observations of R. H. L. and those who opposed the bill its principle was severely reprobated. Mr. Mason and C. M. T. warmly supported it and pronounced it indispensably necessary to preserve the people from ruin and the Country independent. the disposition of the members however was so prevalent for lopping of all business not really necessary that the latter Gentlemen were obliged to submit to its being refd. to the next Session.[3] this bill at least so far as respected british Creditors wod. have had more advocates but for the late period at which it was introduced and because there already exists and will continue in force untill the 1st. of Decr. a law that prohibits suits for or on accot. of British Subjects.[4] The bill Granting revenue to Congress to discharge this states quota of the common debt was taken into consideration yesterday but being very imperfect was postponed untill Monday next.[5] my endeavours to get the impost granted as a general revenue will be fruitless so universal is the opposition to giving it otherwise than to be credited to the States.[6] the collection too must be by the naval officers and by him pd. to the continental receiver quarterly.[7] The land Tax is to be collected by the Sheriffs and paid into the Treasury and by him to the Continental receiver the deficiency if any to be made up out of the poll Tax.[8] If the impost was general these funds wod. be adequate. Our people will not submit the Collectors to be amenable to Congress. If both collections were to be paid to the Continental receiver the bond given payable to Congress and judgments to be moved for by the continental receiver, the revenue could not be well diverted to any other purposes, and wod. answer the object, and nearly come up to the plan of Congress. duplicate receipts or settlements might be lodged with the Treasurer[9] of the amount of the revenues by the respective collectors and the State thereby informed of the proceeds annually independent of the general communication from Congress. The Letter of the Delegates and the report of the Committee respecting the Cession has been read and refd. to a Committee of the whole. this not being the act of Congress a disposition prevails not to take it up.[10] If we have time and the members patience to do it I shall press its being taken up and the Delegates fully instructed to close the matter with Congress if to be effected or the cession be void by a certain day and this I wod. have fixed to some day after the meeting of the next Session.[11] The accounts from the Illinois are before the Executive and a Committee of the House appointed to inspect them. they are at present incompleat and any information of the balance must be altogether conjecture or I shod. mention it.[12] A bill has passed the Delegates establishing funds for paying the interest and sinking the principal of the debt due to our line of the Army for pay & Depreciation including the State Troops eight years is allotted for extinguishing the debt 9d. on salt 4d. on wine 4d. on spirits with some imposts on malt Liqeur and a duty of 10s per Hhd. on Tobacco exported, are the funds which are thot. adequate to pay the interest and extinguish the principal in that time. the deficiency if any is to come out of the poll Tax.[13] We have an empty Treasury or so nearly so as not to have sufficient to pay the Delegates wages and the collection of the Taxes being postponed I think the civil list and Delegates to Congress will be reduced to difficulties.[14] I forgot to mention above, that the report of the Com: on the cession has not fully removed the fears of our people respecting Indian purchases & Grants to companies. their jealousy of Congress on that head is very strong.[15] Mr. Lee tells me he sets out to day for Philadelphia I expect he will be a fortnight at least before he reaches the City. I may spend two or three months there this fall.[16] The new arrangement of the british ministry one would think cannot last long—like oil & water jumbled together they will soon Separate.[17] their existence will I hope be extended to the accomplishment of the definitive Treaty. Hartly appears to have been a friend to its conclusion.[18] several of the banished Scotsmen and some refugees have returned to this Sta[te] three or four to Petersburg of the former, whose presence has so provoked the people of that neighbourhood they were to meet yesterday to order them away.[19] The Cit[izen] bill stands the order of the day for Monday.[20] The opponents of this bill think it premature as the definitive Treaty has not appeared. they also assert it to be unwise and impos[sible] to refuse the admission of these or any others disposed [to] settle in the Country. a descrimination will however if the business is brot. on, take place with respect to refugees whatever may be the fate of the banished Merchants the settlement of this business is the more necessary as there is a very severe law in force agt. British Subjects and th[ose] who have left the Country and joined them, which will not I think be repealed unless the Citizen bill be taken up.[21] This with the revenue bill for the Continental debt, the cession, the alteration proposed in ascertaining the quota of each State[22] & Nathans demand which is to come on next monday[23] are the principal matters remaining to be considered, and will be finished in the course of the next week. I shall leave Richmond this day week. your letters after the receip[t] of this please to direct to Fredericksburg.[24] Monroe will send Mr. Jefferson his letter.[25]

Yr. friend & servt.

Jos: Jones

[1] The contents of JM's missing letter of 10 June to Jones probably resembled those of his letters on that day to Jefferson and Randolph (*qq.v.*).

[2] Between 14 June, when Jones had last written to JM (*q.v.*) and 20 June, both inclusive, the Virginia House of Delegates had put "to sleep" until the session of October 1783 six petitions or bills relating to an individual's grievance or the desire of a particular locality, and five general measures. Of the five the three not mentioned by Jones were: (1) "to indemnify all officers of the armies of the United States, and others, for acts necessarily done in execution of military orders"; (2) "to amend the several acts concerning marriages"; and (3) "to make the half-blood inheritable to lands or slaves descended from, or given by, their common ancestors" (*JHDV*, May 1783, pp. 56, 60, 61, 62, 67, 69). See also for (1), *JHDV*, May 1783, pp. 24, 41; JM Notes, 6 May, and n. 1; 7 May 1783. See also for (3) Randolph to JM, 14 June 1783, and n. 7; Beckley to Randolph, 20 June 1783.

[3] During the session of May 1783 the members of the Virginia General Assembly were sufficiently in accord to defer the collection of several types of taxes but were much divided on the issue of enacting a stay law for the relief of citizens who apparently could not discharge their overdue obligations to private creditors, both domestic and foreign. The county courts, in entertaining suits brought by creditors, varied in their leniency or harshness of judgment and perhaps, too, in the evidence required to validate a debt. Stevens Thomson Mason had already drafted a "Debtors bill," when, on 17 June, he was named by the House of Delegates the chairman of a committee to prepare such a measure. Immediately thereafter, as chairman of the Committee for Courts of Justice, he also introduced, "according to order," a bill "for reforming county courts." Both these proposals, having been referred to a committee of the whole house on the state of the commonwealth, were deferred on 20 June for further consideration until the session of the General Assembly in October 1783. The vote "putting to sleep" the court bill, not having been demanded by a delegate, is not recorded in the journal, but the result was probably similar to the 66–23 division whereby the House of Delegates

tabled the debtors' bill. In that division Jones did not vote, but "R. H. L." (Richard Henry Lee) supported the deferral and "C. M. T." (Charles Mynn Thruston) opposed it (*JHDV*, May 1783, pp. 61, 62, 63, 70). See also Randolph to JM, 9 May, and nn. 4, 5; 15 May, and n. 5; 24 May, and n. 3; Jones to JM, 14 June 1783.

[4] Jones referred to the statute of 1 July 1782, as amended on 22 December 1782 (Hening, *Statutes*, XI, 176–80; *Papers of Madison*, VI, 416, n. 3). See also Harrison to Delegates, 9 May 1783, and n. 6.

[5] On 20 June a committee of the whole house debated the bill "to ascertain certain duties and imposts, and to establish adequate funds for the discharge of this State's quota of the principal and interest of the debt of the United States," but "not having time to go through the same" received permission of the House of Delegates to resume the discussion on 23 June. For the failure of the Senate to pass this bill, see Pendleton to JM, 26 May 1783, n. 11.

[6] For the extensive but ultimately unfavorable attention given to the impost by the House of Delegates during the May session of the General Assembly, see *JHDV*, May 1783, pp. 48, 49, 63, 65, 68, 69, 70, 82, 84–85, 86, 93; Randolph to JM, 15 May, and n. 2; 24 May, and nn. 5, 6; 21 June; 28 June; Jameson to JM, 24 May, and n. 3; Jones to JM, 25 May, and n. 9; 14 June, and n. 7; 28 June; Pendleton to JM, 26 May 1783, and n. 5.

[7] Pendleton to JM, 4 May, and n. 8; Randolph to JM, 15 May, and n. 2; Jones to JM, 14 June 1783, and n. 12. The continental receiver general for Virginia was George Webb.

[8] In this sentence Jones reverted to the bill which he had mentioned three sentences before. For the fate of this measure, see Jones to JM, 28 June 1783. Before adjourning on 28 June, the May session of the General Assembly enacted into law a measure which early in 1784 might yield some financial benefit to Congress. See Pendleton to JM, 26 May 1783, n. 11.

[9] Jacquelin Ambler.

[10] On 19 June Governor Harrison had transmitted to the House of Delegates a copy of the report of a congressional committee on Virginia's offer to cede the lands north and west of the Ohio River (*JHDV*, May 1783, p. 68; JM to Randolph, 10 June, and n. 16; Delegates to Harrison, 17 June, n. 1). See also Randolph to JM, 9 May, and n. 8; 14 June; Jones to JM, 31 May; 14 June, and n. 14; JM Notes, 4 June, and n. 2; 6 June; 10 June 1783.

[11] Instruction to Delegates, 27 June 1783.

[12] In submitting to the House of Delegates on 29 May and 18 and 25 June preliminary and incomplete financial reports from the commissioners to settle western accounts, Governor Harrison commented that many of the claims were fraudulent and their total amount "exceeds conjecture" (Executive Letter Book, 1783–1786, pp. 137, 156, 162, MS in Va. State Library). See also *Papers of Madison*, VI, 475, n. 3; Jones to JM, 8 June; 14 June, and n. 27. On 19 June the report submitted the day before by Harrison was referred to the select committee, George Nicholas, chairman, appointed 16 June, on the claim of Simon Nathan (*JHDV*, May 1783, pp. 60, 64, 68). This committee apparently confined its recommendations concerning the report to the claims of a few individuals, including Simon Nathan and Oliver Pollock (*JHDV*, May 1783, pp. 83, 94, 97).

[13] This bill, which was adopted by the House of Delegates on 20 June and by the Senate four days later, received the signature of the speaker of each chamber on 28 June 1783 (*JHDV*, May 1783, pp. 70–71, 79, 98, 99; Hening, *Statutes*, XI, 196–203). In his summary, Jones omitted the impost duties on snuff, hemp, and cordage. In citing ten shillings per hogshead as the export duty on tobacco, he combined the four shillings stipulated by the law with the inspection tax of six shillings required by another statute enacted at the same session of the General

Assembly. If the annual income derived from the four-shilling export duty and from the imposts fell short of the sum needed to pay the interest and one-eighth of the principal on the certificates issued to the troops, the deficiency was to be covered by revenue derived from the poll tax on slaves. Holders of the interest certificates could use them in lieu of money or commodities for paying taxes (*ibid*., XI, 197, 202, 227–28).

14 Randolph to JM, 14 June 1783, and nn. 5, 6. See also Randolph to JM, 9 May, and n. 4; 24 May, and n. 7; Jones to JM, 31 May 1783.

15 JM to Jefferson, 20 May, n. 5; Jones to JM, 8 June; 28 June; JM to Randolph, 10 June 1783, and n. 16.

16 JM to Randolph, 6 May, n. 9; Jones to JM, 28 June 1783.

17 *Papers of Madison*, VI, 504, n. 3; Jones to JM, 8 June 1783, and n. 22.

18 Pendleton to JM, 4 May, and n. 6; Jones to JM, 8 June 1783, and n. 23.

19 The reopening of ocean-borne trade with the British facilitated, and the provisional treaty of peace appeared to some persons to permit, the return of Loyalists and Scottish merchants to Virginia. Among the "banished Scotsmen" were probably the agents of a Glasgow "tobacco lord," William Cuninghame (d. 1789), who had owned much property in Virginia before 1776 (Robert Renwick, Sir John Lindsay, and George Eyre-Todd, *History of Glasgow* [3 vols.; Glasgow, 1921–34], III, 242, 246–47). Addressing Governor Harrison from Petersburg, these agents, promising to conform with "the Laws of the State," claimed his protection while they sought to re-establish Cuninghame's old commercial ties and reach an accommodation with his numerous debtors (Transcript of the Manuscript Books and Papers of the Commission of Enquiry into the Losses and Services of the American Loyalists . . . in the Public Record Office of England, 1783–1790, LVIII, 421–32, in the New York Public Library). If there was a meeting at Petersburg on 20 June "to order" these agents "away," they may have defied that admonition, but they could not disregard Harrison's proclamation of 2 July, warning all Loyalists and other British subjects to leave Virginia "forthwith" (*ibid*., LVIII, 432; *Cal. of Va. State Papers*, III, 499; Randolph to JM, 12 July 1783, and n. 2).

In the main, the proclamation was enforced impartially, even against so prominent a refugee as Captain John Wormeley (*Papers of Madison*, V, 286, n. 14; *JCSV*, III, 276–77). For the exceptional case of Dr. Philip Turpin, see Randolph to JM, 18 July 1783, and n. 6.

20 Jones's statement makes clear that he wrote the present letter early on 21 June, for he and fifty-five other members of the House of Delegates later that day voted to "put off till the second Monday in October next" a further consideration of the bill "to repeal the act, declaring who shall be deemed citizens of this Commonwealth, and for declaring who shall be deemed such citizens." Carter Braxton, Richard Henry Lee, and Stevens Thomson Mason were among the twenty-seven members who opposed this decision (*JHDV*, May 1783, pp. 21, 22, 76–77). See also *Papers of Madison*, V, 61, n. 11; Jones to JM, 31 May, and nn. 13, 14; 8 June, and n. 27; 14 June 1783.

21 The Virginia Conventions of December 1775 and May 1776 and several sessions of the Virginia General Assembly adopted ordinances or enacted legislation severely punishing Loyalists with fines, imprisonment, confiscation of property, and banishment (Hening, *Statutes*, IX, 101–7, 130–32, 170–71; X, 92–93, 268–70, 310, 386–88, 414). See also *Papers of Madison*, V, 61, n. 12; 81, n. 5; Randolph to JM, 15 May, and n. 5; Jones to JM, 28 June 1783.

22 Pendleton to JM, 26 May, n. 11; Jones to JM, 14 June, and n. 17; Instruction to Delegates, 27 June 1783.

23 On 20 June in the House of Delegates, the committee on the claim of Simon Nathan rendered a report including "several resolutions" and "papers relative to the claim." These were spread on the journal. The next day the recommendation

favoring Nathan's claim, as judged by Joseph Reed and William Bradford, Jr., the two "referees" in Philadelphia, was rejected on the grounds that they had been unaware of some circumstances adverse to the claim. On 24 June the House of Delegates, and on the next day the Senate, agreed that the issue should be submitted to two new arbitrators—one to be appointed by Nathan and the other by the governor and Council of Maryland. Edmund Randolph, as attorney general, was instructed to attend the arbitration. Virginia guaranteed to abide by the outcome. Nathan also was so to pledge under penalty, if he violated his promise, of forfeiting £15,000 to the state of Virginia (*JHDV*, May 1783, pp. 71, 72, 73–75, 81–82, 84). See also *Papers of Madison*, VI, Index, under Nathan, Simon; Delegates to Gálvez, 4 May, ed. n.; JM to Jefferson, 20 May, and n. 4; Jones to JM, 8 June, and n. 19; 14 June; Randolph to JM, 28 June 1783. Nathan, already in financial straits, had been obliged to terminate his lease of Rock-Hall, a "handsome genteel House" in Philadelphia (*Pa. Packet*, 3, 7, and 10 June 1783).

24 The location of the post office nearest to Jones's estate of Spring Hill in King George County.

25 In his missing letter of 10 June to Jones, JM probably had enclosed his letter of the same date to Jefferson (*q.v.*).

From Edmund Randolph

RC (Pennsylvania Historical and Museum Commission). Unsigned and perhaps incomplete. Docketed by JM, "June 21, 1783." Cover addressed to "The honble James Madison jr. esq. of congress Philadelphia."

PETTUS'S[1] June 21. 1783.

MY DEAR FRIEND

Inclosed is a state of the proceedings of the assembly for a week past, and of the expectations of future business.[2] Having been confined at home for ten days by the demands of my clients,[3] I have not been able to collect in person the debates of the legislature. I therefore wrote to the clerk,[4] who has given me the inclosed detail.

The form, in which the impost now appears, amounts to an annihilation of the views of congress. Being reduced to a mode of taxation solely for the benefit of Virginia, it contains no inducement to the other states to adopt it, nor, if it did, would it produce any good.[5]

Mr. Henry left the assembly last saturday, and at the same time the field open to his adversary.[6] He can always recover himself in interest by an exertion, but his sighs for home[7] expose him to a daily loss of his popularity.

1 *Papers of Madison*, IV, 148, n. 2.

2 Beckley to Randolph, 20 June. See also Jones to JM, 21 June 1783, and n. 23.

3 With the adjournment of the courts, the duties of Randolph as attorney general had eased. This lessening of pressure enabled him to turn to his temporarily

neglected private practice as a lawyer. See Randolph to JM, 9 May, and n. 2; 24 May; 14 June 1783, and n. 4.

4 Beckley to Randolph, 20 June 1783, and ed. n.

5 Jones to JM, 21 June, and nn. 6, 7. For a summary of the contents of this bill, see Jones to JM, 28 June 1783.

6 June 14 was "last Saturday." Henry's "adversary" was Richard Henry Lee.

7 Leatherwood, his estate in Henry County (Robert Douthat Meade, *Patrick Henry* [2 vols.; Philadelphia and New York, 1957–69], II, 221–23).

From Theodorick Bland

RC (LC: Madison Papers). Undated and signature clipped. JM later wrote "Theodk. Bland." at the close of the letter. The text is faded almost to the point of illegibility. Letter docketed by JM, "Bland Theodk. June 22. 1783." Cover missing.

[22 June 1783]

Dear Sr.

In consequence of the determination of Congress on Saturday,[1] I took the necessary measures, to put myself in a Situation, to fulfill their intentions as far as concerned myself & Family.[2] I wrote to the President and to Mercer[3]—from the former I have got no decisive answer, from the latter none at all I shall look on it as inglorious, and shamefull to quit my station whilst the majority of Congress shall maintain theirs in Philadelphia, and however imprudent, I as an Individual may deem it that Congress or the members shd trust their persons in the hands of a Mutinous army, without support, if they determine so to do, I on my part shall without hesitation share their fate. It is my wish therefore that you wd as soon as possible let me know their final determination on this point, and particularly how matters stand respecting the determination of the Exe. Council &.c.[4] that I may either return or send for my family accordingly,[5] it being personally perfectly indifferent to me which I do

& you'll oblige

Theodk. Bland

1 JM Notes, 21 June 1783, and n. 5.

2 Although the place to which Bland had gone is not known, he may have been writing from Trenton or Princeton.

3 Elias Boudinot and John Francis Mercer, respectively.

4 JM Notes, 21 June 1783, and n. 7.

5 Mrs. Bland evidently was in Philadelphia. She and her husband had no children. Besides his wife, Bland meant by "family" their household slaves (Charles Campbell, ed., *Bland Papers*, I, viii).

From Edmund Pendleton

Tr (LC: Force Transcripts). In the left margin at the top of the transcription, Peter Force's clerk wrote "MSS McGuire's." See *Papers of Madison*, I, xxii, xxiii.

VIRGA.[1] June 23d, 1783

DEAR SIR

By yr favr of the 10th I find you have at length information that Great Britain is in motion to give the definitive treaty it's force, as well as to settle some general rules for regulating commerce, wch I suppose to be their purpose, & all they can do, 'til your general treaty reaches Europe.[2]

I am glad you think the new Ministry disposed to favour the Peace, as I thought Ld North as little inclined to the measure as any body, however I suppose he was obliged to make that Sacrifice of Sentiments as the price of Coalition, and in such an hetrogenious one many great ones must have been made, if indeed they have any principles beyond ambition & avarice.[3]

I am still in the dark as to what is doing at Richmond on the subject of Finance;[4] I hear they sit closely to hurry home to Harvest, which they will hardly effect, as We are beginning to use the Scythe.[5] What they can adopt of sufficient permanency & not more oppressive in lieu of the impost I cant discover; especially as our efforts will be otherwise Abundantly strain'd to raise the 256 M dollars annually, required beyond the produce of the impost.[6]

I find that Maryland has adopted the measure—some of the Instructions in the Massachusetts, rather appear in opposition.[7] If the measure should be finally agreed to, 'tis pity it could not have operated upon the large importations made & making.[8]

I am Dr Sr Yr Affe &c

EDMD PENDLETON

1 Pendleton was at his estate of Edmundsbury.

2 Although JM's letter of 10 June to Pendleton is missing, the remarks about foreign commerce in his letters of that day to Jefferson and Randolph probably indicate approximately what he had written to Pendleton on the same subject. See JM to Jefferson, 10 June, and nn. 5, 6, 21; JM to Randolph, 10 June 1783.

3 *Papers of Madison*, VI, 504, n. 3; Jones to JM, 8 June, and n. 22; 21 June 1783.

4 Beckley to Randolph, 20 June; Jones to JM, 21 June, and nn. 5, 6, 8; Randolph to JM, 21 June 1783.

5 Probably in the harvest of wheat and other small grains.

6 In the plan for restoring public credit, Virginia's exact quota of the total requisition of $1,500,000 was $256,487. This sum did not include the revenue hoped

for from the impost duties (Pendleton to JM, 26 May, and n. 11; Jones to JM, 8 June, and n. 5; Randolph to JM, 14 June 1783, and n. 9).

7 Pendleton confined his comment to the proposed impost rather than to the revenue plan as a whole. See *Papers of Madison,* IV, 389, n. 16; VI, 296, n. 38; 372, n. 8; 429; 431, n. 3; Jones to JM, 8 June 1783, and n. 9.

8 Randolph to JM, 9 May, and n. 14; 15 May; JM to Randolph, 20 May, and nn. 5, 6, 14; Pendleton to JM, 2 June; 9 June; 16 June, and n. 4; Harrison to Delegates, 7 June 1783, and n. 3.

Virginia Delegates to Benjamin Harrison

RC (Virginia State Library). In the hand of John Francis Mercer, except for JM's signature. Cover franked by Mercer and addressed to "His Excelly. Benja. Harrison Esqr Governor of Virginia." Cover docketed, "Virginia Delegates June 24th 1783 Letter in Cypher." Words italicized were written in the official cipher. Filed with the recipient's copy is a decipherment of the dispatch, docketed, "Letter from Dels: in Congress. rec'd July 4th 1783." On 21 April 1782 Governor Harrison had received the encoding and decoding keys to the official cipher (*Papers of Madison,* IV, 148, n. 9).

EDITORIAL NOTE

This letter is probably the latest in date of the letters to Governor Harrison signed by JM as a delegate in Congress, prior to the expiration of his term on 2 November 1783. For at least a partial explanation of the omission of his signature from the nine remaining letters in this series, see JM to Randolph, 8 July, n. 2; 15 July, and n. 7; JM to Jefferson, 17 July 1783, and n. 10. Assuming as in similar instances that JM authorized the other Virginia delegates to write in his behalf as well as their own, and having much evidence that they kept him informed of their views and their actions at Princeton, the editors will include the nine letters in the present volume. See *Papers of Madison,* IV, 53; 412; VI, 39; 333; 446; 463; 501.

PHILA. June 24. 1783

SIR

In our last to yr Excellen[c]y we convey'd information that a *mutiny* amongst the *troops in Philadelphia* had happily *subsided.*[1] the *event has proved that* appearances were *fallatious. On Friday we received* thro the *executive of this state transmitted* by the *commanding officer at Lancaster* that part *of the troops there* had *set out for this place headed by* their *sergeants.*[2] *Congress immediately appointed a committe*[e] to *confer with the execut*[i]*ve council* & *concert* measures for *preventing a junction. The committe*[e] *reported* from *the executive* that they were *indisposed to call on the militia as they were dou*[b]*tful whether a call would be obeyed. The troops arrived*[,] *formed a junction* when their *officers were obliged to retire.*[3] On *Saturday the state house* whilst *Congress were sitting was surrounded*[4] *by a mutinous and menacing force to the amount of three hundred while detachments took possession of the arsenal and magazine.*[5] *They sent in a written demand* to *to be allowed to appoint officers to redress their grievances* requiring a favorable answer *in twenty minutes* or they *would let in enraged soldiery.*[6] This altho' directed to the *executive council was certainly meant* ultimately *for Congress to whom a memorial had* been previously *presented* signed by *by sergeants of so insolent* a *nature as to forbid any answer.*[7] In this situation *Congress thought it most becoming their character* to take no public *notice of the insult* but to forbear any official *act whatever. By the exertions of General Sinclair and of* individual *members* of *Congress* they were gradually *dive*[r]*ted from their purpose,* altho' inflamed by misrepresentation & *intoxicated with liquor* furnished by *the rabble present.* This *scene continued about twelve to three oclock* when *Congress* retired thro *the soldiers* who themselves shortly after *retired to their barrac*[k]*s.*[8]

At *six oclock Congress reassembled*[9] *and resolved that the comittee* should again wait on *the executives* & *demand a categorical answer* whether they would make exertions to *support government* & to *inform that unless satisfactory measures*[10] *shou*[l]*d be taken to restore the authority to government* (of which *the committe*[e] *and president were to be judges in the reces*[s] of *Congress*) *that then business* should be *summoned to meet at Princetown* or *or Trentown in New Jersey. Of* these *steps General Washington was informed and* directed to *detach a select force for the purpose of quelling the mutiny. The committe*[e] *found the executive* wholly *indecisive* & at their request, gave 'em a *day to deliberate* at the end of which they remained, either *incapable or indisposed to exert the necessary force.*[11] In this state *things now remain the temper and views of mutinears are not yet ascertained* as little are known [of] *the root or extent of the evil*[12]

J. Madison
J F Mercer[13]

1 Delegates to Harrison, 17 June 1783. See also JM Notes, 13 June, and n. 1; JM to Randolph, 17 June 1783, and n. 9.

2 JM Notes, 19 June 1783, and n. 6. Mercer should have encoded "Thursday" rather than "Friday."

[3] JM Notes, 19 June, and n. 7; 20 June 1783. In encoding the first syllable of "preventing," Mercer erroneously wrote 215 rather than 251, signifying "pre." The "*junction*" was with the discontented continental troops stationed in Philadelphia.

[4] By using 267 rather than 93, Mercer encoded "sitting" as "siteing." For "surrounded," he should have written 598. 241. 772. 154. 47 instead of 595. 242. 772. 154. 47, which decodes as a meaningless "shothenceunded."

[5] JM Notes, 21 June 1783, and n. 1.

[6] *Ibid.*, and n. 2. Mercer wrote "to" and then encoded the word.

[7] JM Notes, 13 June, and n. 1; JM to Randolph, 17 June 1783. Mercer repeated "by" in code after writing the word.

[8] JM Notes, 21 June 1783, and nn. 2–4.

[9] Mercer's ciphers for this word decode as "reassemblyre."

[10] Following a correct coding of "sa" in "satisfactory," Mercer erred by writing 759 meaning "save" rather than 758 meaning "ti." Deciphering his 737. 72. 613. 51 results in "moasuees," although Mercer certainly intended to write 713. 113. 751. 51 or another succession or ciphers standing for "measures."

[11] JM Notes, 21 June 1783, and nn. 4–7.

[12] *Ibid.*, and n. 8.

[13] The absence of Theodorick Bland's signature probably indicates that he had not yet returned to Philadelphia (Bland to JM, 22 June 1783, and n. 2).

To Edmund Randolph

RC (LC: Madison Papers). Docketed by Randolph, "J. Madison June 24. 1783." Cover missing.

PHILADA. June 24. 1783

MY DEAR SIR

I cannot break in upon my punctuality so far as to omit acknowledging your favor by yesterday's post,[1] though I can scarce do more than refer you to the official letter to the Govr. and mine to Mr. Jones, which you will see, whether he be absent or present, having addressed it to you on the first contingency.[2] In the former letter Mr. Mercer has related the several circumstances which have resulted from a revolt of the Soldiery at this place, who have recurred to the irregular mode of making redress.[3] Their grievances all terminate as you may [sup]pose in the want of their pay which Congs. are unable to give them;[4] and the information we receive from the States is far from opening any fresh sources for that purpose. Indeed the prospect on the side of the latter compared with the symptoms beginning to appear on the side of the army is to the last degree afflicting to those who love thier Country and aim at its prosperity.[5] If I had leisure to use a Cypher, I could dilate much on the present State of our Affairs; which as it is I must defer to another occasion.

I was prepared by Mr. Jones late letters for the fate to which the Budget of Congs. has been consigned, but the circumstances under which it arrived here gave peculiar pungency to the information.[6] I wish that those who abuse Congs. and baffle their measures, may as much promote the public good as they profess to intend. I am sure they will not do it more effectually tha[n] is intended by some at least of those who promote the measur[es] of Congs.

Adieu.

J. M.

[1] Randolph to JM, 14 June 1783.

[2] JM's letter to Joseph Jones, presumably dated between 21 and 23 June and sent to Randolph for delivery, is missing.

[3] Delegates to Harrison, 24 June 1783, and hdn., nn. 1, 2.

[4] JM Notes, 20 June, and n. 1; 21 June 1783, and nn. 4, 6.

[5] Congress, lacking money, could not quiet its importunate creditors and, lacking effective delegations from six states, could not decide any important issue within its jurisdiction (Jones to JM, 8 June, and n. 9; Burnett, *Letters*, VII, 192–93, 199, 210).

[6] Jones to JM, 8 June, and n. 5; 14 June 1783, and nn. 6, 7, 12, 17.

Instruction to Virginia Delegates *in re* Demobilization of Troops

FC (Virginia State Library). Docketed: "Resolution For advancing three Months pay to the Soldiers of the Virginia line, from the Southern Army 26th June 1783 Copied for Govr."

In the House of Delegates

thursday the 26th. of June 1783

Whereas a body of troops of this States line in the continental service has lately arrived in the town of Richmond from the southward under the command of Captain Parker[1] and other troops of the same line are daily expected to arrive in this State from the South and as no provision that is known to the Legislature hath been made for advancing three months pay to the said troops previous to their being furloughed as hath in like cases been done to the other troops in the service of the United States[2] and the General Assembly considering that it would be very unjust and ungenerous to send those brave troops home after their long dangerous and meritorious services without that reasonable advance of pay which has been extended to all others of the continental troops at the time of furlough have directed a Sum equal to three months pay to be advanced the said troops out of the treasury of this State.[3]

Resolved that it be an instruction to the Delegates of this Commonwealth in Congress to inform that Honorable body of this proceeding and its cause and to move Congress that the Sum so advanced be permitted to be deducted from the next payment to be made by the treasury of this State to the continental receiver here[4] and that this Resolve be transmitted to the Delegates in Congress by the Governor.[5]

1783 June 27th. Teste
Agreed to by the Senate JNO BECKLEY C.H.D.[6]
WILL DREW. C.S.[7]

[1] The word "army" rather than "service" is used in the resolution as printed in *JHDV*, May 1783, p. 86. For Captain Alexander Parker, see *Papers of Madison*, V, 63; 64, n. 6; Fitzpatrick, *Writings of Washington*, XXXI, 79; *Pay Rolls of Militia Entitled to Land Bounties under the Act of Congress of Sept. 28, 1850* (Richmond, 1851), p. 379; *National Intelligencer* (Washington), 4 Sept. 1821.

On 23 June Governor Harrison and the Council of State, in response to Parker's plea on behalf of his command of forty-six soldiers who had marched from Georgia, directed "the Quarter Master" to issue a pair of shoes and some flour to each of the men (*JCSV*, III, 272–73; Pendleton to JM, 26 May, n. 11). On 24 June 1783, having heard that Parker's was only the first contingent of three hundred Virginia troops coming to Richmond from the southern army, Harrison directed Jacquelin Ambler, the treasurer, to "avert the worst of Consequences" by reserving from the commutables received for taxes enough flour to supply those soldiers for twelve days. On the same day, even before the adoption of the present resolution, Harrison expressed to the auditors of the state his earnest hope that they could settle accounts with Parker's band "immediately," so that it could be sent from Richmond before the other troops arrived (Executive Letter Book, 1783–1786, pp. 161, 163, MS in Va. State Library).

[2] *Papers of Madison*, VI, 486, n. 3; JM Notes, 23 May, n. 1; 26 May, and n. 2; 11 June, n. 1; Harrison to Delegates, 31 May, and n. 1; Jones to JM, 31 May; Maryland's Payment to Troops, 28 July 1783, n. 3.

[3] On 25 June the House of Delegates assigned to a committee, Richard Henry Lee, chairman, the task of preparing a bill "for paying the soldiers late from the southern army, belonging to the Virginia continental line, three month's wages." The resolution, which Lee submitted later that day, was adopted on 26 June and delivered by him to the Senate for its concurrence. This was accorded on the following day. The version of the resolution appearing in the journal of the House of Delegates reads "these" rather than "those brave troops" (*JHDV*, May 1783, pp. 83, 85, 93).

[4] George Webb. Perhaps to reinforce the present instruction, Governor Harrison in a letter of 4 July informed Robert Morris, superintendent of finance, that the Virginia continental troops returning from South Carolina were causing the state some expense which would be charged "to the continent" (Executive Letter Book, 1783–1786, p. 166, MS in Va. State Library).

[5] There appears to be no evidence to show that Governor Harrison sent this instruction to the delegates or that they submitted it to Congress. Congress and

Morris, as manifested by the resolutions of the first and the letters of the second, intended that each continental soldier, upon being discharged or furloughed, should receive from a member of the paymaster-general's staff a Confederation treasury note, redeemable in specie in six months, covering three months of his overdue pay. Besides the fact that the printing of sufficient notes had been delayed, the money for their redemption, as well as one month's pay in specie, also promised to each soldier, was to be provided to the continental receiver by the state to which the soldier belonged. Virginia was delinquent in meeting her financial quota. Beyond these considerations, however, both the governor and the Virginia delegates had reason to disregard the instruction (*Papers of Madison*, V, 173–75). See also Maryland's Payment to Troops, 28 July 1783.

[6] Clerk of the House of Delegates.

[7] Clerk of the Senate.

Instruction to Virginia Delegates *in re* ship "Cormorant"

MS (NA: PCC, No. 137, II, 729). Docketed: "Resolution of genl Assembly of Virginia 26 June 1783 Read 23 July Referred so far as relates to the offer of the Ship *Cormorant*, to the Agent of Marine to report."

EDITORIAL NOTE

Unsigned by John Beckley, clerk of the House of Delegates, or by William Drew, clerk of the Senate, this instruction varies in form from that of the instructions usually sent by the Virginia General Assembly to its delegates in Congress. On the FC of the entire document in the Virginia State Library the signatures of both clerks appear, that of Drew beneath his penned notation, "1783 June 27th./ Agreed to by the Senate." Omitted from the copy below was a directive to the "Commissioners superintending the defence of Chesapeake Bay," not involving business with Congress (*JHDV*, May 1783, pp. 86, 90). Governor Harrison probably enclosed the present instruction in his letter of 4 July 1783 to the Virginia delegates (*q.v.*).

IN THE HOUSE OF DELEGATES the 26th. June 1783.

Resolved that the Commissioners superintending the defence of Cheasepeake Bay[1] be directed to sell all the armed vessels belonging to the public except the boats Liberty & Patriot[2] in such manner as they shall think most advantagious first making an offer of the ship Cormorant to Congress[3]

[1] The three commissioners appointed according to the provisions of "An act for defending and protecting the trade of Chesapeake bay," adopted by the Virginia General Assembly on 1 July 1782, were Paul Loyall, Colonel Thomas Newton, Jr., and Thomas Brown (Hening, *Statutes*, XI, 43; McIlwaine, *Official Letters*, III, 297, n. 102, 448–49; *Papers of Madison*, VI, 278, n. 3; 292, n. 2).

[2] Lack of money for sailors' wages and for refitting these two vessels delayed the beginning of their mission against smugglers until the spring of 1786 (*Papers of Madison*, II, 83; 84, n. 7; V, 384, n. 5; *JHDV*, May 1783, pp. 91, 93; *JCSV*, III, 22, 93, 108, 125, 345, 535).

[3] The "Cormorant," which the French had captured from the British in October 1781 and sold to Virginia, was also far from ready for use on Chesapeake Bay, even though she had a copper-sheathed hull and mounted twenty guns. Paul Loyall reported to Governor Harrison early in the summer of 1782 that, being "totally unfit," she probably "wou'd never remove on that service from Appomattox River" (McIlwaine, *Official Letters*, III, 268–69). See also *Papers of Madison*, IV, 44, n. 5; 341, n. 5; 356; 361, n. 33; V, 279, n. 3.

The resolution having been referred on 23 July to Robert Morris, agent of marine, he recommended on 5 August that Virginia's offer be declined on the grounds of lack of money and of the inadvisability of Congress' providing for a "marine" until "the several states shall grant such funds for the construction of ships, docks and naval arsenals, and for the support of the naval service, as shall enable the United States to establish their marine upon a permanent and respectable footing." Congress agreed to this report (*JCC*, XXIV, 444, n. 1, 486). See also Motion of Delegates, 28 July; Harrison to Delegates, 19 Sept.; Delegates to Harrison, 4 Oct. 1783.

Instruction to Virginia Delegates *in re* Cession of Western Lands

RC (NA: PCC, No. 75, fols. 386–87). Docketed: "Resolutions of Assembly of Virginia 27 June 1783 relative to their offer of Cession of lands NW of Ohio Read 23 July to lie on table."

VIRGINIA

IN THE HOUSE OF DELEGATES

Friday the 27th of June 1783

Resolved that it would be improper to determine upon that part of the memorial of the Officers and soldiers of the Virginia line on Continental establishment presented to this Session of Assembly which prays for a grant of Lands on the North Westerly side of the Ohio[1] until it is known whether Congress will accept of the Cession of that Country in the manner proposed by this Commonwealth.[2]

Resolved that as soon as the business of the said Cession shall be finally determined on [,] the consideration of the said memorial ought to be resumed and complied with as far as may consist with the terms of such Cession[3]

Resolved that the Delegates representing this State in Congress be instructed to apply to Congress to agree to such alteration in the terms of Cession as may enable the General Assembly of this Commonwealth to comply with the prayer of the said memorial and that the Executive be desired to transmit this Resolve with a copy of the said Memorial to our Delegates in Congress[4]

1783 June 27th JOHN BECKLEY CHD[5]
Agreed to by the Senate
WILL DREW C S[6]

A Copy
Teste
JOHN BECKLEY C. H. D.

1 For the "memorial," see Jones to JM, 25 May, and n. 12; 31 May; 8 June; 14 June 1783, and n. 14.

2 For the discussion in Congress during May and June of Virginia's offer of 2 January 1781 to cede her lands north and west of the Ohio River to the United States, see Harrison to Delegates, 3 May, n. 4; Randolph to JM, 9 May, and n. 8; JM to Jefferson, 20 May, and nn. 5, 8; JM Notes, 4 June, and nn. 1, 2; 5 June, n. 1; 6 June; 9 June, and nn. 2, 3; 10 June, and nn. 3, 5, 9, 10; 20 June, and nn. 3–5, 8, 10; JM to Randolph, 10 June 1783, and n. 16.

3 The Virginia General Assembly fulfilled the intent of this resolution by enacting on 22 December 1783 a law authorizing "the Delegates of this State in Congress to convey to the United States in Congress assembled all the right of this Commonwealth to the Territory North-Westward of the River Ohio" (*JHDV*, Oct. 1783, pp. 80–81, 82, 83; NA: PCC, No. 75, fols. 388–91). By that date JM was no longer a delegate in Congress.

4 Governor Harrison enclosed a copy of the memorial and of the instruction in his letter of 4 July to the Virginia delegates (*q.v.*). See also Delegates to Gálvez, 4 May, n. 2; to Harrison, 26 July 1783.

5 Clerk of the House of Delegates.

6 Clerk of the Senate.

From Joseph Jones

RC (LC: Madison Papers). Docketed by JM, "June 28. 1783." Cover missing.

RICHMOND. 28th. June 1783.

DEAR SR.

I have your favours by the Post and by the Secretary of War.[1] The day before yesterday the bill for granting a revenue to Congress upon the 3d. reading was ordered to lay on the Table [.] Tas—ll then moved for leave to bring in another under a different Title which was agreed

By His EXCELLENCY

Elias Boudinot, Eſquire,

Preſident of the United States in Congreſs Aſſembled.

A PROCLAMATION.

WHEREAS a body of armed Soldiers in the ſervice of the United States, and quartered in the Barracks of this City, having mutinouſly renounced their obedience to their Officers, did, on Saturday the Twenty-Firſt Day of this inſtant, proceed, under the direction of their Serjeants, in a hoſtile and threatning manner, to the Place in which Congreſs were aſſembled, and did ſurround the ſame with Guards: And whereas Congreſs in conſequence thereof, did on the ſame Day, reſolve, " That the Preſident and Supreme Executive Council of this State " ſhould be informed, that the authority of the United States having been, that Day, groſſly inſulted by the " diſorderly and menacing appearance of a body of armed Soldiers, about the Place within which Congreſs were aſſem-" bled; and that the Peace of this City being endangered by the mutinous Diſpoſition of the ſaid Troops then in the " Barracks; it was, in the Opinion of Congreſs, neceſſary, that effectual Meaſures ſhould be immediately taken for " ſupporting the public Authority:" And alſo whereas Congreſs did at the ſame Time appoint a Committee to confer with the ſaid Preſident and Supreme Executive Council on the practicability of carrying the ſaid Reſolution into due effect: And alſo whereas the ſaid Committee have reported to me, that they have not received ſatisfactory Aſſurances for expecting adequate and prompt exertions of this State for ſupporting the Dignity of the fœderal Government: And alſo whereas the ſaid Soldiers ſtill continue in a ſtate of open Mutiny and Revolt, ſo that the Dignity and Authority of the United States would be conſtantly expoſed to a repetition of Inſult, while Congreſs ſhall continue to ſit in this City, I do therefore, by and with the Advice of the ſaid Committee, and according to the Powers and Authorities in me veſted for this Purpoſe, hereby ſummon the honourable the Delegates compoſing the Congreſs of the United States, and every of them, to meet in Congreſs on Thurſday the Twenty Sixth Day of June inſtant, at Princeton, in the ſtate of New-Jerſey, in order that further and more effectual Meaſures may be taken for ſuppreſſing the preſent Revolt, and maintaining the Dignity and Authority of the United States, of which all Officers of the United States, civil and military, and all others whom it may concern, are deſired to take Notice and govern themſelves accordingly.

GIVEN under my Hand and Seal at Philadelphia, in the ſtate of Pennſylvania, this Twenty-Fourth Day of June, in the Year of Our Lord One Thouſand Seven Hundred and Eighty Three, and of our Sovereignty and Independence the ſeventh.

ELIAS BOUDINOT.

Atteſt,

SAMUEL STERETT, *Private Secretary.*

Philadelphia, Printed by DAVID C. CLAYPOOLE.

PROCLAMATION BY ELIAS BOUDINOT,
PRESIDENT OF CONGRESS, 24 JUNE 1783

JOHN DICKINSON

THOMAS MIFFLIN

to and yesterday it was presented and on the first reading postponed to the next Session of Assembly.[2] The first bill was imperfectly drawn and had undergone such alterations as to be thot. unfit to be enacted into a law. it granted the 5 P Ct. impost and the duty on enumerated articles not as a general fund but to be carryed to the credit of the State and to be in force if Maryland Pensa. & N. Carolina adopted the impost. it granted the land Tax and if any deficiency the poll Tax to furnish the quota of this State if the 1.500.000 doll.[3] the first to be collected by the naval officers the latter by the Sheriffs,[4] the whole appropriated to Congress on account of this States quota of the common debt. The latter bill was drawn to grant the import duty as a general fund the collection under the controul of the Executive but to be paid to the Continental receiver for the use of Congress. the reason of this bill being brot. before the House in that form was the apparent change in many members after discussing the first bill to fall in with the proposition of Congress except as to the mode [of] collecting.[5] this conciliatory disposition was much improved by the arrival of a letter from Genl. Washington on the subject which the Speaker recd. just before the question was about to be taken on the first bill and being read in consequence of the consent of the House to hear the letter before the question was taken had a good effect.[6] but two days alone remaining of the time allotted by the members for finishing the business and the fixed determination to break up at that day (Saturday)[7] suspended all hope of accomplishing any thing effectual this Session. I think if the Members could have been prevailed on to continue a week longer the business wod. have been finished nearly to the wish of Congress. this Session has passed over withot. doing any thing of consequence.[8] Yesterday I suggested to the House an Idea with respect to the cession—to instruct the Delegates to recede from the Guarantee provided Congress wod. agree to the other conditions & limit the time (sometime in Nov. next) when they shod. accept or the c[e]ssion stand revoked.[9] It will be vain to attempt relaxing the clause respecting the Companies. the other parts of the report of the last Com: appear to be agreeable here.[10] The Secretary of War yesterday through the Executive laid before the House a request to be empowered to procure for the U. States abt. ten Acres of land for the purpose of establ[ish]ing a magazine. a bill is ordd. in for the purpose.[11] Resolutions are to be presented to day for furnishing Congress a place of residence—Wmsburg. the public buildings and lands or a tract of territory opposite George Town as may be most agreeable, with a large Sum to erect Hotels for the Delegates, and other necessary buildings will be offered in full Sovereignty. liberal as the offer of Maryland has been our people seem disposed not to be backward in surpassing that liberality where they think a lasting benefit may result to the Community.[12] I wish they could have seen the *plan of Congress* (as to revenue) in the same light and have acted with equal policy and liberality of sentiment [.][13] this day closes the Session. I intend to Mr. Randolphs this evening in my way home where I have not yet been.[14] the heat of the weather and this infernal hole at this Season of the year has almost laid me up. Although Virga. may not grant the funds for discharging their quota of the common debt in the *manner* desired by Congress they are I think determined to furnish ample revenues for the *purpose*. Mr. Laurens gives us no hope of speedily obtaining the definitive Treaty.[15] Nothing has been done in the Citizen bill, it lyes over, and a severe law agt. British subjects coming into this Country, remains in force [.] The Executive may by a proper use of this law until the next Session keep out such as ought not to com[e] among us.[16] After geting home you shall be informed w[hen] I shall see you in Philadelphia. Joe is yet afflicted wi[th] the Spleen and ought to go to the Springs or up the Country. If John Dawson will accompany Mrs. Jones and Joe up the Country I do not know but I may visit f[or] two or three months the City of Phila: during the sickly season.[17]

yr. aff Friend

Jos: Jones

[1] Jones to JM, 31 May, n. 1; JM to Randolph, 17 June, and n. 15; JM Notes, 19 June 1783, and n. 9.

[2] Pendleton to JM, 26 May, and n. 11; Jones to JM, 21 June, and nn. 6, 7. For Henry Tazewell, see Jefferson to JM, 7 May 1783, and n. 9. Following his motion, he was elected chairman of a committee of three, including Jones, to draft a revenue measure for consideration by the House of Delegates (*JHDV*, May 1783, pp. 86, 93).

[3] Jones to JM, 14 June, and n. 7; Randolph to JM, 21 June 1783. The $1,500,000 was the amount to be requisitioned from all the states by Congress in 1783. Of this total, Virginia's quota was $253,500 (*Papers of Madison*, VI, 432; 433, n. 3; 434, nn. 6, 7). Jones should have written "of" rather than "if" immediately after "State."

[4] Pendleton to JM, 4 May, and n. 8; Randolph to JM, 9 May 1783, and n. 5.

[5] Jones to JM, 14 June 1783, and nn. 11, 12.

[6] Between 8 and 21 June Washington addressed a long circular letter to the executive of each state. The copy received by Governor Harrison on 26 June is dated 12 June 1783 (Fitzpatrick, *Writings of Washington*, XXVI, 483, and n. 29, to 496). In the letter Washington devoted a paragraph to praise of the plan for restoring public credit and of the "Address to the United States," drafted by JM. In Washington's words: "no real friend to the honor and Independency of America, can hesitate a single moment respecting the propriety of complying with the just and honorable measures proposed; if their Arguments do not produce con-

viction, I know of nothing that will have greater influence; especially when we recollect that the System referred to, being the result of the collected Wisdom of the Continent, must be esteemed, if not perfect, certainly the least objectionable of any that could be devised; and that if it shall not be carried into immediate execution, a National Bankruptcy, with all its deplorable consequences will take place, before any different Plan can possibly be proposed and adopted; So pressing are the present circumstances! and such is the alternative now offered to the States!" (*ibid*., XXVI, 489).

As "the Legacy of One, who has ardently wished, on all occasions, to be useful to his Country," Washington asked as his "final and only request" that Harrison "communicate these sentiments to your Legislature at their next meeting" (*ibid*., XXVI, 496). Although note of the fact does not appear in the journal, Harrison enclosed Washington's letter to the speaker of the House of Delegates on 26 June 1783 (Executive Letter Book, 1783–1786, p. 163, MS in Va. State Library). See also Randolph to JM, 28 June 1783.

7 Pendleton to JM, 23 June 1783, and n. 5.

8 Pendleton to JM, 26 May, n. 11; Randolph to JM, 14 June 1783, and n. 9.

9 Jones to JM, 14 June; Instruction to Delegates, 27 June 1783, and nn. 2, 3.

10 For the "last Com:" and the issue of the "Companies," see *Papers of Madison*, VI, 502; 503, nn. 4, 6; JM to Jefferson, 20 May, and n. 5; JM Notes, 4 June, and n. 2; 6 June, and n. 1; 10 June, and n. 3; JM to Randolph, 10 June 1783, and n. 16.

11 JM to Randolph, 17 June, n. 10; JM Notes, 19 June 1783, and n. 9. A letter from the governor, enclosing one from Benjamin Lincoln, secretary at war, was referred by the House of Delegates on 27 June to "a committee of the whole House on the state of the Commonwealth." The same day, on the recommendation of that committee, a committee of five members, Charles Mynn Thruston, chairman, was ordered to prepare a bill to enable Congress "to procure ten acres of land in this State, for the public use." Later that day the proposed bill passed two readings and was adopted on 28 June by each house of the General Assembly (*JHDV*, May 1783, pp. 91, 93, 94, 97, 99; Hening, *Statutes*, XI, 288).

12 Instructions to Delegates, 28 June 1783, and nn.

13 Either Jones or JM underlined "plan of Congress" and two italicized words later in the paragraph. JM many years later interlineated "as to revenue" and enclosed the phrase in parentheses.

14 For Randolph's home, see *Papers of Madison*, IV, 148, n. 2. Jones had not been home since at least 18 May (Jones to JM, 25 May 1783, and n. 1).

15 Jones referred to Henry Laurens' dispatch of 15 March, received by Congress on 10 June (NA: PCC, No. 185, III, 66; Wharton, *Revol. Dipl. Corr*., VI, 303–5). JM's missing letter to Jones, enclosed in JM's letter of 17 June to Randolph (*q.v.*, and n. 15), may have mentioned Laurens' dispatch. See also Pendleton to JM, 4 May, n. 6; 23 June; JM to Jefferson, 10 June, and nn. 2, 3, 7; to Randolph, 10 June 1783.

16 Jones to JM, 31 May, and nn. 11–14; 8 June, and nn. 26, 27; 14 June; 21 June 1783, and nn. 20, 21.

17 For Jones's return to Philadelphia, see JM to Randolph, 6 May 1783, n. 9. By "Spleen," Jones probably meant that his son, Joseph, Jr., about three years of age, was either asthmatic or feverish and irritable (Matthew Baillie, *The Morbid Anatomy of Some of the Most Important Parts of the Human Body* [2d ed.; London, 1797], pp. 252–64; *Papers of Madison*, IV, 367, n. 14). By "Springs," Jones may have signified Berkeley Warm Springs (*ibid*., I, 73, n. 2). John Dawson (1762–1814), a brother of the first husband of Jones's wife (Mary Waugh Dawson), was graduated by Harvard College in 1782. He was a delegate from Spotsylvania County in the Virginia General Assembly, 1786–1789, a member of the

convention of his state which ratified the Constitution of the United States in 1788, and a congressman from 1797 to 1814. He served during the War of 1812 as an aide-de-camp of Major General Jacob Brown and Major General Andrew Jackson. Dawson and JM frequently corresponded between 1785 and 1812. See *Papers of Madison*, IV, 261, n. 11.

From Edmund Randolph

RC (LC: Madison Papers). Unsigned but in Randolph's hand. Cover addressed to "The honble James Madison jr. esq. of congress Philadelphia To go by the post." Erroneously docketed by JM, "June 8. 1783."

Pettus's[1] June 28. 1783.

My dear friend

The last post brought, as usual, your esteemed favor.[2]

The friends to the impost, as recommended by congress, finding, that the adoption of that measure in the form of the bill, then depending before the delegates would fix it in a manner averse to continental views, did on thursday last assent to the postponing of it until the next session.[3] It seems now to be the current opinion, that at the next session it will be carried. For my part I perceive no good ground for such an expectation. The opposition is deeprooted in the hearts of the most persevering & most eloquent.[4]

The arrival of Gen: Washington's circular letter excited this hope in the minds of the sanguine:[5] but its effect is momentary, and perhaps it will hereafter be accepted by the assembly with disgust. For the murmur is free and general against what is called the unsolicited intrusion of his advice.

General Lincoln reached Richmond yesterday morning. It was at first believed by those, to whom he was unknown, that he was an ambassador from congress, with a full catalogue in his mouth of the necessities & complaints of the army.[6]

You will readily conceive, how little suited to my feelings a mission is, which I fear will not redound much to the credit of our country nor myself. Nathan's accounts have been the topic of much vehemence in the assembly: and the issue is, that the decision of Reed & Bradf[ord] is annulled and other arbitrators are to be app[oin]ted in Maryland. Before these I am to appear to prop the reputation of Virginia for good faith and to submit to hear just & copious reproaches thrown upon her. The resolution, making this arrangement, assigns as a reason for reversing the award of those gentlemen; that no evidence was before them. It binds Nathan to enter into a bond of £15,000, but leaves the state at liberty to ratify [o]r not what may be the result of their deliberat[ions.][7] If we should not succeed in Maryland, it is possible that I may be honored with a trip to North Carolina; and so on until I visit you in a journey to the states eastward of Phila.[8]

Mr. Jefferson was placed at the head of the delegation, not without his approbation, as I have been informed.[9]

[1] *Papers of Madison*, IV, 148, n. 2.

[2] JM to Randolph, 17 June 1783.

[3] Jones to JM, 28 June 1783, and nn. 2, 3. Although the members of the House of Delegates probably agreed on Thursday, 26 June, to postpone further consideration of the impost, they did not adopt a motion to that effect until the next day (*JHDV*, May 1783, p. 93).

[4] Jones to JM, 14 June; 21 June; Randolph to JM, 14 June 1783, and n. 3.

[5] Jones to JM, 28 June 1783, and n. 6.

[6] *Ibid*., and n. 11.

[7] Jones to JM, 21 June, and nn. 12, 23. The decision, dated 17 February 1783, of William Bradford, Jr. (*Papers of Madison*, I, 73, n. 1), and Joseph Reed, the arbitrators, had fully sustained Simon Nathan's claims against Virginia (*Papers of Madison*, VI, 154; 192, and n. 2; 241; 278; 307; *JHDV*, May 1783, p. 75). On 5 May Governor Harrison submitted a copy of the decision to the House of Delegates of the Virginia General Assembly (*Papers of Madison*, VI, 439; 474; 475, n. 3; Executive Letter Book, 1783–1786, pp. 109, 137, MS in Va. State Library). After rejecting a committee's recommendation of compliance with the decision, the House of Delegates on 24 June and the Senate the next day resolved that Nathan's claims should be arbitrated anew in the manner indicated by Randolph (*JHDV*, May 1783, pp. 72, 75, 81–82, 84; *JCSV*, III, 174, 275). See also Randolph to JM, 23 Aug. 1783.

Joseph Reed (1741–1785), a native of New Jersey, had been graduated by the College of New Jersey (Princeton) in 1757 and admitted to the bar in 1762. Thereafter he had prepared himself further for the practice of law by studying at the Middle Temple in London. Both in Trenton and in Philadelphia, to which he moved in October 1770, he participated prominently in the opposition to Great Britain's colonial policies. After serving as president of the Pennsylvania Provincial Congress early in 1775, as military secretary to Washington in 1775–1776, and as a delegate in Congress in 1777 and 1778, he was president of the Supreme Executive Council of Pennsylvania, 1778–1781. For the earlier connection of Reed and Bradford with the Nathan affair, see *Papers of Madison*, III, 187; 190–91; 192, nn. 3, 4; 284, n. 2.

[8] Randolph's satire reflected his weariness at being further involved in the settlement of a claim which had been frequently troublesome for over three years. For a summary of its history, see Boyd, *Papers of Jefferson*, VI, 321–24.

[9] Jones to JM, 8 June, and n. 10. Jefferson himself, while "in the neighborhood of Richmond," may have informed Randolph of his willingness to become a delegate to Congress (Jefferson to JM, 7 May 1783, and n. 7).

Instructions to Virginia Delegates *in re* Permanent Site for Congress

RC (NA: PCC, No. 46, fols. 55–58). Docketed: "Resolutions of the Genl Assembly of Virginia. Offers to induce Congress to fix their residence in that State. Read July 16. 1783. Copies to be made out & sent to the several States."

VIRGINIA

IN THE HOUSE OF DELEGATES

Saturday June 28th 1783

Whereas[1] the Legislature of Virginia are fully convinced of the advantages that would result to the United States by having some fixed place of residence for Congress[2]

Resolved therefore unanimously that if the Honorable the Congress should esteem the city of Williamsburg in this State to be a fit Place for their session this Assembly will present them on their Removal thereto and during their continuance therein with the Palace the Capitol and all the public buildings[3] and three hundred Acres of land adjoining the said city together with a Sum of money not exceeding one hundred thousand pounds this States Currency to be paid at five annual Installments and to be expended in erecting thirteen Hotels for the Use of the Delegates in Congress.[4]

This Assembly will also cede to Congress during their residence therein a district of Territory contiguous to the said City not exceeding five miles square with such exempt Jurisdiction within the said Limits as the inhabitants residing therein shall consent to yield to Congress to obtain which the Governor with Advice of Council is directed to make application to the said Citizens and when obtained to notify to the Delegates of this State such assent[5]

Resolved unanimously that if the Honorable the Congress should think it more convenient to hold their Sessions at any place on the River Potowmack within this Commonwealth this Assembly will on the above terms cede the like district of Territory at the Place Congress shall so choose and will also appropriate a sum not exceeding one hundred thousand pounds to be paid in five annual installments for the purpose of erecting the said Hotels and will moreover purchase one hundred Acres of Land for the Purpose of erecting such public Buildings as Congress may direct thereon

Resolved unanimously that if the Legislature of Maryland are willing to join in a Cession of territory for the above purpose with this State (the said territory to be on the river Potowmack)[6] that this Assembly will cede to the Honorable the Congress the like District of Territory opposite to that ceded by the State of Maryland freely leaving it with Congress to fix their residence on either Side of the said River as they may see proper: but that if Congress shall reside on the North Side of the said River that then this Assembly will contribute forty thousand Pounds for the aforesaid Purposes in full confidence that the State of Maryland will supply the Deficiency Provided that should Congress thereafter remove from the City of Williamsburg or from the Lands beforementioned that in such Case the lands so ceded with the Buildings shall revert to the Commonwealth

1783 June 28th Teste
Agreed to by the Senate JOHN BECKLEY CHD
WILL DREW CS

A Copy
Teste
JOHN BECKLEY CHD[7]

[1] *Papers of Madison*, VI, 447; 448, nn. 4–7; Harrison to Delegates, 17 May; Delegates to Harrison, 27 May, and n. 2; 17 June 1783, n. 1.

[2] On 12 June, upon receiving from Governor Harrison the Virginia delegates' letter, probably written on 3 June, enclosing copies of the offers made by New York and Maryland, the House of Delegates referred those documents to the "committee of the whole House on the state of the Commonwealth" (Executive Letter Book, 1783–1786, p. 152, MS in Va. State Library; *JHDV*, May 1783, p. 50). Although the present resolutions must have been drafted before 28 June, it was not until then, the final day of the session, that they were submitted by the committee and adopted unanimously by each house of the General Assembly. On 27 June a motion in the House of Delegates asserting that "the seat of government [of Virginia] ought to be removed from the city of Richmond to the city of Williamsburg" failed to carry by a vote of 55 to 39 (*JHDV*, May 1783, pp. 92–93, 96–97, 98).

[3] The Palace, begun in 1706, had been the residence of the royal governors of Virginia until 1775, and then of Patrick Henry and Thomas Jefferson, the first two governors of the Commonwealth. After the removal of the capital to Richmond in 1780, the Palace became a military hospital. The Capitol, the second such building on the site, was in use by 1753. Besides chambers for the House of Burgesses, the Council, and the General Court, it contained committee rooms and offices. Among other public buildings in Williamsburg were the gaol, the powder magazine, and the secretary's office (Marcus Whiffen, *The Public Buildings of Williamsburg, Colonial Capital of Virginia* [Williamsburg, 1958], *passim*).

[4] The "three hundred Acres" may have comprised the "Palace lands adjoining the city of Williamsburg" (Hening, *Statutes*, XI, 406).

[5] For the compliance of the Governor in Council with this request, see Harrison to Virginia Delegates, 4 July 1783, and n. 5.

[6] The offer of the Maryland General Assembly on 30 May had been confined

to Annapolis (NA: PCC, No. 46, fols. 16–23). See also Pendleton to JM, 16 June 1783.

[7] On 1 July Beckley was elected mayor of Richmond (Records of the Common Hall, City of Richmond, 1782–1806 [2 vols.; MS in Va. State Library], II, 42; *Va. Gazette*, 5 July 1783). Harrison enclosed the present copy of the instructions in his letter of 4 July to the delegates (*q.v.*). For the reception of the instructions by Congress see *JCC*, XXIV, 438, n. 2.

From Alexander Hamilton

FC (LC: Hamilton Papers). Lacks salutation and the signature has been excised. Dated by Hamilton, "Princeton June 29. 178[3]," and docketed by him, "1783 29 June—To Mr Madison abt. the removal of Congress."

EDITORIAL NOTE

29 June 1783. Several circumstances appear to warrant the belief that Hamilton did not post this letter: (1) the RC is not among the Madison Papers in the Library of Congress; (2) in his letter of 6 July to Madison on the same subject (*q.v.*), Hamilton omitted mention of this earlier letter but used some of the same phrases appearing in it; (3) JM probably reached Princeton from Philadelphia during the morning of Tuesday, 1 July, thereby enabling Hamilton to communicate the substance of the letter in a conversation (JM to Randolph, 30 June 1783); (4) since the postrider did not travel on Sunday, he could not have picked up the letter in Princeton before 30 June, thus too late for JM to receive it prior to his departure from Philadelphia; and (5) JM's letter of response, dated 16 October 1783 (*q.v.*) is specifically to Hamilton's "favor of the 6th. of July."

Hamilton's letter of 6 July, written in Philadelphia, is less detailed than that of 29 June on the matter at issue. This fact may signify, of course, either that Hamilton knew of the receipt by JM of the earlier letter or, what seems more plausible, that they had talked about the subject when they were together in Princeton on 2 July (*JCC*, XXIV, 411–25, and esp. 422). For two quotations which together comprise most of Hamilton's draft, see Hamilton to JM, 6 July 1783, nn. 5, 6. See also Syrett and Cooke, *Papers of Hamilton*, III, 409, n. 1; Burnett, *Letters*, II, 204, and n. 1.

From Edmund Pendleton

Printed excerpt (Stan. V. Henkels Catalogue No. 694 [1892]).

EDITORIAL NOTE

In LC: Madison Miscellany, a list, probably prepared about 1850 by Peter Force or by his clerk, calendars this letter as follows: "1783, June 30 Virginia To James Madison Virginia rejects Mr. Madison's plan for raising a revenue. Virginia offers the Public buildings and lands and £100,000 if the seat of Government is located at Williamsburg." For Henkels and Force in relation to Madison's papers, see *Papers of Madison,* I, xxii, and nn. 27, 28; II, 22, n. 1; 65–66; 80.

VIRGINIA, June 30, 1783

. . . If the troops were not furlough'd without mutinous behaviour in one instance, and pathetic complaints in general, at a time when they were assured by their beloved Commander that Congress had done everything in their power to do them justice,[1] and they had no reason to doubt the success of their recommendation to the States; what will be their feelings & behaviour when they hear that the plan is rejected? Our Assembly gave a final Negative to the Bill for adopting y'r Propositions, on the 3rd reading, last week.[2]

. . . The Assembly have become bidders to have the session of Congress in this State or in its vicinity. If Williamsburg is accepted they offer all the Public buildings & land there & £100,000, to repair the Palace, build Hotels &c. If any place on Potommack is accepted, they offer diff't sum in conjunction with Maryland, as it shall be on the North or South side of the river. The lands & Jurisdiction which are to accompany the offers I don't distinctly recollect.[3]

[1] Pendleton referred to Washington's address, "To the Officers of the Army," on 15 March 1783 (*Papers of Madison,* VI, 377, nn. 1, 2). See also *ibid.,* VI, 482, n. 14; 486, nn. 2, 3. The address appears in the *Pennsylvania Packet* of 14 June. JM may have enclosed this issue to Pendleton in a missing letter, possibly written on 17 June 1783.

[2] Jones to JM, 14 June, and n. 17; 21 June, and nn. 5, 6, 8; 28 June; Randolph to JM, 14 June, n. 9; 21 June; 28 June 1783, and n. 3.

[3] Instructions to Delegates, 28 June, and nn. 2, 3, 4, 6. See also Harrison to Delegates, 4 July 1783.

To Edmund Randolph

RC (LC: Madison Papers). Unsigned but in JM's hand. Cover franked by JM and addressed to "The honble Edmund Randolph Richmond." Docketed by Randolph, "J Madison June. 30. 1783."

PHILADA. June 30. 1783.

MY DEAR SIR

My last informed you of the mutinous insult which was offered to Congs. on the Saturday preceding.[1] On the Evening after the insult

Congs. met and resolved that the Executive Council sd. be informed that in their opinion effectual measures ought to be immediately taken for suppressing the mutiny & supporting the public authority—that a Come. sd. confer with the Executive and in case no Satisfactory grounds sd. appear of adequate & prompt exertions for those purposes, the Presidt. sd. with the advise of the Come. be authorized to summon the members to meet at Trenton or Princeton in N.J.—that an Express be sent to Genl. Washington for a detachment of regular troops. The Conference with the Executive produced nothing but doubts concerning the disposition of the Militia to act unless some actual outrages were offered to persons or property. They even doubted whether a repetition of the insult to Congs. wd. be a sufficient provocation. Neither the exhortations of the Friends of Presidt. Dickenson nor the reproaches of his enemies could obtain an experiment on the temper of the Militia. During the attendance on the ultimate determinations of the Executive reports from the Barracks were in constant vibration. At one moment the Mutineers were penitent and preparing submissions: the next they were meditating more violent measures. Sometimes the Bank was their object; at other times the seizure of the members of Congress, with whom they imagined an indemnity for their offence might be purchased. On Teusday about two OClock, the efforts of the Govt. being despaired of, and the reports from the Barracks being unfavorable, the Committee advised the President to summon the members to meet in N.J. which he did verbally as to the members present, leaving a general proclamation behind him for the Press.[2] I left Princeton on friday evening when six States only had met. Rhode Islad. made a seventh on Saturday. to day I suppose they will be on business.[3] I shall set out this afternoon, on my return.[4]

Since Congress left the City the Mutiny has been entirely extinguished; the Mutineers having submitted, and most of them accepted furloughs under the Resolution of Congress on that subject. At the time of submission they betrayed their leaders, the chief of whom prove to be a Mr. Carbery a deranged officer, and a Mr. Sullivan a Lieutenant of Horse, both of whom made their escape. Some of the most active Sergeants have also run [?] off. The precise object & plan of the Conspiracy are unascertained.[5]

When I left Princeton no answer had been recd. from Genl. Washington.[6]

The removal of Congs. under the circumstances which gave birth to it, is a subject of much conversation and criticism. Many of Those who condemn it are but partially acquainted with facts. Many of Those who justify it, seem to have their eye remotely on the disgrace of the Executive Councils of the State.[7]

Tell Mr. Ambler that I do not forget him at present,[8] but that being on the point of s[etting out for?] Princeton, I am under the necessity of referring in [this to his?] letter or failing to reach the stage I aim at this evening[.]

[1] JM to Randolph, 24 June 1783.

[2] JM Notes, 19 June, and nn. 6, 7, 8; 20 June, and n. 1; 21 June, and nn. 1–7; Delegates to Harrison, 24 June 1783, and nn. 2, 3.

[3] The absence of entries in the journal for Friday, 27 June, and for 28 June almost certainly signifies that there was no quorum in Congress on either of those days. William Ellery and Jonathan Arnold presented their credentials on 30 June 1783 as delegates from Rhode Island (*JCC*, XXIV, 411). In Princeton on 1 July, Oliver Ellsworth wrote: "We were not able to make a House until Monday, because both of the Rhode Island Members chose to continue in Philadelphia, to shew their courage; and we have now only seven states on the Floor; so that we must have unanimity, which is hardly ever to be expected, or we can do nothing" (Burnett, *Letters*, VII, 209).

[4] Although JM most probably attended Congress on 1 July, he undoubtedly did the next day (*JCC*, XXIV, 421, n. 2, 422).

[5] JM Notes, 21 June, and n. 8. For the "Resolution of Congress" on the subject of "furloughs," see JM Notes, 26 May 1783, and n. 2.

[6] Major General Robert Howe and "about Eleven Hundred of the Massachusetts Line," intending to proceed on 2 July "toward Philadelphia," arrived in Princeton on the evening of 30 June (Burnett, *Letters*, VII, 208, 209). Washington's letter of 24 June, informing President Boudinot that Howe and his detachment would be "put in motion as soon as possible," was read in Congress on 1 July 1783 (Fitzpatrick, *Writings of Washington*, XXVII, 32–35; *JCC*, XXIV, 412 n.).

[7] For items in the *Pennsylvania Packet* and for letters written between 26 June and 15 July defending or blaming Congress for moving from Philadelphia to Princeton, see Burnett, *Letters*, VII, 199–207, 209–10, 211, 212, n. 3, 215–18, 219–24. See also Delegates to Harrison, 5 July; Hamilton to JM, 6 July 1783; Varnum L. Collins, *Continental Congress at Princeton*, pp. 33–36.

[8] JM probably referred to his slowness in replying to Jacquelin Ambler's letter of 14 June (*q.v.*). See also Ambler to JM, 5 July 1783.

Benjamin Harrison to Virginia Delegates

FC (Virginia State Library). In the hand of Thomas Meriwether. Addressed to "Virginia Delegates in Congress."

RICHMOND July 4th. 1783.

GENTLEMEN

Your favor of the 24th. of last Month[1] came safe to hand. I give Congress great Praise for their steadiness on the late trying Occasion,[2] and only wish they had turn'd their Attention to the South rather than the North as it may have some effect on the determination to be had in October next.[3] The enclosed resolution of our Assembly will discover their wishes for the removal of Congress to this State or Maryland, their offers are liberal, and I should think if consider'd impartially the latter would be accepted, as it will certainly be more central on either side of Potowmack than at any of the other Places proposed.[4] I shall write to-day to the Mayor of Williamsburg to know what Jurisdiction the Inhabitants of that City are willing to give to Congress and shall transmit the Answer to you as soon as it comes to hand.[5]

I have the Mortification to enclose you an Act in which you will find a Clause requesting Congress to furnish a guard for our Prison and Military Stores. I shall make no Comment on the request, but leave you to your own reflections, and to take such steps as you may think consistent with the Honor of the State.[6] You have also a Copy of a Memorial from the Officers of the Virginia line to the Assembly and their resolutions founded on it which you'l please to lay before Congress, and obtain their determination against the meeting of the Assembly in October next. It has ever appeared to me unaccountable that this Business has been so protracted if Congress mean to wrest the Land from us by force why do they not tell us so at once. It behoves them now I think to be explicit, as I do not think the Assembly will be triffled with much longer. Our Officers and Soldiers have a just claim on us for Lands, and it seems to be the general wish that they should be gratified with such as they like, and I am convinced the Assembly will grant their request if Congress do not accept of the Cession offer'd them before their next meeting.[7]

The Assembly have directed two armed Boats to be put into Commission to enforce the Payment of Duties laid on our imports and to keep the Trade in some little Order, if you should be of Opinion that the consent of Congress is necessary before they are sent on Duty you'l please to take the proper steps for obtaining it.[8] The resolution of Congress of the 19th. of last Month did not come in Time for the last Assembly. I will take Care to lay it before the next.[9]

I have the Honor to be Yrs. &c.

B. H.

[1] *Q.v.*

[2] That is, the mutiny of troops in Philadelphia (JM Notes, 21 June, and nn.; JM to Randolph, 24 June 1783).

[3] Governor Harrison meant that the Virginia General Assembly at its session of October 1783 might be more disposed to ratify the plan for restoring public

credit if Congress had decided upon leaving Philadelphia to reconvene in Virginia or Maryland rather than in Princeton, N.J.

[4] Instructions to Delegates, 28 June, and nn. 2–7. Besides Princeton, "other Places proposed" had been Kingston, N.Y., Trenton, N.J., and Annapolis, Md. (*Papers of Madison*, VI, 448, n. 4; *JCC*, XXIV, 229, n. 2, 376, 378, n. 2, 422 n.; JM to Jefferson, 17 July 1783, and nn. 7, 9).

[5] In his letter of 4 July, Harrison asked the mayor of Williamsburg without delay "to fall on some Mode" for determining the "Sentiments" of the residents of Williamsburg to the inducement offered to Congress by the Virginia General Assembly to move permanently to that city (Executive Letter Book, 1783–1786, p. 165, MS in Va. State Library).

Mayor William Holt (d. *ca.* 1791) had been a justice of peace of York County and shared prominently in opposing British policies on the eve of the Revolution. On 1 August 1776 he was appointed one of the three judges of the Court of Admiralty and served until 1779 (*JCSV*, I, 103, 105; Williams Armstrong Crozier, ed., *Virginia County Records* [11 vols.; New York, 1905–13], III, 30; Boyd, *Papers of Jefferson*, I, 47, 109). A shipowner, he was also the proprietor, with a partner, of an iron forge in New Kent County and of flour mills in that and James City County (*ibid.*, IV, 332, 385; V, 540; *JCSV*, I, 131, 135; II, 460–61; *Cal. of Va. State Papers*, II, 428, 436, 681; McIlwaine, *Official Letters*, I, 21, and n. 37; *Tyler's Quarterly Historical and Genealogical Magazine*, VII [1925–26], 285; *William and Mary Quarterly*, 1st ser., V [1896–97], 20–22; XI [1902–3], 153; XXII [1913–14], 70; XXIII [1914–15], 137). In a tax list of 1782, Holt was recorded as owning thirty-nine slaves (Augusta B. Fothergill and John M. Naugle, comps., *Virginia Tax Payers, 1782 87*, p. 62). See also Harrison to Delegates, 12 July 1783, and n. 3.

[6] Instruction to Delegates, 20 June 1783, and nn. 1, 3.

[7] Instruction to Delegates, 27 June 1783, and nn. 2, 3.

[8] Instruction to Delegates *in re* "Cormorant," 26–27 June, and nn. 1, 2; Motion *in re* Armed Vessels, 28 July 1783, and ed. n.

[9] Harrison referred to a circular letter from President Elias Boudinot on 20 June, enclosing a copy of the resolution of Congress of 19 June and other documents concerning paying and furloughing of continental troops (JM Notes, 19 June, n. 10; Burnett, *Letters*, VII, 192–93). On 20 October Harrison forwarded these papers to the speaker of the House of Delegates, but its first quorum was on 4 November (Executive Letter Book, 1783–1786, p. 218, MS in Va. State Library; *JHDV*, Oct. 1783, p. 7).

From Jacquelin Ambler

RC (LC: Madison Papers). Cover addressed to "The Honobl. James Madison of Congress Philadelphia." Docketed by JM, "July 5. 1783."

RICHMOND. 5th. July 1783.

DEAR SIR

I still hope the Gentlemen in Congress will enable me to adjust the Accounts of the Treasury in a regular mode, by transmitting a Certificate expressing the share of each, of the Remittances made in the course of this Year, & directing the Auditors to issue warrants accordingly.[1]

I have made no use of the partial Certificates hitherto sent, and the Gentlemen may rely on my restoring them on receipt of a general one.[2] I have been & stil am unhappy that this business is not adjusted—an Accident may happen to me, & if there should—my Accounts must appear erroneous. You mention the sum of £200. as received from the Sheriff of Accomack. Mr. Jones was here when the Sheriff settled & informed me that £203. .15. .9. was paid by young Satchell, & for so much the Sheriff has credit.[3] will you my Dear Sir take the trouble to run over my Letters (if those are in being which covered the Bills transmitted on the general Account of the Deputation both last year & this) & send me a memo. of the Bills distinguishing the dates & Sums.[4] two Days ago a draft signed by yourself Colo. Bland & Mr. Mercer for 80 Dollars in favor of Hyam Solomon dated 20. March. was presented.[5] I have paid it on my private Account: I could not out of the public Money, as the Law requires I should produce an Auditors Warrant for every sum paid out of the Treasury;[6] & indeed I could not know how this sum was divided, & of course how to carry it to account. You will be so good as to consider this also in the General Certificate.

Some days ago the Commissioners for the defence of Chesapeak[7] lodged in the Treasury two Bills of Excha. on Messrs. Lacaze & Mallet Merchts. in Phila. one for £683. .19. .2. & one for £550. Virga. Curry. as there is little probability of Money's coming into the Treasury to any amount before the next Spring (the collection of Taxes being postponed)[8] I could wish these Bills should be applied to yours & the use of the other Gentlemen in Congress, our Delegates. to enable me to do this the Gentlemen will please to authorize their friends here to take from the Auditors Office Warrants on their respective Accounts to the amount of one or both the Bills.[9]

Mr. Jones & Mr. Lee were both clearly of opinion the loss sustained in negotiating the Bills sent formerly may be, with the greatest propriety, debited in their respctive Accounts.[10] I am with great regard

Dear Sir Yr. affect. Servt.

J. AMBLER

1 Ambler to JM, 17 May, and n. 6; 24 May, and n. 2; 7 June; 14 June, and n. 3; JM to Mercer, 16 July 1783. On 1 July the Governor in Council, having received the resignation of John Boush, auditor, appointed John Pendleton, Jr., ad interim to serve with the other auditors, Bolling Stark and Harrison Randolph, until the Virginia General Assembly convened. On 20 November that legislature confirmed the executive's choice by electing Pendleton to the position (*JCSV*, III, 276; *JHDV*, Oct. 1783, pp. 22, 25, 26). For Pendleton, see *Papers of Madison*, I, 188; 190, n. 8.

[2] Summary of Accounts, 28 May, and n. 5; Delegates to Auditors, 28 May; Statement of Receipts, 28 May, and nn.; Ambler to JM, 14 June 1783.

[3] Statement of Receipts, 28 May, and n. 1; Ambler to JM, 14 June 1783. "Young Satchell" was either the sheriff's son Charles Stockley Satchell (d. 1805) or his son William Satchell III (d. 1823) (Northumberland County Court Records, Will Book 29, pp. 282–83, 284–85; Will Book 32, pp. 470–71; Will Book 36, pp. 162–66, microfilm in Va. State Library; *Norfolk Gazette and Public Ledger*, 30 Oct. 1805).

[4] *Papers of Madison*, IV, 108–10; V, 72–73; 73, nn. 3–5; 95; 182; 186; 205, n. 2; 266, and n. 1; VI, 405; JM to Mercer, 16 July 1783. See also the first three citations in n. 2, above. Ambler's further correspondence, if any, with JM during 1783 is missing. For this reason it is not clear whether JM complied with Ambler's request prior to his return to Virginia in December (Ambler to JM, 1 June 1783, n. 4).

[5] *Papers of Madison*, IV, 108, n. 2; 109. For other examples of the delegates' dependence upon Haym Salomon, see *ibid.*, III, 327; IV, 19, n. 2; V, 87; 170; 206, n. 4; 308.

[6] Hening, *Statutes*, IX, 199–200, 536–37.

[7] Instruction to Delegates *in re* "Cormorant," 26–27 June 1783, n. 1.

[8] Randolph to JM, 9 May, n. 4; Ambler to JM, 17 May 1783, n. 2.

[9] Ambler to JM, 10 May, and nn. 1, 2; JM to Mercer, 16 July; Jones to JM, 28 July; 4 Aug. 1783. JM probably did not use the good offices of Randolph in this instance, for he apparently received on 5 September 1783 £246 15*s*. as his share of those bills of exchange "remitted by" Ambler (Ambler to JM, 1 June 1783, n. 4).

[10] Summary of Accounts, 28 May, n. 3; Ambler to JM, 14 June 1783, and n. 4. See also *Papers of Madison*, VI, 405.

Virginia Delegates to Benjamin Harrison

RC (Virginia State Library). The misdatings of "June 5th," both in date line and docket, were apparently corrected soon after the letter's receipt. The letter was drafted and signed by Theodorick Bland, although he obviously was also writing on behalf of JM and John Francis Mercer, his two colleagues from Virginia then in Congress. Docketed: "Virginia Delegates Letter Theo Bland one of the Virginia Delegates, justifying the adjournment of Congress to prevent their invasion by the Mutineers. 1783 July 5th." See Delegates to Harrison, 24 June 1783, ed. n.

PRINCETON June [July] 5th 1783

SR:

Your Excellency's favor with its enclosures reachd us at this place,[1] where, you will have learnt from the Public Prints, Congress thought it both prudent and proper to adjourn on the 26th of June. The Causes which induced them to take that resolution your Excellency will find fully Explaind in the report of their Committe herewith enclosed.[2] We have little doubt but that the step will meet with the General approbation of our Constituents, when it is considered what pernicious Instruments Congress might have been made in the hands of a Lawless band of Armd Desperado's, and what fatal consequences might have ensued to the Union in General, had they remaind impotent and Passive Spectators of the most outrageous Insult to the Government, and to the Authority which is vested in them by the Federal Compact. On the part of Congress the most vigorous, and Immediate Exertions were made to preserve their Dignity and restore the Mutineers to that obedience due to Law and Government. A detachment was Immediately ordered from the Army to Suppress the Mutiny and restore order which passed by this place two days ago for Pennsylvania under the Command of Majr. Genl. Howe. we have Since heard that the Mutineers have returnd to their obedience[3] but that most of the Ring leaders (among whom we are told were unhappily Six Commissd officers) have fled. the Names of the Officers who have fled are Sullivan and Carberry. those who remaind are Christie, Steel and two others,[4] all of which accepted Commissions from a board of Sergeants, to compell a compliance of Govermt. with their demands at the risque of their lives.[5]

We have laid before Congress the Several Resolutions enclosed in Yr. Excellencys letter and also the application of Mr. Cooper the Pilot, and shall in due time inform you of the Steps which Congress may take thereon.[6] we are with the most perfect respect

Yr. Excelly's most obedt. Serts

THEOK: BLAND

[1] Harrison to Delegates, 20 June 1783, and nn. 1, 4.

[2] The eight folios enclosed in the present letter provided Harrison with copies of congressional resolutions, committee reports, letters, and instructions, dated between 19 June and 1 July 1783, relating to the mutiny. The eighth of these pages is signed, "Extract from the minutes Chas Thomson Secy." An additional page is docketed: "Honble Mr. Bland Resolutions of Cong. & Report of Committee from June 1st to July 1st 1783. on the insult to Cong by Troops of Pensylvania belo[nging] to the Army of the U.S. June 21st."

[3] JM Notes, 19 June, and nn. 6, 7; 20 June, and n. 1; 21 June, and nn. 1–7; Delegates to Harrison, 24 June; JM to Randolph, 24 June; 30 June 1783, and n. 6. After encamping his troops "within a few miles of Town," where he deemed it "best to keep them," General Robert Howe reached Philadelphia late in the evening of 3 July (NA: PCC, No. 38, fols. 85–87, 89–92; *Pa. Archives*, 1st ser., X, 66; *Colonial Records of Pa.*, XIII, 619). Although by then the mutiny was over, Howe remained there until September, taking charge of all continental troops in or near that city, of searching for the alleged mutineers who had fled, and of trying by courts-martial those who had been captured. By late in that month only a small number of those soldiers who had been detached in June under his command from Washington's main army were still stationed in or near Philadelphia (Fitzpatrick, *Writings of Washington*, XXVII, 42, and n. 70, 45, 47–48. 100, 114, 147, 162, 170; Burnett, *Letters*, VII, 217–18; JM to Randolph, 8 July; to Jefferson, 17 July 1783).

[4] For Captain Henry Carbery (Carberry, Carbury) and Lieutenant John Sullivan, see JM Notes, 21 June 1783, and n. 8; NA: PCC, No. 38, fols. 119–21; No. 185, III, 70, 72; *JCC*, XII, 1109; XVIII, 843; Fitzpatrick, *Writings of Washington*,

XV, 188, and n.; XXV, 382, and n. Also accused of being implicated in the mutiny were Captain James Christie (Chrystie) (d. 1807) and Lieutenant William Houston (Huston) (d. 1834) of the 2d Pennsylvania Regiment (Heitman, *Historical Register Continental*, pp. 154, 303), Captain Jonas Simonds (Simons, Simmons, Symonds) (d. 1848) of the 4th Continental Artillery Regiment (*Lineage Book of the National Society of the Daughters of the American Revolution*, CXXXVII [1934], 159), and Captain John Steele (Steel) (1758–1827), supernumerary of the 1st Pennsylvania Regiment (*Pa. Mag. of Hist. and Biog.*, LIII [1929], 381–82; *American Historical Register and Monthly Gazette of the Patriotic-Hereditary Societies of the United States of America* [5 vols.; Philadelphia, 1895–97], III, 644–49). For further information about these four officers, consult Fitzpatrick, *Writings of Washington*, index, vols. XXXVIII and XXXIX; *Colonial Records of Pa.*, XIII, 610, 612, 658, n., 664–65, 772; *Pa. Archives*, 1st ser., X, 135, 209; *JCC*, VIII, 427, 464; XII, 1225; Burnett, *Letters*, VII, 212, 223, n. A general court-martial acquitted Christie, Simonds, and Houston (NA: PCC, No. 38, fols. 105–6; No. 185, III, 77; *JCC*, XXV, 565–66; Burnett, *Letters*, VII, 297). Steele apparently was released from confinement without being tried.

[5] JM Notes, 21 June, and nn. 1, 8; Delegates to Harrison, 24 June 1783. Among the members of the "board" were Sergeants Christian Nagle (Nogle) and John Morrison of the 3d Pennsylvania Regiment, William Robinson (alias Taylor), John (?) Smith, Solomon Townsend, and Sergeant Major James Bennett of an artillery corps. Nagle and Morrison, after being condemned to death by the court-martial, petitioned Congress for mercy, strengthened their plea with endorsements from Dr. Benjamin Rush and other prominent Philadelphians, and received "a full, free and absolute pardon" from Congress on 13 September (NA: PCC, No. 38, fols. 105–6, 109, 185–87, 189–91; No. 185, III, 74, 75, 76, 77; *JCC*, XXIV, 509–10, 514 n., 517 n.; XXV, 565–66; Burnett, *Letters*, VII, 226, 263 n., 264 n.; *Pa. Archives*, 1st ser., X, 63, 67, 69, 72).

As for Robinson and Townsend, the "prime agents" of Captain Carbery and Lieutenant Sullivan in fomenting the mutiny, General Howe stated on 2 September in a letter to Washington that Robinson "demonstrably" had fled to Europe and that Townsend "many think has also left the Continent." Smith also appears to have eluded capture (NA: PCC, No. 38, fols. 105–6, 119–21; Fitzpatrick, *Writings of Washington*, XXIV, 310–11; XXV, 90–91, 252). Bennett, who at the time of the mutiny had acted as secretary of the board of sergeants, goes unmentioned in the primary sources after 23 June 1783 (*Diplomatic Correspondence of the United States*, I, 24–25, 36; Burnett, *Letters*, VII, 193, n. 2).

[6] Instruction to Delegates, 4 June, and n. 4; 17 June, and n. 2; Harrison to Delegates, 20 June, and nn. 1–4; Delegates to Harrison, 14 Aug. 1783.

From Alexander Hamilton

RC (LC: Madison Papers). Unsigned but in Hamilton's hand. Cover missing. Docketed by JM, "Alex. Hamilton Philadelphia July 6h. 1783."

6 July 1783

On my arrival in this city[1] I am more convinced than I was before of the necessity of giving a just state of facts to the public. The current runs strongly against Congress and in a great measure for want of information. When facts are explained they make an impression and incline to conclusions more favourable to us[2]—I have no copy of the reports in my possession, which puts it out of my power to publish them: Will you procure and send me one without loss of time? Without appearing I intend to give them to the public with some additional explanations. This done with moderation will no doubt have a good effect.[3]

The prevailing idea is that the actors in the removal of Congress*[4] were influenced by the desire of getting them out of the city, and the generality of the remainder by timidity—some say passion; few give a more favourable interpretation.[5]

I will thank you in your letter to me to answer the following question.

What appeared to be my ideas and disposition respecting the removal of Congress—did I appear to wish to hasten it, or did I not rather show a strong disposition to procrastinate it?[6]

I will be obliged to you in answering this question to do it fully. I do not intend to make any public use of it, but through my friends to vindicate myself, from the insinuation I have mentioned, and withal to confute the supposition that the motive assigned did actuate the members on whom it fell to be more particularly active.[7]

1 The time of Hamilton's arrival in Philadelphia is unknown. He had been in Princeton on 2 July (*JCC*, XXIV, 424; Syrett and Cooke, *Papers of Hamilton*, III, 411).

2 JM to Randolph, 30 June, n. 7. For additional evidence that the removal of Congress to Princeton was a subject of sharp criticism, and rarely of defense, by residents of Philadelphia, see *Pa. Packet*, 28 June, 3 July; *Pa. Gazette*, 9 July; *Pa. Journal*, 28 June, 5 July, 12 July; JM to Randolph, 8 July 1783.

3 The *Pennsylvania Packet* of 10 July and the *Pennsylvania Journal* of 12 July published copies of resolutions, committee reports, letters, and instructions of Congress or President Elias Boudinot relating to the mutiny of the troops and dating between 19 and 23 June 1783. The editor of the *Pennsylvania Packet* stated that a "correspondent" had furnished these documents. If the "correspondent" was Hamilton, he apparently did not accompany them with "additional explanations."

4 A postscript to which this asterisk seemingly refers may have been excised by the unknown person who clipped Hamilton's signature from the letter.

5 In the draft of his letter to JM of 29 June, probably withheld from the post, Hamilton wrote:

"I am informed that among other disagreeable things said about the removal of Congress from Philadelphia it is insinuated that it was a contrivance of some members to get them out of the state of Pennsylvania into one of those to which they belonged—and I am told that this insinuation has been pointed at me in particular.

"Though I am persuaded that all disinterested persons will justify Congress in quitting a place where they were told they were not to expect support (for the conduct of the Council amounted to that) yet I am unwilling to be held up as having had an extraordinary agency in the measure for interested purposes—when the fact is directly the reverse. As you were a witness to my conduct and opinions through the whole of the transaction, I am induced to trouble you for your testimony upon this occasion."

6 In his draft mentioned in n. 5, Hamilton elaborated upon this question as follows:

"Did that part of the resolutions which related to the removal of Congress originate with me or not?

"Did I as a member of the Committee appear to press the departure; or did I not rather manifist a strong disposition to postpone that event as long as possible, even against the general current of opinion?

"I wish you to be as particular & full in your answer as your memory will permit. I think you will recollect that my idea was clearly this—that the mutiny ought not to be terminated by negotiation—that Congress were justifiable in leaving a place where they did not receive the support which they had a right to expect; but as their removal was a measure of critical and delicate nature—might have an ill appearance in Europe—and might from events be susceptible of an unfavorable interpretation in this country—it was prudent to delay it 'till its necessity became apparent—not only 'till it was manifest there would be no change in the spirit which seemed to activate the council, but 'till it was evident complete submission was not to be expected from the troops—that to give full time for this, it would be proper to delay the departure of Congress 'till the latest period which would be compatible with the idea of meeting in Trenton or Princeton on thursday—perhaps even 'till thursday morning."

For "the Committee" and the measures to which Hamilton referred, see JM Notes, 19 June, and nn. 6, 7; 20 June, and n. 1; 21 June, and nn. 1–7. Although Hamilton may not have originated the committee's recommendation that Congress "assemble at Princeton or Trenton on Thursday the 26 instant," the entire report of the committee, including that recommendation, is in his hand. Hamilton's position in the present letter is consistent with his seconding on 2 July, when he and JM were together in Congress, an abortive motion by Mercer to adjourn "to meet at the City of Philadelphia on conformable to their said intention till they shall determine on the place of their permanent residence agreeable to their resolution of" 4 June 1783. In a letter, probably written late in September 1783 to President John Dickinson of Pennsylvania, Hamilton described at length his own views and activities during the mutiny; particularly mentioned his close association with JM at that time; and said that Richard Peters and Oliver Ellsworth, his colleagues on "the Committee," had overcome his own "opposition" to the removal of Congress from the city (*JCC*, XXIV, 381–82, 416–21, 421, nn. 1, 2, 424; Syrett and Cooke, *Papers of Hamilton*, III, 399–407, 401, n. 1; 438–58, and esp. 448; Burnett, *Letters*, VII, 233–34).

7 By what JM would call "singular ill luck," the present letter did not reach him until 15 October (JM to Hamilton, 16 Oct. 1783). Hamilton was then in New York, having left Congress at Princeton about 27 July (Syrett and Cooke, *Papers of Hamilton*, III, 418–19). JM appears to have been in Philadelphia between 6 and 16 July 1783.

To Edmund Randolph

RC (LC: Madison Papers). Unsigned but in JM's hand. Cover franked by him and addressed to "Edmund Randolph Esqr. Richmond." Docketed by Randolph, "J Madison July 8. 1783."

PHILADA. July 8. 1783.

MY DEAR FRIEND

Yours of the 28. of June like the preceding one[1] found me at this place, where my preparations for leaving Congs. will keep me much of the remainder of my time.[2] The footing on which the Impost is placed by the Assembly is not an eligible one, but preferable to a total rejection.[3] It is to be regretted that immediate use was not made of the impression of the letter from Genl. W.[4] The interval preceding the next Session will give full scope to malignant insinuations. The reversal of the award in the case of Nathan may possibly be just in itself, but it will require all your eloquence I fear to sheild the honor of the State from its effects. The Agency which the Delegation had in the affair will impart no small share of the mortification to them. I suppose the feelings of Mr. Jefferson & Mr. Harrison also will not be much delighted by it.[5]

Genl. How is here with a corps of N. England troops detached by Gl. W. for the purpose of quelling the Mutiny. His only employment will now be to detect & punish the promoters of it.[6] Congs. remain at Princeton. Their removal from that place will soon become an interesting question.[7] Not a few maintain strenuously the policy of returning to this City in order to obviate suspicions abroad of any disaffection in the mass of so important a State to the fœderal Govt. and to restore mutual confidence with a State which has of late been so firm in adhering to fœderal measures.[8] It is supposed too that a freer choice might here be made amg the permanent seats offered by the States, than at a place where the necessity of a speedy removal wd. give undue advantage to an offer which happened to be in greatest readiness for immediate use.[9] The Citizens here in general regret the departure of Congs. disavow the idea that they were unwilling to take arms in defence of Congs. and will probably enter into some declaration tending to invite their return.[10]

We hear nothing from our Ministers in Europe.[11] The evacuation of

N. York as to the time seems as problematical as ever.[12] The sending off the negroes continues to take place under the eyes & remonstrances of the Inspectors of Embarkations.[13]

[1] Randolph to JM, 21 June; 28 June 1783 (*qq.v.*).

[2] Although JM had an almost perfect record of attending Congress from 20 March 1780 to 24 June 1783, he was frequently absent from the sessions at Princeton during the remainder of his service as a delegate (*JCC*, XVI, 268; JM Notes, 21 June 1783, n. 5). From 30 June, when a quorum first assembled in Princeton, to 31 October, when his term expired, Congress convened on 94 of the 107 days, not counting the seventeen Sundays. The journal records 94 tallied polls, all taken on 38 of the 94 days. Arthur Lee voted in 82 of the polls, Mercer in 80, Bland in 56, JM in 43, and Jones in 32. The journal and JM's correspondence make clear that he rarely attended in July and August, except near the close of each of those months, and that in September and October he probably shared in congressional business only from 1 to 4 and 12 to 25 September and on 2, 6 to 13, 16 to 18, and 22 October.

Among the reasons impelling JM to spend so much time in Philadelphia, where he continued to keep all his "papers" and to stay in Mrs. House's boardinghouse, were his wish or need to complete some "writing," engage in "close reading," transact "private business" preparatory to "leaving Congress," enjoy as long as possible the "agreeable & even instructive society" of the city, and avoid the cramped quarters in which he was obliged to live when in Princeton (JM to Randolph, 15 July; 5 Aug.; 12 Aug.; 8 Sept.; 13 Sept.; to Jefferson, 7 May, and n. 14; 17 July; 20 Sept.; to James Madison, Sr., 30 Aug.; 8 Sept.). The "thinness" of attendance in Congress during July and most of August blocked decisions on important issues; Virginia was always effectively represented by at least two delegates; and JM returned to Princeton upon notification that his presence in Congress would be "of essential utility" (JM to Jefferson, 17 July; 11 Aug.; to Randolph, 21 July; Hawkins to JM, 9 Aug.; Mercer to JM, 14 Aug.; JM to James Madison, Sr., 30 Aug. 1783).

[3] Randolph to JM, 15 May, and nn. 3, 4; 14 June, n. 9; 21 June; 28 June; Jones to JM, 25 May, and nn. 5, 8; 28 June; Pendleton to JM, 26 May 1783, n. 11.

[4] Jones to JM, 28 June, and n. 6; Randolph to JM, 28 June 1783.

[5] At Harrison's request, JM and the other Virginia delegates in Congress had arranged in Philadelphia for the arbitration of Simon Nathan's financial claims against Virginia. The evidences of debt held by him were the outcome of contracts made with him and others by Jefferson when governor. The arbitrators' decision, favorable to Nathan, had been rejected by the Virginia General Assembly. Harrison no doubt was mortified by the result of the arbitration probably the more so because his own oversight had prevented an important document, adverse to Nathan's claim, from reaching the arbitrators before they rendered their judgment. On 5 May 1783, having reviewed at length the case of Nathan in a letter addressed to the speaker of the House of Delegates, Harrison stated, "Tho' I am dissatisfied with the Award yet I think we are now bound to pay it, and I hope the Assembly will provide a fund" (Executive Letter Book, 1783–1786, p. 110, MS in Va. State Library). See also *Papers of Madison*, VI, 14; 15, n. 8; 29–30; 30, nn. 4, 8; 154; 241; 307; 474; 475, n. 3; 502; Randolph to JM, 28 June 1783, and nn. 7, 8.

[6] Delegates to Harrison, 5 July 1783, and nn. 3, 4.

[7] JM to Randolph, 30 June 1783, and n. 7; Burnett, *Letters*, VII, 215–17, 217, n. 5.

[8] Hamilton to JM, 6 July 1783, and n. 6.

[9] *Papers of Madison*, VI, 447; 448, nn. 4–7; Harrison to Delegates, 17 May; 4 July,

and n. 5; Delegates to Harrison, 27 May, and n. 2; JM to Randolph, 10 June, and n. 14; Instructions to Delegates, 28 June; Hamilton to JM, 6 July 1783, n. 6.

10 JM to Mercer, 16 July 1783, and n. 4.

11 Subsequent to 8 July the first important dispatch from "our Ministers" was Franklin's of 7 March, regarding the treaty with Sweden, received by Congress on 16 July (NA: PCC, No. 185, III, 71). See also *Papers of Madison*, VI, 335; 339, n. 21; JM to Jefferson, 10 June, and n. 24; 17 July 1783, and n. 2.

12 Pendleton to JM, 4 May 1783, n. 5.

13 Walke to Delegates, 3 May, nn. 5, 7; Delegates to Harrison, 20 May, n. 3; JM Notes, 23 May, n. 4; 26 May 1783, n. 1; *JCC*, XXIV, 436.

Benjamin Harrison to Virginia Delegates

FC (Virginia State Library). In the hand of Thomas Meriwether. Addressed to "The Virginia Delegates in Congress."

In Council July 12th. 1783.

Gentlemen

I had not the pleasure of your usual favor by the last post the reason of which I expect was explain'd by a proclamation of your President for the removal of Congress to Prince Town,[1] a step that has given general Satisfaction here, indeed I think nothing could justify your staying so long after the various insults you have received but the Advantages derived from the Bank during the war.[2] In my last I forwarded to you the invitation of our Assembly to this State and then promised to send by this Post the Determination of those who are to be affected if Williamsburg should be the Place fixed on respecting the Jurisdiction they were willing to give to Congress, I now fulfil my Promise as far as it rested with me, tho' you will collect nothing from it, but that we are still jealous of our Liberty and are unwilling to give up any part of it even to Congress,[3] however when your desires on the Subject are made known which I wish to be as speedily as possible I doubt not but they will by their Moderation remove the Apprehensions the Inhabitants of the District may be under of a loss of any part of their Liberty, and perhaps quiet some of the grave ones, on the score of the Luxury your Attendants will probably introduce.[4] You have also two Depositions proving the illbehavior of a French Officer who was prize Master to the Brig Lord Cornwallis taken by the rode Island fleet and sent here, respecting some Cannon and Military Stores carried off by him, if you think they or their value can be recovered you'l please to take the necessary steps for doing it, but if it will be attended with

Trouble or give uneasiness I by no means press it on you, it being of too trifling a Nature to bring on any serious Altercation.[5]

A report prevails here said to come from Philadelphia that our worthy General is become so unpopular in his Army that no Officer will dine with him, the report is so improbable that I give no Credit to it yet I am anxious to hear from you on the Subject,[6] and also to know in what state the definitive Treaty is, and what now obstructs the signing of it.[7]

I am with respect Gent. Yrs &c.

B. H.

1 Harrison could not have received the delegates' letter of 5 July (*q.v.*), which almost certainly would have been written four days earlier, if Congress had remained in Philadelphia.

2 Harrison's comments reflect his reading of the delegates' letter of 24 June (*q.v.*), and also, no doubt, of the *Virginia Gazette* of 12 July. That issue includes a copy of Elias Boudinot's proclamation of 24 June 1783. For the Bank of North America, located in Philadelphia, see *Papers of Madison*, III, 173; 175, n. 16; VI, 495, n. 7.

3 Instructions to Delegates, 28 June, hdn., n. 2; Harrison to Delegates, 4 July, 1783, and n. 5. Residents of Williamsburg and of the countryside, within five miles of the town, at a meeting, with George Wythe, chairman, resolved unanimously that, although Congress had not made its extent of required control clear, they were "willing to submit to any such jurisdiction as may be compatible with their political welfare, and worthy of generous minds either to demand or yield" (NA: PCC, No. 46, fols. 89–92). Upon receiving a copy of these proceedings from the Virginia delegation on 23 July, Congress referred them to a committee which had been appointed five days earlier "to report what jurisdiction may be necessary for Congress in the place where they shall fix their permanent residence." This committee by 23 July was composed of James Duane (N.Y.), chairman, James Wilson, Jacob Read, James McHenry, JM, and, beginning 3 September, Samuel Huntington, and Richard Peters (NA: PCC, No. 186, fol. 112; *JCC*, XXIV, 444, n. 1; XXV, 537). See also JM to Randolph, 28 July; Motion *in re* Permanent Site, 22 Sept. 1783, n. 1.

4 *JCC*, XXV, 603–4, 647–60; JM to Randolph, 13 Oct. 1783.

5 The "two Depositions" have not been found. The acknowledgment of them by the Virginia delegates on 26 July states that the alleged "illbehavior" had been by a "Cap'n Camm." In February 1781 Captain Arnaud Le Gardeur de Tilly, commanding a squadron comprising two frigates and the sixty-four gun "L'Éveille," on which the Marquis H. Le Camus was a junior officer, captured in Chesapeake Bay several enemy vessels, including the privateer brig "Lord Cornwallis" (Baron Ludovic de Contenson, *La Société des Cincinnati de France et la Guerre d'Amérique, 1778–1783* [Paris, 1934], p. 211; *Papers of Madison*, II, 315; 316, n. 7; III, 4, n. 6; 42, n. 2; Wharton, *Revol. Dipl. Corr.*, IV, 271; Edwin Martin Stone, *Our French Allies . . . in the Great War of the American Revolution* [Providence, R.I., 1884], p. 354). After acquiescing to a request to leave his prizes at Yorktown, Tilly and his ships rejoined the French fleet based at Newport, R.I. Governor Thomas Nelson, Jr., of Virginia appears to have loaned the French prizes, among them the "Lord Cornwallis," at least "four Guns 4 pounders and 100 Boulets" (cannon balls), belonging to the state, to enable them more effectively to co-operate with Virginia's ships in defending Chesapeake Bay and the neighboring rivers

against British privateers and other enemy warcraft (Boyd, *Papers of Jefferson*, IV, 659, 678; V, 306 n.).

On 4 April 1781 Washington wrote to Nelson, informing him that Ensign Le Camus, the bearer of the letter, had been ordered by the commander of the French fleet at Newport to proceed to Virginia and take charge of "an armed Vessel in York River." Probably reaching Virginia later that month, at about the time of Lafayette's arrival with his division of continental troops, Le Camus reported to the marquis and then assumed his command of the "Lord Cornwallis" at or near West Point on the York River (Fitzpatrick, *Writings of Washington*, XXI, 415; Louis Gottschalk, *Lafayette and the Close of the American Revolution*, pp. 219, 290, 296). Besides this vessel, Le Camus was commander of several other small ships before the close of the campaign in October 1781 (Fitzpatrick, *Writings of Washington*, XXIII, 215, 225). See also Delegates to Harrison, 26 July 1783.

[6] The Hessian Major Carl Leopold Baurmeister, who returned to New York City on 16 July 1783 following a mission to Philadelphia, ascribed Washington's declining prestige to his subserviency to the unpopular Congress. Baurmeister also understood that the faction devoted to the political fortunes of former President Joseph Reed of Pennsylvania was "active" in spreading discontent with Washington throughout the state (Bernard A. Uhlendorf, trans. and ed., *Revolution in America: Confidential Letters and Journals, 1776–1784, of Adjutant General Major Baurmeister of the Hessian Forces* [New Brunswick, N.J., 1957], p. 576). See also *Papers of Madison*, VI, 266; 269, n. 18; 286; Randolph to JM, 28 June, n. 7; Delegates to Harrison, 27 July 1783.

[7] Delegates to Harrison, 26 July; 1 Aug. See also Pendleton to JM, 4 May, n. 6; *Va. Gazette*, 12 July 1783.

From Edmund Randolph

RC (LC: Madison Papers). Unsigned but in Randolph's hand. Addressed by him to "The honble James Madison jr. esq of congress Princeton New Jersey." Docketed by JM, "July 12. 17[83]."

RICHMOND July 12. 1783

MY DEAR FRIEND

Your flight to Princeton has, I presume, been the cause of the post of thursday bringing no letter from you.[1]

The proclamation, issued by the executive last week, has occasioned much uneasiness in the minds of those, whose british friends are affected by it. Indeed it wants precision to so great a degree, as to subject it to the justest and severest criticism. After a description of the persons, who are to be expelled, it prohibits the return *as well of those, as of all others coming within the like description.* It does no more, than *to prohibit the return and direct the departure of those persons*, and yet commands all officers civil and military to obey it. In what?—It also forbids the return of traitors. Can any act prevent a traiterous citizen from risquing his head upon a trial?[2] It is true, that the penalties of the law are not yet removed from the return of these people: but the proclamation carries the disagreeable idea, that the executive have adopted the spirit of the resolutions of the committees to the northward, who act, as if the treaty were within their power of repeal.[3]

By the next post, I probably shall be able to inclose to you a copy of Colo. Meriwether Smith's pamphlet on british debts. It is now in the press.[4]

It is whispered, that C—ss repent of their abandonment of Phila.[5] I cannot believe, that passion would have dictated the measure, and therefore I presume, that the intelligence of your contrition has passed thro' the impure channel of some interested pen.

Adieu

1 In his letter of 18 July, Randolph acknowledged the receipt in the "last mail" of JM's "favors of June 30. & July 8." (*qq.v.*). Although directed to Princeton, the present letter reached JM in Philadelphia on 21 July (JM to Randolph, 21 July 1783).

2 In the proclamation of 2 July, issued by Harrison with the advice of the Council of State, the governor declared that, contrary to law, "many evil disposed persons" had come to Virginia and "many others would follow their example." He commanded "all Officers, civil and military" and "all others concerned" to compel those persons "forthwith to depart the State." Among "those persons" were some who had "voluntarily left this country" since 19 April 1775 and "adhered to the enemy"; some who had been expelled by legislative act or executive order; some who as "natives" had returned to Virginia, without permission, after serving in the British armed forces; and "all others coming within the like description" (*Va. Gazette*, 5, 12, 19 July; *Va. Gazette, and Weekly Advertiser*, 5 July 1783). Besides believing, along with JM, Pendleton, and Randolph, that the signing of the preliminary articles of peace had not ended "the *state* of war," Harrison evidently assumed that an ordinance of 1776 and two statutes of 1780 and 1782, respectively, which were to continue in force "during the war," and which the Virginia General Assembly in its session of May 1783 had refused to repeal, amply justified the contents of his proclamation (*Papers of Madison*, VI, 365; 439; 456; 458, nn. 2, 3; Pendleton to JM, 4 May; 17 May; Randolph to JM, 9 May; Jones to JM, 31 May, and n. 14; 21 July 1783, and n. 6; Hening, *Statutes*, IX, 170–71; X, 268–70; XII, 136–38).

On the other hand, as Randolph suggested, Harrison in the proclamation was vague, illogical, and seemingly heedless of the provisions of the statutes just mentioned, and even of Virginia's Form of Government and Declaration of Rights (*ibid.*, IX, 109, 110, 112, 115–16). Whom, except those persons referred to earlier in the proclamation, could he mean by "all others coming within the like description"? By what methods were "all Officers, civil and military," and "all others concerned" expected to compel the "evil disposed" individuals "forthwith to depart"? Did not he thereby arrogate to himself and also delegate to "others" the arbitrary power of forcibly ejecting or excluding a suspected person from the state, thus denying him the rights guaranteed both in the Declaration of Rights and in the laws, cited above, of being heard in his own defense and tried before a jury? Furthermore, by prescribing banishment for offenses of less gravity than treason, Harrison unwarrantably had added to the punishments stipulated in those laws.

[3] Papers of Madison, V, 182, n. 5; 282; 286, n. 14; 409–10; VI, 370; Harrison to Delegates, 3 May, and n. 2; 9 May, and n. 6; Randolph to JM, 15 May; 13 Sept., and n. 1; Jones to JM, 8 June, and nn. 26, 27; 14 June; 21 June, and nn. 4, 19; 28 June; *JCSV*, III, 279. For "the resolutions" of New England towns, see Pendleton to JM, 10 May, and n. 4; Delegates to Harrison, 23 Aug. 1783, and n. 2.

[4] On 4 August JM received Randolph's missing letter of 25 July, enclosing Meriwether Smith's pamphlet, *Observations on the Fourth and Fifth Articles of the Preliminaries for a Peace with Great Britain* (Richmond, 1783). Smith, a member of the Virginia Council of State at that time, opposed the payment of private debts and the return of confiscated property to British subjects, including Loyalists, until Great Britain had executed all the stipulations favorable to the United States in the preliminary articles of peace and in the definitive treaty. As late as November 1787 Smith still adhered to this position. See Jones to JM, 8 June 1783, and n. 26; Boyd, *Papers of Jefferson*, VII, 117 n.; Kate Mason Rowland, *The Life of George Mason, 1725–1792* (2 vols.; New York, 1892), II, 205.

[5] Delegates to Harrison, 5 July; Hamilton to JM, 6 July, and n. 2; JM to Randolph, 8 July; JM to Jefferson, 17 July 1783.

From Joseph Jones

RC (LC: Madison Papers). Undocketed and cover missing but undoubtedly written to JM.

FREDERICKSBURG 14th: July 1783.

DR. SIR.

Your favor of the 30th. ult. I have duly recd. giving the history of the proceedings that brought about the removal of Congress to Princeton.[1] that two of the members of the Comtee: were disposed to advise the Predsident to the Measure which his inclination encouraged them to adopt I have no doubt,[2] but why so important a step shod. rest with the Com: and the president I am at a loss to comprehend unless Congress were so intimidated by the conduct of the soldiery as to fear mischievous consequences from their coming together, and so left the business to the Com: & President.[3] Mr. H—'s excuse for concuring in the measure is by no means satisfactory. to be indifferent in a matter of such consequence or to yield oneself up to the guidance of others is a conduct in my judgment reprehensible and has precipitated that Body into a situation I apprehend not very agreeable as well as exposed them to censure and ridicule.[4] altho' judging by the event is not a fair conclusion, it is but too commonly the case and on the present occasion will give force to the censures of those who wish to divert them from the Executive of the State, who from the report of the Com: were justly blameable for declining to give those assurances of support which the circumstances of the case and the dignity of Government required. I wish Congress had shewn more firmness in their conduct with respect to the Soldiery, especially as no just cause of personal danger presented itself and had remained in Philadelphia, notwithstanding the refusal of support by the Executive,[5] and have afterwards taken up the matter of indignity and disrespect on the part of the State with temper and coolness, and have made that the ground of serio[us] removal to one of the places tendered them by the other States.[6] the public opinion wod. have gone with them more generally than as the affair has been conducted. they are now thought to have been too timid, at the same time that the Executive are blamed for their remissness. To return to Phila is I suppose now out of the question. princeton I presume cannot long serve the purpose. where then will you fix? pray inform me what is likely to be done in the matter & how you are accommodated in Princeton. If I visit you can a tolera[ble] birth be procured. The sickly Season is approaching and if I move at all it will be in abt. a fortnight or three weeks especially if Mr. Treasurer can furnish the needfull.[7] Mr. L. we hear is to be Minister for foreign affairs.[8] Heaven smiles upon us this year, as the Crops are in general very promising.[9] Mrs. Jones begs her Compliments.

Yr. Friend & Servt. JOS: JONES.

[1] The contents of JM's missing letter of 30 June to Jones probably resembled those of the one JM wrote to Randolph on the same day (*q.v.*). The present letter and Jones's letter of 21 July 1783 (*q.v.*) may have reached JM simultaneously.

[2] Jones inadvertently misspelled "President." Of the committee composed of Hamilton, chairman, Richard Peters, and Oliver Ellsworth (*JCC*, XXIV, 405, n. 1), Jones probably excepted Peters, whose estate, Belmont, was near Philadelphia (Harold Donaldson Eberlein and Horace Mather Lippincott, *The Colonial Homes of Philadelphia and Its Neighbourhood* [Philadelphia, 1912], pp. 141–49). JM was reported as telling Jared Sparks in 1830 that when Peters was informed that only "a *flash in the pan*" had threatened Congress in Philadelphia, Peters replied, "Yes, but they *went off*" (*Va. Mag. of Hist. and Biog.*, LX [1952], 262). Hamilton, on the other hand, would have excluded himself (Hamilton to JM, 6 July, n. 6). For President Elias Boudinot's "inclination" to have Congress move to his own state, see JM Notes, 21 June 1783, n. 7. Two months later Charles Thomson wrote to his wife that Elizabethtown, N.J., had been "talked of" at the president's "table as a proper place" for Congress to meet. Boudinot, Thomson continued, had a house of twenty rooms there, and if Congress acceded to the suggestion, "the value of his estate will be increased and he will have an opportunity of letting his house at a good rent" as the residence of the president (Burnett, *Letters*, VI, 270–71; Delegates to Harrison, 23 Aug. 1783, n. 7).

[3] Jones's supposition was well warranted. On 21 June after "the authority of the United States" had "been this day grossly insulted by the disorderly and menacing appearance of a body of armed soldiers" outside the State House, Congress adopted

resolutions submitted by the committee empowering and directing Boudinot "on the advice of the committee" to call upon "the members of Congress to meet on Thursday next at Trenton or Princeton." Opponents of the move could plausibly hold that by 24 June, when Boudinot issued the proclamation, the mutiny was virtually at an end. Jones's complaint that "so important a step" should not have been entrusted to the judgment of four men was reasonable, except that effective delegations of seven states, let alone nine, could probably not have been assembled on 21, 22, 23, or 24 June (*JCC*, XXIV, 407, 410; JM Notes, 21 June, nn. 1–8; JM to Randolph, 30 June 1783, and n. 3).

[4] Although the resolutions of the committee are in Hamilton's hand, he insisted that he had not originated the portion of them providing, in case of a prolongation of the emergency, for Congress to leave Philadelphia, and that he had objected to the issuance of the proclamation on 24 June (Hamilton to JM, 6 July, and nn. 2, 5). See also Delegates to Harrison, 5 July; JM to Randolph, 8 July; Harrison to Delegates, 12 July, and n. 2; Randolph to JM, 12 July 1783.

[5] Boudinot, JM, and many other members of Congress would have challenged the truth of Jones's statement that they were in no "personal danger" between 21 and 24 June (JM Notes, 21 June, and nn. 1–6; Bland to JM, 22 June; Delegates to Harrison, 24 June; 5 July 1783; Burnett, *Letters*, VII, 195).

[6] Offers of a permanent site for the capital of the Confederation had been made to Congress by New York, Maryland, New Jersey, and Virginia. See Instructions to Delegates, 28 June, and n. 6; Harrison to Delegates, 4 July, and n. 2; 12 July, and n. 3; JM to Randolph, 8 July 1783; *JCC*, XXIV, 422 n., 438, n. 2.

[7] JM to Randolph, 8 July, n. 2. Having been provided with funds by "Mr. Treasurer," Jacquelin Ambler, early in August, Jones reached Philadelphia about the eighteenth of that month. See JM to Randolph, 6 May, n. 9; 18 Aug.; Ambler to JM, 1 June, and n. 4; Jones to JM, 4 Aug. 1783.

[8] "Mr. L." was probably Arthur Lee, even though Jones should have realized how unlikely it was that Congress would elect an anti-Gallican to the office. He could hardly have meant Robert R. Livingston. See *Papers of Madison*, VI, 224, n. 7; JM Notes, 10 June, and n. 12; JM to Jefferson, 10 June; Livingston to JM, 19 July 1783, n. 6.

[9] *Papers of Madison*, VI, 280; Pendleton to JM, 10 May, 23 June, and 14 July, 1783.

From Edmund Pendleton

Summary (LC: Madison Miscellany). The summary is in a calendar, probably prepared about 1850 by Peter Force's clerk. He noted that the letter was addressed "To James Madison" and that the manuscript consisted of "2 pages 4°."

1783, July 14 VIRGINIA

The offence of the soldier to Congress. The neglect of the Executive of Pennsylvania. The flight of Congress.[1] Speculation in Continental Money. Mr. Pendleton's views of the public liability for the paper money issues.[2] The crops.[3]

[1] Pendleton obviously commented on the mutiny in Philadelphia between 19 and 24 June (JM Notes, 21 June, and nn.; Delegates to Harrison, 5 July, and nn. 2, 5; Pendleton to JM, 21 July 1783, and n. 1).

[2] These topics could have been suggested to Pendleton if he recently had read Meriwether Smith's pamphlet on the debts owed by Americans to British subjects (Randolph to JM, 12 July, and n. 4). See also Pendleton to JM, 2 June; 16 June 1783, and n. 10. For the speculation in continental currency and loan-office certificates, see *Papers of Madison*, VI, 166, n. 14; 172, n. 6; 250; 251, n. 7; 264–65; 267, n. 7; 490–91; 493.

[3] On the subject of "crops," Pendleton may have agreed with Joseph Jones in his letter of 14 July (*q.v.*). See also Pendleton to JM, 10 May 1783.

To Edmund Randolph

RC (LC: Madison Papers). Unsigned but in JM's hand. Cover franked by him and addressed to "Edmund Randolph Esqr. Richmond." Docketed by Randolph, "J. Madison July. 15. 1783." Many years later, after recovering this letter, JM wrote "1783" on the docket under Randolph's indistinct notation of that year.

PHILADA. July 15. 1783.

MY DEAR SIR

Yesterdays post brought me no letter from you.[1] The Contents of the inclosed paper make up every thing of consequence which I have for a subject at present.[2] The enquiry into the Mutiny has not advanced far enough to bring forth any discoveries.[3] An address is circulating & will be generally signed by the Citizens here reciting to Congress the proofs they have heretofore given of attachmt. to the fœderal govt. professing a continuance of that attachmt. and declaring their readiness to support the dignity & privileges of Congs. in case the conveniency of this place for transacting the public affairs sd. give it a preference to others untill a final residence shall be fixed.[4]

Mr. Lee arrived here the day before yesterday and goes to Princeton today.[5] Mr. Mercer's indisposition, carries him to the Sea board of N. Jersey.[6] My absence not producing any chasm in the Representation and some private business requiring my stay here, I shall not return to Princeton for 7 or 8 days.[7]

[1] If Randolph wrote to JM on or about 4 July, the letter is missing.

[2] The paper was probably the *Pennsylvania Packet* of 15 July. Among the items "of consequence" in that issue, JM may have included those about the many British and Hessian troops, as well as Loyalists, sailing from New York City to Canadian ports of debarkation; the announcement by inhabitants of a town in New York warning Loyalists not to return there, for they would be treated "with

the greatest contempt" and not permitted to stay; the counterfeit "halfpence" circulating in Philadelphia; and the erroneous report that "two American gentlemen" were in Madrid on 6 May to negotiate a treaty of amity and commerce with the court of Spain. For the "halfpence," see *Colonial Records of Pa.*, XIII, 643–44, 650.

3 Delegates to Harrison, 5 July 1783, nn. 3–5.

4 JM to Randolph, 8 July 1783, and citations in n. 10.

5 JM to Randolph, 6 May 1783, n. 9.

6 JM to Mercer, 16 July 1783, and n. 7.

7 JM appears to have attended Congress from 22 through 26 July (JM to Randolph, 21 July; 5 Aug. 1783; *JCC*, XXIV, 443, 444, n. 1; Syrett and Cooke, *Papers of Hamilton*, III, 414).

From David Jameson

RC (NA: PCC, No. 78, XIII, 285–88). Cover missing. Addressee uncertain but probably JM. Docketed by Charles Thomson, secretary of Congress, "Letter 16 July 1783 David Jameson."

EDITORIAL NOTE

Lacking the cover or mention of the addressee in the text, this letter may have been written to someone in Congress other than JM. Although Jameson calls his correspondent "my friend," this designation serves only to make certain that he was not addressing the Virginia delegates as a group. JM was Jameson's "friend" (*Papers of Madison*, I, 217, n. 2), but presumably he also so considered Theodorick Bland, Arthur Lee, John Francis Mercer, and Joseph Jones. The last of these was still in Virginia on the date of this letter, but Jameson may have thought him to be in Philadelphia. No one of the Virginia delegates, other than JM, is known to have been a correspondent of Jameson. Jameson had never served in Congress. For this reason it is unlikely that he would have addressed President Elias Boudinot or Charles Thomson and referred to either of them as "my friend."

July 16th. 1783

Dear Sir

Before this reaches you, I suppose you will have received from the Governor a resolution of the last Assembly requesting a Sum of Money from Congress to level the works at York; which I do most earnestly wish may be granted.[1] The people of that place were much distressed by the British, and really are not able to do so great a work themselves. Nor do I imagine any person will think that after all their sufferings, the burthen of leveling those works (kept up & much enlarged for the defence of the French Army) should fall on them, or that they ought to bear at their very doors Mounds of Earth which prevent a free circulation of the Air, and Ditches of stagnant putrid water. General Lincoln has said that the Soldiers for three years still in the pay of the Continent might with propriety be sent to York to level the Works.[2] Should this measure be proposed to Congress give me leave my Friend to offer some reasons against it. Nearly half the number of Houses in the Town were entirely destroyed by the British, and many of those they left standing were much injured by them, by the shels & Balls, by the French Army, or by our own Soldiers, so that it is with difficulty the inhabitants who remained in Town, and who have since the siege & the departure of the French Army returned there; can be tolerably accomodated. it will then follow that there is not room to Barrack or Billet the Soldiers. As soon as it was known that preliminaries of Peace were agreed on, the Soldiers then stationed at York became very licentious, and no vigilence or exertions of the officers could keep them within bounds.[3] very few nights passed without Robbery or gross insult being committed by them. Some of the Men still in pay have already shewn that they will not obey Command. what hope can the inhabitants of York have, that the little remains of their property will be safe from the spoils of a set of abandoned Men who observe no law but their brutish Will? I would propose an expedient—let these Men be discharged.[4] And with much less money than their pay and rations would amount to the work may be done by hiring Negroes who will obey Command, will require fewer conveniencies And an equal number of them will finish it in less than half the time. I mean to include the Works at Gloucester[5] as well as those at York. with great esteem & respect

I am Dr Sir Your Obedt hb. Servt

David Jameson

[1] Instruction to Delegates, 17 June, and n. 2; Harrison to Delegates, 20 June 1783, and n. 4; Donald O. Dewey, ed., ". . . To Level the Works at York . . . a Letter of David Jameson," *Va. Mag. Hist. and Biog.*, LXXI (1963), 150–52.

[2] Jameson, a member of the Virginia Council of State, had perhaps heard Benjamin Lincoln suggest this on his visit to Richmond late in June. See JM Notes, 21 June, and n. 5; Jones to JM, 28 June 1783, n. 11. See also *Papers of Madison*, VI, 186, n. 7.

[3] The "Soldiers" had been members of the Virginia state line and militia (McIlwaine, *Official Letters*, III, 254, 265, 267, 269, 401, 421). For the departure of the French army, see *Papers of Madison*, IV, 395; 397, n. 7; 399; 401, nn. 6, 7; 414.

[4] By "these Men" Jameson apparently meant "the Soldiers for three years still in the pay of the Continent," as suggested by Lincoln. See McIlwaine, *Official Letters*, III, 427, 457; Executive Letter Book, War Office, 1783–1786, p. 43, MS in Va. State Library.

[5] *Papers of Madison*, III, 268, n. 2; IV, 406, n. 1.

To John Francis Mercer

RC (Historical Society of Pennsylvania). Cover addressed to, "The Honble J. F. Mercer. Blackpoint N. Jersey." Docketed by Mercer, "Jas. Madison July 16. 1783."

PHILADA. July 16 1783

DR SIR

The lucky arrival of our brother Lee who is gone on to Princeton has relieved me from the necessity of obeying your summons by Mr. Hawkins.[1] You will not therefore expect any Congressional news by this conveyance.

A letter by the post from Mr. Ambler repeats his request that warrants in form may be sent by all the Delegates for the amount of their respective shares of his remittances. He adds that two bills one for £500, the other for upwards of £600 Va. Curry. have unexpectedly come into the Treasy. & that the Delegates may have the benefit of the good fortune by authorizing their friends in Va. to take out warrants for such propertions of one or both as they may settle among themselves.[2] This is the best and indeed the only news contained in my letters.

The Ct. Martial being not yet opened for enquir[i]ng into the Mutiny, I can say nothing on that head.[3] The Address from the Philadns. to Congress is likely to meet with a very general subscription. They seem to calculate with much assurance on its efficacy.[4] I send you all the Newspaper[s] of this morning.[5] Those from Va. contain nothing that requires that they sd. be superadded.[6] Wishing you a speedy redemption from the Muskettoes of Black point and refitment for your political functions,[7] I bid you for the present adieu.

Done in bed in my Chamber in the Hotel at the Corner of Market & 5 Streets in the City of Philada. at ½ after 6 oClock, on the 16 of July annoque Dom: 1783.[8]

J. MADISON JR.

[1] JM to Randolph, 6 May, n. 9; 15 July 1783. Whether Benjamin Hawkins, a delegate in Congress from North Carolina, had written to JM from Princeton, as he did on 9 August 1783 (*q.v.*), or, coming to Philadelphia, had conveyed Mercer's summons orally, is not known. See *Papers of Madison*, IV, 273, n. 4; JM to Randolph, 8 July 1783, n. 2. With JM, Jones, and Lee absent, Mercer's departure from Princeton would have reduced the Virginia delegation attending Congress to Bland only. The "lucky" arrival of Lee enabled him and Bland, provided that their positions on an issue were attuned, to cast an effective vote on behalf of their state.

GEORGE III, KING OF ENGLAND

ALEXANDER HAMILTON

[2] Ambler to JM, 10 May, and nn. 1, 2; 5 July 1783, and n. 9.

[3] Delegates to Harrison, 5 July 1783, and nn. 3–5.

[4] The "address of the Citizens of Philadelphia and the Liberties thereof," drafted by Thomas Paine and signed by 873 residents, was submitted on 23 July and referred by Congress on that day to a committee with Hugh Williamson as chairman and Arthur Lee among the other four members. The committee reported five days later (NA: PCC, No. 43, fols. 312–31; *JCC*, XXIV, 444, n. 1, 452; Burnett, *Letters*, VII, 253). See also *ibid.*, VII, 233–35, 240–41; JM to Jefferson, 17 July; Jones to JM, 21 July, n. 4; JM to Randolph, 28 July 1783, and n. 3; Varnum L. Collins, *Continental Congress at Princeton*, pp. 263–69.

[5] The newspapers of Philadelphia, published each Wednesday, including 16 July 1783, were the *Pennsylvania Gazette*, the *Pennsylvania Journal*, and the *Freeman's Journal*.

[6] JM probably referred to the 5 July issues of the *Virginia Gazette* and of the *Virginia Gazette, and Weekly Advertiser*. He had been on the mailing lists of these newspapers for well over a year (*Papers of Madison*, IV, 80–81).

[7] JM to Randolph, 15 July 1783. Black Point, on the Navesink River, near Shrewsbury, Monmouth County, N.J., had been during the Revolution a favorite landing place of Loyalist (refugee) raiders from Sandy Hook or New York City. Mercer probably was recuperating in James White's "noted Tavern" which, judging from frequent advertisements in the *Pennsylvania Packet*, provided patrons with a "genteel Bathing-House" as well as "a constant supply of the best Fish, with Lobsters, Oysters, and Clams; also Liquors of the best quality" (*Pa. Packet*, 28 June 1783; *New Jersey Archives*, 1st ser., XXVII, 370, 649).

[8] The "Hotel" was Mrs. Mary House's boardinghouse.

To Thomas Jefferson

RC (LC: Madison Papers). Cover missing. JM docketed the letter, upon recovering it many years later, "Madison, Jas. July 17. 1783."

PHILADA. July 17th. 1783.

DEAR SIR

Your two favors of the 1 & 17 of June, with the debates of Congress and the letter for Miss Floyd and the Cyphers inclosed in the former, and your amendments to the Constitution inclosed in the latter, have been duly recd. The latter came by yesterday's mail.[1] I feel too sensibly the value of these communications to omit my particular acknowledgments for them.

The usual reserve of our Ministers has kept us in entire suspence since my last with regard to the definitive Treaty and every thing else in Europe.[2] The only incident produced in this interval has been that which removed Congress from this City to Princeton. I have selected the Newspaper which contains the Report of a Committee on that subject, from which you will collect the material information.[3] Soon after the removal of Congs. the Mutineers surrendered their arms and impeached some of their officers, the two principal of whom have escaped to sea.[4] Genl. Howe with a detachment of Eastern troops is here and is instituting an enquiry into the whole plot, the object & scheme of which are as yet both involved in darkness.[5] The Citizens of this place seem to disavow the alledged indisposition to exert force agst. insults offered to Congress, and are uniting in an address rehearsing the proofs which they [have] given of attachment to the fœderal authority, professing a continuance of that attachment, and declaring the utmost readiness on every occasion, to support the dignity and privileges of Congs. if they sd. deem this place the fittest for transacting the public business until their permanent residence shall be fixed.[6] What effect this address backed by the scanty accomodations of Princeton will have on Congress is uncertain. The prevailing disposition seemed to be that a return to their former residence as soon as the way sd. be decently opened would be prudent in order to prevent any inferences abroad of disaffection in the mass of so important a State to the revolution or the fœderal governmt.[7] Others suppose that a freer choice among the Seats offered to Congress could be made here than in a place where the necessity of a speedy removal[8] wd. give an undue advantage to the seat happening to be in greatest readiness to receive them. The Advocates for Anapolis appear to be sensible of the force of this consideration, and probably will if they can, detain Congs. in Princeton until a final choice be made. N. Jersey will probably be tempted to concur in the plan by the advantage expected from actual possession. other Members are extremely averse to a return to Philada. for various reasons.[9]

I have been here during the week past engaged partly in some writing which, my papers being all here cd. not be so well done elsewhere, partly in some preparations for leaving Congress. The time of my setting out depends on some circumstances which in point of time are contingent.[10] Mr. Lee arrived here two days ago and proceeds to day to Princeton.[11] Mr. Mercer is gone to the Sea-board in N. Jersey for his health.[12] I shall probably return to Princeton next week, or sooner if I sd. have notice of any subject of consequence being taken up by Congress.[13] Subjects of consequence, particularly a ratification of the Treaty with Sweeden have been long waiting on their table for 9. states.[14]

I am Dr. Sir Yr. sincere friend

J Madison Jr.

[1] Jefferson to JM, 1 June, and nn. 4–8; 17 June 1783, and nn. 6, 7. Why the second of these letters took so long to reach JM is not known.

[2] For earlier remarks by JM about the infrequency with which "our Ministers" wrote to Congress, see *Papers of Madison*, IV, 448; 450, n. 17; V, 70; 86–87; VI, 326; 327, n. 3; JM to Jefferson, 10 June, and n. 9. Except for Franklin's dispatch, already mentioned (JM to Randolph, 8 July, n. 11), letters from them, relating to "every thing else," including the current negotiations of a definitive peace treaty, were not received by Congress until 11 and 12 September (NA: PCC, No. 183, III, 71, 78–80). These many dispatches had been written, of course, weeks before the commissioners of the United States and Great Britain signed that treaty on 3 September 1783.

[3] Hamilton to JM, 6 July, n. 3. See also for the "Committee" and its "Report," JM Notes, 19 June, and n. 7; 20 June, and n. 1; 21 June, and nn. 5–7; *JCC*, XXIV, 412–21.

[4] JM Notes, 21 June, and n. 8; JM to Randolph, 30 June 1783, n. 6.

[5] Delegates to Harrison, 5 July, and nn. 3–5; JM to Randolph, 8 July; 15 July; to Mercer, 16 July 1783.

[6] JM to Randolph, 30 June, and n. 7; 8 July, and n. 2; 15 July; Hamilton to JM, 6 July, and n. 2; JM to Mercer, 16 July 1783, and n. 4.

[7] JM to Randolph, 8 July, and n. 2. Although Congress had received letters, resolutions, or addresses of welcome to New Jersey from Governor William Livingston, the "House of Assembly," the "Governours and Masters of the College" of New Jersey, the "inhabitants of Princeton and vicinity," the "inhabitants of Trenton and vicinity," and from particular residents of Princeton offering the use of their houses, and would soon receive similar resolutions from Newark, New Brunswick, and residents of Hunterdon, Somerset, and Middlesex counties, the delegates responded to this cordiality with general expressions of gratitude, unaccompanied by any commitment not to return eventually to Philadelphia (Hamilton to JM, 6 July 1783, n. 6; *JCC*, XXIV, 412 n., 421, n. 2, 422 n., 423–24, 425, and n. 1, 439, 445, 501–2). Failure to return to that city, which, except during its occupancy by the British army, had been viewed overseas as the capital of the United States ever since 1776, might adversely affect the reputation of the Confederation abroad at a time when commissioners of Congress were negotiating a definitive treaty of peace and treaties of commerce, and seeking further loans from Louis XVI of France.

[8] That is, in Philadelphia rather than in Princeton.

[9] Residents of Princeton and its vicinity, although recognizing that their town lacked the facilities to be the permanent capital of the Confederation, naturally sought to "detain Congs." there as long as possible. Besides Philadelphia, whose citizens wished Congress to return, and Williamsburg, whose citizens declined to pledge to Congress an indefinite extent of jurisdictional powers, Annapolis obviously was better able to provide ample accommodations than the other sites (Kingston, N.Y., Georgetown, Md., Trenton, and along the Delaware River in "the Township of Nottingham in the County of Burlington," N.J.) which had been offered (NA: PCC, No. 46, fols. 35–49; *JCC*, XXIV, 229, n. 2, 376, 378, n. 2, 422 n., 428, 438, n. 2, 439, and n. 1; *Papers of Madison*, VI, 447; 448, nn. 4, 6, 7; Harrison to Delegates, 17 May; 4 July, and n. 5; 12 July, and n. 3; Delegates to Harrison, 27 May, n. 2; Instructions to Delegates, 28 June 1783).

[10] For the probable nature of at least some of JM's "writing" and "preparations," see *Papers of Madison*, V, 232; VI, 293, n. 15; JM to Randolph, 8 July 1783, n. 2. The contingent circumstances probably included the undetermined date of his expected marriage to Catherine Floyd, the precarious state of his mother's health, and perhaps also his lack of assurance that if he left for Montpelier prior to 2

November, when his term expired, Virginia would still have an effective delegation of at least two members in Congress. See JM to Jefferson, 11 Aug.; to James Madison, Sr., 30 Aug. 1783.

[11] JM to Randolph, 6 May, n. 9; 15 July 1783.

[12] JM to Mercer, 16 July 1783, and n. 7.

[13] JM to Randolph, 15 July 1783, and n. 7.

[14] On 18 June Congress referred the treaty of commerce, concluded at Paris on 3 April, to a committee composed of JM, chairman, Stephen Higginson, and Hamilton. The committee's report, drafted by JM, was submitted on 24 July, when only six states were effectively represented in Congress. Five days later, although JM apparently was absent, Congress ratified the treaty, for the number of effective delegations had increased to nine (NA: PCC, No. 185, III, 68; No. 186, fol. 108; *JCC*, XXIV, 457–77, 477, n. 1, 478–79; Treaty with Sweden, 24 July 1783).

From Edmund Randolph

RC (LC: Madison Papers). Unsigned but in Randolph's hand. Cover addressed by him to "The honble James Madison esqr Congress Princeton." Docketed by JM, "July 18. 1783."

RICHMOND July 18. 1783.

MY DEAR FRIEND

I have received by the last mail your two favors of June 30. & July 8.[1] They satisfy me of what was before problematical, the propriety of the removal of congress to Princeton. But with what decency can you retreat from thence without concessions, worthy the acceptance of sovereignty, and, on the other hand, how much have the southern states to fear from the convenience of Osopus,[2] when the permanent seat of congress shall be the subject of discussion?

Betsey and myself fear the effect of your removal to Princeton on the finances of Mrs. H—se.[3]

The assembly no sooner leave us than we sink into a dull, tho' eager people after money. Were it not for the breeze, which the late proclamation of the governor has stirred,[4] we should have nothing to agitate us. It draws forth every hour men, who seemed to have fixed themselves in all the rights of citizenship, to supplicate a little time, until they can arrange their domestic affairs.[5] Among these is a Doctor Turpin, the possessor of the most valuable lots for the purposes of government within the city. He is a native, was taken at York with a medical commission, as I am told, in his pocket, and has been suffered to remain here without interruption ever since; And yet the act determining, who shall be citizens, does not, I believe, exclude him from obtaining a domicil here.

However, there may be some reason to favor both him and many other natives, which the law does not allow. He was sent abroad for his education, during his infancy. He was there surprized by the war, while the purposes of his errand were incomplete. He made several attempts to reach his country, but was so often baffled as to be obliged to enter into the british service, as a surgeon, for subsistence. A departure from hence with the single view of assuming arms against his country would be malignant indeed. But much toleration is due to those, who merely to avoid famine; to the danger of which they have been subjected by the prosecution of their studies, and to gain a fair opportunity of coming to his native country, have submitted to enter into the british service.[6]

The governor has been dangerously ill: and his disorder tho' somewhat soothed for the present, is probably firmly fixed.[7] The symptoms indicate it to be a stone in the gall bladder.

The assembly have directed a revision and collection into one code of all the laws since the revolution. A step absolutely necessary, as scarcely one magistrate understands what the law is, so far as the knowledge of the law is to be found in them.[8]

[1] *Qq.v.*

[2] Randolph should have written "Esopus," or Kingston, N.Y. (*Papers of Madison*, VI, 447; 448, n. 4).

[3] Mrs. Edmund Randolph and Mrs. Mary House (*Papers of Madison*, VI, 430; 431, n. 8; JM to Randolph, 10 June, and n. 2; Mercer to JM, 14 Aug. 1783).

[4] Randolph to JM, 12 July 1783, and nn. 2, 3.

[5] For five examples of "men" who petitioned "for a little time," see Executive Letter Book, 1783–1786, pp. 129, 169, 172, MS in Va. State Library; *Papers of Madison*, VI, 208, n. 12; *JCSV*, III, 256, 260, 277; *Cal. of Va. State Papers*, III, 509.

[6] Dr. Philip Turpin (*ca.* 1743–1828), Jefferson's first cousin, owned land on Shockoe Hill in Richmond (Chesterfield County Court Records, Will Book 11, pp. 320–22, microfilm in Va. State Library; Minute Book, House of Delegates, May 1782, p. 57, MS in Va. State Library; *JCSV*, III, 147, 221, 232, 342; Hening, *Statutes*, XII, 617–18). Turpin was graduated with the degree of M.D. by the University of Edinburgh in 1774. Although he continued to allege adherence to the cause of the United States in the Revolution, he appears to have rejected opportunities to return to Virginia as late as 1778. He served, moreover, as surgeon on a British transport and was with Cornwallis' army at the time of the surrender at Yorktown in October 1781. Thereafter Turpin was permitted to remain in his native state as a prisoner of war on parole. A few weeks after writing this letter Randolph became considerably less willing to grant that the doctor had been obliged to render medical service to the enemy. In response to his petition, the Virginia General Assembly on 22 December readmitted Turpin to full rights as a citizen of the state, an action not recorded in the journal. He subsequently lived at Salisbury, his estate in Chesterfield County (Boyd, *Papers of Jefferson*, I, 23–25; VI, 324–33; Randolph to JM, 23 Aug. 1783; *JHDV*, Oct. 1783, pp. 48, 59–60, 71, 73, 83; Hening, *Statutes*, XI, 316; Francis Earle Lutz, *Chesterfield, an Old Virginia County* [Richmond, 1954], p. 140).

In the manuscript journal of the House of Delegates for the session of October 1783, John Beckley, clerk of the House, concluded the entries for the final day of session, Monday, 22 December, with the notation, "The Speaker then signed the following Inrolled Bills" (Journal, House of Delegates, Oct. 1783, p. 218, MS in Va. State Library). This entry, with editorial emendations, is in the printed journal, followed by the note, "[*Here the Clerk omitted recording any further proceedings of this session.*]" (*JHDV*, Oct. 1783, p. 83). The only other day on which the speaker of the House of Delegates signed enrolled bills into law was on Friday, 5 December, and those five bills are listed by their respective titles (*JHDV*, Oct. 1783, p. 49). All other bills, twenty-seven in number, were probably signed on 22 December 1783, although their titles were then "omitted."

[7] Probably due to illness, Harrison did not summon the Council of State to meet between 15 and 21 July and was not present at the sessions of the Council on 31 July, and 1 and 2 August 1783 (*JCSV*, III, 280, 282). See also Executive Letter Book, 1783–1786, p. 176, MS in Va. State Library, in which Harrison on 19 July mentioned his "very severe indisposition."

[8] On 13 and 16 June, the House of Delegates and the Senate, respectively, of the Virginia General Assembly adopted a resolution drafted by Randolph, first introduced on 26 May, instructing "The Executive to cause the several acts of the General Assembly, subsequent in date to the revisal" of 1769, "and the ordinances of Convention which are now in force, to be collected into one code, with a proper index and marginal notes, to be revised and examined by any two judges of the High Court of Chancery." The resulting code was to be printed and "covered with paste-board"—the "whole expense" not to exceed £750 (*JHDV*, May 1783, pp. 21, 53, 58; Beckley to Randolph, 20 June 1783). See also *Papers of Madison*, VI, 109, entry No. 278 an.

Deciding that John Blair, Edmund Pendleton, and George Wythe, the three judges of the High Court of Chancery, were most highly qualified to "undertake the whole of the Business," Governor Harrison wrote to each of them on 19 June 1783, asking them to consult together on a mode of operations and "favor me with the result" (Executive Letter Book, 1783–1786, pp. 157–58, 240, MS in Va. State Library). The outcome of the jurists' labors, considerably delayed in completion, was printed in Richmond by Thomas Nicolson and William Prentis in 1785. Usually known as *The Chancellors' Revisal*, the volume is titled in full *A Collection of All Such Public Acts of the General Assembly, and Ordinances of the Conventions of Virginia, Passed Since the Year 1768, As Are Now in Force; with a Table of the Principal Matters. Published under the Inspection of the Judges of the High Court of Chancery, by a Resolution of the General Assembly, the 16th Day of June 1783* (David John Mays, *Edmund Pendleton*, II, 212–14, 390, n. 53; *idem*, ed., *The Letters and Papers of Edmund Pendleton, 1734–1803* [2 vols.; Charlottesville, 1967], pp. 457, 459–60).

From Robert R. Livingston

RC (LC: Madison Papers). Cover missing. Docketed by JM over the date line, "Livingston R. R," and in the right margin at the close of the letter, "Rob. Livingston July 19. 1783." The draft copy, among the Robert R. Livingston Papers in the New-York Historical Society, frequently varies in text from that received by JM.

CLER MOUNT[1] 19th. July [1]783

DEAR SIR

I have this moment been informed that the definitive treaty is concluded,[2] & in consequence of it give you this trouble. I believe I mentioned to you before I left Philadelphia[3] that if Congress should make no appointment of a secretary before the arrival of the treaty it would give me great pleasure to be permitted to sign it in that character & thus conclude my political careir.[4] How far I may with propriety indulge the hope that Congress will admit me to this honor, I know not, & therefore I confide this wish only to you, satisfied that if you should find it improper you will discourage it without permitting it to be urged to my disadvantage. If you should believe that Congress will not find it improper[,] as the grand treaty which sets the seal to our independance should not want the usual forms, & as several little matters may be necessary in consequence thereof, perhaps they may be induced to recite that their removal & their want of a full representation having prevented their supplying the plac[e] of the late Secretary for foreign affairs[5] that it would be agreeable to them that he resume the direction of the department *till the ratification of the definitive treaty*. I should write to Coll. Hamilton with whom I have had some conversation on this subject, but that I presume he must by this time be upon his return[6] if however he should be still with you as I have the fullest confidence in his friendship I pray you to shew him this, as well as to Mr. Izard Mr. Rutledge[7] or any other Genr. who have honoured me with their esteem.

I congratulate you upon your escape from Philadelphia, nothing less than an armed force could ever have drawn you from that Capua[8] I wish to know what will be your future destination & whether I may hope to see you contribute to restore the lost splendor of my native place?[9] or whether you are so inamoured with the pure air of the country as to continue Villagers? I will not declare my wishes on this subject least my partialities should betray my want of judgment.

Some letters have passed between Gen. Carleton on the subject of several infractions of the treaty that deserve the attention of Congress & should be attended to in the instructions to ou[r] ministers.[10] The Govr. is gone with Genl Washington to the northward, or I should have send you copie[s] of them they may be obtained thro' our delega[tes.][11]

The servant that delivers this will wait your orders & return with your answer, as the business I have sent him upon will be finished when he delivers this.[12] I am Dr. Sir

with g[reat] respect & esteem Your Most Ob hum: servt

R R LIVINGSTON

[1] Livingston's manorial estate near the Hudson River and Dobbs Ferry, N.Y.

[2] Livingston had been misinformed (JM to Jefferson, 17 July 1783, n. 2; Syrett and Cooke, *Papers of Hamilton*, III, 414, 415, n. 3, 419).

[3] Livingston had terminated his service as secretary for foreign affairs on 5 June (JM Notes, 4 June, and n. 5; JM to Jefferson, 10 June 1783, and n. 16).

[4] Neither on 13 December 1783 nor on 14 January 1784, when Congress received and ratified, respectively, the definitive treaty of peace, was there a secretary for foreign affairs (*JCC*, XXV, 812; XXVI, 22–31; JM Notes, 4 June 1783, n. 3). The "instrument of ratification" and the proclamation announcing the ratification were signed by Thomas Mifflin, president of Congress, and Charles Thomson, secretary (Hunter Miller, ed., *Treaties and Other International Acts*, II, 151–57; Wharton, *Revol. Dipl. Corr.*, VI, 755–57). Livingston's national public career was far from being concluded. See, for example, *JCC*, XXVII, 663.

[5] Livingston.

[6] Alexander Hamilton left Congress at the close of July and was in New York City by 2 August. On 23 July, while still in Princeton, he informed Livingston by letter: "It happens My Dear Sir that both Mr. Maddison and myself are here. We have talked over the subject of your letter to him, and need not assure you how happy we should both be to promote your wish; but the representation continues so thin, that we should have little hope that any thing which is out of the ordinary course and has somewhat of novelty in it could go through. We therefore have concluded it would be to no purpose to make the experiment in the present state of things; but shall *sound* towards a more full representation; though we fear the strictness of the ideas of many Gentlemen will be a bar to the success of the measure. You shall hear from me further on the subject. Mr Maddison does not write himself as this letter contains both our ideas but he presents his compliments and the assurances of his esteem" (Syrett and Cooke, *Papers of Hamilton*, III, 414).

Writing to Livingston from Albany on 13 August 1783, Hamilton added: "The subject you wrote to Maddison and myself about we have since attended to; but we found that nothing could be done in it. Such a thing would always be difficult there; and unluckily it is to be feared that a certain influence has of late increased not friendly to that line of thinking and acting which we call proper" (*ibid.*, III, 431). Although Hamilton did not reveal the nature of the "certain influence," he may have touched on it on 25 July 1783, when he wrote to John Jay, "The road to popularity in each state is to inspire jealousies of the power of Congress" (*ibid.*, III, 416–17).

[7] In his draft copy Livingston wrote "the Gentl. of your late family" instead of Izard and Rutledge. Livingston of course assumed that JM had moved from Mrs. House's boardinghouse to Princeton.

[8] In the draft of his letter Livingston interlineated "Capua" above a deleted "Circian Isle." Ancient Capua, proverbial for its luxury and gladiators, was sixteen miles north of Naples.

[9] Livingston, having been born in New York City, evidently hoped that Congress would choose to move there, following its evacuation by the British armed forces. Congress did convene in New York but not until 11 January 1785 (Edmund Cody Burnett, *The Continental Congress* [N.Y., 1941], p. 618).

[10] General Sir Guy Carleton, in spite of repeated protests from Governor George Clinton of New York, continued to control a larger area, including Long Island, in the southern part of that state "than is necessary for the Convenience, and Security of his Britannic Majesty's Troops, and Stores." By mid-July, although Carleton had released to their owners some estates on Staten Island and Long Island, he still, in Clinton's opinion, occupied too much land and, contrary to Article VII of the preliminary articles of peace, had not returned "Archives, Records, Deeds and Papers" (Hugh Hastings and J. A. Holden, eds., *Public Papers of George Clinton*, VIII, 184–86, 203–4, 207–10, 211–16; Fitzpatrick, *Writings of Washington*, XXVI, 447–48, 499–501; XXVII, 9, 10, 26–28). See also Delegates to Harrison, 23 Aug. 1783, and n. 2.

[11] Washington, accompanied by Clinton, left Newburgh on 18 July. They traveled as far north as Forts Crown Point and Ticonderoga, and as far west as Fort Schuyler on the Mohawk River. Washington again reached his headquarters in Newburgh on 5 August 1783 (Fitzpatrick, *Writings of Washington*, XXVII, 65–67, 71, n. 8). Besides Hamilton, James Duane was the only delegate from New York attending Congress. On 7 August, about a week after Hamilton's departure, Ezra L'Hommedieu joined Duane as the New York delegation (*JCC*, XXIV, 492).

[12] Livingston omitted the closing passage of his draft copy, reading: "I had some thing to say to you on the subject of my arrears but I suppose the time improper when it is otherwise I know you will lend me every necessary assistance in procuring the discharge of them." In his letter of 23 July, cited in n. 6, above, Hamilton assured Livingston that, whenever effective delegations from nine or more states should attend Congress, "I will not forget the money commission you gave me." On this subject, Hamilton commented further to Livingston in a letter of 13 August 1783, "I left in charge with several of my friends who have promised their attention to it, the business of an extra-allowance" (Syrett and Cooke, *Papers of Hamilton*, III, 415, 432). For the basis of his claim for an "extra-allowance," see *Papers of Madison*, VI, 420, n. 4.

From Joseph Jones

RC (LC: Madison Papers). Lacks docket and cover.

Spring Hill. 21. July 1783

Dr. Sir.

I find mine to you of the last week was not in Town in time for the Mail which it seems is now made up at ten o'Clock in the forenoon and is rather inconvenient for those of the Country near the Town as they cannot receive and answer letters the same week unless in Town. my letter will I presume go forward this week.[1] I did suppose Congress wod. not again return to the City[2] and shod. be sorry to hear they had done so unless invited or some step taken by the Executive to atone for the slight put on that Body.[3] had I been present I shod. have opposed the removal at the time but having done so and the cause assigned I shod. not consent to return untill some concession or act of contrition on the part of the offenders authorised the measure the act of the Executive must be deemed the act of the state untill disclaimed or censured by the supreme authority and it is not probable this will be the consequence considering the composition of the present Assembly unless this conduct of Mr. D. shod. lessen the attachment of some of his adherents.[4]

I know not yet whether I shall visit congress if I do I shall depart hence the begining of next month. I shall feel the inconvenience of the removal in the want of su[ch] good accommodations as I hoped and expected to get at my friend Mrs. House's where if Congress have retd. or shall return I depend upon quarters of which the next post shall convey notice.[5] The proclamation of ou[r] Executive has I am told given offence to the B. party and threats have been thrown out of calling for the council Books next Session with a view to censure the advisers of the measure. I am no prophet, but will venture to foret[ell] the person who attempts it will fail in his project and meet rather the censure than applause of the people.[6] If the definitive treaty arrives before the meeting in the fall, I except we shall then have a long and warm Session.[7] My Compliments to the Gents. of the Delegation[8]

Yr aff Friend

JOS: JONES.

1 Jones to JM, 14 July 1783. The "Town" was Fredericksburg, the post office stop nearest to Jones's estate of Spring Hill in King George County, Va.

2 Philadelphia.

3 The "Executive" was President John Dickinson and the Supreme Executive Council of Pennsylvania. See JM to Randolph, 30 June, and citations in n. 2; Hamilton to JM, 6 July 1783, n. 5.

4 Jones to JM, 14 July, and n. 3; JM to Mercer, 16 July, and n. 4; JM to Jefferson, 17 July 1783. Neither Dickinson and the Supreme Executive Council nor "the supreme authority" ("the State of Pennsylvania in General Assembly") ever explicitly expressed "contrition" for the failure of the civil authorities to act vigorously against the mutineers. Although assuring Congress on 3 July of readiness to co-operate in apprehending the ringleaders, the executive of the state voiced to Congress on 14 July the hope that the rank-and-file continental troops of Pennsylvania who had shared in the uprising would be pardoned (NA: PCC, No. 38, fols. 147, 151).

On 13 August Dickinson and the Council "authorized" the Pennsylvania delegation "to declare in the most respectful Terms to Congress that their return to Philadelphia" would be "an Event" which would afford the executive of the state "the greatest satisfaction" (NA: PCC, No. 69, fol. 1155). In resolutions unanimously adopted on 29 August 1783, the General Assembly, besides making known its wish that a site in Pennsylvania would become Congress' permanent home, guaranteed that if Congress should decide to return temporarily to Philadelphia, its former accommodations would be available there and "effective measures" would be taken "to enable the Executive of the State to afford speedy and adequate support and protection to the honor and dignity" of Congress (NA: PCC, No. 69, fols. 451–52). See also *JCC*, XXIV, 432–33, 442, n. 2, 451, n. 1, 452–53, 484–85, 506–8; XXV, 580–81; *Pa. Archives*, 1st ser., X, 69, 72; JM to Mercer, 16 July, and

n. 4; to Randolph, 5 Aug. 1783; Burnett, *Letters*, VII, 217, 253–54, 255, and n. 2, 266, 274, 279, 293.

[5] Jones to JM, 14 July, and n. 7; 28 July. Upon Jones's arrival late in August in Princeton, he and JM shared an uncomfortably small room, making the accommodations at Mrs. Mary House's boardinghouse in Philadelphia seem palatial by contrast (JM to James Madison, Sr., 30 Aug. 1783).

[6] Randolph to JM, 12 July, and nn. 2, 3; 18 July. Jones's "B" stands for British. At the outset of the message of 20 October to the House of Delegates, Governor Harrison justified his proclamation on the basis of the statute warning citizens against having "free and unrestricted intercourse" with Loyalists and British subjects and prohibiting all erstwhile enemies from remaining in or coming to Virginia (Executive Letter Book, 1783–1786, p. 214, MS in Va. State Library). Although the House of Delegates on 17 November "*Ordered*" that the Governor in Council "lay before the House the journal of their proceedings from the month of October 1782 to the present time," and the governor complied three days later, the journal of the House records no motion relating specifically to the proclamation (*ibid.*, p. 236; *JCSV*, III, 308; *JHDV*, Oct. 1783, p. 21). The journal of the Council of State, by stating that all five of the counselors present on 2 July had "advised" Harrison to issue the proclamation "forthwith," thus presented any would-be critics with a united front (*JCSV*, III, 276–77). The Virginia General Assembly, besides re-electing Harrison governor on 27 November, enacted on 22 December a law in place of the ones which had warranted his proclamation, extending to all residents of the United States on 19 April 1775 who thereafter had not borne arms voluntarily against the United States, had not been even part owners of enemy privateers or other armed vessels, or had not served on or under the direction of "the Board of Refugee Commissioners of New York," full "rights of citizenship in Virginia," except those of voting "for members to either house of assembly" and holding "any office of trust or profit, civil or military" (*JHDV*, Oct. 1783, pp. 36, 42, 47, 50, 53, 56, 60, 69, 70, 83; Randolph to JM, 18 July 1783, n. 6; Hening, *Statutes*, XI, 324–25).

[7] On 3 February 1784, over seven weeks after Congress on 13 December 1783 had received the definitive treaty, a copy of that treaty, as ratified by Congress on 14 January 1784, reached Governor Harrison (*JCSV*, III, 326; *JCC*, XXV, 812; XXVI, 23).

[8] JM, Theodorick Bland, and John Francis Mercer.

From Edmund Pendleton

Printed excerpt (Stan. V. Henkels Catalogue No. 694 [1892], pp. 93–94).

EDITORIAL NOTE

About 1850 the present letter was calendared, probably by a clerk of Peter Force, as follows:

"1783, July 21 Virginia
To James Madison

"More about the Soldier offence. Williamsburg the most convenient place for Congress to meet, excepting New York. The temper of an Eastern legislature. Treaty with Sweden. The Definitive treaty. 1 page folio" (LC: Madison Miscellany).

If this is a complete listing of the matters discussed, Henkels omitted from his excerpt whatever Pendleton had written about the last two topics mentioned in the calendar. See Pendleton to JM, 30 June 1783, ed. n. For the "Treaty with Sweden," see *Papers of Madison*, VI, 335; 338, n. 21; Report on Treaty with Sweden, 24 July, and nn. 1, 4, 6; for "The Definitive treaty," Pendleton to JM, 4 May, and n. 6; 16 June 1783.

VIRGINIA, July 21, 1783

. . . With your last fav'r of the 8th came the missing one of June 24th containing the account of the behaviour of the Soldiers in their insult to Congress.[1] I wish the conspiracy may be traced to its real source, and the motives truly investigated, when I still think it will not terminate in Public good, or the redress of real injury in the Army;[2] The citizens I suppose cannot be well pleased either with the company of their military Visitants,[3] or reflections upon their own conduct which made such a Visit necessary, and fix'd a stigma on their public character, as wanting either *inclination* or *courage* to support the members of the great National Council, holding Session in their Metropolis, perhaps the people might want neither, and the fault was in their rulers in not calling forth their exertions, be this as it may, they do not reason badly who Counsel a return to Philad'a either to prevent unfavourable impressions abroad, or that the great question of fixing the Permanent residence of Congress may not be embarrassed, or influenced by temporary convenience.[4] In your state of that question, you take no notice of poor old Williamsburg, and yet I am of opinion that except the City of New York, it is the most convenient place Congress can Assemble at.[5]. . . The temper of an Easter[n] Legislature is really astonishing & alarming, will they censure their Delegates for acceding to a confederation, which their Assembly formerly approved of & directed the assent of the State to be given to, or are they tired of the Union, the moment of its having accomplished their purpose? Did they suffer the Vote for half pay to pass unobjected to, & to operate as a Stimulus to men to continue in an Army under all the discouraging circumstances of want of pay & want of necessaries, until they have performed their severe part of the compact with compleat success to us, and will they protest against that vote?[6] Well says the Psalmist

"When once the firm assurance fails
which public faith imparts
tis time for innocence to flie
from such deceitful Arts"[7]

[1] Both of these letters are missing. Although the contents of JM's letters on 8 July to Randolph (*q.v.*) and to Pendleton probably were similar, JM's letter of 24 June to Pendleton seems to have resembled more closely the detailed account about "the behaviour of the Soldiers" sent by the Virginia delegates on that day to Governor Harrison than the brief mention by JM of that subject in his letter of 24 June 1783 to Randolph (*qq.v.*).

[2] JM Notes, 21 June, n. 8; JM to Randolph, 30 June; 15 July; Delegates to Harrison, 5 July, and nn. 3–5. The "real injury" to the army was, of course, the furloughing or discharge of the continental officers and troops without their pay (JM to Randolph, 24 June; Pendleton to JM, 30 June 1783, and citations in nn. 1 and 2).

[3] For the arrival in or near Philadelphia of General Robert Howe and the continental troops under his command, see JM Notes, 21 June, nn. 4, 8; Delegates to Harrison, 24 June; 5 July, and n. 3; JM to Randolph, 30 June, and n. 6; 8 July; to Jefferson, 17 July 1783.

[4] JM to Randolph, 30 June, and n. 7; 8 July; 15 July; Hamilton to JM, 6 July, and n. 2; Jones to JM, 14 July, and n. 4; JM to Mercer, 16 July, and n. 4; to Jefferson, 17 July 1783.

[5] Pendleton to JM, 30 June, and citations in n. 3; Harrison to Delegates, 4 July, and n. 5; 12 July 1783, and n. 3. By describing Williamsburg as "poor old," Pendleton had in mind the adverse effects upon the town of the removal of the capital of Virginia from there to Richmond in 1780 and the occupation of Williamsburg by British, American, and French troops in 1781 (*Papers of Madison*, I, 300, n. 2; II, 292; 295, n. 9; III, 81, n. 4; 90; 159, n. 5; 182, n. 18; 210, n. 3; 253, n. 3; 263, n. 7; 276, n. 2; Boyd, *Papers of Jefferson*, III, 333–34). As a potential site for the capital of the Confederation, Williamsburg's assets included an approximately midway location between New Hampshire and Georgia, comparatively easy accessibility by water, and comfortable accommodations in vacant public buildings.

[6] Pendleton probably referred to the Massachusetts General Court, although his comment would apply almost as appropriately to the general assemblies of Connecticut and of Rhode Island. See Pendleton to JM, 23 June, and citations in n. 7; JM to Randolph, 21 July. On 26 June 1783 the Massachusetts General Court protested anew to Congress against the guarantee by Congress of full pay for five years to officers of the continental army who had served for at least three years (NA: PCC, No. 65, II, 185–88; *JCC*, XXIV, 483, n. 2; XXV, 607–9; Burnett, *Letters*, VII, 243–44; JM to Randolph, 21 July 1783, and n. 6). For further information about the position of Massachusetts, Rhode Island, and Connecticut, and of their delegates in Congress on this issue, see NA: PCC, No. 65; II, 225–28; No. 66, fols. 240–42, 248–51; *Papers of Madison*, VI, 251, n. 5; 282–83; 284, nn. 2, 4; 298; 299, n. 2; 300–301; 324, n. 10; 348; 370; 371, n. 4; 375; 377, n. 3; Burnett, *Letters*, VII, 164, 168.

[7] Except for writing "tis" instead of "'Tis," "flie" instead of "fly," and "Arts" instead of "arts," Pendleton correctly quoted from the metrical rendering of Psalm 11 in N[ahum] Tate and N[icholas] Brady, *A New Version of the Psalms of David fitted to the Tunes used in Churches* (*ca.* 75th ed.; London, 1771), p. 12. Pendleton may have accurately transcribed if his edition of this oft-printed work, first published in London in 1696, was not the one cited here. Pendleton quoted the metrical version preferred by Whigs. Tories sang the praise of God from the older version of T[homas] Sternhold and J[ohn] Hopkins. For the identification of his source, which had baffled the editors, they are much indebted to the courtesy and perseverance of Atcheson L. Hench, Professor Emeritus, University of Virginia. Following much unrewarding correspondence, he was supplied with the elusive reference by a "'learned friend' of a man in Oxford" University (Letters of Atcheson L. Hench, 9 Apr., 10 Apr. 1970).

To Edmund Randolph

RC (LC: Madison Papers). The fragment of cover is stamped "FREE" and addressed in JM's hand to "Randolph Esqr. Richmond." Docketed by Randolph, "J Madison." Upon recovering the letter many years later, JM added "July. 21. 1783" to the docket.

PHILADA. July 21. 1783.

MY DEAR SIR

This will serve merely to prevent a chasm in my correspondence, having nothing whatever of consequence to make a subject of it. We hear nothing from our Ministers abroad.[1] The Court Martial on the parties to the late Mutiny have come to no decisions as yet.[2] The Address from this City to Congress is I believe gone up pretty generally signed. My next will probably communicate the result of it.[3] Among other conciliating steps they have by voluntary subscriptions given a very splendid & cordial entertainment to the officers of the detachment under Genl. Howe.[4] The Legislature of Massachusetts have in their election for the ensuing year left out all their Delegates now in Congs. as a penalty for their concurrence in the provision lately adopted relative to half pay.[5] Yr. favr. by the post is this moment handed to me.[6] I am on the point of setting off for Princeton[7] to replace Col. Bland whose business keeps him here for a few days. farewell.

J.M.

[1] JM to Jefferson, 17 July 1783, and n. 2.

[2] Delegates to Harrison, 5 July 1783, and nn. 3–5.

[3] JM to Mercer, 16 July, and n. 4; JM to Randolph, 28 July 1783.

[4] At the State House in Philadelphia on 18 July, President John Dickinson of Pennsylvania presided at an "elegant entertainment" tendered by "a number of citizens" to the officers of the "federal army," including Major Generals Horatio Gates, Robert Howe, and Louis Lebègue Duportail. At the banquet, during which "a military band of music" played marches, fourteen "patriotic toasts" were drunk. To each of these, "rounds" from "Two field pieces" were "annexed," varying in number from three to thirteen and totaling 124. The subject of the first toast was "The United-States in Congress" and of the last, "Honor and Immortality to the Principles of Freedom and Virtue, in General WASHINGTON's circular letter." The participants, who were residents of "nearly every State of the Union," acted "in every respect toward each other like members of one great and happy family," including standing with interlocked hands when drinking two of the toasts (*Pa. Packet*, 21 July; *Pa. Gazette*, 23 July; *Pa. Journal*, 23 July). For Washington's "circular letter," see Jones to JM, 28 June 1783, and n. 6.

[5] Pendleton to JM, 21 July, and n. 6. Stephen Higginson and Samuel Holten, the only two delegates from Massachusetts attending Congress on the date of the present letter, had not been re-elected on 27 and 28 June by the General Court

of their state to serve for the year beginning 3 November 1783 (Burnett, *Letters*, VII, lxvii–lxix, 251–52).

[6] Randolph to JM, 12 July 1783.

[7] JM to Randolph, 15 July 1783, and n. 7.

Report on Treaty with Sweden

MS (NA: PCC, No. 29, fols. 323–25). In JM's hand. Docketed: "Rept. of Ratification & Proclamation of Treaty with Sweeden. Mr. Madison Mr. Higginson Mr. Hamilton Q. if the letter of 15 April from Mr. Franklin is returned? Report delivered July 24. 1783 Entd. read. The ratification Passed July 29. 1783 The proclamation postponed Passed Septr. 25th, 1783." The brackets are in the manuscript.

[24 July 1783]

The Come. consisting of Mr Madison, Mr Higgin[son] [Mr Hamilton] to whom was referred the letter from Docr. Franklin of the 15 day of April with an authenticated copy of the Treaty concluded with Sweeden,[1] submit the following forms of a ratification & proclamation of the same:

Ratification

The U.S. of America in Congs. assd. to all who shall see these presents, Greeting

Whereas by our Commission dated at Philada. on the day of [2] B. Franklin Minister Plenipo: &c. was invested with full powers on the part of the U.S. of A. to concert & conclude with a person or persons equally empowered on the part of his Majesty the King of Sweeden[3] a treaty of Amity & Commerce, having for its basis the most perfect equality & for its object the mutual advantage of the parties; we promising, in good faith to ratify whatever sd. be transacted by virtue of the sd. Commission: And Whereas our said Minister, in pursuance of his full powers did at on the day of with Minister Plenipo: named for that purpose on the part of His sd. Majesty the K. of Sweeden, conclude & sign a Treaty of Amity & Commerce[4] in the words following; to wit

[Here insert the Treaty in French][5]

Now Be it known that we the sd. U.S. of A. in Congs. Assd. have accepted & approved, and do by these presents ratify & confirm the sd.

Treaty; and every article & clause thereof: and we do authorise and direct our Minister Plenipo: aforesd. to deliver this our act of ratification, in [exc]hange for the ratification of the said Treaty by His Majesty the K. of Sweeden.[6] In Testimony Whereof, we have &c.

Proclamation

By the U.S. in Congs. assd. &c.

Whereas in pursuance of a Plenipotentiary Commission, given on the 28 day of September 1782 to B.F. &c. a Treaty of Amity & Commerce between his Majesty the K. of S. and the U.S. of A. was on the third day of April 1783 concluded by the sd. B.F. with a Minister Plenipo: named for that purpose by the sd. King: and Whereas the sd. Treaty hath been duly approved & ratified by the U.S. in Congss Assd. and a translation thereof made in the words following to wit

[Here Insert the Translation]

Now therefore to the end that the sd. Treaty may with all good faith be performed & observed on the part of these sd. states, all the Citizens & inhabitants thereo[f] and more especially all officers & others in the service of the U.S. are hereby enjoined & reqd. to govern themselves strictly in all things according to the stipulations above recited.

Done in Congs. &c.[7]

1 On 18 June Congress received Benjamin Franklin's dispatch and appointed the committee (NA: PCC, No. 185, III, 68; No. 186, fol. 108). In his dispatch, addressed to Robert R. Livingston, secretary for foreign affairs until 5 June 1783, Franklin also mentioned that the king of Denmark and Norway "has a strong desire to have a treaty of friendship and commerce with the United States" (Wharton, *Revol. Dipl. Corr.*, VI, 377–80). See also *Papers of Madison*, VI, 224, n. 7; 419, n. 4.

2 28 September 1782 (*JCC*, XXIII, 610–24; *Papers of Madison*, V, 167–68; 168, nn. 2, 3; 186–87; 397).

3 Gustavus III.

4 Franklin and his Swedish counterpart, Gustav Filip, Count Creutz, signed the treaty at Paris on 3 April 1783 (*Papers of Madison*, VI, 338, n. 21; Hunter Miller, ed., *Treaties and Other International Acts*, II, 123–50).

5 The American instrument of ratification is in French with an English translation entered on the lower part of the respective pages, but only the English version was spread on the journal of Congress (*JCC*, XXIV, 457–77). The original instrument in the Swedish archives is in French only (Hunter Miller, ed., *Treaties and Other International Acts*, II, 123, 149 n.).

6 Congress delayed ratifying the treaty until 29 July, because on that day, apparently for the first time since 11 July, effective delegations from nine states, the minimum required by Article IX of the Articles of Confederation for adopting a treaty, were in attendance. The omission of the ratifying poll from the journal probably signifies unanimity. Two tallied divisions on the same day indicate only

eight states present with at least two delegates each (*JCC*, XXIV, 457, 478–79; Burnett, *Letters*, VII, 242–43, 249, 265).

The king of Sweden had ratified the treaty on 23 May 1783. Before exchanging ratifications in Paris on 6 February 1784 with Erik Magnus, Baron de Stael-Holstein, the ambassador of Sweden at the court of King Louis XVI of France, Franklin informed de Stael of Congress' instructions that the terminology in the treaty should be amended so as to delete *Treize* and *Septentrionale* from the title *Treize États Unis de l'Amérique Septentrionale* and to substitute "Delaware" for *les Comtês de New-Castle, de Kent et de Sussex sur la Delaware* (*JCC*, XXIV, 477; Hunter Miller, ed., *Treaties and Other International Acts*, II, 123, 149 n.; Wharton, *Revol. Dipl. Corr.*, VI, 654). See also Burnett, *Letters*, VII, 256.

7 Under the fourth rule of procedure adopted by Congress on 4 May 1781, the report, as noted in the docket, was "delivered" to Charles Thomson on 24 July 1783. On that day he "Entd." the report in his records and "read" it to the delegates (*JCC*, XX, 476; XXIV, 477, n. 1). On 29 July the treaty, which comprised most of the report, was debated and ratified (*JCC*, XXIV, 457–77). The balance of the report consisted of "The proclamation." Nearly two months elapsed before it came again before Congress and "Passed." As adopted, the wording except for minor variations was what JM had proposed. Instead of "&c," the proclamation in its final form closed with "at Princeton, this twenty-fifth day of September, in the year of our Lord one thousand seven hundred and eighty three, and of our sovereignty and independence the eighth" (*JCC*, XXV, 613–14, 989).

Report on Memorial from Merchants of Hamburg

MS (NA: PCC, No. 41, X, 348).

EDITORIAL NOTE

On 20 December 1782 Caspar Voght and Company of the "neutral free and imperial City" of Hamburg, "happily situated upon the *River Elbe*," addressed a memorial to "His Excellency the President, and the Honorable Members of the Congress of the United States of North America, in Council assembled," asking that the attention of American merchants be drawn to the advantages of selling their exports and purchasing manufactured goods in Hamburg. A printed two-page "Specification of Goods, more profitably to be drawn from Hamburg then [*sic*] from any other Market" accompanied the memorial. Voght and Company, after stating that Peter Penet, "Agent for Virginia," who had visited Hamburg, had suggested the memorial, brought it to a close with the words: "We propose, Gentlemen, sending directly an able and intelligent Person to deliver You the Samples &c. and also to receive Your Orders; in case You should please to condescend to the granting us any." For Penet, see Delegates to Gálvez, 4 May, ed. n.; Delegates to Harrison, 6 May 1783, and n. 4.

Charles Thomson's docket of the memorial reads: "Meml. Caspar Voght & Co 20 Decr. 1782. July 26.–to lie on the table" (NA: PCC, No. 41, X, 345–48). Congress referred the memorial to the committee of the week, appointed on 23 July and consisting of JM, chairman, David Howell (R.I.), and Silas Condict (N.J.) (*JCC*, XXIV, 446). JM wrote the report on the docket page of the memorial.

[26 July 1783]

Memorial from   of Hamburg enumerating and recommending the manufactures &c of that place, and praying that they may have the countenance of Congress.

The Committee of the week report that the Memorial lie on the table.[1]

[1] On 18 December 1783 Congress declined to accede to Penet's recommendation that Voght be appointed consul of the United States at Hamburg (*JCC*, XXV, 757–58, 816). See also Burnett, *Letters*, VII, 273, 361, and n. 3. Relations such as Voght and Penet had proposed were not given an official footing until 2 June 1828, when ratifications of a "Convention of Friendship, Commerce, and Navigation" were exchanged at Washington between the United States and the "Free Hanseatic Republics of Lübeck, Bremen, and Hamburg" (Hunter Miller, ed., *Treaties and Other International Acts*, III, 387–404).

Virginia Delegates to Benjamin Harrison

Printed copy (Burnett, *Letters*, VII, 238–39). In or shortly before 1934, Stan. V. Henkels of Philadelphia had possession of the original of this letter (*ibid.*, VII, 238, n. 1). For the date of 27 July as printed in Burnett, *Letters*, see n. 1, below. See also Delegates to Harrison, 24 June 1783, ed. n.

PRINCETON July [26] 27th,[1] 1783

SIR,

We have before us, the two letters with which your Excellency honored us the 4th and 12th of this month.[2] Their enclosures have been laid before Congress, and are referrd for reports.[3]

We shall make due enquiry after Cap'n Camm; and endeavor to retreive the effects he carried off.[4] We have the pleasure to inform your Excellency, that intelligence has been receivd of the arrival of the Definitive treaty at N. York. But Congress have receivd no Advices of it from their Ministers in Europe.[5]

We do not know any colour of reason for the report you mention relative to our Commander in Chief. On the contrary we believe, that his popularity, like his merit, has not suffered the smallest diminution.[6]

We have the honor to be with the greatest respect Yr. Excellencys most obedt. Servts.

THEO'K BLAND JR.
ARTHUR LEE

P.S. Congress has this moment recevd, from Sir Guy Carleton, information, that several persons have been taken up in New York on suspicion of forging the Notes issued by the Superintendant of Finance. It appears from their examinations that this nefarious practice has been carried on to great extent in that City. His Letter dated the 23d makes no mention of the Definitive treaty.[7]

A. L.

[1] Arthur Lee's mention in the postscript (*q.v.*, and n. 7) of Congress' receipt of Carleton's dispatch makes certain that this letter was written on 26 rather than 27 July. In his letter to the delegates on 9 August (*q.v.*), Harrison acknowledged the receipt of their letter of 26 July.

[2] *Qq.v.*

[3] Harrison to Delegates, 4 July, and nn. 4, 6–8; 12 July, and n. 3. With the present letter the delegates enclosed copies of Philadelphia newspapers—probably the 26 July issues of the *Pennsylvania Packet* and of the *Pennsylvania Journal* (Harrison to Delegates, 9 Aug. 1783).

[4] Harrison to Delegates, 12 July 1783, and n. 5.

[5] JM to Jefferson, 17 July, and n. 2. For the origin of this false rumor about the definitive treaty, see JM to Randolph, 28 July, and n. 12; Delegates to Harrison, 1 Aug. 1783.

[6] Harrison to Delegates, 12 July 1783, and n. 6.

[7] In a letter of 24 (not 23) July, delivered by courier to President Elias Boudinot on 26 July and referred by Congress to a committee on that day, General Sir Guy Carleton requested that Congress speedily "appoint persons of their confidence to be present at a Board I mean to constitute to prosecute the inquiries" in New York City concerning "several" alleged "Counterfeiters or passers of certain Notes, commonly called Morris's Notes" (NA: PCC, No. 52, fols. 2–4; No. 185, III, 73; No. 186, fol. 115; *Pa. Packet*, 17 July 1783; *Cal. of Va. State Papers*, III, 512; Hugh Hastings and J. A. Holden, eds., *Public Papers of George Clinton*, VIII, 217–19). The report of the committee drafted by James Duane, chairman, was submitted to Congress on 30 July and, after minor amendment, adopted on 1 August.

The report recommended that Carleton be informed of Congress' "entire confidence" in his intention to bring "to condign punishment" as many of the "atrocious offenders" as were "not amenable to any of these United States" and to deliver to "a guard" all others who were citizens of any American state. The committee further recommended that "the names and places of abode" of the American culprits "be transmitted to the executives of the States to which they respectively belong" (*JCC*, XXIV, 485–86, 486, n. 1; Burnett, *Letters*, VII, 245, 250). With his letters of 13 August and 1 September 1783, Carleton sent Congress copies of many affidavits and of the proceedings of general courts-martial resulting in the acquittal of all persons brought to trial except one British subject and one American citizen (NA: PCC, No. 52, fols. 5–153; *JCC*, XXIV, 509, n. 1; XXV, 533, n. 1; JM to Pendleton, 8 Sept. 1783).

Motion *in re* Armed Vessels of Virginia

MS (NA: PCC, No. 36, II, 195–96). In the hand of Arthur Lee, except that Hugh Williamson wrote the third paragraph and Elias Boudinot the words in the second paragraph between "Defence" and "Pounders," both inclusive. These emendations may not have been made until 3 October or shortly before that date. Docketed: "Motion of Delegates of Virginia July 28 1783 for leave to fit out two Armed Vessels. Passed Oct 4 1783."

EDITORIAL NOTE

JM's undoubted acquaintance with the issue of Virginia's armed vessels, as well as his approval of the action taken by his fellow delegates from Virginia, probably warrants including the motion in this volume, even though JM, after attending Congress on Saturday, 26 July, had returned to Philadelphia (JM to Randolph, 8 July, n. 2; Memorial from Merchants of Hamburg, 26 July 1783).

Arthur Lee presumably introduced the motion. The third paragraph of the motion approximates a recommendation made to Congress on the same day by Secretary at War Benjamin Lincoln in regard to the statute of the Virginia General Assembly "directing the enlistment of Guards for the public prisons and stores" (Instruction to Delegates, 20 June 1783, and nn. 2, 3; *JCC*, XXIV, 455–56). The Virginia General Assembly, although it had instructed the Virginia delegates about these "Guards," had issued no directive to them about "two Armed Vessels." On 27 June, however, the Assembly "*Resolved*, That the Governor, with advice of Council, do appoint some proper person or persons, to procure men, provisions, and other necessaries, for the boats Liberty and Patriot, and to keep them manned and equipped, in such manner as to prevent running of goods subject to duties" (*JHDV*, May 1783, pp. 91, 93). For Governor Harrison's suggestions, which account for the motion, see Harrison to Delegates, 4 July 1783.

[28 July 1783]

Whereas it is provided in the 6th. Art: of the Confederation, that—No Vessels of War shall be kept up, in time of Peace, by any State, except such number only, as shall be deemed necessary by the U.S. in Congress assembled for the defence of such State or its trade[1]—and the Delegates of the State of Virginia having applyd to Congress for their approbation of two armed Vessels being kept up by the said State, at its own expence for the purpose of securing her trade[2]

It is therefore resolved—that the State of Virginia may keep up, at its own expence, two armed vessels, for the Defence of the Trade of that State, provided that the same do not exceed the number of 14 Guns Six Pounders & 75 Men each[3]

That the State of Virginia may keep up at its own Expence to the number of 25 Privates with proper Officers to guard the public Prisons & Stores[4]

[1] Paragraph 4, Article VI of the Articles of Confederation (*JCC*, XIX, 216).

[2] It probably had been on 23 July that the Virginia delegates "applyd to Congress" (NA: PCC, No. 186, fol. 114; *JCC*, XXIV, 444, n. 1; Delegates to Harrison, 26 July 1783).

[3] Instruction to Delegates *in re* "Cormorant," 26–27 June 1783, and n. 3; *JCSV*, III, 369–70.

[4] Although the docket states that Congress adopted the motion on "Oct 4," the journal for the preceding day includes the motion and strongly suggests that it was then agreed to. See Delegates to Harrison, 4 Oct. 1783, and n. 6. JM did not attend Congress on either of those days (*JCC*, XXV, 639–41).

Report on Maryland's Payment to Troops

MS (NA: PCC, No. 19, IV, 411–13). Docketed: "Report of Come. on Lettr. *from Supt of Finance* of June 20. 1783, with the papers inclosed relative to certain proceedings of the State of Maryland. Mr Madison Mr. Hawkins Mr. Duane Delivered July 28. 1783 read." The first three paragraphs of the report are in JM's hand, the last five in that of Benjamin Hawkins.

[28 July 1783]

The Committee to whom was referred a letter of the 20 June 1783, with the papers inclosed report[1]

That it appears from the said papers that the Legislature of the State of Maryland at their last Session directed the intendant of their Revenues to advance five months pay to the Line of that State in the army of the U.S. without the Sanction of any act of Congs.

That in order to supply the means for this advance they at the same time revoked an act appropriating a particular tax towards discharging requisitions of Congs. and ordered the same to be applied to the discharge of the five months pay.[2]

That the Superintendant of Finance has remonstrated in a letter to the Executive of Maryland agst. so unjustifiable a proceeding; has transmitted a copy of the Act of Congs. of the 1st day of October 1782 expressing fully their sense in the case of a similar proceeding on the part of the State of N. Jersey; and has pointed out the alarming tendency of the Act of Maryland to frustrate the later important arrangement for an advance of pay to the Army at large; and to subvert the foundations of public credit.[3]

If Acts of Congress most essential to the common interest and grounded on authority clearly vested by the articles of Union may be defeated by the interference of individual Legislature—If actual grants and appropriations as the Quota due from a State toward the pressing burthens of the public may be revoked and the money applied and expended without the consent or even the knowledge of Congress or their ministers—Vain must be every attempt to maintain a National Character or national credit.[4]

Congress under this apprehension passed the act of the 1st day of October 1782 in a case similar to the present; And on the principles there established no credit can be given to the State of Maryland for any advance made as aforesaid; Nor to any other State for advances which may be made by them; without the allowance of the United States in Congress.

These facts in the opinion of your committee render it the duty of Congress, as guardians of the confederation and of the equal rights of every part of the fœderal army to

Resolve that the Legislature of the State of Maryland be called upon to take into their most serious consideration the pernicious tendency of the measure complained of by the Superintendant of the Finances.

That the State of Maryland be therefore ernestly required to pay into the public Treasury the Quota so appropriated for the use of the United States by their Legislature that Congress may be enabled to do equal justice to the army and the rest of the public creditors by adhering to the Systems which they have on great considerations adopted for the common good.[5]

1 On 1 July Congress referred to a committee, composed of Oliver Ellsworth, chairman, JM, and John Francis Mercer, a letter of 20 June to Congress from Robert Morris, superintendent of finance, enclosing (1) an act of the General Assembly of Maryland, 1 June; (2) a letter from Benjamin Stoddert, president of the Council of Maryland, to Morris on 13 June; and (3) a copy of Morris' reply to Stoddert on 20 June. On 23 July Congress transferred these documents to the reconstituted committee mentioned in the headnote, above (NA: PCC, No. 137, II, 565–77; No. 185, III, 70; No. 186, fol. 110).

2 In his letter of 13 June to Morris, Stoddert enclosed a copy of the Maryland General Assembly's statute of 1 June 1783, which "revoked" so much of the revenue measures of April 1782 as had pledged the proceeds of a 5 per cent tax to the use of Congress. These proceeds were diverted to cover five months' delinquent pay due to the officers and troops of the state's continental line (NA: PCC, No. 137, II, 569–72, 577). The "intendant" was Daniel of St. Thomas Jenifer (Burnett, *Letters*, VII, 281).

[3] In his letter of remonstrance to Stoddert, Morris emphasized that "at the special Request of the United States Congress, and with the solemn Promise of their Support," he had "pledged" his "official Credit by the Issue of a large Sum in Paper" in order that the army "might not be sent Home in a State of absolute Indigence, which from the unparrallelled Neglect of the States was almost unavoidable." He continued: "judge Sir my feelings when I see Revenues sacredly appropriated to the United States suddenly diverted into another Channel. What Ground of Reliance can be formed on Grants liable to such Operations? I shall not presume to examine how far it consists with Justice to take back what has been given." If all other States should follow Maryland's example, the promise of three months' pay by Congress to the continental troops could not be fulfilled, and they would be thrown back for relief upon states which in a year's time had supplied Congress with only meager financial assistance (NA: PCC, No. 137, II, 573–75).

For the "act" of 1 October 1782, drafted by JM, see *Papers of Madison*, V, 173–75. For his expression of opinion, similar to that of Morris when Pennsylvania in January 1783 threatened to pay its own continental troops, see *ibid.*, VI, 145.

[4] In this paragraph, Hawkins referred especially to Article VIII, and in lesser degree to Articles XII and XIII, of the Articles of Confederation (*JCC*, XIX, 217, 221). His warning had been often sounded by JM, Hamilton, and other delegates in Congress.

[5] The following excised paragraphs—of which the second is to some extent a rewriting of the first—are in JM's hand and obviously supplied Hawkins with a part of the phraseology, as well as most of the ideas, embodied by him in the last four paragraphs of the report.

"These facts in the opinion of the Committee render it the duty of Congs. as Guardians of the Confederation and of the equal rights of every part of the fœderal army to resolve & direct that in pursuance of the principles established in the act of the 1st. day of Oct. 1782, no credit be given to the State of Maryland for any advance that may be made as aforesaid; nor to the said nor any other States for any advances that may be made to their respective lines of the army, without the allowance of the U. S. in Congs.

"Resolve that the State of Maryland be called upon to take into their serious reconsideration the irregular measure which they have adopted, and that they be informed that Congs. can not without departing from principles which they solemnly established and countenancing a practice of the most pernicious tendency, permit the State of Maryland or any other State to receive credit for advances made to their respective lines of the army without the allowance of the U. S. in Cong. assd." (NA: PCC, No. 19, IV, 412).

On 28 July Congress took no action on this report after it was submitted, probably by Hawkins, and read (*JCC*, XXIV, 454–55). On 12 August, upon a motion by James McHenry, seconded by Daniel Carroll, which had been introduced on 1 August, Congress resolved: "That the consideration of the report of a committee, to whom was referred a letter of the 20th of June last, from the Superintendant of finance, with the papers enclosed, relative to certain proceedings of the State of Maryland, be postponed, that the delegates from Maryland may have an opportunity to receive information from the legislature, respecting the subject matter thereof" (*JCC*, XXIV, 502–3; Burnett, *Letters*, VII, 249). In the draft of the motion McHenry had justified it by stating that an "immediate approbation" by Congress of the JM-Hawkins report "might be viewed as highly disrespectful to the State whose public act it condemns" (NA: PCC, No. 137, II, 581, 581a). On 3 November 1783 the Maryland delegates sent a copy of the resolution of Congress of 12 August to the General Assembly of their state (Burnett, *Letters*, VII, 368). JM had not attended Congress on either 28 July or 12 August.

From Joseph Jones

RC (LC: Madison Papers). Unsigned and not docketed but in Jones's hand. Spring Hill was his estate.

Spring Hill 28th. July 1783.

Dr. Sr.

Yours of the 7th. inst. came duly to hand.[1] It is strange we have yet no satisfactory accounts of the definitive Treaty. the settlemt. of a British Ministry, I hoped, wod. have speedily brought that important matter to a close; but for any thing we are at present informed the time of its completion is very uncertain.[2] has any step been taken on our part towards a treaty of Commerce. they seem to have moved cautiously in that business. surely we shall not be precipitate, who are, compared to Britain, but novices, very young actors on the Theatre of commerce.[3]

I recollect not giving any intimations to your friends that it wod. be inconvenient for you to take part in the legislative concerns next fall. on the contrary I think I rather encouraged the notion or at least left it quite free for your choice as I hoped and still wish it may suit you to give us your assistance at that time.[4]

I hope such of the Leaders of the late mutiny as shall appear to be guilty will merit the punishment due to their crimes.[5] some of the officers of that line (I mean Pa.) are if we are to judge from former transactions old offenders and having before been pardoned for similar misconduct are the less entitled to favor now.[6] it is to be regretted those princip[ally] concerned have escaped. I doubt whether it wod. be pro[per] for Congress to return to Philada. even upon an address of the Citizens unless couched in terms expressive of the disapprobation of the conduct of the Executive and willingness then as well as at all future times when properly required to turn out in support of the dignity of the fœderal government, which has, (if the report of the Com: deserves credit and we have no reason to doubt any part of it) been grossly disregarded by the Executive Authority of the State. I think at prese[nt] I shod. reluctantly return upon the proposed address and not willingly untill the legislature by some proper resolution paved the way.[7] The Treasurer still leaves me in suspence. whetr. Tomorrows post will produce any thing that will prepare the way to my return [I] cannot now inform you. If I shod. revisit the City my hopes still are I shall see you before your departure.[8]

Yr. aff Friend

[1] JM's letter of 7 July is missing, but, judging from Jones's remarks, its contents may in part have approximated what JM wrote in the last two paragraphs of his letter to Randolph on 8 July (*q.v.*). See also Jones to JM, 31 May 1783, n. 1.

[2] JM to Jefferson, 17 July, and n. 2; Livingston to JM, 19 July, n. 4; Jones to JM, 21 July, and n. 7. The "settlemt. of a British Ministry" refers to the replacement of the Earl of Shelburne's government by that of the Duke of Portland on 1 April (*Papers of Madison*, VI, 504, n. 3; JM to James Madison, Sr., 27 May 1783, n. 9).

[3] *Papers of Madison*, VI, 452–53; 453, n. 5; JM to Jefferson, 13 May, and n. 7; to Randolph, 20 May, and nn. 4–6, 13–14; Instruction to Delegates, 23–24 May 1783, and ed. n. and n. 1.

[4] In this paragraph Jones may have reflected a comment by JM in his missing letter of 7 July. Among "your friends" Jones probably above all included William Moore and Johnny Scott (*Papers of Madison*, I, 148, n. 2), the incumbent delegates in the General Assembly from Orange County. The resignation of either would have provided a vacancy that JM by special election might have filled in time to "take part" in many of "the legislative concerns next fall" (Hening, *Statutes*, IX, 115). JM's evident wish not to commit himself in this regard may signify his lack of certainty about the date of his expected marriage and hence about the date of his return from Philadelphia to Montpelier. JM's engagement to Catherine Floyd, if known to Jones or to Randolph, was never mentioned in the letters of either of them to JM. See Jefferson to JM, 7 May, and nn. 14, 16, 19; JM to Jefferson, 20 May, and n. 10; to James Madison, Sr., 27 May; to Randolph, 3 June; Randolph to JM, 24 May 1783.

[5] JM Notes, 21 June, n. 8; JM to Randolph, 30 June; Delegates to Harrison, 5 July 1783, and nn. 4, 5.

[6] Jones probably referred to the mutinies early in January 1781 and again in June 1781 of Pennsylvania continental troops, even though they did not discreditably involve the officers who would be implicated in the mutiny of June 1783. Captain James Christie, one of those officers, had been reprimanded after being court-martialed for riotous behavior in 1778 (Fitzpatrick, *Writings of Washington*, XII, 256–57). See also *ibid.*, XXI, 55–280, *passim;* XXII, 191; Carl Van Doren, *Mutiny in January: The Story of a Crisis in the Continental Army* . . . (New York, 1943), *passim; Papers of Madison*, II, 279–80; 280, nn. 2, 3; 281, nn. 4, 7–9; 282–84; 287; 301, n. 5. The noncommissioned officers, William Robinson (alias Taylor), John Smith, and Solomon Townsend, who were prominent among the mutineers of June 1783, had all been punished on earlier occasions for serious misconduct, but not for mutiny (Fitzpatrick, *Writings of Washington*, V, 30; VIII, 211; XIII, 137; XXIV, 310–11; XXV, 90–91, 252). Colonel Walter Stewart, who had served ably in helping to suppress the mutiny in January 1781, was among those Pennsylvanians who appear to have stimulated the discontent among some of Washington's officers in the main army at Newburgh in February and March 1783 (*Papers of Madison*, VI, 266; 269, nn. 18, 20; 286; 348; 349, nn. 1, 2; 497, n. 33).

[7] JM to Randolph, 30 June, and n. 7; 8 July; 15 July; 21 July; Delegates to Harrison, 5 July; Hamilton to JM, 6 July, and nn. 5, 7; Jones to JM, 14 July; 21 July, and n. 4; JM to Mercer, 16 July, and n. 4; to Jefferson, 17 July 1783, and nn. 7, 9.

[8] Jones to JM, 14 July, and n. 8; 21 July, and n. 5.

To Edmund Pendleton

Printed excerpts (William Cabell Rives, *History of the Life and Times of James Madison* [3 vols.; Boston, 1859–68], I, 490–91).

EDITORIAL NOTE

These excerpts, except for differences in punctuation, capitalization, abbreviations, and one minor instance of phraseology, are identical with the passage on the same topic in the manuscript of JM's letter to Edmund Randolph on the same date (*q.v.*). If little weight should be accorded to these differences, because Rives was accustomed to alter in the first three respects the texts of the manuscripts from which he quoted, he may have erred in mentioning Pendleton rather than Randolph as the recipient of JM's letter. The fact that almost every letter known to have been posted by JM to Pendleton during 1783 is missing perhaps should strengthen the belief that Rives's attribution was incorrect. The editors have found no other mention of the letter either in JM's day or later.

Circumstantial evidence supporting the accuracy of Rives's citation, however, appears to warrant the inclusion of these excerpts in the present volume. JM often wrote separate letters of overlapping contents to Pendleton and Randolph on the same day (*Papers of Madison*, V, 101–2; 103–5; 157; 158–59; 196–97; 199–200; 209–10; 212–14). Pendleton's letter to JM on 11 August is missing, but a calendar of its contents (*q.v.*), probably made by Peter Force's clerk, indicates that it was wholly or mainly concerned with a site in Virginia for the permanent home of Congress. For that reason the letter from Pendleton seems almost surely to have been a reply to the passage in JM's letter of 28 July 1783 to him.

[28 July 1783]

In order to prepare the way to their permanent residence, Congress have appointed a committee to define the jurisdiction proper for them to be invested with.[1] Williamsburg has asked an explanation on this point.[2] The nearer the subject is viewed, the less easy it is to mark the just boundary between the authority of Congress and that of the State on one side, and, on the other, between the former and the privileges of the inhabitants. May it not also be made a question whether, in constitutional strictness, the gift of any State, without the concurrence of all the rest, can authorize Congress to exercise any power not delegated by the confederation,—as Congress, it would seem, are incompetent to every act not warranted by that instrument, or some other flowing from the same source.[3]

. . . .

Williamsburg[, he says,][4] seems to have a very slender chance, as far as I can discover. Annapolis, I apprehend, would have a greater number of advocates. But the best chance, both for Maryland and Virginia, will be to unite in offering a double jurisdiction on the Potomac.[5]

[1] Harrison to Delegates, 12 July 1783, n. 3.

[2] *Papers of Madison*, VI, 117; 448, nn. 4, 6, 7; Harrison to Delegates, 17 May; 4 July, and n. 5; 12 July, and n. 3; Delegates to Harrison, 27 May, and n. 2; 17 June, n. 1; Pendleton to JM, 16 June, and n. 10; 30 June; Instructions to Delegates, 28 June 1783, and nn. 2, 5–7.

[3] The powers delegated by the Articles of Confederation did not specifically vest in Congress the authority to choose a permanent site for a capital of the United States. Perhaps, by implication, Philadelphia was intended so to be, but the last paragraph of Article IX granted Congress the right "to adjourn to any time within the year, and to any place within the United States" (*JCC*, XIX, 220, 222).

[4] The words "he says" refer to JM and are Rives's interpolation. See ed. n.

[5] For later references to this general issue, see JM to Randolph, 5 Aug.; to Jefferson, 11 Aug.; Pendleton to JM, 11 Aug. 1783.

From Edmund Pendleton

Printed excerpt (Stan. V. Henkels Catalogue No. 694 [1892], p. 94). Below this excerpt the present editors have appended a notation, probably made about 1850 by Peter Force's clerk, of two additional topics mentioned in the letter. The clerk described the manuscript as "1 page folio" (LC: Madison Miscellany).

VIRGINIA, July 28, 1783

I expect that the citizens of Philad'a whilst they are retailing their merit to induce the return of Congress to their City, will feel some remorse for their assumed indifference about their making that the seat of the permanent Session of that body & will enter the list of bidders for the Honour & profit.[1] They may Palliate, but they cant excuse their neglect to suppress a handful of rioters assembled to violate the Laws & to insult either their own Government or that of the State,[2] but we have all reason to practice the divine disposition of forgiving upon repentance.[3]

. . . .

Dry season.[4] Refugees returning with goods[5]

[1] JM to Randolph, 8 July; 15 July; 21 July; Jones to JM, 14 July, and n. 6; 21 July, and n. 4; 28 July; JM to Mercer, 16 July, and n. 4; to Jefferson, 17 July, and nn. 7, 9; to Pendleton, 28 July 1783.

[2] JM Notes, 21 June, and nn. 2, 6, 7; Delegates to Harrison, 24 June; JM to Randolph, 30 June; Hamilton to JM, 6 July 1783, n. 5.

[3] Pendleton to JM, 21 July 1783, and n. 7.

[4] Two weeks earlier Joseph Jones had reported more optimistically that in the vicinity of Fredericksburg "Crops are in general very promising" (Jones to JM, 14 July 1783).

[5] Pendleton to JM, 10 May; 14 July; Randolph to JM, 12 July, and n. 2; 18 July, and nn. 5, 6; Jones to JM, 21 July 1783.

To Edmund Randolph

RC (LC: Madison Papers). Unsigned but in JM's hand. Cover franked "J. Madison Jr.," and addressed by him to "Edmund [Rand]olph Esqr. Richmond." The brackets enclose a syllable which has faded out except for the first stroke of the "R." Docketed by Randolph, "J. Madison July 28 1783."

[PHILADELPHIA, July 28, 1783][1]

MY DEAR SIR

Yesterday's mail brought me no letter from you.[2] The Address from the Citizens of Pa. came before Congs. on thursday and was referred to a Comme. of 5 members. The answer will probably be a very civil one, but will leave open the question touching the return of Congs.[3] This question if decided at all in the affirmative must be preceded by despair of some of the competitors for the permanent residence, almost all of whom now make a common cause agst. Philada.[4] It is not improbable that when the urgency of the scanty accomodations at Princeton comes to be more fully felt,[5] with the difficulty of selecting a final Seat, among the numerous offers, that N.Y. in case of its evacuation[6] may be brought into rivalship with Philada. for the temporary residence of Congress. My own opinion is that it would be less eligible as removing everything connected with Congs. not only farther from the South but farther from the Center, and making a removal to a Southern position finally more difficult, than it would be from Philada. Williamsbg. seems to have a very slender chance as far as I can discover. Annapolis, I apprehend wd. have a greater no. of advocates. But the best chance both for Maryland & Virga. will be to unite in offering a double jurisdiction on the Potowmack.[7] The only dangerous rival in that case will be a like offer from N.J. & Pa. on the Delaware;[8] unless indeed Congs. sd. be carried into N. York befo[re] a final choice be made in which case it wd. be difficult to get them out of the State.

In order to prepare the way to their permanent residence Congs. have appd. a Come. to define the jurisdiction proper for them to be invested with. Williamsbg. has asked our ex[planation] on this point. The nearer the subject is viewed the less easy it is found to mark the just boundary between the authority of C[ongs.] & that of the State on one side & on the other between the former & the privileges of the inhabitants. May it not also be made a question whether in constitutional strictness the gift of any Sta[te] without the Concurrence of all the rest, can authorize Congs. to exercise any power not delegated by the Confederation! As Congs. it would seem they are incompetent to every act not warranted by that instrument or some other flowing from the same source.[9] I wish you could spare a little attention to this su[bject] & transmit your ideas [on i]t.[10] Contrary to my intention I shall be detained here several weeks yet by a disappointmt. in some circumstances which must precede my setting out for Vrg[a.][11]

There is considerable ground to believe that Carlton is possessed of the definitive Treaty.[12] He has lately sent Congs. several depositions relative to forgeries of Mr. Morris' Notes, the authors of which he has confined in N. York & has requested that persons may be sent in to attend the examination.[13]

The Court Martial is still proceeding in the inves[tigation of] the Mutiny but have disclosed no result.[14]

[1] If JM wrote this superscription, it has now faded entirely from the manuscript. Henry D. Gilpin, the editor of the first extensive edition of Madison's writings, perhaps copied this place and date from the manuscript as it appeared in 1840. For this reason the present editors have followed his version. Owing also to fading and to overly close cropping of the right margins of the letter's three pages, the editors, as signified by the brackets in the text, have relied further upon Gilpin, even though he usually extended Madison's abbreviations, added or deleted capitalizations, and altered punctuation.

[2] JM received Randolph's letter of 18 July (*q.v.*) "shortly after" he posted the present letter (JM to Randolph, 5 Aug. 1783).

[3] JM to Mercer, 16 July, and n. 4; to Jefferson, 17 July. The brief acknowledgment by Congress of the "Address" was in the form of a resolution, adopted on 28 July 1783, expressing "great satisfaction in reviewing the spirited and patriotic exertions which have been made by the government and citizens of Pensylvania,

in the course of the late glorious war," and in being assured by the citizens of Philadelphia of their readiness "to aid in all measures which may have a tendency to support the national honor and dignity" (*JCC*, XXIV, 452; Burnett, *Letters*, VII, 241, 253–54). See also JM to Randolph, 5 Aug. 1783, and n. 3.

4 Jones to JM, 14 July, n. 6; JM to Jefferson, 17 July, and nn. 7–9; Delegates to Harrison, 14–15 Aug. 1783; Burnett, *Letters*, VII, 240, 250, 252, 263.

5 Even for the nineteen delegates attending Congress on 30 July, comfortable "accomodations" in the "small Country village," as President Elias Boudinot later described Princeton, were difficult to find. This lack, of course, became almost intolerable with the coming of winter and with the arrival, in response to Boudinot's plea, of more delegates. See Burnett, *Letters*, VII, 229, and second n. 2, 231, 251; JM to Randolph, 5 Aug.; 30 Aug. 1783.

6 The British army did not completely evacuate New York City until 25 November 1783. See Pendleton to JM, 4 May 1783, n. 5.

7 JM to Pendleton, 28 July 1783, and citations in n. 2.

8 JM to Randolph, 13 Oct. 1783; Burnett, *Letters*, VII, 202–3, 326.

9 JM to Pendleton, 28 July, and nn. 3, 5; to Jefferson, 20 Sept. 1783; Burnett, *Letters*, VII, 250, 302, n. 6.

10 Randolph apparently did not comply with this request.

11 The "disappointmt." may have been caused by a letter from Catherine Floyd withdrawing from, or manifesting indecision about continuing, her engagement to marry JM. If he thereupon asked her by letter to renew her promise, he could not expect to receive her reply before "several weeks" had elapsed. See Jefferson to JM, 7 May, n. 16; JM to Jefferson, 17 July, and n. 10; 11 Aug. 1783.

12 Pendleton to JM, 4 May, and n. 6; Delegates to Harrison, 26 July 1783. The "considerable ground" for believing that Carleton had the treaty was a letter to Ralph Izard, written on 21 July by James Rivington, proprietor of the *Royal Gazette* of New York City, stating that the British frigate "Mercury" had brought a copy of the definitive treaty of peace and orders for the British armed forces to evacuate the city and the neighboring waters immediately (Burnett, *Letters*, VII, xxvi, 231, 232, 236, 242–43; *Pa. Packet*, 24 July; 26 July; Delegates to Harrison, 1 Aug. 1783).

13 Delegates to Harrison, 26 July 1783, and n. 7.

14 Delegates to Harrison, 5 July, and nn. 3–5; Mercer to JM, 14 Aug. 1783, n. 8.

Virginia Delegates to Benjamin Harrison

RC (Virginia State Library). In Arthur Lee's hand, except for Theodorick Bland's signature. Addressed to "His Excely. Govr. Harrison." For the absence of JM's signature, see Delegates to Harrison, 24 June 1783, ed. n.

PRINCETON Augt. 1st. 1783

SIR,

Congress have directed the Superintendent of Finance to make public an order he has given to the continental Receivers in the different States, to receive the Notes issued from his Office in payment of the Army, in exchange for hard money, as that shall come to hand. This order having been known to a few only, & not to the Soldiers, & other holders of those notes, it was apprehended that it woud expose them to be speculated upon, & deprivd of the fruits of their toils & sufferings at a very low rate, to their great injury. We think it our duty to give your Excellency this information, that you may make it public if you judge it adviseable.[1]

The discovery of the Forgers of our Paper, in N. York, will it is to be hopd, arrest that nefarious practice in this quarter of the U. S. & as there appear to be many persons concernd in similar practice in Virginia, we trust that government will use every diligence to have them tracd out, & brought to punishment.[2] It woud appear, that the information we had receivd of the arrival of the Definitive treaty at N. York, in the Mercury frigate, tho it came from Rivington who it was conceivd must know, was premature[3]

Nothing has yet been decided relative to the matters we laid before Congress on the part of the State[4]

We have the honor to be, with great respect Yr. Excellency's most Obedt. Servts.

THEOK: BLAND JR
ARTHUR LEE

[1] JM seems to have been absent on all of the days when this matter was before Congress. On 11 July Congress referred to Robert Morris for comment a proposed resolution, drafted by Bland on behalf of a committee of which he was chairman, reading: "That the Superintendant of finance be directed immediately to order the receivers of the continental revenue in each State, to receive the notes issued by his order for the payment of the army, whether signed by himself or Michael Hillegas, treasurer, payable in one, two, three, four, five or six months in discharge of the requisition for eight millions of dollars, for the expence of the year 1782, and that he immediately publish the said order in all the newspapers in the several states." On the same day Morris was further directed to inform Congress of what "measures" he had taken or expected to take "to redeem the notes" which had been or would be issued to the continental officers and troops in accord with the resolution of 26 May (*JCC*, XXIV, 430–32). For that resolution, see *Papers of Madison,* VI, 486, and nn. 2, 3; JM Notes, 20 May, and nn. 1, 2; 26 May, and n. 2; 11–12 June 1783, n. 1.

In his report of 15 July, laid before Congress three days later, Morris stated that he had "long since" instructed the continental receivers to take "in Payment of the Taxes" all the notes signed by him, and to exchange them, on demand, for whatever "public Money" was in "their Hands." Having heretofore treated all varieties of these notes equally, Morris strongly opposed the proposal to confine a public announcement, in regard to an exchange for specie, only to those notes issued "in payment of the Army." To do so, Morris warned, would "destroy what little Credit is at present reposed in the public Servants, and by bringing home immediately all other Notes which have been issued render it impracticable to discharge them, in which Case the Notes issued to the Army could be of no use because no Body would take them" (*JCC*, XXIV, 441–42). In a long letter of 18

July, spread on the journal on 26 July, Morris reminded Congress that eleven days before its resolution of 26 May he had warned a committee of Congress that, lacking the $750,000 required to cover three months' pay for the troops, he would be obliged to resort to notes rather than cash, and that up to 18 July he had furnished the Paymaster General with notes of $500,000 face value. "Congress," continued Morris, "solemnly pledged to me (for the Purpose of inducing my Continuance in Office)" to redeem, by means of "*the vigorous Exertions of the several States in the Collection of Taxes*" and, if possible, "a further Loan of three Million Livres" from Louis XVI of France, "those Notes issued to the Army as well as to fulfill all the other Engagements which I have taken or may take on the public account" (*JCC*, XXIV, 447–51).

The committee, consisting of Bland, chairman, Stephen Higginson, and James McHenry, to which Congress referred Morris' report of 15 July and his letter of 18 July, rendered its first report on 29 July. Following what appears to have been a lengthy debate on that day and the next, Congress agreed, after considerably altering both the language and intent of the committee's report, that "The Superintendant of finance having reported to Congress, 'that the receivers in the several states have long since been instructed to take all notes signed by the Superintendant of finance, in payment of taxes; and also to take up all such notes whenever tendered, if they have public money in their hands;' *Ordered*, That the Superintendant of finance be directed to publish the above information" (*JCC*, XXIV, 477–79, 480–82). Although the avowed purpose of Bland and Higginson was to protect the veterans against speculators, their aim no doubt was also to harass Morris (*Papers of Madison*, VI, 304; 305, n. 4; 306, n. 6; 357; 473, n. 7; Burnett, *Letters*, VII, 123, 166–67, 184, and n. 5, 243–44, 252, and n. 5, 306, n. 6).

In the present letter the delegates conveyed the erroneous impression that the directive to Morris applied only to the notes issued "in payment of the Army." With their letter, however, they evidently enclosed a copy of the congressional resolution. It appeared in the *Virginia Gazette* of 16 August—one day after Harrison, in his acknowledgment to the delegates, assured them that he would acquaint the "public" with the "information" (Harrison to Delegates, 15 Aug. 1783). George Webb was the continental receiver general of taxes in Virginia.

2 Delegates to Harrison, 26 July 1783, and n. 7.

3 JM to Randolph, 28 July 1783, and n. 12.

4 Instructions to Delegates, 23–24 May, and n. 1; 4 and 7 June, and n. 1; 17 June, and n. 2; 20 June, and n. 3; 26–27 June (1st), and n. 3; 27 June; 28 June, and n. 7; Delegates to Harrison, 14–15 Aug. 1783.

From Joseph Jones

RC (LC: Madison Papers). No docket or cover.

Spring Hill 4th. Aug. 1783.

Dr. Sr.

The last post brot. me a Letter from the Treasurer which determines my visit to Congress. He informs me he has bills to the amount of upwards of twelve hundred pounds on Philadelphia which he wishes to apply to the use of the Delegation and had written to you and also to me informing us of it, that our Correspondents, and those of the other Gentlemen, might obtain warrants for our respective proportions of them. he says he expected your answer by the last or this post. I have desired Col. Monroe to obtain a warrant on my accot. if not done, the other Gentlemen will direct their Correspondents to do the same that the bills may be forwarded withot. delay. shod. they arrive before I get up you will be pleased to rec[e]ive my proportion. I am not certain of the day but within a week or ten days at farthest I shall health permiting set out.[1] If Congress shod. be returned to Philadelphia I request a room at Mrs. House's if at Princeton they still remain your assistance to procure me one shall be thankfully acknowledged.[2] Altho I think were I present my voice wod. be opposed to returning to the City for reasons formerly Assigned[3] yet I must confess being in Philadelphia will best suit me on accot. of some private matters I have to attend to, as well as on accot. of more conveni[ent] accommodations an object of some consideration to me [in] my uncertain health and advanced years.[4] I shall return my carriage from Baltimore that Mrs. Jones and Joe may visit the upper Country if she chooses to do so rather than hazard continuing during the sickly season on Rappahannock.[5] from Baltimore I shall ride or take the Stage, as upon inquiry I shall think most agreeable.[6] Th[is] quarter affords no news for your entertainment.

Yr friend & sert.

Jos: Jones

[1] Jacquelin Ambler, the treasurer of Virginia, had informed JM in a letter of 5 July (*q.v.*) that two bills of exchange, totaling £1233 19*s.* 2*d.*, would be made available to the five delegates in Congress. Each of them appears to have taken £246 15*s.* from that amount. JM's reply, if any, to Ambler's letter is missing. Jones's nephew, James Monroe, probably obtained Jones's "warrant" while attending meetings of the Council of State in Richmond on 5 and 6 August (*JCSV*, III, 283). Jones arrived in Philadelphia about the 18th of that month (JM to Randolph, 24 Aug. 1783). He presumably received his allotment on 5 September, the day on which JM noted his own portion in his financial account (Ambler to JM, 5 July 1783, n. 9).

[2] Jones to JM, 25 May, and n. 16; JM to Randolph, 30 Aug. 1783.

[3] Jones to JM, 21 July; 28 July 1783.

[4] Jones was fifty-six years of age. For "his uncertain health," especially during the winter of 1782–1783, see *Papers of Madison*, V, 292, n. 22; 383; 385, n. 9; VI, 17; 18, and n. 4; 21; 22; 155, n. 6; 374, n. 4.

[5] Jones to JM, 14 June, and n. 29; 28 June 1783, and n. 17. Jones's estate was near the Rappahannock River in King George County, Va.

[6] In the *Pennsylvania Packet* of 15 July 1783, the proprietors of the "Baltimore Stages" advertised a five-times-a-week service from Philadelphia to Baltimore and return. The trip of about one hundred miles required two days. A stage accommodated no more than nine passengers, each limited to a maximum of seven pounds of luggage.

From Edmund Pendleton

Summary (LC: Madison Miscellany). The summary is in a calendar, probably prepared about 1850 by Peter Force's clerk. He noted that the letter was addressed "To James Madison" and the manuscript was made up of "2 pages folio."

1783, August 4 VIRGINIA

Contrary reports concerning peace.[1] The debate in the Massachusetts Assembly.[2] Redemption of our obligations. Pay the holder the money he has really advanced and interest.[3]

[1] Pendleton, probably after reading the *Virginia Gazette* of 26 July and 2 August, may have commented upon the conflicting reports stating, on the one hand, that the British military authorities in New York City had received a copy of the definitive treaty of peace between Great Britain and the United States and, on the other hand, that the negotiations in Paris by the peace commissioners of the two countries were still incomplete. See JM to Jefferson, 17 July, and n. 2; JM to Randolph, 28 July 1783, and n. 12.

[2] JM was accustomed to write to Pendleton and Randolph on the same day. In a letter to Randolph on 21 July (*q.v.*, and n. 5) and perhaps also in a missing one to Pendleton on that date, JM mentioned that the Massachusetts General Court had refused to re-elect to Congress their delegates who had voted to grant half-pay for five years to demobilized continental officers.

[3] The general subject of Pendleton's remarks was almost surely the payment of the debt of the United States. He seems to have advocated either that in an instance of a bond being bought with depreciated currency of lower real value than the face value of the bond, the government should repay, with interest, only the specie value of the currency used to purchase the bond, or that speculators, who had bought at a discount the government notes received by veterans or other needy creditors for their services or goods, should be paid by the government only what they had expended in terms of specie, plus interest. At the same time the government should recompense the original holder of the note or his heir with specie equal to the difference between what the speculator had received and the face value of the note. The latter plan may have appealed to JM, who, during the congressional contest in 1790 over funding the national debt, supported a policy of "discrimination" between the original and ultimate holders of the bonds and other government securities (Brant, *Madison*, III, chap. 23). See also Pendleton to JM, 25 Aug. 1783.

To Edmund Randolph

RC (LC: Madison Papers). Cover missing. Docketed by Randolph, "J. Madison Aug: 5. 1783."

PHILADA. Aug: 5. 1783.

MY DEAR FRIEND

Your favor of the 18th. ult. which my last did not acknowledge was in the mail & was shortly after recd.[1] Your succeeding one of the 25th. inclosing the pamphlet came to hand yesterday.[2] The Gazette which I inclose will give you a sight of the Philada. Address to Congress and their answer.[3] Since I left Princeton last I understand the question has been agitated relative to the return of Congs. to this City and a day fixed for its final discussion.[4] There is little reason to suppose that it will be decided in the affirmative by the present composition & thinness of Congs. I rather suppose that no question will be taken when the probability of a negative is fully discovered; though it will be pushed by those who wish to multiply obsticles to a removal South of the Delaware.[5]

The arrival of the definitive Treaty at N. Y. which my last represented as probable, has sunk into a general disbelief.[6] The most sanguine opinion goes no farther now than to the arrival of some preliminary intelligence and instructions touching it.

I am my dear Sir yrs. very affecy.

J. M. JR.

[1] Randolph to JM, 18 July; JM to Randolph, 28 July 1783, and n. 2.

[2] Randolph's letter of 25 July has not been found. The "pamphlet" was undoubtedly that by Meriwether Smith which Randolph had promised about three weeks before to send to JM as soon as it was published (Randolph to JM, 12 July 1783, and n. 4).

[3] JM to Randolph, 28 July, and n. 3. The *Pennsylvania Packet* of 5 August printed the "Address" of the citizens of Philadelphia and the reply thereto by Congress on 28 July 1783.

[4] JM probably had not attended Congress since 26 July (JM to Randolph, 8 July, and n. 2; 15 July, and n. 7). The "reply" mentioned above had not committed Congress either to return or not to return to Philadelphia. On 1 August Congress agreed to delay until 6 August "farther consideration" of a motion to adjourn at Princeton on 8 August for the purpose of meeting in Philadelphia four days later (*JCC*, XXIV, 484–85). Although the issue had been made the order of the day for 6 August, the journal omits mention of renewed discussion of the matter until one week later (*JCC*, XXIV, 506–9). See Delegates to Harrison, 14–15 Aug. 1783.

[5] Of the seven states north of the mouth of the Delaware River, all were effectively represented in Congress on 5 August, except New Hampshire and New York. Of the six south of that stream, Delaware and Georgia had no delegate and Maryland only one in Congress on that day. The arrival in Princeton on 7 August

of Daniel Carroll from Maryland and Ezra L'Hommedieu from New York enabled those states to cast effective votes, provided that the two delegates from each of them concurred in their stand upon a particular issue (*JCC*, XXIV, 484, 492–93).

[6] JM to Jefferson, 17 July, and n. 2; to Randolph, 28 July 1783, and n. 12.

Benjamin Harrison to Virginia Delegates

FC (Virginia State Library). Unsigned. Addressed to "The Honorable Virginia Delegates in Congress." In the hand of Samuel Patteson, appointed temporarily "an Assistant Clerk" by Governor Harrison on 11 August and subsequently "approvd" for regular employment by the Council of State on an unspecified date (*JCSV*, III, 284). The missing RC probably was penned by Archibald Blair, clerk of the Council of State, and the FC entered in the Executive Letter Book by Patteson on or after the date of his temporary appointment.

COUNCIL CHAMBER August 9th: 1783.

GENTLEMEN,

I received your favor of the 26th. of last month with the papers which were very acceptable tho' they contained but little news.[1] I hope the report of Carleton's having received the definitive treaty is true, tho' it seems a little strange that he should have it and you not,[2] as the passage from the ports of France is shorter than from those in England; its arrival would be perfectly agreeable as I earnestly wish to see a free intercourse established with the subjects of all the European powers a very few of our apostate friends excepted which can never take place in this State 'till that event happens and the English shew a disposition to evacuate New York.[3] The british debts I expect will be a subject of much altercation in the next assembly; my own opinion is that the treaty should be strictly adhered to but not unless such of our negroes as are in being are returned and those paid for that were spirited away even tho' they should be dead, as their deaths in a great measure proceeded from a camp fever got in the british army and their being totally neglected when ill.[4] If any thing has lately passed betwixt Congress and Carelton on this subject you'l please to inform me of it.[5] Report says Congress will shortly return to Philadelphia, if they do will they not be blameable after the affronts they have received, or will they ever after remove from thence? I fear not; and therefore most earnestly wish the removal may not take place.[6]

I am &.

1 *Q.v.*, and n. 3.

2 JM to Randolph, 28 July, and n. 12; 5 Aug. 1783.

3 By "a very few of our apostate friends," Harrison meant Virginia Loyalists who had borne arms against the state or the United States. See Instruction to Delegates, 23–24 May, and n. 1; JM Notes, 30 May, n. 1; Jones to JM, 31 May, and nn. 11, 14; 21 June, and n. 21; 28 June. For the evacuation of New York City, see Pendleton to JM, 4 May 1783, n. 5.

4 Harrison to Delegates, 9 May, and n. 6; Jones to JM, 31 May, and citations in n. 15; 21 June, and n. 3; Pendleton to JM, 16 June 1783. On 5 December 1783, the speaker of the House of Delegates signed into law "An act, for further continuing an act, entitled 'an act, to ascertain the losses and injuries sustained from the depredations of the enemy within this Commonwealth' " (*JHDV*, Oct. 1782, p. 50; May 1783, p. 45; Oct. 1783, p. 49; Hening, *Statutes*, XI, 27, 109, 193, 317). The session of October 1783 also extended for about six months the duration of several laws previously enacted "for suspending the issuing of executions on certain judgments" against delinquent debtors (Hening, *Statutes*, XI, 349). Although "camp fever" usually meant typhus or typhoid fever, the term was often employed generically.

5 *Papers of Madison*, VI, 479; 480, n. 7; JM to Jefferson, 13 May, and n. 10; Delegates to Harrison, 20 May, and n. 3; 27 May; JM Notes, 26 May 1783, and n. 1. The three commissioners, appointed by Washington in May to proceed to New York City and, as warranted by the seventh article of the preliminary treaty of peace, "take delivery" of the Negroes and other American property in the possession of British "armies, garrisons and Fleets," quickly found after their arrival that they were reduced to making ineffective remonstrances to General Sir Guy Carleton. He occasionally, through his deputy secretary, replied to their protests about Negroes' overtly leaving the city aboard merchant vessels or ships conveying Loyalists to Nova Scotia, that these departures did not violate the treaty, for it applied only to slaves in the custody of the armed forces. Being apprised of the frustration of the commissioners, Washington on 23 June sent copies of their correspondence with him and with the British authorities to President Elias Boudinot and suggested that they be recalled.

A congressional committee, composed of Hugh Williamson, chairman, JM, and Jacob Read, to which these documents were referred on 2 July, rendered two weeks later an acceptable recommendation, instructing Washington to withdraw the commissioners "unless some change of circumstances shall have occurred, from which he may conclude that further continuance in New York may be productive of some advantage to the citizens of the United States." This instruction probably did not reach Washington until 5 August, when he was again at his headquarters at Newburgh after an absence of eighteen days in northeastern New York and the Mohawk valley. See NA: PCC, No. 152, XI, 345, 349–80; Fitzpatrick, *Writings of Washington*, XXVII, 27–28, and nn. 42 and 44, 71, and n. 8, 83; *JCC*, XXIV, 422, 436; JM to Randolph, 8 July; to Jefferson, 11 Aug., n. 12; Delegates to Harrison, 23 Aug. 1783; Burnett, *Letters*, VII, 166, 279.

On reflection, Washington decided that "some advantage" might accrue from maintaining liaison with British headquarters and thereby even contrived to supply Fort Herkimer on the New York frontier with beef purchased from British and Loyalist merchants in New York City (JM to Jefferson, 11 Aug. 1783, and n. 11). Insofar as the commissioners' prime mission was concerned, he later characterized its discharge as "little more than a farce," for they had "inspected no more property than the British chose they should be witness to the embarkation of" (Fitzpatrick, *Writings of Washington*, XXVII, 27 n., 42, 72, 122–23; XXVIII, 121, 283).

6 Jones to JM, 28 July, and citations in n. 7; JM to Randolph, 28 July, and nn. 3, 5; 5 Aug. 1783, and n. 4.

From Benjamin Hawkins

RC (LC: Madison Papers). Cover missing. Addressed to "The Hon'ble Mr. Maddison." Long after JM received the letter, probably he or someone at his bidding placed a bracket at the close of the fourth paragraph. If JM meant that the first four paragraphs should be included in the earliest published collection of his papers, his wish was disregarded by Henry D. Gilpin, perhaps because the documents edited by him were confined to JM's own writings.

PRINCETON August the 9th. 1783

DEAR SIR.

I thank you for the new publication you sent me.[1] We have letters from Mr. Dana up to the 14th of april O.S. he has communicated his Mission to the vice Chancellor count Osterman and instead of being received, after a second communication, as he expected, he upon invitation visited the count, who made a verbal communication, in substance as follows[2]

1st. That her majesty could not consistent with the character of a mediator receive a minister from the United States 'till the conclusion of the definitive treaty between France, Spain and Great Britain[3]

2nd. That she could not even then do it, consistent with the laws of neutrality while his letter of Credence bore date prior to the acknowledgement of their independence by the king of Great Britain.[4]

3 That she could not do it regularly while his letters of credence bore date before she herself had acknowledged their independence[5]

4 That she could not do it consistently before a minister had been received from the United States in Great Britain.[6]

Mr. Dana mentions something like, his being about to leave Russia as soon as, the season, will admit of traveling, and that he intends to send a memorial to the Count; I assure you I fear, he will take for his guide the conduct of M. J. A. on a similar occasion[7]

I have the honor to be, Dear Sir, Your most obedient & most humble Servant

BENJAMIN HAWKINS

We have ten states, Mass. Rh. Con. N.Y N.J: Pen. Ma. Virgin N & S Carolina[8]

[1] On 4 August JM had received Meriwether Smith's pamphlet. He perhaps gave or loaned his copy to Hawkins. See Randolph to JM, 12 July 1783, and n. 4.

[2] Unnoted in the journal, Congress on 9 August 1783, having received dispatches on the 8th from Francis Dana, minister-designate at the court of St. Petersburg, dated (old style) 6, 11, and 14 April, referred them to a committee composed of Samuel Huntington, chairman, Arthur Lee, and Ralph Izard (NA: PCC, No. 185, III, 73; No. 186, fol. 117). For these dispatches, see Wharton, *Revol. Dipl. Corr.*, VI, 381–82, 390–91, 392–96. In the present letter Hawkins summarized only the latest of these communications. For Ivan Andreievich, Count Osterman (1724–1811), see JM to Randolph, 17 June 1783, n. 5.

[3] *Papers of Madison*, V, 187; 189, n. 13; 235; 236, n. 14; 467; citations in 469, n. 9; VI, 419, n. 3; 427, n. 13; 452; 453, n. 2; Rights of Neutral Nations, 12 June, n. 5; JM to Randolph, 17 June 1783, and n. 5. The separate definitive treaties concluded by Great Britain with France, Spain, and the United States were all signed on 3 September 1783.

[4] Dana's commission was dated 19 December 1780. See *Papers of Madison*, VI, 453, n. 2; Rights of Neutral Nations, 12 June 1783, nn. 6–8.

[5] Russia and the United States delayed entering into formal diplomatic relations until 1809, thirteen years after Tsarina Catherine's death (Samuel Flagg Bemis, *A Diplomatic History of the United States* [New York, 1942], p. 45).

[6] On 1 June 1785 King George III received John Adams as the minister of the United States to the court of St. James (Boyd, *Papers of Jefferson*, VIII, 176).

[7] The "M." before "J. A." may stand for "Monsieur," although Hawkins could have meant "Mr.," "Minister," "Master," or even "Mynheer." Hawkins' abridgment of what Dana wrote is approximately accurate. After stating Osterman's four reasons for the tsarina's refusal to recognize the independence of the United States, Dana summarized his own oral reply, and then added: "An important question arises out of this state of things: What remains to be done on the part of the United States? It belongs to me only to answer what I propose to do further myself, which is to draw a memorial containing this answer, with such observations upon it as shall occur to me, tending to show the futility of the objections which have been made to my immediate reception, and to send it to the vice-chancellor. To such a measure I am advised on a good part." By this last sentence Dana evidently meant the example or counsel of his friend and former chief, John Adams. When minister-designate of the United States at The Hague, Adams had been impatient because of the slowness of the States-General in according him a formal reception. He finally on 19 April 1781 sent one memorial to the States-General and another to the Prince of Orange and Nassau, urging a recognition of American independence. Hawkins neglected to note, however, that Adams' continuing persistence, greatly aided by the pressure of Dutch merchants, the influence of the French ambassador at The Hague, the surrender of Cornwallis, and other circumstances, brought him success on 22 April 1782 (*Papers of Madison*, III, 31, n. 2; 265, n. 2; 282, n. 2; 284; IV, 219; 287, n. 25; 364, n. 3). During the three months following his submission of a memorial to Osterman on 27 April 1783 (old style), Dana received no satisfactory reply. Convinced that his mission was futile and authorized by Congress to abandon it, he thereupon left St. Petersburg to return to Boston (Wharton, *Revol. Dipl. Corr.*, VI, 411–15, 477, 494, 597, 636; *JCC*, XXIV, 226, 227, 267; *Papers of Madison*, VI, 427, n. 14; Rights of Neutral Nations, 12 June 1783).

[8] Hawkins' statement is substantiated by tallied votes recorded in the journal of Congress for 7 and 13 August 1783 (*JCC*, XXIV, 493–94, 505).

To Thomas Jefferson

RC (LC: Madison Papers). Cover missing. After recovering the letter, JM docketed it, "Madison Jas Aug: 11. 1783." Probably also at that time he heavily excised in ink all of his first paragraph except its opening two and closing two sentences. To the partial decipherments of the thirteen obliterated lines by Irving Brant in his biography of Madison (II, 286, 450, n. 7) and Julian P. Boyd in *Papers of Jefferson* (VI, 333, 335 nn.) the present editors have been able to add little.

PHILADA. Aug: 11th. 1783.

MY DEAR SIR

At the date of my letter in April[1] I expected to have had the pleasure by this time of being with you in Virginia. My disappointment has proceeded from several dilatory circumstances on which I had not calculated. One of them was the uncertain state into which the object I was then pursuing had been brought by one of those incidents to which such affairs are liable.[2] The result has rendered the time [of] my return to Virga. less material, as the necessity of my visiting the State of N.Jy: no longer exists.[3] It would be improper by this communication to send particular explanations,[4] and perhaps needless to [trou]ble you with them at any time. An agst is in general an impediment of to them. character will &c. which every the of being demanded of them. Toward the capricious[?] for a profession of indifference at what has happened, I do not forward and have faith in a day of some more propitious turn of fortune[5] My journey to Virga. tho' still somewhat contingent in point of time cannot now be very long postponed. I need not I trust renew my assurances that it will not finally stop on this side of Monticello.[6]

The reserve of our foreign Ministers still leaves us the sport of misinformations concerning the def: Treaty. We all thought a little time ago that it had certainly arrived at N. York. This opinion however has become extinct, and we are thrown back on the newspaper evidence which as usual is full of contradictions.[7] The probability seems to be that the delay arises from discussions with the Dutch.[8] Mr. Dana has been sorely disappointed in the event of his announcing himself to the Court of Russia. His written communications obtain verbal answers only & these hold up the Mediation to which the Empress with the Emperor of G—y have been invited as a bar to any overt transaction with the U.S. and even suggest the necessity of new powers from the latter of a date subsequent to the acknowledgement of their sovereignty by G. B. Having not seen the letters from Mr. Dana myself, I give this idea of them at second hand, remarking at the same time that it has been taken from such passages only as were not in Cypher: the latter being not yet translated.[9] Congs. remain at Princeton utterly undecided both as to their ultimate seat and their intermediate residence. Very little business of moment has been yet done at the new Metropolis, except a ratification of the Treaty with Sweeden.[10] In particular nothing has been [d]one as to a foreign establishment.[11] With regard to an internal peace [es]tablishment, though it has been treated with less inattention, it has undergone little discussion.[12] The Commander [in] cheif has been invited to Princeton with a view to obtain his advice and sanction to the military branches of it, and is every day expected [t]here.[13] The Budget of Congs. is likely to have the fate of many of their other propositions to the States. Delaware is the only one among those which have bestowed a consideration on it that has acceded in toto. Several Legislatures have adjourned without giving even that mark of their [co]ndescension.[14] In the Southern States a jealousy of Congressional usur[p]ations is likely to be the bane of the system:[15] in the Eastern an aversion to the half-pay provided for by it.[16] New Jersey & Maryland have adopted the impost, the other funds recommended being passed for one year only by one of these States, and postponed by the other.[17] Pa. has hitherto been friendly to liberal and fœderal ideas and will continue so, unless the late jar with Congs. sd. give a wrong biass of which there is some danger.[18] Massts. has in the election of delegates for the ensuing year stigmatized the concurrence of those now in place, in the provision for half-pay, by substituting a new representation; and has sent a Memorial to Congs. which I am told is pregnant with the most penurious ideas not only on that subject but on several others which concern the national honor & dignity.[19] This picture of our affairs is not a flattering one; but we have been witnesses of so many cases in which evils & errors have been the parents of their own remedy, that we can not but view it with the consolations of hope.[20] Remind Miss Patsy[21] of my affection for her & be assured that I am Dr Sir

Yr. Sincere friend.

J. Madison Jr.

[1] 22 April 1783 (*Papers of Madison*, VI, 481; 482, n. 7).

[2] Jefferson to JM, 7 May, and n. 16; JM to Jefferson, 17 July, and n. 10; Jones to JM, 28 July, n. 4; JM to Randolph, 28 July 1783, and n. 11.

[3] JM's reference to New Jersey reinforces the supposition that Catherine Floyd had not accompanied her father in May to their home on Long Island but had traveled no farther than New Brunswick, where she stayed with friends or relatives (*Papers of Madison*, VI, 498, n. 2). It is possible that she had spent some time at her home but had arranged with JM to meet him in August or September in New Jersey. Her father, William Floyd, a delegate from New York, did not return to Congress.

[4] Within the context of the society in which he lived, JM meant that committing to paper a matter of personal delicacy, particularly since it involved a lady, would not be in good taste. See Jefferson to JM, 31 Aug. 1783.

[5] So few of the deleted words can be recovered with any confidence that the three or four uncompleted sentences convey little certain meaning. The first sentence may be a further explanation of JM's brief reference to his disappointment –that is, he had always had an aversion against dwelling on personal matters at length. The recovered words in the second sentence do not help to reveal his thought. Perhaps the first clause of the third sentence, especially if "capricious" is what he wrote, adverts to Catherine Floyd's "profession of indifference." The latter part of that sentence seems to have summarized his own outlook.

[6] Jefferson to JM, 7 May, n. 19; JM to Jefferson, 17 July, and n. 10; 20 Sept. 1783.

[7] Delegates to Harrison, 5 July, and nn. 3–5; 26 July; 1 Aug.; JM to Jefferson, 17 July, and n. 2; to Randolph, 28 July, and n. 12; 5 Aug. 1783. Even in the same issue of a Philadelphia newspaper there are contradictory news items under European date lines in May, giving assurance that the definitive peace treaty was or was not "nearly ready for signing" (*Pa. Gazette*, 6 Aug.; *Pa. Packet*, 7 Aug.; *Pa. Journal*, 9 Aug. 1783).

[8] Although the references cited in n. 7 generally agreed that the States-General of the Netherlands, by refusing to accept the terms dictated by the British ministry, was delaying the completion of the definitive treaties, an item in the *Pennsylvania Journal* of 20 August, under a London date line of 7 June 1783, charged that the definitive treaty was being "retarded" by the effort of the American peace commissioners to gain "free egress and regress" for merchant ships of the United States in all French ports, both in Europe and the West Indies. For the conclusion of the definitive treaty between Great Britain and the Netherlands, see Rights of Neutral Nations, 12 June 1783, n. 3.

[9] Hawkins to JM, 9 Aug., and nn. 2–7. Of Dana's three dispatches, dated 6, 11, and 14 April 1783, respectively, only 8 lines of the earliest were encoded (NA: PCC, No. 89, II, 727–42). This passage is not decoded in Wharton, *Revol. Dipl. Corr.*, VI, 382. JM entered the word "Russia" after "Court of" many years later upon recovering the letter. The "Emperor of G––y" was Joseph II, archduke of Austria and Holy Roman Emperor.

[10] JM to Jefferson, 17 July, and n. 14; Jones to JM, 21 July, and n. 4; Treaty with Sweden, 24 July, and hdn., nn. 1, 4, 6, 7; JM to Randolph, 28 July and nn. 3, 5; 5 Aug. 1783, n. 4.

[11] For the reasons delaying decisions concerning American foreign policies, see *Papers of Madison*, VI, 505, and n. 2; JM to Jefferson, 6 May; 10 June, and n. 21; JM Notes, 15 May, and n. 1; 23 May, and n. 7; 10 June, and n. 12; JM to Randolph, 20 May; Jameson to JM, 24 May; Rights of Neutral Nations, 12 June 1783.

[12] For the appointment on 4 April of the committee, including JM, on the peace establishment, see *Papers of Madison*, VI, 432–33; 434, nn. 9, 10; JM to Randolph, 17 June 1783, and n. 10. Besides adopting the plan for establishing public credit, Congress had done little toward formulating a peacetime domestic program, except

to discuss the general problem of the western lands, to instruct Washington to take delivery of military posts from the British, and to request him to submit a plan for a peacetime army (*Papers of Madison*, VI, 442–43; JM Notes, 9 May, and n. 2; 23 May, n. 7; 5 June, n. 1; JM to Randolph, 17 June 1783, and nn. 10–12).

Under authority vested by Article IX of the Articles of Confederation, Congress also instructed the committee "to report on the establishment of a mint" (*Papers of Madison*, VI, 434, n. 10). To report on this subject only, Congress on 23 July named JM a member of a reconstituted committee, Thomas FitzSimons, chairman, which had been appointed originally on 23 April (*JCC*, XXIV, 273, and n. 3, 443). Although this committee on 5 August recommended that Robert Morris be directed to submit "an Estimate which will attend the Establishment of a mint," Congress permitted the issue to lapse during the remainder of 1783 (*JCC*, XXIV, 487; Clarence L. Ver Steeg, *Robert Morris*, pp. 88–89, and nn. 24–26; Boyd, *Papers of Jefferson*, VI, 522, 528).

With the approval of Congress, following an oral report by a committee of which JM was chairman, Washington dispatched Major General Baron von Steuben on 12 July to northern New York and the Old Northwest on what turned out to be, insofar as the principal aim of his mission was concerned, an unsuccessful effort to induce General Frederick Haldimand, commander-in-chief of the British army in those areas and Canada, to evacuate the forts and other military installations within the United States (*JCC*, XXIV, 427, n. 2; Burnett, *Letters*, VII, 214, and n. 2; Fitzpatrick, *Writings of Washington*, XXVII, 48, 61–64, 120–21; Delegates to Harrison, 8 Sept. 1783). Washington's own tour, already mentioned, was partially designed to ascertain how the American defenses in upstate New York could be strengthened (Harrison to Delegates, 9 Aug., n. 5; Fitzpatrick, *Writings of Washington*, XXVII, 84–86). On 27 August 1783 Congress declined to adopt Bland's motion for a committee of the whole to discuss what powers Congress had to create "a military peace establishment." JM voted to postpone consideration of the issue (*JCC*, XXIV, 524–26).

13 On 28 July Congress directed President Elias Boudinot to inform Washington "that his attendance at Congress is requested as soon as may be convenient, after his return from the northward." Delayed by the illness of his wife, Washington left his headquarters at Newburgh on 18 August, arrived in Princeton on 23 August, and was tendered a formal reception by Congress three days later (*JCC*, XXIV, 492, 521–23; Burnett, *Letters*, VII, 243, and n. 2; Fitzpatrick, *Writings of Washington*, XXVII, 102–3, 111, 116–17, and n. 79; Delegates to Harrison, 23 Aug. 1783, n. 8).

14 "The Budget of Congs." was the plan for restoring public credit, adopted on 18 April (*Papers of Madison*, VI, 471; 473, n. 7). In his circular letter of 9 May, enclosing to the executive of each state a copy of the plan, President Boudinot urged that the proposals be given "the most speedy attention" and that "If this should not find the Legislature sitting or likely so to do in a very short Time, I am expressly commanded by Congress earnestly to request it may be summoned with all possible expedition" (Instruction to President, 9 May; Burnett, *Letters*, VII, 160). "Legislatures" which had "adjourned" were those of New Hampshire, Massachusetts, Rhode Island, Connecticut, and Georgia (U.S. Library of Congress, comp., *A Guide to the Microfilm Collection of Early State Records* [Washington, 1950], pp. 21–207, *passim;* JM to Randolph, 12 Aug.; 18 Aug. 1783; Burnett, *Letters*, VII, 269, and n. 4). For Delaware's adoption of the plan on 21 June, see Jones to JM, 8 June 1783, n. 9.

15 Pendleton to JM, 4 May; Instruction to President, 9 May; JM to Randolph, 20 May; 27 May 1783, and n. 8.

16 Pendleton to JM, 21 July, and n. 6; JM to Randolph, 21 July 1783, and n. 5; Burnett, *Letters*, VII, 243–44.

17 Of the revenue articles, the New Jersey General Assembly on 11 June agreed to the impost but limited to one year's duration its sanction of the rest of them. Six days later that Assembly also agreed to the proposed alteration in the method of apportioning congressional requisitions. In the same month the Maryland General Assembly ratified the impost but postponed action on the other financial items until the next session (NA: PCC, No. 75, fols. 191–92, 194; Burnett, *Letters*, VII, 192).

18 By the "late jar," JM referred to the failure of the Pennsylvania executive to protect Congress vigorously at the time of the mutiny (JM Notes, 21 June, and nn.; Delegates to Harrison, 24 June; JM to Randolph, 24 June 1783, and nn. 6, 7). See also Jones to JM, 8 June 1783, and n. 9.

19 Pendleton to JM, 21 July, n. 6; JM to Randolph, 21 July, and n. 5; 12 Aug. 1783. The "Memorial" of the Massachusetts General Court, dated 11 July, was read in Congress on 31 July, discussed by four successive committees and finally spread on the journal on 25 September (*JCC*, XXIV, 483, n. 2; XXV, 571–73; 577–80, 581–85, 586–87, 606–9; Burnett, *Letters*, VII, 243–44, 271–72, 294–97, 316–17; JM to Pendleton, 8 Sept.; to Randolph, 8 Sept.; Memorial of Massachusetts General Court, 19 Sept. 1783). On 20 October 1783 the Massachusetts General Court ratified the impost (NA: PCC, No. 74, fols. 197–203).

20 Upon recovering this letter many years later, JM or someone at his bidding placed a bracket at the close of this sentence. There is no matching bracket at the outset of the paragraph, but JM probably meant that all the paragraph except the terminal sentence should be included in the first edition of his writings. Henry D. Gilpin so interpreted the instruction (Madison, *Papers* [Gilpin ed.], I, 560–62).

21 Jefferson to JM, 7 May 1783, n. 1.

From Edmund Pendleton

Summary (LC: Madison Miscellany). The summary is copied from a calendar, probably prepared about 1850 by Peter Force's clerk He noted that the letter was addressed "To James Madison" and the manuscript consisted of "2 pages 4°."

1783, August 11 VIRGINIA

Williamsburgh as a seat of Government. Some seat on the Potomac. The jurisdiction of Congress over the territory aquired for a seat of Government.[1]

1 For the probability that Pendleton was replying to JM's missing letter of 28 July to him, see JM to Pendleton, 28 July 1783, ed. n., and nn. 1, 3. For "seat on the Potomac" and "jurisdiction of Congress," see *Papers of Madison*, VI, 447; 448, n. 6; Harrison to Delegates, 17 May; 4 July; 12 July, n. 3; Instructions to Delegates, 28 June, and nn. 6, 7; Pendleton to JM, 30 June 1783.

To Edmund Randolph

RC (LC: Madison Papers). Unsigned but in JM's hand. Cover franked by "J. Madison Jr." and addressed by him to "Edmund Randolph Esqr. Richmond." Docketed by Randolph, "J. Madison Aug: 12, 1783."

PHILADA. Aug: 12. 1783.

DEAR SIR

The arrival of yesterday's mail has not enabled me to acknowledge the rect. of a favor. perhaps the post office may be again in fault.[1]

Our[2] late belief of the arrival of the Defin: Treaty at N. York has become utterly extinct. From the tenor of the Newspapers the delay seems to be the effect of discussions with the Dutch.[3] The inclosed letter from our friend Hawkins provides for the article of Russian intelligence. I understand from Mr. Mercer who is here on [b]usiness as well as myself that Mr. Dana's despatches were in part undecypher'd when Mr. Hawkin's transcript was made.[4] The Legislature of Masts. have sent a Memorial to Congress wearing a very unpropitious aspect on the grant of 1/2 pay to the army and in other respects breathing a penurious spirit which if indulged will be fatal to every establishment that requires expence. They profess great poverty, and have declined any decision on the Revenue propositions of Congs.[5] Rhode Island did not even bestow a consideration on them. Mr. H—l from the latter State after being informed of the course taken by Va. said that her backwardness very much emboldened the States that were disinclined to a Genl. Revenue.[6] Congs. have voted Genl. W. an elegant Bronze Statue.[7] He has been invited to Princeton as well to relieve him from the tedium which he suffers on the North River as to make use of his Counsel in digesting a peace Establishmt.[8] We shall probably be reinforced by Mr. Jones in a few days.[9] I shall give you notice when my departure will make it proper for your correspondence to be discontinued.[10]

[1] Being in Baltimore as a representative of Virginia in an effort on 10 August to arbitrate the claims of Simon Nathan against that state, Randolph did not write to JM between 26 July and 22 August, both inclusive (JM to Randolph, 5 Aug., n. 2; Randolph to JM, 23 Aug.). See also Randolph to JM, 28 June 1783, and nn. 7, 8.

[2] JM or someone by his direction placed a bracket at the opening of this paragraph and another after "Establishmt" near the close of the letter, thus signifying the passage to be included in the first edition of his writings. See Madison, *Papers* (Gilpin ed.), I, 562–63.

[3] JM to Randolph, 28 July, and n. 12; 5 Aug.; 13 Sept., n. 2; to Jefferson, 11 Aug. 1783, and nn. 7, 8.

4 Hawkins to JM, 9 Aug.; JM to Jefferson, 11 Aug. 1783, and n. 9. Hawkins' letter included a summary of Francis Dana's dispatches rather than a "transcript" of them. John Francis Mercer's "business" in Philadelphia may have included the procuring of credit for the further operation of his unprosperous Virginia plantations (*Va. Mag. of Hist. and Biog.*, LIX [1951], 190–91; Robert Mercer to John Francis Mercer, 9 Sept. 1783, MS in Va. Historical Society). For at least a portion of JM's business, see JM to Randolph, 28 July, and n. 11; to Jefferson, 11 Aug. 1783, and n. 3.

5 JM to Jefferson, 11 Aug. 1783, and n. 19.

6 The Virginia General Assembly at its session of May 1783 declined to approve the plan for establishing public credit (Pendleton to JM, 26 May, n. 11; Jones to JM, 8 June, n. 5; JM to Jefferson, 11 Aug., and n. 14). On 30 June 1783 David Howell presented to Congress his credentials as a delegate from Rhode Island (*JCC*, XXIV, 411; Burnett, *Letters*, VII, 279).

7 On 6 May Congress, upon adopting Arthur Lee's motion "to prepare a plan for an Equestrian Statue of his Excellency George Washington, Esqr. to be erected where Congress shall fix their residence," named Lee, Oliver Ellsworth, and Thomas Mifflin a committee to recommend a method of achieving the purpose of the resolution (JM Notes, 6 May; *JCC*, XXIV, 330, and n. 1). Among the committee's proposals, first made on 8 May and unanimously adopted after amendment on 7 August 1783, was that Benjamin Franklin, upon being furnished with "the best resemblance of the face and person of General Washington that can be procured," should commission the "best artist" in Europe to execute a bronze statue. On a marble pedestal bearing representations in bas-relief of his principal military successes, Washington should be portrayed "in a Roman dress" with a laurel wreath encircling his head and "holding a truncheon in his right hand" (*JCC*, XXIV, 494–95; Burnett, *Letters*, VII, 260).

8 JM to Jefferson, 11 Aug. 1783, and nn. 12, 13.

9 Jones to JM, 4 Aug. 1783, and n. 1.

10 JM, who apparently did not notify Randolph by letter, may have conveyed to him through Joseph Jones the approximate date of departure from Philadelphia (JM to Randolph, 13 Oct. 1783).

Virginia Delegates to Benjamin Harrison

RC (Virginia State Library). Cover missing. In the hand of Arthur Lee, except for the signatures of the other two delegates and the first sentence of the postscript, written by Mercer. Addressed to "His Excellency The Govr. of Virginia." Docketed, "Virga Delegates L. Augt 14th 1783." For the absence of JM's signature, see Delegates to Harrison, 24 June 1783, ed. n.

Lee's draft of the letter, differing frequently in phraseology but not in substance, and lacking the complimentary close and postscript, is in the library of Harvard University.

PRINCETON Augt. 14th. 1783

SIR,

It is three posts since we have had the honor of hearing from your Excellency, which alarms us about your health.[1]

The Assembly in their last Session passd an Instruction to us, which we have not receivd. It relates to the Accounts of Mr. Finie.[2]

It is now a year since a Commissioner was appointed to settle the Accounts of the State with the U. S. We shoud be obligd to your Excellency for information whether any such Commissioner has been in the State, and whether the Accounts are ready for Settling.[3]

Congress have not yet determind any of the points submitted to them on the part of the State.[4] No Advices from our Ministers abroad relative to the definitive treaty, have reachd us.[5] The Empress of Russia has declind receiving our Minister as inconsistent with her character as Mediatrix, 'till the definitive treaty shall have been signd. A Minister receivd in G. B. from the U. S. & letters of Credence sent bearing a date subsequent to the acknowlegment of our Independence by G. B.[6]

The question for adjourning to Philadelphia, after long debate & mature consideration, was carried in the negative by Six States to two. We have the honor of inclosing a copy of the yeas & nays on this important question.[7]

Two of the ring-leaders in the late Mutiny, have been condemn'd to death by their Courts-martial.[8]

We have the honor to be, with the greatest respect, your Excellency's most obedt[?] Servts.

Theok: Bland jr.
Arthur Lee
John F. Mercer

P. S. Augt. 15th. 1783

A Letter is just recd from Mr. Laurens, dated London June 17. 1783 informs that the Mission of Mr. Hartley will not in all likelihood terminate in a commercial treaty. that the present Ministry is tottering & the restoration of Ld. Shelburne as prime Minister he apprehend woud embarrass the Negociation. The british Court he says has very much changd its tone with regard to reciprocity in commercial stipulations, & seem inclind to have them all in their own favor. He makes no mention of the definitive treaty. But Mr. Fox assurd him that orders were actually sent for the evacuation of N. York.[9]

A. Lee

[1] Governor Harrison's letter of 9 August, not yet received by the delegates, was the first written by him to them since 12 July. For Harrison's illness, see Randolph to JM, 18 July 1783, and n. 7.

[2] The delegates were under a misimpression. The instruction of 4–7 June related to "Accounts" in general, including those of William Finnie but not specifically

mentioning him (Instruction to Delegates, 4 and 7 June, and n. 1; Harrison to Delegates, 20 June, and n. 4; 28 Aug. 1783).

3 By resolutions on 20 and 27 February 1782, Congress provided for the appointment to each state, upon nomination by Robert Morris and subsequent approval by the executive of that state, of a "Commissioner" to concert with executive officers of the state in settling its public accounts with the Confederation treasury. That "Commissioner" is to be distinguished from the five commissioners, one for each of the departments of the armed forces, also authorized by those resolutions to settle the private claims for goods provided, or other services rendered, to the continental army and marine (*JCC*, XXII, 83–86, 102–4; XXIII, 590–91; *Papers of Madison*, IV, 55; 56, n. 6; 71; 72, nn. 1, 3; 333, n. 2; 431, n. 1; V, 58, n. 4; 293, and n. 2; 349, n. 5; 356–57; 459; VI, 215, n. 14; 468, and n. 1; 469, n. 5).

In May 1782 Morris selected Zephaniah Turner of Maryland as his agent for Virginia. Although the Virginia General Assembly on 2 July 1782 extended to Turner "the necessary Aid" of a legal nature to enable him to fulfill his duties effectively, the executive of Virginia by August of the next year had not assembled, and in many instances, owing to the destruction of public papers by the British, could never assemble, all the vouchers and other written evidence required for determining how much the United States and Virginia owed each other (*Cal. of Va. State Papers*, III, 174; *JCSV*, III, 112; McIlwaine, *Official Letters*, III, 253; Hening, *Statutes*, XI, 32–33; *Va. Gazette*, 23 Aug. 1783; Executive Letter Book, 1783–1786, p. 202, MS in Va. State Library). In a letter of 25 September Governor Harrison stated that Turner had arrived in Richmond. Leighton Wood, the solicitor general of Virginia, had been designated by the Virginia General Assembly as the official to work with Turner (Executive Letter Book, 1783–1786, pp. 202, 206).

4 Delegates to Harrison, 1 Aug. 1783, citations in n. 4.

5 JM to Jefferson, 11 Aug. 1783, and nn. 7, 8.

6 Hawkins to JM, 9 Aug., and nn. 2–7; JM to Jefferson, 11 Aug. 1783, and n. 9.

7 JM to Randolph, 5 Aug., and nn. 4, 5. Lee enclosed an accurate copy of the tallied poll entered in the journal of Congress for 14 August. The Pennsylvania and Maryland delegates voted unanimously in the affirmative. Preceding the poll, David Howell's motion to postpone "farther consideration" of the issue failed to carry by a vote of 5 ayes to 3 noes. Bland and Lee, the only Virginia delegates attending Congress on that day, voted "no" in both polls (*JCC*, XXIV, 508–9). In a letter of 14 August to a friend in Virginia, Bland wrote that his vote was alleged to be "contrary to the sense of the State—is it so?" (Burnett, *Letters*, VII, 264). See also Harrison to Delegates, 12 July; Jones to JM, 14 July; 21 July; Randolph to JM, 18 July 1783. Although Mercer had not participated in the polls, he wrote to JM on 14 August (*q.v.*, and n. 2), criticizing Bland for "making a motion with an intention of voting agt. it." In fact, Bland had not made but seconded, and then voted against, David Howell's motion of 11 August. For comments of JM on Howell's, Bland's, and Lee's actions in Congress on the issue, see JM to Randolph, 18 Aug. 1783, and nn. 3, 4.

8 JM Notes, 21 June, n. 8; Delegates to Harrison, 5 July, n. 5; Mercer to JM, 14 Aug. 1783, n. 8.

9 Upon receiving Henry Laurens' letter of 17–18 June, unnoted in the journal, Congress referred it to a committee, Stephen Higginson, chairman, for consideration and report. With the letter Laurens enclosed: "Copy of Articles proposed [29 Apr.] by Amr. Ministers for openg. intercourse or Commerce wth. G. Britain"; "Art: proposed by Mr Hartly—Observations & propositions made [21 May] by Mr. Hartly relative to a free intercourse between G. B. & the Ud. States"; and "Copy Order of the King & Council 14th May allowing unmanufactd goods or Merchandize to be imported into G. B. from America" (NA: PCC, No. 185, III,

75; No. 186, fol. 118; Wharton, *Revol. Dipl. Corr.*, VI, 396–97, 442–44, 491–93). Contrary to the encouraging tenor of the enclosures, Laurens noted in his letter: "Reciprocity appears now to mean enjoyment on one side and restrictions on the other. This change may have been wrought by the sudden and unexpected arrival of divers ships and cargoes from different ports in the United States." "Hence," continued Laurens, "I infer that the last instructions to Mr. Hartley are either calculated for gaining further time, or are such as the American ministers can not accede to" (*ibid.*, VI, 492). See also JM to Randolph, 18 Aug.; 30 Aug. 1783, and n. 12.

On 26 August Congress dismissed the FitzSimons committee, including JM, that had been appointed on 6 May and reconstituted on 5 August for the purpose of submitting a plan of a commercial treaty with Great Britain and suggestions of other commercial treaties to be negotiated. Having been charged on 26 August with these unfulfilled directives, the Higginson committee reported on 1 September (JM to Randolph, 20 May, n. 4; 8 Sept. 1783, and n. 4; NA: PCC, No. 186, fols. 99, 116; *JCC*, XXV, 531–32).

For David Hartley, see JM to Jefferson, 10 June, and n. 8. For Charles James Fox and the evacuation of New York City by British troops, see Pendleton to JM, 4 May, n. 5; JM to Jefferson, 10 June, n. 7. For the fall of the Shelburne ministry and the duration of the Portland-North coalition ministry, see JM to Jones, 8 June, n. 22; to Jefferson, 10 June 1783, n. 4.

From John Francis Mercer

RC (LC: Madison Papers). Cover franked by Mercer and addressed to "Honble James Madison Esq. Philadelphia." Cover docketed twice by JM—once, "Mercer J. F Aug. 11 1783," and once, "Augst. 14. 1783. Jno. F. Mercer."

[PRINCETON 14 August 1783]

DEAR SIR

Before I left Phila. I made enquiry for a Bill on me for 200 Dollars & wch had been presented & accepted but by whom had entirely escaped my recollection. according to the perverse order of human affairs a Letter waiting here informs me of what I wished to know there. it is in the hands of a Mr. J. Ross whom I have directed to apply to you & request the favor of you to discharge it.[1]

The Question for the return to Phila. had been decided in the negative prior to my arrival I must think a worthy colleague hurried this matter on with an unbecoming precipitation, & I am at a loss to reconcile with his professed candor & openness, his making a motion with an intention of voting agt. it, supported by Mr. Howell the inventer of this ingenious & Honourable device.[2] This said worthy Gentleman Mr. Howell, made a motion seconded by our other colleague Mr. Lee, to strike out Government after cofœderal & insert Union, in an Act of Congress.[3] this will give you the complexion of our affairs.[4]

Mr. Laurens writes us from London dated the 17th of June, & suggests that there is no prospect that the mission of Mr. Hartley wd terminate either in a commercial or definitive Treaty.[5]

It will be well for you to advise Mrs. House what steps she shoud take. had I any Idea that the sentiment of Congress coud be so absurdly fixed I woud not hesitate to give my opinion that she shoud remove to where they may plan their residence. I am no doubt disposed by my desire of living with her myself.[6] Does my friend Mrs. Trist pursue the plan of her Indies expedition I wish she wd. write me when she hears from Havanna.[7]

My best respects to Genl. Howe & the Gentn. of his family. the Gnl. will receive official notice of the present aims of Congress which supersedes the propriety of my writing.[8] Come & bring Mr. Jones. your presence wd. be of essential utility.[9]

I am with respect [&] esteem Dr Sir, Yr. mo: Ob. St

JOHN F. MERCER

1 JM to Randolph, 12 Aug., and n. 4; Receipt of Mercer, 11 Oct. For John Ross of Philadelphia, see JM to Bland, 6 May, and n. 1; Statement of Receipts, 28 May 1783.

2 Delegates to Harrison, 14–15 Aug., and n. 7; JM to Randolph, 18 Aug. 1783, and n. 3. Mercer's "worthy colleague" was Theodorick Bland (*JCC*, XXIV, 506, and n. 2, 509).

3 The journal of Congress does not fully sustain Mercer's statement. On 12 August in a reply suggested by a committee to "an address from the inhabitants of New Brunswick and its vicinity" appeared the words "affection and respect for the federal government" (*JCC*, XXIV, 501–2). On 13 August David Howell, seconded by William Ellery, not by Arthur Lee, moved that the word "union" be substituted for "government." Thereupon David Howell "required" a tallied poll to be taken "on the question for re-considering" whether the substitution should be made. In the poll the move to reconsider failed by a vote of 7 to 1. Of the twenty-four delegates who shared in the poll, only Ellery, Holten, Howell, and Lee voted "ay." Mercer was reporting what someone had told him, for he was not in Congress on 13 August 1783 (*JCC*, XXIV, 504–5).

4 By "complexion of our affairs." Mercer probably meant the divisiveness within the ranks of the congressional delegation from Virginia, and perhaps, too, the refusal of a few members of Congress even to designate that assemblage as a "government."

5 Delegates to Harrison, 14–15 Aug. 1783, and n. 9.

6 JM had retained his accommodations in Mrs. Mary House's boardinghouse, but the move of Congress from Philadelphia to Princeton vacated many of her rooms and also reduced her income from providing meals for her tenants. See JM to Mercer, 16 July 1783, and n. 8; Boyd, *Papers of Jefferson*, VI, 375.

7 Mercer referred to Mrs. Nicholas Trist, the daughter of Mrs. House. For at least six years, beginning in 1770, Mrs. Trist's husband was a medical officer in the Eighteenth (or Royal Irish) Regiment of Foot of the British Army. This regi-

ment, shattered by the Battle of Bunker Hill and further worn down in the siege of Boston, left the American states in the summer of 1776 and for the rest of the war was stationed in England and the Channel Islands. Trist, however, appears to have remained in America (Worthington C. Ford, comp., *British Officers Serving in the American Revolution*, pp. 4, 11, 174; G[eorge] Le M[esurier] Gretton and Stannus Geoghegan, *The Campaigns and History of the Royal Irish Regiment. From 1684* [*to 1922*] [2 vols.; Edinburgh and London, 1911–27], I, 83–85, 87).

In 1783 Mrs. Trist was most anxious to rejoin her husband, who by then had settled or expected to settle in or near New Orleans. Although in August she hoped to reach him by going first to Havana, this evidently proved to be impracticable, for in December 1783 she left Philadelphia for New Orleans by way of Pittsburgh. Upon her arrival on the "Accadian Coast Mississippi" early in the summer of the next year, she was told that Dr. Trist had died. The exact date and place of his death have not been ascertained. She returned to Philadelphia in August 1785 (Boyd, *Papers of Jefferson*, VI, 375–76, 383 n., 418; VII, 86–87, 289, 447, 583; VIII, 581; XI, 404; JM to Randolph, 8 Sept.; Jefferson to JM, 11 Dec. 1783).

[8] Mercer's acquaintance with General Robert Howe and "the Gentln. of his family" was probably recent, for during Mercer's military service, he and Howe had been in different geographical "departments." Mercer either wrote this final paragraph on 15 August or he anticipated that a motion introduced on the preceding day, but not brought to a vote, would be adopted by Congress. On 15 August President Boudinot was directed to inform Howe of "the pleasure of Congress" to suspend "the execution of the sentences against the several offenders who have been convicted of mutiny" until "ten days after a full report of all the proceedings of the said court-martial" should be laid before Congress (*JCC*, XXIV, 509–10, 510, n. 1). See also Delegates to Harrison, 5 July 1783, n. 5.

[9] JM and Joseph Jones were in Congress on 27 August, and may have been in attendance two days before (*JCC*, XXIV, 521, n. 1, 525). See also JM to Randolph, 8 July 1783, and n. 2.

Benjamin Harrison to Virginia Delegates

FC (Virginia State Library). In the hand of Samuel Patteson. Addressed to "The Honorable Virginia Delegates in Congress."

Council Chamber August 15th. 1783.

Gentlemen,

I received your favor of the 1st. instant[1] and shall most assuredly use every endeavor to apprehend any forgers of Morris's notes that may be in this country and beg you to give me any information respecting them that may come out in the course of the examination of those that have been taken up in New York and Pensylvania.[2] That the practice is nefarious and injurious to the public is most certain and yet we have no law in this State to punish them but as cheats, the assembly were fully informed that the practice obtained here and yet to my surprize left the matter as they found it.[3]

I have ordered Mr. Morris's directions to be made public and wish good may result from the measure, tho' I have my doubts on that head, if there was money to take all the notes up it would certainly be the case but as only a small proportion can be expected favorites may be prefered by the officers at a distance from the financier to the prejudice of a great number not so circumstanced and thereby raise a clamor that will make the matter worse than it is at present, if the receivers had been ordered to exchange the money with the paymasters only and they enjoined and forced to divide it equally amongst the Soldiers it might have had a good effect.[4]

I am &c.

[1] *Q.v.*

[2] Delegates to Harrison, 26 July, and n. 7; 1 Aug.; JM to Pendleton, 8 Sept.; *Va. Gazette*, 23 Aug. 1783. For the promissory notes of Robert Morris, superintendent of finance, see *Papers of Madison*, IV, 104, n. 1.

[3] Counterfeit notes of Morris had been current in Virginia for at least ten months (*ibid.*, V, 271; 430; 431, n. 4; VI, 302; 303, n. 2; 346; 423; 424, n. 9).

[4] Delegates to Harrison, 1 Aug. 1783, and n. 1.

From Edmund Pendleton

Printed excerpt (Stan. V. Henkels Catalogue No. 694 [1892], p. 94).

EDITORIAL NOTE

In LC: Madison Miscellany, a list, probably prepared about 1850 by Peter Force or by his clerk, calendars this letter as follows: "1783 August 18 Virginia To James Madison The address of the Citizens of Philadelphia to Congress. Prospect of return from Prince Town . . . 1 page foli[o]."

VIRGINIA, August 18, 1783

The Address of the Citizens of Philad'a would have been clearer if fewer Egotisms had appear'd in it. Some were excusable as an evidence of their attachment to the Federal Government, and I am inclined to think that a Majority were ready to have protected Congress from & resented the insult, and that I formerly hinted the true source of the neglect. Be that as it may, that body are polite & civil in their answer, and properly avoided any declaration on the subject of returning.[1]

[1] The subject of this excerpt suggests that JM, as was his custom, had written both to Pendleton and to Randolph on 5 August, mentioning the "Address" and the "answer" of Congress thereto, and enclosing to each of them a copy of the *Pennsylvania Packet* of that date (JM to Randolph, 5 Aug., and nn. 3, 4). See also JM to Randolph, 28 July 1783, and n. 3.

To Edmund Randolph

RC (LC: Madison Papers). Docketed by Randolph, "J. Madison Aug: 18. 1783."

PHILADA. Aug. 18. 1783.

DEAR SIR

I have not this week any more than the last the pleasure of acknowledging a favor from you.[1] Perhaps I may find one at Princeton when I get there.[2] On thursday a question for returning to Philada. was put and decided in the Negative by a large majority. The friends of the measure foreseeing its fate, and supposing that a negative declaration cd. answer no good purpose and might an ill-one, withdrew it. The more moderate opponents concurred in the inexpediency of proclaiming unnecessarily an aversion in Congs to Philada. But some of this class were so keen in their hostility, that a motion was made by two of them to return, who on the question voted agst. their own motion. The public will not I believe fix on this proceeding as one of the brightest pages of the Journals! The abuses to which such an artifice may be extended are palpable. The merit of it in this application belongs to Mr. Howel of R. I. & Mr. B—d of V. The motion was first made by Mr. L. but in the course of the transaction devolved on Mr. Howel.[3] I know of none that will read with pleasure this affair unless it be the Executive of Pa. and those who wish to refer the removal of Congs. to *other motives* than the national dignity & welfare.[4]

Congs. have letters from Mr. Laurens of the 17th. June but they decide nothing as to the definitive Treaty. We have no reason however to impute the delay to any cause which renders the event suspicious. It is said that the British Councils grow more & more wary on the subject of a Commercial Treaty with the U. S. and that the spirit of the Navigation act is likely to prevail over a more liberal system.[5]

S. Carolina we learn has agreed to the Impost on condition only that the revenue be collected by her own officers, & be credited to her own quota. It is supposed that she will agree to exchange the valuation of land for the proposed rule of numbers: But on this point R. I., is even more inflexible than on that of the Impost.[6] I pity from my heart the officers of the Eastern line[7] who are threatened by these prospects with disappointments which the Southern officers have no Idea of. From much conversation which I have lately had with some of the former, and from other information, there appears great reason to believe th[at] if no *Continental provision* be made for them they will not only be docked of their half pay, but will run great hazard of being put off with regard to a great share of their other pay on the pretence of their States that they have already advanced beyond their proportion[8]

I expect Mr. Jones every moment.[9]

[1] JM to Randolph, 12 Aug., and n. 1; Randolph to JM, 23 Aug. 1783. JM inadvertently repeated "the" before "last."

[2] Mercer to JM, 14 Aug. 1783, n. 9. Many years later JM or someone at his bidding inserted a bracket immediately following this sentence and a matching bracket at the close of the letter's second paragraph. Brackets also enclose the last paragraph. These brackets were to designate the portions of the letter to be published in the first extensive edition of JM's writings (Madison, *Papers* [Gilpin ed.], I, 564–66).

[3] Delegates to Harrison, 14–15 Aug. 1783, and n. 7. As recorded in the journal, the sequence of motions and countermotions concerning the meeting place of Congress began on 31 July and culminated on 14 August. On the earlier of these dates, Jacob Read, seconded by James McHenry, moved, "That on the the President shall adjourn Congress, to meet at Philadelphia, on there to continue until the last Monday in October next, at which time the President shall adjourn Congress, to meet at Annapolis on the Friday following, unless Congress shall before that time have determined otherwise." On 1 August Bland, seconded by Howell, moved to fill the first blank with 8 August and the second blank with 12 August. Immediately thereafter they introduced a second motion to strike out all the words in the Read motion following the second blank. The outcome of a tallied vote was to delete those words–their retention being supported by the effective vote of South Carolina alone. In this poll, Bland voted to excise the words and Arthur Lee to retain them. Congress then adopted a motion by Lee, seconded by Samuel Holten, to give the Read motion "farther consideration" on 6 August (*JCC*, XXIV, 484–85).

It was not until 13 August, however, that "Agreeable to the order of the day," Congress considered a Howell-Bland motion, offered on 11 August, for adjourning on 15 August and reconvening in Philadelphia on 21 August. Read, seconded by Daniel Carroll, moved that consideration of the motion be postponed "in order to take up" a new recommendation. Prefacing it with a "Whereas" paragraph to the effect that a continued stay in Princeton was no longer "necessary or expedient," because the mutiny which obliged Congress to move there had been suppressed, Read then repeated the Howell-Bland proposal, but with the supplement "that on the second Monday in October next," Congress adjourn to meet in Annapolis one week later, "unless Congress shall in the mean time order otherwise." The attempt to substitute this motion failed by a vote of 3 to 5. On this poll both Bland and Lee, the only Virginia delegates in attendance, voted "no." Congress adjourned after debating the Howell-Bland motion and entering on the journal a motion of the Pennsylvania delegates expressing the desire of the executive of their state that Congress return to Philadelphia (*JCC*, XXIV, 506–8, 508, n. 2; Jones to JM, 21 July 1783, n. 4).

On Thursday, 14 August, the "friends" of the Howell-Bland motion, recognizing that it could not pass, sought to postpone its "farther consideration." The motion to postpone, introduced by James Duane of New York, failed to carry by a vote of 5 to 3. Bland, Lee, and Howell, also presumably "friends," were against postponement. On the poll to agree to the Howell-Bland motion, those three delegates all voted "no." The motion failed, with only the Pennsylvania and Maryland delegates being unanimously in its favor (*JCC*, XXIV, 508–9; Varnum L. Collins, *Continental Congress at Princeton*, pp. 168–72; Burnett, *Letters*, VII, 262–63, 268,

n. 2, 272; Delegates to Harrison, 14–15 Aug., and n. 7; Mercer to JM, 14 Aug. 1783).

4 The outcome of the poll made clear that, although the offense to "the national dignity & welfare" was the official reason announced on 24 June by President Elias Boudinot for the move of Congress to Princeton, political considerations reflecting individual, state, and sectional rivalries had also influenced the decision and had gradually eclipsed in importance more worthy motives during the eight weeks which had elapsed since the adjournment at Philadelphia. Thus appeared to be confirmed what public officials of Pennsylvania and delegates in Congress had hinted, and prominent citizens of Philadelphia had openly charged even before Congress left that city (Varnum L. Collins, *Continental Congress at Princeton*, pp. 33–37; Burnett, *Letters*, VII, 199, n. 2, 201, second n. 2, 205, n. 3, 209, 212, n. 3, 233–34, 252, 260–61, 266; JM Notes, 21 June, n. 7; JM to Randolph, 8 July; 28 July; 5 Aug. 1783).

5 *Papers of Madison*, VI, 452; 453, n. 5; 495, n. 13; JM to Randolph, 17 June, n. 6; Delegates to Harrison, 14–15 Aug., and n. 9; Mercer to JM, 14 Aug. 1783.

6 JM to Jefferson, 11 Aug., and citations in n. 15; to Randolph, 12 Aug. 1783. JM's information about South Carolina perhaps had been furnished by one or more of the passengers, including General Anthony Wayne, who had arrived at Philadelphia on 13 August by ship from Charleston (*Pa. Packet*, 14 Aug.). The news, whatever may have been its source, was inaccurate, for the South Carolina General Assembly delayed acceding to the proposed impost until the spring of 1784 (Boyd, *Papers of Jefferson*, VII, 130). For the proposal to allocate financial quotas among the states on the basis of population rather than land valuations as stipulated by Article VIII of the Articles of Confederation, see *Papers of Madison*, VI, 26, n. 3; 297, n. 44; 406; 407, and n. 2; 491–92. The South Carolina delegates had opposed the suggested change (*Papers of Madison*, VI, 24, and n. 8; 173).

7 That is, the officers from the New England states in the continental army.

8 For the opposition of the New England states to the pledge by Congress of full pay for five years to the officers of the continental line who had become supernumeraries or served for the duration of the war, see JM to Jefferson, 11 Aug. 1783, and citations in nn. 16 and 19.

9 Mercer to JM, 14 Aug. 1783, n. 9.

Virginia Delegates to Benjamin Harrison

RC (Virginia State Library). In the hand of Theodorick Bland. Docketed, "Letter Hon Virga Del: 23d August 83." A different hand, possibly that of an unknown archivist, continued the docket: "1783 Aug: 23d Containing among other Matters, Sir Guy Carletons reasons for delaying the evacuation of. and informing the Govr. that Congress by resolution had demanded the records and State papers pertaining to Virginia from Great Britain." For the absence of JM's signature, see JM to Randolph, 8 July 1783, and n. 2.

Prince Town Augt. 23d 1783

Sr.

We have been honor'd with Yrs. of the 9th Inst.[1]

Sr. Guy Carleton writes in a letter to Congress dated Augt. 17th. that the June Packet lately arrived has brought him orders for evacuating that Place, and that he shall loose no time in fulfilling his Majesty's commands, but he adds, that notwithstanding his orders are urgent to accelerate the *Total* evacuation, the difficulty of assigning the Precise time for that event is of late greatly encreased, which he attributes to the effects which the Proceedings of the Committes &.c. have had on the Loyalists, who concieve, he says, the safety both of their property and their lives depends on their being removed by him. for this he appeals to the Gazettes, and daily publications in the U. S. and he further adds, he should shew an Indifference to the feelings of humanity as well as to the honor and Interest of the Nation he serves to leave any of the Loyalists that are desirous to quit the Country, a prey to the violence they concieve they have so much reason to apprehend, on which grounds he appears to Justify himself for any delay in the evacuation which may take place. he also expresses his Surprise that Congress have not officially interposed their authority to restrain the Violences he speaks of, and taken other steps to carry into execution the terms of the Treaty.[2] he appears however to think that no blame is imputable to himself, in the glaring infringement of the 7th Article in suffering so large a Number of Negroes to be carried off under the flimsy pretext that they were declared free by the Proclamation of his predecessors, previous to his arrival and the Signature of the treaty from whence he draws this Singular conclusion that they could not possibly be the objects of the negotiation.[3] The official information of the evacuation being soon to take place however, suggested to us the propriety of hastening a demand of the records, papers &.c. belonging to our State and its Citizens, which Congress agreed to in the form of a General resolution comprizing those of all the other States[.] we have no doubt but yr. Excelly. will take the necessary steps to avail Yr self of the demand as far as it concerns the State of Virginia[4]

There seems to be no expectations of the difinitive treaty being speedily concluded.[5] The Powers of Europe seem to have their attention fixd on the War between the two Imperial Courts and the Porte,[6] and on forming Peace establishments, which indeed are so large with respect to their Marine that it may be calld, not improperly Arming for peace.

With respect to the return of Congress to Philadelphia which Yr. Excelly. seems to fear, I believe you may be perfectly at ease on that score, as all Ideas of that sort seem to have vanished, since the great

Majority appeard on the Vote we had the honor to transmit you on that Question in our last.[7] we have the Honor to be

Yr. Excellys. most obedt. Servts

THEOK: BLAND JR. J. F. MERCER A. LEE

P.S.

We are this day honord with the Compy. of his Excelly Genl. Washington, who will remain some time here at the request of Congress.[8]

We could wish yr. Excelly. wd. be pleased to transmit a Succinct State of the Sums Granted by our assembly to Congress, together with Sessions or dates of each grant, and the requisitions under which they were granted, and the purposes to which they have been appropriated in the several grants[9]

THEOK: BLAND JR.

[1] *Q.v.*

[2] Bland accurately summarized Carleton's letter to President Elias Boudinot, enclosing copies of depositions from Loyalists and of letters dating between April and July 1783 from Washington, Governor George Clinton of New York, and Robert R. Livingston, secretary for foreign affairs, tending to support Carleton's charges that, contrary to the provisional articles of peace and in spite of the "pacific" disposition "of the Court of Great Britain," Congress and the state governments seemed unwilling or unable to prevent "Committees formed in various Towns, Cities and districts, and even in Philadelphia" from "barbarous menaces" to the property and often to the lives of "their Countrymen" who had not favored the American cause but wished to remain in the United States. Carleton pointed out that this emigration, which he was resolved to facilitate, could be greatly lessened, and thereby the evacuation of British troops could be much expedited, if Congress and the state executives would fulfill their duty to protect these Loyalists (NA: PCC, No. 52, fols. 217–23, 225–67).

If Carleton had wished to document his mention of "the Proceedings of the Committes &.c.," he needed only to cite many of the issues of the *Pennsylvania Packet* between April and July, both inclusive. For Portsmouth, N.H., see the issue of 24 July; for Boston, Cambridge, Lexington, Malden, Marblehead, Roxbury, and Worcester, Mass., the issues of 15 and 29 April, 20 May, and 5, 10, 19, and 28 June; for Newport, R.I., the issue of 24 May; for New Haven, Conn., the issues of 22 and 29 April; for Amenia, Cambridge, the Canajoharie and Mohawk districts of Tryon County, Poughkeepsie, Rhinebeck, and Scarsdale Manor, N.Y., the issues of 20 May, 3 and 26 June, and 3, 15, and 19 July; for Bucks County, Germantown, and Philadelphia, Pa., the issues of 24 and 31 May, 17 and 19 June, and 8 July; for the militia of Kent County, Del., the issue of 26 June; for Baltimore and Elk-Ridge, Md., the issues of 26 June and 8 July; for Portsmouth, Va., and the proclamation on 2 July of Governor Harrison, the issues of 17 June and 17 July; and for Charleston, S.C., the issue of 24 July 1783. See also Pendleton to JM, 10 May, and n. 4; Jones to JM, 21 June, and n. 20; 28 June; 21 July, n. 6; Randolph to JM, 12 July, and n. 2; 18 July 1783, and nn. 5, 6

[3] Walke to Delegates, 3 May, and nn. 2, 3, 5, 7; JM to Randolph, 6 May, n. 6; to Jefferson, 13 May; JM Notes, 23 May, and n. 4; 26 May, and n. 1; Jones to JM, 25 May; Pendleton to JM, 2 June, n. 3; 16 June 1783.

[4] JM to Randolph, 8 July, and citations in n. 13; Livingston to JM, 19 July, and n. 10; Harrison to Delegates 9 Aug., and nn. 4, 5; 13 Sept. 1783, and n. 3. On 21 August Congress adopted, after amendment, two resolutions, introduced by Arthur

Lee and seconded by Bland, to request the British commanders-in-chief in New York and Quebec "to order the immediate delivery to persons authorized to receive them, of all archives, records, deeds and papers belonging to any of the United States or to any of their Citizens which may have fallen into the hands of any of his Britannic Majesty's Officers during the course of the war." These resolutions, which Congress directed to be sent to the several states, also requested Washington "to make application" to the two British commanders-in-chief for the return of the manuscripts (*JCC*, XXIV, 517–18, 518, n. 1). As early as 28 April, by instructions from General Sir Guy Carleton, Adjutant General Oliver De Lancey, Jr., had called upon "all persons" having papers of the types just mentioned to deposit them in the secretary's office of the army's headquarters in New York City (*Pa. Packet*, 6 May 1783).

[5] JM to Jefferson, 17 July, and n. 2; 11 Aug., and nn. 7, 8; Delegates to Harrison, 14–15 Aug. 1783, and n. 9.

[6] For the war against Turkey by the "Imperial Courts" of Russia and Austria, see *Papers of Madison*, IV, 97; 99, nn. 7, 9, 12; *Va. Gazette*, 23 and 30 Aug., 6, and 13 Sept. 1783.

[7] Delegates to Harrison, 14–15 Aug., and n. 7; JM to Randolph, 18 Aug. 1783, and nn. 3, 4. On 25 August Congress referred to a committee, James Duane, chairman, and JM among the other four members, resolutions of "Inhabitants of Elizabethtown," N.J., offering that town as the site of the capital of the United States. The committee reported on 10 September (NA: PCC, No. 46, fol. 103; *JCC*, XXV, 548). See also Jones to JM, 14 July 1783, n. 2.

[8] JM to Jefferson, 11 Aug. 1783, and n. 13. Rockingham, the residence provided by Congress for Washington's use during his stay from 23 August to 9 November 1783, was a house of twenty rooms, situated on an estate of 120 acres fronting the Millstone River at Rocky Hill, about five miles from Princeton (Fitzpatrick, *Writings of Washington*, XXVII, 114–237, *passim; Pa. Packet*, 28 Sept. 1783).

[9] Harrison to Delegates, 10 Oct. 1783. The wish of the delegates to be provided with these data recalls the request of the Virginia General Assembly to be furnished with a detailed financial accounting by Robert Morris, superintendent of finance (Instruction to Delegates, 4 and 7 June, and n. 1; Harrison to Delegates, 20 June 1783, and n. 4).

From Edmund Randolph

RC (LC: Madison Papers). Unsigned, but in Randolph's hand. Cover addressed to "The honorable James Madison jr esq. of congress now in Philadelphia." Docketed by JM, "August 23. 1783."

RICHMOND[1] August 23. 1783.

MY DEAR FRIEND.

My trip to Baltimore, from which I returned last sunday, has occasioned the chasm in my correspondence.[2]

Mr. Nathan met me according to appointment, with an elaborate argument, prepared on paper by Mr. Sargent. In this he pressed the decision of the former arbitrators,[3] first as conclusive, and afterwards, at least as a reasonable guide for the judgment of the Maryland referees.[4] These topics not being received with much countenance, he insisted upon the efficacy of the bills as draughts for specie—upon the obligation, arising from the assumpsit—and upon the obligation arising from the delay in renouncing that assumpsit.[5] But before we had proceeded further in the inquiry, the arbitrators asked Mr. Nathan and myself for some evidence of the currency of Virginia bills at New Orleans.[6] Neither being able to produce it, and the hurry of their own business not suffering them to spend as much time in the discussion as might be necessary, they declined all further interference at present; fixing the third tuesday in december for the resumption of the affair at Alexandria.[7]

The effect of the assumpsit and the subsequent delay are indeed thorns in the path. But if right could be made to prevail, I should expect Nathan's condemnation This however is hardly to be hoped: and Virginia will probably receive no other satisfaction from my trips to Alexandria and Baltimore, than to learn that a Jew merchant, unconnected with America, took up bills on Virginia from pure magnanimity, or affection for her.[8]

The governor's proclamation, expelling the obnoxious adherents to british interest, continues to give great disquiet to the friends of those, who fall within that description.[9] Mr. Jefferson has taken Dr. Turpin by the hand, and in a long letter to him attempted to shew, that his case belongs not to the offensive class. The Dr: went to Scotland in his infancy for his education. He was surprized there by the American war, with his studies incomplete. He made various attempts to return to Virginia; but being disappointed in his efforts for this purpose, and unable as he says to support himself by other means, he entered as surgeon on board of a british ship of war. While in the service he was captured at York. From these facts, tenderness is due to Turpin. But I cannot admit, that the necessities of that gentleman would protect him from the operation of the law as it now stands; because they do not seem to have been incapable of being supplied thro channels, which were not hostile. Mr. J. doubts whether surgeons ought to be ranked among the instruments of hostility, and refers to a proposition from Carlton to consider them as exempt from the rights of war.[10] But I believe, that he might find more examples than one of a surgeon being executed for treason in joining the king's enemies.[11]

1 In the *Virginia Gazette* of 6 September 1783, Randolph, after stating that he planned to move to Richmond, advertised for sale his property of 470 acres located on the Brook road about six miles from that town. He added that the approximately 80,000 "corn hills" on the two hundred acres of cleared land "will soon be in wheat." This was the estate known as Pettus's, which Randolph, having for a

time rented, later bought from Dabney Pettus (*Papers of Madison*, IV, 148, n. 2).

[2] JM to Randolph, 12 Aug. 1783, n. 1.

[3] For Simon Nathan, Jonathan Dickinson Sergeant, and the long background of Nathan's claim against the state of Virginia, see *Papers of Madison*, III, 20; 21, n. 2; 22, nn. 3, 4; also the other citations under Nathan in the index of that volume, and the indexes of volumes V and VI. For the "appointment" in Baltimore and the reason for Randolph's trip there, see Jones to JM, 21 June, nn. 12, 23; Randolph to JM, 28 June, and nn. 7, 8; JM to Randolph, 8 July 1783, and n. 5; *JCSV*, III, 282; Boyd, *Papers of Jefferson*, VI, 319–21.

[4] The names of the "Maryland referees" of the arbitration scheduled to begin on 10 August are unknown. On 9 July Daniel Dulany (1722–1797) of Annapolis had been requested to represent Virginia, but receiving no reply from him, the governor and Council on 24 July "authorized and empowered" Randolph himself "to nominate and appoint" an arbitrator for the state (*JCSV*, III, 275; Executive Letter Book, 1783–1786, pp. 171, 179–80, MS in Va. State Library).

[5] The matter at issue, involving many thousands of dollars, was whether some of the bills of exchange drawn against Virginia, which Nathan apparently had bought for specie either in Havana or from Oliver Pollock in New Orleans in 1779 and 1780, were for amounts in depreciated currency or in "hard money." For Pollock, see *Papers of Madison*, III, 99, n. 1; 256, n. 6; 344, n. 2; IV, 377–78; V, 208, n. 5; VI, 439; 474; 475, nn. 4, 5; 476, nn. 6, 7; 502; Delegates to Gálvez, 4 May, and nn. 2, 3; JM to Jefferson, 20 May, n. 4; Jones to JM, 14 June 1783, n. 28.

Thomas Jefferson, when governor of Virginia, and the Council of State had accepted the sums mentioned on the bills as being a public debt to be paid in specie or its equivalent in tobacco. This, in the terminology of 1783, was an assumpsit, or "contract not under seal," which, if unfulfilled within the time specified on the bills, made at least a private debtor subject to suit for breach of contract (an action in assumpsit) by the creditor. At the close of 1780, having been assured that in 1779 Virginia paper money was heavily discounted in terms of specie in the district of Kentucky, the Illinois country, and the lower Mississippi Valley, and hence that Pollock had listed most if not all of his charges for goods in depreciated currency, Jefferson, the Council of State, and soon the Virginia General Assembly joined "in renouncing that assumpsit." Jefferson wrote on 1 January 1781, "as our Assumpsit was on Mr. Nathans own Word we do not think that any Error into which we have been led by want of Information or Misinformation can in Equity be irrevocable" (Boyd, *Papers of Jefferson*, III, 315, 320, 322–33; IV, 283).

[6] That is, whether Virginia paper money had been current in New Orleans and, if so, at what varying rates of depreciation on the dates of Pollock's bills.

[7] Randolph used "interference" in the sense of intervention or arbitration between two or more parties in conflict. The "third tuesday in december" was 16 December 1783. Randolph's written report of the meeting at Baltimore, including the decision to resume the conference in December, was approved by Governor Harrison and the Council of State on 22 October. Two days earlier, with his message to the Virginia General Assembly, Harrison had enclosed Randolph's report and Nathan's request "that funds may be provided to discharge what may be awarded him" in December (*JCSV*, III, 298; Executive Letter Book, 1783–1786, pp. 221–22, MS in Va. State Library). Upon being laid before the House of Delegates on 4 November, the first day a quorum assembled, these papers were referred to the committee of the whole on the state of the commonwealth (*JHDV*, Oct. 1783, p. 7). This committee presented no report on the subject during the rest of the session. In June 1784 Randolph reported to the Virginia House of Delegates that "accident" had prevented the arbitration in December 1783 (*JHDV*, May 1784, pp. 56–57).

[8] Randolph meant that when Nathan purchased the controversial bills of exchange he was a Spanish subject living in Havana rather than a resident of Philadelphia (Boyd, *Papers of Jefferson*, III, 320).

[9] Randolph to JM, 12 July, and n. 2; 18 July, and n. 5; Jones to JM, 21 July 1783, and n. 6.

[10] *Ibid.*, n. 6. Perhaps Randolph had been furnished by Jefferson with a copy of his long letter of 29 July to Philip Turpin, or Turpin had shown the letter to Randolph (Boyd, *Papers of Jefferson*, VI, 324–33, and esp. p. 328). For General Sir Guy Carleton's letter of 7 July 1782 to Washington, and the latter's reply on 18 August 1782, see *Papers of Madison*, V, 42–43; Fitzpatrick, *Writings of Washington*, XXV, 26, 38, 196.

[11] Treason had been defined by the Virginia General Assembly as levying "war against this commonwealth in the same," or as adhering "to the enemies of the commonwealth within the same, giving to them aid and comfort in the commonwealth or elsewhere." The accused person, if "legally convicted of open deed by the evidence of two sufficient and lawful witnesses, or their [his] own voluntary confession," was sentenced to "death without benefit of clergy," and would "forfeit his lands and chattels to the commonwealth, saving to the widows of such offenders their dower in the lands." Pardon of the traitor could be extended only by the General Assembly (Hening, *Statutes*, IX, 168). This law, which did not except surgeons from its provisions, clearly made Dr. Philip Turpin subject to trial for treason. He had been born in Virginia and served as a surgeon with the British in that state during its invasion by Cornwallis' army (Randolph to JM, 18 July 1783, n. 6).

Randolph's surmise was correct. With sufficient data available, he might from many "examples" have noted that of Dr. Archibald Campbell (1707–1753), attainted for participation in the Jacobite uprising in Scotland in 1745. Eventually captured, the doctor was tried, sentenced, and executed, despite the fact that he had ministered to the needs of "several of the king's troops that fell wounded" ([Thomas] B[ayly] Howell, comp., *A Complete Collection of State Trials and Proceedings for High Treason and Misdemeanors* . . . [34 vols.; London, 1816–28], XIX, cols. 733–46). Another proscribed participant in the rebellion, young Dr. Hugh Mercer (*ca.* 1725–1777), escaped to America, settled at Fredericksburg, Va., and died from wounds received at Princeton while leading a brigade of "the king's enemies" (Joseph M. Waterman, *With Sword and Lancet: The Life of General Hugh Mercer* [Richmond, 1941]).

To Edmund Randolph

RC (LC: Madison Papers). Cover franked by "J Madison Jr" and addressed to "Edmund Randolph Esqr. Richmond." Docketed by Randolph, "J. Madison Aug: 24. 1783." Beneath this docket is written in an unknown hand, "Letters of the honble J Madison (of Congress)," probably signifying that at one time the cover was at the top of a packet of JM's letters.

PHILADA. Aug: 24. 1783

MY DEAR SIR

Mr. Jones who arrived the beginning of the week[1] acquainted me with your abortive mission to Maryland which I had not before heard of. To this absence from Richmond I impute your silence by the late mails. I hope for the pleasure of a line by the mail now on its way,[2] which will not however be acknowledged till the ensuing week, as I am about returning to Princeton where it will find me too late for the post of this week.[3] All that I have now to tell you is that Sr G. Carlton has notified to Congs. his having recd. orders for the evacuation of N. York; but he specifies no time fixed either by the orders or by his own plans. He repeats his lamentations touching the Loyalists and insinuates that the proceedings of the people agst. them are a proof that little or no Govt. exists in the U. States.[4]

With great affection I am Yr. frd & Svt

J. M Jr

[1] In 1783 the twenty-fourth of August was a Sunday. For this reason, JM could have written "to-day" rather than "the beginning of the week," but he probably meant that Joseph Jones had been in Philadelphia for about a week (Jones to JM, 4 Aug., and n. 1; JM to Randolph, 18 Aug. 1783).

[2] JM to Randolph, 12 Aug., and n. 1; Randolph to JM, 23 Aug. 1783, and nn. 3–8.

[3] JM almost certainly received Randolph's letter of 23 August, but he did not acknowledge it in any letter known to the editors.

[4] Delegates to Harrison, 23 Aug., and n. 1; 4 Oct. 1783. Many years later JM or someone at his bidding placed a bracket at the end of the paragraph. Although the bracket may have been to signify that the entire letter, except for its complimentary close, should be published in the first extensive edition of his writings, only the last two sentences of the paragraph appear in Madison, *Papers* (Gilpin ed.), I, 566.

From Edmund Pendleton

Summary (LC: Madison Miscellany). The summary is copied from a calendar, probably prepared about 1850 by Peter Force's clerk. He noted that the letter was addressed "to James Madison" and the manuscript consisted of "1 page folio."

1783, August 25 VIRGINIA

Mr. Pendleton's reply to Madisons objection to his plan of paying public creditors.[1] Consuls and Superintendents of Trade preferable to Foreign Ministers.[2]

[1] JM's "objection" to Pendleton's "plan" had probably been expressed in a missing letter to Pendleton on or about 12 August. The general nature of the plan is suggested in the summaries of Pendleton's letters of 14 July (*q.v.*) and 4 August 1783 (*q.v.*, and n. 3).

[2] Perhaps Pendleton believed that, following the ratification of the definitive peace treaty, the relationships between the United States and Europe should be almost exclusively commercial in nature. This position would also accord with his stress upon the virtues of an economical and simple government, unthreatened at its capital by the corruptive presence of a diplomatic corps (Pendleton to JM, 26 May; 16 June 1783, and n. 10).

From the Reverend James Madison

RC (LC: Madison Papers). Docketed by JM, "Madison Js Augst. 27. 1783." Cover missing.

WILLIAMSBURG AUG. 27h. 1783.

I have not written to you, my good Friend, for some Time past,[1] because I expected you would have been in Virga. soon after the last I recd. from you; but as I have not heard of your Arrival, suppose you to be still in Congress.[2] If so, I shall continue to tax you even without your Consent.

Is there the least Probability that Congress will fix upon this Place, as their Residence? I promised our Friend M'C to ask you this Question some Time past. When is it proposed finally to determine this Matter? What ever Motives may principally influence the Determination, I am sure pacific Considerations shd. operate as strongly in Favour of this, as any other whatever.[3] I am also interested in the Choice to be made, for then it is probable you wd. once more form a Part of our Society, which I shall always consider as adding materially to our Happiness.[4]

However gloriously the Contest may have been terminated for America, I fear a Patriot in Congress cannot at present be free from much Anxiety, & the deepest concern. Every one here has recd. the Insult offered to the Supremacy of their common Country with Indignation. How much is it to be lamented that such Conduct shd. cloud the bright Morning of our political Day, or rather that the different Legislatures shd. not by their Prudence, have prevented the Cause wh. produced it.[5] I fear we are politicians only in Theory—the practical Part will be more difficult. I have seen with much Pleasure the Pamphlet from Cong. in wh. you have born an active part.[6] It was well calculated to direct the Mind to important Objects, and if Ama. be just & wise, she will not fail to profit from it.

We are here invaded by our annual Enemy—Ague & Fever who never fails to make his Approach, at this Season. The Weather hot, but I believe it is seldom attended with the Effects I see mentioned in Phila. The Therm. I am sure has not been above 90. It was not more than 86, at the Time referred to in Phila.[7]

My Wife[8] wishes you all Happiness, and no one more sincerely than

J MADISON

When you write let me know if you see or hear of any capital Books from Europe of late Publication, or any thing in this way to the Northward.

[1] The Reverend James Madison apparently had last written to JM on 4 June 1783 (*q.v.*).

[2] Except for one transcription, all letters written by JM to the Reverend James Madison have probably been destroyed (JM to the Rev. James Madison, 2 Oct. 1783). In his letter to JM on 15 April 1783, the Reverend James Madison had remarked, "Your Stay at Congress must be nearly at an End" (*Papers of Madison*, VI, 464, and n. 6).

[3] "Friend M'C" was Dr. James McClurg. See JM to Randolph, 10 June 1783, and citations listed in n. 13. In JM's opinion, the possibility that Congress would establish its permanent residence at Williamsburg was "very slender" (*Papers of Madison*, VI, 448, nn. 4, 6, 7; Jones to JM, 28 June; Instructions to Delegates, 28 June, and nn. 2, 5–7; Harrison to Delegates, 4 July, and n. 5; 12 July, and n. 3; Pendleton to JM, 21 July, and n. 5; JM to Randolph, 28 July; 18 Aug. and nn. 3, 4; Delegates to Harrison, 14–15 Aug., and n. 7; 23 Aug. 1783, and n. 7).

[4] With the capital of Virginia at Williamsburg in 1776, when JM was a member of the Convention and, later in that year, of the General Assembly, and again in 1778–1779, when he was a member of the Council of State, he roomed most of the time in the home of his second cousin, the Reverend James Madison (*Papers of Madison*, I, 165–323, *passim*, and esp. 222–23; 224, n. 2; 311, n. 1; 316; 317, n. 11).

[5] The reference is to the mutiny of the Pennsylvania troops between 17 and 25 June, caused mainly by the inability of Congress, owing to the failure of the states to forward their financial quotas, to provide the soldiers with a portion of their long-overdue pay. After being insulted by the mutineers and refused adequate protection from them by the executive of the state, Congress had moved from Philadelphia to Princeton (JM Notes, 19 June, and nn. 6, 7; 20 June, and n. 1; 21 June 1783, and nn.).

[6] JM's "Address to the States," which was among the enclosures sent to the executive of each state along with the congressional plan for restoring public credit, also drafted by JM (*Papers of Madison*, VI, 471; 487–94). For a brief article praising the "Address," see *Pa. Packet*, 16 Aug. 1783.

[7] The Reverend James Madison may have seen the *Pennsylvania Packet* of 26 July and 5 August 1783. The earlier of these issues noted that "Within these few days past, several persons in and about the city have died by the excessive heat of the weather. Others have lost their lives by imprudently drinking cold water when they were very much heated."

[8] On 28 April 1779 the Reverend James Madison married Sarah Taite (d. 1815) of Williamsburg (*Va. Gazette* [Williamsburg, Dixon and Hunter], 1 May 1779; *Daily Compiler* [Richmond], 21 Aug. 1815).

Benjamin Harrison to Virginia Delegates

FC (Virginia State Library). Addressed to "The Honorable Virginia Delegates in Congress." In the hand of Samuel Patteson.

COUNCIL CHAMBER August 28th. 1783.

GENTLEMEN,

Many thanks to you for your kind concern for my health I was so extremely ill that the doctors advised my leaving the fogs of Richmond for some time as absolutely necessary for my recovery.[1] I have received much benifit from the trip short as it was but am not quite recovered and shall therefore set out for the shores of the bay to morrow and shall not return 'till the twelfth of next month, 'till which day you will not hear from me again.[2]

I have never heard of any instructions to you from the assembly relative to Finnie in particular: I sent you a general one which you laid before Congress, who referred it to the financier to which I have received his answer and that of the comptroller. the demand was so extensive that it could not be complyed with under a great length of time: they therefore wrote to me for an explanation of the wishes of the assembly which I obtained thro' the Speaker of the house of delegates and have transmitted it to them. by this it appears that an affair of Finnies which was referred to a committee had been the occasion of the instructions and I suppose is what you allude to.[3] if there should be any thing more I will direct the clerk to the assembly to forward it to you.[4]

No Commissioner has ever yet appeared in this State to settle our continental accounts the state they are in will appear by the inclosed answer of the Solicitor to me to which I refer you.[5]

I am &c.

B. H.

[1] Randolph to JM, 18 July, and n. 7; Delegates to Harrison, 14–15 Aug. 1783.

[2] Perhaps Harrison had gone on his brief "trip" to his estate of Berkeley on the James River in Charles City County. In September he spent almost two weeks in Gloucester on the shores of Chesapeake Bay (Harrison to Delegates, 13 Sept.; 10 Oct. 1783).

[3] Delegates to Harrison, 14–15 Aug. 1783, and citations in n. 2. The "financier" was Robert Morris; the "comptroller," James Milligan; and the "Speaker of the house of delegates," John Tyler (*Papers of Madison*, IV, 30, n. 2; VI, 410, n. 3).

[4] John Beckley was clerk of the House of Delegates of the Virginia General Assembly (*ibid.*, I, 318, n. 2).

[5] Delegates to Harrison, 14–15 Aug. 1783, and n. 3. Although a copy of the "inclosed answer" to Harrison from Solicitor General Leighton Wood has not been identified with certainty, it may have been Wood's letter of May (?) 1783, reporting, among other financial data, "the amount of expences incur'd by the state of Virginia for continental purposes." Harrison had submitted this letter to the Virginia General Assembly at its session of May 1783 (Executive Letter Book, 1783–1786, p. 122, MS in Va. State Library).

To James Madison, Sr.

RC (LC: Madison Papers). Cover missing. The docket, "Madison Js Aug. 30. 1783," is in JM's hand, but he apparently added it at a later date. This letter may have been carried to Virginia by Captain Merry Walker (*Papers of Madison*, III, 208, n. 5). See also JM to James Madison, Sr., 8 Sept. 1783.

PRINCETON Aug: 30. 1783

HOND SIR

I recd. great pleasure from your's recd. by the last post which removed the apprehensions excited by your preceding one regarding the state of my Mother's health.[1] I hope this will find her still further recovered. The time of my setting out for Virga. is still somewhat precarious; several matters being before Congs. which I wish to see first decided.[2] An answer to this if not delayed will probably find me here.[3]

The definitive Treaty is not yet come over.[4] Sr. G. Carlton has notified to Congs. his receipt of final orders for the evacuation of N. York, but fixes no time at which they are to be carried into execution.[5] Genl. Washington has been here some days at the invitation of Congs. & will be consulted on the provision necessary in time of peace for the security of this Country.[6] I inclose you one of the latest papers containing the address of the Presidt. to the Assembly of Pena.[7] The latter have unanimously acceded to the late recommendations of Congs. with respect to revenue, and a change of the rule for apportioning the common burdens.[8] It is said they are also about to address Congs. on the event which occasioned their removal, & to provide especially for the protection of Congs. in case they sd. deem Philada. the fittest place for the transaction of business untill a final residence shall be chosen. What effect this may have is uncertain.[9] We are exceedingly crowded in this place; too much so both for our own comfort & for the dispatch of business. Mr. Jones & my self are in one room scarcely ten feet square & in one bed.[10] With my best regards for all the family

I am yr. dutiful son

J. MADISON JR.

[1] No letter written to JM by his father prior to 1784 appears to exist. For references to his mother's health, see *Papers of Madison*, I, 48, n. 15; 113; 162, n. 11; 223; JM to James Madison, Sr., 27 May; to Jefferson, 17 July 1783, and n. 10.

[2] Among these "matters" were decisions about the permanent site for Congress, the offer of cession of Virginia's lands west and northwest of the Ohio River, and the peace "establishments" in domestic and foreign affairs. Probably JM wished also to delay his return home until after the arrival of the definitive treaty of peace with Great Britain.

[3] This suggests that JM expected to remain in Princeton or Philadelphia for at least another month. For his departure from Philadelphia and arrival at Montpelier, see Jefferson to JM, 7 May, n. 19; JM to James Madison, Sr., 5 June 1783, n. 7.

[4] Pendleton to JM, 4 May, n. 6; JM to Jefferson, 17 July 1783, n. 2.

[5] Delegates to Harrison, 23 Aug. 1783, and n. 2.

[6] *Ibid.*, and n. 8.

[7] Probably the *Pennsylvania Packet* of 26 August 1783, which includes the message of President John Dickinson and the Supreme Executive Council on 18 August to the Pennsylvania General Assembly. They strongly recommended the adoption of the congressional plan for restoring public credit and the presentation to Congress of such proposals "as will evince, that no state can be more sincerely disposed to consult the dignity of that honorable body, and the convenience of the union, than this commonwealth."

[8] JM should have written that a bill had been introduced for these purposes in the Pennsylvania General Assembly on 25 August. The Assembly did not enact the law until 23 September (*JCC*, XXIV, 526–27; JM to Jefferson, 11 Aug. 1783, n. 18).

[9] Although the resolutions adopted by the Pennsylvania General Assembly on 29 August, and submitted to Congress three days later, omitted mention of the mutiny, they assured "speedy and adequate support and protection to the honor and dignity" of Congress if it decided to return temporarily to Philadelphia, and "commodious and agreeable" accommodations if Congress should make clear "what jurisdiction" it required for establishing its "permanent residence" in that state (*JCC*, XXV, 530–31). On 6 October, in a tallied vote on a motion to return to Pennsylvania, only the delegates from that state were unanimously in the affirmative. Repeated efforts in Congress to decide upon a place of residence, other than Princeton, failed during the next two weeks (*JCC*, XXV, 651–52, 653–76, *passim*, 697–99, 706–14, *passim*).

[10] The "place" in which Joseph Jones and JM shared a room has not been identified.

To Edmund Randolph

RC (LC: Madison Papers). Unsigned, but in JM's hand. Cover franked by "J. Madison Jr" and addressed by him to "Edmund Randolph Esqr. Richmond." Docketed by Randolph, "J. Madison Aug: 30. 1783."

Princeton Aug. 30. 1783.

My dear Sir

We hear nothing from Europe that can be depended on relative to the definitive Treaty, nor any thing from N. York as to the time of its evacuation.[1] A Pamphlet has lately come over from G. Britain which appears to be well adapted to retard if not prevent a commercial Treaty, & which is said to be much attended to. It urges an adherence to the principle of the Navigation Act by which American Vessels will be excluded from the trade between the separate parts of the Empire, and from all intercourse with the dependent territories. It undertakes to shew from an enumeration of the produce of the U.S. & the manufactures consumed by them that those of G. B. recommended by the superior credit which her merchant[s] can give, will be sufficiently sure of a preference in the American Market. And lastly it maintains that the interests of the States are so opposite in matters of Commerce, & the authority of Congs. so feeble that no defensive precautions need be feared on the part of the U.S. and threatens that in case they should refuse to let British Vessels exclusively carry on a Commerce between the U.S. and the W. Indies as far as the interest of the Islands may require, the Vessels of one State shall not be permitted to carry the produce of another to any British Port.[2] The whole tenor of the reasoning supposes that France will not permit Vessels of the U.S. to trade with their Islands, in which there is *good reason* to believe they are not mistaken. The object of the French Administration is said to be to allow a direct trade between the U.S. & their W. India possessions, but to confine it to French Bottoms.[3]

The Legislature of Penna. have unanimously adopted the Recommendations of Congs. both as to Revenue & a change of the fœderal rule for apportioning the common burdens.[4] They will also present an invitation to Congs. we understand, to resume their Sessions at Philada. if that place be judged most fit for the despatch of public business untill a permanent seat be chosen & prepared; giving at the same time explicit assurances of support in case it should on any occasion be needed. What effect this conciliatory proposition may have on the temper of Congs. is precarious.[5] With some the complaisance shewn to the late recommendations of Congs. will be far from softening the dislike. With others Philada. will ever be obnoxious while it contains and respects an *obnoxious Character*.[6] Annapolis has siezed the present occasion to forward her views with respect to Congs. and has courted their presence in the most flattering terms.[7] During this contest among the rival seats, we are kept in the most awkward situation that can be imagined; and it is the more so as we every moment expect the Dutch Ambassador.[8] We are crowded too much either to be comfortable ourselves or to be able to carry on the business with advantage. Mr. Jones & myself on our arrival were extremely put to it to get any quarters at all, and are at length put into one bed in a room not more than 10 feet square.[9]

[1] JM to James Madison, Sr., 30 Aug. 1783, and citations in nn. 4 and 5.

[2] JM referred to John Baker Holroyd (1735–1821), Baron, 1st Earl (1816 ff.) of Sheffield and Viscount Pevensey, *Observations on the Commerce of the American States with Europe and the West Indies: including the Several Articles of Import*

and Export; and on the Tendency of a Bill now Depending in Parliament (75 pp.; London: J. Debrett, 1783). This may have been among the pamphlets received by Congress from overseas on 18 August (NA: PCC, No. 185, III, 75). Later editions, of which at least the sixth had been published before the close of 1784, were enlarged by adding extensive appendixes. Sheffield, a leading authority on agriculture and commerce, was a persuasive champion of mercantilism, alleging that to repeal the Navigation Acts, as advocated by the free-trade followers of Adam Smith, would be economically ruinous to Great Britain. Both by his pamphlet and his speeches as the member from Bristol in the House of Commons, Sheffield may have induced Lord Shelburne by the summer of 1783 to abandon his support, given earlier that year, of a commercial treaty which would have opened to American merchantmen many avenues of trade prohibited to them by the Navigation Acts (JM to Jefferson, 13 May, nn. 6, 7, 9; 10 June, nn. 5, 6, 8, 21; Rights of Neutral Nations, 12 June, n. 4; Delegates to Harrison, 14–15 Aug., and n. 9; JM to Randolph, 18 Aug. 1783). On 15 April 1783 in the House of Commons, Sheffield concluded a speech in regard to "opening the trade with America" by remarking that the framing of a treaty to that end would be "the most important subject for negociation the country had ever known. It was to decide whether we were to be ruined by the independence of America or not. The peace, in comparison, was a trifling object" (*Hansard's Parliamentary Debates*, XXIII, col. 764).

Although the *Pennsylvania Packet* in its issue of 4 September published excerpts from Sheffield's pamphlet, that newspaper in its issues of 28 and 30 August and 6 and 13 September copied from the *London Public Advertiser* of 16 June 1783 a free-trade essay entitled, "Upon the American Commerce and Commerce in General," signed "A By-Stander." In the *Pennsylvania Packet* of 28 August also appeared, under a London, 16 June 1783, date line, the statement, "The commercial treaty between this country and America is not likely to be ratified for some considerable time." A "considerable time," of course, would not be until 19 November 1794, when John Jay's Treaty of Amity, Commerce, and Navigation was signed in London; and finally, on 29 February 1796, proclaimed to be in force (Hunter Miller, ed., *Treaties and Other International Acts*, II, 245–74).

3 JM's information, although from a source unknown to the editors, appeared to be confirmed by John Adams' dispatches of 3, 11, and 18 July, received by Congress on 12 September 1783 (NA: PCC, No. 185, III, 79; Wharton, *Revol. Dipl. Corr.*, VI, 512, 540–41, 552; William E. O'Donnell, *Chevalier de La Luzerne*, pp. 238–40; Burnett, *Letters*, VII, 304–5, 353, 366–67, 389–90; Delegates to Harrison, 20 Sept. 1783). In the report of a committee, to which Congress referred these and other dispatches, is the statement: "although the Court of France hath not yet explicitly disclosed her intentions with respect to our future intercourse with her Colonies, there is too much reason to apprehend that she will restrain it to those articles of import and export which do not interfere with her own exports or consumption, and which are in fact of very inconsiderable value" (*JCC*, XXV, 587–88, 629).

4 For a correction of this statement, see JM to James Madison, Sr., 30 Aug. 1783, n. 8.

5 *Ibid.*, n. 9.

6 The "obnoxious Character" may not have been John Dickinson, whom Edmund C. Burnett believed him to be, but Robert Morris, whom influential members of Congress, including Theodorick Bland, Arthur Lee, Samuel Osgood, and Stephen Higginson, especially disliked (*Papers of Madison*, IV, 386; VI, 207; 304; 305, n. 4; 306, n. 6; 347, n. 4; 357; 409, n. 1; Burnett, *Letters*, VII, xl, 77, 156, and n. 2, 167, 252, n. 5, 272, 282, and first n. 3, 299–300).

[7] Jefferson to JM, 7 May, n. 19; Delegates to Harrison, 27 May, n. 2; 14–15 Aug., and n. 7; Pendleton to JM, 16 June; JM to Jefferson, 17 July, and n. 9; to Randolph, 18 Aug. 1783, and n. 23.

[8] JM to Jefferson, 10 June, and n. 23; to Randolph, 13 Oct. 1783.

[9] JM to James Madison, Sr., 30 Aug. 1783, and n. 10. Many years later JM or someone by his direction placed a bracket at the close of the paragraph to signify that the letter should be included in the first extensive edition of his writings. See Madison, *Papers* (Gilpin ed.), I, 566–68.

From Thomas Jefferson

RC (LC: Madison Papers). Addressed to "The Honble James Madison of the Virginia delegation in Congress." Docketed by JM, "August 31. 1783." Another hand wrote "Mr. Jefferson" below that date and, to the right of it, "Th. Jefferson Augst 31. 1783." Under this second dating, William Cabell Rives, the first major biographer of Madison, wrote, probably late in the 1850's, "our allusions in this letter to our affairs of the heart of Mr. Madison." See *Papers of Madison,* I, xxiii–xxiv; William C. Rives, *History of the Life and Times of James Madison,* I, 522–23.

MONTICELLO Aug. 31. 1783.

DEAR SIR

Your favour of July 17.[1] which came to hand long ago remains still unacknoleged, as from the time of it's receipt I had constant hope that you would be on the road for Virginia before an answer could reach you. that of the 11th. inst.[2] I received yesterday, and leaves the time of your visit as unfixed as ever, and excites some fear that I shall miss of you. I propose to set out for Congress about the middle of October, unless they should be returned to Philadelphia in which case I shall take at home the week I meant otherwise to pass at Philadelphia on my way to Congress.[3] I wish it had been possible for your journey to have been so timed as that your return could have been when I go: for I still Suppose you mean to pass the winter there as you told me at a time when it seemed to have no object but that of prosecuting your studies more at leisure.[4] I sincerely lament the misadventure which has happened, from whatever cause it may have happened.[5] should it be final however, the world still presents the same & many other resources of happiness, and you possess many within yourself. firmness of mind & unintermitting occupations will not long leave you in pain. no event has been more contrary to my expectations, and these were founded on what I thought a good knowlege of the ground,[6] but of all machines ours is the most complicated & inexplicable.—either here or in Philadelphia I must ask a perusal of your Congressional notes with leave to take notes from them, as they will better than any thing else possess me of the business I am to enter on.[7] what is become of the mutineers?[8] what of the Secretaryship of foreign affairs?[9] what of the commercial treaty with Gr. Britain?[10] these and many other questions I hope for the pleasure of having answered by you at Monticello. be so good as to present my compliments to mrs. House & mrs. Trist and to ask whether the pleasure of lodging in their house may be counted among the circumstances which will render Philadelphia agreeable to me in case of the return of Congress thither.[11] should Congress not return thither, would it be possible for you to engage me a tolerable birth wherever they are? a room to myself, if it be but a barrack, is indispensable.[12] in either event of my being or not being in Philadelphia I propose to place Patsy there; and will ask the favor of mrs. Trist to think for me on that subject, and to advise me as to the person with whom she may be trusted. some boarding school of course, tho' I am not without objections to her passing more than the day in such a one.[13]—the want of public occurrences worth detailing has filled my letter you find with private & unimportant subjects. I wish you every possible felicity and am with sincere esteem Dr. Sir

Your friend & servt.

TH: JEFFERSON[14]

1 *Q.v.*

2 *Q.v.* The *Virginia Gazette* of 30 August 1783 announced that among the letters remaining unclaimed in the Richmond post office were eighteen for Jefferson.

3 Jefferson to JM, 7 May 1783, and n. 19.

4 The "time" almost surely was between 26 February and 12 April 1783, when Jefferson and JM were together in Philadelphia (*Papers of Madison*, VI, 243, n. 5; 327, n. 6).

5 The breaking by Catherine Floyd of her engagement to marry JM (JM to Jefferson, 11 Aug. 1783, and nn. 3–5).

6 *Papers of Madison*, VI, 180; 182, n. 28; 459; 481.

7 *Ibid.*, V, 231–34; JM to Jefferson, 20 Sept. 1783.

8 JM Notes, 21 June, and n. 8; JM to Randolph, 30 June; to Jefferson, 17 July; 20 Sept.; Mercer to JM, 14 Aug. 1783, n. 8.

9 JM to Randolph, 17 June; Livingston to JM, 19 July 1783, nn. 3, 4.

10 Delegates to Harrison, 14–15 Aug., and n. 9; JM to Randolph, 30 Aug. 1783, and n. 2.

11 Mercer to JM, 14 Aug., and nn. 6, 7; JM to Jefferson, 30 Sept. 1783.

12 JM to Jefferson, 20 Sept.; 30 Sept. 1783.

13 "Patsy" was Jefferson's daughter Martha (JM to Jefferson, 30 Sept. 1783; Boyd, *Papers of Jefferson*, VI, 359–60).

14 JM did not receive this letter until 19 September (JM to Jefferson, 20 Sept. 1783).

From Edmund Pendleton

Summary (LC: Madison Miscellany). The summary is in a calendar, probably prepared about 1850 by Peter Force's clerk. He noted that the letter was addressed "To James Madison" and that the manuscript consisted of "1 page folio."

1783. September 1 VIRGINIA

Congress declines to return to Philadelphia.[1] The question of the protection of Congress and foreign ministers. Congress should control the territory where it sits.[2] But to make Congress the legislature for a people who are not concerned in their election is a violation of fundamental rights, and introduces despotism.[3]

[1] In his letter of 18 August to Randolph (*q.v.*), JM commented upon the decision of Congress on 14 August against "returning to Philada." Being accustomed to write to Pendleton and to Randolph on the same day, JM may have also informed Pendleton of this decision in a letter, now missing. If JM did so, Pendleton would naturally resume his discussion of a subject which had much interested him. See Pendleton to JM, 14 July; 21 July; 28 July; 11 Aug.; 18 Aug. 1783.

[2] JM to Pendleton, 28 July, and nn. 1, 3; JM to James Madison, Sr., 30 Aug., and n. 9; to Randolph, 30 Aug. For an indication of the nature of Pendleton's comments on "control," see JM to Pendleton, 8 Sept. 1783.

[3] Pendleton stated forthrightly a viewpoint earlier expressed more indirectly by the citizens of Williamsburg (Harrison to Delegates, 12 July, and n. 3; Motion *in re* Permanent Site, 22 Sept. 1783).

Virginia Delegates to Benjamin Harrison

RC (Virginia State Library). In the hand of John Francis Mercer, except for the signatures of Theodorick Bland, Jr., and Arthur Lee. Docketed, "Virginia Delegates Sept. 8th. 1783." For the absence of JM's signature, see Delegates to Harrison, 24 June 1783, ed. n.

PRINCETON Septr. 8th. 1783

SIR

This Post brought us no Letter from your Excellency,[1] & little has ocurred with us since our last communications, worthy your attention.

A recent letter recd. by the Secretary of War from Genl. Irvine, commanding at Fort Pitt informs that a body of abt 400 Men, from the Western Frontier of Virginia, had passed the Ohio, in order to establish a settlement on the Muskingum. The General apprehends, that an immediate Indian War, will be among the first of the many evil consequences that must result from such lawless measures.[2]

Intelligence received by a missionary, lately sent in order to communicate the substance of the Articles of pacification to the Indian nations, gives great weight to the surmises of General Irvine. This Person was well received by Brigr. Genl. McClene, the british officer commdg. at Detroit, (altho prevented from holding a council with the Indians,) Who communicated to him the purport of intelligence which he had recd. by an Indian runner from our Western Country, & which he had transmitted to General Haldimand. The substance of this was that the Virginians had passed the Ohio, & had committed many wanton & unprovoked acts of cruelty that had in some measure produced retaliation[3]

Baron Steuben is just arriv'd here from Canada whither he had been sent, in order to make arrangements with General Haldimand, for the reception of the Posts ceded on our north western Frontier. The purposes of his mission have been totally frustrated, as that Officer, (who met him at Sorrel) alledged he had recd: no orders from his Court except to cease hostilities. And that he considered the late pacification so far conditional untill a definitive Treaty that he did not think himself authorized to permit the Baron even to visit the Posts. which (it seems) cannot now (were orders recd. for that purpose) be evacuated untill the ensuing Season.[4]

The evacuation of New York advances rapidly notwithstanding, the number of those inhabitants whose fears have of late determined them, to accompany the Garrison Their apprehensions exaggerated by doubt on one hand by the policy of the enemy & on the other by the publications which have of late appeared in the American Papers, will probably terminate in the sudden establishment of a very rich & powerful neighbour to the United States & certainly a very inimical one.[5]

A Committee was appointed by the Legislature of Virginia at a former session, to state their claim to the Western territory. This business we believe now rests with Mr. Randolph & we wish to be informed of the progress which that Gentleman has made in it,[6]

We have the honor to be with great respect & esteem Yr. Excellency's Most obedient & very humble Servants

JOHN F MERCER
THEOK: BLAND JR.
A. LEE

[1] Harrison to Delegates, 28 Aug. 1783, and n. 2.

[2] In a letter of 17 August to Benjamin Lincoln, secretary at war, Brigadier General William Irvine, commander of the continental troops at Fort Pitt, stated:

"great numbers of Men have crossed the Ohio, and have made actual settlements in different places from the River Muskingham to Wabash, this will in all probability renew the Indian War." Upon receiving the letter on 3 September, Congress referred it to a committee of five delegates, including James Duane, chairman, and Arthur Lee (NA: PCC, No. 149, III, 179–80; *JCC*, XXIV, 534, n. 2).

From the confluence of the Muskingum and Ohio rivers in the southeast of the future state of Ohio to the confluence of the Wabash and Ohio rivers at the southwestern tip of the future state of Indiana is a great distance, especially when measured along the meanderings of the Ohio River. For this reason the four hundred Virginians, chiefly from Yohogania and Ohio counties, who were said to have built their cabins north of that stream, seem few in proportion to the expanse of territory within which they had settled. Probably there were many more than "four hundred" whites (*Cal. of Va. State Papers*, III, 529–30, 536; Executive Letter Book, 1783–1786, pp. 197, 217, MS in Va. State Library). The movement of squatters into the lower Muskingum River valley had quickened in 1782, immediately after the Delaware Indians were expelled from that area. This renewed incursion by the whites soon led the Delawares and other Indian tribes, abetted by the British at Detroit and in their posts along the Lake Erie fringe of the Ohio country, to attack the settlers. The conflict continued with varying intensity until the Treaty of Greenville in 1795 and the ratification of Jay's Treaty at about the same time (C[onsul] W[illshire] Butterfield, ed., *Washington-Irvine Correspondence. The Official Letters which Passed between Washington and Brig.-Gen. William Irvine* . . . [Madison, Wis., 1882], pp. 193–94, n. 3). See also Harrison to Delegates, 19 Sept.; 26 Sept.; Delegates to Harrison, 4 Oct. 1783.

3 On 1 May 1783 Congress ordered Benjamin Lincoln to "take the most effectual measures to inform the several Indian Nations, on the frontiers of the United States" that the war with Great Britain had ended; that the British-held forts within the United States "will speedily be evacuated"; and that Congress, although "disposed to enter into friendly treaty with the different tribes," would take the "most decided measures to compel them thereto," unless "they immediately cease all hostilities against the citizens of these states" (NA: PCC, No. 186, fols. 98, 99; *JCC*, XXIV, 319–20; *Pa. Archives*, 1st ser., X, 45, 46; *Papers of Madison*, VI, 432–33; 434, n. 10; 444, n. 2; Harrison to Delegates, 13 Sept. 1783, and n. 4). In fulfillment of this directive, Lincoln appointed Colonel John Bull (1730–1824) of Philadelphia County, Pa., who had been a prominent negotiator of treaties with the Indians in both the French and Indian War and the Revolution, to be the "missionary" to the Iroquois tribes in upper New York State (*Pa. Mag. Hist. and Biog.*, III [1879], 197, 422; XXIV [1900], 345–47; Fitzpatrick, *Writings of Washington*, IV, 347, and n., 350, 383). At about the same time, Lincoln named Ephraim Douglass (d. 1833), also a Pennsylvanian, who was soon to retire in the grade of major at the Fort Pitt garrison commanded by his friend General Irvine, to undertake a similar mission to the Indians in the Ohio country (Heitman, *Historical Register Continental*, p. 202).

As an aide-de-camp of General Lincoln in 1777, Douglass had been captured by the British and held a prisoner for over three years (*JCC*, V, 753; *Pa. Mag. Hist. and Biog.*, I [1877], 44–54; *Colonial Records of Pa.*, XVI, 447; Fitzpatrick, *Writings of Washington*, IX, 429, and n.). By December 1783, following his return from his mission, Douglass was appointed by President John Dickinson and the Supreme Executive Council of Pennsylvania to several administrative offices in the newly created Fayette County, and settled at Uniontown, the county seat. Thereafter until at least 1808 he held a succession of appointive or elective positions in that county and village (NA: PCC, No. 78, VIII, 35; No. 149, III, 187, 191; *JCC*, XXV, 536, n. 1, 699, n. 1; *Pa. Archives*, 1st ser., X, 118, 262, 553–56, 588, 696; *Colonial*

Records of Pa., XIII, 705; XVI, 447; Franklin Ellis, ed., *History of Fayette County, Pennsylvania, with Biographical Sketches of Many of its Pioneers and Prominent Men* [Philadelphia, 1882], pp. 130–33, 135, 150, 151, 153, 155, 302).

Although Mercer's allusion to Irvine and Detroit referred to the reports of Bull and an associate received by Congress on 6 and 12 August, respectively, his reference to Brigadier General Allen Maclean (1725–1784) as "the british officer commdg. at Detroit" shows that he had confused the reports of the mission there with the similar report by Douglass, received by Congress on 19 August. Lieutenant Colonel Arent Schuyler DePeyster (1736–1822) was the British commandant at Detroit (*Collections of the Illinois State Historical Library*, I [1903], 552). Maclean commanded at Niagara. At the time of Mercer's letter, the committee, with Duane as chairman, to which these narratives and accompanying documents were referred, had not yet reported.

DePeyster and Maclean had prevented Bull and Douglass from carrying out their orders to address the Indian tribes in person, but the envoys had been impressed by their courteous reception at the garrisons and by the apparent determination of commanding officers to restrain the tribes from attacking the settlers. The Indians were largely dependent for their economic well-being upon the British and comprised an important part of the garrison at Niagara. Lieutenant General Frederick Haldimand, commander-in-chief of the British forces in Canada and the Old Northwest, had not ordered the evacuation of the posts south of the Great Lakes and evidently did not plan to do so in the near future (NA: PCC, No. 149, III, 61–69, 109–10, 135–74, 187–94; No. 185, III, 73, 74, 76; No. 186, fols. 112, 118, 119, 120; *JCC*, XXIV, 517, n. 1; *Pa. Archives*, 1st ser., X, 62–64, 70–71, 80–90; *Pa. Packet*, 11 Sept. 1783; Worthington C. Ford, *British Officers Serving in the American Revolution*, pp. 59, 86, 120).

4 On 2 September Congress received and referred to a committee, including Ralph Izard, chairman, Duane, and Arthur Lee, a letter of 30 August from Washington, enclosing the report by General Steuben on his conference with Haldimand at Sorel, Canada, between 8 and 12 August. Acting under the authority of Congress, conferred by a resolution on 12 May, Washington had directed Steuben to survey the British posts within the United States after arranging with Haldimand for their early evacuation. Steuben's report, accompanied by Haldimand's written statement, reconfirmed what Bull and Douglass had learned at Detroit and Niagara. Lacking orders from King George III, Haldimand chose to regard the preliminary articles of peace as merely warranting a cessation of hostilities rather than as an equivalent of a definitive treaty of peace. For this reason he refused to "evacuate an inch of ground," or to allow Steuben to negotiate with the Indians or to visit the British garrisons south of the Canadian border (NA: PCC, No. 152, XI, 449–75; No. 185, III, 77; *JCC*, XXIV, 337–39; XXV, 532, n. 1; Fitzpatrick, *Writings of Washington*, XXVII, 39–40, 48, and n. 83, 61–65, 118, 120–24). See also Harrison to Delegates, 13 Sept., and n. 3; 26 Sept. 1783.

5 Delegates to Harrison, 23 Aug., and n. 2; JM to James Madison, Sr., 30 Aug. General Sir Guy Carleton had promised bounty lands in Nova Scotia to Loyalists who served in the British armed forces. The *Pennsylvania Packet* of 4 and 6 September announced that between 12,000 and 15,000 Loyalists would embark in the New York City area for Nova Scotia, New Brunswick, or the Great and Little Abaco Islands in the Bahama archipelago. See also *Pa. Packet*, 21, 23, 26 Aug., 9 Sept. 1783. Many of the émigrés were persons of considerable wealth and social prominence (Thomas Jefferson Wertenbaker, *Father Knickerbocker Rebels: New York City during the Revolution* [New York, 1948], pp. 248–66).

6 *Papers of Madison*, IV, 91, n. 4; 198, n. 7; 305; 306, n. 3; V, 308–9; 312, n. 18; VI, 245, n. 5; Harrison to Delegates, 27 Sept. 1783.

To James Madison, Sr.

RC (LC: Madison Papers). Docketed by James Madison, Sr., "Sep 8 1783." Cover missing.

PHILADA. Sepr. 8. 1783.

HOND SIR

Mr. Jones & myself being here transacting some private business which brought us from Princeton the end of last week, I here receive[d] your letter of the 22d. ulto.[1] The favorable turn of my Mothers state of health is a source of great satisfaction to me, and will render any delay in my sitting out for Virga. the less irksome to me.[2] I shall return to Princeton tomorrow; my final leaving of which will depend on events, but can not now be at any very great distance.[3] On a view of all circumstances I have judged it most prudent not to force Billey back to Va. even if could be done; and have accordingly taken measures for his final separation from me.[4] I am persuaded his mind is too thoroughly tainted to be a fit companion for fellow slaves in Virga. The laws here do not admit of his being sold for more than 7 years.[5] I do not expect to get near the worth of him; but cannot think of punishing him by transportation merely for coveting that liberty for which we have paid the price of so much blood, and have proclaimed so often to be the right, & worthy the pursuit, of every human being.[6]

We have no later advices from Europe than when I wrote by Merry Walker.[7]

[1] James Madison, Sr.'s letter of 22 August 1783 to JM has not been found. Cashing bills of exchange from Jacquelin Ambler was at least part of the "business" (Jones to JM, 4 Aug.; JM to Randolph, 8 Sept. 1783).

[2] For his "Mothers state of health," see JM to James Madison, Sr., 30 Aug. 1783, and citations in n. 1.

[3] Jefferson to JM, 7 May, n. 19. If JM left Philadelphia on 9 September, he probably reached Princeton the next day. He did not vote in tallied polls taken in Congress on 10 and 11 September. Although no session on 12 September is recorded in the journal, Congress convened and JM probably attended, for he was appointed to a committee on that day (NA: PCC, No. 186, fol. 123). There is no doubt that he shared in the deliberations of 13 September (*JCC*, XXV, 542–45, 552–53, 559).

[4] In 1759 Billey (b. 1759) had been deeded to James Madison, Sr., in trust for JM, then a minor, by JM's grandmother, Rebecca Catlett Conway Moore, in her will (*Va. Mag. Hist. and Biog.*, LII [1944], 66–67; *Papers of Madison*, IV, 396; 398, n. 19).

What "measures" JM had taken have not been discovered. It would appear that under the provisions of the Pennsylvania Emancipation Act of 1780, prudence might have dictated his "registering" Billey and, by establishing the slave's identity, have safeguarded him against possible false charges of being an "absconding or runaway negroe" returnable to a professed master in a state from which he had allegedly fled (*Pa. Packet*, 29 Dec. 1779). Presumably such registration would have been entered with the clerk of the Court of Record of the City of Philadelphia; but the present city archivist of Philadelphia states that no such records are in his custody (letter from Whitfield J. Bell, Jr., 17 Dec. 1969). At the same time, an "extended search" undertaken by the curator of the Historical Society of Pennsylvania of pertinent collections in that institution has been no more rewarding (letter from John D. Kilbourne, 26 Jan. 1970). From these facts it is at least inferable that JM took one of two "measures." He may have covered Billey's identity in a bill of sale made out to a Pennsylvanian, probably a Philadelphian, for the six months that the slave's services would have been legally available if Billey remained in the state, and left the burden of registration to the unknown purchaser. Second, he may have "covenanted" Billey to "personal servitude or apprenticeship" for the legal limit of seven years. In his will, dated 17 September 1787, James Madison, Sr., stated that after he transferred to JM a "good right and title" to Billey, JM "has since sold" the slave (Orange County Court Records, MS in Va. State Library). The word "sold" obviously does not bar the possibility that JM received money for relinquishing his title to Billey by consigning him to a master who kept him as an indentured servant for seven years. In a letter of 6 September 1788, written from New York City to his father, JM made clear, without specifying the place, that he knew where Billey then was (LC: Madison Papers).

[5] *Papers of Madison*, V, 28, n. 5; 97.

[6] *Ibid*., II, 209; 210, n. 1.

[7] JM to James Madison, Sr., 30 Aug. 1783, hdn.

To Edmund Pendleton

RC (Manuscript Division, the New York Public Library: Astor, Lenox, and Tilden Foundations). Docketed by Pendleton, "James Madison jr. Sepr. 8. 1783."

PHILADA. Sepr. 8. 1783.

DEAR SIR

Your favor of the 1st. found me here whither Mr. Jones & myself had been called by some private business for a day or two. I thank you for your remarks on the jurisdiction necessary for Congress within the limits which may be ceded for their permanent residence. They seem to comprise all the alternatives among which a choice is to be made.[1]

We have recd. no advices from Europe since my last.[2] The light in which Sr. G. Carlton places his delay in evacuating N.Y. will be seen in the inclosed paper.[3] He has made report to Congs. of the result of inquiry into the forgery of Morris' Notes, which did not capitally convict any of the authors of the villany but brought forth all the implements made use of not only for that purpose, but for the various forgeries which have issued from N.Y. in the course of the war, and fully verify the charges on that head. These implements were sent to Congress with the Trial. The accused pleaded the countenance of authority for former experiments in this way, and wonder'd at the change of system which had dictated prosecutions for the present. You will wonder I dare say at the facility with which Sr. G. C. has exposed the dishonorable but no doubt secret measures of his predecessors. His military powers might easily have stifled the enquiry & discoveries if he had chosen to do so.[4]

The Legislature of this State have in addition to the other steps rehearsed in the inclosed, made German Town a Candidate for the permanent abode of Congress.[5] The Eastern States are in great perturbation on the subject of the half pay. The violent opposition of the people to that Constitutional demand is considered by those who have been witnesses of it, as of so serious a nature as to threaten very inauspicious effects.[6]

With sincere regd. I am Dr. Sir Yr. friend & servt.

J. MADISON JR.

[1] JM to Randolph, 28 July; Pendleton to JM, 1 Sept. 1783, and nn. 2, 3. The committee on "the jurisdiction necessary" had been appointed by Congress on 18 July and enlarged on 23 July and 3 September (JM to Pendleton, 28 July, and nn. 1–3). The committee's report, drafted by James Duane, was submitted to Congress on 5 September, read thirteen days later, and first discussed on 22 September (NA: PCC, No. 186, fols. 112, 121; Motion *in re* Permanent Site, 22 Sept. 1783).

[2] JM's comment on this subject in his missing letter to Pendleton, on or about 30 August, probably resembled that in his letter of 30 August to Randolph (*q.v.*).

[3] In view of this subject together with the one mentioned at the outset of the letter's third paragraph, JM probably enclosed either the *Pennsylvania Packet* of 2 and 4 September or the *Pennsylvania Journal* of 3 and 6 September. See also Delegates to Harrison, 8 Sept. 1783, and n. 5.

[4] Delegates to Harrison, 26 July, and n. 7; JM to Randolph, 28 July; Harrison to Delegates, 15 Aug. 1783, and n. 3; Burnett, *Letters*, VII, 250.

[5] JM to James Madison, Sr., 30 Aug., and n. 9; to Randolph, 30 Aug. 1783, and n. 6. Congress on 26 July had received from a property owner in Germantown, Pa., an offer of land for its use (*JCC*, XXIV, 451, n. 1, 537). There was read in Congress on 11 September an invitation, dated 4 September, and signed by about 420 residents of Germantown, to choose for the "grand Council of the Nation" the ample accommodations of that town, with their attendant advantages of a "beautiful situation, Salubrious Air, excellent Water, plentiful Market, extensive Pastures, fertile Soil and Contiguity to one of the most flourishing commercial Cities in the Union." The invitation omitted reference to the troublesome issue of

jurisdiction (NA: PCC, No. 46, fols. 117–21; *JCC*, XXV, 553, n. 1). See also Pendleton to JM, 6 Oct. 1783.

6 Pendleton to JM, 4 Aug., and n. 2; JM to Jefferson, 11 Aug., and n. 19; to Randolph, 12 Aug.; 18 Aug. 1783; Burnett, *Letters*, VII, 288, 296, 316–17. JM referred particularly to the protest of 13 July of the Massachusetts General Court. Congress, having received this document on 31 July, referred it to a committee which reported on 2 September. A new committee on the issue reported six days later. Thereupon Congress revived the report of 2 September and referred it on 18 September to a committee comprising JM, chairman, Mercer, and Duane (*JCC*, XXIV, 483, n. 2; XXV, 578–80, 581–85, 584, n. 1). See also Memorial of Massachusetts General Court, 19 Sept. 1783.

To Edmund Randolph

RC (LC: Madison Papers). In JM's hand but lacks complimentary close and signature. Cover franked by "J. Madison Jr," and addressed to "Edmund Randolph Esqr. Richmond." Docketed by Randolph, "J. Madison Sep. 8. 1783."

PHILADA. Sepr. 8. 1783.

MY DEAR SIR

Mr. Jones & myself having come down to this City the end of the past week for the purpose of negociating some pecuniary matters, I am here to date my acknowledgment of your favor of the 30th. ulto.[1] We return again tomorrow.[2]

The delay of the definitive Treaty altho not fully explained to Congress, excites less disquietude here than I find it does in Virginia.[3] Our latest official advices were from Mr. Laurens of the day of June. The Conduct of the British administration was far from explicit, according to his State of it, but probably proceeded more from the discordant materials of which it is composed & doubts as to the commercial footing on which America ought to be placed, than from any insidious views.[4] Why indeed a Commercial Treaty should be made to clog the Treaty of peace is left to conjecture. Perhaps the fact may not be true & the delay of the latter may be owing still to the old cause, to wit, a discussion of the intricate points with the Dutch.[5] The situation of G.B. is such that nothing but some signal change in the aspect of things in this hemisphere can inspire a fresh disposition for war; notwithstandg the menacing tone of Sr. G. Carlton[6]

The Legislature of Pa. have taken every possible step to expiate the default of the Executive short of an impeachment of its members, which the rigor of some members of Congs. included among the terms of reconciliation with the State. They have expressly invited Congs: back, assured them of honorable protection, and given up the State-House with the appendages for their temporary use. They have also made German Town a competitor for the permanent abode of Congress.[7]

The opposition in the N. England States to the Grant of half pay instead of subsiding has increased to such a degree as to produce almost a general anarchy. In what shape it will issue is altogether uncertain. Those who are interested in the event look forward with very poignant apprehensions. Nothing but some continental provision can obtain for them this part of their reward.[8]

The lady whose husband makes a subject of one of your paragraphs has lately recd. letters from him which breathe a warm affection for her, state the impracticability of his coming for her, or leaving that Country altogether at present, and press her to lose no time in getting to him, which she means to attempt in the course of next month. Some traits in his character which were related to you, have come to my knowledge through other channels, particularly his attachment to pelf; But in other respects he has been represented as a man of honesty & worth. His Medical profession is not entirely usurped, being founded on a partial education in that line. My friendship for her estimable qualities makes me regret upon the whole that her prospect of happiness is not more flattering. The removal of Congress has been of some disadvantage to the old Lady, but the established reputation of her House will always command the means of support.[9] She has lately too had the good fortune to have with her one of her sons whom she had not heard of for 4 or 5 years. He has engaged to accompany his sister in her voyage to her husband.[10]

Why did not the Assembly stop the sale of land warrants? They bring no profit to the public Treasury, are a source of constant speculation on the ignorant, and and will finally arm numbers of Citizens of other States & even foreigners with claims & clamors against the faith of Virginia. Immense quantities have from time to time been vended in this place at immense profit, and in no small proportion to the subjects of our Ally. The credulity here being exhausted I am told the land Jobbers are going on with their commodity to Boston & other places to[o?][11]

[1] Not found.

[2] JM to James Madison, Sr., 8 Sept. 1783, and nn. 1, 3.

[3] This statement may reflect JM's reading of Harrison to Delegates, 9 August, and of the issues of the *Virginia Gazette* for 2, 16, and 30 August. See also JM to Randolph, 13 Sept. 1783, and nn. 2, 3.

[4] For Henry Laurens' dispatch of 17 and 18 June, insofar as it concerned a treaty of commerce and a definitive treaty of peace with Great Britain, see Delegates to Harrison, 14–15 Aug., and n. 9; Mercer to JM, 14 Aug.; JM to Randolph, 18 Aug.; 30 Aug. 1783, and n. 2. Congress on 1 September took no action on the report offered by a committee to which Laurens' dispatch had been referred on 15 August. On 12 September, however, the report was consigned to a newly appointed committee, James Duane, chairman, instructed "to consider the dispatches from the ministers of the United States at Foreign Courts." Thirteen days later Congress agreed to the Duane committee's proposal that it was "highly necessary that the Report already made on Mr. Laurens' letters should be taken into consideration and proper instructions dispatched to our ministers to enable them to pursue the very important objects recommended in that report"—that is, the report on 1 September. The "objects" were to commission Adams, Franklin, Jay, and Laurens "or any two of them to negotiate a treaty of amity and commerce" with Great Britain "upon terms of the most perfect reciprocity" (NA: PCC, No. 186, fol. 123; *JCC*, XXV, 531–32, 532, n. 1, 587–88, 588, n. 1, 620, and n. 1). See also *JCC*, XXV, 821, 824–25; JM to Randolph, 13 Sept. 1783, and n. 1.

Commenting upon the Portland-Fox-North ministry, which had taken office on 1 April about five weeks after the resignation of the ministry of the Earl of Shelburne, Laurens wrote: "I have just received an intimation of the tottering state of the present ministry, from their own quarter. Should the late premier recover the reins, which were plucked out of his hands, I apprehend everything in his power will be attempted to embarrass our proceeding" (Wharton, *Revol. Dipl. Corr.*, VI, 493). See also Jones to JM, 8 June, and n. 22; JM to Jefferson, 10 June 1783, and n. 4.

[5] Rights of Neutral Nations, 12 June, nn. 3, 4; JM to Jefferson, 11 Aug., and n. 8; JM to Randolph, 30 Aug. 1783, and n. 2.

[6] Delegates to Harrison, 23 Aug., and n. 2; JM to Randolph, 24 Aug.; JM to Pendleton, 8 Sept. 1783

[7] JM to James Madison, Sr., 30 Aug., and n. 9; JM to Pendleton, 8 Sept. 1783, and n. 5. Among the members of Congress who apparently favored the impeachment of President John Dickinson and the Supreme Executive Council was Oliver Ellsworth. In a letter of 7 August, he expressed the belief that the Pennsylvania General Assembly should "explicitly condemn" their "highly culpable" conduct during the mutiny (Burnett, *Letters*, VII, 253–54). See also *ibid.*, VII, 275.

[8] By "them" in the last sentence of this paragraph, JM referred to the officers of the continental army from New England, and probably above all from Massachusetts (*ibid.*, VII, 288, 296; JM to Pendleton, 8 Sept. 1783, and n. 6). Many years later JM or someone by his direction placed a bracket at the close of the paragraph to signify that the first four paragraphs of the letter should be included in the earliest extensive edition of his writings, but Henry D. Gilpin, either by oversight or choice, published the second, third, fourth, and sixth paragraphs (Madison, *Papers* [Gilpin ed.], I, 569–70).

[9] The "old Lady" was Mrs. Mary House (*Papers of Madison*, II, 92, n. 8; 123, n. 7; Mercer to JM, 14 Aug., and n. 7; Jefferson to JM, 31 Aug. 1783).

[10] JM referred to Samuel House, a trader in the western counties of Virginia who later became a shopkeeper in Philadelphia. Although it is not certain where House had been "for 4 or 5 years," he may have been a ranger on the Pennsylvania

frontier (*Pa. Archives*, 3d ser., XXXIII, 245, 247, 351; Brant, *Madison*, II, 16; Boyd, *Papers of Jefferson*, VI, 373; VIII, 169). If House accompanied his sister, Mrs. Nicholas Trist, in December 1783 when she began her journey to New Orleans, he went with her no farther than Fort Pitt (*ibid.*, VII, 393).

11 After "ignorant," JM inadvertently repeated the word "and."

On 23 and 25 June 1779 the House of Delegates and the Senate, respectively, of the Virginia General Assembly passed legislation "for adjusting and settling the titles of claimers to unpatented lands under the present and former government" and for opening a land office (*JHDV*, May 1779, pp. 63, 66; Hening, *Statutes*, X, 35–65). That office was empowered to issue assignable warrants for land to many varieties of past and future "claimers," including veterans of the French and Indian War and the Revolutionary War, shareholders in the Loyal Company of colonial origin, settlers along the "Western waters" prior to 1763, owners of "headrights" for transporting at their own expense indentured servants from Europe before the Revolution, squatters who had gained or should gain pre-emption rights by living on and improving public land unencumbered by earlier private titles, and persons not in any of these categories who wished to purchase land and could demonstrate that, no matter whether American or foreign-born, they were friendly to the patriot cause in the war. To make these two laws widely known, the Virginia General Assembly provided that printed copies of both should be distributed throughout all the counties of the state, and that one hundred copies of the land-office law should also be sent to the Virginia delegates in Congress, accompanied by a request from Governor Thomas Jefferson that they "take the most speedy and effectual measures for dispersing and publishing the same in the different States" (*JHDV*, May 1779, pp. 63, 68, 69).

From 23 October 1779, when Jefferson signed the first warrant, until the time of the present letter the Virginia land office issued warrants or patents for many thousands of acres in spite of early protests both from Congress and Washington. The boundaries of these grants often overlapped not only in an area, such as Kentucky, undoubtedly owned by Virginia, but, much more seriously for promoting discord among the states, in acreage claimed by Maryland or Pennsylvania or by land speculators resident therein (*JCC*, XV, 1223–24, 1226–30; McIlwaine, *Official Letters*, II, 4, n. 1; Boyd, *Papers of Jefferson*, III, 147, 206–8, 262, 266–67; VI, 640; *Papers of Madison*, I, 189, n. 2; II, 74–76; 100–101; V, 119, n. 20; 286, n. 16; VI, 472, n. 3; Jones to JM, 25 May, n. 12; JM Notes, 20 June 1783, n. 10; Thomas P. Abernethy, *Western Lands and the American Revolution*, pp. 224–25, 228–29).

By 1780 the patents, and especially the warrants issued by the Virginia land office, had become a "source of constant speculation," often by purchasers fated to discover that the validity of their titles could be contested by other claimants to the same acreage. With the close of the war greatly accelerating the westward movement of settlers and the issuance of transferable military-bounty land warrants to needy Virginia veterans, who often had little choice but to sell them for a pittance, the pace and amount of speculation, centering chiefly at Philadelphia, rapidly increased (*ibid.*, pp. 250, 263–64, 368–69; *Papers of Madison*, I, 298, n. 2; II, 65, n. 1; III, 275, n. 8; 349, n. 9). For advertisements by Virginia and Pennsylvania dealers offering Virginia "treasury Land Warrants" and military-bounty land warrants, located in Kentucky, the "Ohio Country," or "any county in the state of Virginia," see *Pennsylvania Packet*, 3, 7, 14, 19, 21, 23, 30 Aug., 2 and 6 Sept. 1783. Most of these same issues also contained notices by the Illinois Land Company and the Wabash Land Company, which, mainly on the basis of titles derived from Indian tribes, claimed large acreages north of the Ohio River in territory within the charter-based boundaries of Virginia.

From Elnathan Haskell

RC (LC: Madison Papers). Salutation, "The Honbl Mr. Madison." Cover addressed to "The Honorable Mr. Madison Princeton. Honored by Major Sergant." Docketed by JM, "Institution of the Cincinnati from E. Haskill Sepr. 12. 1783." "Sergant" was probably Major Winthrop Sargent (1753–1820). Between 1787 and 1801 he was successively the surveyor, secretary, and governor of the Northwest Territory. Enclosed with the letter are twelve folios docketed, "Institution of *the Cincinnati*." Below this, JM added, "inclosed by Majr. Haskell in his letter of Sepr. 12. 1783." The designation of Haskell as "Majr." suggests that JM wrote this portion of the docket on or after 30 September 1783 (n. 3, below).

DEAR SIR — PHILADELPHIA 12th Septr 83.

I procured from a friend of mine a sight of the Institution of the Cincinnati and from it have made a copy which I beg you to accept.[1]

Major Jackson[2] acquainted me yesterday that at the moment of his leaving Princeton a member of Congress had mentioned to him that my affair was referred to the war office, but that it had not reached it. Whether it is at this or any other Stage I shall be obliged by your attention to it.[3]

I am Dear Sir Your most obdt Sert

E. HASKELL

[1] The "copy" is in Captain Haskell's hand. The unidentified "friend" was probably an officer with the main army at West Point, who perhaps had come to Philadelphia for the express purpose of informing officers in General Robert Howe's command of the formation of the Society of the Cincinnati. Elnathan Haskell (1755–1825), aide-de-camp to General Howe, had risen from sergeant to captain in the Massachusetts line. At the time of his removal to South Carolina in 1789, Washington characterized him as "a worthy man" (Bradford Adams Whittemore, *Memorials of the Massachusetts Society of the Cincinnati* [Boston, 1964], p. 239; Fitzpatrick, *Writings of Washington*, XXX, 173; JM Notes, 21 June, and n. 4; JM to Randolph, 30 June, n. 6; 8 July; Delegates to Harrison, 5 July 1783, and n. 3).

The enclosure, which is headed "Cantonment of the American Army on Hudsons River 10th May 1783," includes: (1) note of a meeting on that day, presided over by "Major General Baron De Steuben" and attended by other "General Officers" and representatives of "the several regiments of the respective lines." This meeting, after discussing "Proposals for establishing a Society" to be composed of "officers of the American Army," referred them for revision to a committee of four, Major General Henry Knox, chairman; (2) note of a similar meeting three days later at which the committee's report, in the form of an "Institution" for the society, was adopted; (3) the "Institution" of "the Society of the Cincinnati," embracing paragraphs successively setting forth the cause for forming an hereditary organization; its name and the reason for choosing it; the "immutable" guiding "principles" to shape policies; the federative organization and the means of maintaining close liaison among the state branches; the officers, their tenure and how chosen; the procurement and use of funds "for the relief of the unfortunate members, or their widows and orphans"; rules of eligibility for membership, including a limited number of distinguished American civilians, as well as French military officers and a few French diplomats closely associated with the Revolution; the society's colors and "medal," with a description of its obverse and reverse, including the mottoes, *Omnia relinquit servere Rempublicam* ("He abandons everything in order to serve the republic"), *Virtutio Premium* ("First in valor"), *Esto perpetua* ("May it endure forever"); and a resolution prescribing the pledge to which "the officers of the respective State Lines," who desired to become members, must agree when they signed their names below the copy of the "Institution" to be provided the "Senior officer of each State Line." The "Institution" has been printed often—e.g., Edgar Erskine Hume, *Sesquicentennial History and Roster of the Society of the Cincinnati in the State of Virginia, 1783–1933* (Richmond, 1934), pp. 26–41.

[2] Major William Jackson, assistant secretary at war (*Papers of Madison*, IV, 37, n. 1).

[3] In Philadelphia on 1 September, Haskell wrote to Theodorick Bland: "When I had the pleasure of seeing you last, you may remember I mentioned my intention of soliciting Congress for the rank of major, and the principles on which I should make the request. Since that I have had an opportunity of explaining myself more fully to Mr. Madison, who does me the honor of handing to the President [Elias Boudinot] my petition, and who will, I believe, bring forward the question" (MS in Bland Papers, Va. Historical Society). Although unmentioned in the journal, this may have been done by JM between 25 and 30 August, when he was attending Congress in Princeton (*JCC*, XXIV, 521, n. 1, 525; JM to Randolph, 30 Aug. 1783).

General Howe supported Haskell's plea by writing on 4 September to General Benjamin Lincoln, secretary at war. Since Lincoln was "at the northward" inspecting military posts, Congress the next day referred Howe's letter to Jackson for report (NA: PCC, No. 149, III, 119–21; No. 185, III, 77; No. 186, fol. 122). On 22 September Jackson proposed that Haskell be promoted to the brevet rank of major in recognition of his several "extra-confidential" staff missions, "which it appears that he has discharged with honor to himself and benefit to the service." On 30 September 1783, five days after listening to Jackson's report, Congress adopted his recommendation (NA: PCC, No. 149, 199–202; *JCC*, XXV, 541, 634, and n. 1). Although JM was in Congress on 25 September and may have spoken on that day in favor of Haskell's petition, he did not attend on 5 and 30 September (*JCC*, XXV, 537, 613, 635).

Virginia Delegates to Benjamin Harrison

Letter not found.

EDITORIAL NOTE

13 September 1783. In a letter of 26 September to the Virginia delegates in Congress (*q.v.*), Governor Harrison acknowledged receipt of their letter dated thirteen days earlier. This letter, now missing, was written by Joseph Jones on behalf of the Virginia delegation and forwarded by Harrison on 20 October to John Tyler for submission by him to the Virginia General Assembly (Delegates to Harrison, 20 Sept., and n. 1; Executive Letter Book, 1783–1786, p. 219, MS in Va. State Library; *JHDV*, Oct. 1783, p. 7). In his letter to Tyler, Harrison stated that the delegates' communication "encloses the terms on which Congress will accept the cession of our back country and gives some insight into the policy of Great Britain in laying restrictions on our trade." For the terms of cession, see JM to Jefferson, 20 Sept., and n. 3. For Great Britain's trade policy, see JM to Randolph, 8 Sept., and n. 4; 13 Sept., and nn. 3, 5, 6; to Jefferson, 20 Sept., and nn. 13, 14; Harrison to Delegates, 3 Oct.; 18 Oct., and n. 2; Delegates to Harrison, 4 Oct. 1783, and n. 10.

Benjamin Harrison to Virginia Delegates

FC (Virginia State Library). In the hand of Samuel Patteson. Addressed to "The Honorable Virginia Delegates in Congress."

COUNCIL CHAMBER September 13th. 1783.

GENTLEMEN,

I arrived here yesterday after a very pleasant trip of a fortnight which has perfectly restored my health.[1] It gives me pleasure to find by your favor that positive orders are given to General Carelton to remove from New York, the sooner he goes the better, as I never can think an unrestrained intercourse ought to take place till he is gone.[2] I shall take proper steps to recover our records &c. if they are not destroyed which I think is the case as the whole conduct of the enemy whilst in this State was a series of wanton cruelty.[3] We have had no late arrivals nor is there a word of domestic news except that I have received intelligence which I can depend on that the indians tho' much inclined to peace will continue the war at every hazard if the Pensylvanians carry on their settlements beyond the ohio. if my advice had been followed, to Keep them within their real chartered bounds they would not have had it in their power thus to disturb the quiet of their neighbors.[4]

I am &.

B.H.

[1] Harrison to Delegates, 28 Aug. 1783, and n. 2.

[2] Delegates to Harrison, 23 Aug. 1783, and n. 2. Harrison undoubtedly believed that "unrestrained intercourse" with the enemy contained elements of danger. As late as 20 October 1783 he advised the Virginia General Assembly that the British were still powerful in New York City and, with an unfavorable turn of events in Europe, might constitute a renewed military menace (Executive Letter Book, 1783–1786, p. 214, MS in Va. State Library).

[3] Delegates to Harrison, 23 Aug. 1783, and n. 4. Although the destruction of public records rather than their sequestration had characterized the British invasions of the state between 1779 and 1781, one of Governor Jefferson's letter books

found its way to London (*Papers of Madison*, I, 284, n. 4; II, 288, n. 3; III, 59, n. 4; 183, n. 27; 272, n. 4; IV, 378, and n. 6; V, 284, n. 9; 350, n. 19; 459; *Catalogue of Additions to the Manuscripts in the British Museum in the Years MDCCCCXI–MDCCCCXV* [London, 1925], p. 176).

4 General William Irvine had charged Virginians rather than "Pensylvanians" with aggravating Indians to the point of war by moving north and west of the Ohio River (Delegates to Harrison, 8 Sept. 1783, and n. 2). This factual disagreement partially stemmed from Irvine's designation of at least some of the white intruders as Virginians because, having originally settled in Yohogania County, Va., they declined to continue living there after an allegedly inaccurate survey of the southwestern and western boundary of Pennsylvania had placed them under the jurisdiction of that state—thus imperiling their political privileges and the validity of their land titles.

Governor Harrison contended that if the surveyors, in determining the southwestern boundary of Pennsylvania, had measured, as the Pennsylvania charter of 1681 appeared to intend, five degrees of longitude due west from the meanders of the Delaware River rather than from its most westerly bend, almost all the settlers along the Youghiogheny River would have been found to live within Virginia's rightful jurisdiction. Furthermore, in Harrison's view, many of the trespassers along the Ohio River below Fort Pitt should have been restrained by the government of Pennsylvania, for they were agents of land speculators resident in Philadelphia (Executive Letter Book, 1783–1786, pp. 143, 153–55, 179, 193–95, 197–98, MS in Va. State Library; *Cal. of Va. State Papers*, III, 520–21; McIlwaine, *Official Letters*, III, 351; *Pa. Archives*, 1st ser., IX, 564–66, 585; X, 56, 72, 95–96; *Colonial Records of Pa.*, XIII, 644–45, 685–86; *Papers of Madison*, I, map facing p. 212; V, 74; 75, nn. 10, 11; 276; 277, nn. 4, 5, 8, 9; 440; Jones to JM, 31 May, n. 17; Harrison to Delegates, 19 Sept.; 26 Sept. 1783).

To Edmund Randolph

RC (LC: Madison Papers). Unsigned. Cover franked by JM and addressed to "Edmund Randolph Esqr. Richmond." Docketed by Randolph, "J. Madison. Sep: 13. 1783."

PRINCETON Sepr. 13. 1783.

MY DEAR SIR

Our Ministers in Europe have made some amends for their long silence by voluminous despatches brought down to 27th. July. They were recd. yesterday by Congress.[1] No definitive treaty had then been signed by any of the parties, though all had been ready except Holland & America. The fo[rmer] is said to have settled her difficulties.[2] The American Ministers have been endeavoring to incorporate some important commercial stipulations, but in vain; and in case of emergency must come forward with the provisional articles to be signed as the definitive Treaty.[3] The Conduct of G.B. in the negociation with America has shewn great unsteadiness if not insidiousness on the subject of commerce:[4] and the inclosed proclamation of the 2d. of July is a proof that some experiment is intended on the wisdom, firmness & union of the

States, before they will enter into a Treaty in derogation of her Navigation Act.[5] Congress will probably recommend some defensive plan to the States.[6] If it sd. meet with the fate of former recommendations, it will not probably be owing to Rhode Island whose staple interest more than that of any others lies in carrying between U.S. & the West Indies.[7] If it fails at all it will prove such an inefficacy in the Union as will extinguish all respect for it & reliance on it. My situation here for writing is so incommodious, that you must excuse my brevity.[8]

[1] JM to Randolph, 8 Sept. 1783, n. 4. On 12 September Congress referred to a committee—James Duane, chairman, and four other delegates—thirty dispatches: two, dated 18 and 27 July, from the American commissioners for negotiating peace; sixteen, dated between 14 April and 18 July, from John Adams; one of 22–25 July from Franklin; four, dated between 7 April and 20 July, from Jay; three, dated between 27 June and 2 August, from Laurens; three, dated between 15 May and 6 June, from Dana; and one of 23 June from Dumas (NA: PCC, No. 185, III, 78–80; No. 186, fol. 123; Wharton, *Revol. Dipl. Corr.*, VI, 364, 368, 373–74, 432–33, 455–56, 464–65, 477, 494–570, *passim*, 576, 580–91, 600–606, 628–29). Although the journal of Congress omits mention of the receipt of these dispatches on 12 September 1783, see *JCC*, XXV, 531, 587–88, 588, n. 1.

[2] JM's source of misinformation about the state of the negotiations between the Netherlands and Great Britain appears to have been the *Pennsylvania Packet* of 9 and 11 September. These issues included news items, under Paris date lines of 20 and 25 June and 11 July, giving assurance that those two countries had reached an accord, and that at the Coco Bar in Paris the betting odds were 7 to 4 that all the definitive treaties between Great Britain and her foes would be "signed before the middle of August." In their dispatch of 27 July 1783, the American peace commissioners wrote, "The Dutch preliminaries are not yet agreed on" (Wharton, *Revol. Dipl. Corr.*, VI, 600). See also *ibid.*, VI, 529; JM to Jefferson, 11 Aug. 1783, and n. 8.

[3] In his dispatch of 7 July, virtually repeating what he had written in one of 27 June, Adams stated: "We cannot as yet obtain from Mr. Hartley, or his principals, an explicit consent to any one proposition whatever. Yet England and France, and England and Spain, are probably agreed, and Holland, I suppose, must comply. Our last resource must be to say we are ready to sign the provisional treaty, *totidem verbis*, as the definitive treaty" (Wharton, *Revol. Dipl. Corr.*, VI, 504–5, 517; Jones to JM, 8 June, n. 23; JM to Jefferson, 10 June 1783, and n. 8).

In their dispatch of 27 July, the American peace commissioners wrote: "we are of opinion that finally we shall find it best to drop all commercial articles in our definitive treaty, and leave everything of that kind to a future special treaty, to be made either in America or in Europe, as Congress shall think fit to order" (Wharton, *Revol. Dipl. Corr.*, VI, 600). For the long background of the effort to include in the definitive treaty "important commercial stipulations" and other additions to, or modifications of, the preliminary articles of peace, see *Papers of Madison,* V, 437, n. 4; 476, and n. 2; 477, nn. 4, 5; VI, 356; 357, n. 17; 395; 449, n. 10; 453, n. 7; 495, n. 13; JM Notes, 6 May, and n. 3; 30 May, n. 3; JM to Jefferson, 13 May, and nn. 6–9; 10 June, and nn. 5, 6, 8, 21, 26; Instructions to Peace Commissioners, 20 May; JM to Randolph, 20 May, and nn. 4–6, 13, 14; 10 June; 17 June, n. 6; 30 Aug., and n. 2; 8 Sept., and n. 4; Instruction to Delegates, 23–24 May, and n. 1; Harrison to Delegates, 31 May, n. 2; Delegates to Harrison, 14–15 Aug. 1783, and n. 7.

[4] *Papers of Madison,* VI, 452; 453, n. 5; 495, n. 13; Jones to JM, 8 June; Delegates

to Harrison, 14–15 Aug.; 20 Sept., n. 25; JM to Jefferson, 20 Sept. 1783, and n. 13.

[5] The proclamation of King George III of Great Britain, of which one copy was enclosed by Adams in his dispatch of 14 July and another copy by the American peace commissioners in theirs of 27 July, had been published in the *Pennsylvania Packet* of 11 September (Wharton, *Revol. Dipl. Corr.*, VI, 540–42, 600; *JCC*, XXV, 587). This proclamation sought to confine most of the trade with the British West Indies to "British subjects in British-built ships, owned by his majesty's subjects." They alone could transport naval stores, lumber, livestock, vegetables, grain, flour, bread, and biscuits originating in the United States to "any of his Majesty's West India Islands" and carry "to any port or place within" the United States return cargoes of "rum, sugar, molasses, coffee, cocoa-nuts, ginger, and pimento." As Adams noted in his dispatch: "One of the most remarkable things in this proclamation is the omission of salt-fish, an article which the islands want as much as any that is enumerated. This is, no doubt, to encourage their own fishery, and that of Nova Scotia, as well as a blow aimed at ours."

[6] On 29 September 1783 Congress adopted the portion of the report of the committee, mentioned in n. 1, recommending the appointment of a committee "who shall prepare an address to the States upon the subject of Commerce, stating to them the Regulations which are prevailing in Europe, the evils to be apprehended therefrom, and the steps proper to be taken to guard against and to Counteract them" (*JCC*, XXV, 617–18, 628–29). The proposed address, in the hand of Thomas FitzSimons, was submitted on 9 October 1783, but was not adopted by Congress before the close of that year (*JCC*, XXV, 661–64, 664, n. 1).

[7] By "former recommendations," JM meant the refusal of the Rhode Island General Assembly to approve the proposed 5 per cent impost amendment of the Articles of Confederation and the plan for restoring public credit (Randolph to JM, 15 May, n. 2). One of the most important industries of Rhode Island was the distilling of rum from sugar and molasses of West Indian origin (*Papers of Madison*, V, 375, n. 15; 414–15; VI, 168, n. 28; 298–99; JM to Randolph, 27 May 1783, and citations in n. 5).

[8] JM to Jefferson, 17 July, and n. 9; Jones to JM, 21 July, n. 5; JM to James Madison, Sr., 30 Aug. n. 10; to Randolph, 30 Aug. 1783.

From Edmund Randolph

RC (Harvard College Library: Dearborn Papers). Addressed in the hand of a clerk, probably George Hay, "To James Madison. Sept 13th: 1783," and almost certainly enclosed by Randolph in his longer letter of the same date to JM (*q.v.*).

RICHMOND Sepr. 13. 1783.

DEAR SIR

If your attention to congressional business, and your cramped situation will allow you to shew civilities to a new acquaintance, I must consign Mr. Francis Corbin to them. He is the youngest son of Colo. Corbin of this state, has lately returned from G. Britain, where he has resided for twelve years for his education, and became intimate with men of the purest American principles, being himself zealous and indeed enthusiastic.[1] A letter from my father[2] recommends him to my attention, and at the same time vouches, that he has at no time been wanting in the warmest professions of attachment to the new state.[3]

Yrs. mo. afftely

EDM: RANDOLPH

[1] After being graduated by the College of William and Mary, Richard Corbin (1714–1790) of Laneville, King and Queen County, served prior to 1776 as a justice of the peace, burgess, member of the royal governor's council, and receiver general of the province. Highly regarded for his ability and probity, he had many influential friends, including Governor Harrison and George Washington. Being in poor health and unsympathetic with the American cause, Corbin retired to his plantations at the onset of the Revolution. Neither his person nor his property was molested during the war (*Papers of Madison*, I, 145, n. 5; Elizabeth C. Johnson, "Colonel Richard Corbin of Laneville," *Bulletin of the King and Queen Historical Society of Virginia*, No. 22 [Jan. 1967], pp. 2–4).

During his ten, not twelve, years of residence in England, Francis Corbin (1759–1821) studied at Cambridge University and the Inner Temple in London. He was a delegate from Middlesex County in the Virginia General Assembly for a decade beginning in 1784, and an influential member of the Virginia Convention of 1788 which ratified the Federal Constitution. Although elected on 20 February 1792 to the Congress of the United States, he declined to serve. JM, who esteemed Corbin highly for his character and ability, frequently corresponded with him from 1788 until his death (*Cal. of Va. State Papers*, III, 511; V, 448; Swem and Williams, *Register*, pp. 20 42, *passim; Va. Mag. Hist. and Biog.*, XXX [1922], 80–85, 315–18).

[2] For John Randolph, Edmund's father, see *Papers of Madison*, IV, 162, n. 8; VI, 185, n. 5.

[3] JM to Randolph, 30 Sept. 1783.

From Edmund Randolph

RC (LC: Madison Papers). Unsigned, but in Randolph's hand. Cover addressed by him to "The honble James Madison jr. esq of Congress Princeton." Docketed by JM, "Sepr. 13. 1783 E.R." The bracketed letters are those excised from the manuscript by an overly close cropping, especially along the right margin of the second folio.

RICHMOND Sep: 13. 1783

MY DEAR SIR

Norfolk and its neighbourhood are I fear, doomed to perpetual dissensions. Under the former government, their inhabitants were in the most bitter enmity on account of the small pay. the war has carried the irritating distinction of whig and tory to a very unhappy height, and the governor's proclamation has added fresh fuel to these disturbances. The generality of the third description has given room to one party to expel, or sentence to expulsion, many of the citizens of the other, who are suspected of having adhered to the enemy: Some of those very men too, who have been tried and acquitted. The governor has declared by letter, what the genuine interpretation of the proclamation ought to be, and will by this means, I hope, restrain the violence, now in agitation.[1]

The tories have spread a report, that congress have instructed the American commissioners to obtain a revocation of the preliminary article, which provides for the payment of british debts, and have resolved not to ratify the definitive treaty without the abolition of that article.[2] The report is scarcely attended to; but there is some reason to believe, (tho' it cannot be asserted with any certainty) that it was circulated to aid the pamphlet, forwarded to you some time ago.[3] I doubt the more of its having risen from the patrons of nonpayment, as I do not see the effect, which, if credited, it can have upon their doctrines.

The society of the Cincinnati have for their object what i[s] truly laudable. But at some distant day may it not be a[bus]ed from its present praiseworthy views to something ha[rm]ful? Is it not a mode of assembling on any occasion those, who belong to the army, from North to South, and to keep alive a distinction, between the cit[izen] and soldier? Much better would it have been for the [se]veral states to do justice to their officers, and thus to rend[er] an association for the support of their families unnecess[ary.][4]

I should feel most sensibly f[or] congress at the expectation of a new ambassador, if he did not come from Holland: But even at Princeton you ca[n] surely give him a better reception, and better fare, tha[n] the representative of a nation will require, whose negoc[ia]tors at Munster drew out stinking cheese from the[ir] satchels, and were clad in coarse doublets.[5]

[1] Few, if any, coastal towns in the United States suffered from the war as much as Norfolk. Largely destroyed by fire in December 1775 and January 1776 during the fighting attending the expulsion of Lord Dunmore, the royal governor, the town was also occupied several times between May 1779 and October 1781 by British troops or bombarded by British ships. For a decade before the Revolution, Parliament's restrictive economic legislation and the resistance to it in the form of non-importation, non-exportation, and non-consumption agreements had injured Norfolk's commerce, depressed the wages of her artisans and seamen, and embittered them against the Scottish merchants and other pro-British residents of the town and neighborhood. For these reasons, as well as the ruinous effects during the war of the frequent blockade of Chesapeake Bay by the British navy, the depredations by Loyalist "cruisers," and the removal of slaves by the British army, every erstwhile "tory" who returned to the area in 1783 was greeted with hostility. Governor Harrison's proclamation of 2 July encouraged these expressions of enmity (*Papers of Madison*, I, 273, n. 4; 284, n. 4; 295, n. 5; II, 152, n. 2; 245, n. 3; 296, n. 6; III, 12, n. 7; 16, n. 8; 17, n. 10; 69, n. 2; 80; 120, n. 1; 194, n. 4; V, 90, n. 2; 310, n. 6; VI, 209, n. 12; 239, n. 22; Randolph to JM, 12 July, and n. 2; Delegates to Harrison, 23 Aug. 1783, n. 2; Thomas Jefferson Wertenbaker, *Norfolk: Historic Southern Port* [Durham, N.C., 1931], pp. 58–83).

Probably while serving as attorney general during the session of the state Court of Admiralty, which convened in Williamsburg on 3 September, Randolph gathered much of his information about the "disturbances" in Tidewater Virginia (*Va. Gazette, and Weekly Advertiser*, 20 Sept. 1783). These were by no means confined to Norfolk and neighboring Hampton and Portsmouth. On 18 September 1783 Thomas Smith, a justice of the peace in Gloucester County, wrote to Governor Harrison that, in view of the seeming conflict between the preliminary articles of peace and the laws of Virginia, he did not know how to proceed "with Legality & Propriety" against "such noxious Vermine," as the "infamous" Loyalists and other "truly British subjects," who had "within a few days presumed to make their appearance among us" (*Papers of Madison*, I, 229, n. 4; *Cal. of Va. State Papers*, III, 530–31). Five days later Harrison replied that Smith should let all British subjects remain "except natives who have adhered to the enemy and been actually in arms against America" (Executive Letter Book, 1783–1786, pp. 200–201, MS in Va. State Library). Harrison's earlier letter or letters on this subject have not been found. See also *Va. Gazette*, 27 Sept. 1783, for the letter by "a True Whig" excoriating the Loyalists.

[2] Congress had instructed the American commissioners of peace to seek from the British a modification, rather than "a revocation," of the article to which Randolph referred but had not resolved to reject the definitive treaty of peace unless the change was made (JM Notes, 30 May, and n. 3; JM to Jefferson, 10 June 1783).

[3] Randolph to JM, 12 July 1783, and n. 4.

[4] Haskell to JM, 12 Sept. 1783, and n. 1.

[5] JM to Jefferson, 10 June, and n. 23; to Randolph, 30 Sept. 1783. Randolph's reference was to the "negociators" representing the Estates General of the Netherlands at Münster in 1648 near the close of the Thirty Years War. So desolated by the war was the little German town and its rural environs that a Frenchman labeled it "Swines-ville," and a diplomat dated a dispatch "from Münster, behind the pig-sty" (Friedrich Heer, *The Holy Roman Empire*, trans. Janet Sondheimer [New York, 1968], pp. 211, 212). Insofar as the "cheese" is concerned, the tale may have some basis in fact. Professor Karl J. Weintraub of the University of Chicago kindly furnished the editors with the following translation of a passage from a monograph on the Treaty of Münster in Westphalia largely based upon contemporary manuscripts in the Dutch archives at The Hague: "Jointly these gentlemen received 300 guilders for keeping house. This was in addition, of course, to the cost of the provisions they took with them to inhospitable Westphalia—that is to say, wine and beer valued at 2,000 guilders and 5,000 guilders worth of such good Dutch articles as 'butter, cheese, salt, soap, dried codfish, salted codfish, herring, spices, lard for lacing, vinegar, oil, wax and tallow candles, and all sorts of other necessities.' We learn, by the way, that by 22 May, thus four months after their arrival, all of these provisions had been consumed" (Jan Joseph Poelhekke, *De Vrede van Munster* [The Hague, 1948], p. 224).

Note on "The North-American," No. 1 and No. 2

EDITORIAL NOTE

17 September and 8 October 1783. In the *Pennsylvania Journal, and the Weekly Advertiser* (Philadelphia) of 17 September and 8 October there are two essays, respectively entitled "The North-American, No. 1" and "The North-American, No. 2." With some reservations, Edmund C. Burnett attributed these anonymously written articles to James Madison.[1] Irving Brant is completely convinced that JM was their author.[2] Julian P. Boyd, on the other hand, deems that "an equally good argument could be made for attributing these essays to someone from one of the eastern commercial states (a Philadelphian or a New Yorker) or to someone from one of the small states having no western land claims (Maryland or New Jersey)," a conclusion that he has found no cause to revise.[3] The present editors are of the opinion that JM most probably was not the "North-American." For this reason they have not included the essays in this volume, but their inability to concur with JM's most eminent biographer impels them to justify the omission.

The following paragraphs summarize the contents of the essays, present the evidence supporting and opposing the belief that JM wrote them, and suggest who the "North-American" may have been. For convenience, the citations to the articles in the notes refer the reader to Brant's edition of them in the *William and Mary Quarterly*, but quotations from their texts are taken from the *Pennsylvania Journal*.

"The North-American, No. 2" opens with the statement: "The object of the Author's first address to his countrymen, was to develop those causes of civil dissention, which if not early checked, would put a period to their domestic tranquillity."[4] Basic among "those causes," as expounded in "The North-American, No. 1," were the "separate sovereignties of our respective States," each with a defective government "framed in the moment of turbulence and war," and each jealously guarding its own political power and economic well-being against encroachments by another state or by Congress. History had demonstrated that this "competition of interests and the desires of rulers to exalt their respective communities have laid the foundation of those wars which have desolated the world and entailed misery on the human race."[5] By rejecting the plan for restoring public credit, by withholding from Congress the funds required to honor its pledges to creditors at home and abroad, by beginning "to depreciate the merit of France" during the Revolution, by defending the unwillingness of several states largely unscathed by the war's devastation to share proportionately the extraordinary expenses of the other states in a conflict that had won independence for all of them, and by upholding the refusal of six states to cede to Congress their claims to vast western areas wrested from Great Britain at a heavy cost of the common "blood and treasure," many Americans were thoughtlessly inviting internecine conflict and intervention by European powers.[6] The threat of civil war was the greater because "the northern and middle states, among whom most of the paper money, and other continental securities now rest, might be tempted by their naval superiority to pay themselves out of the rich commerce of the Southern States, who would necessarily seek the protection of foreign nations."[7]

To avert this tragic fate, so different from "the happy state of civil society" in the thirteen colonies as long as Great Britain's rule was "mild and gentle," the "authors of the revolution, who now survive," must complete their work by establishing a government of the United States adequate for assuring "those blessings to which the virtues, sacrifices and sufferings of America have an undeniable claim."[8]

In "The North-American, No. 2," the author's purposes were "to unfold" the "relative situation" which the thirteen states "have assumed, as one of the nations of the earth," and the fearful consequences which would follow their refusal to form a stronger constitutional union.[9] Before developing these themes he levied upon history to contrast the wisdom of the ancient Romans "who rested the defence of their rights on the firm basis of power," with their "degenerate successors" who, having invented "the much boasted political balance," became "a divided prey to numberless petty tyrants" and victims "of the contentions, success or misfortunes of their potent neighbours." "On the continent of Europe," continued the author, "we have seen in our own day the great inland powers dividing the fairest of all regions—one of her most powerful kingdoms [Poland], and prostrating the rights of its citizens, whose discord and anarchy had rent asunder the bonds of Empire."[10]

The "North-American" warned his readers that, no matter how strong each of them esteemed his own state to be, it was impotent and insignificant compared with any European power possessing a formidable navy. Recognizing this weakness, Great Britain had already begun to discriminate against American shipping and "to disseminate those seeds of disunion" among the thirteen states by tempting each of them to outbid the others in its eagerness to gain trade concessions from the government at London. Although Great Britain recently had been their enemy, France and the Netherlands, concerned about maintaining their commerce with the United States and recovering their financial loans to Congress, would be obliged to follow the British example. These economic policies, so menacing to America's "internal tranquility," could succeed only if the states continued to withhold from Congress an authority to make duties on imports and possibly on exports uniform throughout the union.[11]

In Europe, moreover, where the maintenance of a balance of power was the principal aim of statecraft, the king of Sweden, although disposed to be a friend of the United States, would be unable to avoid an alignment with one of the maritime powers. Striking from its Canadian base, now the more hostile because of the many Loyalists in Nova Scotia, Great Britain easily could reduce the disharmonious thirteen states to their former colonial status and deprive Americans of their "natural right" to share in the Newfoundland fisheries. Adjoining the southern and western borders of the United States, absolutistic Spain, fearing lest the successful outcome of the Revolution stimulate its own colonists to rebel, would be inclined to ally militarily with Great Britain against an almost defenseless America.[12]

"The prospect which lies before us of domestic confusion and foreign war," the "North-American" lamented, "is both gloomy and solemn." Yet he added, "still there is a light, although it glimmers at a distance." This note of hope pervades the author's grandiloquent conclusion: "Liberty! thou emanation from the all-beauteous and celestial mind! to Americans thou hast committed the guardianship of the darling rights of mankind,—leaving the Eastern world where indolence has bowed the neck to the yoke of tyranny; in this Western hemisphere hast thou fixed thy sacred empire; whilst the sons of Europe shackled with the manacles of oppression, sigh for thy safety, and pant for thy blessings; the band of patriots who are here thy votaries, cemented by thy invisible power, will be bound to the partners of their toil and dangers, by ties more close than those of kindred, more sacred than those of friendship. Inspired by the virtuous nations, who are now the pride and will be ever the boast of America, will instil this holy truth into the infant minds of their children, and teach them to hold it sacred, even as the divine aphorisms of religion, that the SAFETY OF AMERICA will be found in her UNION."[13] With this emphatic conclusion JM, though much less prone to apostrophize, thoroughly agreed.

Most of the other points of view set forth in these essays were also ones generally favored by JM. During 1783 he, too, realized the need to amend the state constitutions as well as the Articles of Confederation, recognized the impracticability of the land-valuation basis stipulated by those Articles for allotting financial quotas among the states, opposed the adoption of theoretical policies divorced from actuality, deplored the increase in the number of inexperienced delegates who were replacing the time-tested older members of Congress, viewed with mounting alarm the growing stress by each state upon its absolute sovereignty, at least in domestic affairs, and most probably subscribed to the "North-American's" generalization that how to preserve domestic tranquillity "is the most important inquiry."[14]

Advocating a centralized control over foreign trade and reliable, independent sources of revenue for Congress, JM could applaud the unqualified criticism by "North-American" of several state legislatures, and especially the Rhode Island General Assembly, for refusing to ratify the proposed impost amendment of the Articles of Confederation.[15] JM, who had been the chief architect of the congressional plan for restoring public credit and the author of the accompanying "Address to the States," agreed with the anonymous essayist's censure of most of the states, including Virginia, for not ratifying that plan.[16] Both men believed that justice to those states upon which the war had borne most heavily required that the war debt of all thirteen states should be merged into a "common mass" and added to the debt of the Confederation. Elementary considerations of honesty, good faith, national honor, and even of national survival, should impel the states to assure Congress of funds ample enough to pay the yearly interest on that debt and the administrative expenses of the Confederation government. How, otherwise, could the interest on and the principal of the foreign loans, which Congress rather than the individual states had borrowed, ever be paid?[17]

JM and the "North-American" apparently differed little in their endorsement of the just claim of any civilian creditor of Congress; in their blame of Massachusetts and other New England states for opposing the congressional pledge to reward the officers of the continental army with full pay for five years; in their concern about how General Moses Hazen's regiment and similar units of the continental army, not attached to the line of any states, would be paid; and in their sympathy for all other unpaid continental troops.[18]

Although JM realized that the aid extended by France during the war had not been wholly unselfish in its motivation, he could join the essayist in steadfastly upholding the Treaty of Alliance between that country and their own, in referring to King Louis XVI in highly complimentary terms, and in deploring the growing tendency of some congressional delegates in 1783 either to take that sovereign to task for refusing to make additional loans or to belittle his earlier contributions toward the winning of independence by the United States.[19] JM and the "North-American" lacked sympathy for Loyalists, resented British discrimination against American commerce, feared that Great Britain might bar Americans from the Newfoundland fisheries, expected that country in other ways to foment disunion among the thirteen states with the hope of resuming dominion over them, and regretted the unwillingness of France to open all of its West Indian ports to American trade. In their respective discussions of the hostile attitude of Parliament and King George III toward American traffic in goods with Great Britain and its Caribbean colonies, both JM and the essayist had been influenced by reading the future Earl of Sheffield's pamphlet entitled, *Observations on the Commerce of the American States with Europe and the West Indies*.[20]

Except for some provisos, not mentioned in the essays and perhaps not favored by their author, JM shared the firm belief of "North-American" that the "landed" states, and particularly Virginia, should surrender to Congress as soon as possible their claims to the territory between the Appalachian Mountains and the Mississippi River.[21]

Besides these points of view shared by JM and the author of the essays, several circumstances may also support the belief that JM wrote them. The two articles appeared in the *Pennsylvania Journal*, published by Thomas Bradford, the brother of William Bradford, attorney general of Pennsylvania and probably JM's closest friend when they were fellow students at the College of New Jersey.[22] During much of the summer of 1783 JM remained in Philadelphia. While there on 17 July he remarked in a letter to Jefferson (*q.v.*): "I have been here during the week past engaged partly in some writing which, my papers being all here cd. not be so well done elsewhere." His "writing," which almost surely dealt with public issues, has not been identified with certainty, and hence may have been the essays. Although the letter to Jefferson omits mention of any topic discussed in the essays, other letters of JM, dated in that summer or early in the autumn and cited in the documentation of this editorial note, exhibit his concern about many of the issues emphasized by the "North-American."

A word analysis of the essays produced a list of thirty-eight words, other than articles and connectives, which recur five or more times.[23] As probably was to be expected, all the entries, with the exception of "eye" and "hand," are those which anyone, including JM, normally would employ in a discourse on politics. The thirty-eight, with "despot," "man," and "virtue" as somewhat surprising exceptions, are found in JM's letters and other papers dating in 1783. The many pages of them, as contrasted with the few pages of the essays, may lend significance to the fact that JM, unlike the "North-American," proportionally used very seldom thirteen of the thirty-eight words, namely, "claims," "enlighten," "eye," "fortune," "mind," "risk," "sacrifice," "superior," "support," "success," "true," "wise," and "union.[24]

A representative sample of the more conspicuous words in these political essays is as follows: "abortive" (used three times), "aphorism" (once), "artifice" (once), "birthright" (once), "blush" (once), "burthen" (three times), "calculate" (once), "clime" (once), "concertion" (once), "confederal" (once), "convulsive" (once), "ebullition" (once), "espouse" (once), "exigency" (twice), "fashionable" (once), "fastidious" (once), "flatter" (twice), "frigid" (twice), "imbecility" (twice), "impotence" (three times), "infant" (once), "instrument" (twice), "languid" (once), "maxim" (twice), "meteor" (once), "Phantom" (once), "press" (four times), "prognostic" (once), "pulse" (once), "reciprocal" (twice), "rouse" (twice), "scourge" (once), "sentiment" (twice), "sophistry" (once), "speculatists" (once), "splendor" (four times), "stipulate" (once), "sycophants" (once), "systems" (three times), "vaunt" (once), "venerate" (twice), "vigour" (once), "votaries" (once), and "zeal" (twice).

The frequency of JM's use of each of these forty-four words during 1783 is as follows: "abortive" (once), "aphorism" (none), "artifice" (twice), "birthright" (none), "blush" (none), "burthen" (spelled "burden," and used at least 13 times), "calculate" (four times), "clime" (none), "concertion" (seven times but as "concert"), "confederal" (none), "convulsive" (once, but as "convulsions"), "ebullition" (none), "espouse" (four times), "exigencies" (fourteen times, but almost always as "exigences"), "fashionable" (once), "fastidious" (none), "flatter" (five times), "frigid" (none), "imbecility" (four times), "impotence" (three times), "infant" (once), "instrument" (five times), "languid" (none), "maxim" (twice), "meteor" (none), "Phantom" (none), "press" (fourteen times), "prognostic" (twice, in the form "prognosticate"), "pulse" (once), "reciprocal" (twice), "rouse" (none), "scourge" (none), "sentiment" (nine times), "sophistry" (none), "speculatists" (six times, but only as "speculator" or "speculation"), "splendor" (twice), "stipulate" (at least twenty-eight times), "sycophants" (none), "systems" (eleven times), "vaunt" (none), "venerate" (none), "vigour" (none), "votaries" (once), "zeal" (once).

In summary, eighteen of the words were not used by JM in his writings of 1783. To these probably should be added the strange nouns, "concertion," "prognostic," and "speculatists," also avoided by him. He, furthermore, except in one instance wrote "burden" instead of "burthen," and, except in two instances "exigences" instead of "exigencies." Although these two word checks are by no means conclusive, their outcome provides very frail support, if any, to a claim that JM and the "North-American" were the same person.

Given below are quotations from the essays, accompanied wherever possible by identical or somewhat analogous quotations from JM's writings in 1783. The blanks in the column on the right signify that no parallel, even slightly similar, has been found. With the exception of a few portions of JM's "Address to the States," his correspondence and other papers of 1783 are not oratorical in style and do not differentiate verb tenses by using archaically strong forms. For these reasons, most of the numerous expressions of that genre have been excluded from the column on the left. The Roman numeral and the succeeding Arabic numeral after each item cite, respectively, either "The North-American," No. I or No. II, and the page in *William and Mary Quarterly*, 3d ser., III (1946), on which the quotation appears. In the column on the right, each item is followed either by the relevant page number in *Papers of Madison*, VI, or by the relevant item in the present volume. "A to S" designates JM's "Address to the States."

Expressions in "The North-American"	*Nearest corresponding expressions, if any, in JM's writings in 1783*
1. accession of power, II, 581	unanimous accession, 312
2. artifice of intrigue, II, 581	intriguing in order to, 348
3. attended with success, II, 587	attended with . . . difficulties, 491 (A to S)
4. blazing meteor, II, 587	
5. blood and treasure, I, 572, 578	blood and services, 33
6. cause of freedom, II, 584	cause of liberty, 494 (A to S)
7. common benefit, I, 578	common good, Md. Payment to Troops, 28 July 1783
8. common cause, I, 579	common cause, 393, 394
9. confederal rule, I, 579	fœderal rule, JM to Jefferson, 20 May 1783
10. convulsive strength, I, 579	internal convulsions, 31
11. decisive means, II, 586	decisive measures
12. derive no benefit, I, 578	derive advantages
13. discord and anarchy, II, 581	sow discords, 393
14. divided prey, II, 581	prey on, 287
15. divine aphorisms, II, 587	
16. dreams and Phantoms, I, 572	
17. ease and happiness, II, 586	easy & equal, 24
18. enlightened mind, I, 571	enlightened and disinterested, 430
19. essential interests, I, 578	essential to the public interest, 170
20. fail to recollect, II, 586	duty to recollect, 492 (A to S)
21. faith . . . plighted, I, 577	plighted faith, 492 (A to S)
22. flattering delusion, II, 584	flatter myself, 440
23. freedom and tranquility, I, 572	harmony and tranquility, 488 (A to S)
24. frigid maxims, I, 579	strict maxims, 489, 490
25. general plan, I, 574	general plan, 382
26. human nature, I, 579, II, 586	human nature, 493, 494
27. impending ruin, II, 585	
28. in a degree, I, 575	a degree, 55
29. ingratitude and injustice, I, 579	injustice and discontents, 491
30. injury or insult, II, 582	after the insult, JM to Randolph, 30 June 1783
31. interests and the desires, I, 573	interest and the ease, 488 (A to S)
32. joint efforts, I, 578	
33. justice and good faith, I, 577	justice & good faith, 481, 490, 492, 494 (A to S)
34. little prospect, I, 579	little prospect, 120
35. magnanimous exertion, I, 580	magninimity [*sic*] and friendship, 493 (A to S)
36. mark of, I, 579	mark(s) of, 430
37. measure of proportion, I, 575	respective proportions, 397
38. mortifying and useless, II, 585	mortifying it might be, 25, 148
39. mutual confidence, I, 574	mutual concessions, 492 (A to S)

Expressions in "The North-American"	*Nearest corresponding expressions, if any, in JM's writings in 1783*
40. object of, II, 586	object of, 430
41. *partial* view, I, 574	partial provision, 490 (A to S)
42. patience and with fortitude, I, 575	patiently borne, 493 (A to S)
43. peace and social happiness, I, 572	peace and private citizenship, 493 (A to S)
44. poverty or their wretchedness, I, 576	poverty & imbecility, 25
45. precarious rights, II, 581	precarious basis, 285
46. present state, I, 571	present state, 18
47. press him to, II, 584	pressed with, 491 (A to S)
48. pressing exigencies, I, 575	critical exigences, 488 (A to S)
49. pride and . . . boast, II, 587	pride and boast, 493 (A to S)
50. public affairs, I, 579	public affairs, 488 (A to S)
51. put a period to, II, 580	put a stop to, 233
52. real situation, I, 573	real plan, JM to Jefferson, 20 Sept. 1783
53. regular . . . mode, I, 580	irregular mode, JM to Randolph, 24 June 1783
54. render them superior, II, 583	render it, 443, 462
55. rights of mankind, II, 587	rights of mankind, 494 (A to S)
56. sad prognostic, I, 574	with certainty prognosticate, 504
57. secret intentions, II, 580	secret nature, 25
58. seeds of disunion, II, 582	seeds of discords, 394
59. set an example, II, 587	set the example, 465
60. solemn assertions, II, 580	solemn deliberations, 488 (A to S)
61. solid systems, I, 572	solid considerations, 489 (A to S)
62. splendid rising, II, 584	splendid . . . entertainment, JM to Randolph, 21 July 1783
63. stamped his character, II, 587	indelible stain on our character, 383
64. superior . . . advantages, II, 583	superior credit, JM to Randolph, 30 Aug. 1783
65. to the ends of, I, 572	
66. tottering beam, II, 583	
67. true Whigs, I, 580	spotless Whig, 44
68. unbounded commerce, I, 579	unbounded freedom has accrued to commerce, 489 (A to S)
69. under these circumstances, I, 579	under these circumstances, 230
70. unequal load, I, 575	
71. unhappy circumstances, I, 574	fortunate circumstance, JM to Randolph, 10 June 1783; several circumstances, JM to Randolph, 24 June 1783
72. unliquidated Accounts, I, 574	unliquidated . . . claims, 401
73. varying interests, II, 582	variety of sentiments, 457
74. vigor and enterprise, II, 585	vigor & resource, 25

Expressions in "The North-American"	*Nearest corresponding expressions, if any, in JM's writings in 1783*
75. voice of truth, I, 578	voice of humanity, 493 (A to S)
76. votaries of despotism, II, 583	votaries of tyranny, 494 (A to S)
77. want of, I, 14, II, 581	want of, 141
78. western wilds, I, 576	Western Country, 442
79. wisdom and decision, II, 584	wisdom firmness & union, JM to Randolph, 13 Sept. 1783
80. without enthusiasm, II, 583	

Of the quotations from "North-American," fourteen are identical with those used by JM in 1783; forty-eight are nearly identical; and eighteen were either not employed by him or too faintly resemble phrases in the essays to be counted as parallels. All the fourteen, and over half of the forty-eight, are trite expressions which might appear in the writings on public affairs of any man. It may be significant, however, that four of the identical quotations, and eighteen of the nearly identical were used by JM in his "Address to the States" of 25 April 1783. This address, along with the plan for restoring public credit and other documents relevant thereto, was quickly published by order of Congress, and the "Address" and "plan" were also printed in many newspapers.[25] For this reason, the words and phrases in both items were readily available for the anonymous author of "The North-American" essays to use. This consideration, as well as the figures given earlier in this paragraph, obviously bars an emphasis upon the above listing as evidence in support or in refutation of a claim that JM wrote the essays.

In the postscript of his letter to Jefferson on 30 September 1783 (*q.v.*), JM commented: "As the latest papers are very barren I inclose a former one containing No. 1. of N. American, leaving the Author to your conjectures." The last six words of this quotation may be interpreted as a broad hint that JM had written the essay. The anonymous author, at the outset of its sequel, assured his readers that "they will never know him." If JM was that author, he apparently never divulged the secret, nor was he ever so designated by anyone else during his lifetime. Perhaps he held his authorship in strictest confidence because he would have been much embarrassed politically between 1783 and 1785 and after 1791, both within and outside of Virginia, by the unsparing assault upon state sovereignty in the essays.[26]

The assumption that JM's postscript is strong evidence that he was the "North-American" is highly questionable. If this was the case, why had he not enclosed the *Pennsylvania Journal* of 17 September in his letter written three days later to Jefferson (*q.v.*), instead of waiting another ten days? The observation that, being in Princeton on 20 September, he could not have sent it, is not convincing because congressional delegates in that college town received Philadelphia newspapers the day after their publication. Unless the postscript was written hurriedly, as many postscripts no doubt are, JM would be expected, if he wrote "North-American, No. 1," to mention a forthcoming sequel. Perhaps, on the other hand, the "No. 1" made obvious the forthcoming appearance of at least a "No. 2." The words "to your conjectures" are by no means a certain indication of JM's authorship of the essay. Even if Jefferson upon reading the letter regarded that expression as a clue pointing to JM, he almost surely concluded that he had been misled after noting the un-Madisonian style, phraseology, and emphases in the essay itself. By using the plural rather than the singular of "conjecture," JM may have meant to imply that Jefferson would find "North-American's" identification a puzzle which he might or might not be able to solve. In May 1783, when JM sent a copy of his "Address to the States" to several of his friends in Virginia, he had not needed to name or even to hint at the name of the author. The wording of that anonymous address was for them an equivalent of his signature.[27]

To conclude that JM, being the author and fearing that he would be politically injured, took great pains to keep his authorship a secret is vulnerable for several reasons. In the first place it rests upon the unproven premise that he was the "North-American." In the second, it assumes on his part a policy of caution in this instance contrary to his simultaneous criticism of the General Assembly of his state for refusing to ratify the plan for restoring public credit. Earlier in 1783 JM had declared in Congress that he would risk the "personal consequences" of maintaining his advocacy of the proposed impost amendment to the Articles of Confederation, even though the legislature of Virginia had rescinded its ratification of that amendment.[28] Although he spoke in closed session, he did so in the presence of Arthur Lee, an opponent of the measure and a member of the Virginia House of Delegates. JM thereby risked that his defiance would be reported by Lee to the legislature of their state. If, as has been claimed, JM began the writing of "The North-American" essays in the second week of July 1783, he by then had made known his refusal to have his congressional term extended after its expiration at the close of October. When he allegedly was drafting "North-American, No. 1," he expected to marry Catherine Floyd in the autumn. He apparently wrote no letter during the summer of 1783 indicating a willingness to stand in a special election that fall, or in the regular elections the following spring, for membership in the Virginia House of Delegates.[29]

Much weight has been given to the fact that because JM was preparing something of a public nature during the second week of July 1783, the "something" must have been the essays. This conclusion is clearly a *non sequitur*. In the same letter of 17 July conveying the information that, assisted by his "papers," he had been "during the week past engaged partly in some writing," he also acknowledged to Jefferson the receipt, presumably about mid-June, of Jefferson's letter of 1 June (*q.v.*), enclosing a copy of the Declaration of Independence and of notes on the debates in the Second Continental Congress in 1776 leading to the adoption of that document. Although the subject of JM's writing is not conclusively known, an inference that it must have been the "North-American" essays is surely not as plausible as the belief, endorsed by his own recollection, that, having expressed an intention of preparing an edition of the state papers of the American Revolution, he was initiating that project.[30]

If JM wrote the essays—unstudied as they are in their lack of mention of obscure places, persons, dates, and events—he would not have needed the aid of his source material for their preparation. They could have been drafted by any literate person of oratorical bent possessing a general knowledge of European history beginning in ancient times and a more detailed knowledge of American events occurring between about 1750 and 1783. For this reason, it is difficult to understand why, if JM started to prepare "North-American, No. 1" about 10 July, he either took so long to finish it or, completing it reasonably soon thereafter, waited so many weeks before seeking to have it published.[31] Certainly the delay could not have been owing to the number of manuscripts submitted to any newspaper editor, for to judge from the Philadelphia gazettes of July and August 1783, the publishers were apparently hard pressed for materials with which to fill their columns.

The claim that JM wrote these essays rests in considerable degree upon the assumption that, out of prudential considerations, he not only shielded himself behind a pseudonym but also further masked his authorship by adopting an uncharacteristic style of writing. This style, a mixture of ordinary prose discourse and vivid depictions of America's ominous crisis, occasionally embellished with apostrophes suffused with extravagant emotion and imagery, is illustrated by this typical passage from "North-American, No. 2."

". . . They [the British] cut off one of the most profitable branches of our commerce—cramp all and check that bold and adventerous spirit of enterprize, which promised to carry the flag of these States to the remotest corners of the globe, and was (we fondly hoped[)] a sure and happy presage of a rising Navy of America, that might protect her commerce from injury or insult.

"Presumptuous nation, secure in our disunion, thou hast ever been too eager, and thy premature violence has been the parent of our wisdom—catching at the glittering shadow—may the substance ever elude thy fangs."[32]

The suggestion that in these essays JM reverted in tone to the sophomoric poetry of his student days at the College of New Jersey and foreshadowed the manner of his writing in "Who Are the Best Keepers of the People's Liberties?" published on 20 December 1792 in Philip Freneau's *National Gazette* (Philadelphia), cannot be accepted. The kinship, if any, linking even the most oratorical portions of the "North-American" articles with JM's collegiate doggerel or his simulated colloquy between a "Republican" and an "Anti-Republican" about "the People's Liberties" is most remote and indistinct.[33]

If JM was the "North-American," he stepped entirely out of character in more respects than the style of composition. Among other means of disguising his handiwork, he apparently decided to omit altogether, or use only very sparingly, the words he usually favored when discussing political affairs. Among these are "advert," "animadvert," "authenticate," "contravene," "contravert," "espouse," "exigences," "expediency," "inexpedient," "insidious," "interposition," "invidious," "promulge," "propriety," "retrospective," and "superadd."[34] As indicated earlier in this editorial note, JM seems to have resolved for the same reason to employ conspicuous words which he rarely, if ever, had included in his writings. To mask his identity still more securely, he included in the essays "have ever went hand in hand" and "could only have sprang"—thus even abandoning his usual care in the use of the present perfect tense.[35]

Probably the most extreme manifestation of JM's alleged anxiety to conceal his alleged authorship was the fabrication of several trips he never made. "The eye of him whose hand now writes these lines," he exclaimed, "has often traced" the route of the continental troops "on the cold snow, with the blood of their bare feet."[36] If JM was "North-American," he in these essays for the only time in his public career, insofar as is known, resorted to a contrived style and a deliberate falsification of episodes in his life. These manifold devices designed to assure that "his fellow citizens . . . will never know him" seem not only completely un-Madisonian in their nature but also far more elaborate than was needed to avert the slight political peril of having the views expressed in these essays associated with his name.[37]

Although most of these views correspond in a general way with those advocated by JM, they fail to reflect the important qualifications upon them emphasized by him in his remarks in Congress and in his correspondence. These differences oblige anyone claiming that he revealed his true feelings in the essays[38] to explain why he withheld them simultaneously from Jefferson, Randolph, and other friends in Virginia. In view of these contrasts in position, it is hard to understand, if JM was the "North-American," why he should want his authorship of "No. 1" to be known only by Jefferson. If JM was not the "North-American," this dilemma disappears. It seems most unlikely that for several years, in frequent and intimate letters to his closest political acquaintances, he would dissemble his real position on some of the major issues before Congress. Perhaps, however, it was not until the summer of 1783 that his discouragement over the trend of public affairs led him to the "emotional pitch" of extreme nationalism manifested in the essays. If this is so, and if he wrote these essays, it is remarkable that his change of stand is not evident in letters written by him during the latter half of that year.[39]

Granting that the "North-American" can be taken at his word, he was a strong nationalist who, even in his emphasis upon the distresses of war-ravaged New York, saw eye to eye with Alexander Hamilton. The essayist insisted that a "firm ground of power," a "union of force," a "coercive hand of authority," and a "superiority" over every subordinate unit of government were indispensable to "the welfare" of any nation. Otherwise, its life would be fleeting—a victim of its inability to preserve "good faith," to enforce justice, to defend its rights against aggression, and to avoid a dependence upon a foreign country for financial or military assistance. The future of the "nominal union" of thirteen "separate sovereignties," each of them striving to gain an economic upper hand over its neighbors and to contribute as little money as possible to the support of Congress, could only be an increasing "discord" and "confusion" culminating in "never ceasing war." Although these contentions accounted for most of America's woes in 1783, they also made clear the way to end them. Let each state so amend its "imperfect" constitution as to transfer its supreme authority to a central government for all the states, and let the constitution of that government be so altered as to reflect this concentration of sovereignty. To impress his readers the more deeply with the "awful" fate in store for the United States unless this was done, the author depicted the bloodshed and misery which had plagued Europe for centuries following the invention and application of a doctrine of statecraft requiring the maintenance of "the much boasted political balance" among the ambitious and jealous sovereign powers on that continent.[40]

Although JM no doubt agreed with the author's diagnosis of America's ills, he certainly dissented from the suggested remedy as being too drastic. His aim in 1783, as it would be during the rest of his life, was first of all to achieve and thereafter to cherish the goal opposed by the "North-American," that is, a political balance of power between each state and the central government. He recognized that the survival of the United States hinged upon Congress' being delegated a monopoly of control over foreign and interstate commerce and adequate sources of revenue immune from interference by the states. Assuming that the powers inherent in sovereignty could be divided, JM advocated an allocation to the central government of whatever fields of authority were requisite for promoting the general welfare, and a retention by each state or its people of the remaining powers of sovereignty. Far from being "contemptuous of state sovereignty," as has been claimed, he sought to achieve an effective distribution of powers, or a balance of power, between the thirteen parts and the whole and resisted having a concentration of all sovereignty either in each state or at the nation's capital. During all his later career, however much he conspicuously shifted from time to time in his views of the correct weight of power to keep in each scale of the balance, he remained a proponent of a federal union and not of one wherein the states were merely administrative subdivisions of a sovereign central government. For this reason, and for other reasons, the claim that the "thinking" of JM and the "North-American" in the summer and autumn of 1783 was "thoroughly in harmony" cannot be sustained.[41]

JM and the "North-American" were of the same mind in emphasizing that considerations of national honor and public credit obliged Congress as soon as possible to redeem at face value the continental paper money and loan-office certificates, privately owned in disproportionately large amounts by citizens of "the commercial states" as compared with the holdings elsewhere, and that justice required Congress, both by "abatements" and an "assumption of war-incurred debts," varying greatly in their totals among the states, to aid especially those which had been main theaters of the war.[42]

In his discussion of the western lands, the essayist warned that needy war veterans of the six "landless" states, finding that neither those states nor Congress, in spite of its pledges of bounty lands, could give them their due in this respect, might forcibly occupy tracts within the trans-Appalachian country claimed by Virginia and the six other "landed" states. For this reason and many others, the issue of the West was "one of the most fertile sources of endless discord and war" among the states. With this comment JM probably would agree, even though by the summer of 1783, when "North-American, No. 1" may have been written, he was more hopeful than he had been earlier that a main aspect of the problem, involving the terms of the offer by his state to cede its lands north and west of the Ohio River, would be solved by Congress and the Virginia General Assembly compromising their sharp differences over the issue.[43]

He could also generally endorse the rest of the author's exposition of this critical matter. More than a year earlier JM had conceded in Congress, over the dissent of his two fellow delegates from Virginia, that although the title of his state to the Northwest Territory was sound, the United States would also acquire a valid title to the same area if Great Britain relinquished it in the treaty of peace. This indisputable title and also the prior and equally legal titles of the "landed" states, which had been acknowledged by Congress in 1777 and by "the unanimous concurrence of the States" in the Articles of Confederation, were set forth in balanced fashion by the essayist. He then severely criticized Rhode Island for its inconsistency in adamantly opposing the claims of the "landed" states to the West and at the same time, out of a selfish concern for its own economic profit rather than for the welfare of the Union, stubbornly refusing to ratify the proposed impost amendment to the Articles of Confederation.[44]

The essayist offered no definite solution of the western-lands issue, but he no doubt wished his readers to conclude that the deadlock, which eventually might destroy the Union, could be broken only if each of the principal parties receded enough from its inflexible stand to effect a compromise acceptable to both. JM was of the same opinion. To claim that he was the "North-American" and would have been injured politically in Virginia, if the views about the West expressed in the essays became associated with his name, is not credible. Long before the essays appeared he had informed Virginians, both orally and in writing, that he recognized the need to take into account the undisputed title of the United States to the West, wanted the General Assembly of Virginia to abandon some of the restrictions included in its offer of cession, spoke at the same time in Congress for a moderation of its hostile response to that offer, regarded as minimal the possibility of large economic advantage accruing to Virginia from a retention of the lands north of the Ohio River, and viewed a concentration in the Confederation of the title to those lands as one important means of uniting the discordant states.[45]

If JM was the anonymous essayist, his failure to present publicly his solution of this difficult problem is puzzling. In other respects, also, the articles, although embodying some of his viewpoints about the West, present them in a manner characteristically different from his own. He frequently criticized Rhode Island for witholding its sanction of the impost amendment, but he seems never to have paired that state's refusal with its demand upon Virginia to cede the western lands to Congress.[46] The essayist mentioned "the principle which requires a division of unappropriated western lands between the States." James Wilson of Pennsylvania had advanced that "principle" in Congress on 18 April 1783, but its impracticability appears to have denied it support by even the other delegates from the "landless" states.[47]

In the two essays are other statements about miscellaneous matters which warrant doubt whether JM would have written them. At the outset of "North-American, No. 1," for example, is a paragraph eulogizing Great Britain's "mild and gentle forms of government" exercised over the thirteen colonies "prior to the late revolution." Although JM as a child may have experienced such a regime of "freedom and tranquility," some of his earliest papers reflect a dislike of Americans who defended the legislation of Parliament.[48] In both essays there are warnings that if the United States defaulted in the payment of the interest on, and the principal of, the loans extended by King Louis XVI and Dutch bankers during the Revolution, France and the Netherlands might be driven to recover the debt by levying high tariffs, or even by raids, on American commerce. If, too, the states in the Union which were competing one against the others for a preferred position in ocean shipping felt obliged by British pressures to discriminate against France and the Netherlands in their carrying trade, those friends of America might become perforce its enemies at sea. JM was realistic in his understanding of the circumstances impelling France to enter a military alliance with the United States in 1778, but he retained so deep a feeling of gratitude to France, that merely for the purpose of appealing to the fear of his readers, he hardly would have portrayed the French as potential enemies.[49]

Spatially the "North-American" sometimes allotted his emphasis in a manner uncharacteristic of JM's writings of 1783. Although the ideas and phraseology of the plan for restoring the public credit are diffused throughout the essays, reference to the plan itself is confined to less than one sentence. The fate of the plan, along with the movement to and the lingering in Princeton by Congress, entirely unmentioned by the "North-American," was a dominant theme in JM's correspondence during the summer of 1783.[50] It is no difficult achievement, on the other hand, to extract from the essays the thought that not an amendment of the Articles of Confederation, but the adoption of a new federal constitution, was demanded by the times. If JM shared this thought, he not only refrained from expressing it in 1783 but even, according to Stephen Higginson of Massachusetts, "much opposed" in that year "the Idea of a special Convention, for the purpose of revising the Confederation, and increasing the powers of the Union."[51]

Beyond that, if JM was the "North-American" and wrote with no more than ordinary haste, he failed now and again to manifest his characteristic display of sound logic. Although in the first essay the author dismissed "the callous multitude, who are secured from the effects of their resentment, by their imbecility" (which, if penned by JM, leaps from the record as being unique), in the second he asserted that "the people at large," who presumably included the selfsame multitude, "want but information to render them superior to the machinations of intrigue, and the snares of treachery."[52] In the second essay the writer proved himself capable both of eulogizing King Louis XVI of France for having "sacrificed his pleasures to public avocations, and his pomp and splendor to the ease and happiness of his people," and of stating that the "sons of Europe," among whom must have been those of France, were "shackled with the manacles of oppression."[53]

A century and a half seems to have elapsed after 1783 before anyone claimed that JM probably had written the essays. The only primary source material then cited to support this attribution was JM's postscript in his letter to Jefferson on 30 September of that year.[54] Irving Brant, the author of the most comprehensive and scholarly biography of Madison, later defended his own firm belief in JM's authorship by adducing much circumstantial evidence drawn from both the context and the contents of the essays. The present editors have endeavored to summarize Mr. Brant's arguments dispassionately and thereafter to present their own reasons for concluding that JM almost certainly did not write the articles. Among Mr. Brant's premises is one which apparently assumes a threefold variety of passages in the essays: (1) those patently oratorical, including a bit of fictitious autobiography, designed chiefly to mask the author's identity; (2) those in which he reaffirmed opinions previously expressed in his correspondence and in his speeches, reports, and motions in Congress; and (3) those in which he embodied certain deep convictions, calculated to injure him politically and hence never before frankly revealed, but included in the articles because his identity was hidden behind a pseudonym.

Although the present editors cannot agree with Mr. Brant's implication that upon anyone declining to accept JM as the essayist rests the burden of disproving the unprovable,[55] they have examined the matter on their own terms. In doing so, they have applied a standard of judgment almost the reverse of Mr. Brant's. To them it seems more reasonable to assume that the "North-American," although determined to remain anonymous, did not fabricate bits of autobiography and uncharacteristic word choices and literary style, but rather, being uninfluenced by political considerations relating to his future career, confined his opinions to those he had previously made known. He also was expected to have reflected his background of experience by the amount of space and the degree of emotional fervor he allotted among the various topics included in the essays.

By confronting the problem with these assumptions, it is possible to reach tentative conclusions about the author. He was acquainted with the history of Europe, ancient, medieval, and modern,[56] an ardent patriot, and well versed in the course of the American Revolution, including the civil and military issues of 1783. His obvious anxiety about the effect of the prevalent disorder and confusion of that year upon the future of the Confederation may account in part for his stress upon the peace and good order of the colonies under Great Britain's rule in the mid-eighteenth century.[57] Although his sympathy for the civil and military creditors of Congress was unqualified, it above all was manifested emotionally for the unpaid continental troops and their officers.[58] This may signify that he either was one of them or had been closely associated with them during the conflict. His interest in America's ocean-borne commerce suggests his possible vocation or at least his close relationship with merchants and shipowners.[59] His genuine gratitude to France for its military and monetary help was tempered by a realistic, even a somewhat cynical, appraisal of what that country in defense of its national interest might be compelled to do, if its loans were not repaid by Congress, or if the states meekly yielded to Great Britain a commanding position in their commerce.[60] He despised the Loyalists and both feared and scorned "corrupt and languid" Spain, on America's southern border, with its "machinery of monks, officers, and standing armies."[61] Conservative in general outlook, and no democrat,[62] he was an ultra-nationalist, apparently advocating the adoption of new state constitutions and articles of union so as to enhance greatly the authority of the central government.[63]

Taking him further at his word, he sought nothing for himself except the inward satisfaction of hoping that his essays would win support for his constitutional viewpoints.[64] The tenor of the essays, as well as the newspaper in which they were published, strongly points to Philadelphia or its neighborhood as the place of his residence.

Among the considerable number of men who conformed with this general description, Richard Peters (1743–1828) surely was one. Although unable to name him incontrovertibly as the essayist, the editors are confident that his qualifications for that role greatly exceeded those of JM. Through the courtesy of Dr. Nicholas B. Wainright, Director of the Historical Society of Pennsylvania, it has been ascertained that neither "Peters Papers for the latter part of 1783" nor "his memorandum book of 1781–1789" identify him as the "North-American."[65] In this particular, his papers and those of JM are equally unrewarding.

Although the choice by Peters of law as his profession and experimental farming as his avocation probably reflected the influence of his father, from whom he inherited the Belmont estate near Philadelphia in 1771, he often recalled in his later years the inestimable debt he owed to his uncle, the Reverend Richard Peters (1704–1776). Between 1737 and 1762 this redoubtable minister held a succession of civil offices—secretary to the proprietary governor, secretary of the provincial council, and for thirteen years a member of that council. From 1762 until shortly before his death, he was rector of St. Peter's Church in Philadelphia. This kindly and learned mentor inculcated his nephew with a love of Christianity, the classics, and the social stability produced by a strong government justly administered. The opening paragraphs of "North-American, No. 1," with their praise of the "solid systems" of rule established by Great Britain before its officials became "discoloured" by "insolence and barbarity," could well have been written by Richard Peters. JM's earliest writings bearing upon politics criticized rather than complimented British colonial policies.[66]

During his undergraduate days at the College of Philadelphia, Richard Peters had among his fellow students Thomas Bradford, who by 1783 was the proprietor of the *Pennsylvania Journal*. Before that year, Richard's career as a lawyer often brought him into association with Thomas' younger brother William, who probably was JM's closest friend while they both attended the College of New Jersey (Princeton College). If Richard Peters was the "North-American," he even more naturally than JM would choose the *Journal* to publish the two essays. JM's favorite newspaper in Philadelphia was almost surely the *Pennsylvania Packet*.[67]

Congress interrupted the brief field service of Captain Peters with the militia of his state by appointing him secretary to, and after seventeen months a member of, the Board of War, where he served from 13 June 1776 to 29 November 1781. In these capacities he came to know intimately and to view sympathetically the continental soldiers—their shortages of equipment and rations, and their hardships, especially during the winters. In line with his duties he visited Washington's main army and other contingents of American troops. "It is the thing nearest my Heart," he wrote on 6 May 1783, "that the Army should be satisfied." Throughout his later years he often told his friends of the suffering he had witnessed while on these missions. The emotional passage in "North-American, No. 1," mentioning "the blood" from the soldiers' "bare feet," which the author had "often traced" on "the cold snow," would have been a figment of JM's imagination but an authentic part of Peters' experience.[68]

Having been elected by the Pennsylvania General Assembly to Congress on 12 November 1782, Peters presented his credentials six days later. He had frequently met JM while serving as a member of the Board of War, but it was during Peters' first year in Congress, when the two served together on committees, that Peters and JM became warm friends. Both greatly admired Thomas Jefferson, with whom Peters had become closely acquainted in 1775–1776, when Jefferson resided in Philadelphia as a member of the Continental Congress. Mentioning Jefferson as "my old friend," in a letter of 31 December 1807 to JM, Peters added: "We have together *laughed* away, when I was young & playful, many a *little hour*."[69] JM, Jefferson, and Peters, sharing an interest in agriculture, public affairs, the classics, and amusing conversation, naturally enjoyed each other's company. Though their politics came to differ, the cordial relations between JM and Peters continued throughout the long remainder of the Pennsylvanian's life. There is no reason to doubt that JM, in his letter of 20 September 1783 to Jefferson (*q.v.*), included Peters in his reference to the "agreeable & even instructive society" of Philadelphia. It would be strange if Jefferson, during his long visit to that city earlier in the year, had not again enjoyed Peters' company.[70]

When JM in his letter of 30 September (*q.v.*) invited Jefferson's "conjectures" about the author of "North-American, No. 1," his recent association with Peters in Congress or Philadelphia may have led him to surmise that the Pennsylvanian was the essayist. On the other hand, he probably would have been surprised if Jefferson had arrived at the same hypothesis or had concluded from the style of the essay that JM himself was the author. At the close of September JM expected to meet Jefferson either on his way home to Montpelier or in Philadelphia. Although they may have discussed the identity of the "North-American" when they were together for nearly a month beginning on 29 October 1783, they left no record of a conversation on that subject.[71]

Between Peters' arrival in Congress on 18 November 1782 and JM's departure therefrom nearly a year later, they shared in the work of thirteen committees and in the tallied votes of approximately one hundred polls. Insofar as is known, they never seriously differed during the deliberations of a committee. They voted alike in all but about twenty of the polls. A half-dozen of the twenty related to the place of Congress' permanent residence—an issue unmentioned in the anonymous essays.[72] Unlike JM, Peters was a nationalist of the persuasion later designated as "Hamiltonian,"[73] a defender of the companies claiming the validity of titles which derived from the British Crown or from Indian tribes to land west of the Appalachian Mountains,[74] and a friend of the aggrieved speculators who had amassed large amounts of unredeemed currency, loan-office certificates, or other paper evidences of the continental debt.[75] Peters and the "North-American," but not JM, were closely in accord on these subjects.[76]

Peters' differences with JM were often ones of detail about the contents of a measure, or about which of several proposals simultaneously before Congress should be given the first or the more extended consideration. Although Peters at first had vigorously defended the title of the United States to the western territory and the right of the "landless" states to share in it, he ultimately supported the compromise between Congress and Virginia leading to acceptable terms of cession by that state. Although JM had never expressed concern about the interest of the "landless" states individually, he had conceded that Great Britain in the preliminary peace treaty gave the United States a title to the West, and he helped effect the accommodation finally reached by his state with Congress.[77]

Peters and JM favored "abatements" in the largely unpaid financial quotas of states overrun by the enemy.[78] Although Peters cannot conclusively be shown to have supported JM in his advocacy of "assumption," neither can it be demonstrated that Peters was present in Congress on 17 April 1783 when "Virginia was the only state" to vote for the measure.[79] The departure of experienced delegates from Congress led Peters to criticise most of their replacements because they were ultra-state-sovereignty in viewpoint, but JM censured them for seeking to overturn earlier decisions of Congress effected with great difficulty.[80] By midsummer of 1783, when "North-American, No. 1" is said to have been written, Peters was "extremely disgusted" by the frequent lack of a quorum in Congress, its paucity of accomplishments, and refusal to return to Philadelphia. JM also regretted this state of public affairs, but, unlike Peters, he was still sanguine that several of the major problems would be solved before the close of his term.[81] Not long thereafter Peters became further disheartened by "the late transactions" overseas, whereby the United States had aroused the "contempt" of Great Britain and dampened "the enthusiasm which was rising in Europe in our favor." JM also resented Great Britain's discrimination against American commerce, but he did not share Peters' apprehension that the French, Dutch, and Swedes to any dangerous extent would abandon their friendship for the United States.[82]

Except that the anonymous essays omit mention of the dispute over the residence of Congress, they reflect Peters' views on all others of these matters. The alarmist tone of "North-American" was obviously designed to frighten American readers into a realization that their only hope of remedying domestic ills, averting intervention by European powers, and preserving their own country would be by stripping each state of its sovereignty and concentrating it in the central government. This, Peters too, but not JM, could wholly applaud.[83] Peters, who was absent from Congress frequently in the latter half of September and for some days in October, announced, with an evident feeling of longing to be rid of politics, that he was retiring from Congress and would decline re-election thereto.[84]

Although the influence of the recommendations of 6 March, drafted by JM for his fellow members of the committee on restoring public credit, is apparent in the essays, it is not important evidence, as has been contended, that he was the "North-American." The report, printed at once, was frequently debated and amended in Congress during the next seven weeks. Peters or any other delegate could have levied upon the rcommendations for words or phrases to use in writing the essays. The same comment applies to the matured plan for restoring public credit and to JM's "Address to the States," adopted by Congress on 18 and 26 April 1783, respectively.

Earlier in this note, samples of words and phrases in the essays were compared with those found in the approximately two hundred documents written by JM in 1783. Although four hundred documents of Peters, dating between 1776 and 1826, have been analyzed for their conspicuous words and phrases, only thirty of the documents, or about one-seventh the number of JM's were written in 1783.[85] To offset this disparity, words and phrases drawn from the two hundred and eighteen examined items of Peters' writings between 1777 and 1816 have been compared with the same samplings from the "North-American" articles which were employed to test those of JM. The Peters' individual word comparison will not be given here, for its outcome was similar in its ambiguity to that of JM's in relation to the problem of authorship. The result of the following test of Peters' phrases is somewhat more rewarding.

Expressions in "The North-American"	*Nearest corresponding expressions, if any, in Richard Peters' writings*
1. accession of power	Accession of Strength, NA: PCC, No. 147, VI, 304 (15 Mar. 1781)
2. artifice of intrigue	artifice than Conviction, *Pa. Mag. Hist. and Biog.*, VII, 109 (9 Mar. 1783)
3. attended with success	attended with Consequences, Burnett, *Letters*, VII, 375 (16 Nov. 1783)
4. blazing meteor	erratic meteor, *ibid.*, VII, 343 (20 Oct. 1783)
5. blood and treasure	
6. cause of freedom	freedom and happiness, speech of 1816, p. 16
7. common benefit	general Benefit, NA: PCC, No. 147, VI, 290 (8 Mar. 1781)
8. common cause	common cause, NA: PCC, No. 147, I, 323 (19 Aug. 1777)
9. confederal rule	confederal plans, Burnett, *Letters*, VII, 224 (15 July 1783)
10. convulsive strength	convulsed at home, *ibid.*, VII, 225 (15 July 1783)
11. decisive means	decided measures, *JCC*, XXIV, 184 (17 Mar. 1783)
12. derive no benefit	derived from, speech of 1816, p. 8
13. discord and anarchy	disunion and anarchy, *ibid.*, p. 23
14. divided prey	fall a prey, Burnett, *Letters*, VII, 225 (15 July 1783)
15. divine aphorisms	divine injunction, speech of 1816, p. 7

Expressions in "The North-American"	*Nearest corresponding expressions, if any, in Richard Peters' writings*
16. dreams and Phantoms	to the phantom, Burnett, *Letters*, VII, 344 (20 Oct. 1783)
17. ease and happiness	ease and fortune, *JCC*, XXI, 1173 (29 Nov. 1781)
18. enlightened mind	mind can be enlightened, speech of 1816, p. 31
19. essential interests	essential Services, NA: PCC, No. 147, V, 141 (18 May 1781)
20. fail to recollect	do not certainly recollect, Burnett, *Letters*, VII, 375, n. 3 (26 Dec. 1783)
21. faith . . . plighted	pledge my faith, *JCC*, XXIII, 829 (23 Dec. 1782)
22. flattering delusion	mislead or flatter, *JCC*, VII, 344 (20 Oct. 1783)
23. freedom and tranquility	freedom and happiness, speech of 1816, pp. 14, 16
24. frigid maxims	
25. general plan	general Regulation, NA: PCC, No. 147, V, 265 (3 June 1781)
26. human nature	public Nature, NA: PCC, No. 147, V, 59 (2 May 1781)
27. impending ruin	impending misfortunes, NA: PCC, No. 147, IV, 285 (7 Mar. 1780)
28. in a degree	in any degree, NA: PCC, No. 148, II, 407 (19 Oct. 1781)
29. ingratitude and injustice	
30. injury or insult	insult and cruelty, *Pa. Mag. Hist. and Biog.*, XIII, 68–70 (23 May 1778)
31. interest and the desires	interest and welfare, *JCC*, XXIV, 234 (10 Apr. 1793); interests and happiness, Peters, *Agricultural Enquiries*, p. vii
32. joint efforts	joint endeavor, speech of 1816, p. 23
33. justice and good faith	Justice and Good Faith, Burnett, *Letters*, VII, 225 (15 July 1783)
34. little prospect	little prospect, *ibid.*, VII, 224 (15 July 1783)
35. magnanimous exertions	magnanimity exhibited, *ibid.*, VII, 375 (16 Nov. 1783); magnanimity to be the first in their Exertions, *ibid.*, VII, 225 (15 July 1783)
36. mark of	marks of, *ibid.*, VII, 375 (16 Nov. 1783)
37. measure of proportion	justly proportioned, NA: PCC, No. 147, IV, 11 (2 Feb. 1781)

Expressions in "The North-American"	*Nearest corresponding expressions, if any, in Richard Peters' writings*
38. mortifying and useless	mortifying to hear, Burnett, *Letters*, VII, 343–45 (20 Oct. 1783)
39. mutual confidence	mutually agreed on, *JCC*, XXIII, 738 n. (19 Nov. 1782)
40. object of	object of, Burnett, *Letters*, VII, 344 (20 Oct. 1783)
41. *partial* view	partial knowledge, speech of 1816, p. 29
42. patience and with fortitude	fortitude and patience, *JCC*, XII, 1178 (30 Nov. 1778)
43. peace and social happiness	
44. poverty or their wretchedness	
45. precarious rights	precarious Manner, NA: PCC, No. 147, VI, 303 (15 Mar. 1781)
46. present state	present State, *ibid.*, No. 147, VI, 305 (15 Mar. 1781)
47. press him to	pressed to, Burnett, *Letters*, VII, 344 (20 Oct. 1783)
48. pressing exigencies	present Exigencies, NA: PCC, No. 148, II, 417 (26 Oct. 1781)
49. pride and . . . boast	pride and boast, speech of 1816, p. 7
50. public affairs	affairs of a great nation, Burnett, *Letters*, VII, 344 (20 Oct. 1783)
51. put a period to	put to, *ibid.*, VII, 344 (20 Oct. 1783)
52. real situation	real State, *ibid.*, VII, 235 (26 July 1783)
53. regular . . . mode	regular Method, NA: PCC, No. 78; XVIII, 267 (24 Feb. 1779)
54. render them superior	render them incapable, *ibid.*, No. 147, VI, 289 (8 Mar. 1781)
55. rights of mankind	affairs of mankind, Burnett, *Letters*, VII, 224 (15 July 1783)
56. sad prognostic	prognostics, *ibid.*, VII, 345 (20 Oct. 1783)
57. secret intentions	in their nature deemed secret, *JCC*, XXIII, 829 (23 Dec. 1782)
58. seeds of disunion	disunion and anarchy, speech of 1816, p. 23
59. set an example	in precept and example, *ibid.*, p. 9
60. solemn assertions	solemn manner, *JCC*, XXIII, 829 (23 Dec. 1782)
61. solid systems	solid systems, Peters to JM (24 Aug. 1789) in LC: Madison Papers; solid principles, Burnett, *Letters*, VII, 225 (15 July 1783)

Expressions in "The North-American"	*Nearest corresponding expressions, if any, in Richard Peters' writings*
62. splendid rising	rose with so much splendor, Burnett, *Letters,* VII, 343 (20 Oct. 1783)
63. stamped his character	Stamps a Value upon my Services, NA: PCC, No. 78, XVIII, 473 (21 Dec. 1781)
64. superior . . . advantages	superior advantages, speech of 1816, p. 23
65. to the ends of	to the end that, *JCC,* XXV, 747 (24 Oct. 1783)
66. tottering beam	tottering Union, Burnett, *Letters,* VII, 225 (15 July 1783)
67. true Whigs	
68. unbounded commerce	
69. under these circumstances	under these circumstances, NA: PCC, No. 147, IV, 267 (23 Mar. 1780)
70. unequal load	unequal steps, Burnett, *Letters,* VI, 375 (16 Nov. 1783)
71. unhappy circumstances	disagreeable Circumstances, NA: PCC, No. 148, I, 389 (30 May 1781)
72. unliquidated Accounts	liquidate the accounts, *JCC,* XXIV, 154, n. 1 (28 Feb. 1783)
73. varying interests	varying Success, NA: PCC, No. 147, VI, 304 (15 Mar. 1781)
74. vigor and enterprise	vigor and welfare, speech of 1816, p. 5
75. voice of truth	
76. votaries of despotism	ruthless despotism, speech of 1816, p. 10
77. want of	want of, Burnett, *Letters,* VII, 224 (15 July 1783)
78. western wilds	unsubdued wastes, speech of 1816, p. 20
79. wisdom and decision	Consideration and Wisdom, NA: PCC, No. 148, I, 389 (30 May 1781)
80. without enthusiasm	damp the enthusiasm, Burnett, *Letters,* VI, 344 (20 Oct. 1783)

Of the eighty expressions taken from the essays, Peters also used eleven, came close to using fifty-eight others, and seemingly did not use the remaining eleven with sufficient exactness to be counted. His score is a little higher than JM's in the same test. It is noteworthy that of the sixty-nine phrases of Peters which were the same or nearly the same as those of the essays, twenty-nine were found in his writings of the year 1783, when the anonymous articles appeared, and fourteen others in his speech of 1816—a production similar in its oratorical flavor to that of the articles. Peters' brief letter of 15 July 1783, written at the presumed time of the composition of "North-American, No. 1," includes ten phrases identical with or similar to phrases in that essay or its sequel. The twenty-eight papers of JM dating between 1 July and 30 September 1783 include only four of the same relevance. This fact of itself appears to warrant the conclusion that, insofar as this test of phrases is concerned, Peters rather than JM was probably the "North-American."[86]

Other characteristic aspects of Peters' style of writing, grammar, and spelling reinforce this judgment. The anonymous essayist adorned his paragraphs with many single words, metaphors, or similes taken from the phenomena of nature or from the physical and mental attributes of man. Although these are too numerous to list in their entirety, a representative list follows: "clear as the light," "clouded up the prospect," "fertile sources," "firm ground of power," "glittering shadow," "mists of envy," "seeds of disunion," "blush of indignant shame," "dreams and phantoms," "eye of posterity," "fastidious eye," "feeling mind," "infant fortunes," "a thorn in their side," and "throb of a pulse."[87] Samples of corresponding expressions by Peters, who resorted to phrases reflecting the same two sources much more often than JM, are "be at Sea again," "dawnings of education," "dreary deserts," "gloomy wastes," "open a wide field," "path . . . yet less thorny," "Political Comet," "reap any fruits," "childish Reasons," "conciliate their affections," "deranged situation," "eaten up with spleen," "frittered away to the phantom," "my gall overflows," and "wishes of my heart."[88] Although JM almost never used the antiquated form of the perfect tense, the "North-American" wrote "have ever went hand in hand," "on a sudden has arose," and "could only have sprang." Peters likewise sprinkled his prose with "was broke up," "had broke," "has wrote," and "should have wrote."[89] In contrast with JM, Peters and the essayist always wrote "burthen" instead of "burden," "alledge" instead of "allege," and "farther" when "further" was meant.[90]

To remove all doubt about the identity of the "North-American" obviously would require the discovery of the original manuscript of the articles written in a recognizable hand, a signed statement by the author that the pseudonym was his, or testimony, preferably dating in 1783, of trustworthy contemporaries of the author to that effect. Although no single type of evidence presented in the above paragraphs is determinative of the issue, the combination of all of them, unless shown to fit someone or some persons besides Richard Peters equally well or better, justifies the conclusion that he far more likely than JM was the anonymous essayist.

[1] Burnett, *Letters*, VII, 315, n. 3.

[2] Brant, *Madison*, II, 302–5, 453, nn. 35–37; Brant, ed., "Two Neglected Madison Letters," *William and Mary Quarterly*, 3d ser., III (1946), 569–87; Brant, "Madison, the 'North American,' on Federal Power," *American Historical Review*, LX (1954–55), 45–54; Brant, *The Fourth President: A Life of James Madison* (Indianapolis and New York, 1970), pp. 113–15. For economy in citations, these periodicals will be referred to hereafter in this editorial note as *WMQ*, 3d ser., III; *AHR*, LX.

3 Boyd, *Papers of Jefferson*, VI, 342, n.; letter from Julian P. Boyd, 4 Mar. 1970.

4 *WMQ*, 3d ser., III, 580.

5 *WMQ*, 3d ser., III, 573, 574.

6 *WMQ*, 3d ser., III, 574–76, 577–79.

7 *WMQ*, 3d ser., III, 577.

8 *WMQ*, 3d ser., III, 571, 572.

9 *WMQ*, 3d ser., III, 580–81.

10 *WMQ*, 3d ser., III, 581.

11 *WMQ*, 3d ser., III, 580, 581–83.

12 *WMQ*, 3d ser., III, 585–86.

13 *WMQ*, 3d ser., III, 587.

14 *WMQ*, 3d ser., III, 572, 573, 574, 579, 580, 581; *AHR*, LX, 45; *Papers of Madison*, VI, 16; 144–45; 320, n. 7; 327; 402; 429; 488–89; JM to Randolph, 20 May; Jefferson to JM, 17 June 1783, and n. 6; 20 Feb. 1784, and n. 43.

15 Brant, *Madison*, II, 303–4; *WMQ*, 3d ser., III, 579, 581–82, 583, 587; *AHR*, LX, 45; Brant, *The Fourth President*, p. 113; *Papers of Madison*, V, 289; 331; VI, 55; 147; 156; 481; 489; Jefferson to JM, 7 May; JM to Randolph, 20 May; 27 May; 18 Aug.; 13 Sept. 1783.

16 *WMQ*, 3d ser., III, 574; *Papers of Madison*, VI, 55–56; 147; 156; 311–14; 483; 487–94; JM to Randolph, 20 May; 27 May; 24 June; 12 Aug., and n. 6; to Jefferson, 11 Aug. 1783, and n. 14.

17 *WMQ*, 3d ser., III, 575, 577, 579; *Papers of Madison*, VI, 145; 260; 286–87; 294, n. 17; 298; 310; 313; 401–2; 440; 447; 478, n. 1; Jefferson to JM, 7 May, and n. 3; JM to Jefferson, 20 May, and n. 5; to Randolph, 20 May; 27 May; 17 June; 13 Sept. 1783.

18 *WMQ*, 3d ser., III, 574–77, 580; Brant, *The Fourth President*, p. 114; *Papers of Madison*, VI, 20–21; 31; 39; 146; 286; 442; 443, n. 1; 445, n. 10; 493; JM to Jefferson, 11 Aug.; to Randolph, 12 Aug.; 18 Aug., and nn. 7, 8; 8 Sept.; to Pendleton, 8 Sept., and n. 6; Memorial of Massachusetts General Court, 19 Sept. 1783, and ed. n., n. 4.

19 *WMQ*, 3d ser., III, 570, 571, 580, 586; *Papers of Madison*, V, 441; VI, 24–25; 31; 56, n. 8; 355; 364–65; 369, n. 38; 493; JM Notes, 23 May, n. 1; JM to Jefferson, 10 June, n. 3; Delegates to Harrison, 1 Aug. 1783, n. 1.

20 *WMQ*, 3d ser., III, 577, 581–82, 583, 584–85; Brant, *The Fourth President*, p. 115; *Papers of Madison*, VI, 37; 156; 288; 289; 337, n. 11; JM to Randolph, 20 May; 10 June; 24 Aug.; 30 Aug., and nn. 2, 3; 13 Sept., and n. 5; JM Notes, 30 May, and n. 3; JM to Jefferson, 11 Aug. 1783, and n. 8.

21 Brant, *Madison*, II, 302, 303; *WMQ*, 3d ser., III, 576, 577–78; *AHR*, LX, 49–51; Brant, *The Fourth President*, pp. 113, 114; *Papers of Madison*, VI, 290, and n.; 296, n. 40; 312–13; 400–401; 403, nn. 11, 12; 442; 481; 491; 502; 503, nn. 5, 6; JM to Jefferson, 20 May, and nn. 2, 8; JM to Randolph, 10 June, and n. 16; JM Notes, 10 June; 20 June 1783, and n. 10.

22 Clarence S. Brigham, *History and Bibliography of American Newspapers, 1690–1800* (2 vols.; Cambridge, Mass., 1947), II, 937–38, 1381; *Papers of Madison*, I, 73, and n. 1.

23 In this and the subsequent listings in the present editorial note, all words which have the same base are grouped together and regarded as the same word in counting the frequency of its occurrence either in the essays or in JM's writings of 1783. Thus, "just," "justice," "justly," "justify," "justifiable," "unjust," "injustice," and "unjustifiable" are considered to be eight usages of the root word "just."

24 The routine nature of the other words among the thirty-eight seems to justify omitting mention of each of them. To cite JM's particular letter or other paper in which those words and those in the next paragraph appear would obviously require a prohibitively long footnote.

[25] *Papers of Madison,* VI, 487–94; 494, n. 5; Delegates to Harrison, 6 May, and n. 3; JM to Jefferson, 13 May, and n. 11; JM to James Madison, Sr., 5 June 1783, and nn. 3, 4.

[26] Brant, *Madison,* II, 303; *WMQ,* 3d ser., III, 570, 580; *AHR,* LX, 51; Brant, *The Fourth President,* p. 114.

[27] *AHR,* LX, 46; JM to Jefferson, 13 May, and n. 11; 20 May; to Randolph, 13 May; 20 May; Randolph to JM, 24 May; Rev. James Madison to JM, 27 Aug. 1783.

[28] *Papers of Madison,* VI, 147; 152, n. 32; 156.

[29] JM to Randolph, 3 June, and citations in n. 4; Jones to JM, 8 June, n. 11; 28 July, and n. 4; Jefferson to JM, 31 Aug.; Pendleton to JM, 20 Oct. 1783, and n. 3.

[30] *Papers of Madison,* V, 232–33; *WMQ,* 3d ser., III, 569, 572; *AHR,* LX, 47. In a letter to Noah Webster on 12 Oct. 1804, JM wrote: "I have often had it in idea to make out from the materials in my hands, & within my reach, as minute a chronicle as I could of the origin & progress of the last Revolution in our Govt. I went thro' such a task with respect to the declaration of Independence & the old Confederation, whilst a member of Congress in 1783; availing myself of all the circumstances to be gleaned from the public archives, & from some auxiliary sources" (LC: Rives Collection of Madison Papers; also in Madison, *Writings* [Hunt ed.], VII, 167). The evidence of "such a task" may be the documents copied by JM on 106 pages of an undated notebook (LC: Madison Miscellany).

[31] "The North-American, No. 2," which reflects a reading of Sheffield's pamphlet mentioned above, could not have been written before August 1783, for the pamphlet first became available to Americans in Philadelphia during that month (JM to Randolph, 30 Aug. 1783, and n. 2).

[32] *WMQ,* 3d ser., III, 582–83.

[33] Brant, *Madison,* II, 302; *WMQ,* 3d ser., III, 569; *AHR,* LX, 53; *Papers of Madison,* I, 61–65; Madison, *Writings* (Hunt ed.), VI, 120–23.

[34] To cite all the instances in the earlier writings of JM when he used one or another of these words would require a footnote of exorbitant length.

[35] *WMQ,* 3d ser., III, 579, 586.

[36] *WMQ,* 3d ser., III, 576.

[37] *WMQ,* 3d ser., III, 580.

[38] *AHR,* LX, 45, 50; *WMQ,* 3d ser., III, 569.

[39] *WMQ,* 3d ser., III, 575; *Papers of Madison,* VI, 143; 151, n. 12; 277, n. 28; Livingston to JM, 19 July 1783, n. 6.

[40] *WMQ,* 3d ser., III, 572, 573, 574, 577, 578, 579, 581–82, 584, 585, 586, 587. The "North-American" was not explicit about the channel through which the "one generous effort" to make a central government "adequate to the ends of society" should be exerted (p. 572). If he had in mind a constitutional convention, he agreed with Hamilton but not with JM (*Papers of Madison,* VI, 425; 426, n. 7).

[41] *WMQ,* 3d ser., III, 569; *AHR,* LX, 45; *Papers of Madison,* III, 17–19; 19, n. 5; 71–72; IV, 21, n. 7; 23; 39; 40, n. 9; 87; 299, n. 10; 411; V, 42; 83; 84, n. 6; 415; 416, n. 3; VI, 118; 123, n. 4; 265 n.; 268, n. 11; 270–72; 274, n. 4; 277, n. 28; 314, n. 1; Alexander Hamilton, James Madison, John Jay, *The Federalist Papers* (ed. Clinton Rossiter; New York, 1961), pp. 227, 243–46, 255–300, *passim.*

[42] *WMQ,* 3d ser., III, 574–75; *Papers of Madison,* V, 293–94; 294, n. 1; 362–63; 366, n. 23.

[43] *WMQ,* 3d ser., III, 577; *Papers of Madison,* VI, 481, and nn. 10, 11; JM to Randolph, 10 June; to Jefferson, 20 Sept. 1783, and n. 3.

[44] *WMQ,* 3d ser., III, 578–79; *Papers of Madison,* V, 56–57; 69; VI, 246, n. 7; 272 n.; 287.

[45] *WMQ,* 3d ser., III, 570; Brant, *Madison,* II, 303; *AHR,* LX, 51; Brant, *The Fourth President,* p. 114; *Papers of Madison,* V, 69; 115–16; 118, nn. 15–17; 119,

nn. 19, 20; 292, n. 19; VI, 290, and n.; 296, n. 40; 310; 312–13; 491; JM to Jefferson, 20 May, and n. 8; 20 Sept., and n. 3; to Randolph, 10 June 1783.

[46] *WMQ*, 3d ser., III, 579; *Papers of Madison*, II, 74–76; V, 127; 289; 375, n. 15; VI, 131, n. 7; 291, n.; 295, n. 24; JM to Randolph, 27 May, and citations in n. 5; 18 Aug. 1783.

[47] *WMQ*, 3d ser., III, 579; *Papers of Madison*, VI, 471; 472, n. 4.

[48] *WMQ*, 3d ser., III, 571–72; *Papers of Madison*, I, 50; 101; 105; 106; 112; 114–15; 120–21; 135.

[49] *WMQ*, 3d ser., III, 579–80, 582–83, 586–87; *Papers of Madison*, IV, 370; 391; V, 126–27; 448; 450, n. 5; VI, 31; 56, n. 8; 130, n. 1; 157; 364–65; 391–92; 436; 493; JM to Randolph, 30 Aug.; 20 Sept.; to Jefferson, 20 Sept. 1783.

[50] *WMQ*, 3d ser., III, 575; JM to Jefferson, 17 July; 11 Aug.; JM to Randolph, 21 July; 28 July; 5 Aug.; 12 Aug.; 30 Aug.; 8 Sept. 1783.

[51] *WMQ*, 3d ser., III, 572–73, 577, 581, 583; *Papers of Madison*, VI, 425; 426, n. 9.

[52] *WMQ*, 3d ser., III, 577, 583.

[53] *WMQ*, 3d ser., III, 586, 587.

[54] Burnett, *Letters*, VII, 315, n. 3.

[55] *AHR*, LX, 47.

[56] *WMQ*, 3d ser., III, 572, 581.

[57] *WMQ*, 3d ser., III, 571–72.

[58] *WMQ*, 3d ser., III, 574–76, 577.

[59] *WMQ*, 3d ser., III, 577, 578, 579, 581–82, 583.

[60] *WMQ*, 3d ser., III, 579–80, 586.

[61] *WMQ*, 3d ser., III, 585–86.

[62] *WMQ*, 3d ser., III, 577, 583.

[63] *WMQ*, 3d ser., III, 573, 574, 577, 578, 587.

[64] *WMQ*, 3d ser., III, 580.

[65] Letter from Nicholas B. Wainright, 7 Apr. 1970.

[66] *WMQ*, 3d ser., III, 571–72; *Papers of Madison*, I, 50; 97, and n. 8; 101; 105; 106; 107, n. 4; 112–13; 114–15; articles on the Reverend Richard Peters and Richard Peters in the *Dictionary of American Biography*, Vol. XIV; Thomas P. Abernethy, *Western Lands and the American Revolution*, pp. 18, 36–37, 42; Solon J. Buck and Elizabeth H. Buck, *The Planting of Civilization in Western Pennsylvania* (Pittsburgh, 1939), pp. 54, 137.

[67] Brant, *Madison*, II, 302; Brant, *The Fourth President*, p. 113; Clarence S. Brigham, *History and Bibliography of American Newspapers*, II, 937–38; *Papers of Madison*, IV, 326–30; indexes of *ibid.*, IV, V, and VI, under *Pennsylvania Packet*.

[68] *WMQ*, 3d ser., III, 576; *JCC*, V, 438, 526; VI, 1033; IX, 959, 971; XI, 555; XVII, 747; XXI, 1172–73; Burnett, *Letters*, VI, 216, 217, n. 6, 487, n. 3; VII, 156–57; Fitzpatrick, *Writings of Washington*, VIII, 248; XXIII, 14, n. 28, 28, and n. 48; *Papers of Madison*, VI, 266; 269, n. 15; Samuel Breck, "Eulogy of Richard Peters," 20 Sept. 1828, in Samuel Hazard, ed., *The Register of Pennsylvania . . .*, II (Philadelphia, 1829), 251–56.

[69] Peters to JM, 31 Dec. 1807 (LC: Rives Collection, Madison Papers); Boyd, *Papers of Jefferson*, II, 236, 270; IX, 350, 351 n.; XI, 182–83; *Papers of Madison*, III, 270, n. 2; 306; 307, n. 4; V, 295; 299; 417, n. 8; VI, 265; 453; 458, n. 2; Harrison to Delegates, 12 July 1783, and n. 3; *JCC*, XXIII, 726, 748, n. 3, 751, 798, n. 1, 819, n. 1, 822, 851; XXIV, 93, 153, 160, 185, n. 1, 265–66, n. 1, 268, 269, 283, 428, n. 1, 444, n. 1, 603, 787.

[70] *Papers of Madison*, V, 276, n. 4; VI, 4, n. 4; 132, n. 1; 396.

[71] Notes on Place of Residence, 14 Oct. 1783, ed. n.; Burnett, *Letters*, VII, 494.

[72] *JCC*, XXI, 748, n. 3, 751, 798, n. 1, 819, n. 1; XXIII, 93, 160, 185, 265, 268, 428; XXIV, 958, 977. Although to cite each tallied poll separately would require too long a footnote, see *JCC*, XXIII, XXIV, XXV, *passim*.

73 Burnett, *Letters,* VII, 224, 344; *JCC,* XXIV, 135, 525; XXV, 622.

74 JM Notes, 10 June 1783, nn. 9, 10; *JCC,* XXIV, 256–57, 407; XXV, 642–44.

75 Burnett, *Letters,* VII, 224; *JCC,* XXIV, 39–41, 478, 481.

76 *WMQ,* 3d ser., III, 572, 573–74, 577, 578. 581–82, 587.

77 *Papers of Madison,* V, 56–57; VI, 312–13; 327; 400–401; 441, n. 6; 491; *JCC,* XXIV, 256–57, 406–7; XXV, 552, 559–64.

78 *Papers of Madison,* VI, 291–92; 313; 327; 400; *JCC,* XXIV, 162–63; Burnett, *Letters,* VII, 225.

79 *Papers of Madison,* VI, 467–69; *JCC,* XXIV, 255–56, 256, n. 1.

80 *Papers of Madison,* VI, 16; 286; JM to Randolph, 27 May 1783; Burnett, *Letters,* VII, 344.

81 *WMQ,* 3d ser., III, 569, 573, n. 7; Burnett, *Letters,* VII, 217, 233–34, 344–45; JM to Jefferson, 17 July; 11 Aug.; 20 Sept.; to Randolph, 28 July; 5 Aug.; 30 Aug. 1783.

82 Burnett, *Letters,* VII, 225, 344; JM to Jefferson, 10 June; 20 Sept.; to Randolph, 18 Aug.; 30 Aug.; 8 Sept.; 13 Sept.; 20 Sept. 1783.

83 *WMQ,* 3d ser., III, 574–75, 577–78, 580, 582–83, 585–87.

84 *WMQ,* 3d ser., III, 580; Burnett, *Letters,* VII, lxxiv, 343, 345.

85 To give a specific citation for each of these four hundred items would obviously require an insufferably long footnote. Published or unpublished, they are in NA: PCC, No. 78, Vol. XVIII; No. 147, Vols. I–VI; No. 148, Vols. I and II; LC: Madison Papers, and Rives Collection of Madison Papers; *JCC,* Vols. XXI, XXIII–XXV; *Papers of Madison,* Vols. III and VI; Burnett, *Letters,* Vols. III, VI, and VII; *Pa. Mag. of Hist. and Biog.,* Vols. XII, XIII, XVI, XVII, XX, XXII, XXIII, XXIV, XXVI, XXXII, XL; Franklin Knight, ed., *Letters on Agriculture from His Excellency, George Washington . . . to Arthur Young . . . and Sir John Sinclair . . .* (Washington, 1847), pp. 84–87, 104–12; Richard Peters, *Agricultural Enquiries on Plaister of Paris . . . Published as Much with a View to Invite, as to Give Information* (Philadelphia, 1797); Francis Wharton, ed., *State Trials of the United States during the Administrations of Washington and Adams . . .* (Philadelphia, 1849), pp. 91, 171, 187–88, 198, 535, 584–609, *passim,* 679; Richard Peters, Jr., ed., *Admiralty Decisions in the District Court of the United States, for the Pennsylvania District, by the Hon. Richard Peters* (2 vols.; Philadelphia, 1807), *passim;* William Cranch, ed., *Reports of Cases Argued and Adjudged in the Supreme Court of the United States . . . ,* V (1809), 116–26; Richard Peters, *A Discourse on Agriculture, Its Antiquity, and Importance to Every Member of the Community . . .* (Philadelphia, 1816), pp. 5–37; Samuel Breck, "Eulogy of Richard Peters," in Samuel Hazard, ed., *Register of Pennsylvania,* II, 251–56.

86 Burnett, *Letters,* VII, 224–25. In this comparison of phrases, the weight to be given to two circumstances cannot be known. Unless clearly recording a part of his own remarks, a phrase in JM's "Notes on Debates" may have been quoted by him from what another delegate said. In contrary fashion, whenever Peters in his own writings quoted from the "Address to the States," for example, he borrowed the phrase from JM. It has to be assumed that these two possibilities cancel each other out.

87 *WMQ,* 3d ser., III, 572, 576, 577, 580, 581, 582, 583, 584, 585.

88 NA: PCC, No. 147, VI, 13, 305; Burnett, *Letters,* VII, 225, 233, 344, 345; *JCC,* XXI, 1173; *Pa. Mag. Hist. and Biog.,* XVIII, 120–21; speech of 1816, pp. 7, 10, 14, 17.

89 *WMQ,* 3d ser., III, 579, 585, 586; NA: PCC, No. 147, II, 481; VI, 259; Burnett, *Letters,* VII, 79, 235; *Pa. Mag. Hist. and Biog.,* VII, 108.

90 *WMQ,* 3d ser., III, 575, 576, 578, 586; NA: PCC, No. 147, IV, 741, 59 (at end of reel); V, 9; VI, 13; No. 148, I, 357, 389, 425; *Pa. Mag. Hist. and Biog.,* XXVI, 72; speech of 1816, pp. 21, 22.

Report on Memorial of Massachusetts General Court

MS (NA: PCC, No. 20, I, 155–56).

EDITORIAL NOTE

In a memorial of 11 July to Congress, the General Court of Massachusetts justified its refusal to sanction the impost proposed in the Plan for Restoring Public Credit by protesting against the high salaries paid to Congress' too numerous civil officials and the full pay promised to officers of the continental army for five years. This latter was "more than an adequate reward for their Services and, inconsistent with that Equality which ought to subsist among citizens of free and Republican states." The memorial also emphasized that those measures, besides violating "the spirit and general Design of the Confederation," were so contrary to the ideals of "Frugality and Virtue," inherited by citizens of Massachusetts from "their Ancestry," as to produce "the greatest Concern and uneasiness, and involve the Legislature thereof in no small Embarrassments" (NA: PCC, No. 65, II, 185–88; *JCC*, XXV, 607–8). For comments by JM on this unrest, for the receipt by Congress of the memorial, and for its referral to successive committees, see Pendleton to JM, 21 July, n. 6; JM to Randolph, 21 July, and n. 5; 12 Aug.; 18 Aug., and n. 8; 8 Sept., and n. 8; to Jefferson, 11 Aug., and n. 19; to Pendleton, 8 Sept. 1783, and n. 6.

On 2 September a report on the memorial was submitted by a committee of which James Duane was chairman. Six days later Samuel Huntington, chairman of a new committee, submitted "the first part" of a revised report, dealing only with the issue of the civil officials' salaries. Gaillard Hunt inserted that "part" in the journal of Congress under the date of 16 September, when consideration was resumed (*JCC*, XXV, 571–73). On 17 September 1783 Congress recommitted the Huntington report to a third committee, with Duane again chairman (*JCC*, XXV, 572, n. 1). Thereby and thereafter, the "civil-list" issue, precipitated by the memorial, was usually separated from the issue of the army officers' full pay for five years (NA: PCC, No. 186, fol. 125; *JCC*, XXIV, 483, n. 2; XXV, 571–74, 572, n. 1, 577, 584, 623–25, 625, n. 1; XXVII, 405; Burnett, *Letters*, VII, 296).

On 18 September Congress appointed a committee, composed of JM, chairman, John Francis Mercer, and James Duane, to reconsider the portion of the original Duane committee's report of 2 September dealing with the Massachusetts memorial's protest against the pledge of full pay for five years (*JCC*, XXIV, 483, n. 2; XXV, 582–85, 584, n. 1). Although the report of the Madison committee, submitted on 19 September, is two paragraphs longer than that of the Duane committee, this difference arises mainly from the division of some of the paragraphs in the latter report and the elaboration of the contents rather than from marked changes in the conclusions or in the arguments sustaining them. The first and third paragraphs of the Madison committee's report and the first and second paragraphs of its predecessor are almost identical; the last two paragraphs of both reports, dealing briefly with the civil-list issue, are entirely so (*JCC*, XXV, 582–84, 609–12).

The only manuscript of the Madison committee's report known to exist is a fair copy made by a clerk after Congress had adopted the amended report on 25 September 1783. For this reason, the clerk's copy provides no clue to the identification of the member or members of the committee who drafted one or another portion of that report (NA: PCC, No. 20, fols. 147–48). Filed with the manuscript, however, are two folios in JM's hand, reproduced below, three in Mercer's hand, and three almost entirely in that of Duane (NA: PCC, No. 20, fols. 149–53, 155, 156, 159). The last three are a rough copy of the portions of the Duane committee's report which were incorporated virtually unchanged in that of the Madison committee. Taken together, these eight folios reveal at least most of the contribution by each member of the committee.

[19 September 1783]

The Come. to whom was referred the Report on the Memorial of the Massts. Legislature recommend the following alterations[1]

1st. To prefix to the 2d paragraph these words viz. "That without dwelling on the reasonableness & justice of a provision in favor of those whose former professions pursuits and prospects have in a long course of military service given place to habits & acquirements which on the return of peace, however honorable they may be to the possessor, cease to be a source of profit to him; or urging the example of other nations who have considered such provision as indispensable since war is become a Science & is carried on by regular armies"[2]

2d. after "*Yet*" in line 7 of ¶ 2d.[3] to insert "It is to be considered that the diversity of sentiments and circumstances among the Constituents of Congress must often render partial disapprobations an inevitable consequence of measures which in a collective view have the most salutary tendency, and that[4]

[1] That is, in the report of the Duane committee (*JCC*, XXV, 582–84).

[2] The words beginning with "or urging" and ending with "regular armies" were deleted, evidently in a session of the committee; but with or without this deletion, the words closing with "viz." at the outset of the paragraph mean that the portion of it enclosed in quotation marks was intended to be joined to the "2d paragraph" of the Duane committee's report. In the journal, however, Charles Thomson, secretary of Congress, indented both prefix and paragraph, thus conveying the appearance of two separate paragraphs (*JCC*, XXV, 585, 609).

[3] JM should have written "after '*Yet*' in line 7 of ¶ 3d" rather than "2d." of the manuscript of the Duane committee report (NA: PCC, No. 20, fol. 149). As printed in the journal, the reference becomes line 9 of the fourth indentation, or if a paragraph be accepted in the sense of writing that must end with a completed sentence, the reference is to line 9 of the third paragraph.

[4] In the manuscript a crosshatch, probably exemplifying a decision reached within the committee, cancels JM's suggestion. Besides including JM's first addendum, the Madison committee chiefly altered the Duane committee's report by

inserting between its third and fourth paragraphs three others drafted by Mercer (NA: PCC, No. 20, fols. 151–53).

On 19 September, following the submission of the Madison committee's report to Congress, David Howell, seconded by Silas Condict, moved to strike "constitutionally and" from the passage in the third from last paragraph of the report reading: "yet as it [the commutation] is not now under the arbitration of Congress, but an act constitutionally and finally adopted." An effort to prevent the deletion of these two words was defeated by a tallied vote showing that their retention was desired by only five of the nine states effectively represented in Congress (*JCC*, XXV, 586–87, 612). The clerk's copy of the Madison committee's report omits "constitutionally and" and all other cancellations in the report as submitted to Congress or made necessary by amendments in Congress. For this reason there is no doubt that the clerk's copy was prepared on or after 25 September. See ed. n. On that day, probably after further amending the report, Congress adopted it by a vote of seven to two (Rhode Island and New Jersey). Maryland, having only one delegate present, cast an ineffective "ay" vote. New Hampshire and Massachusetts, also underrepresented, each cast an ineffective "no" vote (*JCC*, XXV, 613; Burnett, *Letters*, VII, 316–17).

The adoption of the report failed to quiet the opposition of Massachusetts, Rhode Island, and Connecticut. Despite the favorable vote of the Connecticut delegates, a protest from the House of Representatives of that state obliged Congress to appoint another committee and consider another report similar in tenor to that of the Madison committee (*JCC*, XXV, 786; XXVI, 100–103, 135, 265–69; XXVII, 397, 404; Burnett, *Letters*, VII, 462, 473, 480, 513, 518).

Benjamin Harrison to Virginia Delegates

FC (Virginia State Library). Addressed to "The Honorable Virginia Delegates in Congress." In the hand of Samuel Patteson.

Council Chamber September 19th. 1783.

Gentlemen,

Yesterday's post brought me none of your favors.[1]

I have nothing to communicate to you but that my advices from our north western frontiers tell me that if the Pennsylvanians continue their settlements on the other side of Ohio a general indian war is to be apprehended which I am sure we are unable to engage in at present, and yet we must take part in it or suffer the depopulation of our Country. how this imprudent step is to be corrected I know not.[2] is there no where a power lodged to prevent any State's acting as they please notwithstanding they may injure their neighbors in ever so great a degree.[3]

The Ship Cormorant is much injured by the length of time that has elapsed since the Commissioners offered her to Congress. if no answer comes shortly she will be sold[4]

I am &.

B. H.

1 In his letter of 26 September to the delegates (*q.v.*), Governor Harrison acknowledged the receipt of their letters of 8 (*q.v.*) and 13 September. The latter has not been found.

2 Delegates to Harrison, 8 Sept., and nn. 2–4; Harrison to Delegates, 13 Sept., and n. 4; 26 Sept., and n. 4. On 3 October the Virginia delegates laid most of the second paragraph of the present letter before Congress (Delegates to Harrison, 4 Oct. 1783, and n. 1).

3 On 20 September Congress rejected the report of a committee which had considered a request of the Pennsylvania General Assembly. The rejected report declared that "Congress have no objection to a conference being held on behalf of the State of Pensylvania, with the Indians on their borders, respecting a purchase to be made by and at the expence of the said State, of lands within the limits thereof," provided that Pennsylvania give Virginia and New York the option of sending commissioners to the conference, and also provided that Pennsylvania at the conference refrain from entrenching upon the power solely vested in Congress to make all "engagements relative to peace or war with the said Indians." Having unanimously opposed three amendments unsuccessfully offered, the whole Virginia delegation (JM, Jones, and Mercer) joined to endorse the report as it stood (*JCC*, XXV, 591–96). They thereby supported Harrison's express desire that peace be maintained and at the same time yielded nothing in respect to Virginia's claim to the lands north and west of the Ohio River, that claim not being a point at issue.

On 28 August Congress elected a grand committee to consider a committee's draft of an "Ordinance prohibiting the settlement and purchase of certain lands," submitted on 13 August. The grand committee's report, in the form of a proclamation written by James McHenry, was laid before Congress on 1 September and adopted, apparently without debate, three weeks later (NA: PCC, No. 186, fol. 120; *JCC*, XXIV, 505–6, 506, n. 1, 528; XXV, 602, and n. 1). Citing the ninth article of the Articles of Confederation as its warrant, Congress barred "all persons from making settlements on lands inhabited or claimed by Indians, without the limits or jurisdiction of any particular State, and from purchasing or receiving any gift or cession of such lands or claims without the express authority" of Congress. The proclamation further declared that "every such purchase or settlement, gift or cession, not having the authority aforesaid, is null and void." See also *JCC*, XXV, 680–95. Thus, not without a touch of irony, Congress adopted in part a policy set forth by Great Britain in the Proclamation of 1763, for which see *Papers of Madison*, IV, 8; 14, nn. 9–10. As Consul W. Butterfield remarked: "No attention whatever was paid to this proclamation. The consequence was that the settlements increased continually–so rapidly indeed that in less than two years the United States found it necessary to drive off the settlers by force" (Butterfield, ed., *Washington-Irvine Correspondence*, pp. 196–97, n. 2).

4 Instruction to Delegates *in re* "Cormorant," 26–27 June, and ed. n., nn. 2–3; Delegates to Harrison, 4 Oct. 1783, and n. 6. On the date of the present letter, Harrison wrote to the Virginia commissioners "for protecting the trade of Chesapeake Bay," assuring them of their authority to dispose of the "british-built" ship to anyone offering a fair price. Along with the schooner "Harrison," the "Cormorant" appears to have been sold at auction in Norfolk on 20 October. In a letter of 6 November Harrison directed the Bay commissioners to deliver to Commodore James Barron, Sr., the two state-owned slaves who had been aboard the "Cormorant" (Executive Letter Book, 1783–1786, pp. 199, 228, MS in Va. State Library; *Va. Gazette*, 11 and 18 Oct. 1783; Robert Armistead Stewart, *The History of Virginia's Navy of the Revolution* [Richmond, 1934], p. 127).

Virginia Delegates to Benjamin Harrison

Printed text (Burnett, *Letters,* VII, 301, and n. 1). Probably written by John Francis Mercer, who signed it, and possibly also signed by Joseph Jones and JM. The original manuscript has not been found, although about 1930 it was among the Executive Papers in the Virginia State Library.

PRINCETON 20th Sept. 1783

SIR,

We refer to a letter subscribed by Mr. Jones the last week to shew the disposition of the British nation with respect to our commerce.[1] altho' we are not informed what is the ultimate determination of France on this Subject, there is reason to apprehend, some indulgences excepted, a policy will be adopted by that nation similar to that of Britain.[2] It hath been communicated to Congress by the minister of his most christian Majesty here, that l'Orient hath been declared a free port for the benefit of the U. States[3] the determination of Congress on the cession of Virga. will soon be officially transmitted.[4]

[1] Delegates to Harrison, 13 Sept. 1783, ed. n. On that day, even though all the Virginia delegates attended Congress, their letter to the governor was signed only by Joseph Jones (*JCC,* XXV, 559).

[2] JM to Randolph, 30 Aug. 1783, and n. 3.

[3] At the request of the Chevalier de La Luzerne, the minister of Louis XVI of France to the United States, Congress appointed a committee on 18 September to receive La Luzerne's "communications." The next day James Duane, chairman of the committee, closed its written report by stating "That the Court had in view the Commerce of the United States, and had ordered a diminution of the duty on the Salt and that the same regulation would take place with respect to Brandy. That his Majesty had declared L'Orient a Free Port, because it is the Port which the Americans have preferred to any other." Congress referred the entire report, which mainly explained how the premature reopening of trade by Americans with Great Britain was retarding a simultaneous conclusion of the definitive treaties of peace between that country and the United States, France, Spain, and the Netherlands, to a committee composed of Samuel Huntington, chairman, Duane, and JM (*JCC,* XXV, 588–89, 589, n. 1; JM to Jefferson, 20 Sept. 1783, and n. 13; Burnett, *Letters,* VII, 303).

[4] President Elias Boudinot or Charles Thomson, secretary of Congress, probably never "officially transmitted" a copy of the resolutions of Congress on 13 September concerning the cession by Virginia (Delegates to Harrison, 13 Sept. 1783, ed. n.). With a letter on 11 December 1783 to the speaker of the House of Delegates of the Virginia General Assembly, Harrison enclosed "a copy of the proceedings in Congress on the cession offered by this State which this moment came to hand in a blank cover from Mr. Mercer" (Executive Letter Book, 1783–1786, p. 243, MS in Va. State Library). Apparently among the two or more enclosures was the copy in the hand of George Bond, "Depy Secy." of Congress, docketed, "(A) Observations of Congress on the proposed cessions of the N. Western Territory, by the State of Virginia" (MS in Va. State Library).

To Thomas Jefferson

RC (LC: Madison Papers). Cover missing. Many years later, after the return of the letter to him, JM wrote "Sepr. 20. 1783" at the top of the last page.

PRINCETON Sepr. 20. 1783.

DEAR SIR

Your favor of the 31 ult:[1] came to hand yesterday. As the reason which chiefly urged my departure for Virga. has ceased[2] I have been led to protract my attendance on Congress by the interest I felt in some measures on foot, and the particular interest which my Constituents have in them. Two of these were the territorial cession and the permanent seat of Congress. The former was a few days ago put into a form which I hope will meet the ultimatum of Virginia.[3] The first monday in next month is fixed for a decision of the latter; after which it may still be necessary to choose a temporary residence untill the permanent one can be made ready. I am utterly unable to foretell how either of these points will be determined. It is not impossible that an effective vote may be found attainable on neither; in which case the winter must be spent in this village where the public business can neither be conveniently done, the members of Congress decently provided for nor those connected with Congress provided for at all.[4] I shall lose no time in looking out for quarters for you & entering into provisional engagements in your favor. Your other request relative to Miss Patsy shall be equally attended to as soon as I go to Philada. which will probably be towards the end of next week.[5]

It will give me real concern if we should miss of one another altogether in the journies before us; and yet I foresee the danger of it. Mr. Jones & myself will probably be on the road by the middle of next month or a few days later. This is the time about which you expect to commence your journey. Unless therefore we travel the same road a disappointment of even an interview will be unavoidable. At present our plan is to proceed thro' Baltimore & Alexandria & Fredericksbg. and we may possibly be at the races of the second place.[6] I am at a loss by what regulation I can obey your wishes with regard to the notes I have on hand; having not yet made any copy of them, having no time now for that purpose, and being unwilling for severa[l] reasons to leave them all behind me.[7] A disappointment however will be of the less consequence, as they have been much briefer & more interrupted since the period at which you ran them over, and have been altogether discontinued since the arrival of Congs. here.[8]

My plan of spending this winter in Philada in close reading was not entirely abandoned untill Congress left that City and shewed an utter disinclination to returning to it.[9] The prospect of agreeable & even instructive society was an original consideration with me;[10] and the subsequent one of having yours added to it would have confirmed my intention after the abortive issue of another plan, had not the solicitude of a tender & infirm parent exacted a visit to Virga. and an uncertainty of returning been thereby incurred.[11] Even at present, if Congs. sd make Philada. their seat this winter & I can decline a visit to Virga. or speedily get away from it my anxiety on the subject will be renewed.

Our last information from Europe is dated the 27th. July. France & Spain were then ready for the definitive signing of the Peace. Holland was on the point of being so. The American Plenipos. had done nothing on the subject and in case of emergency could only sign the provisional Treaty as final.[12] Their negociations had been spent chiefly on commercial stipulations from which G.B. after very different professions & appearances, altogether drew back. The ready admission she found into our commerce without paying any price for it has suggested the policy of aiming at the entire benefit of it, and at the same time saving the carriage of the W. India trade the price she at first bid for it. The supposed contrariety of interests among the States and the impotence of the fœderal Govt. are urged by the ministerial pamphleteers as a safeguard agst. retaliation.[13] The other nations of Europe seem to have more honorable views towards our commerce, sundry advances having been made to our Ministers on that subject.[14]

Congress have come to no decision even as yet on any of the great branches of the peace establishment. The military branch is supported and quickened by the presence of the Commander in chief, but without any prospect of a hasty issue.[15] The department of foreign affairs both internal & external remains as it has long done: The election of a Secy. has been an order of the day for many months without a vote being taken.[16] The importance of the marine department has been diminished by the sale of almost all the Vessels belonging to the U.S. The department of Finance is an object of almost daily attack and will be reduced to its crisis on the final resignation of Mr. M. which will take place in a few months.[17] The War office is connected with the Military establishment & will be regulated I suppose in conformity to what that may be.

Among other subjects which divide Congress, their Constitutional authority touching such an establishment in time of peace is one.[18] Another still more puzzling is the precise jurisdiction proper for Congress within the limits of their permanent seat.[19] As these points may possibly remain undecided till Novr. I mention them particularly that your aid may be prepared.[20] The investigation of the Mutiny ended in the condemnation of several Sergeants who were stimulated to the measure without being apprized of the object by the two officers who escaped. They have all recd. a pardon from Congress. The real plan & object of the mutiny lies in profound darkness.[21] I have written this in hopes that it may get to Monticello before you leave it.[22] It might have been made more interesting if I had brought the Cypher from Philada.[23] tho' my present situation required a great effort to accomplish as much as I have. I am obliged to write in a position that scarcely admits the use of any of my limbs, Mr. Jones & myself being lodged in this room not 10 feet square and without a single accommodation for writing.[24]

I am Dear Sir, Your sincere friend & Obt Servt.

J. MADISON JR.

[1] *Q.v.*

[2] Jefferson to JM, 31 Aug. 1783, and n. 5.

[3] On 4 June 1783 Congress appointed a committee of five delegates, including John Rutledge, chairman, and JM, to consider the report of a committee, submitted 3 November 1781, on the offer by the Virginia General Assembly on 2 January 1781 to cede the territory north and west of the Ohio River to the United States. The committee's report, drafted by Rutledge, was laid before Congress on 6 June 1783 and debated two weeks later (*JCC*, XXIV, 381, and n. 1, 406–9; JM to Randolph, 10 June, and n. 16; JM Notes, 20 June 1783, and nn. 2–5, 10). For the prolonged controversy in Congress, prior to 20 June 1783, over the validity of Virginia's claims and the provisos included in its offer of cession, see the indexes of *Papers of Madison*, Vols. II, III, V, and VI under Continental Congress, actions on western lands, and of Vol. IV under Continental Congress, actions on cessions of land; Jefferson to JM, 7 May, and n. 3; JM to Jefferson, 20 May, and n. 8; JM Notes, 4 June, n. 2; 5 June, n. 1; 9 June, and nn. 2, 3; 10 June 1783.

From 20 June until 11 September, Congress delayed giving further attention to the Rutledge report, although the issue continued to be of much concern to the government in Richmond, the Virginia delegates in Congress, and the influential opponents of Virginia's territorial claims, especially those resident in Pennsylvania, New Jersey, and Maryland (Instruction to Delegates, 27 June, and n. 3; Delegates to Harrison, 8 Sept. 1783). On 13 September, after unsuccessful efforts by the Maryland delegates two days before to delay consideration of the Rutledge report for another week, and by those of Maryland and New Jersey on the thirteenth to substitute for that report a resolution wholly adverse to Virginia's claims, Congress adopted the report by a vote of 8 to 2 (Maryland and New Jersey). Thereby Congress promised to accept Virginia's offer of cession, if the state would recede from three of its eight provisos. Congress refused to declare "absolutely void" all land claims resting solely upon purchases from Indians or from "royal grants" traversing "the chartered rights, laws and customs of Virginia."

Rejected also as "either unnecessary or unreasonable" was the proviso requiring Congress to guarantee to Virginia all its territory not included in the cession. Instead of pledging, as one of Virginia's provisos stipulated, to reimburse the state for all its financial costs "since the commencement of the present war" in the area ceded, Congress proposed that three commissioners should be appointed—one by Congress, one by Virginia, "and another by those two commissioners"—to "adjust and liquidate the account of the necessary and reasonable expenses" in the territory north and west of the Ohio River (*JCC*, XXV, 552–53, 554–64, 563, n. 1).

In a letter of 19 September 1783 to Governor George Clinton, the New York delegates somewhat inaccurately remarked that Congress had accepted Virginia's "hard Terms" so as to gain "an immense Tract of Country" which "might be improved to great public Advantage" and "to silence Questions respecting the Western Territories which have proved a great Obstacle to public Business, and might have been a source of internal Contention and Convulsion" (Burnett, *Letters*, VII, 300–301). See also *ibid.*, VII, 312–13, 325–26; Delegates to Harrison, 20 Sept., and n. 4; Harrison to Delegates, 26 Sept. 1783, and n. 5.

[4] Instructions to Delegates, 28 June, and nn. 6, 7; JM to Jefferson, 17 July, and n. 9; Jones to JM, 21 July, n. 4; JM to Pendleton, 28 July, and nn. 1–3; 8 Sept., and n. 1; to Randolph, 5 Aug., and n. 4; 18 Aug., and nn. 3, 4; 30 Aug.; 8 Sept.; Delegates to Harrison, 23 Aug., and n. 7; JM to James Madison, Sr., 30 Aug. 1783, n. 7. Although 12 September had been scheduled by Congress as the day on which it would choose the "place proper for a temporary residence," it was not until 6 October that the subject was revived, and not until 21 October that a resolution passed directing the president "to adjourn Congress on the 12th day of November next, to meet at Annapolis on the 26th of the same month" (*JCC*, XXV, 649–54, 712).

[5] Jefferson to JM, 31 Aug., and n. 13; JM to Jefferson, 30 Sept. 1783. Upon recovering this letter many years later, JM or someone by his direction placed a bracket after "favor" and another bracket at the beginning of the fourth paragraph to signify that all the text except the last sentence of the first paragraph and all that of the second and third paragraphs should be included in the first extensive edition of his writings. Henry D. Gilpin, the editor, complied (Madison, *Papers* [Gilpin ed.], I, 571–74).

[6] Jefferson to JM, 7 May, n. 19; 31 Aug. The races under the auspices of the Jockey Club of Fredericksburg were scheduled to begin on 6 October, and of the Jockey Club of Alexandria on 21 October (*Va. Gazette*, 23 Aug.). Jones, upon being informed of a death in his family, left Philadelphia alone about 14 October and reached his Spring Hill plantation on 23 October (JM to Randolph, 13 Oct., and n. 3; Jones to JM, 30 Oct. 1783).

[7] Jefferson to JM, 31 Aug. By "notes," JM meant his notes on debates in Congress, 4 November 1782 to 21 June 1783 (*Papers of Madison*, V, 231–35; JM Notes, 21 June 1783, and ed. n.).

[8] Instead of "ran them over," JM at first wrote and canceled, "left Philada." On some occasion or occasions during Jefferson's stay in Philadelphia from 27 December 1782 to 26 January 1783, and from 26 February to 12 April 1783, he had scanned JM's notes (*Papers of Madison*, VI, 4, nn. 2, 4; 243, n. 5; 327, n. 6).

[9] Although Congress last met in Philadelphia on 21 June, President Boudinot delayed for three more days before summoning the delegates to reconvene in Princeton (JM Notes, 21 June, and n. 7). See also JM to Jefferson, 17 July, and n. 7; Mercer to JM, 14 Aug.; JM to James Madison, Sr., 30 Aug. 1783, and n. 9.

[10] JM to Randolph, 8 July 1783, and n. 2.

[11] JM to Jefferson, 17 July, n. 10; to James Madison, Sr., 8 Sept., and citations in n. 2. The other "plan" had been rendered "abortive" by the ending of the engagement of JM and Catherine Floyd to marry.

[12] Livingston to JM, 19 July, n. 4; Hawkins to JM, 9 Aug., n. 3; JM to Jefferson, 11 Aug., and n. 8; to Randolph, 13 Sept. 1783, and nn. 1–3.

[13] Delegates to Harrison, 14–15 Aug., and n. 9; 20 Sept., and n. 3; JM to Randolph, 30 Aug., and n. 2; 13 Sept., and nn. 5, 6; Burnett, *Letters*, VII, 309–10. On 18 September 1783 the Chevalier de La Luzerne informed a committee of Congress "That it seems that the Americans by admitting too precipitately English vessels in their ports have deprived themselves of a powerful weapon to induce England to a conclusion of the Treaty. By a continuation of the former prohibitory Laws until the final settlement of peace it is probable that they would have furnished the most pungent arms to the party who sincerely wishes that the Treaty with America might be concluded. However, the Court [of France] is disposed to believe, that it will not be much delayed" (*JCC*, XXV, 589).

[14] Among the "other nations" reported to be making "advances" for the negotiation of commercial treaties with the United States were Denmark, Portugal, Spain, Tuscany, Austria, and Prussia (*JCC*, XXV, 618, 753–55).

[15] JM to Jefferson, 11 Aug., and n. 12; Delegates to Harrison, 23 Aug. 1783, and n. 8.

[16] JM Notes, 23 May, and n. 7; JM to Randolph, 17 June; Livingston to JM, 19 July, and nn. 3, 4; JM to Jefferson, 11 Aug. 1783, and n. 11.

[17] Among the four ships of considerable size comprising the United States Navy at the cessation of hostilities with Great Britain was the frigate "Bourbon," still on the stocks at Middletown, Conn. Congress on 21 April ordered Robert Morris, agent of marine, to have the frigate "Duc De Lauzun" sold upon her arrival in France. In like manner he was instructed on 16 July to sell the ship "Hague." At his suggestion ten days later, Congress authorized him to dispose of the "Bourbon." By then this frigate was ready for launching but had not been rigged. Thus, when the present letter was written, there remained only the packet "Washington," which had recently docked in Philadelphia with dispatches from France, and the "old" frigate "Alliance," unable to leave port because her hull leaked. On 27 March and 8 April 1784, respectively, Congress ordered the "Alliance" to be made seaworthy and the "Washington" to be sold (NA: PCC, No. 137, III, 45, 49, 131; *Papers of Madison*, II, 9, n. 3; VI, 432–33; 434, n. 9; JM Notes, 15 May, n. 1; JM to Randolph, 17 June 1783, n. 10; *JCC*, XXIV, 263, 438, 446, 447, n. 1; XXV, 536, n. 1, 537–38, 571–72, 573, 622, n. 2, 695, 839–40, 840, n. 1; XXVI, 171, 210).

Although Morris was expected to resign "in a few months," he continued to serve as superintendent of finance until November 1784 (*Papers of Madison*, VI, 306, n. 11). For his frequent harassment by Arthur Lee, Theodorick Bland, and many of the New England delegates, see *ibid.*, VI, 304–5; 305, n. 4; 306, n. 6; 409, n. 1; Delegates to Harrison, 1 Aug., n. 1; JM to Randolph, 30 Aug. 1783, and n. 6; *JCC*, XXV, 506, 536–37, 541–43, 573–77.

[18] JM to Randolph, 17 June, and nn. 10–12; Memorial of Massachusetts General Court, 19 Sept. 1783, and n. 3; *JCC*, XXV, 548–51, 571–72.

[19] N. 4, above; Motion *in re* Permanent Site, 22 Sept. 1783.

[20] Jefferson's term as a delegate from Virginia in Congress began on 3 November 1783 (*JCC*, XXV, 797–99, 803).

[21] JM Notes, 21 June, n. 8; Delegates to Harrison, 5 July, nn. 3–5; Mercer to JM, 14 Aug. 1783, and n. 8; *JCC*, XXV, 564–67; Burnett, *Letters*, VII, 297.

[22] Jefferson on 16 October 1783 left Monticello to attend Congress (Jefferson to JM, 7 May 1783, n. 19).

[23] JM to Jefferson, 10 June 1783, and hdn.

[24] JM's irritation with his and Jones's cramped quarters appears to have caused the size of the room to diminish, for on 30 August he had written to Randolph that the room was "not more than ten feet square" (JM to Randolph, 30 Aug. 1783).

To Edmund Randolph

RC (LC: Madison Papers). Cover missing. Many years later, after recovering the letter, JM docketed it, "Sep: 20. 1783 JM."

PRINCETON. Sepr. 20. 1783.

DEAR SIR

I have nothing to add to my last on the subject of foreign affairs, further than that the Court of France has fixed on L'Orient as a free port for the U. S.[1] The Virga. Cession underwent a decision of Congs. a day or two after my last. The form which they have given it may be seen in the hands of the Executive. I sincerely hope it may meet the Ultimatum of Virga.[2] The circumstances which produced brevity in my last as strongly recommend it at present.[3]

Adieu,

J. M JR.

[1] JM to Randolph, 13 Sept., and nn. 1–6; Delegates to Harrison, 20 Sept. 1783, and n. 3.

[2] Delegates to Harrison, 20 Sept., and n. 4; JM to Jefferson, 20 Sept. 1783, and n. 3. Many years later JM or someone at his bidding placed a bracket at the close of the sentence to indicate that all the letter except its last sentence should be included in the first comprehensive edition of his papers (Madison, *Papers* [Gilpin ed.], I, 574).

[3] Here again, as so often in his letters with a Princeton date line, JM referred to his cramped quarters in that village.

Motion *in re* Jurisdiction of Congress over Permanent Site

MS (NA: PCC, No. 23, fol. 161). Undated and unsigned but in JM's hand.

[22 September 1783]

That the district which may be ceded to & accepted by Congress for their permanent residence, ought to be entirely exempted from the authority of the State ceding the same; and the organization & administration of the powers of Govt. within the sd. district concerted between Congress & the inhabitants thereof.[1]

[1] For background of this motion, see Harrison to Delegates, 12 July, n. 3; JM to Pendleton, 28 July, and nn. 1–3; 8 Sept., and n. 1; to Randolph, 28 July; to Jefferson, 20 Sept. 1783, and n. 4. The report of the committee, which included JM, was drafted by the chairman, James Duane. The report recommended that

Congress "ought to enjoy an exclusive Jurisdiction over the District which may be ceded" and that the size of the district "ought not to exceed the contents of Six miles square nor to be less than three miles Square" (NA: PCC, No. 23, fol. 149). JM's proposal, designed to render the first recommendation of the committee more specific and to assure that the "exclusive Jurisdiction" would not deny "the inhabitants" of the ceded district a share in organizing and administering their own government, appears to have been neither included in the committee's report nor offered separately by JM in Congress.

On 22 September Congress decided to resolve itself three days later "into a committee of the whole" to take the report "into consideration" (*JCC*, XXV, 603, and n. 1). Although the committee of the whole met on 25 September, "made some progress" on the issue, and was granted "leave to sit again to-morrow," no further mention of the report appears in the journal during the remainder of 1783. The subject seems to have remained quiescent until revived on 14 April 1784 by resolutions submitted from the legislature of Rhode Island (*JCC*, XXVI, 221–26).

Benjamin Harrison to Virginia Delegates

FC (Virginia State Library). In the hand of Samuel Patteson. Addressed to "The Honorable the Virginia Delegates in Congress."

COUNCIL CHAMBER Sept. 26th. 1783.

GENTLEMEN,

Your two favors of the 8th.[1] and 13th.[2] instant came to hand by the last post one of them has been detained in the post office which I suppose has also been the case with one of mine.[3] General Irvine's complaint of the virginians crossing the Ohio reached me I suppose on the same day that mine against the Pennsylvanians got to you which of them is right I will not undertake to say, but it is most likely that they are both so I shall use every endeavor to stop the people from this country tho' I am confident I shall not succeed,[4] there being no powers in the Executive to punish any kind of offenders, nor do the assembly incline to give them. I can order the militia to drive the people in and they may refuse obedience to the orders and escape all kinds of punishment; for five shillings in short Virginia will very soon be the Seat of anarchy and confusion unless our law makers find out that Government cannot be supported without lodging powers somewhere to enforce obedience to the laws.[5]

I am not disappointed by the conduct of the english respecting our trade. I always thought they intended to amuse us 'till they could form a judgment of the temper we were in with respect to it, and therefore wished in some measure to curb the violent inclination there seemed to be for opening every avenue to them before a treaty of commerce was entered into. I look on the locusts that are crouding here as so many emissaries sent to sound our inclinations and to poison the minds of our people and if possible bring them back to their old and destructive paths; and I am sorry to say that I fear they will succeed unless Congress interfere.[6]

I shall lay the resolutions of Congress on the proposed session of the back country before the assembly and suppose with you they will approve them as they differ very little from their proposals. the Guaranty required was too humiliating for me.[7]

I am &c.

B H

[1] *Q.v.*

[2] Delegates to Harrison, 20 Sept. 1783, and n. 1.

[3] Delegates to Harrison, 8 Sept. 1783, and citations in n. 1.

[4] The delegates' letter of 8 September to Harrison (*q.v.*, and n. 2), in which they mentioned "Irvine's complaint," probably had been delayed in reaching the governor until about 23 September. On approximately that date the delegates received Harrison's letter of 13 September (*q.v.*, and n. 4), warning that settlements "beyond the ohio" by Pennsylvanians were thwarting efforts to conclude peace with the Indians there. See also Harrison to Delegates, 19 Sept., and n. 3; Delegates to Harrison, 4 Oct. 1783.

[5] The "five shillings" was the amount levied by Virginia law against a private who failed to report for "any muster" (Hening, *Statutes*, IX, 30; XI, 174). In a letter of 20 October 1783, addressed to the speaker of the House of Delegates for presentation to that chamber, Harrison emphasized his lack of legal authority to employ militia to remove the squatters, even though their incursions made Indian hostilities a certainty. He urged the Virginia General Assembly to revise the militia laws so as to enable him effectively to preserve the "tranquility" and thereby "the safety of the Commonwealth" (Executive Letter Book, 1783–1786, p. 217, MS in Va. State Library). On this occasion the governor was probably the more cautious, because, during a similar crisis in August and September 1782 when Indians menaced Fort Pitt, he seems to have been threatened with impeachment if he violated the laws by dispatching militia "out of the state" to the aid of that garrison (*Papers of Madison*, V, 74–75; 75, nn. 8–11; 260, 261, n. 4; 318).

In contrast with Harrison's eagerness to avoid war with the Indians, the Virginia General Assembly on 22 December 1783 enacted a measure directing the survey of military bounty lands both in Kentucky and between the Scioto and Little Miami rivers, northwest of the Ohio River. By this law the executive was required, if necessary, to protect the surveyors with militia, provided that such aid "be from the Kentucky country, and not exceed one hundred men" (*JHDV*, Oct. 1783, pp. 27–28, 40, 47, 57, 59, 61, 63, 67, 83; Hening, *Statutes*, XI, 309–13). Except for this statute, the Virginia General Assembly during its session of October 1783 failed to comply with Harrison's request for more authority over the militia.

The members of the Assembly, besides being unwilling to enhance the powers of the executive, may have concluded that their acquiescence on 19 and 20 December 1783 with the congressional resolutions concerning Virginia's offer to cede, except in the military district just mentioned, its territorial and jurisdictional claims to the Old Northwest would on acceptance transfer from the state to the Confederation the entire burden of maintaining peace in that vast area (*JHDV*, Oct. 1783, pp. 71, 79, 81–82, 83; Hening, *Statutes*, XI, 326–28; NA: PCC, No. 75, fols. 388–90; Harrison to Delegates, 20 Sept., and n. 4; JM to Jefferson, 20 Sept. 1783, and n. 3; Boyd, *Papers of Jefferson*, VI, 414, 428; *JCC*, XXVI, 112–17). If so, they were mistaken, for by August 1784 Congress operated only through a Committee of the States, and the Indians were so aroused that Harrison feared Virginia would soon be plunged into "a most bloody and expensive war, which we are at this time not in any degree able to support or are prepared for" (Executive Letter Book, 1783–1786, pp. 377–78, 379–80, 382, 401–2, MS in Va. State Library; *JCSV*, III, 372; *Cal. of Va. State Papers*, III, 599). In the autumn of 1784 JM was a member of a committee of the General Assembly that successfully introduced a bill "authorizing the Governor, with the advice of the Council, to suspend, when necessary, the surveying of certain lands in the western country" (*JHDV*, Oct. 1784, pp. 11, 22, 24, 36, 109; Hening, *Statutes*, XI, 447–48).

6 Randolph to JM, 12 July, and n. 2; 13 Sept. (2d letter), and nn. 1, 2; Jones to JM, 21 July, and n. 6; Harrison to Delegates, 9 Aug.; 3 Oct.; Delegates to Harrison, 14–15 Aug., and n. 9; 20 Sept., and n. 3; JM to Randolph, 30 Aug., and nn. 2, 3; 13 Sept., and nn. 3, 5, 6; to Jefferson, 20 Sept. 1783, and n. 13.

7 For "the Guaranty," see JM to Jefferson, 20 Sept., n. 3. For the approval by the Virginia General Assembly, see Delegates to Harrison, 4 Oct. 1783, n. 5.

Benjamin Harrison to Virginia Delegates

FC (Virginia State Library). In the hand of Samuel Patteson. Addressed to "The Honorable Virginia Delegates in Congress."

COUNCIL CHAMBER Sepr. 27th. 1783.

GENTLEMEN,

Since I wrote to you yesterday[1] I have seen the Attorney who tells me his performance respecting our claim to the western Country is ready for the inspection of the Committee and that as soon as it meets their approbation it will be transmitted to you.[2]

I am &.

B. H.

1 *Q.v.*

2 On 1 June 1782 the Virginia General Assembly appointed a committee including Attorney General Edmund Randolph and four other men "to collect all Documents" required to establish "the Right of this State" to its "Western Territory," especially that north and west of the Ohio River. Various circumstances thrust this unexpectedly difficult assignment upon Randolph alone. Of his committee colleagues, Thomas Jefferson declined to take "an active part," George Mason refused the appointment but agreed "to contribute his aid privately," and Thomas Walker joined Arthur Lee, whose appointment to Congress obliged him to be in Philadelphia or Princeton much of the time, in persuading Randolph to do all the research and writing (*Papers of Madison*, IV, 90, and n. 4; 147; 154–55; 161; 208; 226; 227; 228, n. 7; 305; 306, n. 3; 389, n. 19; V, 30; 264; 309; 312, n. 18; VI, 244–45; 245, nn. 5, 6; 246, n. 7).

Although about "a third" of the report was "approved" by Mason before its completion in August 1783, none of it seems to have been reviewed by Jefferson or Walker. As late as November in that year, Lee remained unavailable, for, contrary to Randolph's hope, he did not attend the Virginia General Assembly during the session convening on 20 October in Richmond. On 25 November, although still lacking the committee's approval of his draft, Randolph wrote to the speaker of the House of Delegates, accounting for the long delay and requesting authorization to have the report "go into print under the correction of Mr. Mason and myself" (MS in Va. State Library). The next day, after the letter was read, the House "ordered" that it "lie on the table" (*JHDV*, Oct. 1783, p. 35).

This anticlimax to Randolph's extensive labors may reflect the delegates' opinion that, by agreeing to the congressional resolutions concerning Virginia's offer of cession, a detailed defense of the state's title to the Northwest Territory was no longer relevant (JM to Jefferson, 20 Sept., and n. 3; Harrison to Delegates, 26 Sept. 1783, n. 5). Whether the report was ever printed or whether a copy of it was sent by Harrison to the Virginia delegates in Congress is unknown. The manuscript has not been found. Randolph probably retained a personal copy and drew on it in composing his manuscript history of Virginia (Edmund Randolph, *History of Virginia*, ed. Arthur H. Shaffer [Charlottesville, 1970], pp. 8–9, 17–19, 32–35, 61–62, 149, 154, 275, 276, 285; Boyd, *Papers of Jefferson*, VII, 259–60, 293).

From Edmund Pendleton

Summary (LC: Madison Miscellany). Copied from a calendar, probably prepared about 1850 by Peter Force's clerk. He noted that the manuscript of the letter, addressed "To James Madison," consisted of "1 page 4°."

1783, September 29 VIRGINIA

Recovery from illness.[1] Sir Guy Carlton.[2] The people Eastward averse to the half-pay, or commutation.[3] The British restrictive proclamation.[4]

[1] Pendleton probably referred to his own illness. His biographer wrote: "From the time of Pendleton's fall from his horse in the winter of 1777, his health had gone into a gradual decline. There were frequent spells of illness, which troubled him the rest of his life, some of them prolonged" (David J. Mays, *Edmund Pendleton*, II, 208).

[2] Pendleton's comment about General Sir Guy Carleton may have reflected JM's mention of the general in a missing letter to Pendleton, probably dated 24 August. Writing on that day to Randolph, JM had presented Carleton's views in regard to the Loyalists and the evacuation of New York City (JM to Randolph, 24 Aug.). See also JM to Pendleton, 8 Sept. 1783. The letter of 17 August, in which Carleton expressed his views to President Elias Boudinot, was printed in the *Maryland Gazette* (Annapolis) of 11 September, and in the *Virginia Gazette, and Weekly Advertiser* of 20 September 1783. Pendleton may have seen one or both of these weeklies. If a letter was posted by JM on 24 August, it would not have reached Pendleton until about 3 September. His illness seems to have prevented him from writing to JM between 1 and 29 September (Pendleton to JM, 1 Sept. 1783, and n. 1).

[3] JM to Pendleton, 8 Sept. 1783, and n. 6.

[4] JM to Randolph, 13 Sept. 1783, and n. 5.

To Thomas Jefferson

RC (LC: Madison Papers). Cover missing. Addressed to "Honble Thomas Jefferson." Docketed by him, "Madison James of Orange." The brackets in the first paragraph signify words or parts of words which a water stain has obliterated.

PHILADA. Sepr. 30. 1783.

DEAR SIR

My last was written on the supposition that Mr. Jones & myself would be on our way to Virga. by the middle of Ocr. and that my best chance of an interview with you might be at Alexandria at the time of the races.[1] On further thought I fear that you may be led by that suggestion to suspend your setting out longer than you proposed, and that I may not find it practicable to leave this place finally before it will be practicable for you to reach it by pursuing your own plan. One circumstance which increases the uncertainty of my movements is a melancholy event in Mr. Jones family which may [a]ffect his plans, to which I shall as far as necessary make mine su[bservi]ent.[2] It will rather therefore be my wish that you should ha[sten] than retard your journey, if it be a matter of indifference to y[o]u, tho' not that you should do either if it be not so.[3]

I have laid a train at Princeton which I hope will provide as commodious quarters as could be expected.[4] If these sd. become necessary in Philada Mrs. House's disposition towards you will be a sure resource.[5] Mrs. Trist concurs in your idea of a boarding school; that it may be expedient for Miss Patsey for hours of instruction but no farther. She will enquire and think for you on the subject as far as her preparations for a voyage to the Mississippi will admit.[6] She & Mrs. House make a tender of their respectful regards for yourself & Miss Patsey. I have nothing to add to my last on public subjects, nor to the above any thing but that I am Dr. Sir

Yr. sincere friend & obt. Servt.

J. MADISON JR.

As the latest papers are very barren I inclose a former one containing No. 1. of N. American, leaving the Author to your conjectures.[7]

[1] JM to Jefferson, 20 Sept. 1783, and n. 6.

[2] *Ibid.*, n. 7. The "melancholy event" probably was the death of Jones's wife, Mary Waugh Dawson Jones.

[3] *Ibid.*, n. 22.

[4] In his letter of 31 August to JM (*q.v.*), Jefferson stated that "a room to myself" would be "indispensable." Whenever JM and Jones were together in Princeton, they uncomfortably shared a small room (JM to Jefferson, 20 Sept. 1783).

[5] Jefferson had lodged in Mrs. Mary House's boardinghouse for over ten weeks earlier in the year (*ibid.*, n. 8).

[6] Mercer to JM, 14 Aug., and n. 7; Jefferson to JM, 31 Aug., n. 13. "Patsy" was Jefferson's spelling of the familiar name of his daughter Martha. Before Jefferson left Philadelphia in November 1783 to attend Congress in Annapolis, he had arranged for her to be tutored and to live in Philadelphia in the home of Mrs. Thomas Hopkinson, the widowed mother of Francis Hopkinson (Boyd, *Papers of Jefferson*, VI, 359–61).

[7] JM enclosed the *Pennsylvania Journal* of 17 Sept. 1783. See Note on "North-American," 17 Sept. and 8 Oct. 1783, ed. n.

To Edmund Randolph

RC (LC: Madison Papers). Unsigned but in JM's hand. Docketed by Randolph, "J. Madison. Sep: 30, 1783."

PHILADA. Sept. 30. 1783.

MY DEAR SIR

Your favor introducing Mr. Corbin and that by the last weeks post have both been recd.[1] The former did not get to Princeton before Mr. C. had left it, nor did I get to this place before He was so near leaving it that I had no opportunity of manifesting my respect for your recommendations otherwise than by verbal civilities to him.[2] Yesterday's post brought me no letter from you.[3] In answer to your comment in the preceding one on the reception of a Minister from the Oeconomical Republic to which we are allied, it will suffice to inform you, that in pursuance of a commission from him *six* elegant horses are provided for his coach, as was to have been one of the best houses in the most fashionable part of this City.[4] Wherever Commerce prevails there will be an inequality of wealth, and wherever the latter does a simplicity of manners must decline.[5]

Our foreign intelligence remains as at the date of my last[6] I forget whether I mentioned to you that our Ministers unanimously express surprise at the doubt started in America as to the epoch which terminated hostilities on our Coast. They affirm that one month from the date of the instrument was meant & suppose that that exposition will not be contested.[7] pray can your researches inform me 1st. whether prizes made by & from parties not subject to the power before whose maritime courts they are carried, are *provisionally* or *finally* tried? 2d. How far the rules established by the Sovereign of the Captor & those by the Sovereign of the Courts prevail in such trials? 3dly. What difference is made in cases where both the parties concerned in the capture are subject to the same power and where they are subject to different powers.[8]

[1] Randolph to JM, 13 Sept. 1783 (1st letter), and n. 1; (2d letter).

[2] JM probably returned from Princeton to Philadelphia on 26 September. He voted in each session of Congress between 16 and 22 September, both inclusive, and also on 25 September. The journal records no tallied polls on 23 and 24 September, but JM most likely was in Princeton on those days (*JCC*, XXVI, 573, 579–80, 581–82, 586–87, 592–93, 596, 601, 613).

[3] Randolph's letters of 13 September appear to be the last which he wrote to JM in 1783. He may have anticipated an early return by JM to Virginia. Randolph, furthermore, was much occupied early in the autumn with selling his country estate (Pettus'), moving to Richmond, perfecting the text of his defense of Virginia's title to the Northwest Territory, seeking anew to reach an accommodation with his father's creditors, and attending the sessions of the General Court at Richmond during the first four weeks in October (Randolph to JM, 23 Aug., n. 1; Harrison to Delegates, 27 Sept., and n. 1; *Va. Gazette*, 6, 13, 20, 27 Sept., 11 Oct., 1 Nov. 1783).

[4] For the "Oconomical Republic," see Randolph to JM, 13 Sept. (2d letter), and n. 5; for the "Minister" thereof to the United States, see JM to Jefferson, 10 June 1783, and n. 23. The house to which van Berckel moved on 7 November was the one in the South Ward of Philadelphia that President Boudinot had occupied until Congress left for Princeton. From the time of his arrival on 11 October until 7 November, van Berckel stayed at the City Tavern on Second Street near Walnut Street (Varnum L. Collins, *Continental Congress at Princeton*, p. 218; Burnett, *Letters*, VII, 229, 282–83, 352, 371; *Pa. Archives*, 3d ser., XVI, 784; JM to Randolph, 30 Aug.; 13 Oct. 1783). See also Delegates to Harrison, 1 Nov. 1783 (2d letter), and n. 3.

[5] JM's comment somewhat resembles that of Pendleton in his letter of 16 June 1783 to JM (*q.v.*, and n. 10).

[6] JM to Randolph, 20 Sept. 1783.

[7] In their letter of 18 July 1783, John Adams, Franklin, and Jay stated: "We are surprised to hear that any doubts have arisen in America respecting the time when the cessation of hostilities took place there. It most certainly took place at the expiration of one month after the date of that declaration in all parts of the world, whether by land or sea, that lay north of the latitude of the Canaries" (Wharton, *Revol. Dipl. Corr.*, VI, 570). By "declaration" the peace commissioners meant the proclamation of King George III on 14 February, declaring that all hostilities in the above-mentioned area should end one month after the conclusion on 3 February of the preliminary articles of peace between Great Britain and France. Although, after much debate, Congress also stipulated 3 March in the proclamation of 12 April declaring a cessation of hostilities, the time of official termination was hardly satisfactory, for British cruisers hovering off the Atlantic coast had captured many American merchant vessels during the interim between those two dates (*ibid.*, VI, 370–72; *Papers of Madison*, VI, 391, and n. 4; 449; 450, and n. 3; 451, n. 4; Pendleton to JM, 10 May; JM to Randolph, 10 June 1783, and n. 6). See also *JCC*, XXV, 753–54, 757.

[8] Randolph's replies, if any, to these queries may have been oral, following JM's return to Virginia early in December 1783.

To the Reverend James Madison

Tr (Yale University Library: Stiles Papers). The original manuscript is missing. For the reason stated in the editorial note, JM should have dated his letter "Octr 2" rather than "Sept 2."

EDITORIAL NOTE

The editors are indebted to Professor Edmund S. Morgan for his assurance that the date line, salutation, and first thirteen words of this document are in the hand of President Ezra Stiles of Yale College. The remainder of the text, together with the names of JM and the Reverend James Madison, was copied by one of President Stiles's children. The transcription appears in Volume 3, page 609 of Stiles's manuscript "Itinerary." The fact that JM's letter was available for transcribing at Yale College suggests that Isaac Stiles either did not present it to the Reverend James Madison, president of the College of William and Mary, or that the addressee handed it back to the youthful bearer.

In his "Literary Diary," under date of 10 September 1783, the Reverend Ezra Stiles recorded, "Writg Lett. recommendg my Son to &c. in Virginia &c." Noting on 28 September that his "son Isaac" left that day "to go to Maryld or Virginia," the father added on 27 November, "This Eveng. my Son Isaac returned to New Haven from Maryland and Virginia having been absent a little above two Months" (Franklin Bowditch Dexter, ed., *The Literary Diary of Ezra Stiles* [3 vols.; New York, 1901], III, 92, 95, 99). These entries seem conclusive in establishing that JM inadvertently dated his own letter of recommendation a month too early.

PRINCETON Sept [Octr] 2 1783

DR SIR

If you receive this at all it will be from the hands of Mr Isaac Stiles son of the President of Yale College who proposes to seek his fortune in some one of the Southern States.[1] His ultimate object is the profession of the Law;[2] But his wish is to be introduced in the first instance into a Gentleman's family where he may at the same time be employ'd in teaching the Languages & some of the more useful branches of science and may carry on his forensic studies under the auspices of a neighbouring Law[y]er.[3] Being myself unacquaint[e]d with any situation in Virginia w[h]ich could answer these joint purposes, I take the liberty of giving Mr Stiles his introduction, and asking in his behalf such information and advice as you may be able to befriend him with

I am Dr Sir yours Sincer[e]ly

J. MADISON JR

1 President Ezra Stiles had been at least an occasional correspondent of the Reverend James Madison for about three years (*Papers of Madison*, II, 55; 56, n. 10; IV, 338; V, 138; 139, n. 11). Isaac Stiles (1763–1795) was graduated by Yale College in 1783. Late in November of that year, after returning to New Haven from Virginia and Maryland, he appears to have begun the study of law. Following his admission to the bar in April 1785, he moved to Tolland (Windsor), Conn. There he practiced his profession until 1790, when he turned to the sea for a livelihood, perhaps as a supercargo. In the spring of 1795, shortly before his father's death, he sailed in the brig "Eagle" for Santo Domingo but was never heard of again (Abiel Holmes, *The Life of Ezra Stiles* [Boston, 1798], p. 375; Franklin B. Dexter, ed., *Literary Diary of Ezra Stiles*, III, 154, 211, 397, 458, 566).

2 The Reverend James Madison, who was versed in law as well as in theology and "natural and moral philosophy," had given thought early in 1781 to "undergoing a Conversion" by exchanging his academic career for the "more fashionable" and "more profitable" one of practicing law (*Papers of Madison*, I, 224, n. 1; II, 294; 295, n. 10).

3 The misspelling here and three more times before the close of this letter probably signifies errors by the transcriber rather than by JM.

Benjamin Harrison to Virginia Delegates

FC (Virginia State Library). Addressed to "The Honorable Virginia Delegates in Congress." In the hand of Samuel Patteson.

COUNCIL CHAMBER October 3d. 1783.

GENTLEMEN,

Your favor of the 20th of last month came safe to hand.[1] The determinations of the French and English respecting our trade is really alarming and in the end will prove ruinous to us if not counteracted by some spirited conduct on our part;[2] I think the way is plain and easy with the latter; but with the former little can be done as trade has never been an object with the french court tho' the want of it has been severely felt by the nation at large and frequently brought the Kingdom to the brink of ruin.[3] Great Britain knows its intrinsic value and if we prohibit the use of their manufactures or west india commodities except when brought by our own vessels or by those of other nations and thereby oblige them to make their purchases[4] in cash they will very soon come to a compromise. how far the powers of Congress may be competent to bring about this or any other regulation that will better answer the end is not for me to say, but surely they should at least take up the matter and recommend some general regulation to the States unfortunately for us the subject is not well understood here nor is that attention paid to it that its importance requires: yet we are some times reasonable people and can understand things if we please to give them due consideration. it will be your parts therefore to smooth the way by a plain and pointed state of the advantages that will derive to the union by a spirited opposition to the measures of the british ministry[5] I have nothing either new or interesting to communicate to you and have therefore only to add that I am &c.

B. H.

[1] *Q.v.*

[2] JM to Randolph, 30 Aug., and nn. 1–3; 13 Sept., and n. 5; Delegates to Harrison, 20 Sept., and nn. 1, 3; JM to Jefferson, 20 Sept. 1783, and nn. 13, 14.

[3] A. W. Ward *et al.*, eds., *Cambridge Modern History*, VI, 55–56, 168–70, 172–74, 176, 182–83, 185.

[4] That is, of American-produced staples such as tobacco, naval stores, indigo, and rice.

[5] JM to Randolph, 13 Sept., n. 6; Delegates to Harrison, 4 Oct. 1783, and n. 10.

Virginia Delegates to Benjamin Harrison

RC (Virginia State Library). In the hand of Theodorick Bland, except for the signatures of Arthur Lee and John F. Mercer. Docketed: "Letter f'm Virga. Delegates 4th. Oct. 83. inclosg resolve of Congress of 5th August. relative to the offer made by Virga of public Vessels. & of Oct. 3d. on subject of the Govrs. Letter &c. 1783." For the absence of JM's signature, see Delegates to Harrison, 24 June 1783, ed. n.

PRINCE TOWN Octr. 4th 1783

SR.

The last Post brought us your Excellencys favor of the 19th Ultimo. The Information which it Containd relative to the Pennsylvanians setling on the N. W. of the Ohio, we thought it our Duty to lay before Congress, and at the same time moved that it might be recommended to that State to take the most effectual measures to restrain its Citizens from a Measure which your Excellency seemd apprehensive might produce so many Evils to our State in Particular, and which we could not but think might be highly prejudicial to the Union in General.[1] the fate of our Motion by no means answerd our Expectations, as you will see by the Enclosed vote.[2] the Chief Arguments against adopting it were, that Pennsylvania had already used every means in her power for that Purpose, that Congress had Issued a Proclamation prohibiting persons from Setling on Lands within the boundaries of the United States & out of the limits of any of them,[3] That such a resolution wd. reflect on the State of Pennsylvania, as it wd suppose that State to have been at least inattentive to a Subject which nearly concernd her own as well as the Welfare of the States in General, and that Congress had under consideration at this time the General arrangement of Indian affairs in which that Subject would be considered more comprehensively,[4] and only waited for the Confirmation of the acceptance of the Cession by our Assembly to take Vigorous and effectual measures to put a stop to the Evils which wd. result from such irregular Proceedings.[5] We have thought fit to Explain to your Excellency our Conduct in this Matter and hope that our Zeal for the Welfare of the State will apologize for it on the one hand & that the reasons above mentiond, will be deemd Valid on the other[6]

We Enclose Your Excellency the Answers of Congress respecting the Guards & Vessels intended to be kept up, which have but lately passed,[7] owing to the numerous important Subjects which have claimd the attention of Congress. we think it our Duty to transcribe for the Information of the Legislature some Paragraphs (in the Joint letter of our Ministers for treating of Peace) Explanatory of the Sense of some of the Preliminary Articles which have been heretofore P[ub]lishd, which Explanations they have given at the desire of Congress, as follows

Extract from the Joint Letter of Mr. Adams, Mr. Franklin & Mr. Jay dated July 18th 1783.

"The Words—for restoring the Property of *Real* British Subjects were well understood and Explaind between us (viz the Negotiators on both Sides) not to mean or comprehend American Refugees. Mr. Oswald & Mr. Fitzherbert know this to have been the case; and will readily Confess and admit it. this mode of Expression was preferred by them as a more delicate mode of Excluding those refugees and making proper distinctions between them and the Subjects of Britain whose only *Particular* Interest in America consisted in holding Lands and Property there.[8]

The 6th Article viz where it declares that no future Confiscations shall be made &c &c. ought to have fixed the time with greater Accuracy We think the most fair and true Construction is that it relates to the date of the Cessation of Hostilities. We are Surprized to hear that any doubts have arisen in America respecting the time when the Cessation of Hostilities took Place. It most certainly took Place at the Expiration of one month after the date of that declaration in all parts of the World, whether Land or Sea that lays North of the Latitude of the Canaries The Ships afterwards taken from us in the more Northerly Latitudes ought to be reclaimed and given up. we shall apply to Mr. Hartley on this Subject, and also on that of transportation of Negroes from New York contrary to the Words and Intention of the Provisional Articles."*[9]

We Send Yr. Excellency the Papers containing the Proclamations of the King of Great Britain & the W. Indies Calculated to check our growing Commerce & Marine. it is conjectured that France will adopt some measures of a Similar nature. Shd. Britain or any other power, persevere in such a System of Commercial Politics we Imagine Congress will address the States either to adopt themselves or to enable Congress to adopt Regulations to counteract them, but this we do not advance as a certainty.[10] It is easy to perceive how these regulations of Great Britain or France may embarrass our Commerce. It remains to be tried whether they themselves will not first and most Sensibly feel the effects of what we esteem an Ill Judged Policy. we are with the most perfect respect Sr.

Yr Excell'ys most obedt. Servts

THEOK. BLAND
ARTHUR LEE
JOHN F MERCER
except as to the
first paragraph

[1] Harrison to Delegates, 19 Sept. 1783, and nn. 2, 3. On 3 October Bland and Lee laid before Congress a copy of the first two sentences of the second paragraph of the governor's letter (*JCC*, XXV, 640). See n. 6.

[2] On six of the folios "Enclosed," a clerk copied an extract from the journal of Congress for 3 October recording the proceedings, including four tallied votes relating to Indian affairs in the Ohio country or in New York State. On three of those polls, Mercer opposed with his vote the position taken by Bland and Lee. For this reason Mercer indicated by the comment following his signature to the present letter that he did not subscribe to the contents of its first paragraph. The initial vote, which was on the question of ending further debate on the Bland-Lee motion so that Congress could give consideration to "the order of the day," was defeated by a vote of five states to four, with Mercer voting "ay" and Bland and Lee, "no." Congress thereupon, by a vote of eight states to one, and over the opposition of Bland and Lee, adopted Mercer's motion to refer the excerpt from Harrison's letter together with the Bland-Lee motion to a committee.

This action cleared the way for a discussion of "the order of the day," that is, the report of the committee on Indian affairs. Although this committee, when appointed on 12 August, consisted of James Duane, chairman, and two other delegates, it was enlarged a week later by the addition of Benjamin Hawkins and Lee (*JCC*, XXIV, 501, n. 1; XXV, 534, n. 2). For the background and contents of its first report, which related solely to Pennsylvania and Indians, see Harrison to Delegates, 19 Sept., and nn. 2, 3. Its second report, submitted on 3 October, recommended that the legislature of New York be urged to cease granting military

* thus far the Joint letter

bounty lands "at Onandaga and Cayuga," if doing so exposed "these United States to the dangers and calamities of an Indian War." Of the twenty-five delegates attending Congress, only two from New Jersey and one from Pennsylvania voted in favor of the recommendation. On that question Mercer agreed with Bland and Lee.

The debate of 3 October on Indian affairs closed with the untallied adoption of a single paragraph providing that agents "for the northern and western districts" jointly hold "one convention" with the Indians within those districts and "yield to separate conventions" only "in case of inevitable necessity" (*JCC*, XXV, 643). When the committee submitted a more extensive report on 15 October, this paragraph was incorporated as the fifth recommendation of the report (*JCC*, XXV, 687). Bland and Lee had moved on 3 October to amend the paragraph by having Congress notify each state from New Hampshire south to Virginia sufficiently in advance to enable any of those states, at its option, to send "commissioners" to the convention. This amendment was rejected by a vote of 2 to 6. Mercer voted against the proposal (*JCC*, XXV, 643–44). For the background of the issue with the Iroquois Indians in New York, see Delegates to Harrison, 8 Sept., and nn. 3, 4; 1 Nov. 1783 (1st letter), and n. 2.

[3] Harrison to Delegates, 19 Sept. 1783, n. 3; *JCC*, XXV, 602.

[4] *Papers of Madison*, VI, 432–33; 434, n. 10; 444, n. 2; 472, n. 3.

[5] Delegates to Harrison, 20 Sept., and n. 4; JM to Jefferson, 20 Sept. 1783, and n. 3. The Virginia General Assembly on 19 and 20 December confirmed Congress' "acceptance of the Cession," and on 22 December directed Governor Harrison to transmit that "Confirmation" to "the delegates of this State," authorizing them "to convey to the United States in Congress assembled, all the right of this Commonwealth to the territory northwestward of the river Ohio" (*JHDV*, Oct. 1783, pp. 71, 79, 81–83).

[6] In a letter of 20 October 1783 to the speaker of the House of Delegates, Harrison forwarded the present letter with its copy of "the proceedings in Congress." After mentioning their connection with "a question propounded by two of our delegates on a paragraph of a letter of mine," he added that the "apology for the step they have taken" was "indeed necessary as it was never intended for the consideration of Congress but was merely a piece of intelligence communicated for them only and not to bring on a public investigation" (Executive Letter Book, 1783–1786, p. 219, MS in Va. State Library). Harrison thus partially vindicated Mercer's dissent from the action of Bland and Lee.

[7] Instruction to Delegates, 20 June, and n. 3; Instruction to Delegates *in re* "Cormorant," 26–27 June, and n. 3; Harrison to Delegates, 4 July; 19 Sept., and n. 4; Motion *in re* Armed Vessels, 28 July 1783, hdn., ed. n., n. 4. Enclosed in the present letter was a copy in a clerk's hand, except for the signature of Charles Thomson, secretary of Congress, of the resolutions of Congress, dated 3 October 1783, in reply to the two instructions.

[8] On a separate page, enclosed with this letter, Arthur Lee copied this paragraph. Congress had received the peace commissioners' dispatch on 12 September (JM to Randolph, 13 Sept., and n. 1; Wharton, *Revol. Dipl. Corr.*, VI, 569). For Richard Oswald and the British peace commissioners, including Alleyn Fitzherbert, see *Papers of Madison*, V, 154, n. 2; 208, n. 3. For the issue posed by the phrase "*Real* British Subjects" in Article V of the provisional articles of peace, see JM Notes, 9 May, and citations in n. 3; 19 May, and n. 1; 30 May, and n. 1; Beckley to Randolph, 20 June, and n. 7; Wharton, *Revol. Dipl. Corr.*, VI, 98. The word "Refugees" was used as an equivalent of "Loyalists" or "Tories."

[9] Bland wrote the footnote in the left margin of the letter. The first sentence of this paragraph quotes the first sentence of the peace commissioners' paragraph

immediately following the one which Bland had copied. The remainder of his paragraph reproduces the last two paragraphs of the peace commissioners' dispatch (*ibid.*, VI, 569, 570). For the "date of the Cessation of Hostilities," see JM to Randolph, 30 Sept., and n. 7. For David Hartley, see JM to Jefferson, 10 June, and n. 8. The problem of the "transportation of Negroes" has been mentioned frequently in the present volume (Walke to Delegates, 3 May, and nn. 2, 5, 7; JM to Jefferson, 13 May, and n. 10; Jones to JM, 25 May; JM Notes, 26 May, and n. 1; Pendleton to JM, 2 June, and n. 3; Beckley to Randolph, 20 June, n. 7; JM to Randolph, 8 July; Harrison to Delegates, 9 Aug. 1783, and n. 4).

10 The "Proclamations" were probably the one on 2 July of King George III, already summarized, and the one on 23 July of the "lieutenant governor general of Martinique and its dependencies, and commandant general of the French Windward Islands," extending Americans a limited freedom of trade with these Caribbean possessions of France (JM to Randolph, 13 Sept., and nn. 5, 6; Delegates to Harrison, 20 Sept., and n. 3; JM to Jefferson, 20 Sept., and nn. 13, 14; Harrison to Delegates, 26 Sept.; 3 Oct.; *Pa. Packet*, 13 Sept., 30 Sept., 2 Oct.; *Pa. Journal*, 13 Sept.; *Va. Gazette*, 27 Sept. 1783). See also Wharton, *Revol. Dipl. Corr.*, VI, 559, 560–61, 582–83, 592–93.

From Edmund Pendleton

Printed excerpt (Stan. V. Henkels Catalogue No. 694 [1892], p. 94).

EDITORIAL NOTE

About 1850 the present letter was calendared, probably by a clerk of Peter Force, as follows:

"1783, October 6. Virginia

To James Madison

"Garrisons in time of peace. A standing army the bane of society. Should garrisons be Continental or supported by the States where located. German-Town as a seat for the Government merely another name for Philadelphia. Trade with France restricted. Arrival of British ships. Rise in the price of goods. Races at Fredericksburg. 1 page 4°" (LC: Madison Miscellany).

The last four topics are obviously omitted from the Henkels' summary. For trade with France, see Delegates to Harrison, 20 Sept., and n. 3; 4 Oct., and n. 9; Harrison to Delegates, 3 Oct., 1783. Although the Philadelphia and Richmond newspapers fail to mention rising prices, they leave no doubt of the more frequent arrivals of British ships (*Pa. Packet*, 20, 25, 27, and 30 Sept.; *Va. Gazette*, 27 Sept.; 4 Oct. 1783). In a recent letter, JM had mentioned the races at Fredericksburg beginning on 6 October (JM to Jefferson, 20 Sept. 1783, and n. 6). Pendleton may have remarked either that, as a trustee of the Fredericksburg Academy, he had been summoned to be in Fredericksburg on 7 October "upon business of the greatest importance," or, what is more probable, that he was attending the General Court which had begun its sessions on 1 October in Richmond (*Va. Gazette*, 27 Sept.; *Va. Gazette, and Weekly Advertiser*, 4 Oct. 1783; David J. Mays, *Edmund Pendleton*, II, 205, 388, n. 15).

VIRGINIA, October 6, 1783

. . . The question touching Garrisons in time of peace, is in its nature delicate as well as difficult, and therefore I don't wonder there should be diversity of opinions about it. They seem useful & indeed necessary & yet have their certain evils, among which not the least considerable is that they lead to a standing Army, that bane of Society; nor is it less difficult to decide the question, if they are admitted, whether they ought to be Continental, or supported by & under the Government of the respective States where they are kept.[1]

. . . German Town must be named in the competition for the permanent seat of Congress, merely as another name for Philad'a which I suppose they can't name with propriety, for I can't suppose a single man in the United States would prefer that Village to the great City so near it.[2] I have thought for some time that the contest would end in a return to that City, as soon as resentment for their former neglect had a little worn off.[3]

[1] In a letter of 20 September to Jefferson (*q.v.*), JM had mentioned the problem, including its constitutional aspect, of reaching a decision in Congress about the nature of a peacetime army. The reference by Pendleton to the subject may signify that in a letter to him, dated on or about the same day, JM had commented similarly. See also JM to Randolph, 17 June, and nn. 10–12; 12 Aug.; to Jefferson, 11 Aug., and nn. 11, 12. If the excerpt includes all Pendleton's remarks on the subject, he neglected to refer to the garrisoning of posts in the Northwest Territory which were or soon would be outside the boundaries of any state (Harrison to Delegates, 26 Sept. 1783, n. 5).

[2] JM to Pendleton, 8 Sept. 1783, and n. 5.

[3] Pendleton to JM, 1 Sept. 1783, and n. 1. Although the issue of returning to Philadelphia was debated frequently in Congress during the next five years, the outcome failed to fulfill Pendleton's expectation (Edmund C. Burnett, *Continental Congress*, pp. 584–86, 616–18, 690–91, 714–19).

Benjamin Harrison to Virginia Delegates

FC (Virginia State Library). In the hand of Samuel Patteson. Addressed to "The Virginia Delegates in Congress."

COUNCIL CHAMBER Oct: 10th. 1783.

GENTLEMEN,

The last post brought no letter from you.[1] The Clerk of the Council[2] informs me that whilst I was in Gloster[3] you wrote for an account of the several sums of money that had been advanced by this State to the continent.[4] the letter by some means or other has been mislaid. I have therefore to desire a copy of it and to request that you will be very particular in the enumeration of the Kind of grants if you mean to take it in the extensive manner it has been represented to me, it will be a work of time.[5]

I am &c.

B. H.

[1] The delegates may have written to Governor Harrison on or about 27 September, but no such letter or any mention of one has been found.
[2] Archibald Blair.
[3] Harrison to Delegates, 28 Aug. 1783, n. 2.
[4] Delegates to Harrison, 23 Aug. 1783, and n. 9.
[5] The delegates apparently neglected to fulfill this request.

Receipt of John Francis Mercer

MS (Morristown National Historical Park, Morristown, N.J.).

Oct. 11. 1783

Recd fm. Loan of the Honble Jas Madison Six hundred Dollars.

John F Mercer[1]

[1] JM and Mercer were in Princeton on 11 October (*JCC*, XXV, 670–71). The "Dollars" were probably either the currency of Pennsylvania or New Jersey. In a letter of 12 November 1784 to JM, Mercer apologized for his delay in repaying the debt, arranged for the remittance of $400, and promised to discharge the balance as soon as his "Crops can be converted into Cash" (LC: Madison Papers). A part of the debt was still unpaid in 1803 (JM to Mercer, 11 Aug. 1803).

To Edmund Randolph

RC (LC: Madison Papers). Cover franked by JM and addressed to "Edmund Randolph Esqr. Richmond." Docketed by Randolph, "J. Madison October 13. 1783."

Philada. Octr. 13th. 1783

My dear Sir

I returned here yesterday in order to be with Mr. Jones before his departure and make some little arrangements with him of a private nature.[1] The past week has been spent by Congress in deliberating on 1.

their permanent seat, 2. their temporary one. The competition for the former lay between the falls of the Potowmack and those of the Delaware.[2] We hoped at first from the *apparent* views of the Eastern Delegates that they would have given a preference to Potowmack. In the event they joined with Pena. & the intermediate States in favor of the Delaware the consequence of which is that the vicinity of its Falls is to become the future Seat of the fœderal Govt. unless a conversion of some of the Eastern States can be effected.[3] The next point was the abode of Congs. untill their permanent seat could receive them. The expediency of removing from Princeton in order "to the more convenient transaction of the affairs of the U.S. and accomodation of Congs.["] was first determined on, Masssts. Cont. & R.I. alone being opposed to it.[4] Trenton was next proposed, on which Question the votes were divided by the River Delaware.[5] Philada. came next in order. Besides its convenient position in relation to the Permanent seat,[6] superior temporary accomodations for the public business and for Congs., arguments in its favor were drawn from the tendency of passing by these accomodations to others inferior in themselves & more distant from the perman[en]t seat, to denote a resentment unworthy of a Sovereign authority agst. a part of its constituents which had fully expiated any offence which they might have committed: and at the same time to convert their penitential and affectionate temper into the bitterest hatred. To enforce this idea some of the proceedings of Congs. expressive of resentment agst. Philada. were made use of.[7] Great stress also was laid on the tendency of removing to any small or distant place, to prevent or delay business which the honor & interest of the U.S. require sd. be dispatched as soon as possible. on the other side objections were drawn from those sources which have produced dislikes to Philada. and wch. will be easily conjectured by you. on the question N.Y. Pa. Delaware Virga. & N. Carolina were ay; Masts. Cont. R.I. N. Jersey no; and Maryland & S. C[aro]lina divided. If either of the divided States had been in the affirmative it was the purpose of N. Jersey to add a seventh vote in favor of Phil. The division of S. Carolina was owing to the absence of Mr. Rutlidge & Mr. Izard both of whom would have voted for Phila. The State was represented by two members only. The division of Maryland represented by Mr. Caroll & Mr. McHenry was occasioned by the negative of the latter whose zeal for Annapolis determined him to sacrifice every consideration to an experiment in its favr. before he would accede to the vote for Philada. The aversion of the Eastern States was the ground of his coalition with them.[8] The arguments in favor of Annapolis consisted of objections agst. Philada. Those agst. it were cheifly the same which had been urged in preference of Philada. On the question the States were Masts. Cont. R.I. Delaware, Maryland & N.C. ay. N.Y. N.J. Pa. Virga. no. S.C. divided. Virga. was represented by Mr. Lee Mr. Mercer & Mr. M. The first was in the affirmative.[9] Mr. Jones & Mr. Bland were in Philad. The vote of the latter wd. have been in favor of Annapolis of the former in favr. of Philada. The opinion of Mr. L. & Mr. B. in favr. of Annapolis resulted from a dislike to Philada. & the idea that the views of Virga. would be promoted by it.[10] That of their colleagues from a belief that the reasons drawn in favr. of Philada. from the national consideration reqd. a concession of local views, and even that a recision of the permanent vote for Trenton in favor of George Town, the object of Va. would be promoted by placing the Eastern States in Philada. They also supposed that the concurrence of the Eastern States in a temporary vote for Annapolis to take effect some weeks hence, was little to be confided in, since the arrival of a colleague to the Delegate from N. Hamshire would with the accession of Pena. who wd. prefer Trenton to Annapolis & be moreover stimulated by resentment, would make up seven States to reverse the removal to Annapolis.[11] Add to the whole that ex[p]erience has verified the opinion that in any small place Congs. are too dependent on courtesy & favor to be exempt eithe[r] in their purses or their sensibility from degrading impositions. Upon the whole it is most probable that Philada. will be abode of Congs. during the Winter.[12] I must refer to Mr. Jones for explanations on all these points; he will be in Richmond early in the Session.[13] For myself I have engaged to return to Princeton to attend some interesting points before Congs. Having not yet settled my arrangements for the Winte[r,] I must for the pres[ent] be silent as to my [future?] situation. Mr. Van Berkel arrived a few [days ago?] Congs. are in a charming situation to receive him, [being?] in an obscure village, unde[te]rmined where they will spend the Winter, and without a Minister of F.A.[14] After the rect. of this you will stop your correspondence, and probably not hear further from me.[15] I set off tomorrow morning at 3 oClock in the Flying Machine for Princeton, and it is now advancing towards the hour of Sleep.[16] In haste adieu My dear friend and be assured that

I am Yrs. sincerely

J.M Jr.

[1] JM to Jefferson, 20 Sept., n. 6; 30 Sept. 1783, and n. 2. The nature of the "little arrangements" may be suggested by Joseph Jones's remark in his letter of 30 October from Virginia to JM (*q.v.*): "Company has hitherto prevented me since my arrival from packing[?] [the] things you desired and sending them to Mr. Maury." For James Maury, see JM to James Madison, Sr., 27 May 1783, n. 2.

[2] The falls of the Potomac River, a mile and a half long, terminate at the Great Falls, a cataract about ten and a half miles northwest of Georgetown and the Virginia shore opposite thereto; those of the Delaware River are at Trenton, N.J., and the Pennsylvania shore opposite thereto. For the "Neighbourhood of George Town" as a possible site of Congress' permanent residence, see *Papers of Madison*, VI, 447; 448, n. 6; Jones to JM, 28 June; Instructions to Delegates, 28 June; Motion *in re* Permanent Site, 22 Sept. 1783, and n. 1. On 24 June the "citizens of Trenton and its vicinity" invited Congress to move there from Philadelphia to escape the mutiny (*JCC*, XXIV, 424). On 13 October a letter to Congress from five prominent residents of Trenton pledged, on behalf of about thirty householders, to provide accommodations for approximately ninety persons and ninety-four horses, as well as some office space and a room, forty-three by twenty feet in size, in which Congress could meet (NA: PCC, No. 22, fols. 283–86; *JCC*, XXV, 695).

[3] On Monday, 6 October, in accord with the "order of the day," Congress took "into consideration the propositions of several states, respecting a place for the permanent residence of Congress." After two efforts by the delegates of Rhode Island, Massachusetts, and New Hampshire to postpone action upon the issue had met with no other support, Congress proceeded to canvass the opinion of the delegates on each state seriatim, beginning with New Hampshire, as a possible site "for the residence of Congress." The outcome made clear that, in this regard, New Hampshire, Massachusetts, Rhode Island, Connecticut, North Carolina, South Carolina, and Georgia required no further attention. New York drew the approval of only its own two delegates, the two from Connecticut, one of the two from Rhode Island, and the one from New Hampshire. Besides its own delegates, New Jersey was favored by those from Connecticut, Rhode Island, Massachusetts, and New Hampshire. As for Pennsylvania, its delegates' unanimous vote of "aye" was echoed only by Jacob Read of South Carolina. For Delaware, its delegates attracted no allies.

Every delegate from Virginia, except Bland, together with all the delegates from North Carolina and South Carolina joined Daniel Carroll and James McHenry in supporting the choice of Maryland. Those two Maryland delegates, however, refused to reciprocate by favoring Virginia. Only Elbridge Gerry of Massachusetts and Jacob Read united with the five delegates of Virginia in endorsing their state as the site for the capital of the Confederation. The session of 6 October apparently adjourned after resolving that "the fixing on a place for providing and erecting buildings for the residence of Congress, be an order of the day for the morrow" (*JCC*, XXV, 647–54).

On 7 October, after unsuccessful efforts to have "near Trenton," "near George-Town," at Annapolis, or on "the Hudson" made either the definitive or alternative choice for a "permanent seat," Congress by a vote of 7 to 4 (Md., Va., N.C., and S.C.) agreed: "That buildings for the use of Congress be erected on or near the banks of the Delaware, provided a suitable district can be procured on or near the banks of the said river, for a federal town; and that the right of soil, and an exclusive or such other jurisdiction as Congress may direct, shall be vested in the United States." In the three tallied polls preceding the adoption of this resolution, the five Virginia delegates, except Arthur Lee, were for retaining "near Trenton" and near "George-Town" as alternative sites and were unanimously against including "the Hudson" or selecting Annapolis (*JCC*, XXV, 654–57).

Immediately after the resolution carried, the delegates of Delaware, supported by Bland and those of Maryland and South Carolina, tried without success to have it amended by specifying "near Wilmington" in Delaware as the place (*JCC*, XXV, 658). Before adjourning on 7 October, Congress, without a recorded vote, decided that "on or near the banks" of the Delaware meant "near the falls," that a committee of five delegates, Gerry, chairman, should proceed there so as to "report a proper district," and that "to consider of the temporary residence of Congress" should be "an order of the day for to-morrow." On 8 October a motion by Hugh Williamson of North Carolina, seconded by Read, to reconsider the choice just mentioned failed to carry. The delegates from the six states north of Delaware were unanimously against the motion; those from Delaware and the four more southerly states were unanimously in its favor (*JCC*, XXV, 658–60). Following the session of 7 October, Bland apparently was absent from Congress until 22 October (*JCC*, XXV, 659, 719). Jones left Congress after the session of 8 October for the remainder of 1783 (JM to Jefferson, 20 Sept. 1783, n. 6).

[4] On 10 October, over the unanimous opposition of the New England delegates, it was decided that for the better accommodation of Congress, "it is expedient for them to adjourn from their present residence" (*JCC*, XXV, 664–66).

[5] The motion leading to the sectional vote stated by JM was introduced on 10 October by James Duane and seconded by David Howell to amend the motion, introduced by Hugh Williamson and seconded by Richard Peters. Williamson proposed that Congress on 30 October move from Princeton to Philadelphia, continue there until 7 June 1784, and thereafter assemble at Trenton. Following the rejection of the Duane amendment, the vote on 10 October was on "the main question," the recommended return of Congress temporarily to Philadelphia (*JCC*, XXV, 666–67).

[6] That is, at or near the falls of the Delaware River.

[7] Delegates to Harrison, 14–15 Aug., and n. 7; 23 Aug.; JM to Randolph, 18 Aug., and nn. 3, 4; 30 Aug.; to James Madison, Sr., 30 Aug. 1783, and n. 9.

[8] *JCC*, XXV, 667–68. Of the two delegates present on 10 October from South Carolina, Jacob Read voted "ay," and Richard Beresford, "no." JM and John Francis Mercer were the only Virginia delegates who shared in the poll.

[9] The poll, summarized accurately by JM, was upon an amended motion on 11 October by William Ellery, seconded by Samuel Holten, to direct President Boudinot to adjourn Congress on 22 October and convene it at Annapolis nine days later. The motion further provided for Congress to continue at Annapolis until 7 June 1784. It should then adjourn and convene at Trenton two days later. Both Annapolis and Trenton were proposed as sites of "temporary residence" (*JCC*, XXV, 669–72).

[10] The stand of Bland and Lee was consistent with that taken by them in a poll on 14 August (Delegates to Harrison, 14–15 Aug., n. 7; JM to Randolph, 18 Aug. 1783, and nn. 3, 4). Unwillingness to have Congress return to the city in which Robert Morris and his business friends wielded great power was most probably a dominant consideration in determining their vote (*Papers of Madison*, VI, 207; 208, n. 5; 304–5; 306, n. 6; 347, n. 7; 357; 409, n. 1; JM to Jefferson, 20 Sept. 1783, and n. 17; Burnett, *Letters*, VII, 342).

[11] Although JM, Jones, and Mercer, contrary to Lee and Bland, believed that the national welfare argued strongly in favor of Philadelphia over Annapolis as a temporary meeting place of Congress, all five of the Virginia delegates undoubtedly preferred Georgetown to the falls of the Delaware River as the site of the permanent capital of the Confederation. JM and Mercer apparently framed their strategy so that if the New England delegates were obliged against their will to return to Philadelphia, the aversion of those delegates to having the permanent capital within the orbit of that city's influence would deepen sufficiently to ally them with the southern delegates in overturning the decision in regard to the permanent capital by replacing the falls of the Delaware River with those of the Potomac. By so reasoning JM and Mercer discounted the significance of the New England delegates' unanimous vote on 7 October in favor of the Delaware

location. JM's hope in this regard was at least halfway gratified by the marked shift of position by those delegates only one week after the date of the present letter (Delegates to Harrison, 1 Nov. 1783 [1st letter]). Contrary to JM's fear, Abiel Foster, the sole delegate from New Hampshire, was not joined by a colleague during the remainder of 1783.

[12] In this instance JM's prophecy was to be unrealized.

[13] Joseph Jones, a delegate from King George County to the General Assembly, may have reached Richmond before the Virginia House of Delegates mustered its first quorum on 4 November (*JHDV*, Oct. 1783, pp. 4, 7, 12; Jones to JM, 30 Oct. 1783, and n. 5).

[14] JM to Jefferson, 10 June 1783, and n. 23. The position of secretary for foreign affairs remained vacant from early in June 1783 until late in December 1784 (JM Notes, 4 June 1783, n. 3).

[15] JM apparently did not write again to Randolph until 10 March 1784 (LC: Madison Papers). For Randolph's last letter of 1783 to JM, see JM to Randolph, 30 Sept. 1783, n. 3.

[16] The stagecoach named the "New-York Flying Machine" left the Bunch of Grapes Tavern on Third Street between Market and Arch Streets in Philadelphia every Tuesday, Thursday, and Saturday at 4:00 A.M. for Elizabethtown, N.J. The passengers were afforded an opportunity to have breakfast at Bristol, Pa., and dinner at Princeton (*Pa. Journal*, 17 Sept. 1783; *New Jersey Archives*, 2d ser., V, 246, 287–88, 422–23). By "3 oClock" JM probably signified the hour at which he would have to awaken so as to reach the tavern in ample time to assure himself of one of the less uncomfortable seats in the stagecoach.

Notes on Congress' Place of Residence

MS (LC: Jefferson Papers). Undated. Unsigned but in JM's hand.

EDITORIAL NOTE

JM's letter of 13 October 1783 to Randolph (*q.v.*) and this memorandum are sufficiently alike in their contents to suggest that they were written at about the same time. In the paragraph beginning with "Philada" in the margin, JM stated that Congress had resolved to fix its place of permanent residence at "the Falls of Delaware." This decision had been reached on 7 October; hence these notes could not have been prepared before that date. They also appear to reflect the inconclusive debates during the next four days on the choice of a temporary meeting place of Congress. If JM had delayed until 21 October before summarizing the arguments for and against each of the towns or other locations proposed as a suitable site for the ad interim capital of the Confederation, he almost surely would have noted the important resolution adopted on that day (Jones to JM, 30 Oct., n. 5). Furthermore, he probably did not attend Congress on 19, 20, and 21 October (Motion *in re* Preliminary Peace Treaty, 18 Oct. 1783, ed. n.).

It is a reasonable assumption that JM gave these notes to Jefferson between

29 October and 3 November, when Jefferson stopped in Philadelphia before proceeding to Congress in Princeton. The memorandum was designed to inform him about issues which by then had not been entirely settled (Boyd, *Papers of Jefferson*, VI, 349 n.; Delegates to Harrison, 1 Nov. 1783 [1st letter]). In a letter of 11 November 1783 to Governor Harrison, devoted in part to summarizing the earlier competition among the delegates in Congress to have the temporary or permanent capital of the Confederation located at their preferred sites, Jefferson seems to have drawn some of his information from the present memorandum (Boyd, *Papers of Jefferson*, VI, 351–53).

[*ca.* 14 October 1783]

Permanent seat of Congress

North River—recommended for the permanent seat of Congs. chiefly by its security against foreign danger[1]

Falls of Potowmac—By 1. geographical centrality—2. proximity to western Country already ceded—2. inducement to further Cessions from N.C. S.C. & Georgia.[2] 4 remoteness from the influence of any overgrown commercial city.

Falls of Delaware—By 1. centrality with regard to number of inhabitants. 2 centrality as to no. of States & of Delegates. 3 facility of obtaining intelligence from sea.[3]

Temporary seat of Congress

Princeton—in favor of it, 1. its neighbourhood to the Permanent [se]at, 2. inconveniency of a removal.[4] 3. beneficial effect of a frug[al] situation of Congs. on their popularity throughout the States. 4 the risque in case of removal from Princeton of returning under the commercial & corrupt influence of Philada.[5]—against it—1. unfitness for transacting the public business. 2 deficiency of accomodation, exposing the attending members to the danger of indignities & extortions, discouraging perhaps the fitest men from undertaking the service & amounting to a prohibition of such as had families from which they would not part.[6]

Trenton. argts. in favor & agst. it similar to those respecting Princeton. It was particularly remarked that when the option lay with the President & committee between Trenton & Princeton the latter was preferred as least unfit to receive Congs. on their removal from Philada.[7]

Philada. In favor of it. 1. its unrivalled conveniency for transacting the public business, & accomodating Congress. 2 its being the only place where all the public offices particularly that of Finance could be kept under the inspection & controul of & proper intercourse with Congs.[8] 3. its conveniency for F. Ministers, to which, cæteris paribus,[9] some regard would be expected. 4. the circumstances which produced a removal from Philada. which rendered a return as soon as the insult had been expiated, expedient for supporting in the eyes of foreign nations the appearance of internal harmony, and preventing an appearance of resentment in Congs. agst. the State of Pa. or City of Philada.[10] an appearance which was very much strengthened by some of their proceedings at Princeton—particularly by an unnecessary & irregular declaration not to return to Phi[l]a. In addition to these overt reasons, it was concluded by sundry of the members who were most anxious to fix Congs. permanently at[11] the falls of the Potowmac that a temporary residence in Philada. would be most likely to prepare a sufficient number of votes for that place in preference to the Falls of Delaware,[12] and to produce a reconsideration of the vote in favor of the latter[13]—Agst. Philada. were alledged. 1. the difficulty & uncertainty of getting away from it at the time limited.[14] 2. the influence of a large comercial & wealthy city on the public Councils. In addition to these objections, the hatred agst. Mr. M. and hope of accelerating his final r[esigna]tion were latent motives with some, as perhaps envy of the prom[inence of] Philada. and dislike of the support of Pa to obnoxious recomendations of Congs. were with others.[15]

Annapolis—in favor of it. 1st. its capacity for accomodating Congs. and its conveniences for the public business. 2. the soothing tendency of so Southern a position on the temper of the S. States.—agst. it, 1st. the preposterousness of taking a temporary station so distant from the permanent seat fixed on, especially as better accomodations were to be passed by at Philada. which was less than 4/5ths of the distance from the Permanent Seat. 2d. the peculiar force such a step would give to the charge agst. Congs. of being swayed by improper motives.[16] Besides these considerations it was the opinion of some that a removal of Congs. to Annapolis would inspire Maryland with hopes that wd. prevent a cooperation in favor of George town, & favor the commerce of that State at the expence of Virginia[17]

[1] *Papers of Madison*, VI, 447; 448, n. 4; JM to Randolph, 10 June, and n. 14; 28 July, and n. 6; 13 Oct., and n. 3; Livingston to JM, 19 July, n. 9; Pendleton to JM, 21 July 1783. New York had offered the town of Kingston for a permanent residence of Congress. Situated ninety miles up the Hudson River, its capture, unless

by envelopment over rugged terrain, would necessitate control of both New York City and West Point.

[2] Instructions to Delegates, 28 June, and nn. 2, 6; Harrison to Delegates, 4 July, and n. 3; 25 Oct.; Pendleton to JM, 28 July; JM to Randolph, 28 July; 13 Oct. 1783, and nn. 2, 3, 11. By "already ceded," JM meant that the Virginia General Assembly during its session of October 1783 probably would accept the modifications insisted upon by Congress in the offer of cession extended by the Assembly on 2 January 1781 (Delegates to Harrison, 13 Sept., ed. n.; 20 Sept., and n. 4; 4 Oct., n. 5; JM to Jefferson, 20 Sept. 1783, n. 3). He may also have had in mind the cession by New York in 1782 (*Papers of Madison*, V, 201, n. 9; 225; 227, n. 13). For the cessions of western lands by North Carolina and South Carolina, see *ibid.*, IV, 203, n. 16; JM Notes, 19 June 1783, n. 2. Georgia delayed until 1802 before surrendering its western territory to the United States.

[3] JM to Randolph, 28 July; 13 Oct. 1783, and nn. 2, 3, 5, 9, 11. If JM had drawn a parallel of latitude from the Atlantic Ocean through the "Falls of Delaware" and across Pennsylvania, most of the inhabitants in New Jersey would have been north of that line, and, in Pennsylvania, south of it. Counting Pennsylvania with the more southerly states and New Jersey with the more northerly ones, the seven states of the north in 1783 had a population of about 1,370,000, and the six of the south, about 1,018,600 (Evarts B. Greene and Virginia D. Harrington, *American Population before the Federal Census of 1790* [New York, 1932], pp. 7–8). Article V of the Articles of Confederation stipulated that, although each state should not have less than two or more than seven delegates in Congress, each state counted only as one in tallying a vote (*JCC*, XIX, 215). Among the three sites competing to be the place where Congress would locate permanently, New York City, from the standpoint "of obtaining intelligence from sea," obviously was the most advantageously situated, and the "Falls of Potowmac" the least.

[4] Princeton is about ten miles northeast of the "Falls of Delaware." Whenever the permanent capital at these "Falls" should be ready for occupancy, a "removal" there from Princeton would be less inconvenient and expensive than from any other proposed temporary site except Trenton.

[5] The New England delegates, especially, favored Princeton as "a frugal situation," far preferable to returning temporarily to "the commercial & corrupt influence" of Philadelphia (JM to Randolph, 13 Oct. 1783, and nn. 3, 4). See also Pendleton to JM, 16 June, and n. 10; JM to Jefferson, 17 July 1783, and n. 9.

[6] JM to Randolph, 8 July, n. 2; 30 Aug.; 13 Sept.; 13 Oct., and n. 12; to Jefferson, 17 July, and n. 9; 20 Sept. 1783.

[7] JM Notes, 21 June, and n. 7; JM to Jefferson, 17 July, and n. 7; to Randolph, 13 Oct. 1783, and n. 2.

[8] JM to Jefferson, 17 July, and n. 7; Pendleton to JM, 6 Oct., and n. 3; JM to Randolph, 13 Oct. 1783, and n. 11.

[9] Other things being equal.

[10] Hamilton to JM, 6 July, n. 6; JM to Randolph, 8 July; 28 July, and n. 3; 13 Oct., and citations in n. 7; to Jefferson, 17 July 1783, and n. 7.

[11] Immediately after "at," JM wrote and canceled "Georgetown."

[12] Between "Delaware" and the comma, JM wrote and canceled "for the permanent."

[13] Delegates to Harrison, 14–15 Aug., and n. 7; Mercer to JM, 14 Aug., and n. 3; JM to Randolph, 18 Aug., and nn. 3, 4; 30 Aug.; 13 Oct., and n. 2; to James Madison, Sr., 30 Aug., and n. 9; to Jefferson, 20 Sept. 1783.

[14] By "time limited" JM meant either 7 June 1784 or the day when the proposed accommodations at the falls of the Delaware River should be ready for occupancy (JM to Randolph, 13 Oct. 1783, nn. 3, 5, 10).

15 "Mr. M." was Robert Morris, superintendent of finance (JM to Randolph, 30 Aug., and n. 6; Burnett, *Letters*, VII, 378–80). For the termination of his service in that office, see JM to Jefferson, 20 Sept. 1783, n. 17. Among the principal "recommendations" supported by the Pennsylvania delegation, but opposed as "obnoxious" by delegates from some of the other states, had been the proposed impost amendment, and half pay for life or full pay for five years to officers of the continental army who served for the duration of the war. For these issues, consult the index of this volume under Continental Congress, actions on furloughing or discharging troops, plan for restoring public credit; Imposts.

16 JM to Jefferson, 17 July, and n. 9; Pendleton to JM, 28 July; JM to Randolph, 13 Oct. 1783, and nn. 9, 11. Annapolis is about 155 miles from the falls of the Delaware River; Philadelphia, about 30 miles. Immediately following "being," JM wrote and heavily canceled four or five words. Of these only the last two, "by resentment," are discernible.

17 JM to Randolph, 13 Oct. 1783, and n. 3. In 1782 Anne Arundel County, Md., in which Annapolis was the principal town, had 18,081 inhabitants—51.82 per cent of whom were white, and 48.18 per cent were black. In the same year, Fairfax County, with a part of its northern line running the length of the falls of the Potomac, had 8,763 inhabitants, with a white-black ratio of 58.82:41.18 per cent (Stella H. Sutherland, *Population Distribution in Colonial America* [New York, 1936], pp. 173–75). Both Annapolis and Alexandria were busy ports. The sailing distance from the Chesapeake Capes to Annapolis is shorter than to Alexandria.

To Alexander Hamilton

RC (LC: Papers of Alexander Hamilton). Manuscript much frayed along its right edge. In JM's hand, but his signature and part of his complimentary close are missing. In the left margin alongside the first four lines of the letter appears in an old-fashioned script, "A. H. Testifies the opposition of H. to the removal of Congress to Princeton, both before and after the event." Docketed by Hamilton, "Letter from Mr. Maddison."

PRINCETON Octr. 16. 1783

DEAR SIR

Your favor of the 6th of July[1] by some singular ill luck never found its way to my hands till yesterday evening. The only part that now needs attention is a request that I will answer the following Question "What appeared to be my ideas and disposition respecting the removal of Congress—did I appear to wish to hasten it, or did I not rather shew a strong disposition to procrastinate it?"[2] If this request had been recd. at the time it ought it might have been answered as fully as you then wished. Even after the delay which has taken place my recollection enable[s] me with certainty to witness that the uniform strain of yo[ur] sentiments as they appeared both from particular conversations with myself and incidental ones with others in [my] presence was opposed to the removal of Congress excep[t] in the last necessity; that when you finally yielded the measure it appeared to be more in compliance with the peremptory expostulations of oth[ers] than with any disposition of your own mind,[3] an[d] that after the arrival of Congress at Princeton you[r] conversation shewed that you received the removal with regret than with pleasure.[4]

Perhaps this obedience to your wishes may be too [late?] to answer the original object of them; But I could not [let pass?] such an opportunity of testifying the esteem & regard with

[1] *Q.v.*, and n. 7.

[2] This is an accurate quotation of Hamilton's fourth paragraph in his letter of 6 July 1783.

[3] For the context of this matter, see JM Notes, 19 June, and nn. 6–8; 20 June, and n. 1; 21 June, and nn. 1–8; JM to Randolph, 30 June; Hamilton to JM, 29 June; 6 July 1783, and nn. 3, 5, 6; Syrett and Cooke, *Papers of Hamilton*, III, 438–58, and esp. 448–49.

[4] JM and Hamilton were together in Congress at Princeton during the first day or two of July and for several days later that month (*ibid.*, III, 413, 414, 418; Hamilton to JM, 6 July, nn. 1, 7; JM to Randolph, 15 July, n. 7; to Jefferson, 17 July, n. 14; Livingston to JM, 19 July 1783, n. 6).

Motion *in re* Preliminary Peace Treaty

MS (NA: PCC, No. 29, fol. 335). In JM's hand. Undated and undocketed.

EDITORIAL NOTE

Although the journal of Congress omits mention of this motion, it appears to be the one summarized by Charles Thomson in his committee book as a proposal made by a delegate, whom he did not identify, "to transmit Exemplfd. Copies of prelimy. Arts. of peace to the respective States." The doubt whether this entry refers to JM's motion arises from the fact that Congress on 18 October named a committee—James Duane, chairman, William Ellery, and Samuel Huntington—to consider the motion noted by Thomson (NA: PCC, No. 186, fol. 133). As a rule, the author of a motion was chosen to be the chairman of the committee to which it was assigned. In this instance, JM may have asked to be excused from that appointment, for he seems to have been in Philadelphia on 19, 20, and 21 October (*JCC*, XXV, 706–10, 712–13, 718–19). The motion is of the same purport as one introduced by Hamilton in Congress on 14 May and recommitted on 30 May (JM Notes, 14 May, and n. 1; 30 May 1783, and nn. 1, 2).

[*ca.* 18 October 1783]

That an Exemplification of the articles concluded on the day[1] of between the Ministers Plenipo: of the U.S & the K. of G.B. as ratified by Congs. on the day of be[2] transmitted to each of the States & that they be informed that Congress deem it indispensable to the honor of the Confederacy & to the principles of good faith, that every act within the States respectively sd. be foreborne which may tend to render any of the stipulations in the said articles hereafter impracticable on the part of the U.S.[3]

1 30 November 1782.

2 15 April 1783.

3 During the spring of 1783 JM contended unsuccessfully that Congress should not ratify the preliminary articles of peace, and that the state of war would not officially end until the conclusion of definitive treaties of peace by Great Britain with France and its ally, the United States (*Papers of Madison*, VI, 453; 454, n. 9; 465–57; 458, n. 3). He later recognized, however, that the refusal by Virginia and most of the other states to abide by the stipulations in Articles IV and V of the provisional articles for enabling British and Loyalist creditors to collect their "bona fide. Debts" and recover their confiscated "Estates" and "Properties" might hamper the American peace commissioners in negotiating a definitive treaty, and perhaps cause difficulties in procuring the return of American-owned slaves in British possession, the withdrawal of British garrisons from forts on American soil, and the timely evacuation of New York City (*Papers of Madison*, VI, 335; 337, n. 14; 341, n. 5; 423, n. 7; Walke to Delegates, 3 May, nn. 2, 5; Pendleton to JM, 4 May, n. 5; Harrison to Delegates, 9 May, and n. 6; JM Notes, 14 May, and n. 1; 26 May, n. 1; 30 May, and n. 1; Jones to JM, 31 May, and n. 14; 21 June, n. 21; 28 June; Beckley to Randolph, 20 June, n. 7; Delegates to Harrison, 23 Aug., and n. 2; 8 Sept. 1783, and nn. 3, 4).

In the report submitted to Congress on 20 October and adopted two days later, the Duane committee concurred with the aim of the motion but tempered the language in deference to each state's sensitivity about its rights. The committee prepared a circular letter, to be sent by President Boudinot to the state executives, stressing that Congress "consider with deep regret any act which might render it impracticable to give a just efficacy to the provisional articles for the restoration of peace, which are expressly stipulated to be inserted in the Definitive treaty" (NA: PCC, No. 186, fol. 133; *JCC*, XXV, 716–17, 717, n. 1). The Virginia delegates, in their letter to Harrison on 1 November (1st letter) probably enclosed a copy of the circular letter, dated 29 October. The governor seems to have submitted it to the Virginia General Assembly on 13 November (Delegates to Harrison, 1 Nov. [1st letter]; Harrison to the speaker of the House of Delegates, 13 Nov. 1783 in Executive Letter Book, 1783–1786, p. 231, MS in Va. State Library; Burnett, *Letters*, VII, 358).

Benjamin Harrison to Virginia Delegates

FC (Virginia State Library). Addressed to "Delegates in Congress." In the hand of Samuel Patteson.

IN COUNCIL Octo: 18th. 1783.

GENTLEMEN,

I received your favor by the last post with its enclosures which shall be laid before the assembly as soon as they meet which I hope will be next week.[1]

The sooner Congress come to a determination on the subject of trade the better as I expect it will be the first thing of consequence that will be taken under consideration by this assembly[2]

I am &c.

B. H.

[1] Delegates to Harrison, 20 Sept., n. 4; 4 Oct., and nn. 2, 5–10; JM to Randolph 13 Oct. 1783, n. 13.

[2] About a month after JM's tenure in Congress had ended, the Virginia House of Delegates unanimously adopted on 4 December a resolution declaring that Congress "ought to be empowered to prohibit," or "to concert any other mode to be adopted by the States" to prohibit, "British vessels from being the carriers of the growth or produce of the British West India islands to these United States, so long as the restriction" imposed by King George III's proclamation of 2 July on American merchantmen desiring to engage in that trade "shall be continued." A bill embodying that resolution was enacted into law by the Virginia General Assembly on 22 December 1783. On the same day the Assembly directed Governor Harrison to send a copy of the statute to the executive of each state and also to the Virginia delegates for submission to Congress (*JHDV*, Oct. 1783, pp. 46, 50, 53, 55, 83; Hening, *Statutes*, XI, 313–14; Randolph to JM, 18 July 1783, and n. 6).

From Edmund Pendleton

Summary (LC: Madison Miscellany). The summary is in a calendar, probably prepared about 1850 by Peter Force's clerk. He noted that the letter was addressed "To James Madison" and that the manuscript was "1 page 4°."

1783, October 20 VIRGINIA

Madison's retirement from Congress.[1] Congress has fixed its permanent residence in the woods of the Jersies.[2] The importance of Madison taking a seat in the Virginia Assembly.[3]

[1] Jefferson to JM, 7 May, and n. 19; JM to Randolph, 17 June, n. 10; 8 July 1783, n. 2.

[2] Pendleton to JM, 28 July; 11 Aug.; 18 Aug.; JM to Randolph, 13 Oct. 1783, nn. 2–12.

[3] Jones to JM, 28 July, and n. 4. In the session of May 1784 JM was a delegate from Orange County in the Virginia House of Delegates (*JHDV*, May 1784, p. 5).

Benjamin Harrison to Virginia Delegates

FC (Virginia State Library). Addressed to "The Virginia Delegates in Congress." In the hand of Samuel Patteson.

EDITORIAL NOTE

This letter and the one from Harrison on 30 October to the Virginia delegates (*q.v.*) are included in this volume because they are dated before the expiration of the term of JM in Congress on 2 November. Obviously, they could not have reached their destination while he was still a delegate. On the other hand, they probably came to his attention. In Philadelphia JM was with Jefferson, who, as a member of the Virginia delegation, first attended Congress at Princeton on 4 November, the last of its sessions in that village. JM delayed his departure for Montpelier until 22 November in order to accompany Jefferson as far as Annapolis, where Congress had resolved to convene four days later (*JCC*, XXV, 797–98, 803, 807; Boyd, *Papers of Jefferson*, VI, 355, and n.).

Octo: 25th. 1783.

Gentlemen,

I am much disappointed in not receiving a letter from you by the last post,[1] as we are all anxious to know where Congress means to fix its permanent residence, reports say it is to be in the woods near Princeton or on the deleware a little below Trenton.[2] I think it impossible that either can be true, if I should be mistaken it will fix this State in an opinion that there is a decided majority against the southern States, and that they are not to expect that Justice they are entitled to when the interest of the other States shall induce a deviation from it. Tho' great offers were made Congress to remove to us yet I never expected a compliance nor would I have voted for it if not commanded so to do, as the common principles of honor would have forbidden it, Maryland is the central State and there it ought to have been fixed, no great matter in what part of it tho' George town was certainly the most proper.[3] A sufficient [number] of members are not yet met to hold the assembly nor do I think we shall have one before the middle of next week.[4]

I am &ca.

[1] No letters written by the delegates to the governor between 4 October and 1 November have been found (Harrison to Delegates, 30 Oct. 1783).

[2] Harrison probably had gleaned the reports from the *Virginia Gazette* of 25 October 1783.

[3] JM to Jefferson, 20 Sept., and n. 4; Motion *in re* Permanent Site, 22 Sept., and n. 1; JM to Randolph, 13 Oct., and nn. 2–12, esp. nn. 3 and 9; Delegates to Harrison, 1 Nov. 1783 (1st letter). In its resolution offering Williamsburg or a site on the Potomac River, perhaps opposite Georgetown, Md., to Congress for a permanent residence, the Virginia General Assembly had "commanded" Harrison to ascertain the disposition of the citizens of Williamsburg toward the offer and to send the resolution as an instruction to the Virginia delegation in Congress (Instructions to Delegates, 28 June, and hdn., nn. 2–6; Jones to JM, 28 June; Harrison to Delegates, 4 July, and nn. 3, 5; 12 July; JM to Randolph, 28 July 1783).

[4] By "members" Harrison meant the senators and delegates composing the Virginia General Assembly (JM to Randolph, 13 Oct. 1783, n. 13).

Benjamin Harrison to Virginia Delegates

FC (Virginia State Library). Addressed to "Delegates in Congress." In the hand of the clerk Samuel Patteson. See Harrison to Delegates, 25 Oct. 1783, ed. n.

IN COUNCIL Octo: 30th 1783.

GENTLEMEN,

The two last posts brought no letters from you[1] which I am really sorry for as a full account of the proceedings of Congress on the place of their permanent residence was expected.[2]

There are not yet a sufficient number of members to proceed to business.[3]

I am &c.

[1] Harrison to Delegates, 25 Oct. 1783, n. 1.

[2] *Ibid.*, n. 3.

[3] *Ibid.*, n. 4.

From Joseph Jones

RC (LC: Madison Papers). Cover missing. Docketed by JM, "Ocr. 30. 1783."

Spring Hill[1] 30th. Octr. 1783

Dr. Sr.

After two or three interruptions on the road by rainy weather I arrived here the 23d. tolerably well[2] two days after Mr. Hardy and Monroe called on me in their way to Philadelphia by whom you will receive this.[3] they hope to find Congress in the City by the time they get up but by your communication received by the Post this week I gave them little encouragmt. to be so happily situated.[4] It gives me concern to find such indirect methods practiced to carry points, and though in the end George Town should be solely established the seat of Congress, instead of their alternate residence much as I prefer that place I shod. not be very well pleased with the manner of it being accomplished.[5]

Although the conduct of Congress with respect to the western Country may call forth the resentment of some of the legislature of Virginia, yet I trust there will be a sufficient number to close with the terms transmitted by Congress and thereby terminate the disagreeable and dangerous controversy so warmly supported by some of the States agt. ours on the Right to that Country. my endeavours to procure its passage shall not be wanting as I consider the ground on which the cession is now placed beneficial to the State and by proper management may prove very much so to the U States.[6]

From the Temper of the Eastern States with respect to the commutation, if nothing else operated with them, I entertained very slender hopes of their adopting the plan of Congress.[7] the rejection of it by Massachusetts was no more than I expected as well on that account as from some other motives, that are sufficiently known to you. Have they laid Taxes to pay their quota of the national debt by any other mode than the one recommended?[8] or have they in fact refused the Comr. appointed to settle the public accounts permission to proceed upon that Business?[9] Notwithstanding these obstacles I still wish Virga to agree to the proposition and hope to find the legislature disposed to do so.[10] I set off in a few days for Richmond. Company has hitherto prevented me since my arrival from packing[?] up the things you desired and sending them to Mr. Maury. It shall be done before I leave home.[11] Mr. Jefferson must be with you as the Gentl. here inform me he had gone on the upper road.[12] remember me respectfully to him and all inquiring friends, particularly to the good Lady of the House and Mrs. Trist, if she is still with you. tell her Joe says he remembers & thanks her for the sword she was so kind as to send him.[13] the vessell on board which I put my things is not yet arrived I fear she was out in the storm that happened the Saturday night and sunday morning after I left you.[14] very truly I am

Yr. friend

Jos: Jones

[1] Jones to JM, 25 May 1783, n. 1.

[2] JM to Jefferson, 20 Sept. 1783, n. 6.

[3] Although the terms of Samuel Hardy and James Monroe as delegates of Virginia in Congress began on 3 November, they apparently did not attend before 26 November, when Congress was scheduled to convene at Annapolis after adjourning at Princeton on 4 November 1783 (*JHDV*, May 1783, p. 39; *JCC*, XXV, 797–98, 807).

[4] JM's letter, presumably written about 21 October, is missing. He probably informed Jones that Congress, still meeting in Princeton, had not decided upon the date of moving from that town (JM to Randolph, 13 Oct. 1783, n. 4).

[5] *Ibid.*, and nn. 3, 10, 11; Notes on Congress' Place of Residence, 14 Oct. 1783, and nn. 5, 10. Although JM was in Philadelphia on 19 and 20 October, he probably told Jones of the congressional proceedings on the seventeenth, when he had been in Princeton. On that day Elbridge Gerry and Arthur Lee moved that "buildings be likewise erected for the use of Congress, at or near the lower falls of Potomac or Georgetown" as an alternate permanent capital. Abraham Clark and Richard Peters, arguing that the subject was of such "important consequences to the Union" that consideration should be deferred until "the first Monday in April next," when the delegates should have procured instructions from their respective states, vainly offered a motion to that effect. Although New Hampshire was represented only by Abiel Foster, the New England states combined with the southern, from Maryland to South Carolina (Georgia being unrepresented), to overbear the unanimous opposition of New York, New Jersey, Pennsylvania, and Delaware (represented only by James Tilton). It was then decided that consideration of the Gerry-Lee motion be deferred until "Wednesday next," that is, 22 October (*JCC*, XXV, 698–99). An attempt was made on 18 October to have the deferment reconsidered but was blocked by New Jersey under the twenty-second rule of the Rules of Procedure adopted on 4 May 1781 (*JCC*, XX, 480; XXV, 699).

Beyond 18 October JM was probably uninformed as to events in Congress at the time he wrote Jones. On Monday, 20 October, the action of New Jersey having automatically made reconsideration an order of the day (*JCC*, XX, 480; XXV, 702), the matter was returned to the floor but was not resolved until the next day. On the latter date both the original Gerry-Lee motion and an amendment thereto, offered as an addendum by Gerry and John Francis Mercer, and itself amended, were passed by a vote of seven states to one. The amendment provided that "until the buildings to be erected on the banks of the Delaware and Potomac shall be prepared for the reception of Congress," sessions should "be alternately at equal periods of not more than one year, and not less than six months in Trenton and

Annapolis." A further amendment, which was uncontested, provided that Congress be adjourned on 12 November and reconvened at Annapolis two weeks later.

In the eight divisions recorded in the journal for 20 and 21 October, Abiel Foster, on the four occasions that he voted, cast an ineffective ballot in opposition to the stand taken by his New England colleagues; and in one instance Connecticut divided. Otherwise, the New England bloc stood staunchly by the united southern delegations. Overborne, the delegations of New Jersey and Pennsylvania seemed to lose heart for the contest and became steadily less effective as members absented themselves (*JCC*, XXV, 706–14).

"Our public affairs are truly in a disagreable situation," Elias Boudinot wrote to Robert R. Livingston on 23 October. Disgruntled at having the permanent capital located at Trenton, the southern members of Congress had "manoeuvred" with such Machiavellian finesse "as to take in the Eastern Members so completely, as to get them (Mr. Gerry at their head) to conform entirely to their views" (Burnett, *Letters*, VII, 347). Although himself opposed to the result, Foster less irritably informed the president of New Hampshire, Meshech Weare, that the successful coalition had acted because of "the uneasiness of the southern Deligates" at having a permanent capital so far north, and of the New Englanders "that no other measures would prove effectual to prevent the return of Congress to Philadelphia, for a temporary residence" (*ibid.*, VII, 348).

6 Jones to JM, 21 June, and n. 10; 28 June; Instruction to Delegates, 27 June, and nn. 3, 4; Delegates to Harrison, 13 Sept., ed. n.; 20 Sept., and n. 4; 4 Oct., n. 5; JM to Jefferson, 20 Sept., and n. 3; Harrison to Delegates, 26 Sept. 1783, and n. 5.

7 The "plan of Congress" was for restoring public credit (*Papers of Madison*, VI, index under Continental Congress, actions on plan for restoring public credit; Pendleton to JM, 4 May, n. 8; Jones to JM, 8 June, n. 9; 14 June, and n. 7; JM to Jefferson, 11 Aug., and nn. 14, 17–19; to Randolph, 12 Aug. 1783). Massachusetts, Rhode Island, and Connecticut had persistently opposed both the guarantee of full pay for five years and its predecessor, the guarantee of half pay for life to continental officers serving throughout the war (*Papers of Madison*, VI, 187; 190, n. 10; 282; 284, n. 4; 297; 299, n. 2; 300; 370; 371, n. 4; 375; 377, n. 3; JM Notes, 5 June, n. 1; Memorial of Massachusetts General Court, 19 Sept. 1783, and ed. n., n. 4; Burnett, *Letters*, VII, 316–17, 387, 333–35, 334, n. 2).

8 Exclusive of the income expected from imposts, Congress had asked the states for $1,500,000 during 1783. Of this total, Massachusetts' quota was $224,427 (*JCC*, XXIV, 259). On 20 October 1783 the Massachusetts General Court provided by law for beginning the levy of imposts specified by Congress in the plan for restoring public credit as soon as Congress should apprise Massachusetts of the enactment of similar statutes by all the other states (NA: PCC, No. 74, fols. 197–99; *JCC*, XXV, 752; Burnett, *Letters*, VII, 323, 363, 374). At that session the General Court adopted no other legislation to provide Congress with revenue. Massachusetts, along with most of the other states, was greatly in arrears in meeting its financial quota, both of 1782 and 1783 (NA: PCC, No. 137, III, 341, 349; *JCC*, XXVI, 298–309, esp. 309).

9 In December 1782 Robert Morris, superintendent of finance, informed a congressional committee that he had submitted to Massachusetts for approval the name of a person, whom he did not identify to the committee, to be "the Comr." (NA: PCC, No. 137, II, 59–60; *JCC*, XXIV, 49). There appears to be no evidence that during 1783 the governor or the Massachusetts General Court acted upon Morris' recommendation or even acknowledged its receipt. An important complicating circumstance in the financial relations between Massachusetts and Congress was the old continental currency held by prominent citizens to an amount far exceeding the proportion allotted that state to redeem at 40 to 1. Unless Con-

gress agreed to designate the big surplus as a partial offset against Massachusetts' quota delinquencies, the General Court could not yield to the pressure from the holders of the obsolete currency to make it acceptable in payment of new taxes levied to provide funds for the Confederation's treasury (*Papers of Madison,* II, 49, n. 2; 71; V, 321–22; 323, nn. 7, 8; VI, 262, n. 6). In a long letter on 28 October 1783, Governor John Hancock complained to President Elias Boudinot about Congress' neglect of Massachusetts' financial requests. Hancock pointed out that Morris, who clearly was disliked in that state, had included in his analysis of the Confederation debt certain items which were vague and others which were erroneous (NA: PCC, No. 65, II, 225–28; Burnett, *Letters,* VII, 349, n. 2. Oscar Handlin and Mary Flug Handlin, *Commonwealth, a Study of the Role of Government in the American Economy: Massachusetts, 1774–1861* [New York, 1947], pp. 37–42).

[10] On 22 December 1783 the Virginia General Assembly enacted a law "to provide certain and adequate funds for the payment of this state's quota of the debts contracted by the United States." As in the case of the Massachusetts statute, this one provided that the imposts prescribed in it would not be levied until Congress informed the governor that "each and every of the other states in the union" had enacted similar legislation (*JHDV,* Oct. 1783, pp. 62, 65, 70, 78, 81, 83; Hening, *Statutes,* XI, 350–52). See also Randolph to JM, 18 July 1783, n. 6.

[11] JM to Randolph, 13 Oct. 1783, and n. 1. Although Jones may have attended earlier, his name does not appear until 8 November in the journal of the Virginia House of Delegates. A quorum had been attained for the first time on 4 November (*JHDV,* Oct. 1783, pp. 7, 12).

[12] Leaving Monticello on 16 October with his daughter Patsy, Jefferson paid a brief visit to Isaac Zane at Marlboro in Frederick County and then proceeded north on the Great Wagon Road to Philadelphia. He passed through Winchester, Harpers Ferry, Frederick, Tawneytown, McAlistertown, Susquehanna, and Lancaster before arriving in Philadelphia on 29 October 1783 (*Va. Mag. Hist. and Biog.,* LXXVII [1969], 302; Edward Dumbauld, *Thomas Jefferson, American Tourist* [Norman, Okla., 1946], p. 53).

[13] Jones to JM, 28 June, and n. 17; Mercer to JM, 14 Aug., and nn. 6, 7; JM to Randolph, 8 Sept. 1783, and nn. 9, 10.

[14] Jones referred to 18 and 19 October, but the name of "the vessell" is not known (JM to Jefferson, 20 Sept. 1783, n. 6).

Virginia Delegates to Benjamin Harrison

RC (Virginia State Library). Cover missing. Addressed to "His Excellency Benjamin Harrison Esqr." In the hand of John Francis Mercer, except for Arthur Lee's signature. For the absence of JM's signature, see Delegates to Harrison, 24 June 1783, ed. n. The present letter and the other one of the same date from the delegates to Governor Harrison were given a single docket, reading "Delegates letters. Nov. 1st 1783."

IN CONGRESS Novr. 1. 1783.

SIR

We have the honor of transmitting to your Excellency two Resolutions of Congress respecting their permanent & temporary residence.

We consider it as superfluous to enter into a minute detail of the progress of questions, the determinations of which (involving in 'em the general & particular interests of States) were protracted to a tedious length of time in order to give them the most mature deliberation. We therefore submit the result & will only generally remark, (that considering the present population of the Continent, so unfavorable as it is to an exclusive residence of the general Council at George Town & the votes of the Confederacy so unfriendly as they are to a southern station & observing that the negativing any other place, was an affirmative in favor of Princeton in which we sat, a situation every way agreable to the Eastern & middle States) we are led to hope, that our conduct as far as it tended to establish the present votes will be satisfactory to our constituents.[1]

Congress have agreed to a Report on Indian Affairs, which we also enclose to Yr. Excellency.[2] The very critical situation in which we found ourselves, with respect to those Savages, render'd it necessary to decide on a state of Peace or War. They in expectation of our determination in favor of the former, were already assembling in order to hold a Treaty.[3] a moment so favorable was embrac'd in order to exact from 'em as a compensation for their unprovok'd & merciless ravages a district of Country, which might satisfy the claims of the Army & contribute towards alleviating the public burthens. other circumstances were also very pressing. We had before us authentic information of continual & extensive emigrations made into a Country which unless otherwise dispos'd of, wou'd not only remain profitless to the United States, but woud become a prey to lawless banditti & adventurers who must necessarily have involv'd us in continued Indian wars & perhaps have form'd Establishments not only on dissimilar principles to those which form the basis of our Republican Constitutions, but such as might eventually prove destructive to them. It was judg'd that a delay untill the Spring without taking the intermediate steps necessary to the then settling this Country with the Army & others, under the protection, direction & for the use of the United States, wou'd be sacrificing too much to that scrupulous delicacy, which might suggest a passive Conduct to Congress, as proper untill the State of Virginia shou'd have acceded to some alterations in the conditions of her Cession—which were indeed consider'd as of so trivial a nature as not to prevent her Delegates in Congress giving their unanimous assent to them.[4]

To these Reasons which were continually press'd on our minds by the entreaties of the Army, urged by the Commander in Chief may be attributed the Proclamation issued by Congress, respecting the illicit Settlement of these Lands.[5] The Delegates of Virginia were in a delicate situation not convinc'd of the necessity or propriety of their opposing measures generally thought to be for the public good & which perhaps it will be the future policy of the State to direct to be pursued with vigor & effect.[6]

Yr. Excellency will find among the enclosures a state of the payments of the respective States & an account as far as has yet been compleated of the expenditures of Public Monies, with such other papers as we thought woud tend to elucidate our general Affairs.[7]

Congress have had long before them a Report on those arrangements which may be necessary for our security in time of Peace. it is the result of the wisdom & experience of the Commander in Chief assisted by every Officer whose rank & reputation promis'd lights on the subject.[8] the temporary adoption of such part of it, as may be necessary to provide Garrisons for the Western Posts which G. Britain has ceded & the guarding the Continental Stores, which it appears to be the present idea of Congress shou'd be distributed in five equal portions thro' the States from North to South, may not admit of delay,[9] but permanent measures on so important & delicate a subject, will no doubt be postpon'd untill our Constituents have time to deliberate & to express their sense on such plans as may be submitted to their consideration; & even what we are compell'd now to do, we think will have referrence to what *they* may hereafter generally direct.

We also transmit to your Excellency a Copy of a Letter from the Honble Jno: Adams. the subject is so important & interesting & at the same time the reflections made, so very evident & uncontrovertible, that to yr. Excellency all comment wd. be unnecessary. We will still add [?] that we have but too certain grounds to beleive that his prognostications are fast fulfilling.[10] The late ordinance publish'd by the French Governor at Hispaniola (for which we refer to the Paper enclos'd) taken with the British Acts of Council, we cannot but consider as the preludes of a concerted System for imposing pernicious & cruel restrain[t] on our Commerce.[11] Massachusetts as we hear by private Letters, has at length agreed to the Recommendations of Congress.[12] If we once regain the reputation of mutual confidence & concertion, we can no longer dread the resentment of determined foes or the interested policy of undetermined friends & we cannot but rely, on the virtue, wisdom & temper which we know pervade the Continent & which have heretofore rendered us superiour to force, machination or intrigue.

We have the honor to be with every Sentiment of Respect Yr. Excellency's most Obt. Servt.

ARTHUR LEE
JOHN F MERCER

[1] Following "constituents" are four lines of text so heavily deleted with ink as to be illegible. Although the "two Reso'utions," probably those adopted by Congress on 30 October, are missing, they apparently were among the "sundry other papers of consequence" which the delegates enclosed in this and their other letter of 1 November to Harrison, and which he submitted, along with the covering letters, to the Virginia House of Delegates on 13 November (Executive Letter Book, 1783–1786, p. 231, MS in Va. State Library; *JHDV*, Oct. 1783, p. 17). One of those resolutions, in part embodying a motion of Arthur Lee, provided for a committee of five delegates, including Mercer, to proceed "to the lower falls of Potomac, to view the situation of the country in the vicinity of the same, and report a proper district" for locating a permanent site at which Congress should meet. The same resolution instructed the committee, Elbridge Gerry, chairman, appointed on 7 October, "to report as soon as may be" concerning "the most suitable place for erecting buildings for the accommodation of Congress, near the falls of the Delaware" during the other half of each year.

The second resolution, which had been moved by David Howell and seconded by Mercer, instructed President Boudinot to send to the executives of the thirteen states copies of the congressional acts of 7 and 21 October that provided, respectively, for permanent sites at the two places mentioned above. The act of the latter date also stipulated that Congress would adjourn at Princeton on 12 November 1783 and convene two weeks later at Annapolis (*JCC*, XXV, 657, 658–59, 714, 768, 770–71). See also JM to Randolph, 13 Oct., and nn. 2–6, 8–12; Note on Congress' Place of Residence, 14 Oct., and nn. 3–5, 14–17; Harrison to Delegates, 25 Oct., and ed. n., n. 1; Jones to JM, 30 Oct. 1783, and nn. 3–5.

[2] The enclosure, seven pages written by a clerk and signed by "Chas Thomson Secy," and an additional page bearing the notation "To the honbl. Mr. Mercer Oct 1783," is a copy of the report on 14 October of the committee, James Duane, chairman, and Lee among its other four members, first appointed on 19 August to consider Indian and British affairs west of the Appalachian Mountains and on the New York frontier, including the outcome of Ephraim Douglass' mission (NA: PCC, No. 186, fol. 119; Delegates to Harrison, 8 Sept., and n. 3). From the time of its appointment, or at least within a few weeks thereafter, this committee was considered a standing committee to which Congress from time to time referred a variety of particular issues relating to the Indians. Prior to its comprehensive recommendations submitted on 14 October and in part adopted in amended form the next day, the committee had been unable to gain Congress' acceptance of its reports on specific aspects of the general problem (NA: PCC, No. 186, fols. 120, 121, 122, 123, 124; *JCC*, XXV, 591–96, 640–44, 692, and n. 1, 695). See also Harrison to Delegates, 19 Sept., and n. 3; 26 Sept., and nn. 4, 5; Delegates to Harrison, 4 Oct. 1783, and n. 2.

At the outset of its report, which strongly reflected Washington's advice, the committee stated that, although the Indians in the Northwest Territory seemed "seriously disposed to a pacification," they were "not in a temper" to cede land "without further struggles" (Fitzpatrick, *Writings of Washington*, XXVII, 133–40, 192, n. 87). Nevertheless, the tribes which had broken their pledges of neutrality, given in 1775, by allying with the enemy and destroying lives and property should "make atonement" by yielding territory "commensurate to the public wants" of the United States. Congress, lacking money, needed a large area north and west of the Ohio River to provide bounty lands for veterans of the continental army, cash from land sales for paying the Confederation's debts, and home sites for immigrants from Europe, as well as for the increasing "domestic population" of the United States. Although the hostile Indians deserved to be driven "beyond the Lakes" as punishment for their ravages during the Revolution, a war for that purpose would be far too costly, not only because the British probably would aid them, but also because if the United States was victorious, the Indians would divert all their fur trade into Canadian channels. Whether the United States won or lost the struggle, it would be obliged to maintain "numerous garrisons" throughout the Northwest Territory. For these reasons, Congress should prefer "clemency to rigour," strive to convince the Indians that "their true interest and safety must depend upon our friendship," and at the same time demand land from them, as reparations for their "fatal experience" between 1776 and 1783. If the Indians were willing to relinquish some acreage to the United States but not the required amount, Congress should agree to pay for the excess rather than "hazard a War which will be much more expensive."

The committee, therefore, recommended that Congress seek at once to have a commission assemble representatives of all the tribes on the New York frontier and between the Ohio River and Lake Erie in one "Convention." Besides requiring that they immediately release all their prisoners, the commissioners should endeavor to have them by a treaty cede approximately all, except the northwestern portion, of the territory which later would include the state of Ohio. No land, however, should be demanded from the friendly Oneidas and Tuscarawas, nor should the commissioners admit into the treaty any stipulation confirming grants made by Indians "to any Individual or Individuals." The Indians should be assured that, for reasons of trade and other peaceful purposes, they could continue to enter the ceded area, but that any unauthorized white man who ventured into their territory would be guilty of trespass. Although the commissioners should make known "the displeasure of Congress" to all white squatters on either side of the proposed boundary line, they should assure the French settlers everywhere throughout the Northwest Territory that upon professing "allegiance to the United States," Congress would protect their "Liberty" and "just & lawful property." The copy of the report in the Virginia State Library is signed by Charles Thomson and is docketed "For the honbl. Mr. Mercer."

On 15 October, the day that the report was spread on the journal, Congress adopted and referred to a committee, Abraham Clark, chairman, a proposal of the committee on Indian affairs to have an ordinance drafted "for regulating the Indian trade" (*JCC*, XXV, 677–94, and esp. 693). On the same day Congress also entertained a motion by Elbridge Gerry to make clear that "the legislative rights" and "territorial claims" in the area embraced by the committee's proposals would not be traversed by their adoption (*JCC*, XXV, 693). Before adjournment on 15 October, Congress named a committee—Duane, chairman, JM, and Samuel Huntington—to consider the recommendations of the committee on Indian affairs which had not yet been adopted or otherwise disposed of, and also an amended proposal of that committee, first submitted on 14 October, "to erect a district of the western territory into a distinct government." This proposal further recommended that whenever the settlers in the "district" became sufficiently numerous, they should draft a "permanent constitution for themselves" on "republican principles" and "be admitted to a representation in the Union" as "citizens of a free, sovereign and independent State" (*JCC*, XXV, 677, 694–95). JM was among the five members of a committee, Benjamin Hawkins, chairman, appointed on 16 October to report on the state of affairs with "the Cherokees and all the Indians within the United States to the southward of that tribe" (*JCC*, XXV, 692, and n. 1).

Prior to the expiration of JM's term on 2 November, Congress neither received any report from those two committees nor took any further action affecting Indian affairs, except to reject for the "present" a plea from veterans for bounty land allotments in the West and, after much debate, to permit Pennsylvania commissioners, "for the sole purpose" of buying land within that state from the Indians, to attend the expected "convention" (*JCC*, XXV, 717–19, 752, 762–67).

[3] Mercer's "expectation" of an early conference with the Indians, probably the Iroquois tribes in New York, was not fulfilled. Congress delayed until 4 March 1784 before appointing commissioners "to negotiate," and no treaties were concluded with the Iroquois and with the Indians in the Ohio country until October and December, respectively, of that year (*JCC*, XXVI, 124–25; Solon J. Buck and Elizabeth Hawthorn Buck, *Planting of Civilization in Western Pennsylvania*, p. 200). Virginia's agents to the Indians made a treaty of peace with the Chickasaws on 6 November and expected—vainly as it turned out—to confer for the same purpose with the Shawnees at Louisville on 18 November 1783 (MS copy of treaty in Va. State Library; Robert S. Cotterill, "The Virginia-Chickasaw Treaty of 1783," *Journal of Southern History*, VIII [1942], 483–96; *Cal. of Va. State Papers*, III, 536, 539, 544–45, 548; Executive Letter Book, 1783–1786, pp. 189–90, 193–95, 197–98, 222, 229–30, 231–32, MS in Va. State Library). See also Delegates to Harrison, 8 Sept. 1783, n. 2.

[4] Delegates to Harrison, 13 Sept., ed. n.; JM to Jefferson, 20 Sept., n. 3; Harrison to Delegates, 26 Sept., n. 5; Jones to JM, 30 Oct. 1783.

[5] Harrison to Delegates, 19 Sept. 1783, n. 3. Washington, who was residing near Princeton, supported "the entreaties of the Army" for its pay and bounty lands (*Papers of Madison*, VI, 377, n. 2; Delegates to Harrison, 23 Aug., n. 8; JM to Jefferson, 20 Sept. 1783; Fitzpatrick, *Writings of Washington*, XXVII, 136–37, 156, 163–64, 167–68, 172, 188, 224–25, 227, 232–33).

[6] *JCC*, XXV, 591–96, 640–44, 677–80, 717–19, 762–67; Harrison to Delegates, 19 Sept. 1783, n. 3.

[7] Enclosure is missing. Mercer appears to have referred in part to the elaborate report of Robert Morris, superintendent of finance, submitted to Congress on 22 October in fulfillment of its instructions resulting from Lee's motions of 18 and 19 August (*JCC*, XXIV, 512, 514–15; XXV, 715–16; NA: PCC, No. 144, fols. 133, 136, 140, 145, 147, 151–67). As of 14 October 1783 the foreign debt of the United States was $7,907,037, and the domestic, $41,207,861 (NA: PCC, No. 144, fols. 133, 140). Not included in the report was a list "of the payments of the respective States." By the close of 1783, they had paid $1,486,511.71 of a total requisition of $8,000,000. Delaware, North Carolina, and Georgia had forwarded none of their respective quotas. Virginia was $1,192,490.47 in arrears in meeting its quota of $1,307,594.00 (NA: PCC, No. 144, fol. 93).

[8] JM to Randolph, 17 June 1783, and n. 10. On 18 June, after gathering the recommendations of Washington and other general officers, Hamilton, the chairman of the committee on peace arrangements, submitted its detailed report to Congress. Thereafter the matter was in abeyance until 7 August. On that day, knowing that Washington would soon come to Princeton after making an extended visit to the garrisons on the New York frontier, Congress appointed a committee to confer further with him "on the peace arrangement." On 10 September the committee reported the "observations of the General," which somewhat modified his earlier proposals, and was discharged. Congress then appointed another committee on the subject, consisting of James Duane, chairman, and Lee among the other four members (*JCC*, XXIV, 494, 501, n. 1, 522, 523, 524–26; XXV, 549–51). The report, as drafted orginally by Hamilton, was spread on the journal of Congress on 23 October 1783 and referred at once to a committee of the whole (*JCC*,

XXV, 722–44). The next day a recommendation of the Duane committee concerning the purchase of "goods and articles proper and necessary for the Indians" was entered and read (*JCC*, XXV, 747, and n. 2).

[9] Before adjourning its first session on 23 October, the committee of the whole agreed that "some garrisons ought to be maintained in time of peace at the expence of the United States for their security and defense under their present circumstances" (*JCC*, XXV, 745). Thereafter, prior to 2 November 1783, the journal records no further report by this committee. For the recommendation by the Hamilton committee (n. 2, above) of five sites for "Arsenals and Magazines," see JM to Randolph, 17 June 1783, n. 10; *JCC*, XXV, 738.

[10] Enclosure not found, but it probably was a copy of John Adams' dispatch of 18 July 1783. Among Adams' "apprehensions," which he feared would be realized unless Congress possessed power for "governing the trade of the whole" union of states, was that Great Britain and France, separately rather than in concert, would invade "our natural right to the carrying trade." To counter this, continued Adams, negotiations must be undertaken "with the Dutch, Danes, Portuguese, and even with the empires." "If," he concluded, "the United States do not soon show to the world a proof that they can command a common revenue to satisfy their creditors at home and abroad, that they can act as one people, as one nation, as one man, in their transactions with foreign nations, we shall be soon so far despised that it will be but a few years, perhaps but a few months only, before we are involved in another war" (Wharton, *Revol. Dipl. Corr.*, VI, 560–62; *JCC*, XXV, 617–19, 621–22, 628–32, 661–64, 664, n. 1; Burnett, *Letters*, VII, 304–7).

[11] JM to Randolph, 13 Sept., n. 5; to Jefferson, 20 Sept., n. 13; Delegates to Harrison, 4 Oct. 1783, and n. 10. Following "Commerce," about six lines of text are so heavily deleted with ink as to be illegible. The delegates probably enclosed copies of the *Pennsylvania Journal* of 25 October and 1 November. The earlier of these included an item relating to British Orders in Council concerning foreign commerce; the latter published an ordinance, which had become effective on 1 July 1783, stopping "the admission of foreign vessels belonging to neutral powers, into the ports of admiralty" of Haiti and the other French Leeward Islands.

[12] On 20 October the Massachusetts General Court agreed to the impost provisions of the plan for restoring public credit but adjourned without accepting the other recommendations of Congress in that plan (JM to Jefferson, 11 Aug. 1783, n. 19).

Virginia Delegates to Benjamin Harrison

RC (Virginia State Library). Cover missing. Addressed to "His Excellency Benjamin Harrison." In the hand of John Francis Mercer, except for Arthur Lee's signature. For the absence of JM's signature, see Delegates to Harrison, 24 June 1783, ed. n. The present letter and the other one of 1 November from the delegates to Governor Harrison were given a single docket, reading "Delegates letters. Novr. 1st 1783."

In Congress Nov. 1. 1783

Sir

This day the Honourable Peter John Van Berckel Minister plenipotentiary from their High Mightinesses had his first public audience.[1] We do ourselves the honor of transmitting to you a Copy of his Credentials, of his address on delivering them & the answer returned by Congress.[2] The reception & Ceremony were more conformable to present circumstances & embarrassmts than to the Representatives of a Great Nation. Still the characters who were in attendance, & the cordiality with which they were conducted may well compensate for Pomp splendor & shew.[3]

There is just now receiv'd authentic information from Colo. Ogden immediately arriv'd from France, that the Definitive Treaty was signed on the third of Septr.[4] Mr. Adams, Mr. Franklin & Mr. Jay signed on the part of America, & Mr. Thackster Secretary of Mr. Adams had embarked in the L'Orient Packet with an authenticated Copy, & may be daily expected.[5] We beg leave to congratulate Yr. Excellency on the happy event which is not the less important from the delay which has attended it.

We are with great respect & esteem Yr. Excellency's most Obt:

ARTHUR LEE
JOHN F. MERCER

[1] The "audience" was on 31 October, not 1 November 1783 (*JCC*, XXV, 780–86). Following "Mightinesses," Mercer assumed that Governor Harrison would interpolate "the States-General of the United Netherlands." For van Berckel, see JM to Jefferson, 10 June, and n. 23; to Randolph, 30 Aug.; 30 Sept., and n. 4; 13 Oct. 1783.

[2] These enclosures, each correctly dated 31 October 1783, are in Mercer's hand. He obviously made a careful copy of President Boudinot's answer on behalf of Congress from either the manuscript or from the entry in the journal (*JCC*, XXV, 785–86). On the other hand, Mercer's version of van Berckel's "address" and his "Credentials" contrasts considerably in phraseology, but not in meaning, with their translations from the French and Dutch, respectively, as spread on the journal (*JCC*, XXV, 781–84).

[3] The form of the ceremonial is described, and the characters to be invited are listed in *JCC*, XXV, 748–51. See also Varnum L. Collins, *Continental Congress at Princeton*, pp. 218–25, 231–36. Thomas FitzSimons was told by van Berckel that he was "not a little disappointed at his Reception." "He told me very politely," continued FitzSimons, "that the States of Holland, to do honor to their 1st Embassy to the United States had sent their Minister with a Respectable fleet, that when Mr. Adams arrived in Holland the states sent a person to receive him, and provided a proper place for his reception" (Burnett, *Letters*, VII, 370).

[4] Colonel Matthias Ogden, who had disembarked at New York City on 30 October from the ship "Hartford," in which he had returned from England, reached Princeton the next day with unofficial but authentic news of the signing of the definitive treaty of peace between Great Britain and the United States (Varnum L. Collins, *Continental Congress at Princeton*, p. 231). For Ogden, see *Papers of Madison*, I, 159, n. 6; V, 473; VI, 224, n. 5.

[5] Hunter Miller, ed., *Treaties and Other International Acts*, II, 151–57. The

treaty, which was laid before Congress on 13 December 1783 at Annapolis, was not spread on the journal until 14 January 1784 (Jefferson to JM, 11 Dec. 1783, and n. 3; *JCC*, XXV, 812; XXVI, 22–28). John Thaxter, Jr., private secretary to John Adams, arrived in Philadelphia on 22 November with an official copy of the treaty (Burnett, *Letters*, VII, 376–77). For Thaxter, see *Papers of Madison*, IV, 282, n. 19.

From Joseph Chew

RC (LC: Madison Papers). Addressed to "James Madison Esqr. jr." Cover missing. Under the heading of the letter, JM wrote "Chew Jos."

NEW YORK 6th Novr. *1783*

MY DEAR SIR

I[1] find I omitted many things in my Letter of yesterday[2] as I dare say I shall in this let me Request you in the first Place to let me hear from you on the Receipt of that Letter as soon as Possible direct for me to be Left at the Commissry Generals[3] in the Next Place have the goodness to write to me[4] in London and give me as particular Account as you [can?] of the Regulations that may be made with Respect to trade by Congress or any Particular State I Earnestly wish to know the situation of Trade in Virginia & the Demand for British Goods—of this I have wrote to my friend your Father.[5] another matter be so kind as to give me your Opinion how I might Expect to be treated should [I?] Visit Virginia on Either the footing of seeing my friends or that of doing Business.[6] if you could inform your self of these matters, and write me sometime Early in December or by the middle of that month it [would?] be of Essential service to me. in your first Letter Provided I Can Receive it in ten or 12 days from this date[7] Pray be as Particular as you can as to our friends in that you write me to London let What you say be in General Terms for fear of a miscarriage I will not Trouble you further at Present than to Request when you see General Washington Present my Respects to him in a Particular manner, and to assure I am with the Greatest truth my Dear Sir your most Affectionate Kinsman[8] &c

JOS CHEW

upon second thoughts when you write the Letter to m[e] here direct it to be Left at the Post office to the care of John Foxcroft Esq.[9] who in case I should go sooner than I Expect will forward it to me when you write to me in England direct for me

To be Left at the House of James Christee Esq.[10] Pall Mall London

[1] *Papers of Madison*, I, 69, and n. 5; JM to J. Madison, Sr., 27 May 1783, and n. 7. Chew had moved from Virginia to New London, Conn., by 1750. There he was a merchant, a member of the Susquehannah Land Company, and, from 1763 until probably 1775, the postmaster (Leonard W. Labaree, ed., *The Papers of Benjamin Franklin* [12 vols. to date; New Haven, Conn., 1959---], X, 319, n. 3, 362, n. 1; XI, 109, n. 2).

[2] Not found.

[3] In the New York City office of the British Commissary General Brook Watson (1735–1807), Chew was superintendent of the fuel department (Edward E. Curtis, *The Organization of the British Army in the American Revolution* [New Haven, Conn., 1926], pp. 107, and n. 95, 109–10).

[4] If JM answered Chew's letter, his reply is missing.

[5] Chew's letter to James Madison, Sr., has not been found. See Delegates to Harrison, 6 May; Randolph to JM, 9 May, and n. 14; 15 May; 24 May; Pendleton to JM, 2 June, and n. 4; 28 July; Harrison to Delegates, 7 June 1783, and n. 3.

[6] Jones to JM, 31 May; 8 June, and n. 26; 21 June, and n. 19; 28 June; 21 July, n. 6; Randolph to JM, 12 July, and n. 2; 13 Sept. (2d letter), and n. 1; Harrison to Delegates, 9 Aug. 1783, and nn. 3, 5.

[7] Chew probably intended to sail from New York with other Loyalists before or when the last contingents of British troops left that city on 25 November (Thomas J. Wertenbaker, *Father Knickerbocker Rebels*, pp. 267–68).

[8] Chew and James Madison, Sr., were first cousins (*Papers of Madison*, I, 69, n. 5).

[9] John Foxcroft (d. 1790) had been secretary to Lieutenant Governor Francis Fauquier of Virginia from 1758 to 1761. In the latter year Foxcroft was appointed a joint deputy postmaster general of North America. From 1765 to 1775 he served with the same title in the northern district, which included Canada and the other colonies south through Virginia. He and his wife moved from Philadelphia to New York in 1765. After about three years (1776–1778?) as an American prisoner of war, Foxcroft returned to New York City, where he served as royal postmaster general (Historical Manuscripts Commission, eds., *Report on American Manuscripts*, III, 269). In 1783 he became the resident agent in that city for the British packet service (Leonard W. Labaree, ed., *Papers of Franklin*, IX, 378, and n. 7, 379, and n. 1; XII, 89, n. 3, 280–82; *Pa. Mag. Hist. and Biog.*, XXVI [1902], 346; XXVII [1903], 501–2; XXVIII [1904], 122–23; XXXVIII [1914], 246; Fitzpatrick, *Writings of Washington*, VI, 308; VII, 79; *JCC*, V, 841; VI, 875–76, 885, 933).

[10] James Christie (*ca.* 1730–1803), founder of the well-known London auction house, first opened his "Great Auction Room" on Pall Mall on 8 July 1767 (Joint Publishing Committee Representing the London County Council and the London Survey Committee, *Survey of London*, XXIX, Part I [1960], 297). "With an easy and gentleman-like flow of eloquence, he possessed, in a great degree, the power of persuasion, and even tempered his public address by a gentle refinement of manners" (*The Annual Register, or a View of the History, Politics, and Literature, for the Year 1803*, XLV [London, 1805], 462).

To Thomas Jefferson

RC (LC: Madison Papers). Cover missing. In the right margin of the second page, Jefferson wrote in ink, now much faded, what appears to have been "to dispute Buffon theory of temperature." Upon recovering the letter many years later, JM docketed it by inserting "Decr. 10. 1783" between the two lines of Jefferson's comment. Using the JM-Jefferson Code No. 2, JM encoded the words that are italicized in the first paragraph. Jefferson interlineated a decoding of the ciphers.

ORANGE Decemr. 10th. 1783.

DEAR SIR

My journey from Annapolis was so much retarded by rains and their effect on the water courses that I did not complete it till the ninth day after I left you.[1] I took *Col. Mason* in my *way and had an evening's conversation*[2] *with him. I found him much less oppose*[d] *to the general impost*[3] *than I had expected.* Indeed *he disclaimed all opposition to the measure itself but had taken up a vague* apprehension that *if adopted at this crisis it might embarras* the *defence of our trade against British machinations.*[4] *He seemed* upon the whole to *acquiesce in the territoryal cession* but *dwelt much on the* expediency of the *guaranty.*[5] *On the article of a convention* for *revising our form of government, he was sound and ripe and I think would*[6] *not decline a* participation *in the work. His* [he]*terodoxy*[7] *lay chiefly in being too little impressed with* either the *necessity* or the *proper means of preserving* the confederacy.[8]

The situation of the commerce of this country[9] as far as I can learn is even more deplorable than I had conceived. It can not pay less to Philada. & Baltimore if one may judge from a comparison of prices here & in Europe, than 30 or 40 Per Ct. on all the exports & imports, a tribute which if paid into the treasury of the State would yield a surplus above all its wants.[10] If the Assembly should take any steps towards its emancipation you will no doubt be apprized of them as well as of their other proceedings from Richmond.[11]

I am not yet settled in the course of law reading with which I have tasked myself and find it will be impossible to guard it against frequent interruptions.[12] I deputed one of my brothers[13] to Monticello with the draught on your library, but Capt. Key was down at Richmond.[14] As soon as he returns I propose to send again. My Trunk with Buffon

&c. has come safe to Fredg. so that I shall be well furnished with materials for collateral reading.[15] In conversing on this author's Theory of Central heat I recollect that we touched upon, as the best means for trying its validity, the comparative distances from the Earth's center of the summits of the highest mountains and their bases or the level of the sea.[16] Does not the oblate figure of the earth present a much more extensive and perhaps adequate field for experiments? According to the calculations of Martin grounded on the data of Maupertius &c.[17]

The Equatorial diameter of the Earth is	7942.2. Eng: Miles
The polar diam:	7852.4. E.M.
difference between Eq: & pol: diameter	89.8 E.M.[18]

The difference then of the semidiameters is 44.9. E. Miles, that is 1/87.94 of the mean semidiameter.[19] calling this difference in round numbers 45 Miles, and disregarding the small variations produced by the elliptical form of the Earth, the radii will be shortened ½ of a mile by each degree from the Equator to the poles.[20] It would seem therefore that the difference of distance from the center at the Equator & at the highest latitude that may [be] visited must be sufficient to produce a discoverable difference in the degrees of any heat emitted equally in every direction from the center: and the experiments might be sufficiently diversified to guard against illusion from any difference which might be supposed in the intermediate density of different parts of the earth. The distance even between the Equator & the polar circle produces a difference of no less than 33 1/6 miles i.e. 1/119 of the mean distance from the center;[21] so that if the curiosity of the two setts of French Philosophers employed in ascertaining the figure of the earth, had been directed to this question, a very little additional trouble & expence might perhaps have finally solved it.[22] Nay the extent of the U.S. computing from the 31°. of lat: to the 45°. only makes a difference of 7 miles in the distance from the center of the Earth; a greater difference I suppose than is afforded by the highest mountains or the deepest mines or both put together.[23]

On my delivering you the draught on Mr. Ambler I remember you put into my hands a note which I never looked into, supposing it to relate to that circumstance. In examining my papers I perceive that I have lost it and mention it to put you on your guard in case the note sd. fall into bad hands & be capable of being abused.[24] Present my respects to Mr. Mercer & the other gentlemen of the Delegation & be assured that I am Yrs sincerely

J. Madison Jr.

You will be so good as to give the inclosed a safe conveyance to Mrs. House.[25]

[1] JM and Jefferson left Philadelphia on 22 November and arrived in Annapolis three days later (Boyd, *Papers of Jefferson,* VI, 355, and n., 359). How long JM tarried in Annapolis is uncertain. If he stayed there only two nights and one day (26 November), he must have reached Montpelier on 5 December. In his letter of 11 December to JM (*q.v.*), Jefferson remarked that JM left Annapolis in "fine weather" but "immediately" experienced a "tempestuous season." This supports the conclusion that JM set out from Annapolis on 27 November, for on that date there was a violent storm of rain and wind which drove vessels ashore in Delaware Bay and New York Bay (*Pa. Packet,* 12 Dec. [extra issue], and 13 Dec. 1783).

[2] George Mason of Gunston Hall in Fairfax County, Va.

[3] That is, the imposts requested by Congress in the plan for restoring public credit (*Papers of Madison,* VI, 311–12; 350–51; 417; Beckley to Randolph, 20 June 1783).

[4] Mason's "apprehension" appears to reflect his belief that flexible rather than specifically defined imposts would have been preferable for retaliating against present and probably future restrictions by the British upon American commerce. See JM to Randolph, 13 Sept., n. 6; Delegates to Harrison, 4 Oct., and n. 10; Harrison to Delegates, 18 Oct. 1783, and n. 2.

[5] JM to Jefferson, 20 Sept., n. 3; Harrison to Delegates, 26 Sept.; Delegates to Harrison, 4 Oct. 1783, and n. 5.

[6] Although the cipher for "would" is 527, JM wrote 537 meaning "pacification."

[7] JM inadvertently omitted the cipher 247 for "he" in encoding "heterodoxy."

[8] After enciphering "the," JM spelled out the same word. JM's juxtaposition of "revising our form of government" and "preserving the confederacy" mingles two separate subjects. George Mason was obviously much of the opinion held by his nephew Stevens Thomson Mason to "*new model*" the Virginia constitution, a matter close to Jefferson's heart (Jefferson to JM, 7 May 1783, and nn. 11–12), but the older Mason's view in respect to strengthening the powers of Congress, as reported by JM, appears to foreshadow his opposition to the ratification of the Federal Constitution in 1787 and 1788 (Kate M. Rowland, *Life of George Mason,* II, 97–98, chaps. 4–8, *passim*). See also Jefferson to JM, 17 June, and n. 6; JM to Jefferson, 17 July 1783.

[9] Virginia.

[10] JM meant that by controlling so much of the commerce of Virginia, the merchants of Baltimore and Philadelphia were realizing huge profits and thereby diverting them both from the treasury of that state and from the pockets of its citizens.

[11] Although the Virginia General Assembly during the session of October 1783 adopted no legislation specifically designed to effect an "emancipation," it ratified the schedule of impost duties requested by Congress. If the other states also ratified, the resulting uniformity of rates on many commodities of foreign origin might benefit Virginia's commerce more than Maryland's and Pennsylvania's (Jones to JM, 30 Oct. 1783, n. 10).

[12] Soon after beginning "to read Law" in 1773, JM called it a "coarse and dry

study"—evidently much less to his taste than belles lettres or participation in the public affairs of Virginia (*Papers of Madison*, I, 70–71; 100–101; 105). During his first three years of service in Congress, a few of his papers refer to international law but give no warrant for inferring that either that or any other area of law especially attracted him (*ibid*., III, 271–72; IV, 10–11; 16, n. 23; 241; 242, n. 3; 314; V, 436; 437, n. 2). In January 1783, however, he included the works of outstanding legists in his proposed list of books for a congressional library (*ibid*., VI, 66–68; 90–92). For his "law reading" during the winter of 1783–1784, see JM to Jefferson, 11 Feb.; 17 Feb. 1784.

13 Probably William Madison, then twenty-one years of age (*Papers of Madison*, I, 76, n. 3; II, 295, n. 9).

14 As late as 16 March 1784, JM had not sent again to Monticello for books (JM to Jefferson, 16 Mar. 1784, LC: Madison Papers). John Key III, in Albemarle County court records usually designated as "Jr." in order to distinguish him from a living namesake uncle, had been born about 1752 (*Virginia Genealogist*, VIII [Jan.–Mar. 1964], 179) and was Jefferson's steward at Monticello from 1782 to 1784 (Edwin Morris Betts, ed., *Thomas Jefferson's Farm Book, with Commentary and Relevant Extracts from Other Writings* [Princeton, N.J., 1953], p. 149). From the rank of sergeant in the 8th Virginia Regiment, continental line, he rose to that of ensign before resigning his commission in 1778 (Heitman, *Historical Register Continental*, p. 330). Thereafter he served in the Albemarle militia, as captain at the time of the present letter, and subsequently as major (Albemarle County Personal Property-Tax Book, 1810, MS in Va. State Library). In March 1797 he appeared as a witness in a court action against Jefferson, for which appearance the plaintiff was directed to pay Key one dollar (Albemarle County Court Records, Order Book, 1795–1798, p. 252, microfilm in Va. State Library). The disappearance of his name from Albemarle County records after 1811 suggests either that he died intestate or moved from the county. If not Key, at least his "family" is thought to have emigrated to Kentucky or Tennessee (Edgar Woods, *Albemarle County in Virginia* [Charlottesville, 1901], pp. 245–46, 368, 376, 379; Boyd, *Papers of Jefferson*, VI, 354, 358, 567; Gwathmey, *Historical Register of Virginians*, p. 444; *JCC*, XI, 842–43; *Cal. of Va. State Papers*, II, 350).

15 The delivery to Montpelier of the trunk which JM had shipped from Philadelphia, probably to the care of James Maury at Fredericksburg, was delayed until March 1784 (JM to Jefferson, 11 Feb.; also 16 Mar. 1784 in LC: Madison Papers). For Maury, see JM to James Madison, Sr., 27 May 1783, n. 2; for previous references to Georges Louis Leclerc, Comte de Buffon, and his works on natural history, *Papers of Madison*, II, 55; 56, n. 8; V, 16; 18, n. 7.

16 Many years later, after recovering this letter, JM wrote in the left margin of his sentence on "Central heat," "see [?] letter of Feby. 17. 1784 shewing Buffon who [?] had been read to have been misconceived." That is, JM, at the time he wrote the present letter, relied upon what Jefferson had told him about Buffon's "Theory of Central heat." In a letter of 1 January 1784, Jefferson admitted that, upon reflecting "a little more attentively," he had come to realize how "false" an "idea of Buffon's hypothesis" he had given JM in their "conversation." In his letter of acknowledgment on 17 February, after commenting that Jefferson had "rectified my misconception" of the "hypothesis," JM added: "I forbear as I ought perhaps formerly to have done, making any further remarks on it, at least till I have seen the work itself" (Jefferson to JM, 1 Jan., and JM to Jefferson, 17 Feb. 1784). For this reason, JM's marginal comment would have been clearer if, after "had been read," he had added "by Jefferson." The "work" at issue was Georges Louis Leclerc, Comte de Buffon (1707–1788), *Théorie de la terre*. See M. A. Richard

and M. le Baron Cuvier, eds. *Oeuvres complètes de Buffon* (34 vols.; Paris, 1825–31), I, 120–27, 156–58, 175–80; II, 235–393, *passim*.

17 JM refers to Benjamin Martin (1704–1782), a British mathematician and maker of optical instruments, and to Pierre Louis Moreau de Maupertuis (1698–1759), a French mathematician and astronomer.

18 *Oeuvres de Maupertuis* (Nouvelle édition corrigée & augmentée; 4 vols.; Lyon, 1768), III, 51–58, 167–68; IV, 287, 335; Benjamin Martin, *A Plain and Familiar Introduction to the Newtonian Philosophy* (London, 1751), pp. 92, 105, 156; Benjamin Martin, *Philosophia Britannica; or, a New and Comprehensive System of the Newtonian Philosophy, Astronomy, and Geography* (3 vols.; London, 1788), I, 146; III, 290, 295–98, 301, 302.

19 The 87.94 is obtained by dividing "the mean semidiameter" (7942.2 + 7852.4 ÷ by 4) by ½ of 89.8, or 44.9.

20 If the "44.9" is made 45 miles and the "89.8" is made 90 miles, the radius of the earth from its center to its surface would shorten ½ mile for each of the 90 degrees from the equator to the North or South Pole.

21 The equator is separated from the Arctic Circle by 66° 30′ of latitude. If, upon moving north from the equator, the distance from the earth's center to the surface shortens by ½ mile for each degree of latitude, the distance from the earth's center at the Arctic Circle is 33 1/6 miles less than at the equator. To arrive at 1/119, JM first of all added to 7852.4 an extra 11.6 miles—that is, ½ mile for each of the 23° 30′ from the Arctic Circle to the North Pole. The result, 7,864 added to 7,942.2, and their sum quartered, is 3,951.55 miles. This is the "mean distance" from the center of the earth to the surface in the span of 66° 30′ of latitude separating the equator from the Arctic Circle. Taking 3,951.55 and dividing it by 33.1666 produces 119.14.

22 Isaac Newton (1642–1727), of whom both Maupertuis and Martin were followers, had held that the earth was an oblate spheroid, but Jean Dominique Cassini (1625–1712), an Italo-French astronomer, contended that the earth was an oblong spheroid. To determine which scientist was correct, Maupertuis led an expedition to the Arctic Circle in Lapland in 1736–1739, and other French scientists journeyed to the equator in Peru in 1744 (*Papers of Madison*, VI, 114, entry No. 296). By comparing the difference in the diameter of the meridians of the two sites, they demonstrated that Newton had been correct. The earth was an oblate spheroid, sufficiently flattened at the Arctic Circle to make the diameter of a meridian there about 1/200th shorter than at the equator (*Oeuvres de Maupertuis*, I, 66–68; II, 292–98; III, 51–58; IV, 287, 331; Benjamin Martin, *Philosophia Britannica*, III, 294).

23 Approximately all the Atlantic coast of the United States was between 31° and 45° north latitude. If, on moving northward from the equator, the distance from the surface of the earth to its center lessens by ½ mile for each degree of latitude, the southern border of the United States was seven miles farther than its northern border from the earth's center.

Many years later, after recovering this letter, JM or someone by his direction placed a bracket at the close of the paragraph, probably signifying that all he had written to that point should be published in the first extensive edition of his papers; but Henry D. Gilpin, the editor of that edition, printed only the first two paragraphs of the letter (Madison, *Papers* [Gilpin ed.], I, 579–80).

24 Relying on the money owed him for services as a delegate, JM on 26 November loaned Jefferson in Annapolis $333.33 in the form of a draft on Jacquelin Ambler, the treasurer of Virginia. The "note" was an acknowledgment by Jefferson to JM of that sum. Before leaving Philadelphia, JM had also loaned $170 to Jefferson. Jefferson repaid these loans in part by a bill of exchange and in part by purchases,

especially of books, for JM in Philadelphia and later in Paris (Settlement of Accounts, 31 Dec. 1783; Jefferson to JM, 1 Jan.; 20 Feb.; 16 Mar. 1784 in LC: Madison Papers; Boyd, *Papers of Jefferson*, VII, 243–44, 356–57, 536–37).

[25] Mrs. Mary House in Philadelphia. See Jefferson to JM, 11 Dec. 1783; 1 Jan. 1784.

From Thomas Jefferson

RC (LC: Madison Papers). Cover addressed to "James Madison junr. esq. Orange. to the care of mr Jas. Maury Fredericksburg." Docketed by JM, "Ths. Jefferson Dec 11. 1783."

ANNAPOLIS Dec. 11. 1783.

DEAR SIR

Your determination to avail yourself of the fine weather proved I fear a very unfortunate one. I pitied your probable situation in the tempestuous season which immediately succeeded your departure.[1] it is now above a fortnight since we should have met, and six states only appear. we have some hopes of Rhodeisland coming in to-day, but when two more will be added seems as insusceptible of calculation as when the next earthquake will happen.[2] we have at length received the Definitive treaty with a joint letter from all our Commissioners. not a tittle is changed in the treaty but the preamble & some small things which were of course.[3] the Commissioners write that the riot of Philadelphia & departure of Congress thence made the most serious impressions in Europe, and have excited great doubts of the stability of our confederacy, and in what we shall end. the accounts were greatly exaggerated, & it is suspected that Gr. Br. wished to sign no treaty.[4]

You have seen G. M. I hope & had much conversation with him. what are his sentiments as to the amendment of our constitution? what amendments would he approve? is he determined to sleep on, or will he rouse & be active? I wish to hear from you on this subject, & at all times on any others which occupy your thoughts.[5] I see Bradford advertizes Smith's history of N. York. as I mean to write for one for myself, and think I heard you say you had it not, I shall add one for you.[6] our news from the good family we left is not agreeable. mrs. Trist is much agitated by the doubts and difficulties which hang over her & impede her reunion with mr. Trist. they are without lodgers except those we left there, & the ladies we left there propose soon to depart. we hear some circumstances of rudeness in mr. S. inconsistent with the inoffensiveness of character we had given him credit for.[7] I wish you much happiness and am with the sincerest esteem Dr. Sir

Your friend & servt.

TH: JEFFERSON

P.S. I have taken the liberty of putting under cover to you a book for my nephew Peter Carr who is at mr. Maury's in your neighborhood.[8]

[1] JM to Jefferson, 10 Dec. 1783, and n. 1.

[2] A "number of members" insufficient "to proceed to business" met in Annapolis on 26 November, the day scheduled by Congress to convene there after adjourning at Princeton on 4 November. William Ellery and David Howell of Rhode Island having arrived, effective delegations were present on 13 December from seven states, not counting New Hampshire and South Carolina, for they each had only one delegate in attendance (*JCC*, XXV, 807, 809–10). On 29 December the number of delegations dropped to six. Only five were on hand at the close of 1783 (*JCC*, XXV, 814–42, *passim*).

[3] On 13 December Congress received an official copy of the definitive treaty of peace, signed by the commissioners of Great Britain and the United States at Paris on 3 September 1783 (*JCC*, XXV, 812). Article X of the document stipulated that "solemn Ratifications" should "be exchanged between the contracting Parties in the Space of Six Months" (Hunter Miller, ed., *Treaties and Other International Acts*, II, 155–56). Article IX of the Articles of Confederation manifestly connoted that the ratification of a peace treaty required the assent of at least nine states (*JCC*, XIX, 220). On 26 and 27 December 1783, with the deadline only about two months in the future, with only seven states effectively represented in Congress, with little prospect of adding two more, and with a belief prevalent that Great Britain would be glad "to postpone the conclusion of the treaty," the delegates debated but failed to adopt a motion "that 7 states were competent to the ratification" (*JCC*, XXV, 836–37; Burnett, *Letters*, VII, 392–93, 395–96, 399, and n. 3, 403–4, 405–6). Jefferson meant, of course, that the terms of the preliminary and the definitive treaties of peace were in all important respects identical.

[4] John Adams, Benjamin Franklin, and John Jay enclosed the definitive treaty in their dispatch of 10 September 1783 to President Elias Boudinot. The commissioners mentioned, among the news items from the United States which had "diminished the admiration" of Europeans for "the people of America," and possibly helped to account for Great Britain's delay in concluding the treaty, "the exaggerated accounts of divisions among our people and want of authority of Congress," the harsh treatment of Loyalists, "the situation of the army, the reluctance of the people to pay taxes, and the circumstances under which Congress removed from Philadelphia" (Wharton, *Revol. Dipl. Corr.*, VI, 687–91). See also Delegates to Harrison, 1 Nov. 1783 (1st letter), and n. 10.

[5] In his letter to Jefferson on 10 December (*q.v.*), JM had partially answered these questions about George Mason. Fifty-eight years of age in 1783, Mason had declined two years before to continue as a member of the Virginia House of Delegates, stating that "They drove me out of the Assembly with a thorough Conviction that it was not in my Power to do any Manner of Good" (Robert A. Rutland, ed., *The Papers of George Mason* [3 vols.; Chapel Hill, N.C., 1970], II, 768). Between 1785 and 1788, however, in spite of frequent periods of illness, he

resumed his public career. During those years he shared in the Mount Vernon Conference, the Annapolis Convention, four sessions of the House of Delegates, the Federal Constitutional Convention, and the Virginia Convention which ratified the Constitution of the United States (Swem and Williams, *Register*, pp. 24, 26; Kate M. Rowland, *Life of George Mason*, II, 1, 23, 81–297, *passim*).

6 Thomas Bradford, proprietor of a bookstore on Front Street in Philadelphia, announced in the 10 December issue of his *Pennsylvania Journal, and the Weekly Advertiser* that he had for sale, among the volumes "IMPORTED in the last vessels from London," "Smiths History of New-York." The reference is to William Smith, *The History of the Province of New-York, from the First Discovery* . . . (London, 1757; 2d ed.; London 1776). See also *Papers of Madison*, VI, 103, entry No. 256; JM to Jefferson, 11 Feb.; Jefferson to JM, 20 Feb. 1784.

7 In a letter written to Jefferson about 8 December, Mrs. Eliza House Trist, the daughter of Mrs. Mary House, remarked: "Mama pines exceedingly; she has sustaind a heavy loss. It is not likely she will ever have so agreeable a family again for I have not the most distant hope that Congress will ever return to this city. Mr. Harrison and Lady (he is a banished tory from N York) and old Smith who is grown intollarable are all that at present encircles our board. I realy am obliged to be silent and bite my tongue fear of Quarreling I wou'd rather live among Hornets than be obliged to live with Mr. Smith" (Boyd, *Papers of Jefferson*, VI, 375). See also Randolph to JM, 18 July; Mercer to JM, 14 Aug., and nn. 6, 7; JM to Randolph, 8 Sept. 1783.

8 Peter Carr (1770–1815), the eldest son of Jefferson's widowed sister Martha, whose husband, Dabney Carr, had died in 1773, was attending the school of Walker Maury at Orange, not far from Montpelier (*William and Mary Quarterly*, 1st ser., XV [1906–7], 117; *Papers of Madison*, I, 317, n. 10). Jefferson enclosed for Peter a copy of the works of Homer. At least seven weeks before the present letter finally reached JM after a "very tedious conveyance," Maury's pupils had "dispersed" as a result of his decision to move his school to "the Capital" in Williamsburg (*Va. Gazette*, 10 Jan., 20 Mar. 1784). Thereafter Peter's formal education was suspended until the spring of 1785 when, upon JM's recommendation, he enrolled again under Maury's tutelage at Williamsburg (JM to Jefferson, 11 Feb. 1784; Boyd, *Papers of Jefferson*, VI, 166–67, 415–16, 470; VII, 234, 408; VIII, 101; Edgar Woods, *Albemarle County in Virginia*, p. 160; Elizabeth Dabney Coleman, "Peter Carr of Carr's-Brook [1770–1815]," *Papers of the Albemarle County Historical Society*, IV, 5–23).

On the date of the present letter, Jefferson also wrote to Peter Carr, recommending that he "find means to attract the notice and acquaintance of" JM. "His judgment is so sound and his heart so good," Jefferson continued, "that I would wish you to respect every advice he would be so kind as to give you, equally as if it came from me" (Boyd, *Papers of Jefferson*, VI, 380). When in 1784 Jefferson accepted the post of minister plenipotentiary to France, he asked JM to serve as Peter's guardian (*ibid.*, VII, 233–34).

Settlement of Accounts with Virginia

FC (LC: Madison Papers). In JM's hand. Ink faded and some of the writing rendered illegible by water stains. JM's docket appears to read, "Acct. & Recpts. [?] for 1783 as Delegate to Congs. Jan 84"

J. Madison Junr. in Account with the Commonwealth of Virginia

1783	Dr.	£	S	D
March 29.	To cash recd. of Mr. Jones out of a sum recd. by him for use of the Delegates to Congs. from the Sheriff of N. hampton	50	18	11[1]
April	To do. recd. out of bills of exchange on Inglis & Co. for one thousand dollars & Trumbul & Co. for 566⅔ remitted by J. Ambler Esqr. for use of the Delegates	100	—	—[2]
	To do. recd. out of do. on Jno. Ross & Co. for 1666⅔ remitted by J. Ambler Esqr. for use of do.	100	—	—[3]
May	To do. recd. on two bills dated 12 & 14 May 1783 for £100 each on S. Inglis & Co. by D. Cochran in favr. of J. Ambler Esqr & remitted by Foster Webb in consequence of warrants issued on my account	200	—	—[4]
	To. do recd. out of 2 bills for £500 each on Lacaze & Mallet remitted by J. Ambler Esqr. for use of the Delegates	697	18	—[5]
June	To do. recd. in 1 bill dated May 12 for £100 drawn by D. Cochran in favr. of J. Ambler Esqr. remitted by W.[?] in consequence of warrant issued on my acct.	100	—	[6]
Sepr. 5.	To do. recd. out of two bills on Lacaze & Mallet remitted by J. Ambler Esqr. for use of the Delegates in consequence of warrant issued on their[?] acct.	246	15	—[7]
	To do. in consequence of warrant issued	100	—	[8]
		1595—12[9]		

1782	Credt	£	S	D
Decr. 31	By ballance settled	865	8	3[10]
1783	By service as Delegate to Congs. from Jany. 1. to Octr. 25. inclusive 298 days at 8 drs. per day	715—	4—	[11]
	By 12 days returning from Congs at do	28—	16—	[12]
		1609—	8—	3[13]

[1] Statement of Receipts, 28 May 1783, and n. 1. Jones was Joseph Jones, a delegate from Virginia in Congress.

[2] *Ibid.*, and n. 2. Jacquelin Ambler was the treasurer of Virginia. "Trumbul & Co." was probably William Turnbull and Company of Philadelphia.

[3] Summary of Accounts, 28 May, and n. 4; Statement of Receipts, 28 May 1783, and n. 3.

[4] After "May," at the outset of the entry, JM wrote and deleted "27." See JM to Randolph, 27 May; Summary of Accounts, 28 May, n. 5; Statement of Receipts, 28 May, n. 5. For Foster Webb, Jr., see Ambler to JM, 17 May 1783, n. 3.

[5] Ambler to JM, 17 May; Summary of Accounts, 28 May, n. 5; Delegates to Auditors, 28 May, hdn., and n. 3; Statement of Receipts, 28 May 1783, and n. 4.

[6] Statement of Receipts, 28 May, and n. 5; Ambler to JM, 1 June. "W." [?] probably signifies Foster Webb, Jr. (JM to Randolph, 3 June 1783).

[7] JM to Mercer, 16 July; Jones to JM, 4 Aug. 1783, and n. 1.

[8] Ambler to JM, 1 June 1783, n. 4.

[9] JM evidently rounded off the exact total of £1,595 11*s.* 11*d.*

[10] Ambler to JM, 17 May; Summary of Accounts, 28 May 1783, and n. 1.

[11] In his Summary of Accounts, 28 May (*q.v.*, and n. 2), JM claimed per diem pay of $8.00, as stipulated by law, for 140 days from 31 December 1782 to 28 May 1783 (*Papers of Madison*, V, 19, n. 4). The "298 days" obviously includes the 140—thus leaving 158 for the period 29 May to 2 November (not "Octr. 25.") when his term as a delegate expired. During those 158 calendar days, Congress convened on 109, including four (6 June, 31 July, 22 August, and 12 September) unnoted in the journal but recorded by Charles Thomson in his committee book (*JCC*, XXIV, 368–528, *passim;* XXV, 529–794, *passim;* NA: PCC, No. 186, fols. 106, 115, 119, 123). In his financial account of 28 May, JM was careful not to charge for the days when he was absent from Congress (Summary of Accounts, 28 May 1783, and n. 2). In the present statement he claimed $8.00 for every calendar day after 28 May, even though, among the 109, he was not in attendance on about 52—one in June, ten in July, sixteen in August, nine in September, fifteen in October, and one in November. In every instance when he was not present, he appears to have been engaged in work or other pursuits unconnected with his duties as a delegate (Hamilton to JM, 29 June, ed. n.; JM to Randolph, 30 June, and n. 4; 8 July, and n. 2; 15 July, and n. 7; 21 July; 5 Aug., and n. 4; 24 Aug.; 13 Oct.; to Jefferson, 17 July, and n. 14; Motion *in re* Armed Vessels, 28 July, ed. n.; Delegates to Harrison, 1 Aug., and n. 1; 23 Aug., n. 7; Mercer to JM, 14 Aug., and n. 9; JM to James Madison, Sr., 8 Sept. 1783).

The result of multiplying 298 by $8 and dividing the outcome by 3⅓ to change the dollars into pounds is £715 2*s.* rather than £714 4*s.*

[12] JM had also taken twelve days in March 1780 to travel from his home to Philadelphia (*Papers of Madison*, II, 3, and n. 1; JM to Jefferson, 10 Dec. 1783, and n. 1). The result of multiplying 12 by $8 and dividing the outcome by 3⅓ is £28 8*s.*, rather than £28 16*s.* JM charged for only those days he actually traveled and did not count those days when he broke his trip. His return to Montpelier actually took fourteen days.

[13] When JM received the small balance due him is not known. In the Virginia State Library is a memorandum, or perhaps a docket, in Jacquelin Ambler's hand, reading: "July 21st. 1784. Bills drawn by the Honble Jas Madison & A L. Delegates to Congs. Mr. Madison & Mr Walker £40 ea:." From what Virginia owed him as a delegate in Congress, Jefferson may have partially discharged the loan to him of October 1783 from JM by authorizing Ambler to pay £40 to JM (JM to Jefferson, 10 Dec. 1783, n. 24; Boyd, *Papers of Jefferson*, VII, 234, 243–44). "Mr Walker" may have received the £40 on behalf of Arthur Lee.

During his final four months of service as a delegate, JM was clearly less embarrassed financially than in any earlier period of similar length since he had entered Congress. Between March and June he was paid about £1,249 (*ca.* \$4,163) by Virginia, and received £346 15*s.* (*ca.* \$1,155.75) more from the same source in September. To this probably was added an unknown amount gained from disposing of his slave Billey (JM to James Madison, Sr., 8 Sept., and n. 4). From these funds he paid whatever debt he may still have owed Haym Salomon, met the cost of room and board in Philadelphia and of his food and the expensive room he shared with Joseph Jones in Princeton, loaned John Francis Mercer at least \$600, and Thomas Jefferson, \$503 (Ambler to JM, 5 July, and n. 5; Mercer to JM, 14 Aug.; Receipt of Mercer, 11 Oct., and n. 1; JM to Randolph, 13 Oct.; to Jefferson 10 Dec. 1783, n. 24). How much money JM may have had in pocket upon his arrival early in December at Montpelier is not known, but probably it was not a large sum.

From Thomas Jefferson

RC (LC: Madison Papers). Cover missing. Docketed by JM, "Thos. Jefferson Jan 1 1784." Beneath the docket appears in an unknown hand, "Buffons theory respecting the Globe."

ANNAPOLIS Jan. 1. 1784.

DEAR SIR

Your favour of the 10th. Dec. came to hand about a fortnight after its date.[1] It has occasioned me to reflect a little more attentively on Buffon's central heat than I did in the moment of our conversation and to form an opinion different from what I then expressed. the term 'central heat' does of itself give us a false idea of Buffon's hypothesis. if it meant a heat lodged in the center of the earth and diffusing it's warmth from thence to the extremities, then certainly it would be less in proportion to the distance from that center, & of course less under the equator than the poles, on high mountains than in deep vallies. but Buffon's theory is that this earth was once in a state of hot fusion, and that it has been, and still continues to be cooling. What is the course of this process? a heated body being surrounded by a colder one whether solid or fluid, the heat, which is itself a fluid, flows into the colder body equally from every point of the hotter. hence if a heated spheroid of iron cools to a given degree, in a given space of time, an inch deep from its surface, in one point, it has in the same time done the same in any & every other point. in a given time more, it will be cooled all round to double that depth, so that it will always be equally cooled at equal depths from the surface. this would be the case of Buffon's earth if it were a smooth figure without unevennesses, but it has mountains and vallies. the tops of mountains will cool to greater depths in the same time than the sides of mountains & than plains in proportion as the line a.b. is longer than a.c. or d.e. or f.g. in the valley the line h.i. or depth of the same temperature will be the same as on a plain. this

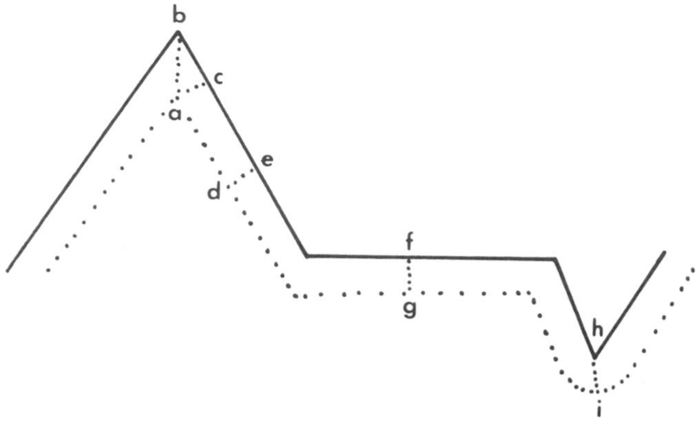

however is very different from Buffon's opinion. he sais that the earth being thinnest at the poles will cool sooner there than under the equator where it is thicker. if my idea of the process of cooling be right his is wrong and his whole theory in the Epochs of nature is overset.[2]

The note which I delivered you contained an acknowledgement of my having borrowed from you a draught for 333 1/3 dollars and a promise to repay it on demand. This was exclusive of what I had borrowed in Philadelphia.[3]

We have never yet had more than 7. states, and very seldom that, as Maryland is scarcely ever present, and we are now without a hope of it's attending till February. consequently having six states only, we do nothing. expresses & letters are gone forth to hasten on the absent states that we may have 9. for a ratification of the definitive treaty. Jersey perhaps may come in, and if Beresford will not come to Congress, Congress must go to him to do this one act. even now it is full late. the critical situation in which we are like to be gave birth to an idea that 7. might ratify, but it could not be supported.[4] I will give you a further account of this when it shall be finally settled.[5]

The letters of our ministers inform us that the two empires have formed a league defensive against Christian powers & offensive agt the Turks. when announced by the Empress to the K. of Prussia he answered that he was very sensible on it as one is when informed of important things. France answered in a higher tone and offered to mediate. if Prussia will join France perhaps it may prevent the war: if he does not, it will be bold for France alone to take the aid of the Turks on herself.[6] Ireland is likely to find employment for England.[7] the United Netherlands are in high fermentation. the people now marshall themselves in arms and exercise regularly under the banners ensigns of their towns. their object is to reduce the powers of the Stadtholder.[8]

I have forwarded your letter to mrs. House. mrs. Trist I expect left Philadelphia about the 18th. of Dec. for Pittsburgh. I had a letter from her in which she complained of your not having written and desired me to mention it to you. I made your excuse on the good grounds of the delays you must have experienced on your journey & your distance from the post road: but I am afraid she was gone before my letter reached Philadelphia.[9] I have had very ill health since I have been here and am getting rather lower than otherwise.[10] I wish you every felicity and am with sincere affection

Your friend & servt.

TH: JEFFERSON

[1] *Q.v.* A letter from Montpelier, which was not on the post road, evidently took four days longer to go to Annapolis than a letter from Richmond to Philadelphia. See, however, Jefferson to JM, 20 Feb. 1784.

[2] JM to Jefferson, 10 Dec. 1783, and n. 16.

[3] *Ibid.*, and n. 24.

[4] *Ibid.*, and n. 3; Jefferson to JM, 11 Dec. 1783, and nn. 2, 3. On 23 December Congress adopted a motion, introduced by Hugh Williamson and seconded by Jefferson, instructing President Thomas Mifflin to inform the executives of New Hampshire, Connecticut, New York, New Jersey, South Carolina, and Georgia "that the ratification of the definitive treaty, and several other matters" involving the national "safety, honor and good faith" now "require the immediate attendance of their delegates" (*JCC*, XXV, 836–37). On the same day Mifflin posted letters in conformance with this resolution. On 24 December 1783 he further emphasized the urgency by having an "Express" rush messages of the same tenor to the governors of Delaware, New Jersey, and Connecticut (Burnett, *Letters*, VII, 395–96).

Beginning on 2 January 1784 and continuing for five weeks thereafter, an effective vote was cast by Maryland, provided that its two delegates were in agreement on an issue. On 2 January 1784 Congress entertained a committee's report, written by Jefferson, chairman, recommending that proposals upon "important" issues, including those relating "to the ratification of the Definitive Treaty," require for their determination "the assent" of at least nine state delegations (*JCC*, XXVI, 2). For a compromise suggestion by Jefferson on this same matter, see Boyd, *Papers of Jefferson*, VI, 439–42. Until 25 February, New Jersey had only one delegate in attendance. Being detained in Philadelphia by illness, Richard Beresford was unable until 14 January to reach Annapolis and join his congressional colleague, Jacob

Read, of South Carolina. On that day, "nine states being present," Congress unanimously ratified the definitive peace treaty with Great Britain (Burnett, *Letters*, VII, lxvi, lxvii, lxx, lxxv, lxxvi; *JCC*, XXVI, 22–23).

[5] Jefferson to JM, 20 Feb. 1784.

[6] Jefferson appears to be referring to John Adams' dispatch of 2 August to Robert R. Livingston, and perhaps also to Lafayette's letter of 7 September 1783 to the president of Congress. This correspondence had been submitted to Congress on 13 December and referred to a committee of which Jefferson was chairman (NA: PCC, No. 185, III, 87, 89; *JCC*, XXV, 812, n. 2, 821–28; Wharton, *Revol. Dipl. Corr.*, VI, 629–31, 679–81).

In 1780 the "two empires" governed by Tsarina Catherine of Russia and Holy Roman Emperor Joseph II of Austria, respectively, had concluded an offensive alliance against Turkey. Soon thereafter Joseph II resumed his policy of expanding the size of his personal domains at the expense of several German states. As countermoves, Frederick the Great of Prussia sought a rapprochement with Louis XVI of France and George III of Great Britain, continued to alienate Catherine the Great by threatening further encroachment upon Poland and by urging Turkey to resist Russian absorption of the Crimea, and in 1785, about a year before his death, succeeded in forming a confederation (*Fürstenbund*) of German princes to block Joseph II's westward push. Turkey delayed until 1787 before declaring war on Russia, supported by Austria (A. W. Ward *et al.*, eds., *Cambridge Modern History*, VI, 708–9).

[7] Although Parliament granted Ireland legislative independence in 1782, the Catholics there continued to demand the repeal of discriminatory legislation against them in the areas of religion, education, the legal profession, and ownership of property (*Hansard's Parliamentary Debates*, XXIII, cols. 17–47, 91–95, 147–51, 322–42, 730–57; A. W. Ward *et al.*, eds., *Cambridge Modern History*, VI, 458–59, 496–505).

[8] Between "the" and "ensigns," Jefferson interlineated "banners," probably to make clear that by "ensigns" he meant flags rather than military officers. He seems to have read Charles G. F. Dumas' missing dispatch from The Hague on 28 September. According to Charles Thomson's record book of incoming letters, this communication dealt with "commotions in Holland" and reached Congress on 27 December 1783 (NA: PCC, No. 185, III, 90). The "commotions" had been caused by the generally unsuccessful demand of Emperor Joseph II that, in spite of the guarantee of the Treaty of Münster (1648), the Dutch should open their primary waterway, the Scheldt, to Austrian shipping (A. W. Ward *et al.*, eds., *Cambridge Modern History*, VI, 642–46).

The efforts of the States-General to reduce the power of the stadtholder, William V, Prince of Orange and Nassau, reflected the dislike by the merchants in the Dutch cities of his partiality for Great Britain and his opposition, 1780–1782, to the conclusion of a treaty of amity and commerce between the Netherlands and the United States (*Papers of Madison*, IV, 220, n. 3; 287, n. 25; 291, n. 19; 292; V, 210; 211, n. 15; 214).

[9] JM to Jefferson, 10 Dec., and nn. 1, 25. For Mrs. Nicholas Trist's letter of *ca.* 8 December to Jefferson, see Boyd, *Papers of Jefferson*, VI, 375–76. In his missing letter of 22 December 1783 to Mrs. Trist, Jefferson probably explained JM's delay in writing (*ibid.*, VI, 418).

[10] In a letter of 15 January 1784 to his daughter Patsy, Jefferson assured her that, although he had been in "very ill health" ever since his arrival in Annapolis, he was feeling "considerably better" (*ibid.*, VI, 465–66).

From Edmund Randolph

RC (LC: Madison Papers). Cover missing. Docketed by JM, "Randolph. Edmd. Jany. 27. 1784."

RICHMOND Jany. 27. 1784.

MY DEAR FRIEND

Altho' your return from congress has brought you nearer in point of distance, it has fixed a wider gulph between us in point of communication by letter. But I do not mean to suffer the danger of miscarrage, to which even a private opportunity is exposed, whensoever any thing, worthy of notice, occurs.[1] At present therefore I break in upon your retirement with the inclosed rough draught. I have not leisure to transcribe it with the alterations, which I made in the copy sent to the governor. Your friendship will excuse the inaccuracies, and you will collect the substance of my ideas, although they abound.[2]

Believe me to be my dear Madison Yr. affte friend

E. R.

[1] JM to Jefferson, 10 Dec. 1783, n. 1; Jefferson to JM, 1 Jan. 1784, n. 1. Not until the 1790's, when a post office was established at Orange Court House, could JM send a letter from, or receive one at, Montpelier unless it was entrusted to a private courier or transmitted through a more distant post office, such as the one at Fredericksburg (Jedidiah Morse, comp., *The American Gazetteer* . . . [2d ed., cor.; London, 1798], p. 618).

[2] On 20 July 1780 George Hancock, Jr. (1754–1820), the son of wealthy George Hancock, Sr. (d. 1782), of South Carolina, was admitted to practice in the county court of Powhatan County, Va., of which county he subsequently became a captain of militia. In September 1781 he married in Botetourt County; was admitted five months later to practice law in its county court; and eventually resided at Santillane, an estate near Fincastle in that county (Powhatan County Court Records, Order Book 1, 1777–1784, p. 60, microfilm in Va. State Library; Boyd, *Papers of Jefferson*, VI, 188; Robert Douthat Stoner, *A Seed-Bed of the Republic: A Study of the Pioneers in the Upper* [*Southern*] *Valley of Virginia* [Roanoke, Va., 1962], pp. 294–96, 407–8).

In the meantime George Hancock, Sr., pleading "the turbulence of the times" in South Carolina, had been permitted to bring sixty-three slaves to Virginia and register them in Henry County (*Cal. of Va. State Papers*, III, 30, 142). At the time of his death he was a resident of Bedford County (Bedford County Court Records, Will Book 1, 1763–1787, pp. 434–35; will printed in Joida Whitten, comp. and ed., *Abstracts of Bedford County, Virginia, Wills, Inventories and Accounts, 1754–1787* [Dallas, Tex., 1968], p. 136). As his father's executor, the son went to the Camden district of South Carolina, where the will was probated. While there on 22 October 1783, he with "fist and switch" violently assaulted Jonas Beard, a planter living along the Saluda River, a colonel of militia, a justice of the peace, a judge of the court of general sessions, and a member of the state legislature (A[lexander] S. Salley, Jr., *The History of Orangeburg County, South Carolina, from Its First Settlement to the Close of the Revolutionary War* [Orangeburg, 1898], pp. 249, 257, 258, 265, 266–69, 276, 278, 293, 346, 469).

In a letter of 16 December 1783 Governor Benjamin Guerard of South Carolina requested Harrison to extradite Hancock for trial in that state, justifying his request by enclosing Beard's affidavit and, more importantly, by citing the paragraph of Article IV of the Articles of Confederation, providing that "If any Person guilty of, or charged with treason, felony, or other high misdemeanor in any state, shall flee from Justice, and be found in any of the united states, he shall, upon demand of the Governor or executive power, of the state from which he fled, be delivered up and removed to the state having jurisdiction of his offence" (*Cal. of Va. State Papers*, III, 549; *JCC*, XIX, 215). Upon receiving Guerard's "extraordinary letter," Harrison on 17 January 1784 sought the advice of Randolph, the attorney general of Virginia. Randolph replied four days later (Executive Letter Book, 1783–1786, p. 262, MS in Va. State Library; *Cal. of Va. State Papers*, III, 556–57).

He enclosed the ten-page, rough draft of that answer in the present letter. The text of the draft contains many deletions and interlineations, occasional abbreviations, and a marginal insert on the eighth page. The Library of Congress may have acquired this document, and perhaps Randolph's brief letter also, from Stan. V. Henkels, a manuscript dealer of Philadelphia (Henkels Catalogue No. 694 [1892]). Jefferson, to whom Randolph and JM wrote separately about the Hancock case, seems to have let it rest without any comments of his own (Boyd, *Papers of Jefferson*, VI, 513–15; VII, 38–39).

Randolph viewed the issue as one "of delicacy and danger." An unqualified refusal of Guerard's request "may produce a rupture of federal harmony," but a complete fulfillment of it "will furnish cause for the most bitter complaint against that authority, which shall transport a citizen to a foreign tribunal, for trial on a penal accusation." Conscious of this dilemma, Randolph sought to find a solution which would avoid either of those extremes. Assuming that each of the states of the United States was sovereign, he believed that their legal relationships fell within the domain of international law. Upon consulting Emmerich de Vattel, *The Law of Nations; or, Principles of the Law of Nature*, he found the author's discussion limited to comity practices among the Swiss cantons. None of them, in Randolph's opinion, had been derived with sufficient certainty from international law to furnish a "precedent" for Harrison's guidance.

Randolph was also impressed by the extent to which American legal terminology, procedures, and safeguards of an accused person's rights reflected British models. He emphasized that the term "high misdemeanor," being linked with "treason" and "felony" in the Articles of Confederation, must mean a crime comparable in gravity with those most reprehensible offenses. In support of this judgment, he cited Sir William Blackstone's *Commentaries on the Laws of England* to the effect that a "high misdemeanor" was confined to "an unequivocal attack against the state." Neither Guerard in his letter nor Beard in his affidavit provided conclusive evidence that Hancock's assault had been more than an "ordinary" one, or had been aggravated in seriousness by being made when Beard was acting in his official capacity as a judge of the "court of general sessions." Randolph therefore held that, in the light of the facts as then known, Harrison justifiably should consider the extradition provision of the Articles of Confederation to be inapplicable.

Arguing further from the same general premise, Randolph asked rhetorically: "if a subject of G. B. commit an offence in F.[,] flee to his own country, and be demanded by the court of Versailles, would G. B. be so perfidious to the peace of her people, as to surrender him without well-searching into his crime, when the meanest of these cannot be imprisoned for a violation of municipal law, before his guilt is fully-weighed?" Answering his own question, Randolph asserted: "France must submit to steps of preparatory inquiry, since it would have taken place in common cases, not affecting foreign nations." "I am aware," he concluded, "that I am here comparing two members of a grand perpetual confederacy, with two nations, disunited except by treaties which may have terminated hostilities. But So. Carolina and Virginia are also disunited from each other in those instances for which the confederation has not provided, expressly or virtually."

The "Full faith and credit" paragraph in Article IV of the Articles of Confederation was one of those legal ties designed "expressly" to unite the states, but it was not in point in the present instance. This was so, Randolph argued, because Guerard's charge, although meriting Harrison's "respect," was neither an equivalent of an attested record of a South Carolina court nor equal in "supremacy" to the "public acts" of Virginia. In this connection, however, Randolph added that the extradition provision of the Articles of Confederation assumed that each state had the sovereign power to decide what act committed within its own borders was "criminal." Hence, if South Carolina forwarded authenticated copies of its law defining a "high misdemeanor," and of the evidence proving Hancock guilty of that offense, Harrison "perhaps" should then return him to South Carolina, even though the nature of his assault did not constitute a "high misdemeanor" under the law of Virginia.

On the above grounds, Randolph advised Harrison not to extradite Hancock. If, however, the governor decided otherwise, he still would not be able to ascertain "the mode of delivery" from a perusal of the Articles of Confederation or any statute of Virginia. At the close of his letter, Randolph recommended that the "mode" should be a notification to "a justice of the peace that the demand" had been "properly made" by South Carolina and he must cause Hancock "to be apprehended."

On 16 February 1784 the Virginia Council of State, including John Marshall, a future Chief Justice of the United States, agreed with Randolph's conclusion by advising Harrison "not to comply with the requisition for the delivery of the said George Hancock." On the same day, observing that delay in answering had been due to bad weather, which had prevented the postrider from going to Charleston, Harrison wrote to Guerard. The refusal of Virginia to extradite Hancock, he explained, had arisen from "no opinion hastily taken up, or from a desire to enter into altercation," but from "maturest consideration and attention to the confederation" on the one hand, and to the rights of every citizen "who is not pointedly and indisputably charged with such a crime as is evidently within the meaning and literal construction" of the Articles of Confederation on the other. After observing that the evidence offered of Hancock's guilt was far from sufficient "in a criminal case" to warrant extradition, Harrison asked Guerard to forward more positive proof. As the matter stood, the charge was "nothing more than a common assault," and the only grounds given for extraditing was Beard's eminence. Did that fact render the assault any different from one made on a man of less distinction? Harrison answered his own question: not unless Beard had been assaulted "whilst in the actual execution of one or other" of his public "trusts," and although Harrison did not so state the matter, Hancock was too shrewd a lawyer to have committed that blunder. The matter had, Harrison concluded, also been put to the attorney general of Virginia, and his reply was "a perfect coincidence of opinion" (Executive Letter Book, 1783–1786, pp. 271–73, MS in Va. State Library; *JCSV*, III, 328).

JM's view of the issue was considerably at variance from that of Randolph and the Council of State (JM to Randolph, 10 Mar. 1784, in LC: Madison Papers; Boyd, *Papers of Jefferson*, VII, 38–39, and n.). On 15 May Randolph informed

Jefferson that the latest reports, though unofficial, were that the legislature of South Carolina had refused to support Guerard and might even have "reprehended" his conduct "as the effect of indelicacy and vehemence of temper" (Boyd, *Papers of Jefferson*, VII, 260).

These developments did not, however, resolve the embarrassment that Harrison foresaw if an unquestionably valid demand for extradition should be made upon a Virginia executive powerless to respond—a matter that he submitted to the General Assembly in a letter of 3 May (Executive Letter Book, 1783–1786, p. 311, MS in Va. State Library). On 1 June the House of Delegates elected a committee, of which JM was a member, that successfully introduced a bill "directing the mode of suing out and prosecuting writs of habeas corpus." Therein provision against a potential cause of future interstate controversy was incorporated, and the bill was signed into law on 30 June 1784 (*JHDV*, May 1784, pp. 30, 38, 39, 66, 69, 81, 89; Hening, *Statutes*, XI, 408–10).

In 1785 George Hancock, Jr., was appointed colonel of Botetourt County militia, and in 1787 county attorney for the commonwealth. From 1784 to 1787 and in 1792 he served as a delegate to the Virginia General Assembly (Swem and Williams, *Register*, pp. 19, 21, 23, 37), and in 1793–1797 as a representative in the Congress of the United States. Later in life he moved to Fotheringay, his estate in Montgomery County. His daughter Julia was the first wife of William Clark, who, with Meriwether Lewis, won fame as an explorer.

To Thomas Jefferson

RC (LC: Madison Papers). Lacks docket and cover.

ORANGE Feby. 11. 1784

DEAR SIR

Your favor of the 11. of Decr. ulto.[1] came safe to hand after a very tedious conveyance. Mr. W. Maury having broken up his school in this Neighbourhood in order to attempt a superior one in Williamsburg & his pupils being dispersed, I have sent the book for Mr. P. Carr into the neighbourhood of Doctr. Walker whence I supposed it would most easily find its way to him.[2] I thank you for the mark of attention afforded by your order for Smith's Hist: of N.Y. for me. If it should be in every respect convenient I could wish a copy of Blairs Lectures to be added to it.[3]

We have had a severer season & particularly a greater quantity of snow than is remembered to have distinguished any preceding winter.[4] The effect of it on the price of grain & other provisions is much dreaded. It has been as yet so far favorable to me that I have pursued my intended course of *law*-reading with fewer interruptions than I had presupposed:[5] but on the other hand it has deprived me entirely of the philosophical books which I had allotted for incidental reading: all my Trunks sent from Philada. both by Myself, & by Mr. House after I left it, being still at Fredericksg.[6]

I have been thinking whether the present situation of the Report of the Revisors of the Laws does not render the printing of it for public consideration advisable. Such a step would not only ensure the preservation of the work & gain us credit abroad, but the sanction which it would probably procure to the Legislature might incline them to adopt it the more readily in the gross. If any material objections occur to you, you will be so good as to mention them[7] I sincerely sympathize with the worthy family left behind us in Philada. but am not without hopes that the vacancies produced by our departure were of short duration. If a visit to Miss Patsy should carry you to Philada. I beg you to remember me in the most affectionate terms to the old lady & to Mrs. Trist if the persecutions of fortune should have so long frustrated her meditated voyage.[8] You will also be so good as to tender my respects to Mr. Mercer if he be at Annapolis & to your other Colleagues, and to be assured of my sincerest wishes for your happiness.[9]

I am Dr. Sir Your friend & servt.

J. Madison Jr.

In the Supplement to the 45. vol. of the Universal Magazine page 373. I find it mentioned by Docr. Hunter that there are in the British Museum grinders of the Incognitum which were found in Brasil & Lima. If I do not misremember your Hypothesis it supposes no bones of that animal to have been met with so far to the South.[10]

[1] *Q.v.*

[2] Jefferson to JM, 11 Dec. 1783, and n. 8. For Dr. Thomas Walker of Castle Hill, Albemarle County, see *Papers of Madison*, I, 241; 242, n. 3; IV, 157, n. 15; 306, n. 3; VI, 416; 417, n. 6; Edgar Woods, *Albemarle County in Virginia*, pp. 271, 334–35; Natalie J. Disbrow, "Thomas Walker of Albemarle," *Papers of the Albemarle County Historical Society*, I (1940–41), 5–18. Mrs. Dabney Carr, the sister of Jefferson and mother of Peter Carr, was living at Monticello (Boyd, *Papers of Jefferson*, I, 98 n.; VI, 199 n.).

[3] Jefferson to JM, 11 Dec. 1783, and n. 6. JM referred to the Reverend Dr. Hugh Blair (1718–1800), *Lectures on Rhetoric and Belles Lettres* (2 vols.; London, 1783). During the next seventy-five years this work appeared in many editions, including translations into French, Italian, Spanish, and Russian. Probably the copy purchased for thirty-five shillings in May 1784 by Jefferson for JM was one

printed "in a beautiful quarto volume, on very fine paper" by Robert Aitken in his bookstore "at Pope's Head, near the Coffee-House, Market Street," Philadelphia (*Pa. Gazette*, 7 Apr. 1784; Boyd, *Papers of Jefferson*, VII, 288, 290 n.).

4 Almost every issue of the weekly *Virginia Gazette* between 17 January and 10 April, with its references to the "extreme severity of the season," "no mail from the north," or travels prevented by ice, high water, or mud, confirms JM's remarks (*Va. Gazette*, 17, 24, and 31 Jan., 7, 14, 21, and 28 Feb., 10 Apr. 1784).

5 JM to Jefferson, 10 Dec. 1783, and n. 12. JM no doubt meant that the impassable condition of the roads had lessened the usual number of winter visits to and from friends.

6 Samuel House (JM to Randolph, 8 Sept., and n. 10). For the arrival of JM's trunks at Montpelier, see JM to Jefferson, 10 Dec. 1783, n. 15.

7 On 24 October 1776 the Virginia General Assembly, responding to a motion offered by Jefferson in the House of Delegates, enacted a statute providing for a "Committee of Revisors." This committee, elected twelve days later by the General Assembly, was composed of Jefferson, chairman, Edmund Pendleton, George Wythe, George Mason, and Thomas Ludwell Lee. Of these, Mason declined to serve and Lee died on 13 April 1778 without sharing in the work. The instructions by the legislature obliged a review of all Virginia statutes for the purpose of recommending repeal of laws "inapplicable to the powers of Government as now organized," or "founded on principles heterogeneous to the republican spirit," or "oppressive to the people." The committee was also directed to propose "certain other laws, which though proved by the experience of other states to be friendly to liberty and the rights of mankind, we have not heretofore been permitted to adopt" (*JHDV* [1828 ed.], Oct. 1776, pp. 10, 13, 14, 16, 26, 28, 41; Hening, *Statutes*, IX, 175–77).

On 18 June 1779 Jefferson and Wythe sent to Benjamin Harrison, then speaker of the House of Delegates, a "catalogue" listing the titles of the "126 bills" proposed by the committee (McIlwaine, *Official Letters*, II, 8; Boyd, *Papers of Jefferson*, II, 301–2). Very few of these were given consideration by the Virginia General Assembly during the next five years. On the other hand, the Assembly at its session of May 1783 provided for a codification of existing laws. Pendleton and Wythe of the "Committee of Revisors" also shared prominently in that work (Randolph to JM, 18 July 1783, and n. 8). For Jefferson's response to JM's suggestion, see Jefferson to JM, 20 Feb.; 25 Apr. 1784 (Boyd, *Papers of Jefferson*, VII, 119–20).

8 JM to Jefferson, 10 Dec., and n. 25; Jefferson to JM, 11 Dec. 1783, and n. 7; 1 Jan. 1784, and n. 9. For Martha (Patsy) Jefferson, see JM to Jefferson, 20 Sept.; 30 Sept. 1783, and n. 6.

9 Although the Virginia delegation consisted of Jefferson, James Monroe, Arthur Lee, John Francis Mercer, and Samuel Hardy, only Jefferson, Monroe, and Lee seem to have been attending Congress during the first half of February. Mercer did not appear until 19 March 1784 (Jones to JM, 8 June 1783, and n. 10; *JCC*, XXVI, 73, 75–78, 150).

10 William Hunter, M.D., F.R.S., "Observations on, with an accurately engraved Copper-plate Representation of the BONES, commonly supposed to be Elephants BONES, which have been found near the River Ohio in America," *The Universal Magazine of Knowledge and Pleasure* . . . (a monthly, published by John Hinton; London, 1st ser., Vols. I–CXIII [1747–1803]), XLV (1769, supplement), 112, 371–75, and esp. 373. See also Jefferson to JM, 20 Feb. 1784.

To Thomas Jefferson

RC (LC: Madison Papers). Undocketed. Cover missing.

ORANGE Feby 17th. 1784.

DEAR SIR

I wrote to you a few days ago by the post acknowledging your favor of the 10th. of Decr.[1] Mr. Maury has since afforded me an opportunity which I cannot omit to acknowledge that of the first of Jany. which has just come to hand, and to express the concern I feel at the account it gives of your ill health. I hope earnestly that this will find it in a better state and that I may soon receive a confirmation of such a favorable change.[2] Your explanation of Buffon's hypothesis has rectified my misconception of it and I forbear as I ought perhaps formerly to have done, making any further remarks on it, at least till I have seen the work itself.[3] I forgot to mention to you in my last that I had recd. a letter from Mazzei dated at *Richmond*, apprising me of a proposed visit to Orange from whence he meant to proceed to Annapolis.[4] As I wish in a little time to make an effort to import som[e] law-books, and shall probably hereafter extend the plan to other books, particularly from France, I must beg the favor of you to obtain the name & address of a fit Bookseller both in London & Paris if the means of such information should at any time fall in your way.[5] I have committed to Mr. Maury's care another letter to my worthy friend Mrs. House, which in case he should not proceed to Philada. he will put into your hand.[6]

I am my dear Sir with the sincerest wishes for the reestablishment of your health and every other happiness, your Obt. friend & servant

J. MADISON JR.

1 Jefferson to JM, 11 (not 10) Dec. 1783; JM to Jefferson, 11 Feb. 1784.

2 Jefferson to JM, 1 Jan. 1784, and n. 10. The bearer of the present letter was probably James Maury of Fredericksburg (Jefferson to JM, 11 Dec. 1783, and hdn.).

3 JM to Jefferson, 10 Dec. 1783, and nn. 15–23; Jefferson to JM, 1 Jan. 1784.

4 For Philip Mazzei's arrival in Virginia from Europe on 23 November 1783, see *Papers of Madison*, VI, 243, n. 1; 244, n. 5. Mazzei's letter to JM has not been found. He visited Montpelier both in March and April 1784 (Boyd, *Papers of Jefferson*, VII, 62–63, 121–22, 124 n.; Richard Cecil Garlick, Jr., *Philip Mazzei, Friend of Jefferson: His Life and Letters* [Baltimore, 1933], pp. 86–87; "Memoirs of Philip Mazzei," trans. E[ugenio] C. Branchi, *William and Mary Quarterly*, 2d ser., X [1930], 7–9). To the news that Mazzei was expected "to proceed to Annapolis," Jefferson responded on 16 Mar. 1784 (LC: Madison Papers).

5 JM to Jefferson, 10 Dec. 1783, and n. 12; Jefferson to JM, 20 Feb. 1784, and nn. 47, 48; Boyd, *Papers of Jefferson*, VII, 31, 37.

6 JM to Jefferson, 10 Dec. 1783, and n. 25.

From Thomas Jefferson

RC (LC: Madison Papers). Unsigned but in Jefferson's hand. Docketed by JM, "Thos. Jefferson. Feb 20th. 1784." The italicized words are those written in the JM-Jefferson Code No. 2.

ANNAPOLIS Feb. 20. 1784:

DEAR SIR

Your favour of the 11th. inst.[1] came to hand this day. I had prepared a multitude of mem[orandu]ms of subjects whereon to write you, but I will first answer those arising from your letter. by the time my order got to Philadelphia every copy of Smith's history of New York was sold.[2] I shall take care to get Blair's Lectures for you as soon as published,[3] and will attend to your presumed wishes whenever I meet with any thing rare & of worth. I wish I knew better what things of this kind you have collected for yourself, as I may often doubt whether you have or have not a thing. I know of no objections to the printing the revisal; on the contrary I think good will result from it.[4] should this be decided I must make a short trip to Virginia, as from the loss of originals I beleive my copies must often be wanting. I had never met with the particular fact relative to the grinders of the incognitum found in Brasil & Lima & deposited in the British museum which you mention from Dr. Hunter.[5] I know it has been said that in a very few instances such bones have been found in S. America. you will find a collection of these in 2. Buff. Epoq. de la nature 187.[6] but they have been so illy attested, so loosely & ignorantly described, and so seldom even pretended to have been seen, that I have supposed their identity with the Northern bones, & perhaps their existence at all not sufficiently established. the authority of Hunter is respectable: but if this be the only well attested instance of those bones brought from S. Amera., they may still be beleived to have been first carried there either previous to the emigration of the Spaniards when there was doubtless a communication between the Indns. of the two continents, or after that emigration when an intercourse between the Spaniards of N. & S. Amera. took place. it would be unsafe to deny the fact; but I think it may well be doubted. I wish you had a thermometer. mr. Madison of the college & myself are keeping observations for a comparison of climate. we observe at Sunrise & at 4. o'clock P.M. which are the coldest & warmest points of the day. if you could observe at the same time it should shew the difference between going

North & Northwest on this continent.[7] I suspect it to be colder in Orange or Albemarle than here.

I think I informed you in my last[8] that an attempt had been made to ratify the Definitive treaty by seven states only, and to impose this under the sanction of our seal (without letting our actual state appear) on the British court.[9] Reade, Williamson & Lee were violent for this, and gave notice that when the question should be put they would call the yeas & nays, and shew by whose fault the ratification of this important instrument should fail, if it should fail.[10] I prepared the inclosed resolution by way of protest & informed them I would place that also on the journals with the yeas & nays, as a justification of those who opposed the proposition. I beleive this put a stop to it.[11] they suffered the question to rest undecided till the 14th. of Jan. when 9. states appeared & ratified.[12] Colo Harmer & Colo Franks were immediately dispatched to take passages to Europe with copies of the ratification.[13] but by the extraordinary severity of the season we know they had not sailed on the 7th. inst. the ratification will not therefore arrive in time.[14] being persuaded I shall be misrepresented within my own state, if any difficulties should arise, I inclose you a copy of the protest containing my reasons. had the question been put there were but two states who would have voted for a ratification by seven. the others would have been in the negative or divided.[15] I find Congress every moment stopped by questions whether the most trifling money propositions are not above the powers of seven states as being appropriations of money. my idea is that the estimate for the year & requisition grounded on that, whereon the sums to be allowed to each department are stated, is the general appropriation which requires 9. states, & that the detailing it out provided they do not go beyond these sums may be done by the subordinate officers of the federal government or by a Congress of 7: states. I wish you to think of this & give me your thoughts on the subject.[16] we have as yet no Secy. of Foreign affairs. *Lee* avows himself a candidate.[17] the plan of Foreign affairs likely to take place is to commission Adams, Franklin & Jay to conclude treaties with the several European powers, and then to return, leaving the feild to subordinate characters.[18] messrs. Adams & Jay have paid a visit to the court of London unordered & uninvited. their reception has been forbidding.[19] *Luzern*[e] *leaves* us in August, whether *recalled* or on *his own request* is not known. this information comes from *himself* tho' is not as yet *spok*[e]*n* of *publicly*.[20] *Lee* finding no *faction* among the *men* here, entered into that among the *women* which rages to a very high degree. a *bal*[l] being appointed by the one party on a certain *night* he undertook to *give* one and fixed it precisely on the same *night.* this of course has placed him in the midst of the mud. he is *courting Miss Sprig* a *young girl* of *seventeen* and of *thirty thousand pound*[s] expectation.[21] I have no doubt from some conversations with *him* that there is a design agitating to sever the *Northern Nec*[k] and add it to this *state. he* supported in conversation with me the propriety & necessity of such a general measure, to wit of enlarging the *small states* to interest them in the *union. he* deserves to be well *watched* in our state. *he* is extremely soured with it and is not cautious in betraying his hostility *against it.*[22] we cannot make up a Congress at all. there are 8. states in town, 6 of which are represented by two members only. of these two members of different states are confined by the gout so that we cannot make a house. we have not sit above 3. days I beleive in as many weeks. admonition after admonition has been sent to the states, to no effect. we have sent one to day. if it fails, it seems as well we should all retire. there have never been 9 states on the floor but for the ratification of the treaty and a day or two after.[23] Georgetown languishes. the smile is hardly covered now when the federal towns are spoken of. I fear that our chance is at this time desperate. our object therefore must be if we fail in an effort to remove to Georgetown, to endeavor then to get to some place off the waters of the Chesapeak where we may be ensured against Congress considering themselves as fixed.[24] my present expectations are, that as soon as we get a Congress, to do business, we shall attend to nothing but the most pressing matters, get through them & adjourn, not to meet again till November, leaving a Commee. of the states. that Commee will be obliged to go immediately to Philadelphia to examine the offices & of course they will set there till the meeting in November. whether that meeting will be in Philada. or Trenton will be the question and will in my opinion depend on the vote of *New York.*[25] did not you once suppose in conversation with me that Congress had no authority to decide any cases between two differing states, except those of disputed territory? I think you did. If I am not mistaken in this I should wish to know your sense of the words which describe those cases which may be submitted to a federal court. they seem to me to comprehend every cause of difference.[26]

We have received the act of our assembly ceding the lands North of Ohio & are about executing a deed for it.[27] I think the territory will be laid out by passing a meridian through the Western cape of the Mouth of the Gr. Kanhaway from the Ohio to L. Erie, and another through the rapids of Ohio from the same river to Michigan & crossing these by the parallels of latitude 37°. 39°. 41°. &c. allowing to each state an extent of 2°. from N. to South. on the Eastern side of the meridn. of Kanhaway will still be one new state, to wit, the territory lying between that meridian, Pennsylva. the Ohio & L. Erie.[28] we hope N. Carola. will cede all beyond the same meridian of Kanhaway, & Virga. also.[29] for god's sake push this at the next session of assembly.[30] we have transmitted a copy of a petition from the people of Kentucky to Congress praying to be separated from Virginia. Congress took no notice of it. we sent the copy to the Governor desiring it to be laid before the assembly.[31] our view was to bring on the question. it is for the interest of Virginia to cede so far immediately because the people beyond that will separate themselves, because they will be joined by all our settlements beyond the Alleghaney if they are the first movers. whereas if we draw the line those at Kentucky having their end will not interest themselves for the people of Indiana, Greenbriar &c. who will of course be left to our management,[32] and I can with certainty almost say that Congress would approve of the meridian of the mouth of Kanhaway and consider it as the ultimate point to be desired from Virginia. I form this opinion from conversation with many members. should we not be the first movers, and the Indianians & Kentuckians take themselves off and claim to the Alleghaney I am afraid Congress would secretly wish them well. Virginia is extremely interested to retain to that meridian: 1. because the gr. Kanhaway runs from North to South across our whole country forming by its waters a belt of fine land which will be thickly settled & will form a strong barrier for us. 2. because the country for 180 miles beyond that is an absolute desart, barren & mountainous which can never be inhabited, & will therefore be a fine separation between us & the next state.[33] 3. because the government of Virginia is more convenient to the people on all the upper parts of Kanhaway than any other which will be laid out. 4. because our lead mines are in that country.[34] 5. because the Kanhaway is capable of being made navigable, and therefore gives entrance into the Western waters to every part of our latitude. 6. because it is not now navigable & can only be made so by expensive works which require that we should own the soil on both sides. 7. because the Ohio and it's branches which head up against the Patowmac affords the shortest water communication by 500. miles of any which can ever be got between the Western waters & Atlantic,[35] & of course promises us almost a monopoly of the Western & Indian trade. I think the opening this navigation is an object on which no time is to be lost. Pennsylva. is attending to the Western commerce. she has had surveys made of the river Susquehanna and of the grounds thro' which a canal must pass to go directly to Philadelphia. it is reported practicable at an expence of £200,000 and they have determined to open it.[36] what an example this is! if we do not push this matter immediately they will be beforehand with us & get possession of the commerce. and it is difficult to turn it from a channel in which it is once established. could not our assembly be induced to lay a particular tax which should bring in 5. or 10,000£ a year to be applied till the navigation of the Ohio & Patowmac is opened, then James river & so on through the whole successively.[37] Genl. Washington has that of the Patowmac much at heart. the superintendance of it would be a noble amusement in his retirement & leave a monument of him as long as the waters should flow. I am of opinion he would accept of the direction as long as the money should be to be emploied on the Patowmac, & the popularity of his name would carry it thro' the assembly.[38] the portage between Yohogania & the N. branch of Patowmac is of 40 or 50 miles. Cheat river is navigable far up. it's head is within 10 miles of the head of the North branch of Patowmac & I am informed offers the shortest & best portage.[39] I wish in the next election of delegates for Congress, Short could be sent. his talents are great & his weight in our state must ere long become principal.[40] I see the best effects produced by sending our young statesmen here. they see the affairs of the Confederacy from a high ground; they learn the importance of the Union & befriend federal measures when they return. those who never come here, see our affairs insulated, pursue a system of jealousy & self interest, and distract the Union as much as they can.[41] Genl. Gates would Supply Short's place in the council very well, and would act. he is now here.[42] what will you do with the council? they are expensive, and not constantly nor often necessary: yet to drop them would be wrong. I think you had better require their attendance twice a year to examine the Executive department & see that it be going on rightly; advise on that subject the Governor or inform the legislature as they shall see occasion. give them 50. guineas for each trip, fill up only 5 of the places, and let them be always subject to summons on great emergencies by the Governor, on which occasions their expences only should be paid. at an expence of 500 guineas you will thus preserve this member of the constitution always fit for use. young & ambitious men will leave it & go into the assembly, but the elderly & able who have retired from the legislative feild as too turbulent will accept of the offices.[43] among other legislative subjects our distresses ask notice. I had been from home four months & had expended 1200 Dollars before I received one farthing. by the last post we received about seven weeks allowance. in the mean time some of us had had the mortification to have our horses turned out of the livery stable for want of money. there is really no standing this. the supply gives us no relief because it was mortgaged. we are trying to get something more effectual from the treasury, having sent an express to inform them of our predicament.[44] I shall endeavour to place as much in the Philadelphia bank as will repay your kindness unless you should alter your mind & chuse to take it in the Virginia treasury.[45] I have hunted out *Chatlux* journal & had a reading of it. I had never so falsely estimated the character of a book. there are about six sentences of offensive bagatelles which are all of them publicly known, because having respected individual characters they were like carrion for the buzzard curiosity. all the rest of the book (and it is a 4to. of 186 pages) is either entertaining, or instructive & would be highly flattering to the Americans. he has visited all the principal feilds of battle, enquired minutely into the detail of the actions, & has given what are probably the best accounts extant of them. he often finds occasion to criticize & to deny the British accounts from an inspection of the ground. I think to write to him, recommend the expunging the few exceptionable passages & publication of the rest.[46] I have had an opportunity here of examining Bynkershoek's works. there are about a fourth part of them which you would like to have. they are the following tracts. Questiones juris publici, de lege Rhodiâ, de dominio maris, du Juge competent des Ambassadeurs, for this last if not the rest has been translated into French with notes by Barbeyrac.[47] I have had from Boinod & Gaillard a copy of Mussenbroeck's cours de Physique.[48] it is certainly the most comprehensive & most accurate body of Natl. Philosophy which has been ever published. I would recommend to you to get it, or I will get that and any other books you want from Boinod or elsewhere. I hope you have found access to my library. I beg you to make free use of it. Key, the steward is living there now & of course will be always in the way.[49] Monroe is buying land almost adjoining me.[50] Short will do the same.[51] what would I not give you could fall into the circle. with such a society I could once more venture home & lay myself up for the residue of life, quitting all it's contentions which grow daily more & more insupportable. think of it. to render it practicable only requires you to think it so. life is of no value but as it brings us gratifications. among the most valuable of these is rational society. it informs the mind, sweetens the temper, cheers our spirits, and promotes health.

there is a little farm of 140 as. adjoining me & within two miles, all of good land, tho' old, with a small indifferent house on it, the whole worth not more than £250. such a one might be a farm of experiment & support a little table & household. it is on the road to Orange & so much nearer than I am. it is convenient enough for supplementary supplies from thence.[52] once more think of it, and Adieu

[1] *Q.v.*

[2] Jefferson to JM, 11 Dec. 1783, and n. 6.

[3] JM to Jefferson, 11 Feb. 1784, and n. 3.

[4] *Ibid.*, and n. 7.

[5] *Ibid.*, and n. 10.

[6] Jefferson may have used the edition of George Louis Leclerc, Comte de Buffon, *Époques de la nature*, the supplement of the *Histoire naturelle, générale et particulière* . . . (Paris, 1778). Buffon stressed Canada and the Ohio River valley rather than South America as the areas in the Western Hemisphere where *ossements d'éléphant* had been found.

[7] The Reverend James Madison, president of the College of William and Mary. See Boyd, *Papers of Jefferson*, VI, 420, 507–8; VII, 31.

[8] Jefferson to JM, 1 Jan. 1784, and n. 4.

[9] That is, affixing the "seal" of "the United States in Congress Assembled" to the copy of an act of ratification to be sent to the peace commissioners in Paris, without revealing to the British that the ordinance had been approved by the delegations of seven states only rather than by the nine or more required by Article IX of the Articles of Confederation (*JCC*, XIX, 220).

[10] Jacob Read, Hugh Williamson, and Arthur Lee. In the much fuller treatment of the ratification issue in his autobiography, Jefferson also mentioned Jeremiah Townley Chase (Md.) (Burnett, *Letters*, VII, 399, n. 3, 407, n. 3). See also *ibid.*, VII, 403–4, 405, 406–8.

[11] For the purpose stated in the present letter, Jefferson on 27 December 1783 drafted a "resolution" comprising a brief preamble and eight numbered paragraphs devoted to presenting as many different reasons why the delegates of "seven states only" were not competent, in view of "the usage of modern nations," the stipulation of the Articles of Confederation, and the "commission and instructions" of the American peace commissioners, to enact a valid ratification of the definitive treaty of peace. The "inclosed" copy in Jefferson's hand is among the Rives Collection of Madison Papers in the Library of Congress. Also in that depository is a "corrected" copy. This is reproduced in Boyd, *Papers of Jefferson*, VI, 424–25, 425 n. Although the two versions are identical in argument, they vary occasionally in punctuation, and the corrected copy includes several additional sentences, clauses, and phrases. For JM's lengthy comment on the issue, see his letter of 16 March 1784 to Jefferson (LC: Madison Papers).

[12] *JCC*, XXVI, 22–29. On 14 January New York and Georgia were not represented in Congress, and New Hampshire and New Jersey each had only one delegate in attendance. Following a unanimous vote, Congress adopted a proclamation announcing the ratification and calling upon the states to enforce the provisions of the treaty. To give added stress to this admonition of "observance," the delegates also agreed to a resolution "earnestly" recommending that, by revising or repealing all legislation adverse to "real British subjects" or to Loyalists "who have not borne arms against" the United States, the state legislatures should subscribe fully to the pledges in the treaty, "so as to render the said laws or acts perfectly con-

sistent, not only with justice and equity, but with that spirit of conciliation, which, on the return of the blessings of peace, should universally prevail" (*JCC*, XXVI, 29–31; Burnett, *Letters*, VII, 439–41).

13 For this mission the journal of Congress for 14 January notes only the appointment of brevet Colonel Josiah Harmar (1753–1813) of Philadelphia (*JCC*, XXVI, 29). President Thomas Mifflin, for whom Harmar had been acting as private secretary, directed him to proceed as expeditiously as possible to the American peace commissioners in Paris (Burnett, *Letters*, VII, 411, and first n. 2, 412). Lieutenant Colonel David Salisbury Franks (*Papers of Madison*, IV, 450, n. 14; VI, 180, n. 6; 236) was instructed on 15 January to carry another copy of the ratification to Europe (*JCC*, XXVI, 34–35). Congress also consigned to Robert Morris, agent of marine, a third copy, "to be forwarded by any good opportunity" (Burnett, *Letters*, VII, 411, and first n. 2, 416, 422, 454).

As an officer of the Pennsylvania continental line from October 1776 until 30 November 1783, Harmar served with distinction both with the main army and in the southern department. Shortly after his a rival in Philadelphia from France on 7 August 1784, Congress appointed him the Indian agent in the Northwest Territory and commanding officer of the "1st. Amer. Regt.," then encamped near Fort Pitt. Harmar was brevetted brigadier general in 1787, and became general-in-chief of the army in the autumn of 1789. In that capacity he was in command on 22 October 1790 during an unsuccessful engagement with the Miami Indians in the Ohio country. In 1793, the year after he resigned his commission in the regular army, he became adjutant general of Pennsylvania and continued to hold that office until 1799.

14 The unusually cold weather had blocked New York Harbor with ice (David M. Ludlum, *Early American Winters, 1604–1820* [Boston, 1966], pp. 151–53). This, as well as other untoward circumstances, delayed both Harmar and Franks from sailing until 17 February. Obviously neither of them could reach his destination by 3 March, the latest date stipulated by Article 10 of the definitive peace treaty for an exchange of ratifications by Great Britain and the United States. Harmar sailed for Lorient in the packet "Le Courier de l'Amérique" and delivered the copy of the act of ratification in his custody to Franklin at Passy on the evening of 29 March. Franks, aboard the American ship "Edward," reached London the next day (NA: PCC, No. 163, fols. 377, 385; *Pa. Packet*, 14 Feb. and 2 Mar. 1784; Burnett, *Letters*, VII, 438–39, 454, 457, 460; Richard B. Morris, *The Peacemakers*, p. 448). Two days earlier, David Hartley, the British peace commissioner, had informed Henry Laurens that "it is not thought necessary, on the part of Great Britain, to enter into any formal convention for the prolongation of the term in which the ratifications of the definitive treaty were to be exchanged." The exchange took place at Paris on 12 May 1784 (Wharton, *Revol. Dipl. Corr.*, VI, 789, 790, 805, 806, 811–13).

15 Jefferson reverted to the draft of his "resolution," already mentioned. One of the "two states" would have been Massachusetts; probably the other would have been either Maryland or South Carolina (Boyd, *Papers of Jefferson*, VI, 426; Burnett, *Letters*, VII, 400–401 n.).

16 Article IX of the Articles of Confederation unequivocally provides that an appropriation of money requires the assent of the congressional delegations of at least nine states (*JCC*, XIX, 220). In a letter of 16 March 1784, JM replied to Jefferson's comments (LC: Madison Papers).

17 *Papers of Madison*, VI, 224, n. 7; JM Notes, 4 June, n. 3; Jones to JM, 14 July 1783, and n. 8.

18 On 7 May 1784, besides amending the instructions of 29 October 1783 to the American peace commissioners to negotiate "treaties of amity and commerce with

the Commercial powers of Europe," Congress elected Jefferson as a minister plenipotentiary to join Adams and Franklin "in concerting drafts or propositions" for that purpose. Although Laurens and Jay also had been bound by the original instructions, they were soon to return to the United States, since Congress, even before October 1783, had acquiesced with their wish to resign (*JCC*, XXIV, 226; XXV, 753–57; XXVI, 356, 357–62; Wharton, *Revol. Dipl. Corr.*, VI, 410–11, 554, 575; JM to Jefferson, 10 June 1783, nn. 8, 21).

[19] Jay and Adams went separately from Paris to London late in October 1783. To transact financial business for Congress, Adams regretfully left England for The Hague on 5 January 1784. In a letter of 14 November 1783 to Charles Thomson, secretary of Congress, Jay wrote that the Tories in the cabinet "persuade themselves that we shall not be able to act as a nation, that our government is too feeble to command respect and our credit too much abased to recover its reputation or merit confidence. I hope better things. We are not without friends in this country, but they have more inclination than power to be friendly" (Wharton, *Revol. Dipl. Corr.*, VI, 683–84, 693, 721, 733, 740; L. H. Butterfield *et al.*, eds., *Diary and Autobiography of John Adams*, III, 146, 149, 152–53). This letter, along with Adams' of 13 November 1783 concerning "English politics," was probably received by Congress on 21 January 1784 (NA: PCC, No. 185, III, 92).

[20] On both 21 April and 13 May the Chevalier de La Luzerne informed President Mifflin that King Louis XVI had granted his request of "last summer" to return temporarily to France (Wharton, *Revol. Dipl. Corr.*, VI, 794–95, 805–6). As reasons for seeking a furlough, La Luzerne mentioned "poor health and the necessity of regulating his private affairs." He embarked at Philadelphia for France on 21 June 1784 and never returned to the United States (William E. O'Donnell, *Chevalier de La Luzerne*, pp. 247–49; Burnett, *Letters*, VII, 484).

[21] Jefferson referred to Arthur Lee and Sophia Sprigg (1766–1812), daughter of Richard Sprigg of Cedar Park, an estate in Anne Arundel County, Md. (John Martin Hammond, *Colonial Mansions of Maryland and Delaware* [Philadelphia, 1914], p. 147; *Maryland Gazette* [Annapolis], 1 Oct. 1812). The "certain *night*" was that of 17 February (Burnett, *Letters*, VII, 443, 498). Lee remained a bachelor. Miss Sprigg married John Francis Mercer in the spring of 1785 and thus became the wife of a future governor of Maryland. Her father was a friend and correspondent of Washington (Boyd, *Papers of Jefferson*, VIII, 79, 134; Fitzpatrick, *Writings of Washington*, XXVIII, 374, 470, 471; XXIX, 193, 281, 378; XXXII, 32; XXXIII, 290, 388). For the social gaiety of Annapolis during Congress' residence there, see Burnett, *Letters*, VII, 389, n. 2, 398, n. 8, 439, 451, 472, 498, 565.

[22] *Papers of Madison*, IV, 144, n. 2; VI, 12, n. 3; Thomas P. Abernethy, *Western Lands and the American Revolution*, pp. 8, 154; Cazenove Gardner Lee, Jr., *Lee Chronicle: Studies of the Early Generations of the Lees of Virginia*, ed. Dorothy Mills Parker (New York, 1957), pp. 313–24. In his reply on 16 March 1784, JM commented upon Jefferson's word of caution (LC: Madison Papers).

[23] The delegations from nine states, which had enabled Congress to ratify the definitive treaty of peace on 14 January, continued to attend during the next two days. Thereafter through 20 February Congress convened on twenty-seven days. Of these sessions, eight states were effectively represented at four, seven states at eight, six states at eight, five states at five, and three states at two (*JCC*, XXVI, 22–88, *passim*). For the first time since 16 January, effective delegations from nine states attended Congress on 1 March (*JCC*, XXVI, 109).

The two delegates absent because of gout appear to have been Edward Lloyd (Md.) and Richard Dobbs Spaight (N.C.) (*JCC*, XXVI, 53, 88; Burnett, *Letters*, VII, 444, n. 2, 445). In his letter of 20 February 1784 to the executives of the seven states without effective delegations in Congress (N.H., N.Y., N.J., Del., Md.,

N.C., and Ga.), President Mifflin stressed that "matters of the highest importance to the safety, honour and happiness of the United States" required "immediate Attention" and added "that the members present are dissatisfied with attending to no purpose and are very impatient under their situation" (Burnett, *Letters*, VII, 444, and n. 2). See also *ibid.*, VII, 427, 438, 443, 446.

[24] For Georgetown as one of the two places at which Congress would assemble annually, see Notes on Place of Residence, 14 Oct., and nn. 2, 17; Jones to JM, 30 Oct., n. 5; Delegates to Harrison, 1 Nov. 1783 (1st letter), and n. 1. In a letter of 2 February, Samuel Osgood, a member of Congress from Massachusetts, commented: "the delegates from the eastward cannot live so far southward as Georgetown. The summers there will either destroy or debilitate our best constitutions" (Burnett, *Letters*, VII, 431). Several of the congressional colleagues of David Howell apparently agreed with his comment that a "perambulatory Congress favors republicanism—a permanent one tends to concentrate power, Aristocracy and Monarchy" (*ibid.*, VII, 397, 414–15, 421–22, 430–32).

[25] *Ibid.*, VII, 408, 415, 418, 420, 423. Between 1 March and 3 June attendance in Congress was sufficiently large to permit decisions to be reached on "the most pressing matters." On 3 June Congress adjourned, after agreeing to reconvene in Trenton on 30 October. As provided by Articles IX and X of the Articles of Confederation, Congress had elected a Committee of the States, composed of one delegate from each state. If at least nine members of this committee were present, it could exercise whatever powers Congress entrusted to it, provided that these powers did not embrace subjects which Congress itself could not legislate about unless nine or more state delegations concurred (*JCC*, XIX, 219, 220, 221; XXVI, 287–96; XXVII, 529, 555–56).

Jefferson was chairman of the committee appointed on 23 January to define the powers to be entrusted to a Committee of the States. The report, drafted by him and submitted a week later, occasioned much debate before being adopted in amended form by Congress on 29 May (Boyd, *Papers of Jefferson*, VI, 516–29; *JCC*, XXVII, 561–64). From 4 June to 13 August, whenever a quorum could be mustered, the Committee of the States held its sessions in Annapolis (*JCC*, XXVII, 561–638, *passim*). During that entire period the committee's member from New York failed to attend; nor did any delegate from that state appear in Congress until a month after it assembled in Trenton on 1 November 1784 (*JCC*, XXVII, 641, 656).

[26] In his reply to Jefferson on 16 March 1784, JM acknowledged that, having "detected the error a few days ago," he was "utterly at a loss to account" for being so mistaken in what he had told his friend (LC: Madison Papers). As Jefferson remarked, the ninth of the Articles of Confederation constituted Congress, acting through "a federal court," as "the last resort on appeals" not only "in all disputes and differences" arising "between two or more states," but also on the petition of either party to the Congress in all "controversies concerning the private right of soil claimed under different grants of two or more states" (*JCC*, XIX, 217–19).

Jefferson probably asked the question because he knew that Colonel George Morgan, "agent for the State of New Jersey," was soon to petition Congress "for a hearing, and to prosecute the said hearing to issue, in the mode pointed out by the Articles of Confederation," to decide whether Virginia should not abandon its claim to land "lying on the river Ohio" owned by Morgan and "the other proprietors" organized as "the Indiana Company." This petition, dated 26 February, was read in Congress on 1 March 1784. After much debate, Congress tabled the petition and adopted a motion to have the delegates of Virginia deliver "the deed," drawn by them in conformance with the act passed by the Virginia General Assembly at its session of October 1783, conveying to Congress "all the right of that Commonwealth, to the territory northwestward of the river Ohio" (*JCC*, XXVI, 110–17; Burnett, *Letters*, VII, 468). The Virginia General Assembly at its session of October 1783 had deleted from the original act of cession of 2 January 1781 the proviso that Congress, upon accepting the cession, must acknowledge "as absolutely void and of no effect" any "purchases and deeds" to land within the ceded area if they had been derived solely from Indians or from "royal grants" which were "inconsistent with the chartered rights, laws and customs of Virginia" (*JHDV*, Oct. 1780, p. 80; JM to Jefferson, 20 Sept. 1783, n. 3). For the Indiana Company and George Morgan, see *Papers of Madison*, II, 176–77; 178, nn. 1–6; 188; III, 47, n. 2; 210, n. 4; 287; 288, n. 5; 290–91; 295, and n. 6; 304, and n. 1; IV, 15, n. 16; 33; 215, n. 2; V, 26, and n. 7; 277, n. 5; George E. Lewis, *The Indiana Company, 1763–1798: A Study in Eighteenth Century Frontier Land Speculation and Business Venture* (Glendale, Calif., 1941).

27 On 16 January 1784 the Virginia delegation in Congress may have received Governor Harrison's letter, written about three weeks before, enclosing a copy of the Virginia General Assembly's act of cession, mentioned in n. 26 (NA: PCC, No. 75, fols. 88–90; *JHDV*, Oct. 1783, pp. 79, 83; *JCSV*, III, 320; Burnett, *Letters*, VII, 427; Boyd, *Papers of Jefferson*, VI, 468–69, 551). As authorized by the act, Jefferson, on behalf of his fellow delegates from Virginia, drafted a deed conveying title to, and right of jurisdiction over, the ceded land to Congress. On 13 February Congress referred that draft, together with a copy of the cession act, to a committee, Roger Sherman (Conn.), chairman (NA: PCC, No. 186, fol. 149; Burnett, *Letters*, VII, 446, 451). Following the refusal of Congress ten days later to approve the committee's report, Jefferson prepared a lengthier deed, incorporating a copy of the act of cession. On 1 March 1784, by the acquiescence of a bare minimum of seven states, with New Jersey and South Carolina in opposition, Congress accepted the cession and the deed of conveyance. Thereupon the deed, in the presence of Congress, was "Sign'd, Sealed, and Delivered" by the Virginia delegates and ordered to be engrossed (*JCC*, XXVI, 89–90, 112–17; Boyd, *Papers of Jefferson*, VI, 571–80; VII, 4–5; Burnett, *Letters*, VII, 457, 463).

28 On 3 February Congress appointed a committee—Jefferson, chairman, Jeremiah T. Chase, and David Howell—to recommend a "temporary governmt. of western territory" (NA: PCC, No. 186, fol. 147). The report of the committee, first submitted on 1 March and later amended, was adopted by Congress on 23 April 1784 (*JCC*, XXVI, 118–20, 247, 248–52, 255–60, 274–79, 279, n. 1; Boyd, *Papers of Jefferson*, VI, 581–615). For charts depicting the boundaries "of each state," see *ibid.*, VI, 588–93. The "Western cape" at the confluence of the Great Kanawha and Ohio rivers is opposite the town of Point Pleasant, W. Va. A meridian drawn northward from that cape would intersect the southern shore of Lake Erie at the approximate site of present-day Lorain, Ohio. A meridian similarly drawn from the rapids of the Ohio River at Louisville, Ky., would converge with the eastern shore at Lake Michigan at approximately the future site of Leland, Mich. The line of 37° north latitude would cross south central Kentucky to approximately the confluence of the Ohio and Mississippi rivers. Huttonsville, W. Va., New Bethel, Ohio, Bloomfield, Ind., and Troy, Mo., are approximately in 39° north latitude. Findlay, Ohio, Star City, Ind., Chebanse, Ill., and Mediapolis, Iowa, are approximately in 41° north latitude. The proposed state last mentioned by Jefferson would embrace about the eastern third of the present state of Ohio.

29 Jefferson not only expressed the hope that North Carolina would cede Congress the territory south of the Great Smoky Mountains and west of Asheville, and the lands to become the state of Tennessee, but that Virginia would yield her claims to Kentucky and approximately the western third of the future state of

West Virginia. For the discontent of settlers in the mountains of North Carolina and its short-lived offer of cession in 1784, see JM Notes, 19 June 1783, and n. 2.

30 Although JM had been urged to seek election as a delegate from Orange County in the Virginia General Assembly, Jefferson's plea is the first certain evidence that JM intended to be, or already was, a candidate for that position (Jones to JM, 28 July, and n. 4; Pendleton to JM, 20 Oct. 1783, and n. 3; Boyd, *Papers of Jefferson*, VI, 429). For JM's brief response to Jefferson on the issue of a further cession of land by Virginia to Congress, see JM to Jefferson, 16 Mar. 1784 (LC: Madison Papers).

31 The petition, signed by about 150 "Inhabitants of Kentuckey Settlement, westeward of the Cumberland Mountains, on the waters empting into the Ohio River," was submitted to Congress on 2 January and apparently tabled (NA: PCC, No. 185, III, 90; *JCC*, XXVI, 3, n. 2). The petitioners, of whom many had their names written for them by others among the signatories, listed numerous grievances. Among these the most stressed were insufficient opportunity to acquire a preemptive right to land improved by, and defended, at a "great loss of their Blood and treasure," against "a barbarous savage enemy"; inadequate help in resisting that foe; engrossment of land, including indispensable "Salt Springs," by absentee owners or a few "affluent" residents; inequable and exorbitant taxes; and the failure of a distant legislature at Richmond, which they could not afford to attend, to enact laws suited to frontier life and its needs. For these reasons, the signers prayed Congress to enable them to "enjoy the Freedom and Blessings of our fellow Citizens" by creating Kentucky "as a free Independent State" (NA: PCC, No. 41, V, 101–2). The Virginia delegates in their letter of 20 February 1784 to Governor Harrison enclosed a copy of the petition and expressed the hope that he would submit it to the General Assembly (Burnett, *Letters*, VI, 446, and n. 2). Harrison replied that he would do "agreeably to your request" (Executive Letter Book, 1783–1786, p. 279, MS in Va. State Library).

32 Burnett, *Letters*, VI, 451–52. Besides this prudential consideration, Jefferson probably also agreed with the principle expressed by the Kentucky petitioners: "It is a well known truth that the riches and strenth of a free country does not consist in property being Vested in a few individuals, but the more generaly it is distributed the more it promotes Industry, Population and frugality, and even morality." The "people of Indiana Greenbriar &c." were those settled in areas claimed by the Indiana Company and the Greenbriar Company. Most of that region is now within the state of West Virginia (*Papers of Madison*, I, map facing p. 212; Thomas P. Abernethy, *Western Lands and the American Revolution*, pp. 7, 8, 37, 39 [chart], 90, 144, 190, 259, 305).

33 The distance Jefferson mentioned would extend approximately from Charleston, on the Great Kanawha River in West Virginia, to Danville, Ky. Obviously "never" was much too long a time for that expanse to remain an uninhabited "absolute desart."

34 The principal lead mines were along the New River in Montgomery County. Others of lesser importance were in Bedford, Chesterfield, and Washington counties (*Papers of Madison*, II, 154, first n. 2; V, 355; 356, n. 5; *JCSV*, I, 6, 9, 65; II, 74; *Cal. of Va. State Papers*, I, 503; McIlwaine, *Official Letters*, I, 8, 235; Hening, *Statutes*, IX, 237; Thomas P. Abernethy, *Western Lands and the American Revolution*, p. 79).

35 *Papers of Madison*, I, map facing p. 212. The advantage of "500. miles" enjoyed by Virginia and Maryland over Pennsylvania, for example, appears true only when the measure of miles begins at Cumberland, Md., on the Potomac River. If "water communication" is interpreted as "commerce," a fairer comparison with Pennsylvania would be between Philadelphia and Alexandria on the Potomac. Using that

town as the starting point and bearing in mind the falls near there and farther northwestward in the Potomac, the "500. miles" is an exaggeration.

[36] In September 1783 the Pennsylvania General Assembly provided for the appointment of six commissioners to report methods and probable cost of improving the navigation of the Schuylkill River from Philadelphia to Reading and "of opening a communication" between the Schuylkill at Reading and an advantageous place on the Susquehanna River. The commissioners were also instructed to examine the west branch of the Susquehanna for the purpose of ascertaining its navigability (*Pa. Archives*, 1st ser., X, 128–30, 312, 334–35; Solon J. Buck and Elizabeth H. Buck, *Planting of Civilization in Western Pennsylvania*, pp. 231–41).

[37] These remarks foreshadow the chartering of the James River Company and the Potowmack Company by the Virginia General Assembly at its session of October 1784 (*JHDV*, Oct. 1784, pp. 109, 110; Hening, *Statutes*, XI, 450–62, 510–25).

[38] The Virginia General Assembly at its session of October 1784 "vested in George Washington, esq. his heirs and assigns, forever," fifty shares in the Potowmack Company and one hundred shares in the James River Company (*JHDV*, Oct. 1784, p. 110; Hening, *Statutes*, XI, 525–26). Washington indeed had the navigation of the "Patowmac much at heart" (Fitzpatrick, *Writings of Washington*, indexes of XXVII and XXVIII under Potomac Navigation Company, and esp. XXVII, 471–80, 480, n. 56).

[39] From Cumberland, Md., on the North Branch of the Potomac River, west-northwest in a straight line to the present Youghiogheny Dam in Pennsylvania is about twenty-eight miles. The Cheat River flows north and northwest through West Virginia to its confluence with the Monongahela River at Point Marion in southwestern Pennsylvania. By "head," Jefferson meant the confluence of Horseshoe Run and Clover Run, which form the Cheat in Tucker County, W. Va. From Port Marion it would be little farther than fifteen miles to present Kempton Junction on the North Branch of the Potomac. The above distances in straight lines do not, of course, allow for the natural obstacles that would increase the distances of portage.

[40] William Short, a member of the Virginia Council of State from June 1783 until his resignation in August 1784 to become private secretary to Jefferson during his diplomatic mission to France (*Papers of Madison*, III, 269–70; Jefferson to JM, 7 May, and n. 15; Jones to JM, 8 June 1783, and n. 13; *JCSV*, III, 267, 374, 375).

[41] JM had viewed "new members" of Congress from a different standpoint (*Papers of Madison*, VI, 16; JM to Randolph, 27 May 1783, and n. 8).

[42] Major General Horatio Gates of Berkeley County, Va., may have stayed in Annapolis until early in April 1784 (Boyd, *Papers of Jefferson*, VII, 62). He was never a member of the Council of State or the Virginia General Assembly. Moving in 1790 to Rose Hill, an estate two or three miles north of New York City, Gates resided there during the last sixteen years of his life (Samuel White Patterson, *Horatio Gates: Defender of American Liberties* [New York, 1941], pp. 367–96).

[43] In his draft of a new Form of Government for Virginia, written in 1783, Jefferson proposed that "executive power" be centered in the governor, and that the status of the Council of State be correspondingly reduced (Boyd, *Papers of Jefferson*, VI, 298–300). JM agreed that the Council was a "grave of useful talents" and its cost exceeded the worth of its services, but he accurately predicted that it probably would be left untouched by the Virginia General Assembly in the session of May 1784 (JM to Jefferson, 16 Mar. 1784, in LC: Madison Papers).

[44] Jefferson probably had five horses at Annapolis (Boyd, *Papers of Jefferson*, VI, 355). In his correspondence between 23 December 1783 and 28 February 1784, the "disgraceful predicament in which the Gentlemen of the Delegation are placed for want of remittances from the State" is frequently mentioned (*ibid.*, VI, 418,

427, 431, 512–13, 534, 538, 539, 540, 544, 565). On 14 February Jefferson received from the treasurer, Jacquelin Ambler, the bill of exchange of Benjamin Harrison on John Holker for 433⅓ dollars. Three days later he sold the bill to John Hopkins Stone and received $100 in part payment (*Maryland Historical Magazine*, XLI [1946], 119).

45 JM replied that, although the place of repayment was "not material" to him, Jefferson should delay returning the loan until his own financial stringency at Annapolis had been eased (JM to Jefferson, 16 Mar. 1784, in LC: Madison Papers). For the origin of the debt, see Boyd, *Papers of Jefferson*, VI, 358; JM to Jefferson, 10 Dec., and n. 24; Settlement of Accounts, 31 Dec. 1783, n. 13; Jefferson to JM, 1 Jan. 1784.

46 François Jean, Chevalier (later Marquis) de Chastellux, *Voyage de Newport à Philadelphie, Albany, &c*, published anonymously at Newport, R.I., in 1781 by the Imprimerie Royale de l'Escadre (*Papers of Madison*, V, 138; 139, n. 9; also *ibid.*, II, 226, n. 7; III, 131, n. 4; IV, 83, nn. 6, 7; 338, n. 11; V, 18, n. 10; 327, and nn. 7, 8; 344, n. 7; Boyd, *Papers of Jefferson*, VI, 550 n.). Not until 24 December 1784, when he was in Paris, did Jefferson write to Chastellux about the book (*ibid.*, VII, 580–81).

47 Cornelius van Bynkershoek (Bijnkershoek), *Questionum juris publici libri duo, quorum primus est de rebus bellicus, secundus de rebus varii argumenti de lege Rhodia de jactu liber singularis, et de dominanio maris dissertatio* (The Hague, 1703; 2d ed.; Leyden, 1737); [*Liber singularis de foro legatorum*] *Traité du juge compétent des ambassadeurs, tant pour le civil, que pour le criminel. Traduit du Latin . . . par Jean Barbeyrac* (The Hague, 1723; 3d ed.; 2 vols.; The Hague, 1746). See *Papers of Madison*, VI, 69, entry No. 30.

48 Daniel Boinod and Alexander Gaillard, "lately from Europe," advertised in the *Pennsylvania Packet* of 3 February 1784 that their catalogue, selling for "¼ a dollar," listed the books available for purchase at their store on Second Street near Vine Street in Philadelphia. Petrus van Musschenbroek (1692–1761), *Cours de Physique expérimentale et mathematique, . . . traduit par M. Sigaud de la Fond* (3 vols.; Paris, 1769). The Latin title of the author's work is *Physicae experimentales et geometricae* . . . (Leyden, 1729).

49 JM to Jefferson, 10 Dec. 1783, and n. 14; JM to Jefferson, 16 Mar. 1784 (LC: Madison Papers).

50 *Ibid.* By "is buying" Jefferson meant "hopes to buy," for on 20 July 1784 Monroe wrote that his negotiations with the owner of the land had been unsuccessful (Boyd, *Papers of Jefferson*, VII, 299–300; also VII, 381, 565; VIII, 150; X, 277). By 1786, still without land near Monticello, Monroe was practicing law in Fredericksburg, Spotsylvania County.

51 Thomas Jefferson, as attorney for William Short, bought the "Indian Camp plantation" in Albemarle County in 1795 from Champe Carter of Blenheim, paying $4,700 for 1,334 acres (Edgar Woods, *Albemarle County in Virginia*, pp. 24, 217; George Green Shackelford, "William Short and Albemarle," *Magazine of Albemarle County History*, XV [1955–56], 21).

52 The property mentioned by Jefferson has not been identified. Jefferson's suggestion may have become less tempting to JM when on 19 August 1784 he was presented by his father, "in Consideration of paternal affection and of five Shillings," with about 560 acres from the Montpelier estate (Orange County Court Records, MS in Va. State Library).

INDEX

Note: Persons are identified on pages cited below in boldface type. Identifications made in earlier volumes are noted immediately after the person's name.

The Papers of James Madison

DESIGNED BY JOHN B. GOETZ
COMPOSED BY THE UNIVERSITY OF CHICAGO PRESS
IN LINOTYPE JANSON WITH DISPLAY LINES IN
MONOTYPE JANSON AND CASLON OLD STYLE
PRINTED BY THE UNIVERSITY OF CHICAGO PRESS
ON WARREN'S UNIVERSITY TEXT, A PAPER WATERMARKED
WITH JAMES MADISON'S SIGNATURE AND MADE EXPRESSLY
FOR THE VOLUMES OF THIS SET
PLATES PRINTED BY MERIDEN GRAVURE COMPANY
BOUND BY A. C. ENGDAHL IN COLUMBIA BAYSIDE LINEN
AND STAMPED IN GENUINE GOLD